CALIFORNIA
REAL ESTATE PRINCIPLES

17th Edition, 2nd Printing

Sherry Shindler Price

Leigh Conway

ALLIED
REAL ESTATE SCHOOLS
A Division of Allied Business Schools

This publication is designed to provide accurate and current information regarding the subject matter covered. The principles and conclusions presented are subject to local, state, and federal laws and regulations, court cases and revisions of same. If legal advice or other expert assistance is required, the reader is urged to consult a competent professional in the field.

Real Estate Publisher
Leigh Conway

Academic Information Analyst
Laura King

Writers
Nicole Thome, Senior Technical Writer
Ben Hernandez, Technical Writer
Sue Carlson, Technical Writer

Editors
Stephanie Pratap
Emily Kazmierski

Production Designer
Susan Mackessy Richmond

©2017 by Allied Real Estate Schools, a division of Allied Business Schools, Inc.
17th Edition, 2nd Printing

Allied Real Estate Schools
22952 Alcalde Drive
Laguna Hills, California 92653

Printed in the United States of America

ISBN: 978-0-934772-74-7

CONTENTS

PREFACE

Whether your purpose is to increase your knowledge as a buyer or seller, or to pass the California Real Estate License Exam, you will find the information presented in this text to be useful. This text is written primarily for the beginning real estate student; however, inquiring consumers and investors will also find answers to their real estate questions.

Each unit in this textbook has been divided into topics. Topic content is reinforced through real-life examples, photographs, illustrations, charts, and tables. Important terms are highlighted in **bold type** in each unit. Each unit ends with a summary.

Review exercises have been designed for each unit. The quiz exercises feature real estate terms and multiple-choice questions. The multiple-choice questions at the end of each unit will help students prepare for the real estate exam. These challenging questions were designed to test higher-level concepts and will often require students to combine information they have learned in different units. After completing a quiz exercise, students can check their answers by reviewing the Answer Key at the end of each unit. Students should be encouraged to review their work often to make sure they understand what they have read.

ABOUT THE AUTHORS

SHERRY SHINDLER PRICE

Sherry Shindler Price has been a California Community College real estate instructor since 1986. Her experience in the real estate profession includes eight years of specialization in investment properties and residential sales. She has authored *Escrow Principles and Practices* and *Real Estate Finance*. In addition, Ms. Shindler Price has reviewed numerous real estate textbooks for major publishers and has written a series of continuing education courses for private real estate schools. Her extensive knowledge in real estate was used to write test questions for state licensing examinations in Nevada, Wisconsin, Minnesota, Maryland, and Iowa. Ms. Shindler Price has a Bachelor of Science degree in Education from Long Beach State College.

LEIGH CONWAY

Leigh Conway brings a rich background in real estate to the creation and production of this text. She is a licensed real estate broker in California with experience in commercial brokerage, residential and commercial property management, syndication, and real estate development. With over ten years of experience in real estate education, she has taught various statutory and continuing education courses. In addition, she co-authored a number of real estate textbooks and wrote several continuing education courses for private real estate schools. Ms. Conway has a Bachelor's Degree from the University of California at Los Angeles.

ABOUT THE TECHNICAL ADVISOR

Ignacio Gonzalez is a Real Estate Coordinator with Mendocino Community College in Ukiah, California. He has over twelve years in real estate education and has taught classes in Real Estate Principles, Real Estate Practices, Appraisal, Finance, Property Management, and Real Estate Economics. In 1999, he received a Mendocino College President's Award for Outstanding Teacher as an Adjunct Instructor. He has authored *California Real Estate Economics*.

Mr. Gonzalez is a Land Use Planner whose specialization is in urban and rural land use planning. This expertise includes subdivision review, zoning administration, community general planning, redevelopment, environmental analysis, transportation planning, coastal review, and natural resource administration.

Mr. Gonzalez has a Bachelor of Arts degree in Planning from Sonoma State University.

ACKNOWLEDGMENTS

The authors would like to thank the real estate professionals and educators who contributed to the earlier editions of this text.

Additionally, the authors would like to acknowledge the California Bureau of Real Estate, California Association of REALTORS®, and others for the forms and contracts found throughout the text.

Cover photos of San Francisco Bay and Napa Vineyard courtesy and copyright of Free Range Stock (freerangestock.com). Photographer - Chance Agrella.

INTRODUCTION

In this Unit, you will learn about California and why it is called the Golden State. You will look at how California's diverse population affects its economic base, sustains the state's economic growth, and how the state's economy influences the national economy. Finally, we will touch on the brokerage business and opportunities in the real estate industry.

Learning Objectives

After completing this Unit, you should be able to:

1A   recall the unique characteristics of California's climate and geography.

1B   characterize California's multicultural demographics.

1C   indicate factors contributing to California's economy and housing market.

ONLY IN CALIFORNIA

Location! Location! Location! Most of you have seen this phrase in a real estate ad describing the perfect neighborhood. All of you reading this, no matter what city you live in, are experiencing the perfect location. No…we are not referring to your specific street, town or county...we are talking about California. California has everything, and usually it is the best! Whoever said, "Less is more" just never lived in California.

California's natural and man-made wonders can only be described with superlatives. California's economy is so large that it actually competes with countries—not just states. Additionally, it is the first state to ever reach a trillion-dollar economy in gross state product. At over 38 million people, California is the most culturally diverse and the most populous state in the country, and has been since 1962. In fact, one out of every eight United States residents lives in California. California is called The Golden State. Some say it is due to its long association with gold mining made famous by the Gold Rush. Others point to the golden grasses that cover our hills in the summer and fall, or the fields of golden poppies that bloom in the springtime. You might call California golden because of our fabulous, golden sunshine and warm climate. In any event, gold has been intertwined with the history and development of California.

Climate and Geography

Where but California could you surf in the morning, play 18 holes of golf, and then enjoy a torch-lit night ski run—all in the same day? California is a beautiful place, blessed with phenomenal natural beauty and a climate free from hurricanes, tornadoes, and blizzards. We definitely enjoy a relatively mild climate.

Climate

Our basic climate is called Mediterranean, characterized by general sun and warmth with rain mainly in the winter. Of course, there are variations based on the distance from the ocean and the elevation. Average rainfall varies from 80 inches in Del Norte County (north coast) to as low as 3 inches in Imperial County (desert).

California has a relatively mild climate

We have five main zones: coastal, desert, foothill, valley, and mountain.

Coastal climate is characterized by mild temperatures with minor annual variations. Most of the state's population lives along the coast.

Desert climate is characterized by high summer temperatures, extremely low humidity, and very little rainfall.

Valley climate is characterized by high temperatures and low humidity in the summer and low temperature and high humidity in the winter. Both the Sacramento and San Joaquin Valleys have this weather pattern.

Foothill climate (1,000 to 3,000 feet in elevation) is similar to the valley regions but with more rain and less fog.

Mountain climate is the only area that gets heavy snow in the winter. Winters are very cold and summers are bright and sunny.

Geography

California is the third largest state in land area (158,693 square miles) with 1,264 miles of coastline and an average width of 175 miles. We have everything here: beautiful beaches, deserts, valleys, foothills, towering mountains, and even a delta with levees.

There are still three active volcanoes in California. In the Cascade Mountain Range are Mt. Lassen (elevation 10,457 feet) and Mt. Shasta (elevation 14,162 feet). Mt. Mammoth (elevation 11,000 feet) is located in the Sierra Nevada Mountain Range.

CALIFORNIA—THE PEOPLE MAGNET

California, with its mild climate and seemingly unending opportunities, continues to draw immigrants today just as it did 150 years ago. We shouldn't be surprised. A recent Harris Poll® conducted online among a nationwide cross section of adults, showed that Americans would like to live here than in any other state. They were asked, "If you could live in any state in the country, except the state you live in now, what state would you choose to live in?" California was the first choice with Florida second and Hawaii third.

Finding California

California was already inhabited by Native Americans in villages and tribes when early explorers touched our coastline and made new claims for foreign countries. Portuguese-born Juan Rodriguez Cabrillo explored the California coastline from San Diego to Santa Barbara and claimed it for Spain. Sir Francis Drake landed north of San Francisco Bay and claimed the territory for England. The Russians established Fort Ross, a trading post near Bodega Bay, and claimed the territory north of San Francisco for Russia.

A few hardy settlers in covered wagons took the perilous trek across the deserts to reach the promise of a better future. But, when gold was discovered in Sutter's Mill in 1848, the Forty-Niners flocked here with strike-it-rich dreams. When Southern Pacific Railroad finally extended its rail system into Los Angeles, it hired real estate developers to tout Southern California as a Mediterranean-like paradise. They were very successful because over 12,000 eager tourists and settlers arrived by railroad each month. In just 20 short years, the population in Los Angeles grew from 11,000 in 1880 to more than 100,000 by 1900. During World War II, the government spent billions of dollars each year in government contracts to build liberty ships and thousands of warplanes. Lured by the promise of work, more than 700,000 workers had come to California by 1943. They located by the defense plants in Los Angeles, Santa Monica, Burbank, Long Beach, El Segundo, and San Diego.

After the war, the California economy continued to boom drawing yet more people. In 1962, California, with a population of more than 17 million, officially surpassed that of New York. Since then people have come here from all parts of the world, drawn to our wonderful climate, stunning landscapes, and economic opportunities.

As of the 2010 U.S. Census, California had an estimated population of 38 million, which is more than 12% of the U.S. population. In addition, Los Angeles County was the nation's most populous county, with 9.8 million residents.

This large population corridor interconnected by economic activity, transportation, and communication linkages creates a megalopolis. A megalopolis is a large, densely populated metropolitan area consisting of a number of major urban areas and smaller surrounding cities. The Southern California **megalopolis** stretches from Santa Barbara to the Mexican border, and is centered around the city of Los Angeles. It is the largest population center and industrial center in the western United States, and the second largest in the nation.

Multicultural California

Because people everywhere have viewed California as a land of opportunity, California has become one of the most ethnically diverse regions of the world. Nearly one-half of Californians speak a language other than English at home, a proportion far higher than in any other state.

Our population reflects virtually every area of the globe, as new arrivals continue to stake their claims to the California dream. Victorian homes in Eureka, New England-style cottages in Mendocino, houseboats in Sausalito, and Spanish-style homes in Southern California remind us of the diversity of our grandparents.

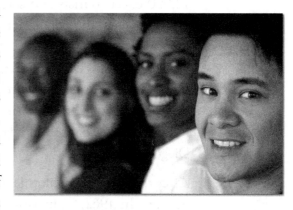

The largest group (more than half of the population) is made up of people whose ancestors came from the British Isles; European countries such as Germany, France, Poland, and Italy; and Scandinavian countries such as Norway and Sweden. More than 1/3 of Californians have ethnic roots in Latin America. The Golden State has more people who speak Spanish than any other state.

About 14% of the state's population is Asian. The Tien Hau Temple in San Francisco is the oldest Chinese temple in the United States. The Bok Kai Taoist temple in Marysville is over 121 years old. African Americans are about 7% of the state's population. Although Native Americans make up less than one percent of the total population, California has about 250 Native American tribes, more than exist in any other state.

One of the best ways to learn about California's ethnic diversity is to enjoy the many festivals and celebrations held up and down the state. In February, the annual San Francisco Chinese New Year Festival and Parade features a huge dancing dragon and brightly lit floats. In early May, Mexican Americans throughout the state celebrate Cinco de Mayo with large fiestas. Native American tribes gather from across the country to perform ceremonial dancing, drumming, and singing at the annual Indian Fair held each June in San Diego. Each July, the French Festival in Santa Barbara celebrates the music, art, dancing, and food of France. The Los Angeles African Marketplace and Cultural Faire celebrate African culture around the world in late summer. The Japanese Cultural Bazaar is held every August in Sacramento and features Japanese food, dancing, art, and Taiko drummers. Every July 4th, Americans, regardless of ethnic ancestry, join together to celebrate our nation's birthday with parades, picnics, and fireworks.

CALIFORNIA'S STRONG ECONOMY

The economic system in America, and therefore California, is a mixed capitalistic system. **Capitalism** is an economic system in which most of the economy's resources are privately owned and managed. The government is asked by its citizens to influence the general economic direction, and to assure reasonable, stable competition. Currently, California has the 7th largest economy in the world. California generates more than 13% of the United States Gross Domestic Product (GDP) and is the nation's number one exporting state. California produces more than $1 trillion worth of goods and services each year.

California is home to more than 2.5 million small businesses. If you've ever eaten at a Denny's, Carl's Jr., Taco Bell, A&W, or Bob's Big Boy, you've eaten at a restaurant chain that started in California. Dick and Mac McDonald opened the first McDonald's restaurant in San Bernardino, California.

The early California economy was based primarily on agriculture, mining, and drilling for oil and gas. Gold and silver mining brought wealth to Northern California. The "black gold" of our oil wells brought capital investment and unbridled growth to Southern California.

The Golden Era of Hollywood captured the imagination of all Americans with movie making and star building and brought more wealth into Southern California. Northern California experienced a new Gold Rush when computer technology made the Silicon Valley a "buzz word" around the world.

Currently, California's top industries include: tourism, manufacturing, construction, agriculture, oil and gas production, telecommunications, engineering services, aerospace, and entertainment (including motion pictures, TV, and recording). The state is geared for the future with continuing advances in microelectronics, biotechnology, and environmental technology.

The Golden Era of Hollywood captured the imagination of many Americans.

California ... where dreams are rewarded.

With the opportunity to work in such a diverse society and consistent economy, no wonder California has such a strong appeal. Where else are dreams so welcomed and so often rewarded?

Economic Firsts

1873 - Levi Strauss & Co., the largest clothing manufacturer in the world, created and patented the world's first blue jeans.

1860 - California's famous mail courier service, the Pony Express, was the first of its kind, connecting California's communication system with the Midwest.

1873 - The world's first cable car rumbled down the streets of San Francisco. Cable cars are still popular today with visitors and residents.

1905 - Eleven-year-old Frank Epperson accidentally invented Popsicles® in San Francisco. He applied for the patent in 1923.

1908 - The "Sultan's Power" was the first complete film made in Los Angeles.

1927 - Lindbergh's plane, "The Spirit of St. Louis", was built in San Diego.

1934 - The first mass-produced commercial aircraft, the DC-2, was built by McDonnell Douglas in Santa Monica.

1935 - A statewide irrigation system was started. Irrigation turned the vast land of the Great Central Valley from semi-arid plains to green croplands. This project is the world's largest water project. Allegedly, according to Susan Sward writing in the Santa Barbara News-Press in March, 1977, "...the astronauts who landed on the moon reported they could see the California project, the only man-made item they could identify from that distance". Today, California is the leading agricultural economy of the United States.

1970 - Security National Bank activated the first automated teller bank in Los Angeles.

1970s - Mountain biking was invented in Mill Valley and first tested on Mount Tamalpais in Marin County.

1977 - The Apple II computer was developed in Silicon Valley.

The Importance of Real Estate in the Economy

The real estate industry is so large that it influences both the state and the national economies. The major roles that real estate plays in our economy are creating net worth, increasing income flow, creating new jobs, and helping control appreciation and inflation.

Net Worth

Real estate in the form of land and improvements makes up a very large portion of the total net worth of the United States as a nation (not to be confused with the government). **Net worth** is the value of all assets minus all liabilities.

Income Flow

The circular flow chart of our economy—money is paid for the use of real estate and for the raw materials, labor, capital, and management used in construction work of all kinds.

The circular flow of the national economy.

Major Employer

The real estate industry (brokerage, construction, management, finance) is a major employer in this country. It provides employment for a large segment of the population, accounting for billions of dollars in national income.

Appreciation and Inflation

Appreciation is the increase in market value of real estate. **Inflation** is measured as an increase in the general price level of goods and services, or as a decrease in purchasing power of the dollar. As the value of the dollar has decreased, passbook savings accounts and other forms of financial savings have lost their appeal as ways to save and invest for the future. As a result, real estate has become a major means by which people save. Particularly in California where property appreciated at such an alarmingly fast rate, it was common for homeowners to consider their home as money in the bank. This is true unless home values depreciate significantly.

California Housing Market

The housing market is shaped mainly by the inventory of available housing, by housing affordability, and by mortgage interest rates. California's inventory of housing units is not enough to meet the demand because our population typically increases faster than our supply of housing. With a shortage of housing, we know there is demand. The next thing to look at is the affordability index. The **affordability index** shows how many households will be able to afford a median-priced home in California. As the affordability index gets lower it means fewer households will be able to buy a home. For example, if the affordability index falls to 19, less than one-in-five households will be able to purchase a median-priced home in California. The higher the affordability index, the more households are able to purchase homes. Finally, we need to look at current mortgage interest rates. Interest rates determine the amount of a loan a borrower can get. The higher the interest, the lower the loan amount, and conversely, the lower the interest, the higher the loan amount.

Based on this, the best housing market would be created with adequate housing inventory, a high affordability index, and low interest rates.

Median Home Prices

The **median home price** is the price that is middle value of a sample of sales, with one-half of the sales below and one-half of the sales above the median home price. It is used by economists to compare home sale prices and measure increases and decreases. The housing market fluctuates with time and location. However, over the last 25 years, all areas of California have shown increases in the median home price. Some areas, however, have increased far more than others.

The **California Association of REALTORS®** (C.A.R.) is a **trade association** that is dedicated to the advancement of professionalism in real estate. C.A.R. tracks the median home sales price for several geographic areas. The following table shows some of the areas and the increase in the median home sales price.

In spite of short-term fluctuation in home prices, as we can see from the following table, the median price of a single-family home in California continues to increase.

Median Home Prices By County		
California Counties	**1983**	**2015**
Kern	$92,700	$217,000
Los Angeles County	$118,500	$502,750
Monterey	$112,600	$517,500
Napa	$94,700	$628,100
Orange	$131,450	$710,000
Riverside	$94,900	$348,000
Sacramento	$76,150	$297,600
San Bernardino	$80,400	$234,000
San Diego	$103,100	$548,000
San Francisco	$133,750	$1,215,620
San Luis Obispo	$104,150	$548,400
Santa Barbara	$131,750	$555,000
Santa Clara	$134,000	$920,000
Ventura	$128,675	$602,000

C.A.R. economists also track other statistics about California. For example, the unemployment rate, job growth, and population change. The unemployment rate is the percentage of the people classified as unemployed as compared to the total labor force. All of these factors affect the real estate market by affecting the demand for housing and the ability to pay for it.

CALIFORNIA ECONOMY			
	2013	**2014**	**2015**
Unemployment Rate	8.9%	7.5%	5.8%
Job Growth	2.7%	3.1%	2.9%
Population Growth	1.0%	1.0%	1.0%

GETTING STARTED IN REAL ESTATE

You may also have heard the saying, "Success Breeds Success." Well, California is highly successful. When you combine that proven success with our fabulous climate and natural beauty, we become a people magnet. Over 25,000 people move here every month. Each person will need housing and that is where you come in. As a licensed real estate broker or salesperson you are in the unique position to help our current and incoming residents to buy homes, rent apartments, get loans, buy businesses, manage properties or buy investments—to help them achieve their dreams.

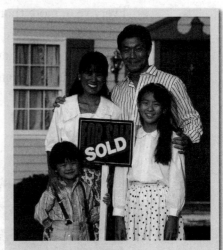

A licensed real estate broker or salesperson is in a unique position to help people achieve their dreams.

In California, if you want to work in a real estate brokerage business you must have a real estate license. There are two types of real estate licenses: a salesperson's license and a broker's license. You will learn more about the licenses and the work that you will do during the course of this text. For now, it is enough to know that a salesperson must put his or her license with a licensed broker who will help you as you get started in the business. Think of it as being a sort of apprenticeship.

This text is designed to help you understand the concepts you need to start your career in real estate. As you read through the units, you will be introduced to real estate concepts and laws regarding real estate transactions. Additionally, it offers practical information and useful tips to help you pass the state exam. You will learn property law, agency law, required disclosures, and contract law. You will study how property is owned and how ownership can be limited; how title is held and how title is transferred. Of course, we will learn about getting financing, valuing property, and the role that escrow and title play in a transaction. Once the basics are covered, we will go over residential real estate brokerage and specialty fields. Finally, we will go over the steps needed to get and keep your real estate license.

After passing the state examination and receiving your license you will probably enter one of the new licensee training programs offered by larger real estate firms. With consistent marketing, persistent prospecting, dedication to client satisfaction, and a strong dose of hard work you can make a good career in real estate.

Every year, more than 400,000 housing units are sold—the majority through a licensed real estate agent. By the time you have finished this text, another 25,000 people will have come to California, and all these newcomers will need help from a real estate professional.

Uniquely California

Floor mosaic of the seal of the state of California, created in the late 1800s. Located in San Francisco's ferry building.

Economy

- California has a vibrant, healthy economy which ranks 7th largest in the world. Only a few other countries, including the United States, are ahead of California in economic production.

- Los Angeles International Airport (LAX) claims to be the world's fifth busiest airport with over 70 million passengers per year.

- California is the first state to ever reach a trillion dollar economy in gross state product.

- The city of Los Angeles is ranked the fourth largest economy in the country compared to other states.

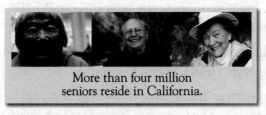

LAX control tower

- The Port of Los Angeles located in San Pedro Bay is one of the world's largest, busiest, and most successful seaports.

- California has the most major military bases and installations in the country.

Demographics

- At over 38 million people, California is the most culturally diverse and the most populous state in the country, and has been since 1962.

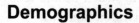

More than four million seniors reside in California.

- California has the largest number of senior citizens living within its borders, with more than four million residents over 60 years of age.

- At only 10 feet wide, the Kaweah Post Office in Tulare is the smallest post office still in operation.

- One out of every eight United States residents lives in California.

- The Little Red Schoolhouse in Solvang, the Danish Capital of America, was built in 1883, and is one of the oldest schoolhouses still in use.

- The Chinese hamlet of Locke is the only rural community in the country built and occupied by Chinese.

- Totaling nearly three million acres, San Bernardino County is the largest county in the country.

Natural Wonders

- Lake Tahoe is the highest lake of its size in the country and the largest alpine lake in North America. It is the second deepest lake in the country and the tenth deepest in the world.

- Sutter Buttes (2,132 feet high) is a mountain range near Sutter and is the world's smallest mountain range.

- The oldest living thing in the world, the Bristlecone Pine tree, grows at an altitude of 11,000 feet in California's White Mountains. Aged at nearly 5,000 years, it is as old as the Great Pyramids of Egypt.

Lake Tahoe

- Yosemite Falls, with its drop of 2,425 feet, has the longest drop for any waterfall in the country.

- At 14,495 feet, Mt. Whitney in Sequoia National Park is the highest elevation point in the contiguous United States. From there you can see Badwater, in Death Valley National Park, which at 282 feet below sea level is the lowest elevation point in the United States.

- California Caverns claims the distinction of being the most extensive system of caverns and passageways in the Mother Lode region of the state.

- The San Francisco Bay is the largest natural harbor on the West Coast of the United States.

- The world's tallest living tree (367.5 feet) is the California Redwood found along the North and Central Coast area.

- The largest trees in the world are the Sequoias and grow in the high Sierra Nevadas. The General Grant Tree in Kings Canyon National Park is famous as "The Nation's Christmas Tree". Its trunk measures 40 feet around at its base and is wider than a three-lane freeway. The General Sherman Tree, in Sequoia National Park, is the biggest living thing on earth. At almost 2.7 million pounds, it would make enough lumber to build 40 five-room houses.

Tunnel log in Sequoia National Park

- The area around Geyserville, just north of San Francisco, is the largest geothermal area in the world.

- Death Valley is recognized as the hottest, driest place in the United States. It is not uncommon for the summer temperatures to reach more than 115 degrees.

- In the center of California, the California Delta has over 1,000 miles of navigable waterways forming a triangle of channels and sloughs from Sacramento (north) to Stockton (south) to Pittsburg (west).

Death Valley National Park

- Once again, Coronado Beach was named among America's Top Ten Beaches.

Ecology

- The Monterey Bay National Marine Sanctuary located along California's central coast encompasses 5,322 square feet, making it the largest marine sanctuary in the country.

- Lake Merritt, a natural saltwater lake in the middle of Oakland, became the country's first state wildlife refuge in 1870.

- Lava Beds National Monument and the adjoining Klamath Basin National Wildlife Refuge in Northeastern California have the most bald eagles in the contiguous United States.

- Anza Borrego Desert State Park is the largest state park in the Southwest, covering 600,000 acres from the edge of the coastal mountains east to the Salton Sea and south almost to the U.S./Mexico border.

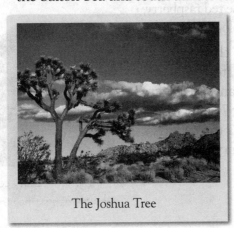

The Joshua Tree

- The Salton Sea north of El Centro has the most diverse bird species of any National Wildlife Refuges in the west.

- California Condors are the largest flying birds in North America.

- The Joshua Tree is the largest of the yuccas and grows only in the Mojave Desert.

Agriculture

- Castroville is known as the Artichoke Capital of the World. In 1947, a young woman named Norma Jean was crowned Castroville's first Artichoke Queen. She went on to become actress Marilyn Monroe.

Orchid

- California has been the number one agricultural state in the country for more than 50 years.

- The largest orchid farm (over 1.5 million square feet of greenhouse space) in the country is in Carpenteria.

- California is the only U.S. commercial producer of almonds, artichokes, dates, figs, olives, persimmons, pistachios, and walnuts.

- California is the second most important rice state in the country, producing about 20% of the nation's crop in a typical year. California supplies about half of Japan's imports of rice.

- California has by far the highest per capita avocado consumption in the country and produces the most, as well.

- Southern California produces over 33% of all lemons grown in the country.

- California leads the nation in tree nut production. Virtually all U.S. almonds, pistachios, and walnuts are California produced.

- The Coachella Valley in Southern California remains the unrivaled date capital of the United States.

- California's most famous farm is probably Knott's Berry Farm, a popular tourist attraction. A new berry, the boysenberry, was created there. It is a cross between the red raspberry, blackberry, and loganberry.

- California is the nation's leading dairy state, producing more milk than any other state. In fact with over 740,000 cows, Tulare County is the country's No. 1 dairy county.

Dairy cows

- California produces the most wine of any other state in the country. In fact, California is the fourth leading wine-producer in the world behind Italy, France, and Spain. Wine grapes are grown in 45 of California's 58 counties.

- Fresno is the Raisin Capital of the World.

- California is the largest producer of grapes, strawberries, peaches, nectarines, and kiwifruit. It is a major producer of a variety of other non-citrus fruit like apples, pears, plums, and sweet cherries.

Natural Resources

- The Mojave Desert is the most important source of boron in the world.

- The tourmaline deposits in Riverside and San Diego Counties have produced more tourmaline, and of greater value, than any other deposits in the Northern Hemisphere.

Mojave Desert

- The Kennedy Mine, located in Jackson, was one of the richest gold mines in the world and the deepest mine in North America.

- By the spring of 1849, California experienced the largest gold rush in American history.

- Redding is the nation's second-sunniest city (Tucson, AZ is first) with an average of more than 320 days of sunshine per year.

Engineering Marvels

Golden Gate Bridge

- Named one of the "Seven Wonders of the Modern World" by the American Society of Civil Engineers, the Golden Gate Bridge in San Francisco is one of the longest single-span suspension bridges ever built. Its two massive towers are the highest bridge towers in the country at 746 feet above the water.

- The longest runway in the world (7.5 miles) is located at Edwards Air Force Base near Lancaster and is used for space shuttle landings.

- The Long Beach Harbor is one of the world's largest man-made harbors.
- The Palm Springs Arial Tramway is the world's largest rotating tramcar, rising up the sheer cliffs of Chino Canyon (2,643 ft.) to the Mountain Station at 8,516 ft. on Mt. San Jacinto.
- The world famous Tehachapi Loop is a feat of civil engineering genius allowing trains from the Central Valley to cross an exceptionally steep section of the Tehachapi mountains in order to reach Los Angeles. It is one of the seven wonders of the railroad world.
- The Shasta Dam spillway, at 487 feet tall, is the world's highest man-made waterfall and is three times the height of Niagara Falls.
- The Altamont Pass by San Francisco still contains the world's largest concentration of wind turbines; however, the wind turbines in the Tehachapi Pass are the largest producers of wind-generated electricity in the country. This is enough electricity to meet the residential needs of more than 500,000 Southern Californians or nearly one million Europeans.

Wind turbines in Tehachapi Pass

- The first cable car in the world went into service in San Francisco.

Entertainment

- California has the most theme parks and amusement parks in the country.
- The largest permanent archery range in North America is at the Olympic Training Center in Chula Vista.
- The largest private zoo in the world was created by William Randolph Hearst on his ranch at San Simeon. Hearst Castle is one of the world's greatest showplaces and one of the largest historic house museums (90,080 square feet) in the country.
- The Hollywood Bowl is the largest outdoor natural amphitheater in the United States.
- San Francisco had the first municipally owned opera house in the country.
- Furnace Creek Inn, built in Death Valley in 1927, has the lowest grass golf course in the world, at 214 feet below sea level.
- Gold Mountain Ski Area, near Graeagle is the oldest reported sport-skiing area in the western hemisphere.

- The largest three-day rodeo in the country is held on the Tehama County Fairgrounds in Red Bluff.

- The "Perilous Plunge" water slide at Knott's Berry Farm in Buena Park is one of the world's steepest, tallest, and wettest water slide.

- Grauman's Chinese Theatre in Hollywood is the most famous movie theatre in the world. Millions of tourists visit each year to see the footprints of the stars. Since opening, it has had more gala Hollywood movie premieres than any other theatre.

Grauman's Chinese Theatre

- Valencia is home to Six Flags Magic Mountain where "Superman: The Escape", which is California's fastest and tallest thrill ride, reaching 100 mph in seven seconds and standing 41 stories high, is located.

- The tallest and biggest thermometer in the world is in Baker.

- The largest roadside dinosaur in the country is a 150-foot long, 150-ton brontosaurus (nicknamed "Dinny") off Interstate 10 in Cabazon. Next to "Dinny" is "Rexxie", a 65-foot tall, 100-ton tyrannosaurus housing a date shop and an observation tower in his jaws.

- For his presidential inauguration, former California Governor Ronald Reagan ordered 3.5 tons of Jelly Belly candies from the Jelly Belly factory in Fairfield. A large portrait of President Reagan made out of jelly beans is displayed at the factory.

- The world's largest yo-yo, weighing 256 pounds and standing 50-inches tall, is at the National Yo-Yo Museum in Chico.

- Tarzana is named after Edgar Rice Burroughs' Tarzana Ranch, the home of "Tarzan".

SUMMARY

California is a diverse state in geography, economic base, and population. There are five main climate zones: coastal, desert, foothill, valley, and mountain.

The strong economy in California is a mixed capitalistic system. Top industries in this state include tourism, manufacturing, construction, agriculture, oil and gas production, telecommunications, engineering services, aerospace, and entertainment.

California's population is a mixed blend of European/Scandinavian/Great Britain Americans, Hispanic Americans, Asian/Pacific Islander Americans, African Americans, and Native Americans.

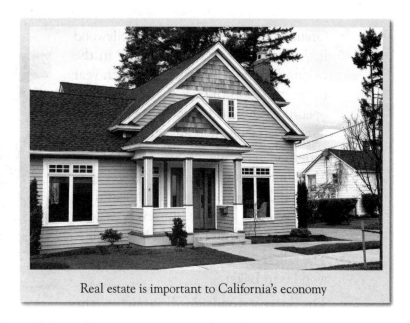

Real estate is important to California's economy

The major roles that real estate plays in our economy are: creating net worth, increasing income flow, creating new jobs, and helping control appreciation and inflation. California's current housing is not enough to meet the demand because the state's population is increasing faster than its supply of housing. Affordability is a concern because less than one-in-five households will be able to purchase a median-priced home in California.

A California real estate license is required in the state of California to sell property. This license can be obtained by passing the state real estate licensing examination.

UNIT 1 REVIEW

■ Matching Exercise

Instructions: Write the letter of the matching term on the blank line before its definition. Answers immediately follow the Multiple Choice Questions.

Terms

A. affordability index	F. demographics	K. median home price
B. appreciation	G. diversity	L. mortgage interest rate
C. black gold	H. gold rush	M. net worth
D. C.A.R.	I. housing inventory	N. trade association
E. capitalism	J. inflation	O. unemployment rate

Definitions

1. _____ An economic system in which most of the economy's resources are privately owned.

2. _____ The value of all assets minus all liabilities.

3. _____ The increase in market value of real estate.

4. _____ The increase in the general price level of goods and services.

5. _____ The price that is middle value of a sample of sales, with one-half of the sales below and one-half of the sales above.

6. _____ Information from a variety of sources used to create a broad profile of any community.

7. _____ A large migration of people to a newly discovered gold field.

8. _____ Housing units that are available for sale or in the process of being made ready for sale.

9. _____ A California trade association representing REALTORS® statewide.

10. _____ The percentage of the people classified as unemployed as compared to the total labor force.

▪ Multiple Choice Questions

Instructions: Circle your response and then check your response with the Answer Key that immediately follows the Multiple Choice Questions.

1. California's economy is so large that it actually competes with:
    a. counties.
    b. countries.
    c. conglomerates.
    d. continents.

2. The most populous state in the country is:
    a. New York.
    b. Ohio.
    c. Florida.
    d. California.

3. A large, densely populated metropolitan area consisting of a number of major urban areas and smaller surrounding cities is called a:
    a. megalopolis.
    b. metrozone.
    c. city.
    d. metropolis.

4. An economic system in which most of the economy's resources are privately owned and managed is called:
    a. capitalism.
    b. socialism.
    c   communism.
    d. Marxism.

5. The increase in market value of real estate defines:
    a. inflation.
    b. net worth.
    c. purchasing power.
    d. appreciation.

6. A decrease in purchasing power of the dollar describes:
    a. inflation.
    b. appreciation.
    c. net worth.
    d. median.

7. The real estate housing market is influenced by:
    a. the inventory of available housing.
    b. the affordability of housing.
    c. mortgage interest rates.
    d. all of the above.

8. The best housing market would be created by all of the following, except:
    a. adequate housing inventory.
    b. a low affordability index.
    c. a high affordability index.
    d. low interest rates.

9. The price that is middle value of a sample of sales, with one-half of the sales below and one-half of the sales above is called:
    a. affordability index.
    b. inflation.
    c. median home price.
    d. appreciation.

10. In California, to work as a real estate salesperson or broker you must have:
    a. a college degree.
    b. a real estate license issued by the California Bureau of Real Estate.
    c. a driver license.
    d. all of the above.

UNIT 1 ANSWER KEY

Answers – Matching

1. E	3. B	5. K	7. H	9. D
2. M	4. J	6. F	8. I	10. O

Answers – Multiple Choice

1. **(b)** California's economy is so large that it actually competes with countries—not just states. [Only in California]

2. **(d)** At over 38 million people, California is the most culturally diverse and the most populous state in the country, and has been since 1962. In fact, one out of every eight United States residents lives in California. [Only in California]

3. **(a)** A megalopolis is a large, densely populated metropolitan area consisting of a number of major urban areas and smaller surrounding cities. [California – The People Magnet]

4. **(a)** Capitalism is an economic system in which most of the economy's resources are privately owned and managed. [California's Strong Economy]

5. **(d)** Appreciation is the increase in market value of real estate. [California's Strong Economy]

6. **(a)** Inflation is an increase in the general price level of goods and services, or as a decrease in purchasing power of the dollar. [California's Strong Economy]

7. **(d)** The housing market is shaped mainly by the inventory of available housing, housing affordability and mortgage interest rates. [California's Strong Economy]

8. **(b)** The best housing market would be created with adequate housing inventory, a high affordability index, and low interest rates. [California's Strong Economy]

9. **(c)** The median home price is the price that is middle value of a sample of sales, with one-half of the sales below and one-half of the sales above the median home price. It is used by economists to compare home sale prices and measure increases and decreases. [California's Strong Economy]

10. **(b)** In California, if you want to work in a real estate brokerage business, you must have a real estate license. There are two types of real estate licenses: salesperson license and broker license. [Getting Started in Real Estate]

Unit 2

INTRODUCTION

Ownership is the basic element of real estate. Owning real estate is considered a basic right in our culture. However, the right to own property did not always exist. Our laws of property ownership began with English Common Law at a time when all property was owned by the current monarch or an appointed noble. No one else was allowed to own property. Upset by their lack of rights, people set powerful forces of change in motion. Eventually, all people gained the right to own real property, now called real estate. Each owner of real estate acquired certain rights along with property ownership. In fact, ownership of real estate is legally described in terms of these rights, and not in terms of what is owned.

Historically, the question has been, "Who owns this property, and what is their interest in it?" As a real estate agent, you will explain to your clients (sellers) and customers (buyers) the ways property may be owned, what kind of ownership may be taken, how ownership is measured, the duration of that ownership and how much is owned.

This section answers these questions about titles and estates, with information that will be used every time you are involved in the transfer of real property.

Learning Objectives

After completing this Unit, you should be able to:

2A   identify the bundle of rights inherent in owning property.

2B   differentiate personal and real property.

2C   specify the types of estates.

2D   distinguish types of real property ownership.

2E   recall the recording process and how it safeguards ownership.

BUNDLE OF RIGHTS

When you buy property, you might think you are buying the physical item; however, what you are buying are the rights to use that property. **Property rights** are the rights someone has in something and are known collectively as the **bundle of rights**. This important package includes the right to own, possess, use, enjoy, borrow against, and dispose of real property. An owner may choose to sell or give away one of the rights and keep the rest. For example, an owner may give away the right of use for a period of time to a tenant, under a lease agreement.

Use:	The right to use property, within the law in any way, or for any purpose.
Possess:	The right to live on the property and the right to keep others out.
Transfer:	The right to sell property, give it as a gift, or dispose of it in any way permitted by law.
Encumber:	The right to borrow money and use property as security for the loan.
Enjoy:	The right to peace and quiet enjoyment without aggravation by others.

Bundle of Rights: Property rights are the rights someone has in something.
Remember the mnemonic UPTEE:
Use, Possess, Transfer, Encumber, and Enjoy.

PROPERTY

Property is anything that may be owned and gained lawfully. Property can be real or personal. Anything that is not real property is personal property.

Property can be real or personal.

Personal Property

Personal property is everything other than real property and is often referred to as movable property, personalty, or chattel. [CC §663]. Personal property can be transferred or sold using a bill of sale and may be pledged as security for a loan. Some examples of personal property include cash, negotiable instruments such as a promissory note, emblements, intangible assets, trade fixtures, cars, bank accounts, insurance policies, and patents.

Real Property

Real property is the land, anything permanently attached to the land (attachments), anything appurtenant to the land (appurtenances), and anything immovable by law. In addition to the physical real estate, real property includes the legal bundle of rights inherent in the ownership of real property. Real property is immovable and is usually transferred or sold by a deed. When real property is sold, anything that has become attached to it goes to the buyer as part of the sale unless other arrangements have been made. [CC §658].

Land

The physical component of real property is land. Land is three-dimensional because **land** includes the surface, limited quantities of airspace above the surface, and the materials and minerals beneath the surface to the center of the earth (subsurface). A good illustration of this concept is an inverted pyramid with the tip at the center of the earth and its base extending out into the sky above the property to a reasonable height.

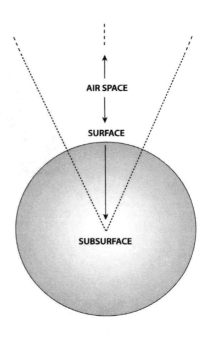

Surface Rights

The surface is the topsoil and the rights to the use of the soil. **Surface rights** include the right to build on the land, grow crops, hunt, fish, and the basic enjoyment of the land. Surface rights also include the right to drill or mine through the surface when subsurface rights are involved. **Water** on the surface, flowing in a stream or underground (**percolating**) is real property. If it is taken and bottled, then it becomes personal property.

Surface Water Rights

Surface water rights depend on whether or not the water is flowing or in a defined channel. A **defined channel** is any natural watercourse, even if it is dry. Water that overflows a defined channel is called **floodwater**. The three types of floodwater are **inundation, sheet overflow,** and **ponding.**

Certain **water rights** that go with the land are considered real property. A person's water rights do not exceed the amount reasonably needed for one's own personal use. Because of the many disputes over the use of water, the law is very clear about the rights of owners. Water cannot be owned, nor can it be channeled or dammed for the benefit of one landowner to the detriment of other property owners. Under the **correlative-rights doctrine**, an owner may take only a reasonable share of underground waters (not to exclude adjoining owners).

The owner of property bordering a stream or river has **riparian rights** (a riparian owner). Riparian property owners have reasonable use of flowing water, providing it does not injure other riparian landowners. Owners of land bordering a lake (**littoral owners**) generally own to the average low water mark or the edge of the lake. The boundary line of land touching the ocean is the ordinary **high tide mark**.

When there is a need for the government to divert water for public use, its right of appropriation is applied. **Appropriation** is the right to use water for a beneficial use by diverting surface water. Typically, beneficial uses include domestic, municipal, agricultural, mining, stock watering, recreation, wildlife, or power generation.

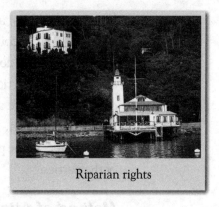

Riparian rights

Air Rights

Air rights are the rights an owner of real property has to the airspace above the property to a reasonable height. As real property, air rights can be sold, leased, or encumbered separately from the land. For example, a developer of high-rise condominiums may sell the airspace as real property.

Subsurface Rights

Subsurface rights are the rights to the natural resources, such as minerals, oil, and gas below the surface. **Minerals** are owned as real property unless they are **fugitive substances**, that is, non-solid, **migratory minerals** such as oil or gas. Oil and gas may not be owned until taken from the ground, at which time they become the personal property of whoever removed them. The rights to the minerals, oil, and gas can be sold or leased separately.

Attachments

Attatchments are items permanently attached to the land are real property and belong to the owner. These items include improvements, fixtures, and natural attachments.

Improvements

Improvements such as houses, garages, fences, swimming pools or anything resting on the land to become permanent are owned as a part of the property.

Fixtures

A **fixture** is anything that is permanently attached to real property. It also includes anything permanently attached to the fixture, such as the door to a cabinet.

Any **growing thing** attached by roots, such as trees, shrubs and flowers are real property except emblements.

Disputes about real and personal property have caused the courts to adopt a set of tests to help them decide ownership rights of disagreeing parties. The five tests to determine a fixture are method of attachment, adaptation, relationship of the parties, intent of the parties, and agreement of the parties.

Method of Attachment

How is the disputed item attached to the property? If it is permanently attached, it is real property. A chandelier wired into the electrical system makes it a fixture, or real property. It would be included in the sale of the house as something attached or affixed to the land unless the sellers specifically mentioned they wanted to take it with them.

Adaptation

Has the item been made especially for the property? For example, have the drapes been custom-made for the windows? Has the carpet been cut especially to fit the rooms? Is the stove built into the counter? If so, each has become a fixture and has lost its status as personal property.

Items permanently attached to land.

> **Five Tests of a Fixture**
> **Mnemonic = MARIA**
>
> **M**ethod of attachment
> **A**daptation
> **R**elationship of the parties
> **I**ntention
> **A**greement of the parties

Relationship of the Parties

In a dispute about fixtures, when there is no convincing evidence of the right of one party, courts will look at whether the parties are landlord-tenant, lender-borrower, or buyer-seller. The court then makes a decision based on the relationship of the parties in the case. Usually the court will favor the tenant over the landlord, the lender over the borrower, and the buyer over the seller.

Intention

If apparent, either in writing or by the actions of either party involved, this is considered to be the most important test of a fixture. Let us look at the tenant who wired special cosmetic lights into the bathroom wall, telling the landlord he intended the lights to remain his personal property. He said he would repair the wall when he moved and would take the lights with him. This was a clear case of a tenant's intention to keep the lights as his personal property. A fixture may remain personal property if all parties are informed. Intention should always be put in writing.

Agreement of the Parties

When there has been a clear agreement between the parties in a dispute about fixtures, the courts will apply this test to determine who is in the right.

> Example: Imagine that you are a prospective buyer. You walk into a house and fall in love with the chandelier hanging from the ceiling in the dining room. You make an offer to buy the house, it is accepted, and the escrow goes through smoothly. The sellers get their money and you get the deed to the house.

> When you arrive with your moving van, your anticipation turns to hostility when you discover a lonely light bulb hanging where the elegant chandelier had been. The former owners wonder why you are annoyed when you call to arrange the return of your chandelier. They tell you it is not your chandelier; it has been in the family for generations. They never intended it to go with the house.

> If you did not know the difference between real and personal property, you might think the sellers had a right to the chandelier.

Part of a real estate agent's job is to make sure all parties involved in a sale know what goes and what stays. In the above case, the listing agent should have asked the sellers if they wanted to keep the chandelier, and notified prospective buyers that it did not go with the house.

Since it was not excluded from the listing, it was reasonable for the buyer to assume it was real property. It had become a fixture and therefore should have gone with the sale. When a buyer makes an offer on a property, there is a section in the offer-to-purchase contract where he or she may request any item of real or personal property.

Exception – Trade Fixtures

Trade fixtures are items of personal property, such as shelves, commercial ovens, or room partitions that are attached to real estate by a tenant, usually used to conduct a business. Tenants retain ownership of the items as personal property when they vacate the premises, but are responsible for repairing any damage that results from replacing the trade fixtures.

Natural Attachments

Natural attachments are growing plants attached by its roots, such as trees, shrubs, and flowers. The two types of natural attachments are *fructus naturales* and *fructus industriales*.

Fructus Naturales

Fructus naturales are naturally occurring plant growth, such as grasses, trees, and shrubs and are considered part of the real property. Therefore, when a home is sold, the planted trees and landscaping are real property and go with the sale.

Fructus Industriales

Fructus industriales are annual crops produced by human labor, such as fruits, nuts, vegetables, and grains. The main difference between cultivated plants and wild plants is that cultivated plants are considered personal property even before they are harvested.

Established trees are considered immovable by law and must be sold with the property. For example, a seller may not sell the property and exclude the orange grove from the sale. The seller may have sold the oranges as personal property, but the actual orange trees are real property and may not be excluded from the sale.

Emblements are a specific type of *fructus industriales*. **Emblements** are annual crops cultivated by tenant farmers and sharecroppers. They lease the land for agricultural use. The crops are the personal property of the farmer—not the landowner. The farmer has an irrevocable license to enter the land to care for and harvest the crop.

Emblements

If a large tract of farmland is being sold, it is important to have a written agreement stating who will retain ownership of the crops that are growing in the field. The emblements rule does not apply to ornamental trees, rose bushes, or any other type of perennial growth.

Appurtenances

An **appurtenance** is anything used with the land for its benefit. Appurtenance means "belonging to" so, an appurtenance does not exist apart from the land to which it belongs. Easements and stock rights in a mutual water company are the two most common appurtenances to real property.

An **easement** is an interest owned by one person in the land of another person, such as a right-of-way across a parcel of land. The easement is appurtenant to the property.

Stock in a mutual water company is real property owned by water users who have organized to form a water company for their mutual benefit. The shares in this water company are appurtenant to the land and go with the sale of the property.

Anything Immovable by Law

Established trees are considered immovable by law and must be sold with the property. A seller may not sell the property and exclude the orange grove from the sale. The seller may sell the crop resulting from the trees as personal property, but the trees are real property and may not be excluded from the sale.

> **Review - Real Property**
> • Land
> • Attachments
> • Appurtenances
> • Anything Immovable by law

TYPES OF ESTATES

An **estate** is the ownership interest or claim a person has in real property. Ownership of the estate is measured by its duration—indefinite or definite. An estate with indefinite duration or that is measured by the length of someone's life is classified as a **freehold estate**. Whereas, an estate with a fixed or determinable duration is classified as a **nonfreehold estate**.

Types of Estates

Freehold Estates

A freehold estate is an estate of indefinite duration. This type of estate continues for an indefinite period of time and is sometimes called an estate of inheritance. The types of freehold estates are estates in fee and life estates.

Estates in Fee

An **estate in fee**, sometimes known as a **fee simple estate**, is the greatest ownership interest in real property. An estate that is unqualified, of indefinite duration, freely transferable, and inheritable. It is known as an **estate of inheritance** or a **perpetual estate** because the owner may dispose of it in his or her lifetime or after death by will. This is the most common type of estate that is transferred in a normal real estate transaction. If the property is transferred or sold with no conditions or limitations on its use, it is known as an estate in **fee simple absolute**.

A property owner may impose qualifications, conditions, or restrictions when transferring title to property. Property restrictions are created by deed or written agreement. If a seller imposes qualifications or conditions that the buyer must do or not do, this is known as a **fee simple subject to condition subsequent**.

Since 1983, a **fee simple subject to condition subsequent** is any fee estate containing a condition that if violated, could lead to the termination of the estate and give the grantor a right of entry. [C.C. §885.020]. Language in a fee simple subject to condition subsequent will describe some condition and, if that condition occurs, the grantor can exercise a right of entry. These conditions typically have words like "until," "unless," "but if" in the condition, so that its occurrence is more clearly a specific event that triggers the right of entry.

With a fee simple subject to a **condition subsequent**, there is something that the owner must not do. If the owner breaks the condition, the property will go back to the former owner.

> Example: A seller may require the property to be used for a specified purpose such as a church or a rehabilitation center. The owner sells the property with the condition that this requirement be met. If the buyer breaches this condition subsequent after the sale, the seller may take possession of the property and regain title.

Life Estates

A **life estate** is one that is limited in duration of a measuring life. The **measuring life** is usually the grantee's life—but it does not have to be. It can even be created on the life of a designated person who has no interest in the property as the measuring life—known as **pur autre vie**, meaning for another's life.

The holder of a life estate is known as the **life tenant**. Since a life estate is a type of freehold estate, the life tenant has all the rights that go with fee ownership except disposing of the estate by will. Life estate holders must pay the taxes and maintain the property. They may collect all rents and keep all profits for the duration of the life estate. They may encumber the property or dispose of it in any way except by will. Any interest the life estate holders may create in the property—extending beyond the life of the person used to measure the estate—will become invalid when that designated person dies.

Remember, the life estate is tied to a designated life, and when that party dies, the estate goes to either the person in reversion or the person in remainder, or their heirs.

Estate in Reversion

Amy grants Bob a life estate with the provision that upon Bob's death, the property reverts to Amy. Bob is then the life tenant and the designated party on whom the life estate is based. Amy holds an estate in reversion.

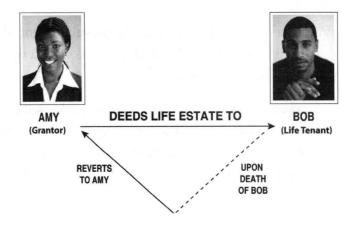

AMY
(Grantor)

DEEDS LIFE ESTATE TO

BOB
(Life Tenant)

REVERTS
TO AMY

UPON
DEATH
OF BOB

Reserving a Life Estate

An elderly couple sells their property to a developer reserving the right to live on the property until their death when the developer will be able to take possession of the property. This is called reserving a life estate.

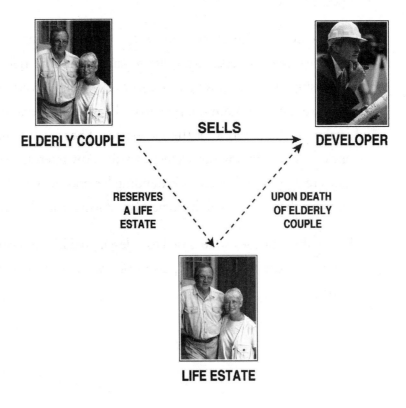

ELDERLY COUPLE

SELLS

DEVELOPER

RESERVES
A LIFE
ESTATE

UPON DEATH
OF ELDERLY
COUPLE

LIFE ESTATE

Pur Autre Vie

Tom grants a life estate to Susan for the life of Elizabeth, with the provision that it goes to Laura when Elizabeth dies. Susan may enjoy the benefits of the life estate as long as Elizabeth is alive. Upon Elizabeth's death, the estate goes to Laura or her heirs.

Estate in Remainder

Instead of keeping a reversionary interest, the grantor can instead identify someone to receive the property when the life tenant dies. That interest is known as a remainder and the person identified in the instrument creating the interest is known as the **remainderman**. A **remainder** is a future interest that takes effect upon the expiration of a life estate when the life tenant dies.

Greg grants a life estate to Linda, with the provision that upon Linda's death, the property goes to a third party, Charles. The interest that Charles holds is known as an estate in remainder.

Nonfreehold Estates

A **nonfreehold estate** is a tenant's possessory estate in land or premises. The nonfreehold estate (also called a **less-than-freehold estate** or leasehold) is owned by renters or tenants. Leaseholds are also called **chattels real** because the lease is personal property (chattel) that concerns real property (real). Remember, anything movable becomes personal property. The **lease** is a movable document describing the temporary possession and use of the property, and thus is personal property. The owner of the leasehold (tenant) has exclusive possession and use of real property for a fixed amount of time. This includes the right to the use and quiet enjoyment of the premises during the term of the lease. They have the right to the exclusive use of the rented property, and to live quietly without privacy invasion.

Types of Leasehold Interests

A leasehold interest in real estate and its duration is known as a **tenancy**. The types of tenancy are tenancy for years, periodic tenancy, tenancy at will, and tenancy at sufferance.

Tenancy for Years

A **tenancy for years** is for a fixed term and definite end date. It does not have to be for only a year, but if a definite end date is stated, it nevertheless is known as a tenancy for years. The lease of office space or a commercial center is commonly a tenancy for years. It is not automatically renewable and does not require notice to quit at the end of the lease (must be renegotiated). It is a less-than-freehold estate.

When an apartment lease mentions an end date, it is considered a tenancy for years. Increasingly, owners of residential income property (apartment buildings) are using this type of an agreement to guarantee that a tenant will stay, at least until the lease expires. The benefit of a tenancy for years to the landlord is that a desirable, long-term tenant may be attracted to the apartment or house. The benefit to the tenant is the assurance that the rent will remain the same over the period of the lease. At the expiration of the lease, terms must be mutually renegotiated.

Periodic Tenancy

A **periodic tenancy** (estate from period-to-period) refers to a leasehold interest that is for an indefinite period of time—usually month to month. This month-to-month tenancy requires 30-days notice to quit. It automatically renews itself unless terminated by landlord or tenant.

Tenancy at Will

A **tenancy at will** is created when a tenant obtains possession of the property with the owner's permission, but without a rental agreement. The tenancy may be ended by the unilateral decision of either party. There is no agreed-upon termination date; however, and either party must give 30-days notice before ending the tenancy.

Tenancy at Sufferance

A **tenancy at sufferance** is often referred to as a **holdover tenancy**. It occurs when the tenant originally obtained possession lawfully, but the tenant's right to remain has expired (as when a lease ends and there is no agreement for an extension or the conversion of that lease to a month-to-month tenancy). If the tenant does not leave, the owner must commence eviction proceedings to remove the tenant.

OWNERSHIP OF REAL PROPERTY

Ownership of land in California began with Spanish explorers who claimed it for the king of Spain in the early 16th century. Since the king technically owned everything, all land was granted to private parties by the military representatives of Spanish rule. Ownership and transfer of land and property rights were determined by local authorities operating under a strict set of civil laws that were given to them by the Spanish king.

This continued until 1822, when Mexico began colonizing California and took over governing the territory. In 1848, the **Treaty of Guadalupe Hidalgo** ended the war with Mexico, and California became a possession of the United States. Land claims that had been granted by Mexico were honored, and confirmed with **patents** to the land, by the U.S. government, to those with proven ownership. Even though Spain or Mexico granted ownership, according to the Roman Civil Law they followed, the laws changed after California became a state in 1850. England's Common Law principles now governs how title to real property is held (**title vesting**).

The title vesting appears on the grant deed and the deed of trust. The manner in which a person holds title may have significant legal and tax consequences. **Title** is the evidence that the owner of land is in lawful possession. It is the proof of ownership, such as a grant deed. Separate ownership and concurrent ownership are the two ways a person or other entity can take title to or own real estate.

Separate Ownership

Separate ownership means ownership by one person or one entity, such as a city or corporation. Property owned by one person or entity is known as sole and separate, or **ownership in severalty**. With separate ownership, the ownership rights are severed from everyone else. A corporation is known to hold title in severalty, because it is a sole entity.

Ownership by one entity (ABC Company) or one person.

Concurrent Ownership

When property is owned by two or more persons or entities at the same time, it is known as **concurrent ownership**, or co-ownership. The title is held jointly and severally. Concurrent ownership has several forms, such as joint tenancy, tenancy in common, community property, and tenancy in partnership. **Tenancy** also refers to a mode or method of ownership or holding title to property.

> **Four Types of Concurrent Ownership**
> 1. Tenancy in common
> 2. Joint tenancy
> 3. Community property
> 4. Tenancy in partnership

Tenancy in Common

When two or more persons, whose interests are not necessarily equal, are owners of **undivided interests** in a single estate, a **tenancy in common** exists. Co-owners take title as a tenancy in common unless some other form of ownership or vesting is mentioned specifically in the deed.

The only requirement of **unity** (equality) for tenants in common is the equal right of possession or undivided interest, as it is called. **Undivided interest** means that each owner has a certain equitable interest in the property (such as one-half interest, or one-fourth interest), but has the right to use the whole property. None of the owners may exclude any co-owner from the property, nor claim any portion of the property for exclusive use.

> ### The Four Characteristics of Tenants in Common
> 1. Tenants in common may take title at different times.
> 2. Tenants in common may take title on separate deeds.
> 3. Tenants in common may have unequal interests.
> 4. Tenants in common have an undivided interest or equal right of possession (one unity).

Any tenant in common may sell, encumber, or will his or her interest, with heirs simply becoming a tenant in common among the others. One tenant in common cannot create an easement on the property without the consent of the other co-owners. A tenant in common must pay a proportionate share of any expenses incurred on the property, including money spent for repairs, taxes, loan payments, and insurance.

This is an example of tenancy in common—have equal possession.

When tenants in common do not agree on matters pertaining to the property, any of the co-owners may file a **partition action** asking the court to decide the fate of the investment.

Joint Tenancy

When two or more parties own real property as co-owners, with the right of survivorship, it is called **joint tenancy**. The **right of survivorship** means that if one of the joint tenants dies, the surviving joint tenant automatically becomes sole owner of the property.

The share of the deceased does not go to his or her estate or heirs, but becomes the property of the co-tenant without becoming involved in probate. Also, the surviving joint tenant is not liable to creditors of the deceased who hold liens on the joint tenancy property.

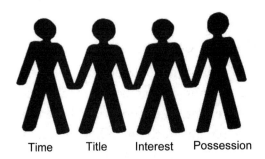

Time   Title   Interest   Possession

This is an example of joint tenancy.

In order to have a joint tenancy, the four unities—time, title, interest, and possession—must exist. If any one of the unities is missing, a tenancy in common is created.

The Four Unities of Joint Tenancy
Mnemonic = T-Tip

Time	become joint tenants at the same time.
Title	take title on the same deed.
Interest	have an equal undivided interest in the property.
Possession	have equal right of possession.

All four items must occur to have a joint tenancy. Co-owners may sell their interest, give it away, or borrow money against it, without consent of the other joint tenants. A joint tenant may sever his or her interest in the joint tenancy by selling it. The new co-owner would become a tenant in common with the remaining joint tenants. The joint tenancy is not severed (broken) if a lien is put against the interest of one of the co-owners. However, a foreclosure on the lien would sever that interest from the joint tenancy.

Example: Stacey, Ken, Catherine, and Dan are joint tenants. Dan sells his interest to Eva. The joint tenancy has been broken regarding the interest Dan had in the property. The new vesting, after the sale of Dan's interest, is Stacey, Ken, and Catherine as joint tenants with equal interests, and the right of survivorship, with Eva as a tenant in common.

Stacey, Ken, Catherine, and Eva, in the above property, wish to restore a joint tenancy with each of the four having the right of survivorship. Eva holds a tenancy in common, so she will have to be added to the joint tenancy. Since all joint tenants must take title at the same time, on the same document, Stacey, Ken, Catherine, and Eva must sign a new deed that lists Stacey, Ken, Catherine, and Eva as joint tenants. Then the property can be deeded to all four parties as joint tenants. All requirements for a joint tenancy—time, title, interest, and possession—will then be fulfilled.

Due to the right of survivorship, a joint tenant may not will his or her share. Joint tenancy is terminated when any one of the four unities ends, such as by sale, gift, or by mutual agreement.

> Example: Audrey, Bob, Carol, and David are joint tenants. David dies and his interest automatically goes to Audrey, Bob and Carol as joint tenants with equal one-third interests.

> Example: Kelly and Roger own a house as joint tenants. Roger dies and Kelly now owns the house as her sole and separate property without probate. Roger's heirs are not entitled to his share because of the right of survivorship. If Kelly wishes to convey title after Roger's death, she will need to record an affidavit of "Death of Joint Tenant" and then record a new deed removing Roger from title. This would allow her to convey the title to the property without Roger.

Community Property

All property acquired by a husband and wife during a valid marriage—except for certain separate property—is called **community property**. Community property excludes property acquired before marriage or during marriage by gift or inheritance. Any income, including wages from either spouse, is considered community property, unless it is income derived from separate property.

Interest is equal (50/50) in community property.

Property Excluded from Community Property Treatment

- Property owned before marriage.
- Property acquired by either of the parties during marriage by gift or inheritance.
- Income derived from separate property.

Community property has one unity—equal interest, with each spouse owning 50%. The one similarity between community property and joint tenancy is the unity of equal interests.

In 2001, California enacted a law allowing a husband and wife to hold title to their property as **community property with right of survivorship**. Holding title as community property provides a stepped-up tax basis for both halves of the property upon the death of the first spouse. Holding title as joint tenants provides for the immediate and automatic transfer of title to the surviving spouse upon the death of the first spouse. This new form of holding title combines the desirable tax features of community property with the right of survivorship of joint tenancy.

If spouses want to maintain the status of their separate property, they must be very careful not to commingle it with their community property. For example, if community property funds are used to offset the negative cash flow of an apartment building that is separate property, the apartment building will become community property.

Community property cannot be sold or encumbered by only one of the partners. Either spouse may lease community property for up to one year or may sign a listing agreement to put a property on the market. Although a listing agreement signed by the husband or wife is enforceable, both must accept and sign any contract to sell the community property (deposit receipt). Either spouse may buy real or personal property without the consent of the other; both are bound by the contract made by either one, unless the new property is bought specifically as separate property with funds from a separate property account.

A married couple in California has three choices when it comes to how they may take title. However, unless otherwise stated, title is presumed community property.

> The first is joint tenancy, which includes the right of survivorship if one of the spouses dies, which may also include a tax liability for the surviving spouse.

> The second is community property, which does not include the right of survivorship, but includes probate after a spouse dies and all the costs involved in that process.

> The third type of vesting is community property with the right of survivorship, which includes the better of the first two types of vesting. There is no particular tax liability because of the death of a spouse and there is no probate with its seemingly endless costs.

When title is taken simply as community property, either party may will one-half of the community property. When vesting is community property, if there is no will, the surviving spouse inherits all community property by **intestate succession**. This is important to know, particularly with multiple marriages, for estate planning. Property may be owned with the intention that it go to one's children, only to learn after the parent's death that children of the first marriage are no longer natural heirs. If there is a subsequent husband or wife and no will has been made, the new spouse will become the natural heir to any property owned or community property.

Regarding separate property, if there is no will, the surviving spouse gets one-half and one child gets one-half. If there is more than one child, the surviving spouse gets one-third and the children get two-thirds.

Do All States Recognize Community Property Law?

Nine states—Arizona, California, Idaho, Louisiana, Nevada, New Mexico, Texas, Washington, and Wisconsin—use the community property system to determine the interest of a husband and wife in property acquired during marriage. If you now live or previously lived in one of these states, you should be aware that some special rules apply to community property. Any property you may have acquired while living in one of these nine states is probably community property even today.

Tenancy in Partnership

Ownership by two or more persons who form a partnership for business purposes is known as **tenancy in partnership**. The rights of each of the partners are subject to a partnership agreement and are described therein.

RECORDING SAFEGUARDS OWNERSHIP

Recording allows (rather than requires) documents that affect title to real property to be filed. Whenever an interest in real property is transferred voluntarily or involuntarily, the new owner should record the transfer instrument to protect his or her legal interests.

The Recording Act of California provides that, after acknowledgment, any instrument or **abstract of judgment** affecting the title to—or possession of—real property may be recorded. **Acknowledgment** is a formal declaration before a notary public or certain public officials, by the person (grantor) who signed (executed) the instrument (deed) that he or she in fact did execute (sign) the document.

A **notary public** (notary) is a licensed public officer who takes or witnesses the acknowledgment. A notary cannot acknowledge any document in which the notary is named a principal. A notary who is an employee of a corporation may notarize a deed involving the corporation so long as he or she does not have a personal interest in the subject matter of the transaction.

Acknowledgment acts as a safeguard against forgery and once acknowledged, a document is accepted as **prima facie** (on its face) evidence in court.

A deed must be acknowledged to be recorded. Recording allows (rather than requires) documents affecting title to real property to be filed.

Recording Process

The process consists of copying the instrument to be recorded in the proper index, and filing it in alphabetical order, under the names of the parties, immediately. To be valid, documents must be recorded by the county recorder in the county within which the property is located.

When the recorder receives a document to be filed, he or she notes the time and date of filing and at whose request it was filed. After the contents of the document are copied into the record, the original document is marked "filed for record", stamped with the proper time and date of recording, and returned to the person who requested the recording.

Constructive Notice

Recording a document as well as possession of the property give **constructive notice** of an interest in real property. Recording gives public notice (constructive notice) of the content of any instrument recorded to anyone who cares to look into the records. Possession is also considered constructive notice. Even the act of taking possession of an unrecorded deed gives constructive notice. A buyer should always check that no one is living on the property who might have a prior claim to ownership. It is the buyer's duty to conduct proper inquiry before purchasing any property. Failure to do so does not relieve the buyer of that responsibility.

> Example: Ann bought a property through her broker, sight unseen. The escrow closed and the deed was recorded. When Ann tried to move into her new home; however, she found George living there. He told her that he bought the property one year ago but had not bothered to record the deed. He then moved in and considered it his home. When she consulted her attorney, Ann found that indeed George—because he was in possession of the property—had given notice to anyone who might inquire. Therefore, George does have legal title because of his possession of the property.

Actual Notice

If a person has direct, express information about the ownership interest of a property, it is called **actual notice**. Actual notice is a fact, such as seeing the grant deed or knowing that a person inherited a property by will.

Priorities in Recording

As we have seen, recording laws are meant to protect citizens against fraud and to give others notification of property ownership. The first valid deed that is recorded determines the owner, unless that person, prior to recording, had either actual or constructive notice of the rights of others. Other information that might influence ownership can be recorded also, such as liens and other encumbrances. **Priority** means the order in which deeds are recorded. Whether it is a grant deed, trust deed or some other evidence of a lien or encumbrance, the priority is determined by the date stamped in the upper right-hand corner of the document by the county recorder. To obtain priority through recording, a buyer must be a good faith purchaser, for a valuable consideration, and record the deed first.

If several grant deeds are recorded against the property, the one recorded first is valid. If several trust deeds are recorded against a property, no mention will be made about which one is the first trust deed, which is the second, and so forth. A person inquiring about the priority of the deeds should look at the time and date the deed was recorded for that information. You will see, as we proceed in our study, the importance of the date and time of recording.

There are certain instruments not affected by the priority of recording rule. Certain liens, such as tax liens and mechanic's liens, take priority even though they are recorded after a deed.

SUMMARY

The **bundle of rights** is an ownership understanding that describes all the legal rights attached to real property. **Property** is anything lawfully owned and is either real or personal. Real property is immovable; personal property is movable. **Personal property** is everything other than real property. **Real property** is the land, anything attached to land, anything appurtenant to the land, or anything lawfully immovable that is transferred or sold with a deed.

An **estate** is the ownership interest or claim a person has in real property. There are two types of estates: **freehold estates** and **nonfreehold estates**.

An individual or other legal entity can own property under **separate ownership** or **concurrent ownership**. The types of concurrent ownership include tenancy in common, joint tenancy, community property, and tenancy in partnership.

UNIT 2 REVIEW

Matching Exercise

Instructions: Write the letter of the matching term on the blank line before its definition. Answers immediately follow the Multiple Choice Questions.

Terms

A. acknowledgment
B. appurtenance
C. bundle of rights
D. chattel
E. constructive notice
F. easement
G. emblements
H. estate
I. estate in fee

J. fee simple absolute
K. fee simple qualified
L. fixture
M. freehold estate
N. less-than-freehold estate
O. life estate
P. littoral
Q. patents

R. personal property
S. prescription
T. quiet enjoyment
U. real property
V. riparian rights
W. severalty
X. title
Y. trade fixture

Definitions

1. _____ A formal declaration to a public official (notary) by a person who has signed an instrument that states that the signing was voluntary.

2. _____ Those rights and improvements that belong to and pass with the transfer of real property but are not necessarily a part of the actual property.

3. _____ An ownership concept describing all the legal rights that attach to the ownership of real property.

4. _____ Interest owned by one person in the land of another person.

5. _____ A legal interest in land; defines the nature, degree, extent, and duration of a person's ownership in land.

6. _____ Personal property affixed to leased property by the tenant for business purposes that may be removed by tenant upon termination of the lease.

7. _____ The rights of a landowner whose land is next to a natural watercourse to reasonable use of whatever water flows past the property.

8. _____ An estate in real property which continues for an indefinite period of time.

9. _____ Annual crops produced for sale by tenant farmers.

10. _____ Anything movable that is not real property.

11. _____ Land bordering a lake, ocean, or sea.

12. _____ Personal property that has become affixed to real estate.

13. _____ Land, anything affixed to the land, anything appurtenant to the land, anything immovable by law.

14. _____ Ownership of real property by one person or entity.

15. _____ Personal property.

16. _____ A leasehold estate; considered to exist for a definite period of time or successive periods of time until termination.

17. _____ An estate that is limited in duration to the life of its owner or the life of some other chosen person.

18. _____ Evidence of land ownership.

19. _____ Notice given by recording a document or taking possession of the property.

20. _____ The right to peace without aggravation by others.

▢ Multiple Choice Questions

Instructions: Circle your response and then check your response with the Answer Key that immediately follows the Multiple Choice Questions.

1. In a technical sense, the term "property" refers to:
   a. rights or interests in the thing owned.
   b. a freehold estate.
   c. personal property only.
   d. land and buildings only.

2. Why do disputes arise regarding ownership of personal property?
   a. Personal property can be pledged.
   b. Personal property can be alienated.
   c. Personal property can be hypothecated.
   d. Personal property can become real property.

3. Which of the following is considered real property?
    a. Timber
    b. Airspace above the land
    c. Unharvested crops under a prior sales contract
    d. Landfill soil being hauled

4. Which of the following is considered personal property?
    a. Minerals
    b. Leases
    c. All improvements to land
    d. Trees growing in a natural forest

5. A running stream is considered:
    a. personal property.
    b. real property.
    c. a fixture.
    d. a chattel.

6. Which of the following statements concerning riparian rights is NOT correct?
    a. Riparian property owners have reasonable use of flowing water.
    b. The owner of property bordering a stream or river has riparian rights.
    c. Riparian property owners own the water and may use as much as they want.
    d. The owner of adjacent land may not lawfully divert all available water and thereby deprive a riparian owner of water.

7. Which of the following is considered personal property?
    a. An easement
    b. Minerals
    c. Trees growing in a forest
    d. An existing mortgage

8. Which of the following is considered appurtenant to land?
    a. Something acquired by legal right and used with the land for its benefit
    b. A right-of-way over another's adjoining land
    c. Stock in a mutual water company
    d. All of the above

9. Of the following, which is not one of five general tests of a fixture?

    a. Method of attachment

    b. Time of attachment

    c. Adaptability of the item

    d. Intention of the parties

10. Which of the following is considered real property?

    a. Bearing wall in a single-family residence

    b. Grape crop that is governed by a sales contract

    c. Trade fixtures installed by a tenant that are removable without damage

    d. Built-in stove in a mobile home with no permanent foundation

11. "Of indefinite duration" is a phrase that describes an:

    a. tenancy for years.

    b. periodic tenancy.

    c. estate of inheritance.

    d. less-than-freehold estate.

12. John conveys a portion of his fee estate to Fred that is for a term less than his own, John's own interest would be:

    a. remainder.

    b. reversion.

    c. vested sufferance.

    d. fee defeasible.

13. Which of the following is a nonfreehold estate?

    a. Life estate

    b. Estate of inheritance

    c. Tenancy for years

    d. Estate in remainder

14. David left his son 2/3 interest and left his son's wife 1/3 interest in real property jointly and without the right of survivorship. They will take title as:

    a. community property.

    b. joint tenancy.

    c. tenancy in common.

    d. severalty.

15. Ownership in severalty would most likely involve:
    a. a fee simple defeasible estate.
    b. tenancy in common.
    c. ownership with other parties.
    d. sole ownership.

16. Baker, Cook, and Turner own equal interests in a parcel of land as tenants in common. Without the consent of the others, Turner leased the entire parcel to Hunter for agricultural purposes. Such a lease would be:
    a. valid and binding for all three co-tenants.
    b. invalid because land owned by multiple owners may not be leased.
    c. valid, provided that the term did not exceed 51 years.
    d. valid, but Hunter takes the property subject to Baker and Cooks right to share in the enjoyment and possession of the property.

17. The words "time, title, interest, and possession" are most closely related to:
    a. severalty.
    b. survivorship.
    c. sole ownership.
    d. adverse possession.

18. How are a joint tenancy interest and a community property interest alike?
    a. Ownership interests are equal
    b. Only a husband and wife are involved
    c. Both owners must join in any conveyance
    d. Both provide the right of survivorship

19. Chris, Bell, and Lyn took title to a property as joint tenants. Chris sold her share to Pat, and then Bell died. Who owns the property now?
    a. Lyn owns 2/3 and Pat owns 1/3 as tenants in common.
    b. Lyn, Pat, and Bell's heirs own the property 1/3 each as joint tenants.
    c. Lyn owns 2/3 and Pat owns 1/3 as joint tenants.
    d. Lyn, Pat, and Bells's heirs own the property 1/3 each as tenants-in-common.

20. A contract to sell community real property made by one spouse only is:
    a. valid.
    b. illegal.
    c. enforceable.
    d. unenforceable.

UNIT 2 ANSWER KEY

Answers – Matching

1. A	5. H	9. G	13. U	17. O
2. B	6. Y	10. R	14. W	18. X
3. C	7. V	11. P	15. D	19. E
4. F	8. M	12. L	16. N	20. T

Answers – Multiple Choice

1. **(a)** Property refers to the bundle (collection) of rights a person has in the thing owned. [Bundle of Rights]

2. **(d)** Personal property becomes real property if it is permanently affixed to land or improvements. [Property]

3. **(b)** Land includes the surface, the space above, and the space beneath for an indefinite distance. Timber, crops, and landfill soil are movable personal property. [Property]

4. **(b)** A lease, also known as a leasehold estate, is a personal property estate of a tenant. [Property]

5. **(b)** Water on the surface, flowing in a stream or underground (percolating) is real property. If it is taken and bottled, then it becomes personal. [Property]

6. **(c)** The owner of property bordering a stream or river has riparian rights (a riparian owner). Riparian property owners have reasonable use of flowing water, providing it does not injure other riparian landowners. Riparian rights have been ruled in court to be real property. Such rights, like most others, are not immune from actions such as prescription and condemnation. [Property]

7. **(d)** Easements, mineral rights, and trees are all real property. [Property]

8. **(d)** An appurtenance is anything used with the land for its benefit, such as easements and stock in a mutual water company [Property]

9. **(b)** In addition to (a), (c), and (d), the other two general tests are the relationship between the parties and an agreement between the parties. [Property]

10. **(a)** Crops that are intended to be harvested and trade fixtures are personal property. A mobilehome not attached to a foundation, including its contents, is considered personal property. [Property]

11. **(c)** Freehold estates are real property estates of ownership. This type of estate continues for an indefinite period and is sometimes called an estate of inheritance. [Types of Estates]

12. **(b)**   The rights of possession and use would return to John, so John has a reversionary interest. A remainder interest would be one that goes to a third party. [Types of Estates]

13. **(c)**   A tenancy for years is one of the four types of nonfreehold estates. Choices (a), (b), and (d) are freehold estates. [Types of Estates]

14. **(c)**   The unequal interests disallow community property or joint tenancy. Severalty is ownership by an individual.   [Types of Estates]

15. **(d)**   Property owned by one person or entity is known as sole and separate, or ownership in severalty.. [Ownership of Real Property]

16. **(d)**   Each tenant-in-common has the right to use the entire property. Therefore, Turner cannot give exclusive possession to Hunter because the other tenants in common did not agree to or sign the lease. Tenants in common are free to sell, convey (sell or lease), or mortgage their own interest. [Ownership of Real Property]

17. **(b)**   These are four unities of a joint tenancy. If formed properly, a joint tenancy creates a right of survivorship. [Ownership of Real Property]

18. **(a)**   A joint tenancy requires equal interests. Community property ownership is also an equal 50/50 interest. [Ownership of Real Property]

19. **(a)**   A person may sell a joint tenancy interest, but may not will it. When Chris sold her interest to Pat, Pat became a tenant in common. Bell and Lyn remained as joint tenants. When Bell died, Bell's third was automatically conveyed to Lyn, So Lyn ends up owning 2/3 and Pat 1/3—both as tenants in common. [Ownership of Real Property]

20. **(d)**   A contract to sell community real property must be signed by both spouses. If it is signed by only one, the contract cannot be enforced. [Ownership of Real Property]

Unit 3

INTRODUCTION

You need an organized system for keeping track of property ownership to determine who owns what, and how ownership can be transferred. Of course, the system, which serves you as a real estate agent and a consumer, must be completely reliable.

In this Unit, you will learn the methods and types of deeds that are used to transfer ownership of real property from one person to another.

Learning Objectives

After completing this Unit, you should be able to:

3A   identify types of encumbrances.

3B   determine how title to real estate is acquired or conveyed.

ENCUMBRANCES: LIMITATIONS ON REAL PROPERTY

An **encumbrance** is a non-possessory interest in real property that is held by someone who is not the owner. Anything that burdens or affects the title or the use of the property is an encumbrance. A property is encumbered when it is burdened with legal obligations against the title. Most buyers purchase encumbered property.

Encumbrances fall into two categories: those that affect the title, known as **financial encumbrances**, and those that affect the use of the property, known as **non-financial encumbrances**. Common types of financial encumbrances are trust deeds and mortgages, mechanic's liens, tax liens, special assessments, attachments, and recorded abstracts of judgment. The types of encumbrances that affect the physical use of property are easements, building restrictions, and zoning requirements and encroachments.

Financial Encumbrances

The financial encumbrances that create a legal obligation to pay are known as liens. A lien uses real property as security for the payment of a debt.

A **lien** is an obligation to pay a financial encumbrance that may be voluntary or involuntary. An owner may choose to borrow money, using the property as security for the loan, creating a **voluntary lien**. A voluntary lien does not have to be recorded.

Typical voluntary liens include trust deeds and mortgages. On the other hand, if the owner does not pay taxes or the debt owed, a lien may be placed against his or her property without permission, creating an **involuntary lien**. Typical involuntary liens include mechanic's liens, recorded abstracts of judgment, tax liens, and attachments.

A lien may be specific or general. A **specific lien** is one that is placed against a certain property, such as a mechanic's lien, trust deed, attachment, property tax lien, and lis pendens. A **general lien** affects all property of the owner, such as a judgment lien or federal or state income tax liens.

> **All liens are encumbrances but not all encumbrances are liens.**

Trust Deeds and Mortgages

Trust deeds and mortgages are both instruments used in real estate financing to create voluntary, specific liens against real property.

Mechanic's Lien

A **mechanic's lien** may be placed against a property by anyone who supplies labor, services, or materials used for improvements on real property and who did not receive payment for the improvements. Therefore, a contractor, a subcontractor, a laborer on a job, any person who furnishes materials, such as lumber, plumbing or roofing, or anyone who furnishes services, such as an architect, engineer, teamster, or equipment lessor is eligible to file a mechanic's lien.

A mechanic's lien must be verified and recorded. The law is very time specific about the recording. The statutory procedure must be followed exactly if the mechanic's lien is to be valid. The four steps to be taken include: (1) the preliminary notice, (2) the notice of completion, (3) no notice of completion, and (4) foreclosure action.

1. **Preliminary Notice:** A preliminary notice is a written notice that must be given to the owner within 20 days of first furnishing labor or materials for a job by anyone eligible to file a mechanic's lien. This document gives owners notice that their property may have a lien placed on it if they do not pay for work completed.

2. **Notice of Completion:** If the owner records a notice of completion within 10 days after the project is finished, the original contractors have 60 days after the notice is filed, and all others have 30 days after the notice is filed, to record a mechanic's lien.

3. **No Notice of Completion**: If the owner does not record a notice of completion when work is finished, all claimants have a maximum of 90 days from the day work was finished to record a mechanic's lien.

4. **Foreclosure Action**: After a mechanic's lien is recorded, the claimant has 90 days to bring foreclosure action to enforce the lien. If he or she does not bring action, the lien will be terminated and the claimant loses the right to foreclose.

If an owner discovers unauthorized work on the property, he or she must file a **notice of non-responsibility**. This is a notice that must be recorded and posted on the property to be valid, stating the owner is not responsible for work being done. This notice releases the owner from the liability for work done without permission. The owner must record this notice within 10 days after discovering the unauthorized work. The notice normally is posted with a commercial lease at the beginning of a job, if a tenant is ordering the job.

Mechanic's Lien Time Line

Here are the major events to be followed, in a timely manner, whenever improvement of real property is done.
1. Work Commences
2. Preliminary 20-Day Notice
3. Work Completed
4. Notice of Completion Recorded
5. Lien Recorded
6. Foreclosure Action and Lis Pendens Recorded
7. Service of Process
8. Court Decision
    a) Judgment
    b) Release of Lien
    c) Dismissed
    d) Foreclosure

Determining the starting date for a mechanic's lien is very important. Mechanic's liens have priority as of the date work began or materials were first furnished for the job. A mechanic's lien has priority over any other liens filed after the commencement of labor or delivery of materials with the exception of government liens (taxes and special assessments). That means if there is a foreclosure action, the mechanic's lien would be paid before any other liens that were recorded after work started on the job.

That includes trust deeds or mortgages recorded prior to the filing of the mechanic's lien, but after the start of the work. Lenders will make a physical inspection of the property to determine that no materials have been delivered and no work has been done before recording a construction loan to assure the priority of their trust deed or mortgage.

In the following example, the mechanic's lien has the priority:

Mechanic's Lien has Priority over Trust Deed
1. Start of work June 15
2. Trust Deed recorded June 18
3. Notice of completion Sept 1
4. Mechanic's Lien recorded September 28

Tax Liens and Special Assessments

If any government taxes, such as income or property taxes are not paid, they become a **tax lien** against the property. **Special assessments** are levied against property owners to pay for local improvements, such as underground utilities, street repair, or water projects. Payment for the projects is secured by a special assessment, which becomes a lien against real property. Property taxes and special assessments are specific liens, whereas other government taxes are general liens.

Lis Pendens

A **lis pendens** (also called a pendency of action) is a recorded notice that indicates pending litigation affecting the title on a property. It clouds the title and gives notice to prospective lenders or buyers that title to the property is disputed. It also does not actually prevent anyone from buying the property, but it warns parties that they could be involved in a lawsuit if they do.

Attachments and Judgments

An **attachment lien** or writ of attachment is the process by which the court holds the real or personal property of a defendant as security for a possible judgment pending the outcome of a lawsuit. An attachment lien is an involuntary, specific lien that is valid for three years. It does not terminate upon death and it may be extended in certain cases.

A **judgment** is the final determination of the rights of parties in a lawsuit by the court. A judgment does not automatically create a lien. A summary of the court decision, known as an **abstract of judgment**, must be recorded with the county recorder. When the abstract of judgment is recorded, it is a general lien on all non-exempt property owned or acquired by the judgment debtor for 10 years, in the county in which the abstract is filed. The court may force the sale of the property to satisfy the judgment by issuing a **writ of execution**. The sale is called an **execution sale**.

Non-Financial Encumbrances

A non-finacial encumbrance is one that affects the use of property, such as an easement, a building restriction, an encroachment, or a lease.

Easements

An **easement** is the right to enter or use someone else's land for a specified purpose. An interest in an easement is non-possessory. That means the holder of an easement can use it only for the purpose intended and may not exclude anyone else from using it. The right to enter onto a property using an easement is called **ingress** (enter). The right to exit from a property using an easement is called **egress** (exit).

Classification of Easements

There are two kinds of easements—appurtenant easements and easements in gross.

Appurtenant Easement

As you recall, an appurtenance is anything used for the benefit of the land. An easement appurtenant has a servient and a dominant tenement. The owner whose land is being used is the one giving the easement and the land is the **servient tenement**. The servient tenement is the one encumbered by the easement. The person's land receiving the benefit of the easement is known as the **dominant tenement**.

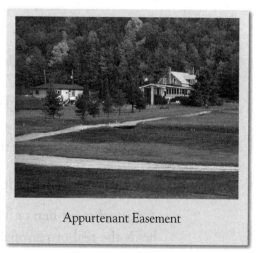

Appurtenant Easement

An easement appurtenant automatically goes with the sale of the dominant tenement. To be valid, the dominant and servient tenements of an appurtenant easement do not have to be mentioned in the deed (*unlocated*), nor do they have to touch each other (abut).

Easement in Gross

Since an unlocated easement is valid, it is possible to have an easement that is not appurtenant to any particular land. Thus, Joe, who owns no land, may have an easement over Sam's land for the purpose of getting to the stream where he regularly fishes. The easement for the path to cross the land does not need to specify where the path is actually located. A commercial camping enterprise may use an easement over private property to take clients to remote sites, which may otherwise be inaccessible.

Public utilities also have easements that are not appurtenant to any one parcel. These easements are known as **easements in gross**, and only have a servient tenement (no dominant tenement). Easements in gross are the most common type of easement.

Make sure you understand the difference between an easement in gross and a license. An easement may not be terminated arbitrarily, as you will see in the following section. A **license** is permission to use property. However, a license to use may be revoked at any time.

Creating Easements

Easements are created in various ways—commonly by express grant or reservation in a grant deed or by a written agreement between owners of adjoining land. An easement always should be recorded to assure its continued existence. It is recorded by the party benefiting from the easement as the dominant tenement.

Express Grant

The servient tenement, or the giver of the easement, grants the easement by deed or express agreement.

Express Reservation

The seller of a parcel who owns adjoining land reserves an easement or right-of-way over the former property. It is created at the time of the sale with a deed or express agreement.

Implied Grant or Reservation

The existence of an easement is obvious and necessary at the time a property is conveyed, even though no mention is made of it in the deed.

Necessity

An **easement by necessity** is created when a parcel is completely land locked and has no access. It is automatically terminated when another way to enter and leave the property becomes available.

Prescription

Prescription is the process of acquiring an interest, not ownership, in a certain property.

An **easement by prescription** may be created by continuous and uninterrupted use, by a single party, for a period of five years. The use must be against the owner's wishes and be open and notorious. No confrontation with the owner is required and property taxes do not have to be paid. The party wishing to obtain the prescriptive easement must have some reasonable claim to the use of the property.

The method used for acquiring property rights through prescription is similar to **adverse possession**, which is discussed later in the unit. The main difference is the payment of taxes. Adverse possession requires the payment of taxes for five continuous years, while prescription does not. Also, remember one acquires title to property through adverse possession, but only a specified interest in property through prescription.

Terminating Easements

The owner of the property with the servient tenement cannot revoke or terminate the easement. Easements may be terminated or extinguished in eight ways:

1. **Abandonment**: Abandonment is the obvious and intentional surrender of the easement. **Non-use**: If a prescriptive easement is not used for a period of five years, the easement is terminated.

2. **Destruction of the servient tenement**: If the government takes the servient tenement for its use, as in eminent domain, the easement is terminated.

3. **Adverse possession**: The owner of the servient tenement may, by his or her own use, prevent the dominant tenement from using the easement for a period of five years, thus terminating the easement.

4. **Merger**: If the same person owns both the dominant and servient tenements, the easement is terminated.

5. **Express release**: The owner of the dominant tenement is the only one who can release an easement. A usual way would be to sign a quitclaim deed.

6. **Legal proceedings**: In order to terminate an easement, the owner of the servient tenement would bring an action to quiet title against the owner of the dominant tenement. A lawsuit to establish or settle title to real property is called a **quiet title action** or an action to quiet title.

7. **Estoppel**: Unless created by express grant, an easement may be terminated by non-use and the property owner has reason to believe that no further use is intended.

   Example: John is a farmer who owns some land. Bob, the son of a neighboring farmer, cuts through John's field on the way to high school. Upon graduation, Bob leaves for college and stops taking the short cut through John's field. Farmer John, seeing that the easement was no longer in use, fenced his field. John's action showed that he relied on Bob's conduct (no longer taking the shortcut). Therefore, the easement terminates through the estoppel.

8. **Excessive use**: Depending on the terms of the easement, excessive use can terminate the easement.

   Example: Dan Smith owns a Victorian style 6-bedroom, 2-story house on 1/2 acre. Even though he has street access, he asked his neighbor Betty if he could use her private dirt road at the back of her 1/2 acre to get to his home because it was faster. Betty agreed and gave him an easement to use her private dirt road. In order to pay for an upcoming trip, Dan decided to rent out all the bedrooms in his home to college students. He rented each room to four students. Therefore, the traffic across the easement increased dramatically. Betty, understandably upset, terminated Dan's easement due to excessive use.

The Requirements for Terminating an Easement
Mnemonic = ADAM E. LEE

Abandonment	Legal proceedings
Destruction of the servient tenement	Estoppel
Adverse possession	Excessive
Merger	
Express release	

Restrictions

A **restriction** is a limitation placed on the use of property. It is usually placed on property to assure that land use is consistent and uniform within a certain area. Restrictions may be placed by a private owner, a developer, or the government. **Private restrictions** are placed by a present or past owner and affect only a specific property or development. **Zoning (public restriction)** is an example of government restrictions that benefit the public.

Private Restrictions

Private restrictions are created in the deed at the time of sale, by other written agreements, or in the general plan of a subdivision by the developer. For example, a developer may use a height restriction to ensure views from each parcel in a subdivision.Restrictions are commonly known as **CC&Rs** or covenants, conditions, and restrictions. The CC&Rs for a new subdivision are listed in a recorded **Declaration of Restrictions** which gives each owner the right to enforce the CC&Rs.

A **covenant** is a promise to do or not do certain things. The penalty for a breach of a covenant is usually money damages or an injunction. An **injunction** is a court order forcing a person to do or not do an act, such as violating a private restriction. An example of a covenant might be that the tenant agrees to make certain repairs, or that a property may be used only for a specific purpose.

A **condition** is much the same as a covenant, a promise to do or not do something (usually a limitation on the use of the property), except the penalty for breaking a condition is return of the property to the grantor. A **condition subsequent** is a restriction, placed in a deed at the time of conveyance, upon future use of the property. It is a condition placed on the property that comes into play subsequent to the transaction. Upon breach of the condition subsequent, the grantor may take back the property. A **condition precedent** requires that a certain event, or condition, occur before title can pass to the new owner. It is a condition that must be taken care of preceding the transaction.

Covenants, conditions, and restrictions are void if they are unlawful, impossible to perform, or in restraint of alienation. Therefore, a deed restriction prohibiting For Sale signs is illegal, but the signs may be limited to a reasonable size.

Public Restrictions

Public restrictions are primarily zoning laws (zoning) which promote public health or general public welfare. Zoning regulates land use with regard to lot sizes, types of structures permitted, building heights, setbacks, and density. Zoning departments use zoning symbols to show types of property use. For example, R-3 is multiple family, R-1 is single family, M-1 is light industrial, and C-1 stands for commercial property.

Changes in zoning may be initiated by a single property owner, developer, or government entity. Commonly, zoning is changed from a high-density use to a lower density use, such as commercial (C-1) or light manufacturing (M-1) to residential (R-1), or from residential to conservation. This is called **downzoning**. Sometimes developers ask for higher density, such as changing from low density residential (R-1) to high density (R-3) in order to build condominiums.

Zoning changes can create **non-conforming** use, for example, farmland rezoned for residential use. All new structures must conform to the new zoning and be for residential use. Existing farms are now non-conforming properties, but may continue to operate because a **grandfather clause** allows an owner to continue to use structures which are now non-conforming with the new zoning laws.

If a person wants to use property in a way that is currently prohibited by zoning laws, he or she may petition to rezone the entire area or petition for a variance for the single piece of land. A **variance** is an allowable difference to the zoning laws for a structure or land use.

Whenever there is a conflict between zoning and deed restrictions, the more restrictive of the two must be followed.

Encroachments

Placing a permanent improvement, such as a fence, wall, driveway or roof, so that it extends over the lot line into adjacent property owned by another, is known as an **encroachment**. This unauthorized intrusion on the adjoining land can limit its use and reduce it in size and value. An owner has three years in which to sue the neighbor to have the unauthorized encroachment removed.

Tree limbs and branches encroach airspace — roots encroach underground

Garage encroaches on neighbor's lot

Portable garden shed encroaching

Misaligned fence encroaches

Patio extends over the property line

Shrubs beginning to encroach on vacant lot

Common Encroachments

Homestead Protection

California has homestead laws to protect families. **Homestead** property is the home (primary residence) occupied by a family that is exempt from the claims of, or eviction by, unsecured creditors. A **homestead exemption** is in effect a lien that protects a certain amount of equity in a person's home by limiting the amount of liability for certain debts against which a home can be used to satisfy a judgment. The amount protected varies depending on the age, marital status, and income of the property owner. A homestead exemption does not stop the sale of the property. Its purpose is to ensure that the homeowner receives the amount of the exemption before the creditors are paid from the sale proceeds.

The first $100,000 of a home's value may not be used to satisfy a judgment against married persons or the head of a household. A mentally or physically disabled person, or someone over the age of 65, is entitled to protection up to $175,000. All others have a homestead exemption of $75,000. A homestead does not protect an owner against foreclosure on a trust deed, mechanic's lien, or lien recorded prior to the filing of the homestead.

Types of Homestead Exemptions

California law provides for two types of homestead exemption—automatic and declared.

Automatic Homestead

The **automatic homestead** is just that—automatic. Anyone living in his or her home has an automatic homestead exemption protecting the equity. A declaration of homestead does not need to be filed. The automatic, or **statutory homestead exemption,** only applies on the forced sale of the property. The homeowner must live continuously on the property from the date the judgment creditor's lien attaches until the date the court determines that the dwelling is a homestead. A **dwelling** is the place where a person resides.

Declared Homestead

A **declared homestead** is the dwelling described in a homestead declaration. A **declaration of homestead** is a recorded notice a property owner files to protect the equity in his or her real property. The declaration of homestead only protects real estate dwellings—not dwellings that are personal property, such as mobilehomes on leased land, houseboats, or other waterborne vessels.

Requirements for a Declaration of Homestead

- Name of the declared homestead owner
- Description of the declared homestead
- Statement that the declared homestead is the principal dwelling of the declared homestead owner.

The declaration of homestead must be signed, acknowledged, and recorded to take effect. Once the declaration of homestead is recorded, the property becomes a homestead. A homestead can be terminated by recording a **notice of abandonment**, by conveying the property, or through an execution and forced sale. An owner must file an **Abandonment of Homestead** form in order to obtain a homestead on a new property. If the owner moves from the homesteaded property and does not wish to file a new declaration of homestead, the

A Homestead

original homestead remains valid. Sale of the property automatically causes the homestead to terminate. However, neither death of the homesteader nor destruction of the property terminates the homestead.

ACQUISITION & CONVEYANCE OF REAL ESTATE

Acquisition and conveyance is also defined as buying and selling. If one person is buying, someone must be selling. This section studies the two functions together. Real property may be acquired and conveyed by will, succession, accession, adverse possession, and transfer.

Will

A **testamentary instrument**, usually in the form of a **will**, disposes of property after death. A **testator** is a person who makes a will. If a person died **testate** it means the person left a valid will. If a person died **intestate** it means the person did not leave a will. A gift of real property by will is a **devise**, while a gift of money or personal property by will is a **bequest** or legacy. The maker, before death, may change a will by a **codicil**.

California recognizes three types of wills: witnessed wills, statutory form wills, and holographic wills. A **witnessed will**, usually prepared by an attorney and signed by the maker (testator) and two witnesses. A **statutory form will** is a "fill-in-the-blanks" will created to meet the requirements of Probate Code §6240. A **holographic will** is written entirely in the handwriting of the testator (maker) and is dated and signed by the testator.

Probate

Probate is the legal process to prove a will is valid. Probate proceedings are held in the superior court to determine creditors' claims and beneficiaries' interests in an estate upon the owner's death. A hearing is held to appoint a representative to handle the estate of the deceased. If that person is named in a will, he or she is referred to as an **executor** or **executrix**. If there is no will or someone named in a will to administer the estate, the court will appoint an **administrator** or **administratrix**.

Estate property may be sold during the probate period at a public or private auction. An administrator or executor may list the property for up to 90 days with court permission. The court confirms the final sale and sets the broker's commission.

Succession

Succession is the legal transfer of a person's interests in real and personal property under the laws of descent and distribution. When a person inherits property as a result of someone dying without a will, it is called **intestate succession**. An intestate decedent's property passes to his or her heirs according to the **laws of descent** in the state where such real property is located. The law provides for disposition of the deceased's property by statute.

If the deceased was married, and died intestate, the surviving spouse receives all community property. Separate property is divided between a surviving spouse and any children. If there is only one child, the separate property is split equally. If there is more than one child, the surviving spouse receives one-third and the children, two-thirds.

Accession

Accession is a process by which there is an addition or reduction to property by the efforts of natural forces. The land itself can be enlarged or reduced by natural forces—gradually through accretion and reliction or quickly through avulsion.

Accretion is the gradual and imperceptible addition of land to a parcel by the natural deposition and accumulation of **alluvium** (or **alluvion**) upon the bank of a stream or river. Another gradual change is **reliction**, which is the process of land adjacent to a watercourse covered by water becoming uncovered because of receding water. It is a slow and imperceptible recession and the recession must be permanent. In both instances, the landowner acquires title to the newly formed or exposed land on the bank. **Erosion** is the gradual wearing away of land by the natural processes of water, wind, or glacial ice. In this context, erosion is the opposite of accretion.

Avulsion is the process by which the action of water causes a sudden, perceptible loss of or addition to land. A large quantity of land is suddenly removed from the land of one person and added to the shore of another person—usually caused by flood or a change in the stream.

Ownership of the land does not change due to avulsive changes, such as a river breaking through the narrow part of an oxbow in a stream or river. If the land can be identified on the opposite bank, avulsion has occurred; otherwise, the courts may presume that accretion has occurred. To establish title to lands lost by avulsion, the original landowner has one year to reclaim the part that was carried away by avulsion. If unclaimed, the original landowner will lose title and it will become part of the new land to which it has attached.

Adverse Possession

Ownership of real property can be acquired by adverse possession. The property must be occupied without the owner's knowledge. It cannot be publicly owned (national and state parks, government buildings, public beaches, and the like). **Adverse possession** is the ability to obtain title by occupying land for a statutory time period without the permission of the owner.

In order for a non-owner to oust the ownership of another through adverse possession, the adverse possessor must meet six requirements. Paying the property taxes is often the most difficult requirement to meet, because in many counties the tax collector will return a second payment on the same piece of property.

Requirements to Acquire Ownership through Adverse Possession

- Open possession (some assertion of control, such as fencing or use)
- Notorious possession (i.e., such as a reasonable owner of the property would otherwise recognize)
- Continuous for a five-year time period
- Pay property taxes on the disputed property for the entire five years of the disputed claim
- Hostile (not with the original owner's permission)
- Adverse to a claim of right (adverse possessor must claim the title)

In addition, the adverse possessor will have to file a lawsuit to **quiet title** against the person who, until that point, had valid title to the property.

Transfer

Property is acquired by **transfer** when, by an act of the parties or law, title is **conveyed**, or transferred, from one person to another by means of a written document. The transfer may be voluntary, such as the sale of a home, or involuntary by act of law, such as a foreclosure sale. Real property may be transferred (**alienated**) by private grant, public grant, public dedication, or operation of law (court action).

Private Grant

When property is transferred by **private grant** a written instrument is used. An **instrument** is a formal legal document, such as a contract, deed or will. The kinds of deeds commonly used for private grants include grant deed, quitclaim deed, gift deed, and warranty deed.

Grant Deed

In California, the **grant deed** is the most frequently used instrument to transfer title. The parties involved in the grant deed are the grantor and grantee. The **grantor** is the person conveying the property, and the **grantee** is the person receiving the property or to whom it is being conveyed.

A grant deed must have a **granting clause** and has two **implied warranties** by the grantor. One is that the grantor has not already conveyed title to any other person, and the other is that the estate is free from encumbrances other than those disclosed by the grantor. If you see the words **et ux**. on a grant deed, it means "and wife."

> ### Review - Grant Deed
> - A written instrument (document) that transfers title to real property.
> - Must contain a granting clause.

The grantor also promises to deed any rights he or she might acquire to the property after conveying it to the grantee. This is called **after-acquired title**, which means any benefits that come to the property after a sale must follow the sale and accrue to the new owner. For example, oil or mineral rights might revert to the property at some time in the future, after the present owner has sold the property.

Requirements for a Valid Grant Deed

- According to the statute of frauds, a deed must be in writing.
- The parties to the transfer (grantor and grantee) must be sufficiently identified and described.
- The grantor must be competent to convey the property (not a minor or incompetent).
- The grantee must be capable of holding title (must be a real living person, not fictitious).
- The property must be adequately described but it does not require a legal description.
- Words of granting, such as grant or convey must be included.
- The deed must be executed (signed) by the grantor. The deed may be signed by a witnessed mark "X".
- The deed must be delivered to and accepted by the grantee.

A deed is void (invalid) if the grantor is a minor or incompetent or if the grantee does not exist. A deed to a deceased person or fictitious person, as ABC Company is void; however, a deed to an actual person using a fictitious name or DBA is valid. A **fictitious business name** or assumed name is a business name other than the name of the person who has registered the business. For example, "ABC Real Estate Brokerage" owned by Jill Jones or "South Coast Property Management" owned by Bill Hernandez. The acronym **DBA** means, doing business as. An example is, Bill Hernandez, DBA "South Coast Property Management".

A grant deed is not effective until it is delivered. It must be the intention of the grantor that the deed is delivered and title be transferred during his or her lifetime. For example, a deed would not be valid if signed and put in a safe place until the death of the grantor, and then recorded. Recording a deed is considered the same as delivery. After a deed has been acknowledged by the grantor, it may be filed with the county recorder, giving **constructive notice** of the sale. An **acknowledgment** is a signed statement, made before a notary public, by a named person confirming that the signature on a document is genuine and that it was made of free will. A deed does not have to be acknowledged to be valid, but must be acknowledged to be recorded.

The purpose of recording a deed is to protect the **chain of title**. This is a sequential record of changes in ownership showing the connection from one owner to the next. A complete chain of title is desirable whenever property is transferred and required by title insurance companies if they are writing a policy on a property.

> Example: Jane Borden, a single woman, owned the house in which she lived, as her sole and separate property. After marrying Sam Jones, she decided to sell the house. However, because the chain of the title showed that Jane Borden owned it, reference had to be made, in the grant deed to the buyer, that Jane Jones, a married woman, previously known as Jane Borden, was conveying her interest in the property. In that way, the chain of title remained unbroken.

The **priority of a deed** is determined by the date it is recorded. In other words, recording establishes a claim of ownership which has priority over any deeds recorded after it. The first to record a deed is the first in right.

> Example: Cal sells his house to Margaret, and, without telling Margaret. He also sells it to Anita. Anita records her deed before Margaret has a chance to record hers. Anita is the owner of record and gets the house. Margaret has a definite cause for a lawsuit against Cal.

However, there are some exceptions to the "first to record is first in right" rule. If the same property is sold to two parties, and the second party knows of the first sale and is aware of the fraud intended by the seller, the original sale is valid, even if it was not recorded first.

Also, as you recall, possession is considered constructive notice, just like recording. So, if a deed is not recorded, but the buyer moves in, that sale has priority over later recorded deeds.

RECORDING REQUESTED BY

WHEN RECORDED MAIL TO

NAME
ADDRESS
CITY
STATE & ZIP

Title Order No.   Escrow No.

SPACE ABOVE THIS LINE FOR RECORDER'S USE

GRANT DEED

The undersigned declares that the documentary transfer tax is   and is

☐ Computed on the full value of the interest or property conveyed, or is

☐ Computed on the full value less the value of liens or encumbrances remaining at time of sale. The land, tenements realty is located in

☐ Unincorporated area of: ☐ City of: and

FOR A VALUABLE CONSIDERATION, receipt of which is hereby acknowledged.

hereby GRANT(S) to

the following described real property in the

County of: , State of:

Dated:

STATE OF:

COUNTY OF: }ss

On _____ before me, the
undersigned, a Notary Public in and for State,
personally appeared

_____

_____

personally known to me or proved to me on the basis of satisfactory evidence to be the person(s) whose name(s) is/are subscribed to the within instrument and acknowledged to me that he/she/they executed the same in his/her/their authorized capacity(ies), and that by his/her/their signature(s) on the instrument the person(s), or the entity upon behalf of which the person(s) acted, executed the instrument.

WITNESS my hand and official seal

Signature _____   (This area for official notary seal)

MAIL TAX STATEMENTS AS DIRECTED ABOVE

Example: Greta sells her house to Victor, who moves in without recording the deed. Greta also sells the house to Alex, telling him to record the deed quickly, making him aware that she had previously sold it to Victor. Due to Alex's knowledge of the prior sale, and Victor's possession and occupancy of the property, which established his right of ownership, Victor gets the house.

A grantee must accept a deed before it is considered effective. Acceptance is automatic if the grantee is an infant or incompetent person. Acceptance may be shown by the acts of the grantee, such as moving onto the property.

The grant deed need not be signed by the grantee. An undated, unrecorded, and unacknowledged grant deed may be valid as long as it contains the essential items required for a valid deed. Here is a list of non-essentials for a grant deed to be valid:

Items a Valid Deed Does Not Require
- Acknowledgment
- Recording
- Competent grantee; may be a minor, felon or incompetent
- Date
- Mention of the consideration
- Signature of grantee
- Habendum clause (to have and to hold)
- Seal or witnesses
- Legal description, an adequate description is sufficient

Quitclaim Deed

A **quitclaim deed** contains no warranties and transfers any interest the grantor may have at the time the deed is signed. It is often used to clear a cloud on the title. A **cloud on title** is any condition that affects the clear title of real property or minor defect in the chain of title, which needs to be removed. A quitclaim is used to transfer interests between husband and wife or to terminate an easement. If a buyer defaults on a loan carried back by the seller, the fastest way to clear title would be for the defaulting buyer to sign a quitclaim deed to the seller.

RECORDING REQUESTED BY

AND WHEN RECORDED MAIL TO

NAME
ADDRESS
CITY
STATE & ZIP

MAIL TAX STATEMENTS TO

NAME
ADDRESS
CITY
STATE & ZIP

Title Order No. _____   Escrow No. _____

SPACE ABOVE THIS LINE FOR RECORDER'S USE

QUITCLAIM DEED

The undersigned grantor(s) declares(s) that the documentary transfer tax is _____ and is

☐ Computed on the full value of the interest or property conveyed, or is

☐ Computed on the full value less the value of liens or encumbrances remaining at time of sale.

☐ Unincorporated area of: _____   ☐ City of: _____   and

FOR A VALUABLE CONSIDERATION, receipt of which is hereby acknowledged.

hereby REMISE(S), RELEASE(S) AND FOREVER QUITCLAIM(S) to

the following described real property in the

County of: _____   , State of: _____

Dated: _____

STATE OF: _____

COUNTY OF: _____   }ss

On _____ before me, the
undersigned, a Notary Public in and for State,
personally appeared

_____

_____

personally known to me or proved to me on the basis of satisfactory evidence to be the person(s) whose name(s) is/are subscribed to the within instrument and acknowledged to me that he/she/they executed the same in his/her/their authorized capacity(ies), and that by his/her/their signature(s) on the instrument the person(s), or the entity upon behalf of which the person(s) acted, executed the instrument.

WITNESS my hand and official seal

Signature _____   (This area for official notary seal)

MAIL TAX STATEMENTS AS DIRECTED ABOVE

Gift Deed

A **gift deed** is used to make a gift of property to a grantee, usually a close friend or relative. The consideration in a gift deed is called **love and affection**.

Warranty Deed

A **warranty deed** is a document containing **express covenants** of title and is rarely used in California because title companies have taken over the role of insuring title to property.

Financing Instruments

Deeds of trust and deeds of reconveyance are primarily financing instruments.

Public Grant

Real property can be transferred by **public grant**, which is the transfer of title by the government to a private individual. In the last century many people moved west and improved land by building and planting crops. As they qualified for ownership under the homestead laws, they received a patent from the government as proof of ownership. A **patent** is the document used by the government to transfer title to land instead of using a deed.

Public Dedication

When real property is intended for public use, it may be acquired as a **public dedication**. There are three means of public dedication: (1) common law dedication, (2) statutory dedication, and (3) deed.

In a **common law dedication**, a property owner implies through his or her conduct the intent that the public use the land. In order to be effective, the dedication must be accepted by public use or local ordinance.

A **statutory dedication** is a dedication made by a private individual to the public. An owner follows procedures outlined in the Subdivision Map Act— commonly used by developers to dedicate streets and common areas to the public.

A **deed** is a formal transfer by a party as in a gift deed where there is no consideration.

Operation of Law

Sometimes property is transferred by the **operation of law**. It is usually an involuntary transfer involving foreclosure or is the result of a judgment or some other lien against the title. There is a variety of situations in which courts establish legal title regardless of the desires of the record owners.

Foreclosure

Foreclosure is the legal procedure lenders use to terminate the trustor or mortgagor's rights, title, and interest in real property by selling the property and using the sale proceeds to satisfy the liens of creditors.

Bankruptcy

The court proceeding to relieve a person's or company's financial insolvency is called **bankruptcy**. A person whose debts exceed assets and who is unable to pay current liabilities is financially insolvent.

In a Chapter 7 bankruptcy, known as a liquidation bankruptcy, title to all of the debtor's real property is vested in a court-appointed trustee. The debtor lists (schedules) all of the debts he or she owes. The bankruptcy judge may discharge the debts or may sell the debtor's property to satisfy the claims of the creditors. Creditors' claims are discharged as of the date of the filing. Although most of the person's or company's debts are forgiven, not all debts can be discharged through bankruptcy. Non-dischargeable debts include income taxes, child support, alimony, student loans, and criminal fines.

Quiet Title Action

Quiet title action is a court proceeding to establish an individual's right to ownership of real property against one or more adverse claimants. It is used to clear a cloud on the title of real property. It is frequently used to clear tax titles, titles based on adverse possession, and the seller's title under a forfeited, recorded land contract.

Execution Sale

An **execution sale** is a forced sale of property under a **writ of execution** with the proceeds used to satisfy a money judgment. A **sheriff's deed** is given to a buyer when property is sold through court action in order to satisfy a judgment for money or foreclosure of a mortgage.

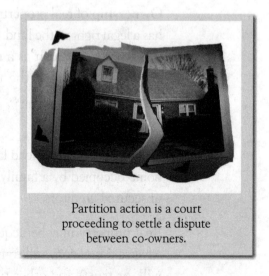

Partition action is a court proceeding to settle a dispute between co-owners.

Partition Action

Partition action is a court proceeding to settle a dispute between co-owners (joint tenants or tenants in common) about dividing their interests in real property. The court can physically divide either the property or the money derived from its sale.

Escheat

Escheat is a legal process in which property reverts to the state because the deceased owner left no will and has no legal heirs. The state must wait five years before trying to claim the property.

Eminent Domain

The power of **eminent domain** is the power of the government to take private property for public use after paying just compensation to the owner. **Just compensation** is fair and reasonable payment due to a private property owner when his or her property is condemned under eminent domain.

Condemnation is the process by which the government acquires private property for public use, under its right of eminent domain. This right is based on the Fifth Amendment of the U. S. Constitution and is not an example of police power or zoning.

Inverse condemnation is the opposite of eminent domain. With inverse condemnation, a private party forces the government to pay just compensation if the property value or use has been diminished by a public entity. For example, if part of a farmer's land is condemned for freeway construction, leaving an unusable piece that is cut off from the rest of the farm, the farmer could sue for inverse condemnation since the small piece that has been effectively taken without just compensation.

SUMMARY

Ownership of real property requires a title. A **title** is evidence that a person has a legal right in the land. An **encumbrance** is anything that affects or limits title to property such as a mortgage. There are two types of encumbrances: (1) those that affect the title to the property (**financial encumbrances**, called liens) and (2) those that affect the use of the property (**non-financial encumbrances**).

California has homestead laws to protect families. **Homestead** property is the home occupied by a family that is exempt from the claims of, or eviction by, unsecured creditors.

Real property may be acquired and conveyed by will, succession, accession, adverse possession, and transfer. Sometimes the transfer is voluntary (by **deed**, **will**, or **trust**) and other times it is involuntary (by the **operation of law** or **court action**).

UNIT 3 REVIEW

Matching Exercise

Instructions: Write the letter of the matching term on the blank line before its definition. Answers immediately follow the Multiple Choice Questions.

Terms

A. abandonment

B. accession

C. accretion

D. alienate

E. avulsion

F. bequest

G. codicil

H. easement in gross

I. encroachment

J. executor

K. grantee

L. grantor

M. homestead

N. instrument

O. intestate

P. license

Q. lis pendens

R. quiet title action

S. reliction

T. succession

Definitions

1. _____ An easement that is not appurtenant to any one parcel.

2. _____ Permission to use a property which may be revoked at any time.

3. _____ The unauthorized placement of permanent improvements that intrude on adjacent property owned by another.

4. _____ Status provided to a homeowner's principal residence that protects the home against judgments up to specified amounts.

5. _____ A gift of personal property by will.

6. _____ Dying without leaving a will.

7. _____ Process by which there is an addition or reduction to property by the efforts natural forces.

8. _____ Gradual buildup of alluvium by natural causes on property bordering a river, lake, or ocean.

9. _____ Occurs when land that has been covered by water is exposed by receding of the water.

10. _____ The act of transferring ownership, title, or interest.

11. _____ The person receiving the property, or to whom it is being conveyed.

12. _____ The person conveying or transferring the property.

13. _____ A document in real estate.

14. _____ It is a court proceeding to clear a cloud on the title of real property.

15. _____ Notice that indicates pending litigation affecting title on a property.

Multiple Choice Questions

Instructions: Circle your response and then check your response with the Answer Key that immediately follows the Multiple Choice Questions.

1. Which of the following is the best definition of encumbrance?
    a. The degree, quantity, and extent of interest a person has in real property.
    b. Anything that affects or limits the fee simple title to or value of property.
    c. The use of property as security for a debt.
    d. Any action regarding property, other than acquiring or transferring title.

2. The form of encumbrance that makes specific property the security for the payment of a debt or discharge of an obligation is called a:
    a. reservation.
    b. fief.
    c. lien.
    d. quitclaim.

3. A recorded abstract of judgment is classified as a(n)_____lien.
    a. equitable
    b. involuntary
    c. inferior
    d. superior

4. Recording a lis pendens:
    a. does not affect the title.
    b. clouds the title but does not affect marketability.
    c. clouds the title and affects marketability.
    d. affects the current owner but not a subsequent owner.

5. The owner of an apartment building does not declare the income from the rental units. The IRS filed a government tax lien, which would be a:

    a. voluntary lien.

    b. general lien.

    c. judgment lien.

    d. none of the above

6. The personal, revocable, unassignable permission to use the property of another without a possessory interest in it is called a(n):

    a. license.

    b. easement.

    c. encroachment.

    d. option.

7. Roger, who owns a ranch, gave Sam who owns no property, a non-revocable right to cross his ranch to fish in the stream. Sam has a(n):

    a. easement in gross.

    b. license.

    c. easement appurtenant.

    d. easement by prescription.

8. Private restrictions on land can be created by deed:

    a. only.

    b. or written agreement.

    c. or zoning ordinance.

    d. or written agreement or zoning ordinance.

9. Alienation of title to real property most nearly means to:

    a. cloud the title.

    b. encumber the title.

    c. record a homestead.

    d. convey or transfer title and possession.

10. To be binding on a buyer and a seller, a deed to transfer real property must be:

    a. recorded.

    b. delivered and accepted.

    c. acknowledged.

    d. all of the above.

11. A grant deed is considered executed when it is:
    a. recorded by the grantee.
    b. signed by the grantor.
    c. acknowledged by the grantee.
    d. delivered by the grantor.

12. Effective delivery of a deed depends on:
    a. the intention of the grantor.
    b. recording the deed.
    c. knowledge of its existence by the grantee.
    d. acknowledgement of the grantor's signature before a Notary Public.

13. Dana sold a property to Kim, who did not record the deed but did occupy the premises. Dana then sold the same property to Lee, who did not inspect the property but did record the deed. After the second sale, who would have legal title to the property?
    a. The title would revert to Dana as the remainderman.
    b. The title would remain with Kim.
    c. The title would be Lee's due to Kim's failure to record his deed.
    d. Lee would be able to sue Kim for his failure to record his deed.

14. An owner of a parcel of real property gave his neighbor a deed conveying an easement for ingress and egress. The easement was not specifically located in the deed. Under the circumstances, the neighbor's right to use the easement is:
    a. enforceable because the location of the easement does not need to be specified.
    b. enforceable only if the easement is an easement in gross.
    c. unenforceable because the location of the easement must be specified.
    d. unenforceable because easements are never created by deed, only by written agreement.

15. Which of the following actions is a quiet title action?
    a. Court action to foreclose
    b. Court action in ejectment
    c. Police action to quiet a noisy neighbor
    d. Court action to remove a cloud on title

UNIT 3 ANSWER KEY

Answers – Matching

1. H	4. M	7. B	10. D	13. N
2. P	5. F	8. C	11. K	14. R
3. I	6. O	9. S	12. L	15. Q

Answers – Multiple Choice

1. **(b)** This is CalBRE's definition of an encumbrance. [Encumbrances]

2. **(c)** A lien creates an obligation on a specific property. [Encumbrances]

3. **(b)** A recorded abstract of judgment creates an involuntary general lien on all real property of the debtor that is located in the county where the judgment was recorded. [Encumbrances]

4. **(c)** Recording a lis pendens creates a cloud on title and warns parties that they could be involved in a lawsuit if the purchase the property, which could affect marketability. [Encumbrances]

5. **(b)** Income tax liens, court judgments, and California Franchise Tax liens are general liens and affect all of the property of the owner in the county where recorded. [Encumbrances]

6. **(a)** The statement of the question is a good definition of a license. [Encumbrances]

7. **(a)** An easement in gross is a personal easement that is not attached to the land, and cannot be revoked. Sam does not have a license because the right is irrevocable. It is not an easement appurtenant because Sam owns no land and it is not an easement by prescription because Roger gave the easement in gross to Sam. [Encumbrances]

8. **(b)** Zoning ordinances are public, not private restrictions. Private restrictions can be created by CC&Rs, deeds, leases, and other written agreements. [Encumbrances]

9. **(d)** The terms alienation, convey, and transfer are used interchangeably when transferring ownership of property from one person to another. [Acquisition & Conveyance of Real Estate]

10. **(b)** Delivery and acceptance are required elements of a valid deed. The deed does not have to be acknowledged or recorded. [Acquisition & Conveyance of Real Estate]

11. **(b)** One of the requirements for a valid deed is that the deed must be executed (signed) by the grantor [Acquisition & Conveyance of Real Estate]

12. **(a)** The grantor must have the intention, during his or her lifetime, that the deed is delivered and title is transferred. [Acquisition & Conveyance of Real Estate]

13. **(b)** Possession is considered constructive notice, just like recording. If a deed is not recorded, but the buyer moves in, that sale has priority over any later recorded deeds. [Acquisition & Conveyance of Real Estate]

14. **(a)** Ingress and egress mean to enter and to exit. An easement may be created by deed or written agreement, which is express grant. An unlocated easement is valid. [Acquisition & Conveyance of Real Estate]

15. **(d)** A lawsuit to establish or settle title to real property is called a quiet title action or an action to quiet title. [Acquisition & Conveyance of Real Estate]

INTRODUCTION

Every time you are involved in a real estate transaction, you will use a contract that transfers or indicates an interest in the property. It is important that you understand the nature of legal agreements, so you are able to explain them to your clients and customers as part of your role as a real estate licensee. This Unit explains what a contract is and how contracts are used to assure the understanding and approval of all parties to an agreement.

Learning Objectives

After completing this Unit, you should be able to:

5A   recall classifications of contracts.

5B   identify the elements needed to create legally binding contracts.

5C   choose the ways to discharge contracts.

5D   specify the purpose of the statute of frauds, the parol evidence rule, and the statute of limitations.

CLASSIFICATION OF CONTRACTS

A **contract** is a legally enforceable agreement made by competent parties, to perform or not perform a certain act. Contracts may be express or implied, bilateral or unilateral, executory or executed, and void, voidable, unenforceable, or valid.

Express or Implied Contracts

A contract may be an **express contract**, in which the parties declare the terms and put their intentions in words, either oral or written. A lease or rental agreement, for example, is an express contract. The landlord agrees to allow the tenant to live in the apartment and the tenant agrees to pay rent in return. A contract may be an **implied contract** in which agreement is shown by act and conduct rather than words. We create a contract when we go into a restaurant and order food, go to a movie, or have a daily newspaper delivered. By showing a desire to use a service, we imply that we will pay for it.

Bilateral or Unilateral Contracts

Contracts may be bilateral or unilateral. A **bilateral contract** is an agreement in which each person promises to perform an act in exchange for another person's promise to perform. In other words, both parties must keep their agreement for the contract to be completed. An example might be a promise from a would-be pilot to pay $2,500 for flying lessons, and a return promise from the instructor to teach him or her to fly. A **unilateral contract** is a contract in which a party promises to perform without expectation of performance by the other party. The second party is not bound to act, but if he or she does, the first party is obligated to keep the promise. An example might be a radio station offering $1,000 to the 100th caller. Some lucky person makes the call and the station pays the money. An option is another example of a unilateral contract.

Executory or Executed Contracts

A contract may be executory or executed. In an **executory contract**, something remains to be performed by one or both parties. An escrow that is not yet closed, or a contract not signed by the parties are examples of executory contracts. In an **executed contract**, all parties have performed completely. One of the meanings of execute is to sign, or complete in some way. An executed contract may be a sales agreement signed by all parties.

Void, Voidable, Unenforceable, or Valid Contracts

Contracts may be void, voidable, unenforceable, or valid. A **void contract** is no contract at all or no legal effect (to lack of capacity, illegal subject matter). A **voidable contract** is valid and enforceable on its face, but may be rejected by one or more of the parties (induced by fraud, menace, duress). An **unenforceable contract** is valid, but for some reason cannot be proved by one or both of the parties (an oral agreement should be in writing because of the statute of frauds). A **valid contract** that is binding and enforceable has all the basic elements required by law.

BASIC ELEMENTS OF VALID CONTRACTS

In order for a contract to be legally binding and enforceable, there are four requirements: (1) legally competent parties, (2) mutual consent between the parties, (3) lawful objective, and (4) sufficient consideration.

Legally Competent Parties

Parties entering into a contract must have **legal capacity** to do so. Almost anyone is capable, with a few exceptions. A person must be at least 18 years of age unless married, in the military, or declared emancipated by the court.

A **minor** is not capable of appointing an agent, or entering into an agency agreement with a broker to buy or sell. Brokers dealing with minors should proceed cautiously and should seek an attorney's advice. A contract with a minor is considered voidable by the minor.

When it has been determined judicially that a person is not legally competent, the contract made by that person is terminated. If it is obvious that a person is not legally competent there can be no contract. In the case of a person who is not legally competent, a court-appointed guardian would have legal capacity to contract. Both minors and people who are not legally competent may acquire title to real property by gift or inheritance. However, any transfer of acquired property must be court approved.

A contract made by a person who is intoxicated or under the influence of legal or illegal drugs can be cancelled when the individual sobers up. Or the contract may be **ratified** (approved after the fact) depending on the parties.

Any person may give another the authority to act on his or her behalf. The legal document that does this is called a **power of attorney**. The person holding the power of attorney is an attorney-in-fact. When dealing with real property, a power of attorney must be recorded to be valid, and is good for as long as the **principal** is competent. A power of attorney can be cancelled by the principal at any time by recording a **revocation**. A power of attorney is useful, for example, when a buyer or seller is out of town and has full trust in that agent to operate on his or her behalf.

Mutual Consent Between the Parties

In a valid contract, all parties must mutually agree. **Mutual consent** (or mutual assent), is sometimes called a **meeting of the minds**. It is an offer by one party and acceptance by the other party.

Offer

An **offer** shows the contractual intent of the **offeror**, or the person making the offer, to enter into a contract. That offer must be communicated to the **offeree**, or the person to whom the offer is being made. Unconditional acceptance of the offer is necessary for all parties to be legally bound. The offer must be definite and certain in its terms, and the agreement must be genuine or the contract may be voidable by one or both parties.

Termination of an Offer

An offeror expects that his or her offer will be accepted in a timely manner and a contract created. An offer is specific, and an offeror does not have to wait indefinitely for an answer.

> **Methods to Terminate an Offer**
> - Lapse of time: an offer is revoked if the offeree fails to accept it within a prescribed period
> - Communication of notice of revocation: notice is filed by the offeror anytime before the other party has communicated acceptance
> - Failure of offeree to fulfill a condition of acceptance prescribed by the offeror
> - A qualified acceptance, or counteroffer by the offeree
> - Rejection by the offeree
> - Death or insanity of the offeror or offeree
> - Unlawful object of the proposed contract

Acceptance

One party must offer and another must accept, without condition. An **acceptance** is an unqualified agreement to the terms of an offer. The offeree must agree to every item of the offer for the acceptance to be complete. If the original terms change in any way in the acceptance, the offer becomes a **counteroffer**, and the first offer terminates. The person making the original offer is no longer bound by that offer, and may accept the counteroffer or not. The counteroffer becomes a new offer, made by the original offeree. Acceptance of an offer must be communicated to the offeror, in the manner specified, before a contract becomes binding between the parties. The seller may rescind an offer prior to acceptance. Silence is not considered to be acceptance.

Genuine Assent

A final requirement for mutual consent is that the offer and acceptance be genuine and freely made by all parties. **Genuine assent** does not exist if there is fraud, misrepresentation, mistake, duress, menace, or undue influence involved in reaching an agreement.

Fraud

An act meant to deceive in order to get someone to part with something of value is called **fraud**. An outright lie, or making a promise with no intention of carrying it out, can be fraud. Lack of disclosure—causing someone to make or accept an offer—is also fraud. For example, failure to tell a prospective buyer that the roof leaks when he or she makes an offer to purchase on a sunny day is fraud. It can make the contract voidable.

Innocent Misrepresentation

When the person unknowingly provides wrong information, **innocent misrepresentation** occurs. Even though no dishonesty is involved, a contract may be rescinded or revoked by the party who feels misled. The **hold harmless clause** protects the broker from incorrect information.

Mistake

In contract law, **mistake** means an agreement was unclear or there was a misunderstanding in the facts. Mistake does not include ignorance, incompetence, or poor judgment. For example, you accepted an offer to purchase a home on what you thought was an all cash offer. Later you found that you had agreed to carry a second trust deed. Even though you made a mistake in reading the sales contract, you now have a binding agreement.

There are times when ambiguity creates a misunderstanding, and ultimately you void the contract. For instance, you were given directions to a friend's beach house, went there on your own, and fell in love with the home. You immediately made an offer, which was accepted, only to discover you had gone to the wrong house. Because you thought you were purchasing a different property than the one the seller was selling, this mistake is a major misunderstanding of a material fact, and therefore would void any signed contract.

Duress

Use of force, known as **duress** or **menace**, which is the threat of violence, cannot be used to get agreement.

Undue Influence

Undue influence or using unfair advantage is also unacceptable. All can result in a contract to be voidable by the injured party.

> **Review - Situations that Negate Genuine Assent**
> - Fraud
> - Misrepresentation
> - Mistake
> - Duress or Menace
> - Undue Influence

Lawful Objective

Even though the parties are capable, and mutually agreeable, the object of the contract must be lawful. A contract requiring the performance of an illegal act would not be valid, nor would one in which the consideration was stolen.

The contract also must be legal in its formation and operation. For example, a note bearing an interest rate in excess of that allowed by law would be void. Contracts may be unenforceable if they are unconscionable, or contrary to law or public policy.

Sufficient Consideration

There are several types of consideration one can use in a contract. Generally, **consideration** is something of value, such as a promise of future payment, money, property, or personal services. For example, there can be an exchange of a promise for a promise, money for a promise, money for property, or goods for services. Legally, all contracts require **acceptable consideration**. Terms that denote acceptable consideration include valuable, adequate, good, or sufficient consideration.

Forbearance, or forgiving a debt or obligation, or giving up an interest or a right, qualifies as valuable consideration. Gifts, such as real property based solely on love and affection are good consideration. They meet the legal requirement that consideration be present in a contract.

In an option, the promise of the offeror is the consideration for the forbearance desired from the offeree. In other words, the person wanting the option promises to give something of value in return for being able to exercise the option to purchase at some specifically named time in the future.

In a bilateral contract, a promise of one party is consideration for the promise of another. For example, in the sale of real property, the buyer promises to pay a certain amount and the seller promises to transfer title.

Note: The earnest money given at the time of an offer is not the consideration for the sale. It is simply an indication of the buyer's intent to perform the contract, and may be used for damages, even if the buyer backs out of the sale.

INTERPRETATION OF CONTRACTS

Once the parties have entered into an agreement, disputes may still arise about how certain terms or phrases in the agreement are to be interpreted. There are a number of principles for the interpretation of contracts, many of which have been enacted into the California Civil Code.

Statute of Frauds

Most contracts required by law to be in writing are under the **statute of frauds**. In California, the statute of frauds requires that certain contracts be in writing to prevent fraud in the sale of land or an interest in land. Included in this are offers, acceptances, loan assumptions, land contracts, deeds, escrows, and options to purchase. Trust deeds, promissory notes, and leases for more than one year also must be in writing to be enforceable. There are a number of agreements subject to the statute of frauds that are beyond the scope of this work. The principal agreements of interest in the real estate business are found in Civil Code §1624.

Contracts That Must Be In Writing

- An agreement for the sale of real property
- An agreement that cannot be performed within a year from its making. This includes a lease for longer than one year
- An agreement to employ an agent, broker, or other person to purchase, sell, or to lease real estate for longer than one year, for compensation or a commission
- An agreement by a purchaser of real property to pay an indebtedness secured by a mortgage or deed of trust upon the property purchased, unless the purchaser's assumption of the indebtedness is provided for in the conveyance of the property

The statute of frauds also affects personal property. Personal property valued at more than $500 must be accompanied by a written bill of sale.

Parol Evidence Rule

When two parties make oral promises to each other, and then write and sign a contract promising something different, the written contract will be considered the valid one. Parol means oral, or by word of mouth. The **parol evidence rule** extends this meaning and prohibits introducing any kind of outside evidence to vary or add to the terms of deeds, contracts or other writings once executed. Under the parol evidence rule, when a contract is intended to be the parties' complete and final agreement, no further outside promises, oral or written, are allowed. Occasionally a contract is ambiguous or vague. Then the courts will allow use of prior agreements to clarify an existing disputed contract.

One of a real estate licensee's main duties is to make sure all contract language conveys the parties' wishes and agreements. Oral agreements have caused much confusion and bad feelings over the years, particularly in real estate. Even a lease for less than one year should be in writing, though the statute of frauds does not require it. (A lease for one or more years must be in writing). It is easy to forget oral agreements. A written contract is the most reasonable way to ensure mutual assent.

Determining Conflicts in a Contract

When preparing a contract, if the parties involved want to make handwritten changes and initial them, those changes control the document.

Order of Resolving Contradictory Statements in Contracts

1. Handwritten content
2. Typewritten content
3. Attached addenda
4. Preprinted material

Handwritten clauses and insertions take precedence over any typewritten content, attached addenda, and preprinted material. Typed clauses and insertions take precedence over any attached addenda and the preprinted material. Attached addenda take precedence over the preprinted material.

DISCHARGE OF CONTRACTS

Discharge of contract refers to the cancellation or termination of a contract. Contracts are discharged by performance, release, assignment, novation, and breach.

Performance

Commonly the discharge of a contract occurs when the contract has been fully performed.

A **tender of performance** is an offer by one of the parties to carry out his or her part of the contract. Usually, a tender is made at the time to close escrow. The person to whom the tender is made must state any objections at that time or they are waived. A **waiver** is the relinquishment or refusal to accept a right. A person must take advantage of his or her rights at the proper time. If they do not, they give up (waive) their rights. A tender of performance by the buyer, for example, by depositing the purchase money into escrow, places the seller in default, if the seller refuses to accept it and deliver a deed. The buyer could rescind the transaction, or sue for breach of contract or for specific performance. **Specific performance** is a court action brought about by one party to force the other (breaching) party to fulfill the conditions of the contract.

Release

The person in the contract to whom an obligation is owed may release the other party from the obligation to perform the contract.

Mutual Rescission

A **mutual rescission** occurs when all parties to a contract agree to cancel the agreement.

Assignment

An assignment will transfer all the interests of the **assignor** (principal) to the **assignee**. The assignee takes over the assignor's rights, remedies, benefits, and duties in the contract. In this situation, the assignor is not completely released from the obligations for the contract and remains secondarily liable.

Novation

If the assignor wants to be released entirely from any obligation for the contract, it may be done by **novation**. That is the substitution, by agreement, of a new obligation for an existing one, with the intent to extinguish the original contract. For example, novation occurs when a buyer assumes a seller's loan, and the lender releases the seller from the loan contract by substituting the buyer's name on the loan.

Breach

Occasionally one party or the other will be unable to live up to the terms of the contract and is in breach of the agreement. A **breach of contract** is a failure to perform on part or all of the terms and conditions of a contract. A person harmed by non-performance can accept the failure to perform or has a choice of three remedies: unilateral rescission, lawsuit for money damages, or lawsuit for specific performance.

Unilateral Rescission

Unilateral rescission is available to a person who enters a contract without genuine assent because of fraud, mistake, duress, menace, undue influence, or faulty consideration. Rescission may be used as a means of discharging a contract by agreement, as we have mentioned.

If one of the parties has been wronged by a breach of contract that innocent party can stop performing all obligations as well, therefore unilaterally rescinding the contract. It must be done promptly, restoring to the other party everything of value received as a result of the breached contract, on condition that the other party shall do the same.

Lawsuit for Money Damages

When a party is a breach-of-contract victim, a second remedy is a **lawsuit for money damages**. If damages to an injured party are expressed in a dollar amount, the innocent party could sue for money damage. This includes the price paid by the buyer, the difference between the contract price, and the value of the property, title and document expenses, consequential damages, and interest.

Lawsuit for Specific Performance

A third remedy for breach of contract is a **lawsuit for specific performance**. This is an action in court by the injured party to force the breaching party to carry out the remainder of the contract according to the agreed-upon terms, price, and conditions. Generally, this remedy occurs when money cannot restore an injured party's position. This is often the case in real estate because of the difficulty in finding a similar property.

> **Review - Discharge of Contracts**
> - Full performance
> - Release by one or all of the parties
> - Assignment
> - Novation
> - Breach of contract

STATUTE OF LIMITATIONS

Under California law, any person filing a lawsuit must follow the time limits in the statute of limitations. The **statute of limitations** places a limit on the length of time a plaintiff has to file a lawsuit. Once the statute of limitations has expired, any lawsuit that could have been brought to enforce one's contractual rights is terminated just as completely as if they had not existed in the first place.

Time Limits for Filing Civil Actions

90 Days	Civil actions to recover personal property, such as suitcases, clothing, or jewelry alleged to have been left at a hotel or in an apartment; must begin within 90 days after the owners depart from the personal property.
6 Months	Action against an officer to recover property seized in an official capacity—such as by a tax collector.
1 Year	Libel or slander, injury or death caused by wrongful act, or loss to depositor against a bank for the payment of a forged check.
2 Years	Action on a contract, not in writing; action based on a policy of title insurance.
3 Years	Action on a liability created by statute; action for trespass on or injury to real property, such as encroachment; action for relief on the grounds of fraud or mistake; attachment.
4 Years	Action on any written contract; includes most real estate contracts.
10 Years	Action on a judgment or decree of any court in the United States.

SUMMARY

A **contract** is a legally enforceable agreement to perform or not perform a certain act. Contracts are classified as express or implied; bilateral or unilateral; executory or executed; and void, voidable, unenforceable, or valid.

There are four requirements for a contract to be legally binding and enforceable: (1) legally competent parties, (2) mutual consent between the parties, a (3) lawful objective, and (4) sufficient consideration.

In a valid contract, all parties must mutually agree **(meeting of the minds)**. One party must offer and another must accept unconditionally. An **acceptance** is an unqualified agreement to the terms of an offer. The offer must be definite and certain in its terms, and the agreement must be genuine or the contract may be voidable by one or both parties. A **counteroffer** becomes a new offer, made by the original party (offeree). Parties can terminate a contract by performance, release, assignment, novation, and breach. All contracts require acceptable consideration.

The **California Statute of Frauds** requires that certain contracts be in writing to prevent fraud in the sale of land or an interest in land.

When using preprinted forms, typed or handwritten clauses and insertions take priority over the preprinted material.

UNIT 4 REVIEW

Matching Exercise

Instructions: Write the letter of the matching term on the blank line before its definition. Answers immediately follow the Multiple Choice Questions.

Terms

A. abrogation
B. addendum
C. assignee
D. assignor
E. consideration
F. counteroffer
G. executory contract

H. express contract
I. forbearance
J. novation
K. offer
L. offeree
M. offeror
N. rescission

O. revocation
P. specific performance
Q. statute of frauds
R. statute of limitations
S. tender
T. waiver

Definitions

1. _____ The rejection of an original offer that becomes a new offer.

2. _____ A presentation or proposal for acceptance to form a contract.

3. _____ Something of value—such as money, a promise, property, or personal services.

4. _____ An offer by one of the parties to carry out his or her part of the contract.

5. _____ The law that requires contracts to be in writing.

6. _____ The relinquishment or refusal to accept a right.

7. _____ The person transferring a claim, benefit, or right in property to another.

8. _____ A court action brought to compel a party to carry out the terms of a contract.

9. _____ A contract in which obligation to perform exists on one or both sides.

10. _____ The canceling of an offer to contract by the person making the original offer.

11. _____ Party to whom a lease is assigned or transferred.

12. _____ Legal action taken to repeal a contract either by mutual consent of the parties or by one party when the other party has breached a contract.

13. _____ The party making an offer.

14. _____ The substitution by agreement of a new obligation for an existing one.

15. _____ Parties declare the terms and put their intentions in oral or written words.

Multiple Choice Questions

Instructions: Circle your response and then check your response with the Answer Key that immediately follows the Multiple Choice Questions.

1. When a promise is given by both parties with the expectation of performance by the other party, it is known as a(n) _____ contract.
    a. unilateral
    b. bilateral
    c. implied
    d. express

2. A contract signed under duress is:
    a. void.
    b. voidable.
    c. illicit.
    d. enforceable.

3. A minor cannot hire a real estate broker using a listing agreement because a minor:
    a. can disaffirm the contract.
    b. is legally incapable.
    c. is incapable of making an adult decision.
    d. cannot do so without parental approval.

4. All of the following are necessary for a valid contract, except:
    a. sufficient writing.
    b. genuine consent.
    c. lawful object.
    d. capable parties.

5. All of the following are necessary for a valid contract except:

    a. payment of money.
    b. genuine consent.
    c. lawful object.
    d. adequate mental capacity of the contracting parties.

6. The following are necessary elements to create a valid contract, except:

    a. consideration.
    b. acceptance.
    c. offer.
    d. performance.

7. The essential element needed to create a binding employment contract for the sale of any right, title, or interest in real property is a(n):

    a. written instrument.
    b. written authorization to accept offers on the property.
    c. written agreement as to the amount of commission.
    d. authorization to accept a deposit.

8. A written contract takes precedence over oral agreements. This principle is expressed by the:

    a. statute of limitations.
    b. statute of frauds.
    c. parol evidence rule.
    d. rule of previous evidence.

9. The relinquishment or refusal to accept a right is known as:

    a. tender.
    b. waiver.
    c. novation.
    d. forbearance.

10. The substitution of an obligation or contract with a new one is called:

    a. recission.
    b. subordination.
    c. novation.
    d. conversion.

11. A bilateral contract is:
    a. a contract in which a party promises to perform without expectation of performance by the other party.
    b. an agreement in which each person promises to perform an act in exchange for another person's promise to perform.
    c. an agreement shown by act and conduct rather than words.
    d. an agreement in which something remains to be performed by one or both parties.

12. Of the following, who would not be considered a legally competent party?
    a. Mary, a 20-year old university student
    b. Bob, a 16-year old emancipated by the court
    c. Alice, a 17-year old who is engaged to be married
    d. Tom, a 17-year old who enlisted in the navy after graduating high school

13. Tom listed his home with broker Barbara. The listing agreement was a standard preprinted form into which Barbara typed the listing information. She typed 90 days as the term of the listing. However, at the listing meeting, Tom changed the term of the listing agreement from 90 to 60 days which he wrote in the contract, initialed the change, and signed the contract. After 60 days, Tom told Barbara he was going to list with another broker, but Barbara told him that he had 30 days remaining on his existing listing agreement. Who is correct, broker Barbara or seller Tom?
    a. Barbara - typed clauses and insertions take precedence over any attached addenda and the preprinted material.
    b. Barbara - preprinted material and typed clauses take precedence over any attached addenda and handwritten clauses.
    c. Tom - handwritten clauses takes precedence over the preprinted material but not typewritten content.
    d. Tom - handwritten clauses and insertions take precedence over any type-written content, attached addenda, and preprinted material.

14. What is the commonality of unilateral rescission, performance, and breach?
    a. They are methods of creating contracts.
    b. They are methods of discharging contracts.
    c. They refer to the statute of frauds.
    d. They are contract classifications.

15. How long is the statute of limitations for a contract to purchase a condominium?
    a. 3 years
    b. 4 years
    c. 5 years
    d. 10 years

UNIT 4 ANSWER KEY

Answers – Matching

1. F	4. S	7. D	10. O	13. M
2. K	5. Q	8. P	11. C	14. J
3. E	6. T	9. G	12. N	15. H

Answers – Multiple Choice

1. **(b)**   A bilateral contract is an agreement in which each person promises to perform an act in exchange for another person's promise to perform. [Classification of Contracts]

2. **(b)**   Duress is unlawful and makes the contract voidable. A voidable contract is valid and enforceable on its face, but may be rejected by the person who signed it under duress, menace, or undue influence. [Classification of Contracts]

3. **(b)**   A listing agreement is an employment contract, so all four elements to create a valid contract must be present to be valid. A minor cannot enter into a valid and binding contract because of incapacity. If capacity is lacking, the contract is void from the start. [Basic Elements of Valid Contracts]

4. **(a)**   A valid contract does not require a sufficient writing. However, according to the statute of frauds, sufficient writing is required for an enforceable real estate contract. The question is asking the valid requirements for a contract not a valid real estate contract. [Basic Elements of Valid Contracts]

5. **(a)**   Choice (a) is correct because consideration is required—not necessarily as money. The following items are essential for a valid contract: capacity, mutual consent, lawful object, and consideration. Choices (b), (c), and (d) are required. [Basic Elements of Valid Contracts]

6. **(d)**   Performance is not essential to create a valid contract. Choices (a), (b), and (c) are required to create a valid contract. [Basic Elements of Valid Contracts]

7. **(a)**   According to the Statute of Frauds, the employment agreement must be in writing to be enforceable. [Interpretation of Contracts]

8. **(c)**   Under the parol evidence rule, when two parties make oral promises to each other, and then write and sign a contract promising something different, the written contract will be considered the valid one. [Interpretation of Contracts]

9. **(b)**   A waiver is the relinquishment or refusal to accept a right. A tender of performance is an offer by one of the parties to carry out his or her part of the contract. Novation is the substitution, by agreement, of a new obligation for an existing one, with the intent to extinguish the original contract. Forbearance is forgiving a debt or obligation, or giving up an interest or a right. [Discharge of Contracts]

10. **(c)**   Novation substitutes one contract for another, by mutual agreement. The intent is to extinguish the former contract and create a new one. [Discharge of Contracts]

11. **(b)**   A bilateral contract is an agreement in which each person promises to perform an act in exchange for another person's promise to perform. [Classification of Contracts]

12. **(c)**   Parties entering into a contract must have legal capacity to do so. A person must be at least 18 years of age unless married, in the military, or declared emancipated by the court. [Basic Elements of Valid Contracts]

13. **(d)**   Handwritten clauses and insertions take precedence over any typewritten content, attached addenda, and preprinted material. Typed clauses and insertions take precedence over any attached addenda and the preprinted material. Attached addenda take precedence over the preprinted material. [Interpretation of Contracts]

14. **(b)**   Contracts are discharged by performance, release, assignment, novation, and breach. [Discharge of Contracts]

15. **(b)**   The statute of limitations is 4 years for actions on any written contract, which includes most real estate contracts. [Statute of Limitations]

Agency Relationships

Unit 5

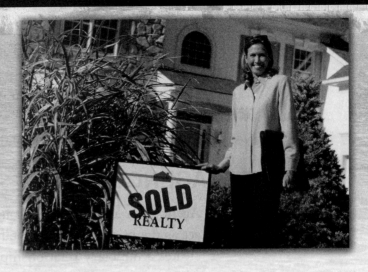

INTRODUCTION

As a real estate licensee, your main job will be to represent someone else in a real estate transaction. When that person gives you the authority to act on his or her behalf, it creates a special legal relationship called agency, which is defined, within Real Estate Law, by a body of laws called agency law. This unit will outline the different types of relationships you as a licensee can form with a client. These relationships are called **agency relationships**. Agency law affects all of your dealings as a licensee—all of your agency relationships.

The purpose of agency law is to make sure you know whom you are representing and what your obligations are when you act for another person. Your success in real estate sales will depend on your knowledge of agency law. Consumers rely on you to explain the law as well as to make sure it is carried out. They want to be assured that you are representing their best interests.

Learning Objectives

After completing this Unit, you should be able to:

4A   recognize the types of agency relationships and methods to create and terminate them.

4B   classify listing and buyer representation agreements used in California.

4C   delineate the duties and rights of the parties in agency relationships.

WHAT IS AGENCY?

Agency is a legal relationship in which a principal authorizes an agent to act as the principal's representative when dealing with third parties. This creates a **fiduciary relationship** between the agent and the principal. A fiduciary relationship implies a position of trust or confidence. The agent is in a position of trust or confidence with the principal and owes the principal certain fiduciary duties. The agent has the fiduciary duty of loyalty, integrity, and utmost care to the principal. This means that the agent bound by agency law acts in the best interests of the principal. There is an obligation always to act fairly and honestly with third parties. The law compares the fiduciary duties owed by the agent to the principal, as to the trustee to a beneficiary, or like a mortgagee to mortgagor.

> **The agent works for the principal and with third parties.**

An agent is either a special agent or general agent. This depends on the scope of authority delegated to the agent by the principal. A **special agent** is employed to perform a specific task, whereas any other agent would be a **general agent**. A real estate broker, for example, who has a contract is a special agent authorized to perform certain acts for a specified time.

The authority given an agent is determined by the principal. If described in a written agreement, it is called **actual authority**. A principal is not responsible for the acts of the agent if those acts are beyond the agent's actual authority. If the principal has not given the agent actual or ostensible (apparent) authority to do the act, a third party cannot hold the principal responsible. An agent may have authority under a power of attorney, allowing him or her to conduct certain business for a principal. A **power of attorney** is a written document that gives a person legal authority to act on behalf of another person. Typically, there are two types used in real estate–special and general. A **special power of attorney** authorizes the agent to do certain specific acts. A **general power of attorney** allows the agent to transact all the business of the principal. The agent is then known as an attorney-in-fact.

Agency Relationships in Real Estate

As we just learned, every agency relationship has a principal, an agent, and a third party. In a real estate transaction the **principal** (buyer or seller), **agent** (real estate broker) and **third party** (customer) are bound together in a legal relationship, with all the duties and rights that go with that connection. Most frequently, the principal is a seller who employs an agent to find a buyer for his or her property. Sometimes the principal is a buyer who employs an agent to locate a property.

The Broker is the Agent

The agent is always a licensed real estate broker. That is why a listing broker is also called a listing agent; a selling broker is also called a selling agent; and a buyer's broker is also called a buyer's agent. When a broker represents only the buyer or the seller in the transaction, it is called **single agency**. A **dual agency** exists if one broker represents both principals in the transaction.

Review – Agency Relationships		
Agent (Broker)	Principal (Client)	Third Party (Customer)
Listing Agent	Seller	Buyer
Subagent	Seller	Buyer
Buyer's Agent	Buyer	Seller
Selling Agent	Seller or Buyer	Buyer orSeller
Cooperating Broker	Seller or Buyer	Buyer or Seller
Dual Agent	Seller & Buyer	No Third Party

Listing Agent

A **listing agent** is a broker who obtains a listing from a seller to act as an agent for compensation. A **listing** is a contract between an owner of real property and an agent who is authorized to obtain a buyer.

Subagent

A **subagent** is a broker delegated by the listing agent (if authorized by the seller) who represents the seller in finding a buyer for the listed property.

Buyer's Agent

A **buyer's agent** is a broker employed by the buyer to locate a certain kind of real property.

Dual Agent

A **dual agent** is a broker acting as agent for both the seller and the buyer in the same transaction. A broker can legally be the agent of both the seller and the buyer in a transaction, but the broker must have the informed, written consent of both the seller and the buyer. The dual agent is a broker who may be working independently or through an associate licensee. A real estate broker who has a listing agreement with a seller may establish an agency with a buyer as well. In this case, whether the broker is the actual agent of both the seller and the buyer, or the agent of the seller and the ostensible or implied agent of the buyer, the broker is acting as a dual agent. Dual agency commonly occurs when two associate licensees employed by the same broker represent two or more parties to a transaction. The real estate broker is then a dual agent.

A real estate broker who represents both buyer and seller must act with extreme care because the broker owes fiduciary duties to both principals. The broker would have conflict with the negotiation of price and terms between seller and buyer and the negotiation of loan amount and terms between lender and borrower. A real estate broker functioning as a dual agent may not disclose to the seller that the buyer is willing to pay more than the buyer's written offer to purchase. A dual agent cannot disclose to the buyer that the seller will take less than the listing agreement, without the express written consent of the party authorizing the disclosure.

Selling Agent

A **selling agent** is the broker who finds a buyer and obtains an offer for the real property. Usually a cooperating broker, the selling agent (broker) may act as a subagent of the seller, as an agent of the buyer, or as a dual agent.

Cooperating Broker

A **cooperating broker** is a selling agent who assists another broker by finding a buyer. A cooperating broker participates in the multiple listing service (MLS), and finds a buyer for a property listed in MLS. A cooperating broker may represent either the seller or the buyer.

Is the Cooperating Broker a Subagent?

Most property is sold through a local association of brokers called a multiple listing service. A **multiple listing service (MLS)** is a cooperative listing service conducted by a group of brokers, usually members of a real estate association. Listings are submitted to a central bureau where they are entered into a computerized system and printed regularly in a multiple listing book that is available to the members. The MLS maintains an inventory of all the available, listed properties in the area. Any MLS member may view the listed properties and obtain offers from buyers for these properties even though he or she is not the listing broker.

A broker who brings an offer to the listing broker in this way is called a cooperating broker. The cooperating broker receives a part of the commission at the close of escrow.

Since a cooperating broker finds the buyer, an issue that can be confusing is the question of whether the cooperating broker represents the seller or the buyer. Buyers commonly believe that the cooperating broker represents the buyer. Others assume that the cooperating broker is a subagent of the listing broker and represents the seller.

A **subagent** is defined as the agent of someone who is already the agent of the principal. If authorized by the seller, the listing agent can delegate another broker to be a subagent who will also represent the seller. Therefore, subagents take on the same fiduciary duties as primary agents. If the cooperating broker is a subagent for the seller, then the cooperating broker owes a fiduciary duty and loyalty to the seller. If the cooperating broker represents the buyer, the fiduciary duty is to the buyer.

Nothing in the listing agreement compels the cooperating broker to represent the seller. A seller authorizes the listing broker to cooperate in any manner with other brokers in showing the property, but the seller must give specific authorization for subagency. If authorized, the listing broker may offer subagency to a cooperating broker, and the cooperating broker may accept or decline the offer. (Acceptance could be in writing or by the conduct of the cooperating broker).

Thus, a cooperating broker does not automatically become a subagent when he or she shows a listed property. As long as complete disclosure is made about agency relationships, the cooperating broker can represent either the seller or the buyer.

Cooperating brokers should choose to be either the seller's agent or the buyer's agent, and make sure their actions conform to their choice. They should be aware of the practical and legal consequences of this choice to avoid a conflict of loyalties or a violation of Real Estate Law.

In general, if the cooperating broker is acting like the agent of the buyer, he or she is the agent of the buyer. An agency relationship is created between the broker and the buyer by implication. The buyer becomes the cooperating broker's principal, and the seller becomes the third party. When the buyer makes an offer, he or she signs the Confirmation of Agency form and confirms the agency relationship in writing. Until that point, there is no clear rule about when the fiduciary relationship starts between the cooperating broker and the buyer. It is safe to assume that the agency relationship starts as soon as the cooperating broker begins acting in the best interest of the buyer.

**The Orange County Association of REALTORS®
addresses the optional nature of subagency in Rule 7.12**

Rule 7.12 Unilateral Contractual Offer; Subagency Optional. In filing a property with the MLS, the broker participant makes a blanket unilateral contractual offer of compensation to the other MLS broker participants for their services in selling the property. A broker participant must specify some compensation to be paid to either a buyer's agent or a subagent and the offer of compensation must be stated in one, or a combination of the following forms (1) a percentage of the gross selling price; or (2) a definite dollar amount. At the broker participant's option, a broker participant may limit his or her offer of compensation to buyer's agents only, to subagents only, or make the offer of compensation to both. Any such limitations must be specified on the property data form and in the MLS. The amount of compensation offered to buyer's agents or subagents may be the same or different but must be clearly specified on the property data profile sheet. Broker participants wishing to offer subagency to the other MLS participants must so specify on the property data profile sheet and on the MLS; otherwise, the offer of compensation does not constitute an offer of subagency.

Agents Working for the Broker

A **sales associate** (also called an **associate licensee**) is a licensed real estate salesperson or broker whose license is held by an employing licensed broker. The sales associate works for an employing broker, and the employing broker is responsible for the acts of the sales associate. A sales associate is the agent of his or her employing broker and must deal fairly with the broker's customers. Sales associates are not agents of the buyer or seller in a real property transaction.

> Example: Rose, a sales associate in the employ of broker Dan, listed a property owned by Jose Miranda. Under the law, the agency has been created between Jose Miranda and broker Dan. Rose is bound by the agency because she represents Dan.

Review - Agency
- **In a real estate transaction, the agent is always a broker.**
- **In a listing agreement:**
  - the agent of the seller (principal) is the listing agent or listing broker.
  - a subagent represents the seller.
  - a broker who works with the buyer (third party) can be the selling agent or cooperating broker.
- **The broker who represents and works for both buyer and seller is a dual agent.**
- **In a buyer representation agreement:**
  - the agent of the buyer is the buyer's agent or buyer's broker.

Disclosing the Agency Relationship

Traditionally, the principal in a real estate transaction was a seller, represented by the listing broker. The selling broker might have represented the principal as a subagent. Then, as now, the selling broker was legally bound by a fiduciary duty to the seller. So who represented the buyer when the listing broker wrote up the offer? Who represented the buyer when a selling broker wrote up the offer and presented it to the seller? The answer is—no one. Legally, the buyer had no representation, even though it appeared to be the licensed agent showing the property and writing up the offer.

The requirement to disclose agency and reveal what relationship the parties have with each other came out of public demand for assurance of representation in all real estate dealings.

As of January 1, 1988, the **Agency Relationship Disclosure Act** became effective in an attempt to clarify the agency relationships among sellers, agents, and buyers. It applies to every residential property transaction of one-to-four units. The law requires that an agent supply a written document, called Disclosure Regarding Real Estate Agency Relationships, explaining the nature of agency. This disclosure must be made **prior** to taking a listing or writing an offer.

Disclosure Process

The steps in the disclosure process are disclose, elect, and confirm. (Mnemonic DEC).

Disclose the Relationship

The Disclosure Regarding Real Estate Agency Relationships document describes the obligations of an agent as seller's agent, buyer's agent, or dual agent. At this point, all parties are made aware that they do have a choice of who is to represent them as their own agent.

Who Presents a Written Disclosure?

- Listing agent (or his or her sales associate) must deliver the form to the seller before entering into a listing agreement.

- Selling agent (who may also be the listing agent) must provide the form to the buyer before the buyer makes an offer to purchase.

- Selling agent (if different from the listing agent) must provide the form to the seller before the offer to purchase is accepted.

Elect the Agency

The second part of the agency disclosure form requires all parties involved to confirm that they understand the agent's role. In other words, the first part of the disclosure reveals that the agent may represent only the buyer, only the seller, or both. All parties acknowledge their understanding at this point.

Confirm the Agency

All parties to the transaction (buyer, seller, and agents) are required to acknowledge that they understand who is representing whom, and sign the agency confirmation form. One more time, the relationship will be confirmed in the sales contract, which is signed by all parties.

DISCLOSURE REGARDING
REAL ESTATE AGENCY RELATIONSHIP

(Listing Firm to Seller)
(As required by the Civil Code)
(C.A.R. Form AD, Revised 12/14)

☐ (If checked) This form is being provided in connection with a transaction for a leasehold interest exceeding one year as per Civil Code section 2079.13(k) and (l).

When you enter into a discussion with a real estate agent regarding a real estate transaction, you should from the outset understand what type of agency relationship or representation you wish to have with the agent in the transaction.

SELLER'S AGENT

A Seller's agent under a listing agreement with the Seller acts as the agent for the Seller only. A Seller's agent or a subagent of that agent has the following affirmative obligations:

To the Seller: A Fiduciary duty of utmost care, integrity, honesty and loyalty in dealings with the Seller.

To the Buyer and the Seller:

(a) Diligent exercise of reasonable skill and care in performance of the agent's duties.

(b) A duty of honest and fair dealing and good faith.

(c) A duty to disclose all facts known to the agent materially affecting the value or desirability of the property that are not known to, or within the diligent attention and observation of, the parties. An agent is not obligated to reveal to either party any confidential information obtained from the other party that does not involve the affirmative duties set forth above.

BUYER'S AGENT

A selling agent can, with a Buyer's consent, agree to act as agent for the Buyer only. In these situations, the agent is not the Seller's agent, even if by agreement the agent may receive compensation for services rendered, either in full or in part from the Seller. An agent acting only for a Buyer has the following affirmative obligations:

To the Buyer: A fiduciary duty of utmost care, integrity, honesty and loyalty in dealings with the Buyer.

To the Buyer and the Seller:

(a) Diligent exercise of reasonable skill and care in performance of the agent's duties.

(b) A duty of honest and fair dealing and good faith.

(c) A duty to disclose all facts known to the agent materially affecting the value or desirability of the property that are not known to, or within the diligent attention and observation of, the parties.

An agent is not obligated to reveal to either party any confidential information obtained from the other party that does not involve the affirmative duties set forth above.

AGENT REPRESENTING BOTH SELLER AND BUYER

A real estate agent, either acting directly or through one or more associate licensees, can legally be the agent of both the Seller and the Buyer in a transaction, but only with the knowledge and consent of both the Seller and the Buyer.

In a dual agency situation, the agent has the following affirmative obligations to both the Seller and the Buyer:

(a) A fiduciary duty of utmost care, integrity, honesty and loyalty in the dealings with either the Seller or the Buyer.

(b) Other duties to the Seller and the Buyer as stated above in their respective sections.

In representing both Seller and Buyer, the agent may not, without the express permission of the respective party, disclose to the other party that the Seller will accept a price less than the listing price or that the Buyer will pay a price greater than the price offered.

The above duties of the agent in a real estate transaction do not relieve a Seller or Buyer from the responsibility to protect his or her own interests. You should carefully read all agreements to assure that they adequately express your understanding of the transaction. A real estate agent is a person qualified to advise about real estate. If legal or tax advice is desired, consult a competent professional.

Throughout your real property transaction you may receive more than one disclosure form, depending upon the number of agents assisting in the transaction. The law requires each agent with whom you have more than a casual relationship to present you with this disclosure form. You should read its contents each time it is presented to you, considering the relationship between you and the real estate agent in your specific transaction. **This disclosure form includes the provisions of Sections 2079.13 to 2079.24, inclusive, of the Civil Code set forth on page 2. Read it carefully. I/WE ACKNOWLEDGE RECEIPT OF A COPY OF THIS DISCLOSURE AND THE PORTIONS OF THE CIVIL CODE PRINTED ON THE BACK (OR A SEPARATE PAGE).**

☐ Buyer ☐ Seller ☐ Landlord ☐ Tenant _____ Date _____

☐ Buyer ☐ Seller ☐ Landlord ☐ Tenant _____ Date _____

Agent _____ BRE Lic. # _____
              Real Estate Broker (Firm)

By _____ BRE Lic. # _____ Date _____
    (Salesperson or Broker-Associate)

Agency Disclosure Compliance (Civil Code §2079.14):
- When the listing brokerage company also represents Buyer/Tenant: The Listing Agent shall have one AD form signed by Seller/Landlord and a different AD form signed by Buyer/Tenant.
- When Seller/Landlord and Buyer/Tenant are represented by different brokerage companies: (i) the Listing Agent shall have one AD form signed by Seller/Landlord and (ii) the Buyer's/Tenant's Agent shall have one AD form signed by Buyer/Tenant and either that same or a different AD form presented to Seller/Landlord for signature prior to presentation of the offer. If the same form is used, Seller may sign here:

        (SELLER/LANDLORD: DO NOT SIGN HERE)   **(SELLER/LANDLORD: DO NOT SIGN HERE)**

Seller/Landlord _____ Date _____   Seller/Landlord _____ Date _____

Reviewed by _____ Date _____

🏠 EQUAL HOUSING OPPORTUNITY

AD REVISED 12/14 (PAGE 1 OF 2)

DISCLOSURE REGARDING REAL ESTATE AGENCY RELATIONSHIP (AD PAGE 1 OF 2)

Phone: Fax:

Produced with zipForm® by zipLogix 18070 Fifteen Mile Road, Fraser, Michigan 48026 www.zipLogix.com

CIVIL CODE SECTIONS 2079.24 (2079.16 APPEARS ON THE FRONT)

2079.13 As used in Sections 2079.14 to 2079.24, inclusive, the following terms have the following meanings: **(a)** "Agent" means a person acting under provisions of Title 9 (commencing with Section 2295) in a real property transaction, and includes a person who is licensed as a real estate broker under Chapter 3 (commencing with Section 10130) of Part 1 of Division 4 of the Business and Professions Code, and under whose license a listing is executed or an offer to purchase is obtained. **(b)** "Associate licensee" means a person who is licensed as a real estate broker or salesperson under Chapter 3 (commencing with Section 10130) of Part 1 of Division 4 of the Business and Professions Code and who is either licensed under a broker or has entered into a written contract with a broker to act as the broker's agent in connection with acts requiring a real estate license and to function under the broker's supervision in the capacity of an associate licensee. The agent in the real property transaction bears responsibility for his or her associate licensees who perform as agents of the agent. When an associate licensee owes a duty to any principal, or to any buyer or seller who is not a principal, in a real property transaction, that duty is equivalent to the duty owed to that party by the broker for whom the associate licensee functions. **(c)** "Buyer" means a transferee in a real property transaction, and includes a person who executes an offer to purchase real property from a seller through an agent, or who seeks the services of an agent in more than a casual, transitory, or preliminary manner, with the object of entering into a real property transaction. "Buyer" includes vendee or lessee. **(d)** "Commercial real property" means all real property in the state, except single-family residential real property, dwelling units made subject to Chapter 2 (commencing with Section 1940) of Title 5, mobilehomes, as defined in Section 798.3, or recreational vehicles, as defined in Section 799.29. **(e)** "Dual agent" means an agent acting, either directly or through an associate licensee, as agent for both the seller and the buyer in a real property transaction. **(f)** "Listing agreement" means a contract between an owner of real property and an agent, by which the agent has been authorized to sell the real property or to find or obtain a buyer. **(g)** "Listing agent" means a person who has obtained a listing of real property to act as an agent for compensation. **(h)** "Listing price" is the amount expressed in dollars specified in the listing for which the seller is willing to sell the real property through the listing agent. **(i)** "Offering price" is the amount expressed in dollars specified in an offer to purchase for which the buyer is willing to buy the real property. **(j)** "Offer to purchase" means a written contract executed by a buyer acting through a selling agent that becomes the contract for the sale of the real property upon acceptance by the seller. **(k)** "Real property" means any estate specified by subdivision (1) or (2) of Section 761 in property that constitutes or is improved with one to four dwelling units, any commercial real property, any leasehold in these types of property exceeding one year's duration, and mobilehomes, when offered for sale or sold through an agent pursuant to the authority contained in Section 10131.6 of the Business and Professions Code. **(l)** "Real property transaction" means a transaction for the sale of real property in which an agent is employed by one or more of the principals to act in that transaction, and includes a listing or an offer to purchase. **(m)** "Sell," "sale," or "sold" refers to a transaction for the transfer of real property from the seller to the buyer, and includes exchanges of real property between the seller and buyer, transactions for the creation of a real property sales contract within the meaning of Section 2985, and transactions for the creation of a leasehold exceeding one year's duration. **(n)** "Seller" means the transferor in a real property transaction, and includes an owner who lists real property with an agent, whether or not a transfer results, or who receives an offer to purchase real property of which he or she is the owner from an agent on behalf of another. "Seller" includes both a vendor and a lessor. **(o)** "Selling agent" means a listing agent who acts alone, or an agent who acts in cooperation with a listing agent, and who sells or finds and obtains a buyer for the real property, or an agent who locates property for a buyer or who finds a buyer for a property for which no listing exists and presents an offer to purchase to the seller. **(p)** "Subagent" means a person to whom an agent delegates agency powers as provided in Article 5 (commencing with Section 2349) of Chapter 1 of Title 9. However, "subagent" does not include an associate licensee who is acting under the supervision of an agent in a real property transaction.

2079.14 Listing agents and selling agents shall provide the seller and buyer in a real property transaction with a copy of the disclosure form specified in Section 2079.16, and, except as provided in subdivision (c), shall obtain a signed acknowledgement of receipt from that seller or buyer, except as provided in this section or Section 2079.15, as follows: **(a)** The listing agent, if any, shall provide the disclosure form to the seller prior to entering into the listing agreement. **(b)** The selling agent shall provide the disclosure form to the seller as soon as practicable prior to presenting the seller with an offer to purchase, unless the selling agent previously provided the seller with a copy of the disclosure form pursuant to subdivision (a). **(c)** Where the selling agent does not deal on a face-to-face basis with the seller, the disclosure form prepared by the selling agent may be furnished to the seller (and acknowledgement of receipt obtained for the selling agent from the seller) by the listing agent, or the selling agent may deliver the disclosure form by certified mail addressed to the seller at his or her last known address, in which case no signed acknowledgement of receipt is required. **(d)** The selling agent shall provide the disclosure form to the buyer as soon as practicable prior to execution of the buyer's offer to purchase, except that if the offer to purchase is not prepared by the selling agent, the selling agent shall present the disclosure form to the buyer not later than the next business day after the selling agent receives the offer to purchase from the buyer.

2079.15 In any circumstance in which the seller or buyer refuses to sign an acknowledgement of receipt pursuant to Section 2079.14, the agent, or an associate licensee acting for an agent, shall set forth, sign, and date a written declaration of the facts of the refusal.

2079.16 Reproduced on Page 1 of this AD form.

2079.17 (a) As soon as practicable, the selling agent shall disclose to the buyer and seller whether the selling agent is acting in the real property transaction exclusively as the buyer's agent, exclusively as the seller's agent, or as a dual agent representing both the buyer and the seller. This relationship shall be confirmed in the contract to purchase and sell real property or in a separate writing executed or acknowledged by the seller, the buyer, and the selling agent prior to or coincident with execution of that contract by the buyer and the seller, respectively. **(b)** As soon as practicable, the listing agent shall disclose to the seller whether the listing agent is acting in the real property transaction exclusively as the seller's agent, or as a dual agent representing both the buyer and seller. This relationship shall be confirmed in the contract to purchase and sell real property or in a separate writing executed or acknowledged by the seller and the listing agent prior to or coincident with the execution of that contract by the seller. **(c)** The confirmation required by subdivisions (a) and (b) shall be in the following form.

_____
(DO NOT COMPLETE. SAMPLE ONLY) is the agent of (check one): ☐ the seller exclusively; or ☐ both the buyer and seller.
(Name of Listing Agent)

_____
(DO NOT COMPLETE. SAMPLE ONLY) is the agent of (check one): ☐ the buyer exclusively; or ☐ the seller exclusively; or
(Name of Selling Agent if not the same as the Listing Agent) ☐ both the buyer and seller.

(d) The disclosures and confirmation required by this section shall be in addition to the disclosure required by Section 2079.14.

2079.18 No selling agent in a real property transaction may act as an agent for the buyer only, when the selling agent is also acting as the listing agent in the transaction.

2079.19 The payment of compensation or the obligation to pay compensation to an agent by the seller or buyer is not necessarily determinative of a particular agency relationship between an agent and the seller or buyer. A listing agent and a selling agent may agree to share any compensation or commission paid, or any right to any compensation or commission for which an obligation arises as the result of a real estate transaction, and the terms of any such agreement shall not necessarily be determinative of a particular relationship.

2079.20 Nothing in this article prevents an agent from selecting, as a condition of the agent's employment, a specific form of agency relationship not specifically prohibited by this article if the requirements of Section 2079.14 and Section 2079.17 are complied with.

2079.21 A dual agent shall not disclose to the buyer that the seller is willing to sell the property at a price less than the listing price, without the express written consent of the seller. A dual agent shall not disclose to the seller that the buyer is willing to pay a price greater than the offering price, without the express written consent of the buyer. This section does not alter in any way the duty or responsibility of a dual agent to any principal with respect to confidential information other than price.

2079.22 Nothing in this article precludes a listing agent from also being a selling agent, and the combination of these functions in one agent does not, of itself, make that agent a dual agent.

2079.23 A contract between the principal and agent may be modified or altered to change the agency relationship at any time before the performance of the act which is the object of the agency with the written consent of the parties to the agency relationship.

2079.24 Nothing in this article shall be construed to either diminish the duty of disclosure owed buyers and sellers by agents and their associate licensees, subagents, and employees or to relieve agents and their associate licensees, subagents, and employees from liability for their conduct in connection with acts governed by this article or for any breach of a fiduciary duty or a duty of disclosure.

Published and Distributed by:
REAL ESTATE BUSINESS SERVICES, INC.
a subsidiary of the California Association of REALTORS®
525 South Virgil Avenue, Los Angeles, California 90020

Reviewed by _____ Date _____

AD REVISED 12/14 (PAGE 2 OF 2)

DISCLOSURE REGARDING REAL ESTATE AGENCY RELATIONSHIP (AD PAGE 2 OF 2)

Produced with zipForm® by zipLogix 18070 Fifteen Mile Road, Fraser, Michigan 48026 www.zipLogix.com   Untitled

CALIFORNIA
ASSOCIATION
OF REALTORS®

**CONFIRMATION OF REAL ESTATE AGENCY
RELATIONSHIPS**
(As required by the Civil Code)
(C.A.R. Form AC, Revised 04/08)

Subject Property Address _____

The following agency relationship(s) is/are hereby confirmed for this transaction:

LISTING AGENT: _____
(Print Firm Name)

is the agent of (check one):

❏ the Seller/Landlord exclusively; or

❏ both the Buyer/Tenant and Seller/Landlord

SELLING AGENT: _____
(Print Firm Name)

(if not the same as Listing Agent)

is the agent of (check one):

❏ the Buyer/Tenant exclusively; or

❏ the Seller/Landlord exclusively; or

❏ both the Buyer/Tenant and Seller/Landlord

I/WE ACKNOWLEDGE RECEIPT OF A COPY OF THIS CONFIRMATION.

Seller/Landlord _____ Date _____

Seller/Landlord _____ Date _____

Buyer/Tenant _____ Date _____

Buyer/Tenant _____ Date _____

Real Estate Broker (Selling Firm) _____

By _____ Date _____

Real Estate Broker (Listing Firm) _____

By _____ Date _____

**A REAL ESTATE BROKER IS QUALIFIED TO ADVISE ON REAL ESTATE. IF YOU DESIRE LEGAL ADVICE,
CONSULT YOUR ATTORNEY.**

This form is available for use by the entire real estate industry. It is not intended to identify the user as a REALTOR®. REALTOR® is a registered collective membership mark which may be used only by members of the NATIONAL ASSOCIATION OF REALTORS® who subscribe to its Code of Ethics.

The copyright laws of the United States (17 U.S. Code) forbid the unauthorized reproduction of this form by any means, including facsimile or computerized formats.
Copyright © 1987 - 2008, CALIFORNIA ASSOCIATION OF REALTORS®

REBS
INC®

Published and Distributed by:
REAL ESTATE BUSINESS SERVICES, INC.
a subsidiary of the California Association of REALTORS®
525 South Virgil Avenue, Los Angeles, California 90020

EQUAL HOUSING
OPPORTUNITY

Reviewed by _____ Date _____

CONFIRMATION REAL ESTATE AGENCY RELATIONSHIPS (AC PAGE 1 OF 1)

Agent:	Phone:	Fax:	Prepared using WINForms® software
Broker:			

Review - Basic Requirements of the Agent in the Disclosure of Agency

- A fiduciary duty of utmost care, integrity, honesty, and loyalty in dealings with the agent's principal
- Reasonable skill and care in performance of agent's duties
- A duty of honesty, fair dealing, and good faith
- A duty to disclose all facts known to the agent materially affecting the value or desirability of the property not known to the other parties

In case you are wondering why all this repetition and paperwork, the agency disclosure is probably one of the most important documents available to the consumer. After years of ambiguity, the law is clear about who is legally representing whom. Buyers or sellers

Steps in the Disclosure Process
Mnemonic = DEC
Disclose
Elect
Confirm

can be confident that their best interests are being represented by an agent on their side in the negotiations.

As a licensee, you must use the Disclosure Regarding Real Estate Agency Relationships form and be able to explain it to your clients and customers. The law is very clear about your responsibility for full disclosure. Misunderstanding or ignorance of the law is not a defense. A real estate license may be revoked or suspended for violation of the agency disclosure law.

Review - Disclosure of Agency Law

- An agent is either the agent of the seller, the buyer, or both buyer and seller.
- A listing broker who is also a selling broker is a dual agent and may not be the agent for the buyer only.
- A dual agent may not tell the seller that the buyer is willing to pay more, nor may a dual agent tell the buyer that the seller will take less without the express written consent of the parties.
- An agency relationship can exist even though no compensation is received from the party with whom the agency relationship is established.

Creating an Agency Relationship

An agency relationship is created between an agent and principal, by agreement, ratification, or estoppel. It is created by an express or implied, written or oral contract. Brokers are fiduciaries whether the agency is created by oral agreement or by **express** (written) **agreement**.

> **Review - Creation of Agency Relationship**
> - Agreement
> - Ratification
> - Estoppel (Ostensible or Implied Agency)

Agency by Agreement

An agency relationship may be created by **agreement**, with or without a written contract. However, a real estate agreement must be in writing to be enforceable in a court of law. The two common ways to create agency with a written real estate contract are through a listing agreement or a buyer representation agreement.

Listing Agreements

A **listing agreement** is a written contract by which a principal, or seller, employs a broker to sell real estate. Depending on its wording, a listing agreement may be considered a bilateral or a unilateral contract. When the seller signs an exclusive authorization and right to sell listing agreement promising payment for service by the listing broker and the broker promises to use due diligence in finding a buyer, it is a **bilateral contract**—in that a promise is given in exchange for a promise.

> **Review - A listing agreement is the most common way to create an agency relationship.**

The listing agreement a contract in which the seller promises to pay a commission upon presentation of a ready, willing, and able buyer who meets all the terms of the listing. A **ready, willing,** and **able** buyer is prepared to enter into a purchase contract, is ready to buy, and meets the financing requirements of purchase. A listing agreement gives the broker the right to be paid only after doing the job, or producing results. Think of it as simply an employment contract between the seller and the broker.

Under agency law, the listing broker is a special agent who deals in the name of the principal to negotiate the sale of property. The broker does not have control over the property itself, while acting within the course of a special agency, but only has the right to represent that principal. The seller is not promising to sell the house, nor can the seller be forced to sell even after signing a listing agreement. The seller is promising to pay a commission to the broker if he or she brings a ready, willing, and able buyer.

> Example: Ellen, a licensed real estate broker, spoke to everyone in her area at least once a month. Since she was well known, when owners wanted to sell their homes, they called Ellen. She would then meet with the owners to complete the listing agreement. An agency by express, written agreement had been created.

Buyer Representation Agreements

As a single agency becomes more prevalent, more brokers represent the buyer to locate a property rather than represent the seller. Typically, an agency relationship is created through the Exclusive Right to Represent Buyer Agreement. The listing agreement is to the seller as the buyer representation agreement is to the buyer. As with all exclusive agreements, a definite termination date is specified. Also, the manner of the broker's compensation is described, stating that all real estate commissions are negotiable.

Agency by Ratification

Ratification means acceptance of an act already performed. Ratification of an agency relationship is created by approving acts after they are done. For example, a seller can accept an offer presented by a licensee and agree to pay a commission, even though no agency has been approved. The seller is creating an agency by ratification by accepting the actions of the agent, after the fact.

> Example: As Ellen walked through the neighborhood talking to people, she became familiar with most of the homes in the area. One day, she answered the office phone and talked to a caller who described the type of home he wanted to buy. She knew of one just like his description, but it was not listed for sale. She called the owner of the house, who told her she could show it to the prospective buyer. Afterward, she presented an offer from the buyer, which included a request to pay Ellen a commission. The owner accepted the offer and agreed to pay Ellen a commission—thus an agency by ratification was created.

Agency by Estoppel

Finally, an agency relationship can be created by estoppel. **Estoppel** is a legal bar that prevents a person from asserting facts or rights that are not consistent with what was implied by the person's previous behavior. That's why this is also called an **implied** or **ostensible** (apparent) agency. Agency is created when the principal causes a third party to believe another person is the principal's agent. What the principal has implied by his or her behavior is barred, or estopped, from being denied. Authority is given when a principal allows a third party to believe that another person is the agent, even if the third party is unaware of the appointment.

> Example: If a seller allows a buyer to believe, a broker represents the seller, and the buyer believes that to be so, the existence of an agency cannot be denied by the seller, who will be bound by the actions of the broker. This is known as the Doctrine of Estoppel.

Ostensible or Implied Agency

A licensee must be aware that an agency relationship can result from one's conduct, even though no express employment contract has been signed, or possible payments established. This is a subject where great care must be taken to assure that the agent is operating correctly, under the law.

When a broker takes a listing, he or she promises to represent the seller while finding a buyer. The broker has a fiduciary duty to conduct negotiations in the best interest of the seller in dealing with buyers who are interested in the property. However, in California, the distinction of who represents whom can get blurred unintentionally.

As the seller's agent, a broker has the duty of utmost care, integrity, honesty, and loyalty in dealings with the seller. Yet the law also requires that the broker exercise reasonable skill and care, honest and fair dealing, and full disclosure of all material facts to all parties. It is difficult for an agent to live up to fiduciary duty to a seller and at the same time meet general obligations to a buyer.

A seller's agent may provide the following services to a buyer without becoming the ostensible or implied agent of the buyer.

Seller's agent may:

- show the buyer properties meeting the buyer's requirements and describe to the buyer a property's amenities, attributes, condition, and status.

- complete a standard purchase contract by inserting the terms of the buyer's offer in the form's blanks and transmit all offers of the buyer to the seller on a timely basis.

- inform the buyer about the availability of financing, legal service, inspection companies, title companies, or other related services desired or required by the buyer to complete the transaction.

While performing the above tasks, it is very difficult not to establish an implied agency with the buyer. A seller's agent must be very alert and conscious of his or her role at all times to avoid becoming a dual agent by implication or conduct.

Listing brokers would violate their agency relationships with their sellers if they made these types of comments to buyers:

- "Leave it all up to me. I can get you the house at the price you want."

- "I'm sure I can get the seller to agree to this price and get the financing you need."

- "I know the seller personally, and I'm sure they won't counter at that price."

- "The house has been for sale for more than eight months and I think it is listed too high. Let's make a lower offer to see if they take it."

- "If the sellers insist on their asking price, I'll remind them that the heating system is old; the carpet is not exactly designer quality; and the whole place needs repainting. That should convince them to reduce their price."

- "I'll write up the offer for you and present it to the seller. If they don't like it, I can always try to find out their bottom line and we can go from there."

Terminating an Agency Relationship

At any time during the agency, the principal or agent may **terminate the agency**, except in an agency coupled with an interest. An agency is also terminated by the expiration of its term, the full performance of the terms of the agency, the destruction of the property, or the death or incapacity of either principal or agent.

> **Review - Termination of Agency Relationship**
> - Full performance
> - Expiration of its term
> - Agreement of the parties
> - Acts of the parties
> - Destruction of the property
> - Death, incapacity, or insanity of the broker or principal
> - Bankruptcy of the principal

Since the relationship between a principal and agent is a personal one, the principal has the right to revoke the agency at any time. If the cancellation is without good reason, the seller may be liable for breach of contract and may be liable to pay a commission to the listing broker. A seller cannot terminate a listing agreement if it is coupled with an interest. An **agency coupled with an interest** is one in which the agent gets an interest in the subject of the agency, which is the property. For example, a broker might advance funds to pay for a defaulted loan on the property to keep it out of foreclosure. The seller cannot revoke the listing after the broker has cured the loan.

An agency agreement must be in writing for the agent to enforce a commission claim based upon a breach of contract.

TYPES OF LISTING AGREEMENTS

In California, there are four commonly used listing agreements: exclusive right to sell listing, exclusive agency listing, open listing, and net listing.

The California Association of REALTORS® (C.A.R.), a dominant provider of real estate forms, has renamed its listing forms to the following:

- **Residential Listing Agreement - Exclusive (Form RLA)**, formerly named Exclusive Authorization and Right to Sell Agreement

- **Residential Listing Agreement - Agency (Form RLAA)**, formerly named Exclusive Agency Listing Agreement

- **Residential Listing Agreement - "Open" (Form RLAN)**, formerly named Non-Exclusive ("Open") Agency Residential Listing Agreement

Exclusive Authorization and Right-to-Sell Listing

An **exclusive authorization** and **right-to-sell listing** is an exclusive contract where the seller must pay the listing broker a commission if the property is sold within the time limit by the listing broker, any other person, or even by the owner. It is a bilateral contract because both parties exchange promises to perform. If the broker brings the seller a mirror offer, or an offer that matches exactly all terms in the listing, the seller does not have to accept the offer. However, under the terms of the listing, the seller must pay the broker a commission. In this listing, the phrase "right to sell" means right to find a buyer. It does not authorize the broker the right to convey any property belonging to the principal unless the agent has a power of attorney to do so.

> **Every exclusive listing must specify a definite termination date.**

Exclusive Agency Listing

An **exclusive agency listing** is an exclusive contract where the seller must pay the listing broker a commission if any broker sells the property. Initially, it is a unilateral contract because nothing is owed unless the broker produces a buyer. It becomes a bilateral contract if and when the broker produces a buyer because at that point both parties have obligations that must be fulfilled and can be enforced. However, the seller has the right to sell the property without a broker and pay no commission. Every exclusive listing must specify a definite termination date.

Open Listing

An **open listing** is a listing agreement that gives any number of brokers the right to sell a property. It is not exclusive and may be given to any number of agents at the same time. An open listing agreement is a unilateral contract because only one party (the seller) is obligated to act if and when an agent produces a buyer. The first broker to obtain a buyer who meets the terms of the listing, and whose offer is accepted by the seller, earns the commission. That agent is known as the procuring cause of the sale. **Procuring cause** refers to a broker who produces a buyer ready, willing, and able to purchase the property for the price and on the terms specified by the seller, regardless of whether the sale is completed. Unlike an exclusive listing agreement, an open listing does not require a specific termination date. The owner may sell the property without an agent, owing no commission.

Net Listing

A **net listing** is an employment contract in which the commission is not definite. Instead, the broker receives all the money from the sale of the property that is in excess of the selling price set by the seller. The broker must disclose the selling price to both buyer and seller within 30 days after closing the transaction.

Option Listing

An **option listing** gives the broker the right to purchase the property that is listed. A broker with an option is acting as a principal as well as an agent. Prior to exercising the option, the seller must be informed of the full amount of the broker's profit and agree to it in writing.

CALIFORNIA
ASSOCIATION
OF REALTORS®

RESIDENTIAL LISTING AGREEMENT
(Exclusive Authorization and Right to Sell)
(C.A.R. Form RLA, Revised 12/15)

Date Prepared: _____
1. EXCLUSIVE RIGHT TO SELL: _____ ("Seller")
hereby employs and grants _____ ("Broker")
beginning (date) _____ and ending at 11:59 P.M. on (date) _____ ("Listing Period")
the exclusive and irrevocable right to sell or exchange the real property described as _____
_____, situated in _____ (City),
_____ (County), California, _____ (Zip Code), Assessor's Parcel No. _____ ("Property").
☐ This Property is a manufactured (mobile) home. See addendum for additional terms.
☐ This Property is being sold as part of a probate, conservatorship or guardianship. See addendum for additional terms.

2. LISTING PRICE AND TERMS:
　A. The listing price shall be: _____
_____ Dollars ($ _____).
　B. Listing Terms: _____
_____

3. COMPENSATION TO BROKER:
Notice: The amount or rate of real estate commissions is not fixed by law. They are set by each Broker individually and may be negotiable between Seller and Broker (real estate commissions include all compensation and fees to Broker).
　A. Seller agrees to pay to Broker as compensation for services irrespective of agency relationship(s), either ☐ _____ percent of the listing price (or if a purchase agreement is entered into, of the purchase price), or ☐ $ _____,
AND _____ , as follows:
　　(1) If during the Listing Period, or any extension, Broker, cooperating broker, Seller or any other person procures a ready, willing, and able buyer(s) whose offer to purchase the Property on any price and terms is accepted by Seller, provided the Buyer completes the transaction or is prevented from doing so by Seller. (Broker is entitled to compensation whether any escrow resulting from such offer closes during or after the expiration of the Listing Period, or any extension.)
　　OR (2) If within _____ calendar days (a) after the end of the Listing Period or any extension; or (b) after any cancellation of this Agreement, unless otherwise agreed, Seller enters into a contract to sell, convey, lease or otherwise transfer the Property to anyone ("Prospective Buyer") or that person's related entity: (i) who physically entered and was shown the Property during the Listing Period or any extension by Broker or a cooperating broker; or (ii) for whom Broker or any cooperating broker submitted to Seller a signed, written offer to acquire, lease, exchange or obtain an option on the Property. Seller, however, shall have no obligation to Broker under paragraph 3A(2) unless, not later than the end of the Listing Period or any extension or cancellation, Broker has given Seller a written notice of the names of such Prospective Buyers.
　　OR (3) If, without Broker's prior written consent, the Property is withdrawn from sale, conveyed, leased, rented, otherwise transferred, or made unmarketable by a voluntary act of Seller during the Listing Period, or any extension.
　B. If completion of the sale is prevented by a party to the transaction other than Seller, then compensation which otherwise would have been earned under paragraph 3A shall be payable only if and when Seller collects damages by suit, arbitration, settlement or otherwise, and then in an amount equal to the lesser of one-half of the damages recovered or the above compensation, after first deducting title and escrow expenses and the expenses of collection, if any.
　C. In addition, Seller agrees to pay Broker: _____ .
　D. Seller has been advised of Broker's policy regarding cooperation with, and the amount of compensation offered to, other brokers.
　　(1) Broker is authorized to cooperate with and compensate brokers participating through the multiple listing service(s) ("MLS") by offering to MLS brokers out of Broker's compensation specified in 3A, either ☐ _____ percent of the purchase price, or ☐ $ _____.
　　(2) Broker is authorized to cooperate with and compensate brokers operating outside the MLS as per Broker's policy.
　E. Seller hereby irrevocably assigns to Broker the above compensation from Seller's funds and proceeds in escrow. Broker may submit this Agreement, as instructions to compensate Broker pursuant to paragraph 3A, to any escrow regarding the Property involving Seller and a buyer, Prospective Buyer or other transferee.
　F. **(1)** Seller represents that Seller has not previously entered into a listing agreement with another broker regarding the Property, unless specified as follows: _____
　　(2) Seller warrants that Seller has no obligation to pay compensation to any other broker regarding the Property unless the Property is transferred to any of the following individuals or entities: _____
_____
　　(3) If the Property is sold to anyone listed above during the time Seller is obligated to compensate another broker: (i) Broker is not entitled to compensation under this Agreement; and (ii) Broker is not obligated to represent Seller in such transaction.
4. A. ITEMS EXCLUDED AND INCLUDED: Unless otherwise specified in a real estate purchase agreement, all fixtures and fittings that are attached to the Property are included, and personal property items are excluded, from the purchase price.
　　ADDITIONAL ITEMS EXCLUDED: _____ .
　　ADDITIONAL ITEMS INCLUDED: _____ .

Seller's Initials (_____) (_____)

RLA REVISED 12/15 (PAGE 1 OF 5)

EQUAL HOUSING
OPPORTUNITY

RESIDENTIAL LISTING AGREEMENT - EXCLUSIVE (RLA PAGE 1 OF 5)

Property Address: _____ Date: _____

Seller intends that the above items be excluded or included in offering the Property for sale, but understands that: (i) the purchase agreement supersedes any intention expressed above and will ultimately determine which items are excluded and included in the sale; and (ii) Broker is not responsible for and does not guarantee that the above exclusions and/or inclusions will be in the purchase agreement.

    B. **(1) Leased Items:** The following items are leased:
      ☐ Solar power system   ☐ Alarm system   ☐ Propane tank   ☐ Water Softener
      ☐ Other _____

      (2) Liened Items: The following items have been financed and a lien has been placed on the Property to secure payment:
      ☐ Solar power system   ☐ Windows or doors   ☐ Heating/Ventilation/Air conditioning system
      ☐ Other _____
    Seller will provide to Buyer, as part of the sales agreement, copies of lease documents, or other documents obligating Seller to pay for any such leased or liened item.

5. MULTIPLE LISTING SERVICE:

A. Broker is a participant/subscriber to _____ Multiple Listing Service (MLS) and possibly others. Unless otherwise instructed in writing the Property will be listed with the MLS(s) specified above. That MLS is (or if checked ☐ is not) the primary MLS for the geographic area of the Property. All terms of the transaction, including sales price and financing, if applicable, (i) will be provided to the MLS in which the property is listed for publication, dissemination and use by persons and entities on terms approved by the MLS and (ii) may be provided to the MLS even if the Property was not listed with the MLS.

BENEFITS OF USING THE MLS; IMPACT OF OPTING OUT OF THE MLS; PRESENTING ALL OFFERS

WHAT IS AN MLS? The MLS is a database of properties for sale that is available and disseminated to and accessible by all other real estate agents who are participants or subscribers to the MLS. Property information submitted to the MLS describes the price, terms and conditions under which the Seller's property is offered for sale (including but not limited to the listing broker's offer of compensation to other brokers). It is likely that a significant number of real estate practitioners in any given area are participants or subscribers to the MLS. The MLS may also be part of a reciprocal agreement to which other multiple listing services belong. Real estate agents belonging to other multiple listing services that have reciprocal agreements with the MLS also have access to the information submitted to the MLS. The MLS may further transmit listing information to Internet sites that post property listings online.

EXPOSURE TO BUYERS THROUGH MLS: Listing property with an MLS exposes a seller's property to all real estate agents and brokers (and their potential buyer clients) who are participants or subscribers to the MLS or a reciprocating MLS.

CLOSED/PRIVATE LISTING CLUBS OR GROUPS: Closed or private listing clubs or groups are not the same as the MLS. The MLS referred to above is accessible to all eligible real estate licensees and provides broad exposure for a listed property. Private or closed listing clubs or groups of licensees may have been formed outside the MLS. Private or closed listing clubs or groups are accessible to a more limited number of licensees and generally offer less exposure for listed property. Whether listing property through a closed, private network - and excluding it from the MLS - is advantageous or disadvantageous to a seller, and why, should be discussed with the agent taking the Seller's listing.

NOT LISTING PROPERTY IN A LOCAL MLS: If the Property is listed in an MLS which does not cover the geographic area where the Property is located then real estate agents and brokers working that territory, and Buyers they represent looking for property in the neighborhood, may not be aware the Property is for sale.

OPTING OUT OF MLS: If Seller elects to exclude the Property from the MLS, Seller understands and acknowledges that: (a) real estate agents and brokers from other real estate offices, and their buyer clients, who have access to that MLS may not be aware that Seller's Property is offered for sale; (b) Information about Seller's Property will not be transmitted from the MLS to various real estate Internet sites that are used by the public to search for property listings; (c) real estate agents, brokers and members of the public may be unaware of the terms and conditions under which Seller is marketing the Property.

REDUCTION IN EXPOSURE: Any reduction in exposure of the Property may lower the number of offers and negatively impact the sales price.

PRESENTING ALL OFFERS: Seller understands that Broker must present all offers received for Seller's Property unless Seller gives Broker written instructions to the contrary.

    Seller's Initials (_____ **)(** _____ **)**   **Broker's/agent's Initials (** _____ **)(** _____ **)**

B. MLS rules generally provide that residential real property and vacant lot listings be submitted to the MLS within 2 days or some other period of time after all necessary signatures have been obtained on the listing agreement. Broker will not have to submit this listing to the MLS if, within that time, Broker submits to the MLS an appropriate form signed by Seller.
    ☐ Seller elects to exclude the Property from the MLS as provided by C.A.R. Form SELM or the local equivalent form.

Seller's Initials (_____) (_____)

RESIDENTIAL LISTING AGREEMENT - EXCLUSIVE (RLA PAGE 2 OF 5)

Property Address: _____   Date: _____

C. MLS rules allow MLS data to be made available by the MLS to additional Internet sites unless Broker gives the MLS instructions to the contrary. Seller acknowledges that for any of the below opt-out instructions to be effective, Seller must make them on a separate instruction to Broker signed by Seller. Specific information that can be excluded from the Internet as permitted by (or in accordance with) the MLS is as follows:

(1) Property Availability: Seller can instruct Broker to have the MLS not display the Property on the Internet.

(2) Property Address: Seller can instruct Broker to have the MLS not display the Property address on the Internet.

Seller understands that the above opt-outs would mean consumers searching for listings on the Internet may not see the Property or Property's address in response to their search.

(3) Feature Opt-Outs: Seller can instruct Broker to advise the MLS that Seller does not want visitors to MLS Participant or Subscriber Websites or Electronic Displays that display the Property listing to have the features below. Seller understands (i) that these opt-outs apply only to Websites or Electronic Displays of MLS Participants and Subscribers who are real estate broker and agent members of the MLS; (ii) that other Internet sites may or may not have the features set forth herein; and (iii) that neither Broker nor the MLS may have the ability to control or block such features on other Internet sites.

(a) Comments And Reviews: The ability to write comments or reviews about the Property on those sites; or the ability to link to another site containing such comments or reviews if the link is in immediate conjunction with the Property display.

(b) Automated Estimate Of Value: The ability to create an automated estimate of value or to link to another site containing such an estimate of value if the link is in immediate conjunction with the Property display. ☐ Seller elects to opt out of certain Internet features as provided by C.A.R. Form SELI or the local equivalent form.

6. SELLER REPRESENTATIONS: Seller represents that, unless otherwise specified in writing, Seller is unaware of: (i) any Notice of Default recorded against the Property; (ii) any delinquent amounts due under any loan secured by, or other obligation affecting, the Property; (iii) any bankruptcy, insolvency or similar proceeding affecting the Property; (iv) any litigation, arbitration, administrative action, government investigation or other pending or threatened action that affects or may affect the Property or Seller's ability to transfer it; and (v) any current, pending or proposed special assessments affecting the Property. Seller shall promptly notify Broker in writing if Seller becomes aware of any of these items during the Listing Period or any extension thereof.

7. BROKER'S AND SELLER'S DUTIES:

A. Broker agrees to exercise reasonable effort and due diligence to achieve the purposes of this Agreement. Unless Seller gives Broker written instructions to the contrary, Broker is authorized, but not required, to (i) order reports and disclosures including those specified in 7C as necessary, (ii) advertise and market the Property by any method and in any medium selected by Broker, including MLS and the Internet, and, to the extent permitted by these media, control the dissemination of the information submitted to any medium; and (iii) disclose to any real estate licensee making an inquiry the receipt of any offers on the Property and the offering price of such offers.

B. Seller agrees to consider offers presented by Broker, and to act in good faith to accomplish the sale of the Property by, among other things, making the Property available for showing at reasonable times and, subject to paragraph 3F, referring to Broker all inquiries of any party interested in the Property. Seller is responsible for determining at what price to list and sell the Property.

C. Investigations and Reports: Seller agrees, within 5 (or ___) Days of the beginning date of this Agreement, to pay for the following pre-sale reports: ☐ Structural Pest Control ☐ General Property Inspection ☐ Homeowners Association Documents ☐ Other _____.

D. Seller further agrees to indemnify, defend and hold Broker harmless from all claims, disputes, litigation, judgments attorney fees and costs arising from any incorrect or incomplete information supplied by Seller, or from any material facts that Seller knows but fails to disclose.

8. DEPOSIT: Broker is authorized to accept and hold on Seller's behalf any deposits to be applied toward the purchase price.

9. AGENCY RELATIONSHIPS:

A. Disclosure: The Seller acknowledges receipt of a ☒ "Disclosure Regarding Real Estate Agency Relationships" (C.A.R. Form AD).

B. Seller Representation: Broker shall represent Seller in any resulting transaction, except as specified in paragraph 3F.

C. Possible Dual Agency With Buyer: Depending upon the circumstances, it may be necessary or appropriate for Broker to act as an agent for both Seller and buyer, exchange party, or one or more additional parties ("Buyer"). Broker shall, as soon as practicable, disclose to Seller any election to act as a dual agent representing both Seller and Buyer. If a Buyer is procured directly by Broker or an associate-licensee in Broker's firm, Seller hereby consents to Broker acting as a dual agent for Seller and Buyer. In the event of an exchange, Seller hereby consents to Broker collecting compensation from additional parties for services rendered, provided there is disclosure to all parties of such agency and compensation. Seller understands and agrees that: (i) Broker, without the prior written consent of Seller, will not disclose to Buyer that Seller is willing to sell the Property at a price less than the listing price; (ii) Broker, without the prior written consent of Buyer, will not disclose to Seller that Buyer is willing to pay a price greater than the offered price; and (iii) except for (i) and (ii) above, a dual agent is obligated to disclose known facts materially affecting the value or desirability of the Property to both parties.

D. Confirmation: If the Property includes residential property with one-to-four dwelling units, Broker shall confirm the agency relationship described above, or as modified, in writing, prior to or concurrent with Seller's execution of a purchase agreement.

E. Potentially Competing Sellers and Buyers: Seller understands that Broker may have or obtain listings on other properties, and that potential buyers may consider, make offers on, or purchase through Broker, property the same as or similar to Seller's Property. Seller consents to Broker's representation of sellers and buyers of other properties before, during and after the end of this Agreement. Seller acknowledges receipt of a ☒ "Possible Representation of More than One Buyer or Seller - Disclosure and Consent" (C.A.R. Form PRBS).

Seller's Initials (_____) (_____)

Property Address: _____ Date: _____

10. SECURITY AND INSURANCE: Broker is not responsible for loss of or damage to personal or real property, or person, whether attributable to use of a keysafe/lockbox, a showing of the Property, or otherwise. Third parties, including, but not limited to, appraisers, inspectors, brokers and prospective buyers, may have access to, and take videos and photographs of, the interior of the Property. Seller agrees: (i) to take reasonable precautions to safeguard and protect valuables that might be accessible during showings of the Property; and (ii) to obtain insurance to protect against these risks. Broker does not maintain insurance to protect Seller.

11. PHOTOGRAPHS AND INTERNET ADVERTISING:
   A. In order to effectively market the Property for sale it is often necessary to provide photographs, virtual tours and other media to buyers. Seller agrees (or ☐ checked, does not agree) that Broker may photograph or otherwise electronically capture images of the exterior and interior of the Property ("Images") for static and/or virtual tours of the Property by buyers and others for use on Broker's website, the MLS, and other marketing materials and sites. Seller acknowledges that once Images are placed on the Internet neither Broker nor Seller has control over who can view such Images and what use viewers may make of the Images, or how long such Images may remain available on the Internet. Seller further assigns any rights in all Images to the Broker and agrees that such Images are the property of Broker and that Broker may use such Images for advertising, including post sale and for Broker's business in the future.
   B. Seller acknowledges that prospective buyers and/or other persons coming onto the property may take photographs, videos or other images of the property. Seller understands that Broker does not have the ability to control or block the taking and use of Images by any such persons. (If checked) ☐ Seller instructs Broker to publish in the MLS that taking of Images is limited to those persons preparing Appraisal or Inspection reports. Seller acknowledges that unauthorized persons may take images who do not have access to or have not read any limiting instruction in the MLS or who take images regardless of any limiting instruction in the MLS. Once Images are taken and/or put into electronic display on the Internet or otherwise, neither Broker nor Seller has control over who views such Images nor what use viewers may make of the Images.

12. KEYSAFE/LOCKBOX: A keysafe/lockbox is designed to hold a key to the Property to permit access to the Property by Broker, cooperating brokers, MLS participants, their authorized licensees and representatives, authorized inspectors, and accompanied prospective buyers. Broker, cooperating brokers, MLS and Associations/Boards of REALTORS® are not insurers against injury, theft, loss, vandalism or damage attributed to the use of a keysafe/lockbox. Seller does (or if checked ☐ does not) authorize Broker to install a keysafe/lockbox. If Seller does not occupy the Property, Seller shall be responsible for obtaining occupant(s)' written permission for use of a keysafe/lockbox (C.A.R. Form KLA).

13. SIGN: Seller does (or if checked ☐ does not) authorize Broker to install a FOR SALE/SOLD sign on the Property.

14. EQUAL HOUSING OPPORTUNITY: The Property is offered in compliance with federal, state and local anti-discrimination laws.

15. ATTORNEY FEES: In any action, proceeding or arbitration between Seller and Broker regarding the obligation to pay compensation under this Agreement, the prevailing Seller or Broker shall be entitled to reasonable attorney fees and costs from the non-prevailing Seller or Broker, except as provided in paragraph 19A.

16. ADDITIONAL TERMS: ☐ REO Advisory Listing (C.A.R. Form REOL) ☐ Short Sale Information and Advisory (C.A.R. Form SSIA)
   ☐ Trust Advisory (C.A.R. Form TAL) _____
   _____
   _____
   _____
   _____
   _____

17. MANAGEMENT APPROVAL: If an associate-licensee in Broker's office (salesperson or broker-associate) enters into this Agreement on Broker's behalf, and Broker or Manager does not approve of its terms, Broker or Manager has the right to cancel this Agreement, in writing, within **5 Days** After its execution.

18. SUCCESSORS AND ASSIGNS: This Agreement shall be binding upon Seller and Seller's successors and assigns.

19. DISPUTE RESOLUTION:
   A. MEDIATION: Seller and Broker agree to mediate any dispute or claim arising between them regarding the obligation to pay compensation under this Agreement, before resorting to arbitration or court action. Mediation fees, if any, shall be divided equally among the parties involved. If, for any dispute or claim to which this paragraph applies, any party (i) commences an action without first attempting to resolve the matter through mediation, or (ii) before commencement of an action, refuses to mediate after a request has been made, then that party shall not be entitled to recover attorney fees, even if they would otherwise be available to that party in any such action. THIS MEDIATION PROVISION APPLIES WHETHER OR NOT THE ARBITRATION PROVISION IS INITIALED. **Exclusions from this mediation agreement are specified in paragraph 19C.**
   B. ARBITRATION OF DISPUTES:
   Seller and Broker agree that any dispute or claim in Law or equity arising between them regarding the obligation to pay compensation under this Agreement, which is not settled through mediation, shall be decided by neutral, binding arbitration. The arbitrator shall be a retired judge or justice, or an attorney with at least 5 years of residential real estate Law experience, unless the parties mutually agree to a different arbitrator. The parties shall have the right to discovery in accordance with Code of Civil Procedure §1283.05. In all other respects, the arbitration shall be conducted in accordance with Title 9 of Part 3 of the Code of Civil Procedure. Judgment upon the award of the arbitrator(s) may be entered into any court having jurisdiction. Enforcement of this agreement to arbitrate shall be governed by the Federal Arbitration Act. Exclusions from this arbitration agreement are specified in paragraph 19C.

Seller's Initials (_____) (_____)

RLA REVISED 12/15 (PAGE 4 OF 5)

RESIDENTIAL LISTING AGREEMENT - EXCLUSIVE (RLA PAGE 4 OF 5)
Produced with zipForm® by zipLogix 18070 Fifteen Mile Road, Fraser, Michigan 48026 www.zipLogix.com

Property Address: _____ Date: _____

"NOTICE: BY INITIALING IN THE SPACE BELOW YOU ARE AGREEING TO HAVE ANY DISPUTE ARISING OUT OF THE MATTERS INCLUDED IN THE 'ARBITRATION OF DISPUTES' PROVISION DECIDED BY NEUTRAL ARBITRATION AS PROVIDED BY CALIFORNIA LAW AND YOU ARE GIVING UP ANY RIGHTS YOU MIGHT POSSESS TO HAVE THE DISPUTE LITIGATED IN A COURT OR JURY TRIAL. BY INITIALING IN THE SPACE BELOW YOU ARE GIVING UP YOUR JUDICIAL RIGHTS TO DISCOVERY AND APPEAL, UNLESS THOSE RIGHTS ARE SPECIFICALLY INCLUDED IN THE 'ARBITRATION OF DISPUTES' PROVISION. IF YOU REFUSE TO SUBMIT TO ARBITRATION AFTER AGREEING TO THIS PROVISION, YOU MAY BE COMPELLED TO ARBITRATE UNDER THE AUTHORITY OF THE CALIFORNIA CODE OF CIVIL PROCEDURE. YOUR AGREEMENT TO THIS ARBITRATION PROVISION IS VOLUNTARY."

"WE HAVE READ AND UNDERSTAND THE FOREGOING AND AGREE TO SUBMIT DISPUTES ARISING OUT OF THE MATTERS INCLUDED IN THE 'ARBITRATION OF DISPUTES' PROVISION TO NEUTRAL ARBITRATION."

Seller's Initials _____ / _____	Broker's/agent's Initials _____ / _____

C. **ADDITIONAL MEDIATION AND ARBITRATION TERMS:** The following matters shall be excluded from mediation and arbitration: (i) a judicial or non-judicial foreclosure or other action or proceeding to enforce a deed of trust, mortgage or installment land sale contract as defined in Civil Code §2985; (ii) an unlawful detainer action; (iii) the filing or enforcement of a mechanic's lien; and (iv) any matter that is within the jurisdiction of a probate, small claims or bankruptcy court. The filing of a court action to enable the recording of a notice of pending action, for order of attachment, receivership, injunction, or other provisional remedies, shall not constitute a waiver or violation of the mediation and arbitration provisions.

20. **ENTIRE AGREEMENT:** All prior discussions, negotiations and agreements between the parties concerning the subject matter of this Agreement are superseded by this Agreement, which constitutes the entire contract and a complete and exclusive expression of their agreement, and may not be contradicted by evidence of any prior agreement or contemporaneous oral agreement. If any provision of this Agreement is held to be ineffective or invalid, the remaining provisions will nevertheless be given full force and effect. This Agreement and any supplement, addendum or modification, including any photocopy or facsimile, may be executed in counterparts.

21. **OWNERSHIP, TITLE AND AUTHORITY:** Seller warrants that: (i) Seller is the owner of the Property; (ii) no other persons or entities have title to the Property; and (iii) Seller has the authority to both execute this Agreement and sell the Property. Exceptions to ownership, title and authority are as follows: _____
_____ .

☐ **REPRESENTATIVE CAPACITY:** This Listing Agreement is being signed for Seller by an individual acting in a Representative Capacity as specified in the attached Representative Capacity Signature Disclosure (C.A.R. Form RCSD-S). Wherever the signature or initials of the representative identified in the RCSD appear on this Agreement or any related documents, it shall be deemed to be in a representative capacity for the entity described and not in an individual capacity, unless otherwise indicated. Seller (i) represents that the entity for which the individual is signing already exists and (ii) shall Deliver to Broker, within 3 Days After Execution of this Agreement, evidence of authority to act (such as but not limited to: applicable trust document, or portion thereof, letters testamentary, court order, power of attorney, resolution, or formation documents of the business entity).

By signing below, Seller acknowledges that Seller has read, understands, received a copy of and agrees to the terms of this Agreement.

Seller _____ Date _____

Address _____ City _____ State _____ Zip _____
Telephone _____ Fax _____ E-mail _____

Seller _____ Date _____

Address _____ City _____ State _____ Zip _____
Telephone _____ Fax _____ E-mail _____

Real Estate Broker (Firm) _____ Cal BRE Lic. # _____
Address _____ City _____ State _____ Zip _____
By _____ Tel._____ E-mail _____ CalBRE Lic.# _____ Date _____
By _____ Tel._____ E-mail _____ CalBRE Lic.# _____ Date _____

☐ Two Brokers with different companies are co-listing the property. Co-listing Broker information is on the attached Additional Broker Acknowledgement (C.A.R. Form ABA).

Published and Distributed by:
REAL ESTATE BUSINESS SERVICES, INC.
a subsidiary of the California Association of REALTORS®
525 South Virgil Avenue, Los Angeles, California 90020

Reviewed by _____ Date _____

RLA REVISED 12/15 (PAGE 5 OF 5)

RESIDENTIAL LISTING AGREEMENT -EXCLUSIVE (RLA PAGE 5 OF 5)

OBLIGATIONS AND RIGHTS OF AGENTS AND PRINCIPALS

Agency law binds listing brokers and sellers. In a real estate agency relationship, both parties have legal obligations.

Duties an Agent Owes to a Principal

A real estate agent owes loyalty and confidentiality to his or her principal. The agent is a fiduciary and may not personally profit from the agency relationship except through the agreed-upon commission. As a fiduciary, the agent is bound by law to show good faith, loyalty, and honesty to the principal. Remember the mnemonic COALD — Care, Obedience, Accounting, Loyalty, and Disclosure.

A broker must present all offers to his or her principal before closing unless expressly instructed otherwise or the offer is patently frivolous. When handling multiple written offers, the listing broker often presents them to the seller in the order they were received.

Under the law of agency, the listing broker is a special agent who deals in the name of the principal to negotiate the sale of property. The broker does not have control over the property itself. He or she acts within the course of a special agency, and only has the right to represent that principal.

A listing contract does not give the listing broker the right to convey any property belonging to the principal unless the agent has a power of attorney to do so.

Listing Violations

If an agent does not comply with the following obligations, the punishment may be suspension or revocation of the real estate license:

- Every exclusive listing must specify a **definite termination date**.

- A listing broker must give a copy of the listing to the seller at the time the seller signs it.

- A listing broker cannot accept a deposit from a buyer unless specifically authorized to do so in the listing agreement. When a listing broker does so without authorization from the seller, he or she is acting as an agent of the buyer and not the seller. Any misappropriation of these funds by the listing broker would result in loss to the buyer and not the seller. Most listing agreements, however, do allow the broker to receive the buyer's deposit on behalf of the seller. This authority given to the broker also applies to any subagents, unless the subagent is working as the agent of the buyer.

- A listing broker may not return a buyer's deposit after the seller accepts the offer, without the consent of the seller.

- The acceptance of a check, rather than cash or a promissory note, as an earnest money deposit must be disclosed to the seller at the time the offer is presented.

- Also, if the buyer instructs the listing broker to hold the check uncashed until the offer is accepted, the fact must be disclosed to the seller when the offer is presented. The check may be held until the offer is accepted and then placed in escrow but only when directed to do so by the buyer.

- Any agent who puts a client's money in his or her own personal bank account is guilty of commingling. **Commingling** is the illegal practice of depositing client's funds in a broker's personal or general business account. Checks must be deposited within 3 business days after receiving them, either into a trust account or a neutral escrow account (unless being held uncashed). If a broker uses the client's money, it is known as **conversion**.

Duties an Agent Owes to Third Parties

In addition to those duties to the seller, the listing broker owes a duty of fair and honest dealing to the buyer, including the duty of full disclosure. The duty to disclose requires that the listing broker conduct a reasonably competent and diligent inspection of the property and note anything that would affect its value or desirability.

A listing broker may not withhold any material facts that are known to the seller or broker from a prospective buyer. A **material fact** is any fact that would seem likely to affect the judgment of the principal in giving consent to the agent to enter into the particular transaction on the specified terms. As a result of the Easton decision (*Easton v. Strassburger*, 1984), real estate agents can be held liable, not only for defects they know about, but for defects about which they should have known as a result of careful investigation.

Occasionally, the line between truth and fiction is blurred, sometimes innocently, sometimes with malice intended. It is easy for an agent to misrepresent a fact to a third party if the agent is not careful.

Misrepresentation

Misrepresentation is making a false statement or concealing a material fact. There are three types of misrepresentations: (1) innocent misrepresentations, (2) negligent misrepresentations, and (3) fraudulent misrepresentations.

Innocent Misrepresentations

Innocent misrepresentations are statements not known to be untrue at the time they are made, and usually carry no criminal liability for an agent. However, a buyer or seller could cancel a contract as a result.

Negligent Misrepresentations

Negligent misrepresentations are untrue statements made without facts to back them up in circumstances where care should have been taken.

Fraudulent Misrepresentations

Untrue statements made by an agent who knows that he or she is not telling the truth. The agent may be liable for committing fraud.

Puffing

Puffing is a statement of opinion that is not factual about a piece of property. Puffing describes an opinion made by an agent who honestly believes that the inflated statement about the condition of a property is just another innocent way to make a sale. If a prospective buyer believes the statement to be true, the agent may be guilty of misrepresentation and may be held liable.

Tort

A **tort** is a violation of a legal right or a civil wrong, such as negligence, libel, or nuisance. An agent is not liable for torts committed by the principal, only his or her own torts.

> Example: If a seller does not disclose to the listing broker that the shower floor has dry rot or that the roof leaks, the listing broker is not responsible for lack of disclosure by the seller.

Duties a Principal Owes to an Agent

A seller cannot be forced to sell, even after signing a listing agreement. However, he or she can be forced to pay a commission if the broker finds a buyer (even if the seller refuses to sell to that buyer). When the broker has fulfilled the obligations of the listing agreement, he or she is entitled to the agreed-upon commission.

Negotiating the Commission

The amount of commission is decided by the seller and the broker, and included in the listing agreement. Usually it is a percentage of the sales price, but does not necessarily have to be mentioned in this manner. The amount of commission is not set by law and is always negotiable between sellers and brokers.

Agreements between cooperating brokers for dividing commissions are normally made. Usually the listing broker is the one who receives the commission as a result of his or her contract with the seller. Commonly, the broker agrees to a 50-50 split with the cooperating, or selling, broker. The payment ordinarily is made through escrow at the closing.

> **Review - Commissions**
> - The amount of commission is not set by law and is always negotiable.
> - It is a violation of the Sherman Anti-Trust Law for brokers to discuss or set commission rates in a community.

When Does the Agent Earn the Commission?

The obligation to pay compensation to the broker must be in writing. A broker has earned a commission once he or she produces a buyer who is ready, willing, and able to purchase the property according to the price and terms of the listing agreement or any price and terms acceptable to the seller. Thus, if buyer and seller enter into a valid contract, the broker is entitled to a commission even though the sale is never completed.

During the term of the listing, if a broker presents an accepted offer to the seller, the broker has earned the commission. If, after a listing has expired, a buyer and seller complete a sale on the exact terms of those presented and rejected during the term of the listing, the broker has earned a commission.

Procuring Cause

Procuring cause refers to a broker who produces a buyer ready, willing, and able to purchase the property for the price and on the terms specified by the seller, regardless of whether the sale is completed. A procuring cause is that which produces the desired results. The broker must be the procuring cause of the sale to earn a commission.

Occasionally, determining who the procuring cause of a sale is becomes a matter of great dispute between real estate agents. When more than one agent has shown a prospective buyer a property, with or without the knowledge of the other agent's involvement, each may feel he or she has earned the commission when the buyer finally authorizes one of them to write up an offer, which is accepted by the seller.

The law states that the broker who is the procuring cause of the sale, or the one who actually wrote the offer and presented it to the seller for acceptance, has earned the commission. The others were unable to bring the buyer to the point of sale and, therefore, did not earn a commission.

Safety Clause

Most listing agreements have a safety clause, sometimes called a protection clause. The **safety clause** protects the listing broker's commission, if the owner personally sells the property to someone who was shown the property or made an offer during the term of the listing. At the time the listing is signed, the seller and broker need to agree on a length of time for the protection period. The protection clause applies only if the broker has given the seller a list containing the names of the protected buyers within three calendar days of expiration of the listing. This prevents a seller from waiting for a listing to end before accepting an offer and then refusing to pay the original broker (the procuring cause) a commission.

The agent produces a ready, willing, and able buyer to purchase on the seller's terms and asking price.

> **Review - An Agent's Commission is Earned When:**
> - The agent produces a ready, willing, and able buyer to purchase on the terms and at the price asked by the seller.
> - The agent secures from a prospective buyer a binding contract with terms and conditions that are accepted by the seller.

SUMMARY

Agency is a legal relationship created when principals (sellers or buyers) give an agent (licensed broker) the authority to represent them in a real estate transaction. A broker representing either a buyer or a seller is a **single agent**, representing both, a **dual agent**.

A real estate agency can be created by express agreement, ratification, and estoppel. Usually an **agency relationship** is created by a listing contract between the seller and broker. A contract between a broker and a buyer is called the **buyer representation agreement**.

An agent must disclose to both the buyer and seller who the agent is representing and the duties involved in that representation. California requires that all parties read and sign the Disclosure Regarding Real Estate Agency Relationships document.

The agent has the duties of full disclosure and loyalty to the principal, and the duties of honesty and good faith dealing with all parties. The principal's duties include good faith dealing with the agent, as well as responsibility for all the actions the agent takes within the agency relationship.

Common agency violations include incomplete disclosure, commingling, **misrepresentation**, false promise, trust fund problems, and problems with commissions.

Termination of agency can be made at any time by the principal or the agent, unless it is an agency coupled with an interest. Agency can also be terminated by expiration of terms, full performance of terms, destruction of the property, or the death or incapacity of either principal or agent.

UNIT 5 REVIEW

▢ Matching Exercise

Instructions: Write the letter of the matching term on the blank line before its definition. Answers immediately follow the Multiple Choice Questions.

Terms

A. agency relationship	J. general agent	S. real estate salesperson
B. agent	K. listing agreement	T. RLA – exclusive form
C. associate licensee	L. misrepresentation	U. safety clause
D. attorney-in-fact	M. net listing	V. single agency
E. commingling	N. principal	W special agent
F. conversion	O. procuring cause	X. subagent
G. customer	P. puffing	Y. third party
H. dual agent	Q ratification	
I. fiduciary relationship	R. ready, willing, and able	

Definitions

1. _____ The approval of a previously authorized act, performed on behalf of a person, which makes the act valid and legally binding.

2. _____ When a broker represents only the buyer or only the seller in the transaction.

3. _____ A person employed to perform a specific task.

4. _____ A buyer who is prepared to enter a purchase contract, who really wants to buy, and who meets the financing requirements of purchase.

5. _____ A relationship that implies a position of trust or confidence.

6. _____ Another term used for a licensed real estate salesperson employed by a licensed real estate broker.

7. _____ A broker who represents both parties in a transaction.

8. _____ Depositing client funds in the broker's personal account or general business account.

9. _____ An employment contract in which the commission is not definite.

10. _____ Exaggerated comments or opinions not made as representations of fact, thus not grounds for misrepresentation.

11. _____ The appropriation of property belonging to another as in a broker using a client's funds.

12. _____ A person with a real estate license and employed by a real estate broker—agent of the broker—not the seller or buyer.

13. _____ In a real estate transaction, the one (seller) who hires the broker to represent him or her in the sale of the property.

14. _____ A person who acts for and in the place of another, called a principal, for the purpose of affecting the principal's legal relationship with third persons.

15. _____ A prospective buyer of real estate; not to be confused with a property seller, who is the listing broker's client.

16. _____ A written contract by which a principal, or seller, employs a broker to sell real estate.

17. _____ Clause that protects the listing broker's commission, if the owner personally sells the property to someone who was shown the property or made an offer during the term of the listing.

18. _____ The new C.A.R. name for the Exclusive Authorization and Right to Sell Listing Agreement.

19. _____ A person who would be considered the customer in an agency relationship.

20. _____ The broker who produces a buyer ready, willing, and able to purchase the property for the price and on the terms specified by the seller, regardless of whether the sale is completed.

Multiple Choice Questions

Instructions: Circle your response and then check your response with the Answer Key that immediately follows the Multiple Choice Questions.

1. Every agency relationship has a principal, an agent, and a third party. In a real estate transaction the agent is the:

   a. buyer.

   b. seller.

   c. broker.

   d. customer.

2. An enforceable listing contract for the sale of real property must be:

   a. in writing.

   b. acknowledged and recorded.

   c. in writing and recorded.

   d. in writing, acknowledged, and recorded.

3. The usual listing contract authorizes a broker to:

   a. find a purchaser and bind his or her principal to a contract to sell.

   b. find a purchaser and receive an offer to purchase accompanied by a deposit.

   c. assure a prospective purchaser that an offer meeting the terms of the listing will be accepted by his or her principal.

   d. convey the real property that is being listed.

4. Seller Sam signed a listing contract with broker Baker. If Baker brings the seller a full price offer:

   a. Sam must accept the offer.

   b. Sam does not have to accept the offer.

   c. the prospective buyer can force Sam to accept the offer under specific performance.

   d. the doctrine of caveat emptor requires Sam to pay Baker a commission.

5. An agency relationship may be terminated by all of the following, except:

   a. a fire destroying the property that is the subject of the agency contract.

   b. the principal's refusal of an offer to purchase that was presented in the name of a third party.

   c. mutual agreement of both the principal and the agent before the original term expires.

   d. the renunciation of the agency by the agent.

6. Broker Davis signed an exclusive right-to-sell listing to sell John's $365,000 house. Davis diligently advertised the sale of the house. One week before the listing was to expire, the house was sold through John's own efforts to a friend. Under current rules and regulations, Davis is most likely to receive:

    a. no commission.
    b. half of the commission.
    c. the costs of advertising the house.
    d. the commission stated in the listing agreement.

7. In an exclusive listing, as a matter of law, a listing between the broker and seller:

    a. must have a definite termination date.
    b. is three months.
    c. is 90 days after the listing agreement is signed.
    d. has no specified term.

8. Wes hired Horn to sell a property through a 90-day exclusive agency listing. Thirty (30) days later the house had not sold, so Wes sent Horn a certified letter ending the agency listing which Horn accepted. A few days later, another broker sold the house through an open listing. Under such circumstances:

    a. Horn is owed a commission.
    b. only the open agent is owed a commission.
    c. Wes was not entitled to cancel the exclusive agency listing.
    d. the exclusive agent and the open agent are both entitled to a commission.

9. Seller Janet signs a memorandum for an open listing with a broker authorizing the sale of her house for $165,000. The broker expends considerable time and money advertising and showing the house and obtains several offers. However, Janet rejects the offers and instead sells the house to a friend. The broker:

    a. is not entitled to a commission because of the open listing.
    b. would be entitled to half the agreed commission.
    c. could probably collect the full commission in a civil lawsuit.
    d. should file for arbitration with the Real Estate Commissioner.

10. To be entitled to a commission, a broker must show that he or she was the procuring cause of the sale under all of the following types of listing agreements, except a(n) _____ listing.

    a. net
    b. open
    c. exclusive agency
    d. exclusive right-to-sell

11. An agent receives an offer. The agent gives the offer to the seller, who asks to consider it for 24 hours. At 6 p.m. the same day, the agent receives two more offers. The agent believes the seller will not accept any of the three offers. The agent should:

    a. not convey the two new offers.
    b. convey the two new offers by 10 a.m. the next day.
    c. convey the two new offers at the same time.
    d. hold the offers for 24 hours before conveying them to the owner.

12. A listing broker received a bona fide offer and a personal check as a deposit. The prospective buyer asked the listing broker to hold the check uncashed until the end of the week. The listing broker must:

    a. deposit the check within 24 hours.
    b. inform the seller.
    c. follow the buyer's instructions to the letter.
    d. refuse to accept the check.

13. A listing broker is relieved of the obligation to present an offer to purchase real property to his or her principal when the:

    a. offer contains more than three contingency clauses.
    b. offer is for the purchase of nonresidential property.
    c. broker is acting on written instructions from the principal or the offer is patently frivolous.
    d. broker notifies the seller in writing of his or her decision not to present the offer.

14. If a listing broker acts as an agent, the broker owes to the seller a fiduciary duty. What does the broker owe to the buyer?

    a. The same fiduciary duty
    b. A duty of fair and honest dealing
    c. A duty to answer all questions
    d. A duty to disclose all information regarding the selling price only

15. A broker is most likely to earn a commission when the broker:

    a. attempts to bind the principal to the contract.
    b. secures an offer with a substantial deposit.
    c. communicates the buyer's offer to the seller.
    d. communicates the seller's acceptance to the buyer.

UNIT 5 ANSWER KEY

Answers – Matching

1. Q	5. I	9. M	13. N	17. U
2. V	6. C	10. P	14. B	18. T
3. W	7. H	11. F	15. G	19. Y
4. R	8. E	12. S	16. K	20. O

Answers – Multiple Choice

1. **(c)** Every agency relationship has a principal, an agent, and a third party. In a real estate transaction the principal (buyer or seller), agent (real estate broker), and third party (customer) are bound together in a legal relationship, with all the duties and rights that go with that connection. [What is Agency]

2. **(a)** A real estate agreement must be in writing to be enforceable in a court of law. This includes listing agreements. However, listing agreements are not recorded, and therefore not acknowledged. [What is Agency]

3. **(b)** Almost all listing agreements give the broker express authority to accept a deposit as an agent of the owner. It does not authorize the broker to convey property on behalf of a principal or legally bind the seller to make a deal. [What is Agency]

4. **(b)** A seller cannot be forced to sell, even after signing a listing agreement. [What is Agency]

5. **(b)** At any time during the agency, the principal or agent may terminate the agency, except in an agency coupled with an interest. An agency is also terminated by the destruction of the property or by the parties to terminate the agency. In Choice (b) the seller's refusal to accept an offer does not terminate the agency. [What is Agency]

6. **(d)** An exclusive authorization and right-to-sell listing is an exclusive contract in which the seller must pay the listing broker a commission if the property is sold within the time limit by the listing broker, any other broker, or even by the owner. [Types of Listing Agreements]

7. **(a)** Every exclusive agency agreement must have a definite termination date. [B&P Code 10176(f)]. [Types of Listing Agreements]

8. **(b)** Under an exclusive agency or an open listing, Wes could sell the property himself and owe no commission. Wes cancelled Horn's listing prior to accepting the offer from another broker, so Horn is not entitled to a commission. However if another agent sold the property during Horn's listing agreement, Wes could be liable for two full commissions. [Types of Listing Agreements]

9. **(a)** In an open listing, the seller may sell the property without paying the broker a commission. [Types of Listing Agreements]

10. **(d)** The types of listing agreements in choices (a), (b), and (c) require the broker to prove he or she was the procuring cause. In the exclusive right-to-sell listing agreement, the broker is entitled to a commission regardless of who sells the property. [Types of Listing Agreements]

11. **(c)** The agent must act in the best interests of the seller and must present all offers, unless patently frivolous. It is best to present them at the same time. [Types of Listing Agreements]

12. **(b)** The listing broker's fiduciary duty requires full disclosure of material facts. If the buyer instructs the listing broker to hold the check uncashed until the offer is accepted, this material fact must be disclosed to the seller when the offer is presented. [Obligations & Rights of Agents and Principals]

13. **(c)** A listing agent must present all written offers to the owner before closing unless expressly instructed otherwise or unless the offer is patently frivolous (not a serious offer). [Obligations & Rights of Agents and Principals]

14. **(b)** A listing broker has the duty of fair and honest dealings with third parties—the buyer. This duty includes full disclosure of all material facts. [Obligations & Rights of Agents and Principals]

15. **(d)** Communication of the seller's acceptance to the buyer shows that the broker is the procuring cause of the sale and that the broker has found a ready, willing, and able buyer. [Obligations & Rights of Agents and Principals]

Unit 6

INTRODUCTION

In this Unit, you will review the basic elements of a contract and learn about real estate contracts. Real estate contracts discussed include:

- agreements employing a broker to market and sell real estate for compensation.

- agreements employing a broker to locate real estate for compensation.

- contracts for the purchase of real property, or of an interest therein.

- contracts for the option of real property, or of an interest therein.

- agreements for leasing realty for more than a year.

Real estate contracts must have all the elements of a valid contract. Additionally, they must be in writing, according to the statute of frauds, and must be signed by the parties.

Learning Objectives

After completing this Unit, you should be able to:

5E   identify clauses in the Residential Purchase Agreement and Joint Escrow Instructions.

5F   recall the purpose of counteroffers and options.

5G   classify leases, lease terms, and responsibilities of the parties to a lease.

LISTING AND BUYER REPRESENTATION AGREEMENTS

Listing agreements and buyer representation agreements were discussed in the previous Unit.

A listing is a contract by which a principal, or seller, employs a broker to sell real estate. Primarily, a listing agreement is an employment contract between a seller and a broker. It is a bilateral agreement in which the seller agrees to pay a commission if the broker finds a buyer, and the broker promises to use due diligence to procure a buyer.

A buyer representation agreement is an employment contract between a buyer and a broker. It is a single agency agreement in which the broker agrees to represent a buyer in purchasing a property.

PURCHASE AGREEMENT

In California, most real estate agents use the Residential Purchase Agreement and Joint Escrow Instructions, commonly known as a **purchase agreement** or **purchase offer** because it is an offer to purchase real property. Some licensees refer to the purchase agreement as the **deposit receipt** because it acts as the receipt for earnest money given by the buyer to secure an offer. A purchase agreement is the original agreement between the buyer and seller. Once the seller agrees to the offer and the buyer is informed of the seller's acceptance, the purchase agreement is a legally binding contract. Once all parties **execute** (sign) the purchase agreement it becomes a bilateral contract.

Upon writing an offer to purchase real property, a buyer may give some consideration, such as a personal check, commonly in the amount of 1% of the purchase price, as a sign that he or she is serious about making the offer. The check is made out to an escrow company or the listing broker. The real estate agent holds the check. If the seller refuses the offer, the check is returned to the buyer. If the seller accepts the offer, the buyer's check is deposited into an escrow account or into the broker's trust account within three business days after receiving it.

The purchase agreement covers more than just the purchase price and closing date. It covers contingencies, various inspections, mandatory disclosures, and buyer's rights to investigate the property, how the buyer will take title, damages and dispute resolution, escrow instructions, compensation to the brokers, and acceptance of the offer. The purchase agreement, as the original contract between the buyer and seller, may become the actual escrow instructions. Usually there are terms in the contract that must be met during the escrow period; therefore, the contract is considered executory until all the terms are completed and escrow closes.

California Residential Purchase Agreement and Joint Escrow Instructions

In most cases, a standard California Residential Purchase Agreement and Joint Escrow Instructions (RPA-CA) contract is used by real estate agents when a buyer makes an offer anywhere in California. It was created by the California Association of REALTORS® (C.A.R.). The Bureau of Real Estate does not officially recommend this form; nor is any type of specific form required by law. Real estate agents do have alternatives, depending on the custom in their area of the state. Real estate practices differ significantly in different parts of California and some of those differences are not reflected in the commonly used purchase agreement. Alternate forms are available to real estate agents who desire features not included in the other form.

The Main Clauses Included in the Purchase Agreement
- Date of the agreement
- Names and addresses of the parties to the contract
- Description of the property
- The consideration or price
- Financing and terms
- Date and place of closing
- Signatures of buyer and seller

CALIFORNIA
RESIDENTIAL PURCHASE AGREEMENT
AND JOINT ESCROW INSTRUCTIONS
(C.A.R. Form RPA-CA, Revised 12/15)

Date Prepared: _____

1. OFFER:
   A. THIS IS AN OFFER FROM _____ ("Buyer").
   B. THE REAL PROPERTY to be acquired is _____ , situated in
       _____ (City), _____ (County), California, _____ (Zip Code), Assessor's Parcel No._____ ("Property").
   C. THE PURCHASE PRICE offered is _____
       Dollars $ _____ .
   D. CLOSE OF ESCROW shall occur on ☐ _____ (date)(or ☐ _____ **Days** After Acceptance).
   E. Buyer and Seller are referred to herein as the "Parties." Brokers are not Parties to this Agreement.

2. AGENCY:
   A. DISCLOSURE: The Parties each acknowledge receipt of a ☒ "Disclosure Regarding Real Estate Agency Relationships"
      (C.A.R. Form AD).
   B. CONFIRMATION: The following agency relationships are hereby confirmed for this transaction:
      Listing Agent _____ (Print Firm Name) is the agent of (check one):
      ☐ the Seller exclusively; or ☐ both the Buyer and Seller.
      Selling Agent _____ (Print Firm Name) (if not the same as the
      Listing Agent) is the agent of (check one): ☐ the Buyer exclusively; or ☐ the Seller exclusively; or ☐ both the Buyer and Seller.
   C. POTENTIALLY COMPETING BUYERS AND SELLERS: The Parties each acknowledge receipt of a ☒ "Possible
      Representation of More than One Buyer or Seller - Disclosure and Consent" (C.A.R. Form PRBS).

3. FINANCE TERMS: Buyer represents that funds will be good when deposited with Escrow Holder.
   A. INITIAL DEPOSIT: Deposit shall be in the amount of . . . . $ _____
      (1) Buyer Direct Deposit: Buyer shall deliver deposit directly to Escrow Holder by electronic funds
      transfer, ☐ cashier's check, ☐ personal check, ☐ other _____ within 3 business days
      after Acceptance (or _____);
      OR **(2)** ☐ **Buyer Deposit with Agent:** Buyer has given the deposit by personal check (or _____)
      to the agent submitting the offer (or to _____), made payable to
      _____ . The deposit shall be held uncashed until Acceptance and then deposited
      with Escrow Holder within **3 business days** after Acceptance (or _____).
      Deposit checks given to agent shall be an original signed check and not a copy.
      (Note: Initial and increased deposits checks received by agent shall be recorded in Broker's trust fund log.)
   B. INCREASED DEPOSIT: Buyer shall deposit with Escrow Holder an increased deposit in the amount of . . . . $ _____
      within ____ **Days** After Acceptance (or _____).
      If the Parties agree to liquidated damages in this Agreement, they also agree to incorporate the increased
      deposit into the liquidated damages amount in a separate liquidated damages clause (C.A.R. Form
      RID) at the time the increased deposit is delivered to Escrow Holder.
   C. ☐ **ALL CASH OFFER:** No loan is needed to purchase the Property. This offer is NOT contingent on Buyer
      obtaining a loan. Written verification of sufficient funds to close this transaction IS ATTACHED to this offer or
      ☐ Buyer shall, within **3 (or _____) Days** After Acceptance, Deliver to Seller such verification.
   D. LOAN(S):
      (1) FIRST LOAN: in the amount of . . . . $ _____
      This loan will be conventional financing or ☐ FHA, ☐ VA, ☐ Seller financing (C.A.R. Form SFA),
      ☐ assumed financing (C.A.R. Form AFA), ☐ Other _____ . This loan shall be at a fixed
      rate not to exceed _____ % or, ☐ an adjustable rate loan with initial rate not to exceed _____ %.
      Regardless of the type of loan, Buyer shall pay points not to exceed _____ % of the loan amount.
      (2) ☐ **SECOND LOAN** in the amount of . . . . $ _____
      This loan will be conventional financing or ☐ Seller financing (C.A.R. Form SFA), ☐ assumed
      financing (C.A.R. Form AFA), ☐ Other _____ . This loan shall be at a fixed rate not to
      exceed _____ % or, ☐ an adjustable rate loan with initial rate not to exceed _____ %. Regardless of
      the type of loan, Buyer shall pay points not to exceed _____ % of the loan amount.
      (3) FHA/VA: For any FHA or VA loan specified in 3D(1), Buyer has **17 (or _____) Days** After Acceptance
      to Deliver to Seller written notice (C.A.R. Form FVA) of any lender-required repairs or costs that
      Buyer requests Seller to pay for or otherwise correct. Seller has no obligation to pay or satisfy lender
      requirements unless agreed in writing. A FHA/VA amendatory clause (C.A.R. Form FVAC) shall be a
      part of this Agreement.
   E. ADDITIONAL FINANCING TERMS: _____
      _____
   F. BALANCE OF DOWN PAYMENT OR PURCHASE PRICE in the amount of . . . . $ _____
      to be deposited with Escrow Holder pursuant to Escrow Holder instructions.
   G. PURCHASE PRICE (TOTAL): . . . . $ _____

Buyer's Initials (_____) (_____)   Seller's Initials (_____) (_____)

RPA-CA REVISED 12/15 (PAGE 1 OF 10)
CALIFORNIA RESIDENTIAL PURCHASE AGREEMENT (RPA-CA PAGE 1 OF 10)

Property Address: _____ Date: _____

H. VERIFICATION OF DOWN PAYMENT AND CLOSING COSTS: Buyer (or Buyer's lender or loan broker pursuant to paragraph 3J(1)) shall, within **3 (or ____) Days** After Acceptance, Deliver to Seller written verification of Buyer's down payment and closing costs. (☐ Verification attached.)

I. APPRAISAL CONTINGENCY AND REMOVAL: This Agreement is **(or ☐ is NOT)** contingent upon a written appraisal of the Property by a licensed or certified appraiser at no less than the purchase price. Buyer shall, as specified in paragraph 14B(3), in writing, remove the appraisal contingency or cancel this Agreement within **17 (or ____) Days** After Acceptance.

J. LOAN TERMS:

(1) LOAN APPLICATIONS: Within **3 (or ___) Days** After Acceptance, Buyer shall Deliver to Seller a letter from Buyer's lender or loan broker stating that, based on a review of Buyer's written application and credit report, Buyer is prequalified or preapproved for any NEW loan specified in paragraph 3D. If any loan specified in paragraph 3D is an adjustable rate loan, the prequalification or preapproval letter shall be based on the qualifying rate, not the initial loan rate. (☐ Letter attached.)

(2) LOAN CONTINGENCY: Buyer shall act diligently and in good faith to obtain the designated loan(s). Buyer's qualification for the loan(s) specified above **is a contingency** of this Agreement unless otherwise agreed in writing. If there is no appraisal contingency or the appraisal contingency has been waived or removed, then failure of the Property to appraise at the purchase price does not entitle Buyer to exercise the cancellation right pursuant to the loan contingency if Buyer is otherwise qualified for the specified loan. Buyer's contractual obligations regarding deposit, balance of down payment and closing costs **are not contingencies** of this Agreement.

(3) LOAN CONTINGENCY REMOVAL:
Within **21 (or ____) Days** After Acceptance, Buyer shall, as specified in paragraph 14, in writing, remove the loan contingency or cancel this Agreement. If there is an appraisal contingency, removal of the loan contingency shall not be deemed removal of the appraisal contingency.

(4) ☐ NO LOAN CONTINGENCY: Obtaining any loan specified above is NOT a contingency of this Agreement. If Buyer does not obtain the loan and as a result does not purchase the Property, Seller may be entitled to Buyer's deposit or other legal remedies.

(5) LENDER LIMITS ON BUYER CREDITS: Any credit to Buyer, from any source, for closing or other costs that is agreed to by the Parties ("Contractual Credit") shall be disclosed to Buyer's lender. If the total credit allowed by Buyer's lender ("Lender Allowable Credit") is less than the Contractual Credit, then (i) the Contractual Credit shall be reduced to the Lender Allowable Credit, and (ii) in the absence of a separate written agreement between the Parties, there shall be no automatic adjustment to the purchase price to make up for the difference between the Contractual Credit and the Lender Allowable Credit.

K. BUYER STATED FINANCING: Seller is relying on Buyer's representation of the type of financing specified (including but not limited to, as applicable, all cash, amount of down payment, or contingent or non-contingent loan). Seller has agreed to a specific closing date, purchase price and to sell to Buyer in reliance on Buyer's covenant concerning financing. Buyer shall pursue the financing specified in this Agreement. Seller has no obligation to cooperate with Buyer's efforts to obtain any financing other than that specified in the Agreement and the availability of any such alternate financing does not excuse Buyer from the obligation to purchase the Property and close escrow as specified in this Agreement.

4. SALE OF BUYER'S PROPERTY:

A. This Agreement and Buyer's ability to obtain financing are NOT contingent upon the sale of any property owned by Buyer.

OR B. ☐ This Agreement and Buyer's ability to obtain financing are contingent upon the sale of property owned by Buyer as specified in the attached addendum (C.A.R. Form COP).

5. ADDENDA AND ADVISORIES:

A. ADDENDA:

	☐ Addendum # _____ (C.A.R. Form ADM)
☐ Back Up Offer Addendum (C.A.R. Form BUO)	☐ Court Confirmation Addendum (C.A.R. Form CCA)
☐ Septic, Well and Property Monument Addendum (C.A.R. Form SWPI)	
☐ Short Sale Addendum (C.A.R. Form SSA)	☐ Other

B. BUYER AND SELLER ADVISORIES:

	☒ Buyer's Inspection Advisory (C.A.R. Form BIA)
☐ Probate Advisory (C.A.R. Form PA)	☐ Statewide Buyer and Seller Advisory (C.A.R. Form SBSA)
☐ Trust Advisory (C.A.R. Form TA)	☐ REO Advisory (C.A.R. Form REO)
☐ Short Sale Information and Advisory (C.A.R. Form SSIA)	☐ Other

6. OTHER TERMS: _____
_____
_____

7. ALLOCATION OF COSTS

A. INSPECTIONS, REPORTS AND CERTIFICATES: Unless otherwise agreed in writing, this paragraph only determines who is to pay for the inspection, test, certificate or service ("Report") mentioned; it **does not determine who is to pay for any work recommended or identified in the Report.**

(1) ☐ Buyer ☐ Seller shall pay for a natural hazard zone disclosure report, including tax ☐ environmental ☐ Other: _____ prepared by _____.

(2) ☐ Buyer ☐ Seller shall pay for the following Report _____ prepared by _____.

(3) ☐ Buyer ☐ Seller shall pay for the following Report _____ prepared by _____.

Buyer's Initials (_____) (_____)   Seller's Initials (_____) (_____)

Property Address: _____ Date: _____

B. GOVERNMENT REQUIREMENTS AND RETROFIT:

    (1) ☐ Buyer ☐ Seller shall pay for smoke alarm and carbon monoxide device installation and water heater bracing, if required by Law. Prior to Close Of Escrow ("COE"), Seller shall provide Buyer written statement(s) of compliance in accordance with state and local Law, unless Seller is exempt.

    (2) (i) ☐ Buyer ☐ Seller shall pay the cost of compliance with any other minimum mandatory government inspections and reports if required as a condition of closing escrow under any Law.

    (ii) ☐ Buyer ☐ Seller shall pay the cost of compliance with any other minimum mandatory government retrofit standards required as a condition of closing escrow under any Law, whether the work is required to be completed before or after COE.

    (iii) Buyer shall be provided, within the time specified in paragraph 14A, a copy of any required government conducted or point-of-sale inspection report prepared pursuant to this Agreement or in anticipation of this sale of the Property.

C. ESCROW AND TITLE:

    (1) (a) ☐ Buyer ☐ Seller shall pay escrow fee _____ .

    (b) Escrow Holder shall be _____ .

    (c) The Parties shall, within **5 (or ___) Days** After receipt, sign and return Escrow Holder's general provisions.

    (2) (a) ☐ Buyer ☐ Seller shall pay for **owner's** title insurance policy specified in paragraph 13E _____ .

    (b) Owner's title policy to be issued by _____ .

    (Buyer shall pay for any title insurance policy insuring Buyer's **lender**, unless otherwise agreed in writing.)

D. OTHER COSTS:

    (1) ☐ Buyer ☐ Seller shall pay County transfer tax or fee _____ .

    (2) ☐ Buyer ☐ Seller shall pay City transfer tax or fee _____ .

    (3) ☐ Buyer ☐ Seller shall pay Homeowners' Association ("HOA") transfer fee _____ .

    (4) Seller shall pay HOA fees for preparing documents required to be delivered by Civil Code §4525.

    (5) ☐ Buyer ☐ Seller shall pay HOA fees for preparing all documents other than those required by Civil Code §4525.

    (6) Buyer to pay for any HOA certification fee.

    (7) ☐ Buyer ☐ Seller shall pay for any private transfer fee _____ .

    (8) ☐ Buyer ☐ Seller shall pay for _____ .

    (9) ☐ Buyer ☐ Seller shall pay for _____ .

    (10) ☐ Buyer ☐ Seller shall pay for the cost, not to exceed $ _____ , of a standard (or ☐ upgraded) one-year home warranty plan, issued by _____ , with the following optional coverages: ☐ Air Conditioner ☐ Pool/Spa ☐ Other: _____ . Buyer is informed that home warranty plans have many optional coverages in addition to those listed above. Buyer is advised to investigate these coverages to determine those that may be suitable for Buyer.

    OR ☐ **Buyer waives the purchase of a home warranty plan. Nothing in this paragraph precludes Buyer's purchasing a home warranty plan during the term of this Agreement.**

8. ITEMS INCLUDED IN AND EXCLUDED FROM SALE:

    A. NOTE TO BUYER AND SELLER: Items listed as included or excluded in the MLS, flyers or marketing materials are **not** included in the purchase price or excluded from the sale unless specified in paragraph 8 B or C.

    B. ITEMS INCLUDED IN SALE: Except as otherwise specified or disclosed,

    (1) All EXISTING fixtures and fittings that are attached to the Property;

    (2) EXISTING electrical, mechanical, lighting, plumbing and heating fixtures, ceiling fans, fireplace inserts, gas logs and grates, solar power systems, built-in appliances, window and door screens, awnings, shutters, window coverings, attached floor coverings, television antennas, satellite dishes, air coolers/conditioners, pool/spa equipment, garage door openers/remote controls, mailbox, in-ground landscaping, trees/shrubs, water features and fountains, water softeners, water purifiers, security systems/alarms and the following if checked : ☐ all stove(s), except _____ ; ☐ all refrigerator(s) except _____ ; ☐ all washer(s) and dryer(s), except _____ ;

    (3) The following additional items: _____

    (4) Existing integrated phone and home automation systems, including necessary components such as intranet and Internet-connected hardware or devices, control units (other than non-dedicated mobile devices, electronics and computers) and applicable software, permissions, passwords, codes and access information, are (☐ are NOT) included in the sale.

    (5) LEASED OR LIENED ITEMS AND SYSTEMS: Seller shall, within the time specified in paragraph 14A, (i) disclose to Buyer if any item or system specified in paragraph 8B or otherwise included in the sale is leased, or not owned by Seller, or specifically subject to a lien or other encumbrance, and (ii) Deliver to Buyer all written materials (such as lease, warranty, etc.) concerning any such item. Buyer's ability to assume any such lease, or willingness to accept the Property subject to any such lien or encumbrance, is a contingency in favor of Buyer and Seller as specified in paragraph 14B and C.

    (6) Seller represents that all items included in the purchase price, unless otherwise specified, (i) are owned by Seller and shall be transferred free and clear of liens and encumbrances, except the items and systems identified pursuant to 8B(5) and ____ _____ , and (ii) are transferred without Seller warranty regardless of value.

    C. ITEMS EXCLUDED FROM SALE: Unless otherwise specified, the following items are excluded from sale: (i) audio and video components (such as flat screen TVs, speakers and other items) if any such item is not itself attached to the Property, even if a bracket or other mechanism attached to the component or item is attached to the Property; (ii) furniture and other items secured to the Property for earthquake purposes; and (iii) _____

_____ . **Brackets attached to walls, floors or ceilings for any such component, furniture or item shall remain with the Property (or** ☐ **will be removed and holes or other damage shall be repaired, but not painted).**

Buyer's Initials (_____) (_____)   Seller's Initials (_____) (_____)

Unit 6   Real Estate Contracts   **147**

Property Address: _____ Date: _____

9. CLOSING AND POSSESSION:

A. Buyer intends (or ☐ does not intend) to occupy the Property as Buyer's primary residence.

B. **Seller-occupied or vacant property:** Possession shall be delivered to Buyer: (i) at 6 PM or (_____ ☐ AM/☐ PM) on the date of Close Of Escrow; (ii) ☐ no later than ____ calendar days after Close Of Escrow; or (iii) ☐ at _____ ☐ AM/☐ PM on _____ .

C. **Seller remaining in possession After Close Of Escrow:** If Seller has the right to remain in possession after Close Of Escrow, (i) the Parties are advised to sign a separate occupancy agreement such as ☐ C.A.R. Form SIP, for Seller continued occupancy of less than 30 days, ☐ C.A.R. Form RLAS for Seller continued occupancy of 30 days or more; and (ii) the Parties are advised to consult with their insurance and legal advisors for information about liability and damage or injury to persons and personal and real property; and (iii) Buyer is advised to consult with Buyer's lender about the impact of Seller's occupancy on Buyer's loan.

D. **Tenant-occupied property: Property shall be vacant** at least **5 (or _____) Days** Prior to Close Of Escrow, unless otherwise agreed in writing. **Note to Seller: If you are unable to deliver Property vacant in accordance with rent control and other applicable Law, you may be in breach of this Agreement.**

OR☐ **Tenant to remain in possession** (C.A.R. Form TIP).

E. At Close Of Escrow: Seller assigns to Buyer any assignable warranty rights for items included in the sale; and Seller shall Deliver to Buyer available Copies of any such warranties. Brokers cannot and will not determine the assignability of any warranties.

F. At Close Of Escrow, unless otherwise agreed in writing, Seller shall provide keys, passwords, codes and/or means to operate all locks, mailboxes, security systems, alarms, home automation systems and intranet and Internet-connected devices included in the purchase price, and garage door openers. If the Property is a condominium or located in a common interest subdivision, Buyer may be required to pay a deposit to the Homeowners' Association ("HOA") to obtain keys to accessible HOA facilities.

10. STATUTORY AND OTHER DISCLOSURES (INCLUDING LEAD-BASED PAINT HAZARD DISCLOSURES) AND CANCELLATION RIGHTS:

A. **(1)** Seller shall, within the time specified in paragraph 14A, Deliver to Buyer: (i) if required by Law, a fully completed: Federal Lead-Based Paint Disclosures (C.A.R. Form FLD) and pamphlet ("Lead Disclosures"); and **(ii)** unless exempt, fully completed disclosures or notices required by sections 1102 et. seq. and 1103 et. seq. of the Civil Code ("Statutory Disclosures"). Statutory Disclosures include, but are not limited to, a Real Estate Transfer Disclosure Statement ("TDS"), Natural Hazard Disclosure Statement ("NHD"), notice or actual knowledge of release of illegal controlled substance, notice of special tax and/or assessments (or, if allowed, substantially equivalent notice regarding the Mello-Roos Community Facilities Act of 1982 and Improvement Bond Act of 1915) and, if Seller has actual knowledge, of industrial use and military ordnance location (C.A.R. Form SPQ or ESD).

(2) Any Statutory Disclosure required by this paragraph is considered fully completed if Seller has answered all questions and completed and signed the Seller section(s) and the Listing Agent, if any, has completed and signed the Listing Broker section(s), or, if applicable, an Agent Visual Inspection Disclosure (C.A.R. Form AVID). Nothing stated herein relieves a Buyer's Broker, if any, from the obligation to (i) conduct a reasonably competent and diligent visual inspection of the accessible areas of the Property and disclose, on Section IV of the TDS, or an AVID, material facts affecting the value or desirability of the Property that were or should have been revealed by such an inspection or (ii) complete any sections on all disclosures required to be completed by Buyer's Broker.

(3) Note to Buyer and Seller: Waiver of Statutory and Lead Disclosures is prohibited by Law.

(4) Within the time specified in paragraph 14A, **(i)** Seller, unless exempt from the obligation to provide a TDS, shall, complete and provide Buyer with a Seller Property Questionnaire (C.A.R. Form SPQ); **(ii)** if Seller is not required to provide a TDS, Seller shall complete and provide Buyer with an Exempt Seller Disclosure (C.A.R. Form ESD).

(5) Buyer shall, within the time specified in paragraph 14B(1), return Signed Copies of the Statutory, Lead and other disclosures to Seller.

(6) In the event Seller or Listing Broker, prior to Close Of Escrow, becomes aware of adverse conditions materially affecting the Property, or any material inaccuracy in disclosures, information or representations previously provided to Buyer, Seller shall promptly provide a subsequent or amended disclosure or notice, in writing, covering those items. **However, a subsequent or amended disclosure shall not be required for conditions and material inaccuracies** of which Buyer is otherwise aware, or which are **disclosed in reports provided to or obtained by Buyer or ordered and paid for by Buyer.**

(7) If any disclosure or notice specified in paragraph 10A(1), or subsequent or amended disclosure or notice is Delivered to Buyer after the offer is Signed, Buyer shall have the right to cancel this Agreement within **3 Days** After Delivery in person, or **5 Days** After Delivery by deposit in the mail, by giving written notice of cancellation to Seller or Seller's agent.

B. **NATURAL AND ENVIRONMENTAL HAZARD DISCLOSURES AND OTHER BOOKLETS:** Within the time specified in paragraph 14A, Seller shall, if required by Law: **(i)** Deliver to Buyer earthquake guide(s) (and questionnaire), environmental hazards booklet, and home energy rating pamphlet; **(ii)** disclose if the Property is located in a Special Flood Hazard Area; Potential Flooding (Inundation) Area; Very High Fire Hazard Zone; State Fire Responsibility Area; Earthquake Fault Zone; and Seismic Hazard Zone; and **(iii)** disclose any other zone as required by Law and provide any other information required for those zones.

C. **WITHHOLDING TAXES:** Within the time specified in paragraph 14A, to avoid required withholding, Seller shall Deliver to Buyer or qualified substitute, an affidavit sufficient to comply with federal (FIRPTA) and California withholding Law (C.A.R. Form AS or QS).

D. **MEGAN'S LAW DATABASE DISCLOSURE:** Notice: Pursuant to Section 290.46 of the Penal Code, information about specified registered sex offenders is made available to the public via an Internet Web site maintained by the Department of Justice at **www.meganslaw.ca.gov.** Depending on an offender's criminal history, this information will include either the address at which the offender resides or the community of residence and ZIP Code in which he or she resides. (Neither Seller nor Brokers are required to check this website. If Buyer wants further information, Broker recommends that Buyer obtain information from this website during Buyer's inspection contingency period. Brokers do not have expertise in this area.)

E. **NOTICE REGARDING GAS AND HAZARDOUS LIQUID TRANSMISSION PIPELINES:** This notice is being provided simply to inform you that information about the general location of gas and hazardous liquid transmission pipelines is available to the public via the National Pipeline Mapping System (NPMS) Internet Web site maintained by the United States Department of Transportation at **http://www.npms.phmsa.dot.gov/.** To seek further information about possible transmission pipelines near the Property, you may contact your local gas utility or other pipeline operators in the area. Contact information for pipeline operators is searchable by ZIP Code and county on the NPMS Internet Web site.

F. **CONDOMINIUM/PLANNED DEVELOPMENT DISCLOSURES:**

(1) SELLER HAS: 7 (or _____) Days After Acceptance to disclose to Buyer if the Property is a condominium, or is located in a planned development or other common interest subdivision (C.A.R. Form SPQ or ESD).

Buyer's Initials (_____) (_____)   Seller's Initials (_____) (_____)

RPA-CA REVISED 12/15 (PAGE 4 OF 10)

CALIFORNIA RESIDENTIAL PURCHASE AGREEMENT (RPA-CA PAGE 4 OF 10)

Produced with zipForm® by zipLogix 18070 Fifteen Mile Road, Fraser, Michigan 48026 www.zipLogix.com

Property Address: _____ Date: _____

(2) If the Property is a condominium or is located in a planned development or other common interest subdivision, Seller has **3 (or ___) Days** After Acceptance to request from the HOA (C.A.R. Form HOA1): **(i)** Copies of any documents required by Law; **(ii)** disclosure of any pending or anticipated claim or litigation by or against the HOA; **(iii)** a statement containing the location and number of designated parking and storage spaces; **(iv)** Copies of the most recent 12 months of HOA minutes for regular and special meetings; and **(v)** the names and contact information of all HOAs governing the Property (collectively, "CI Disclosures"). **(vi)** private transfer fees; **(vii)** Pet fee restrictions; and **(viii)** smoking restrictions. Seller shall itemize and Deliver to Buyer all CI Disclosures received from the HOA and any CI Disclosures in Seller's possession. Buyer's approval of CI Disclosures is a contingency of this Agreement as specified in paragraph 14B(3). The Party specified in paragraph 7, as directed by escrow, shall deposit funds into escrow or direct to HOA or management company to pay for any of the above.

11. **CONDITION OF PROPERTY:** Unless otherwise agreed in writing: **(i)** the Property is sold (a) "AS-IS" in its PRESENT physical condition as of the date of Acceptance and (b) subject to Buyer's Investigation rights; **(ii)** the Property, including pool, spa, landscaping and grounds, is to be maintained in substantially the same condition as on the date of Acceptance; and **(iii)** all debris and personal property not included in the sale shall be removed by Close Of Escrow.
    A. Seller shall, within the time specified in paragraph 14A, DISCLOSE KNOWN MATERIAL FACTS AND DEFECTS affecting the Property, including known insurance claims within the past five years, and make any and all other disclosures required by law.
    B. Buyer has the right to conduct Buyer Investigations of the Property and, as specified in paragraph 14B, based upon information discovered in those investigations: (i) cancel this Agreement; or (ii) request that Seller make Repairs or take other action.
    C. **Buyer is strongly advised to conduct investigations of the entire Property in order to determine its present condition. Seller may not be aware of all defects affecting the Property or other factors that Buyer considers important. Property improvements may not be built according to code, in compliance with current Law, or have had permits issued.**

12. **BUYER'S INVESTIGATION OF PROPERTY AND MATTERS AFFECTING PROPERTY:**
    A. Buyer's acceptance of the condition of, and any other matter affecting the Property, is a contingency of this Agreement as specified in this paragraph and paragraph 14B. Within the time specified in paragraph 14B(1), Buyer shall have the right, at Buyer's expense unless otherwise agreed, to conduct inspections, investigations, tests, surveys and other studies ("Buyer Investigations"), including, but not limited to: **(i)** a general physical inspection; **(ii)** an inspection specifically for wood destroying pests and organisms. Any inspection for wood destroying pests and organisms shall be prepared by a registered Structural Pest Control company; shall cover the main building and attached structures; may cover detached structures; shall NOT include water tests of shower pans on upper level units unless the owners of property below the shower consent; shall NOT include roof coverings; and, if the Property is a unit in a condominium or other common interest subdivision, the inspection shall include only the separate interest and any exclusive-use areas being transferred, and shall NOT include common areas; and shall include a report ("Pest Control Report") showing the findings of the company which shall be separated into sections for evident infestation or infections (Section 1) and for conditions likely to lead to infestation or infection (Section 2); **(iii)** inspect for lead-based paint and other lead-based paint hazards; **(iv)** satisfy Buyer as to any matter specified in the attached Buyer's Inspection Advisory (C.A.R. Form BIA); **(v)** review the registered sex offender database; **(vi)** confirm the insurability of Buyer and the Property including the availability and cost of flood and fire insurance; and **(vii)** review and seek approval of leases that may need to be assumed by Buyer. Without Seller's prior written consent, Buyer shall neither make nor cause to be made: invasive or destructive Buyer Investigations, except for minimally invasive testing required to prepare a Pest Control Report; or inspections by any governmental building or zoning inspector or government employee, unless required by Law.
    B. Seller shall make the Property available for all Buyer Investigations. Buyer shall **(i)** as specified in paragraph 14B, complete Buyer Investigations and either remove the contingency or cancel this Agreement, and **(ii)** give Seller, at no cost, complete Copies of all such Investigation reports obtained by Buyer, which obligation shall survive the termination of this Agreement.
    C. Seller shall have water, gas, electricity and all operable pilot lights on for Buyer's Investigations and through the date possession is made available to Buyer.
    D. **Buyer indemnity and seller protection for entry upon property:** Buyer shall: **(i)** keep the Property free and clear of liens; **(ii)** repair all damage arising from Buyer Investigations; and **(iii)** indemnify and hold Seller harmless from all resulting liability, claims, demands, damages and costs. Buyer shall carry, or Buyer shall require anyone acting on Buyer's behalf to carry, policies of liability, workers' compensation and other applicable insurance, defending and protecting Seller from liability for any injuries to persons or property occurring during any Buyer Investigations or work done on the Property at Buyer's direction prior to Close Of Escrow. Seller is advised that certain protections may be afforded Seller by recording a "Notice of Non-Responsibility" (C.A.R. Form NNR) for Buyer Investigations and work done on the Property at Buyer's direction. Buyer's obligations under this paragraph shall survive the termination of this Agreement.

13. **TITLE AND VESTING:**
    A. Within the time specified in paragraph 14, Buyer shall be provided a current preliminary title report ("Preliminary Report"). The Preliminary Report is only an offer by the title insurer to issue a policy of title insurance and may not contain every item affecting title. Buyer's review of the Preliminary Report and any other matters which may affect title are a contingency of this Agreement as specified in paragraph 14B. The company providing the Preliminary Report shall, prior to issuing a Preliminary Report, conduct a search of the General Index for all Sellers except banks or other institutional lenders selling properties they acquired through foreclosure (REOs), corporations, and government entities. Seller shall within 7 Days After Acceptance, give Escrow Holder a completed Statement of Information.
    B. Title is taken in its present condition subject to all encumbrances, easements, covenants, conditions, restrictions, rights and other matters, whether of record or not, as of the date of Acceptance except for: **(i)** monetary liens of record (which Seller is obligated to pay off) unless Buyer is assuming those obligations or taking the Property subject to those obligations; and **(ii)** those matters which Seller has agreed to remove in writing.
    C. Within the time specified in paragraph 14A, Seller has a duty to disclose to Buyer all matters known to Seller affecting title, whether of record or not.
    D. At Close Of Escrow, Buyer shall receive a grant deed conveying title (or, for stock cooperative or long-term lease, an assignment of stock certificate or of Seller's leasehold interest), including oil, mineral and water rights if currently owned by Seller. Title shall vest as designated in Buyer's supplemental escrow instructions. THE MANNER OF TAKING TITLE MAY HAVE SIGNIFICANT LEGAL AND TAX CONSEQUENCES. CONSULT AN APPROPRIATE PROFESSIONAL.

Property Address: _____   Date: _____

E. Buyer shall receive a CLTA/ALTA "Homeowner's Policy of Title Insurance", if applicable to the type of property and buyer. If not, Escrow Holder shall notify Buyer. A title company can provide information about the availability, coverage, and cost of other title policies and endorsements. If the Homeowner's Policy is not available, Buyer shall choose another policy, instruct Escrow Holder in writing and shall pay any increase in cost.

14. TIME PERIODS; REMOVAL OF CONTINGENCIES; CANCELLATION RIGHTS: The following time periods may only be extended, altered, modified or changed by mutual written agreement. Any removal of contingencies or cancellation under this paragraph by either Buyer or Seller must be exercised in good faith and in writing (C.A.R. Form CR or CC).

A. SELLER HAS: 7 (or _____) Days After Acceptance to Deliver to Buyer all Reports, disclosures and information for which Seller is responsible under paragraphs 5, 6, 7, 8B(4), 10A, B, C, and F, 11A and 13A. If, by the time specified, Seller has not Delivered any such item, Buyer after first Delivering to Seller a Notice to Seller to Perform (C.A.R. Form NSP) may cancel this Agreement.

B. (1) BUYER HAS: 17 (or _____) Days After Acceptance, unless otherwise agreed in writing, to: (i) complete all Buyer Investigations; review all disclosures, reports, lease documents to be assumed by Buyer pursuant to paragraph 8B(5), and other applicable information, which Buyer receives from Seller; and approve all matters affecting the Property; and (ii) Deliver to Seller Signed Copies of Statutory and Lead Disclosures and other disclosures Delivered by Seller in accordance with paragraph 10A.

(2) Within the time specified in paragraph 14B(1), Buyer may request that Seller make repairs or take any other action regarding the Property (C.A.R. Form RR). Seller has no obligation to agree to or respond to (C.A.R. Form RRRR) Buyer's requests.

(3) By the end of the time specified in paragraph 14B(1) (or as otherwise specified in this Agreement), Buyer shall Deliver to Seller a removal of the applicable contingency or cancellation (C.A.R. Form CR or CC) of this Agreement. However, if any report, disclosure or information for which Seller is responsible is not Delivered within the time specified in paragraph 14A, then Buyer has **5 (or _____) Days** After Delivery of any such items, or the time specified in paragraph 14B(1), whichever is later, to Deliver to Seller a removal of the applicable contingency or cancellation of this Agreement.

(4) **Continuation of Contingency:** Even after the end of the time specified in paragraph 14B(1) and before Seller cancels, if at all, pursuant to paragraph 14D, Buyer retains the right, in writing, to either (i) remove remaining contingencies, or (ii) cancel this Agreement based on a remaining contingency. Once Buyer's written removal of all contingencies is Delivered to Seller, Seller may not cancel this Agreement pursuant to paragraph 14D(1).

(5) **Access to Property:** Buyer shall have access to the Property to conduct inspections and investigations for **17 (or _____) Days** After Acceptance, whether or not any part of the Buyer's Investigation Contingency has been waived or removed.

C. ☐ **REMOVAL OF CONTINGENCIES WITH OFFER: Buyer removes the contingencies specified in the attached Contingency Removal form (C.A.R. Form CR). If Buyer removes any contingency without an adequate understanding of the Property's condition or Buyer's ability to purchase, Buyer is acting against the advice of Broker.**

D. SELLER RIGHT TO CANCEL:

(1) **Seller right to Cancel; Buyer Contingencies:** If, by the time specified in this Agreement, Buyer does not Deliver to Seller a removal of the applicable contingency or cancellation of this Agreement, then Seller, after first Delivering to Buyer a Notice to Buyer to Perform (C.A.R. Form NBP), may cancel this Agreement. In such event, Seller shall authorize the return of Buyer's deposit, except for fees incurred by Buyer.

(2) **Seller right to Cancel; Buyer Contract Obligations:** Seller, after first delivering to Buyer a NBP, may cancel this Agreement if, by the time specified in this Agreement, Buyer does not take the following action(s): (i) Deposit funds as required by paragraph 3A, or 3B or if the funds deposited pursuant to paragraph 3A or 3B are not good when deposited; (ii) Deliver a notice of FHA or VA costs or terms as required by paragraph 3D(3) (C.A.R. Form FVA); (iii) Deliver a letter as required by paragraph 3J(1); (iv) Deliver verification, or a satisfactory verification if Seller reasonably disapproves of the verification already provided, as required by paragraph 3C or 3H; (v) In writing assume or accept leases or liens specified in 8B5; (vi) Return Statutory and Lead Disclosures as required by paragraph 10A(5); or (vii) Sign or initial a separate liquidated damages form for an increased deposit as required by paragraphs 3B and 21B; or (viii) Provide evidence of authority to sign in a representative capacity as specified in paragraph 19. In such event, Seller shall authorize the return of Buyer's deposit, except for fees incurred by Buyer.

E. NOTICE TO BUYER OR SELLER TO PERFORM: The NBP or NSP shall: (i) be in writing; (ii) be signed by the applicable Buyer or Seller; and (iii) give the other Party at least **2 (or _____) Days** After Delivery (or until the time specified in the applicable paragraph, whichever occurs last) to take the applicable action. A NBP or NSP may not be Delivered any earlier than **2 Days** Prior to the expiration of the applicable time for the other Party to remove a contingency or cancel this Agreement or meet an obligation specified in paragraph 14.

F. EFFECT OF BUYER'S REMOVAL OF CONTINGENCIES: If Buyer removes, in writing, any contingency or cancellation rights, unless otherwise specified in writing, Buyer shall conclusively be deemed to have: (i) completed all Buyer Investigations, and review of reports and other applicable information and disclosures pertaining to that contingency or cancellation right; (ii) elected to proceed with the transaction; and (iii) assumed all liability, responsibility and expense for Repairs or corrections pertaining to that contingency or cancellation right, or for the inability to obtain financing.

G. CLOSE OF ESCROW: Before Buyer or Seller may cancel this Agreement for failure of the other Party to close escrow pursuant to this Agreement, Buyer or Seller must first Deliver to the other Party a demand to close escrow (C.A.R. Form DCE). The DCE shall: (i) be signed by the applicable Buyer or Seller; and (ii) give the other Party at least **3 (or _____) Days** After Delivery to close escrow. A DCE may not be Delivered any earlier than **3 Days** Prior to the scheduled close of escrow.

H. EFFECT OF CANCELLATION ON DEPOSITS: If Buyer or Seller gives written notice of cancellation pursuant to rights duly exercised under the terms of this Agreement, the Parties agree to Sign mutual instructions to cancel the sale and escrow and release deposits, if any, to the party entitled to the funds, less fees and costs incurred by that party. Fees and costs may be payable to service providers and vendors for services and products provided during escrow. Except as specified below, **release of funds will require mutual Signed release instructions from the Parties, judicial decision or arbitration award.** If either Party fails to execute mutual instructions to cancel escrow, one Party may make a written demand to Escrow Holder for the deposit. (C.A.R. Form BDRD or SDRD). Escrow Holder, upon receipt, shall promptly deliver notice of the demand to the other Party. If, within 10 Days After Escrow Holder's notice, the other Party does not object to the demand, Escrow Holder shall disburse the deposit to the Party making the demand. If Escrow Holder complies with the preceding process, each Party shall be deemed to have released Escrow Holder from any and all claims or liability related to the disbursal of the deposit. Escrow Holder, at its discretion, may nonetheless require mutual cancellation instructions. **A Party may be subject to a civil penalty of up to $1,000 for refusal to sign cancellation instructions if no good faith dispute exists as to who is entitled to the deposited funds (Civil Code §1057.3).**

Buyer's Initials (_____) (_____)   Seller's Initials (_____) (_____)

RPA-CA REVISED 12/15 (PAGE 6 OF 10)

CALIFORNIA RESIDENTIAL PURCHASE AGREEMENT (RPA-CA PAGE 6 OF 10)

Produced with zipForm® by zipLogix 18070 Fifteen Mile Road, Fraser, Michigan 48026   www.zipLogix.com

Property Address: _____ Date: _____

15. FINAL VERIFICATION OF CONDITION: Buyer shall have the right to make a final verification of the Property within **5 (or ☐ ___) Days** Prior to Close Of Escrow, NOT AS A CONTINGENCY OF THE SALE, but solely to confirm: **(i)** the Property is maintained pursuant to paragraph 11; **(ii)** Repairs have been completed as agreed; and **(iii)** Seller has complied with Seller's other obligations under this Agreement (C.A.R. Form VP).

16. REPAIRS: Repairs shall be completed prior to final verification of condition unless otherwise agreed in writing. Repairs to be performed at Seller's expense may be performed by Seller or through others, provided that the work complies with applicable Law, including governmental permit, inspection and approval requirements. Repairs shall be performed in a good, skillful manner with materials of quality and appearance comparable to existing materials. It is understood that exact restoration of appearance or cosmetic items following all Repairs may not be possible. Seller shall: **(i)** obtain invoices and paid receipts for Repairs performed by others; **(ii)** prepare a written statement indicating the Repairs performed by Seller and the date of such Repairs; and **(iii)** provide Copies of invoices and paid receipts and statements to Buyer prior to final verification of condition.

17. PRORATIONS OF PROPERTY TAXES AND OTHER ITEMS: Unless otherwise agreed in writing, the following items shall be PAID CURRENT and prorated between Buyer and Seller as of Close Of Escrow: real property taxes and assessments, interest, rents, HOA regular, special, and emergency dues and assessments imposed prior to Close Of Escrow, premiums on insurance assumed by Buyer, payments on bonds and assessments assumed by Buyer, and payments on Mello-Roos and other Special Assessment District bonds and assessments that are now a lien. The following items shall be assumed by Buyer WITHOUT CREDIT toward the purchase price: prorated payments on Mello-Roos and other Special Assessment District bonds and assessments and HOA special assessments that are now a lien but not yet due. Property will be reassessed upon change of ownership. Any supplemental tax bills shall be paid as follows: **(i)** for periods after Close Of Escrow, by Buyer; and **(ii)** for periods prior to Close Of Escrow, by Seller (see C.A.R. Form SPT or SBSA for further information). TAX BILLS ISSUED AFTER CLOSE OF ESCROW SHALL BE HANDLED DIRECTLY BETWEEN BUYER AND SELLER. Prorations shall be made based on a 30-day month.

18. BROKERS:

    A. COMPENSATION: Seller or Buyer, or both, as applicable, agree to pay compensation to Broker as specified in a separate written agreement between Broker and that Seller or Buyer. Compensation is payable upon Close Of Escrow, or if escrow does not close, as otherwise specified in the agreement between Broker and that Seller or Buyer.

    B. SCOPE OF DUTY: Buyer and Seller acknowledge and agree that Broker: **(i)** Does not decide what price Buyer should pay or Seller should accept; **(ii)** Does not guarantee the condition of the Property; **(iii)** Does not guarantee the performance, adequacy or completeness of inspections, services, products or repairs provided or made by Seller or others; **(iv)** Does not have an obligation to conduct an inspection of common areas or areas off the site of the Property; **(v)** Shall not be responsible for identifying defects on the Property, in common areas, or offsite unless such defects are visually observable by an inspection of reasonably accessible areas of the Property or are known to Broker; **(vi)** Shall not be responsible for inspecting public records or permits concerning the title or use of Property; **(vii)** Shall not be responsible for identifying the location of boundary lines or other items affecting title; **(viii)** Shall not be responsible for verifying square footage, representations of others or information contained in Investigation reports, Multiple Listing Service, advertisements, flyers or other promotional material; **(ix)** Shall not be responsible for determining the fair market value of the Property or any personal property included in the sale; **(x)** Shall not be responsible for providing legal or tax advice regarding any aspect of a transaction entered into by Buyer or Seller; and **(xi)** Shall not be responsible for providing other advice or information that exceeds the knowledge, education and experience required to perform real estate licensed activity. Buyer and Seller agree to seek legal, tax, insurance, title and other desired assistance from appropriate professionals.

19. REPRESENTATIVE CAPACITY: If one or more Parties is signing this Agreement in a representative capacity and not for him/herself as an individual then that Party shall so indicate in paragraph 31 or 32 and attach a Representative Capacity Signature Disclosure (C.A.R. Form RCSD). Wherever the signature or initials of the representative identified in the RCSD appear on this Agreement or any related documents, it shall be deemed to be in a representative capacity for the entity described and not in an individual capacity, unless otherwise indicated. The Party acting in a representative capacity (i) represents that the entity for which that party is acting already exists and (ii) shall Deliver to the other Party and Escrow Holder, within **3 Days** After Acceptance, evidence of authority to act in that capacity (such as but not limited to: applicable portion of the trust or Certification Of Trust (Probate Code §18100.5), letters testamentary, court order, power of attorney, corporate resolution, or formation documents of the business entity).

20. JOINT ESCROW INSTRUCTIONS TO ESCROW HOLDER:

    A. The following paragraphs, or applicable portions thereof, of this Agreement constitute the **joint escrow instructions of Buyer and Seller to Escrow Holder,** which Escrow Holder is to use along with any related counter offers and addenda, and any additional mutual instructions to close the escrow: paragraphs 1, 3, 4B, 5A, 6, 7, 10C, 13, 14G, 17, 18A, 19, 20, 26, 29, 30, 31, 32 and paragraph D of the section titled Real Estate Brokers on page 10. If a Copy of the separate compensation agreement(s) provided for in paragraph 18A, or paragraph D of the section titled Real Estate Brokers on page 10 is deposited with Escrow Holder by Broker, Escrow Holder shall accept such agreement(s) and pay out from Buyer's or Seller's funds, or both, as applicable, the Broker's compensation provided for in such agreement(s). The terms and conditions of this Agreement not set forth in the specified paragraphs are additional matters for the information of Escrow Holder, but about which Escrow Holder need not be concerned. Buyer and Seller will receive Escrow Holder's general provisions, if any, directly from Escrow Holder and will execute such provisions within the time specified in paragraph 7C(1)(c). To the extent the general provisions are inconsistent or conflict with this Agreement, the general provisions will control as to the duties and obligations of Escrow Holder only. Buyer and Seller will execute additional instructions, documents and forms provided by Escrow Holder that are reasonably necessary to close the escrow and, as directed by Escrow Holder, within **3 (or ___) Days,** shall pay to Escrow Holder or HOA or HOA management company or others any fee required by paragraphs 7, 10 or elsewhere in this Agreement.

    B. A Copy of this Agreement including any counter offer(s) and addenda shall be delivered to Escrow Holder within **3 Days** After Acceptance (or _____). Buyer and Seller authorize Escrow Holder to accept and rely on Copies and Signatures as defined in this Agreement as originals, to open escrow and for other purposes of escrow. The validity of this Agreement as between Buyer and Seller is not affected by whether or when Escrow Holder Signs this Agreement. Escrow Holder shall provide Seller's Statement of Information to Title company when received from Seller. If Seller delivers an affidavit to Escrow Holder to satisfy Seller's FIRPTA obligation under paragraph 10C, Escrow Holder shall deliver to Buyer a Qualified Substitute statement that complies with federal Law.

Buyer's Initials (_____) (_____)   Seller's Initials (_____) (_____)

Property Address: _____ Date: _____

C. Brokers are a party to the escrow for the sole purpose of compensation pursuant to paragraph 18A and paragraph D of the section titled Real Estate Brokers on page 10. Buyer and Seller irrevocably assign to Brokers compensation specified in paragraph 18A, and irrevocably instruct Escrow Holder to disburse those funds to Brokers at Close Of Escrow or pursuant to any other mutually executed cancellation agreement. Compensation instructions can be amended or revoked only with the written consent of Brokers. Buyer and Seller shall release and hold harmless Escrow Holder from any liability resulting from Escrow Holder's payment to Broker(s) of compensation pursuant to this Agreement.

D. Upon receipt, Escrow Holder shall provide Seller and Seller's Broker verification of Buyer's deposit of funds pursuant to paragraph 3A and 3B. Once Escrow Holder becomes aware of any of the following, Escrow Holder shall immediately notify all Brokers: **(i)** if Buyer's initial or any additional deposit or down payment is not made pursuant to this Agreement, or is not good at time of deposit with Escrow Holder; or **(ii)** if Buyer and Seller instruct Escrow Holder to cancel escrow.

E. A Copy of any amendment that affects any paragraph of this Agreement for which Escrow Holder is responsible shall be delivered to Escrow Holder within 3 Days after mutual execution of the amendment.

21. REMEDIES FOR BUYER'S BREACH OF CONTRACT:

A. Any clause added by the Parties specifying a remedy (such as release or forfeiture of deposit or making a deposit non-refundable) for failure of Buyer to complete the purchase in violation of this Agreement shall be deemed invalid unless the clause independently satisfies the statutory liquidated damages requirements set forth in the Civil Code.

B. LIQUIDATED DAMAGES: If Buyer fails to complete this purchase because of Buyer's default, Seller shall retain, as liquidated damages, the deposit actually paid. If the Property is a dwelling with no more than four units, one of which Buyer intends to occupy, then the amount retained shall be no more than 3% of the purchase price. Any excess shall be returned to Buyer. Except as provided in paragraph 14G, release of funds will require mutual, Signed release instructions from both Buyer and Seller, judicial decision or arbitration award. AT THE TIME OF ANY INCREASED DEPOSIT BUYER AND SELLER SHALL SIGN A SEPARATE LIQUIDATED DAMAGES PROVISION INCORPORATING THE INCREASED DEPOSIT AS LIQUIDATED DAMAGES (C.A.R. FORM RID).

Buyer's Initials _____ / _____   Seller's Initials _____ / _____

22. DISPUTE RESOLUTION:

A. **MEDIATION:** The Parties agree to mediate any dispute or claim arising between them out of this Agreement, or any resulting transaction, before resorting to arbitration or court action through the C.A.R. Real Estate Mediation Center for Consumers (www.consumermediation.org) or through any other mediation provider or service mutually agreed to by the Parties. The Parties also agree to mediate any disputes or claims with Broker(s), who, in writing, agree to such mediation prior to, or within a reasonable time after, the dispute or claim is presented to the Broker. Mediation fees, if any, shall be divided equally among the Parties involved. If, for any dispute or claim to which this paragraph applies, any Party **(i)** commences an action without first attempting to resolve the matter through mediation, or **(ii)** before commencement of an action, refuses to mediate after a request has been made, then that Party shall not be entitled to recover attorney fees, even if they would otherwise be available to that Party in any such action. THIS MEDIATION PROVISION APPLIES WHETHER OR NOT THE ARBITRATION PROVISION IS INITIALED. **Exclusions from this mediation agreement are specified in paragraph 22C.**

B. **ARBITRATION OF DISPUTES:**

The Parties agree that any dispute or claim in Law or equity arising between them out of this Agreement or any resulting transaction, which is not settled through mediation, shall be decided by neutral, binding arbitration. The Parties also agree to arbitrate any disputes or claims with Broker(s), who, in writing, agree to such arbitration prior to, or within a reasonable time after, the dispute or claim is presented to the Broker. The arbitrator shall be a retired judge or justice, or an attorney with at least 5 years of residential real estate Law experience, unless the parties mutually agree to a different arbitrator. The Parties shall have the right to discovery in accordance with Code of Civil Procedure §1283.05. In all other respects, the arbitration shall be conducted in accordance with Title 9 of Part 3 of the Code of Civil Procedure. Judgment upon the award of the arbitrator(s) may be entered into any court having jurisdiction. Enforcement of this agreement to arbitrate shall be governed by the Federal Arbitration Act. Exclusions from this arbitration agreement are specified in paragraph 22C.

"**NOTICE: BY INITIALING IN THE SPACE BELOW YOU ARE AGREEING TO HAVE ANY DISPUTE ARISING OUT OF THE MATTERS INCLUDED IN THE 'ARBITRATION OF DISPUTES' PROVISION DECIDED BY NEUTRAL ARBITRATION AS PROVIDED BY CALIFORNIA LAW AND YOU ARE GIVING UP ANY RIGHTS YOU MIGHT POSSESS TO HAVE THE DISPUTE LITIGATED IN A COURT OR JURY TRIAL. BY INITIALING IN THE SPACE BELOW YOU ARE GIVING UP YOUR JUDICIAL RIGHTS TO DISCOVERY AND APPEAL, UNLESS THOSE RIGHTS ARE SPECIFICALLY INCLUDED IN THE 'ARBITRATION OF DISPUTES' PROVISION. IF YOU REFUSE TO SUBMIT TO ARBITRATION AFTER AGREEING TO THIS PROVISION, YOU MAY BE COMPELLED TO ARBITRATE UNDER THE AUTHORITY OF THE CALIFORNIA CODE OF CIVIL PROCEDURE. YOUR AGREEMENT TO THIS ARBITRATION PROVISION IS VOLUNTARY.**"

"**WE HAVE READ AND UNDERSTAND THE FOREGOING AND AGREE TO SUBMIT DISPUTES ARISING OUT OF THE MATTERS INCLUDED IN THE 'ARBITRATION OF DISPUTES' PROVISION TO NEUTRAL ARBITRATION.**"

Buyer's Initials _____ / _____   Seller's Initials _____ / _____

C. **ADDITIONAL MEDIATION AND ARBITRATION TERMS:**

(1) EXCLUSIONS: The following matters are excluded from mediation and arbitration: **(i)** a judicial or non-judicial foreclosure or other action or proceeding to enforce a deed of trust, mortgage or installment land sale contract as defined in Civil Code §2985; **(ii)** an unlawful detainer action; and **(iii)** any matter that is within the jurisdiction of a probate, small claims or bankruptcy court.

Buyer's Initials (_____) (_____)   Seller's Initials (_____) (_____)

CALIFORNIA RESIDENTIAL PURCHASE AGREEMENT (RPA-CA PAGE 8 OF 10)

Property Address: _____ Date: _____

    (2) **PRESERVATION OF ACTIONS: The following shall not constitute a waiver nor violation of the mediation and arbitration provisions: (i) the filing of a court action to preserve a statute of limitations; (ii) the filing of a court action to enable the recording of a notice of pending action, for order of attachment, receivership, injunction, or other provisional remedies; or (iii) the filing of a mechanic's lien.**

    (3) **BROKERS: Brokers shall not be obligated nor compelled to mediate or arbitrate unless they agree to do so in writing. Any Broker(s) participating in mediation or arbitration shall not be deemed a party to this Agreement.**

23. **SELECTION OF SERVICE PROVIDERS:** Brokers do not guarantee the performance of any vendors, service or product providers ("Providers"), whether referred by Broker or selected by Buyer, Seller or other person. Buyer and Seller may select ANY Providers of their own choosing.

24. **MULTIPLE LISTING SERVICE ("MLS"):** Brokers are authorized to report to the MLS a pending sale and, upon Close Of Escrow, the sales price and other terms of this transaction shall be provided to the MLS to be published and disseminated to persons and entities authorized to use the information on terms approved by the MLS.

25. **ATTORNEY FEES:** In any action, proceeding, or arbitration between Buyer and Seller arising out of this Agreement, the prevailing Buyer or Seller shall be entitled to reasonable attorney fees and costs from the non-prevailing Buyer or Seller, except as provided in paragraph 22A.

26. **ASSIGNMENT:** Buyer shall not assign all or any part of Buyer's interest in this Agreement without first having obtained the separate written consent of Seller to a specified assignee. Such consent shall not be unreasonably withheld. Any total or partial assignment shall not relieve Buyer of Buyer's obligations pursuant to this Agreement unless otherwise agreed in writing by Seller. (C.A.R. Form AOAA).

27. **EQUAL HOUSING OPPORTUNITY:** The Property is sold in compliance with federal, state and local anti-discrimination Laws.

28. **TERMS AND CONDITIONS OF OFFER:**

    This is an offer to purchase the Property on the above terms and conditions. The liquidated damages paragraph or the arbitration of disputes paragraph is incorporated in this Agreement if initialed by all Parties or if incorporated by mutual agreement in a counter offer or addendum. If at least one but not all Parties initial, a counter offer is required until agreement is reached. Seller has the right to continue to offer the Property for sale and to accept any other offer at any time prior to notification of Acceptance. The Parties have read and acknowledge receipt of a Copy of the offer and agree to the confirmation of agency relationships. If this offer is accepted and Buyer subsequently defaults, Buyer may be responsible for payment of Brokers' compensation. This Agreement and any supplement, addendum or modification, including any Copy, may be Signed in two or more counterparts, all of which shall constitute one and the same writing.

29. **TIME OF ESSENCE; ENTIRE CONTRACT; CHANGES:** Time is of the essence. All understandings between the Parties are incorporated in this Agreement. Its terms are intended by the Parties as a final, complete and exclusive expression of their Agreement with respect to its subject matter, and may not be contradicted by evidence of any prior agreement or contemporaneous oral agreement. If any provision of this Agreement is held to be ineffective or invalid, the remaining provisions will nevertheless be given full force and effect. Except as otherwise specified, this Agreement shall be interpreted and disputes shall be resolved in accordance with the Laws of the State of California. **Neither this Agreement nor any provision in it may be extended, amended, modified, altered or changed, except in writing Signed by Buyer and Seller.**

30. **DEFINITIONS:** As used in this Agreement:

    A. **"Acceptance"** means the time the offer or final counter offer is accepted in writing by a Party and is delivered to and personally received by the other Party or that Party's authorized agent in accordance with the terms of this offer or a final counter offer.

    B. **"Agreement"** means this document and any counter offers and any incorporated addenda, collectively forming the binding agreement between the Parties. Addenda are incorporated only when Signed by all Parties.

    C. **"C.A.R. Form"** means the most current version of the specific form referenced or another comparable form agreed to by the parties.

    D. **"Close Of Escrow"**, including "COE", means the date the grant deed, or other evidence of transfer of title, is recorded.

    E. **"Copy"** means copy by any means including photocopy, NCR, facsimile and electronic.

    F. **"Days"** means calendar days. However, after Acceptance, the last **Day** for performance of any act required by this Agreement (including Close Of Escrow) shall not include any Saturday, Sunday, or legal holiday and shall instead be the next Day.

    G. **"Days After"** means the specified number of calendar days after the occurrence of the event specified, not counting the calendar date on which the specified event occurs, and ending at 11:59 PM on the final day.

    H. **"Days Prior"** means the specified number of calendar days before the occurrence of the event specified, not counting the calendar date on which the specified event is scheduled to occur.

    I. **"Deliver", "Delivered"** or **"Delivery"**, unless otherwise specified in writing, means and shall be effective upon: personal receipt by Buyer or Seller or the individual Real Estate Licensee for that principal as specified in the section titled Real Estate Brokers on page 10, regardless of the method used (i.e., messenger, mail, email, fax, other).

    J. **"Electronic Copy"** or **"Electronic Signature"** means, as applicable, an electronic copy or signature complying with California Law. Buyer and Seller agree that electronic means will not be used by either Party to modify or alter the content or integrity of this Agreement without the knowledge and consent of the other Party.

    K. **"Law"** means any law, code, statute, ordinance, regulation, rule or order, which is adopted by a controlling city, county, state or federal legislative, judicial or executive body or agency.

    L. **"Repairs"** means any repairs (including pest control), alterations, replacements, modifications or retrofitting of the Property provided for under this Agreement.

    M. **"Signed"** means either a handwritten or electronic signature on an original document, Copy or any counterpart.

31. **EXPIRATION OF OFFER:** This offer shall be deemed revoked and the deposit, if any, shall be returned to Buyer unless the offer is Signed by Seller and a Copy of the Signed offer is personally received by Buyer, or by _____, who is authorized to receive it, by 5:00 PM on the third Day after this offer is signed by Buyer (or by ☐ _____ ☐ AM/ ☐ PM, on _____ (date)).

☐ One or more Buyers is signing this Agreement in a representative capacity and not for him/herself as an individual. See attached Representative Capacity Signature Disclosure (C.A.R. Form RCSD-B) for additional terms.

Date _____ BUYER _____

(Print name) _____

Date _____ BUYER _____

(Print name) _____

☐ Additional Signature Addendum attached (C.A.R. Form ASA).

Seller's Initials (_____) (_____)

RPA-CA REVISED 12/15 (PAGE 9 OF 10)

CALIFORNIA RESIDENTIAL PURCHASE AGREEMENT (RPA-CA PAGE 9 OF 10)

Property Address: _____ Date: _____

32. ACCEPTANCE OF OFFER: Seller warrants that Seller is the owner of the Property, or has the authority to execute this Agreement. Seller accepts the above offer, and agrees to sell the Property on the above terms and conditions. Seller has read and acknowledges receipt of a Copy of this Agreement, and authorizes Broker to Deliver a Signed Copy to Buyer.

☐ **(If checked) SELLER'S ACCEPTANCE IS SUBJECT TO ATTACHED COUNTER OFFER (C.A.R. Form SCO or SMCO) DATED:**
_____.

☐ One or more Sellers is signing this Agreement in a representative capacity and not for him/herself as an individual. See attached Representative Capacity Signature Disclosure (C.A.R. Form RCSD-S) for additional terms.

Date _____ SELLER _____

(Print name) _____

Date _____ SELLER _____

(Print name) _____

☐ Additional Signature Addendum attached (C.A.R. Form ASA).

(_____/_____) **(Do not initial if making a counter offer.) CONFIRMATION OF ACCEPTANCE:** A Copy of Signed Acceptance was
(Initials) personally received by Buyer or Buyer's authorized agent on (date) _____ at _____
☐ AM/ ☐ PM. **A binding Agreement is created when a Copy of Signed Acceptance is personally received by Buyer or Buyer's authorized agent whether or not confirmed in this document. Completion of this confirmation is not legally required in order to create a binding Agreement; it is solely intended to evidence the date that Confirmation of Acceptance has occurred.**

REAL ESTATE BROKERS:
A. Real Estate Brokers are not parties to the Agreement between Buyer and Seller.
B. Agency relationships are confirmed as stated in paragraph 2.
C. If specified in paragraph 3A(2), Agent who submitted the offer for Buyer acknowledges receipt of deposit.
D. **COOPERATING BROKER COMPENSATION:** Listing Broker agrees to pay Cooperating Broker **(Selling Firm)** and Cooperating Broker agrees to accept, out of Listing Broker's proceeds in escrow, the amount specified in the MLS, provided Cooperating Broker is a Participant of the MLS in which the Property is offered for sale or a reciprocal MLS. If Listing Broker and Cooperating Broker are not both Participants of the MLS, or a reciprocal MLS, in which the Property is offered for sale, then compensation must be specified in a separate written agreement (C.A.R. Form CBC). Declaration of License and Tax (C.A.R. Form DLT) may be used to document that tax reporting will be required or that an exemption exists.

Real Estate Broker (Selling Firm) _____ CalBRE Lic. # _____
By _____ CalBRE Lic. # _____ Date _____
By _____ CalBRE Lic. # _____ Date _____
Address _____ City _____ State _____ Zip _____
Telephone _____ Fax _____ E-mail _____
Real Estate Broker (Listing Firm) _____ CalBRE Lic. # _____
By _____ CalBRE Lic. # _____ Date _____
By _____ CalBRE Lic. # _____ Date _____
Address _____ City _____ State _____ Zip _____
Telephone _____ Fax _____ E-mail _____

ESCROW HOLDER ACKNOWLEDGMENT:
Escrow Holder acknowledges receipt of a Copy of this Agreement, (if checked, ☐ a deposit in the amount of $ _____),
counter offer numbers _____ ☐ Seller's Statement of Information and _____
_____, and agrees to act as Escrow Holder subject to paragraph 20 of this Agreement, any supplemental escrow instructions and the terms of Escrow Holder's general provisions.

Escrow Holder is advised that the date of Confirmation of Acceptance of the Agreement as between Buyer and Seller is _____

Escrow Holder _____ Escrow # _____
By _____ Date _____
Address _____
Phone/Fax/E-mail _____
Escrow Holder has the following license number # _____
☐ Department of Business Oversight, ☐ Department of Insurance, ☐ Bureau of Real Estate.

PRESENTATION OF OFFER: (_____) Listing Broker presented this offer to Seller on _____ (date).
 Broker or Designee Initials

REJECTION OF OFFER: (_____) (_____) No counter offer is being made. This offer was rejected by Seller on _____ (date).
 Seller's Initials

Published and Distributed by: Buyer Acknowledges that page 10 is part of this Agreement (_____)(_____)
REAL ESTATE BUSINESS SERVICES, INC.   Buyer's Initials
a subsidiary of the CALIFORNIA ASSOCIATION OF REALTORS®
525 South Virgil Avenue, Los Angeles, California 90020   Reviewed by
RPA-CA REVISED 12/15 (PAGE 10 of 10)   Broker or Designee _____

CALIFORNIA RESIDENTIAL PURCHASE AGREEMENT (RPA-CA PAGE 10 OF 10)
Produced with zipForm® by zipLogix 18070 Fifteen Mile Road, Fraser, Michigan 48026 www.zipLogix.com

Remember, the purchase agreement is probably the most important real estate document you—as an agent—will have to understand. Consumers rely on your knowledge, and your commission depends on your ability to explain a sometimes-difficult transaction to them. It is important that you read the entire California Residential Purchase Agreement and Joint Escrow Instructions (purchase agreement).

The offer covers more than just the purchase price and closing date. It covers contingencies, various inspections, mandatory disclosures, buyer's rights to investigate the property, how the buyer will take title, damages and dispute resolution, escrow instructions, compensation to the brokers, and acceptance of the offer.

The first line on the contract to be filled in is the date and place the contract is signed by the buyer. As you read through the contract pay particular attention to the clauses listed.

Offer: This paragraph shows the name of the buyer, describes the property to be purchased, the offered purchase price, and the closing date for escrow.

Finance Terms: This section addresses whether the purchase will be an all cash offer or an offer based on obtaining financing. If the buyer must obtain financing to complete the transaction, the finance terms should state if the purchase of the property is contingent upon the buyer's ability to get financing. The amounts of the **initial deposit**, any **increased deposit** and the loans are listed and added to total the amount of the purchase price. Remember, any earnest money or deposits received by an agent are trust funds and handled as prescribed by the Commissioner's Real Estate Law and Regulations.

Allocation of Costs: Since there are many inspections, reports, and tests associated with purchasing a property, it is important for both buyer and seller to agree about who will be responsible for their payment. Also, buyer and seller select the escrow and title provider and allocate the payment responsibility.

Closing and **Possession**: This section covers the intent of the buyer to occupy the property as a primary residence, the date the seller (or tenant) will turn over possession of the property to the buyer, and if the buyer is allowed to take possession of the property prior to close of escrow. In order to protect the rights and obligations of both seller and buyer, an **Interim Occupancy Agreement** should be used if a buyer wants early possession of the property. The new C.A.R. form contains wording that prohibits a landlord from demanding that rent be paid in cash.

Statutory Disclosures: A seller is required by law to give a buyer several disclosures about the property and surrounding area, which may affect the buyer's decision to purchase the property.

Items Included In or Excluded from Purchase Price: Sometimes sellers plan to take an appliance, window coverings, and light fixtures with them when they sell the property. Unless personal property items are excluded in the listing agreement, buyers may assume that what they see in the property is included in the sale. Some buyers will list items to be sure that they are included in their offering price. Listing agents need to discuss which personal property, if any, sellers may want to exclude from the sale.

Title and Vesting: Explain the importance of reviewing the preliminary title report with the buyer. Check for any undisclosed liens or easements that may affect the use of the property. Because the property is still owned by the seller, any existing trust deeds will be shown with the seller as the trustor. Once the property is sold, the new title insurance policy will show the buyer's loan. The manner in which a buyer takes title to real property (**vesting**) can have unforeseen legal and tax ramifications. Always direct the buyer to an attorney and/or tax professional to get advice on vesting.

Time Periods; Removal of Contingencies: Buyers and sellers are given specific amounts of time to meet the various conditions written in the contract.

Prorations: Since most real estate offices use the C.A.R. Purchase Agreement and Joint Escrow Instruction contract, this clause tells escrow the buyers' and sellers' wishes regarding the prorations (allocation) of property tax, interest, assessments, and any other charge normally prorated in escrow.

Breach of Contract: Parties to a contract may decide in advance the amount of damages to be paid, should either party breach the contract. In fact, the offer to purchase, or sales contract, usually contains a printed clause that says the seller may keep the deposit as liquidated damages if the buyer backs out without good reason. In the event the buyer defaults on the contract, the liquidated damages cannot exceed 3% of the purchase price if the property is a single-family residence.

Dispute Resolution: Even when the utmost care is taken in a transaction, disputes may arise. To try to settle any disputes amicably, the contract offers both mediation and arbitration. Both buyer and seller must agree to be bound by mutual arbitration in order for the clause to be effective.

Time is of the Essence: Time is often significant in a contract; indeed, its performance may be measured by the passage of time. By law, if no time is required by the contract, a reasonable time is allowed. If the act can be done instantly—as in the payment of money—it must be done at once.

Expiration of the Offer: If the offer is not accepted by the seller within the time frame, the offer is revoked and any deposit is returned to the buyer. A deposit may be refunded by agreement, judgment, or arbitration.

Acceptance of the Offer: Once the purchase agreement is accepted and signed by the seller it becomes a legally binding contract. Death or incapacity does not automatically cancel a contract. After acceptance of the offer, if the seller dies or becomes incapacitated, the seller's heirs must complete the sale.

Termination of Offer

An offer may be terminated for a number of reasons. The buyer may withdraw the offer before the seller accepts it. Since the seller has not accepted the offer, there is no contract, so the buyer would get his or her deposit back. An offer ends when the time limit given in the offer for acceptance expires. If the buyer dies before the seller accepts the offer, the offer terminates. The original offer expires if the seller gives the buyer a counteroffer.

COUNTEROFFER

In a real estate transaction, a **counteroffer** is the rejection of an original purchase offer and the submission of a new and different offer. If a seller rejects the offer and submits a counteroffer, the original offer automatically terminates.

OPTION

An **option** is a contract to keep open, for a set period of time, an offer to purchase or lease real property. The person who owns the property (seller, lessor) is the **optionor**. The person who wants to purchase or lease (lessee) the property is called the **optionee**. An optionor is to an optionee as an assignor is to an assignee. An option is a written, unilateral contract between the owner of real property and a prospective buyer, stating the right to purchase, a fixed price, and time frame. The price and all other terms should be stated clearly, as the option may become the sales agreement when the optionee exercises the right to purchase. If the option is exercised by the optionee, it does not necessarily require a separate sales contract. A real estate broker earns commission on an option when it is exercised.

SELLER COUNTER OFFER No. 1
May not be used as a multiple counter offer.
(C.A.R. Form SCO, 11/14)

Date _____

This is a counter offer to the: ☐ Purchase Agreement, ☐ Buyer Counter Offer No.___ , or ☐ Other _____ ("Offer"),
dated _____ , on property known as _____ ("Property"),
between _____ ("Buyer")
and _____ ("Seller").

1. **TERMS:** The terms and conditions of the above referenced document are accepted subject to the following:
   A. Paragraphs in the Offer that require initials by all parties, but are not initialed by all parties, are excluded from the final agreement unless specifically referenced for inclusion in paragraph 1C of this or another Counter Offer or an addendum.
   B. Unless otherwise agreed in writing, down payment and loan amount(s) will be adjusted in the same proportion as in the original Offer.
   C. **OTHER TERMS:** _____
   _____
   _____
   _____
   _____
   _____
   _____
   _____
   _____
   D. **The following attached addenda are incorporated into this Seller Counter offer:** ☐ Addendum No. _____
   ☐ _____

2. **EXPIRATION:** This Seller Counter Offer shall be deemed revoked and the deposits, if any, shall be returned:
   A. Unless by 5:00pm on the third Day After the date it is signed in paragraph 4 (if more than one signature then, the last signature date)(or by _____ ☐ AM ☐ PM on _____ (date)) (i) it is signed in paragraph 5 by Buyer and (ii) a copy of the signed Seller Counter Offer is personally received by Seller or _____ , who is authorized to receive it.
   OR B. If Seller withdraws it anytime prior to Acceptance (CAR Form WOO may be used).
   OR C. If Seller accepts another offer prior to Buyer's Acceptance of this counter offer.

3. **MARKETING TO OTHER BUYERS:** Seller has the right to continue to offer the Property for sale. Seller has the right to accept any other offer received, prior to Acceptance of this Counter Offer by Buyer as specified in 2A and 5. In such event, Seller is advised to withdraw this Seller Counter Offer before accepting another offer.

4. **OFFER: SELLER MAKES THIS COUNTER OFFER ON THE TERMS ABOVE AND ACKNOWLEDGES RECEIPT OF A COPY.**
   Seller _____ Date _____
   Seller _____ Date _____

5. **ACCEPTANCE: I/WE** accept the above Seller Counter Offer **(If checked ☐ SUBJECT TO THE ATTACHED COUNTER OFFER)** and acknowledge receipt of a Copy.
   Buyer _____ Date _____ Time _____ ☐ AM/☐ PM
   Buyer _____ Date _____ Time _____ ☐ AM/☐ PM

CONFIRMATION OF ACCEPTANCE:

(_____ / _____) (Initials) **Confirmation of Acceptance:** A Copy of Signed Acceptance was personally received by Seller, or Seller's authorized agent as specified in paragraph 2A on (date) _____ at _____ ☐ AM/☐ PM. **A binding Agreement is created when a Copy of Signed Acceptance is personally received by Seller or Seller's authorized agent whether or not confirmed in this document.**

Published and Distributed by:
REAL ESTATE BUSINESS SERVICES, INC.
a subsidiary of the California Association of REALTORS®
525 South Virgil Avenue, Los Angeles, California 90020

Reviewed by _____ Date _____

SCO 11/14 (PAGE 1 OF 1)

SELLER COUNTER OFFER (SCO PAGE 1 OF 1)

Phone: Fax:
Produced with zipForm® by zipLogix 18070 Fifteen Mile Road, Fraser, Michigan 48026 www.zipLogix.com

Elements of a Valid Option

An option must be in writing and must have actual monetary consideration paid to the owner (optionor). The consideration may be in the form of cash, a check, or something else of value. In a lease option, payment of rent and the provisions of the lease are acceptable as the consideration.

Rights of the Optionor and Optionee

An option contract actually restricts the rights of the seller (optionor) because he or she cannot sell or lease the property during the option period. If the optionee decides not to buy the property during the term of the option, the consideration remains with the optionor.

The buyer (optionee) is the only one who has a choice, once the contract is signed and the consideration given. The option does not bind the optionee to any performance—he or she does not have to exercise the option. It merely provides the right to demand performance from the optionor, who must sell if the optionee decides to buy the property during the course of the option. The option does not give the optionee a legal interest in the title and the optionee does not have any right to use the land. The optionee may assign or sell the option without the permission of the optionor during the term of the option. The optionee may find another buyer for the property to exercise the option.

LEASES

A **lease** is a contract between a property owner, (lessor or landlord) and a renter (lessee or tenant) which gives the tenant a tenancy. **Tenancy** is defined as the interest of a person holding property by any right or title. For example, an arrangement by formal lease or informal agreement in which the owner (landlord) allows another (tenant) to take exclusive possession of land in consideration for rent, is

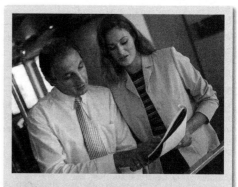

A lease lists the rights and options of the property manager and the lessee.

a type of tenancy. Normally, under a lease, the tenant takes possession and use of a property in return for rent payment. The lease is usually a written agreement that transfers the right of exclusive possession and use of real estate for a definite time period. Another name for lease is **rental agreement**.

OPTION AGREEMENT
(To be used with a Purchase Agreement. May also be used with a Lease.)
(C.A.R. Form OA, Revised 11/12)

Date _____, at _____, California
_____ ("Optionor"), grants to
_____ , ("Optionee"),
on the following terms and conditions, an option ("Option") to purchase the real property and improvements situated in
City of _____, County of _____,
California, described as _____ ("Property") on the terms and
conditions specified in the attached: ☐ Real Estate Purchase Agreement or dated _____ ("Purchase Agreement")
☐ Other _____, which is incorporated by reference as a part of this Option.

1. **OPTION CONSIDERATION:**
   A. _____ Dollars ($ _____),
      payable upon acceptance of this Option, or, if checked, ☐ _____ ,
      by ☐ cash, ☐ cashier's check, ☐ personal check, or ☐ _____ ,
      made payable to _____ .
   OR B. ☐ (If checked) Mutual execution of the attached Lease specified in paragraph 2A.
   OR C. ☐ (If checked) Both 1A and 1B.

2. ☐ **LEASE (If checked):**
   A. The attached Lease Agreement, dated _____ , between Optionee as Tenant and Optionor, as Landlord,
      ("Lease") is incorporated by reference as part of this Option.
   B. If the Option is exercised, the Lease shall terminate on the earliest of (i) the date scheduled for Close Of Escrow under the
      Purchase Agreement, or as extended in writing, (ii) the Close Of Escrow of the Purchase Agreement, or (iii) mutual cancellation
      of the Purchase Agreement.

3. **OPTION PERIOD:** The Option shall begin on (date) _____ , and shall end at 11:59 p.m.
   (or at ☐ _____), on (date) _____ .

4. **MANNER OF EXERCISE:** Optionee may exercise the Option **only** by delivering a written unconditional notice of exercise, signed
   by Optionee, to Optionor, or to _____ , who is authorized to receive it.
   A copy of the unconditional notice of exercise shall be delivered to the Brokers identified in this Agreement.

5. **NON-EXERCISE:** If the Option is not exercised in the manner specified, within the option period or any written extension thereof,
   or if it is terminated under any provision of this Option, then:
   A. The Option and all rights of Optionee to purchase the Property shall immediately terminate without notice; and
   B. All Option Consideration paid, rent paid, services rendered to Optionor, and improvements made to the Property, if any, by
      Optionee, shall be retained by Optionor in consideration of the granting of the Option; and
   C. Optionee shall execute, acknowledge, and deliver to Optionor, within **5 (or** ☐ _____ **) calendar Days** of Optionor's request,
      a release, quitclaim deed, or any other document reasonably required by Optionor or a title insurance company to verify the
      termination of the Option.

6. **EFFECT OF DEFAULT ON OPTION:**
   A. Optionee shall have no right to exercise this Option if Optionee has not performed any obligation imposed by, or is in default of,
      any obligation of this Option, any addenda, or any document incorporated by reference.
   B. In addition, if a lease is incorporated by reference in paragraph 2A, Optionee shall have no right to exercise this Option if
      Optionor, as Landlord, has given to Optionee, as Tenant, two or more notices to cure any default or non-performance under
      that lease.

7. **OPTIONOR DISCLOSURE:**
   A. Unless exempt, if the Property contains one-to-four residential dwelling units, Optionor shall within **7 (or** _____ **) Days After**
      entering into this Option provide to Optionee (i) a Real Estate Transfer Disclosure Statement, a Natural Hazard Disclosure
      Statement, a Notice of Private Transfer Fee and other disclosures required by Civil Code §§1102 and 1103 et seq.,
      (ii) ☐ a preliminary title report, and (iii) ☐ _____ .
   B. If any disclosure or notice specified in 7A (i) is delivered to Optionee after the Option is Signed, Optionee shall have the right to
      cancel this Option within **3 Days After** delivery in person or **5 Days After** delivery by deposit in the mail by giving written notice
      of cancellation to Optionor or Optionor's agent.

Optionee and Optionor acknowledge receipt of copy of this page.

Optionee's Initials (_____) (_____)   Optionor's Initials (_____) (_____)

OA REVISED 11/12 (PAGE 1 OF 3)

Reviewed by	Date

OPTION AGREEMENT (OA PAGE 1 OF 3)

Agent:	Phone:	Fax:	Prepared using zipForm® software
Broker:			

The **lessor** (landlord) owns the property and signs the lease to give possession and use to the lessee (tenant). The lessor keeps the right to retake possession of the property after the lease term expires. The right of the landlord to reclaim the property is known as the **reversionary right**. The lessor's interest is called a **leased fee estate**. The **lessee** (tenant) has the use, possession and the right of quiet enjoyment of the property for the duration of the lease. The lessee's interest is a **less-than-freehold estate** in real property.

A lease can be described in any number of ways, as long as the names of the parties, description of the property, rent amount, and duration of lease are included. Sometimes the words "to let" or "to **demise**", (another way to say "to rent"), will be found in a rental agreement, but those words are optional.

Leases for longer than one year (1 year plus 1 day) must be in writing, according to the California statute of frauds. However, it is common practice, and makes common sense to produce all lease agreements in writing. It must be signed by the lessor, but not necessarily by the lessee. Again, it is common practice for the lessee to sign the lease, but the law requires only that the lease be delivered to the lessee for it to be binding. The tenant's acceptance of the lease signed by the landlord or the tenants paying rent and taking possession of the property binds both parties to the terms of the agreement.

Facts About Leases

- If more than 1 year, must be in writing

- Signed by lessor (landlord)

- Lessee (tenant) does not have to sign lease

- Reversionary right belongs to the lessor

- Possessory right belongs to the lessee

- A rental is presumed to be month to month unless specified otherwise

- Agricultural lease limited to maximum of 51 years

- Urban lease limited to maximum of 99 years

- Mineral, oil, and gas leases are limited to a maximum of 99 years

Classifications of Leases

There are many varieties of lease contracts. If a lessee and lessor agree on terms that differ from the law, both will be required to meet the terms of their written agreement. For example, a new two-page lease agreement adopted by the California Association of REALTORS® only requires a four-hour notice for a landlord to inspect a leased property. California statutory law states that 24 hours is necessary, unless landlord and tenant have a different written agreement.

Leases are generally classified in one of the following three ways: (1) type of real estate, (2) length of term, or (3) method of payment.

Type of Real Estate

Leases based on type of real estate would include office leases, ground leases, proprietary leases, and residential leases. A **ground lease** is a lease for only the land. A **proprietary lease** is used in co-op apartment buildings. The lessee is also a stockholder in the corporation that owns the building. A **residential lease** is used for all residential property including single-family homes, duplexes, and multiple-family dwellings.

Length of Time

Leases based on length of time would include short-term and long-term leases. An apartment lease is an example of a short-term lease. An example of a long-term lease is a major tenant in a shopping center that has multiple-renewal rights.

Method of Rent Payments

Leases are also classified by method of rent payments, such as gross, net, and percentage leases.

Gross lease: A gross lease is also called a flat, fixed, or straight lease. The tenant pays an agreed-upon sum as rent and the landlord pays any other expenses, such as taxes, maintenance, or insurance. Residential leases are usually gross leases with fixed, level payments, usually due on the 1st of each month.

Net lease: In a net lease, the tenant pays an agreed-upon sum as rent, plus certain agreed-upon expenses per month (i.e., taxes, insurance, and repairs). The benefit of a net lease to the lessor is that it creates a fixed income. Net leases are categorized as a single net (N) lease, a double net (NN) lease, or a triple net (NNN) lease.

Percentage lease: A percentage lease is a lease in which the tenant pays a percentage of gross monthly receipts in addition to a base rent. Usually the higher the gross receipts, the lower the percentage **rate**. A percentage lease typically is used for retail stores in shopping centers or malls.

CALIFORNIA
ASSOCIATION
OF REALTORS®

RESIDENTIAL LEASE OR
MONTH-TO-MONTH RENTAL AGREEMENT
(C.A.R. Form LR, Revised 12/15)

Date _____ , _____ ("Landlord") and
_____ ("Tenant") agree as follows:

1. PROPERTY:
   A. Landlord rents to Tenant and Tenant rents from Landlord, the real property and improvements described as: *4091 1st street, ,* _____
                                                                                    ("Premises").
   B. The Premises are for the sole use as a personal residence by the following named person(s) **only**: _____
   C. The following personal property, maintained pursuant to paragraph 11, is included: _____ .
                                          or ☐ (if checked) the personal property on the attached addendum.
   D. The Premises may be subject to a local rent control ordinance _____

2. TERM: The term begins on (date) _____ ("Commencement Date"), **(Check A or B):**
   ☐ **A.** **Month-to-Month:** and continues as a month-to-month tenancy. Tenant may terminate the tenancy by giving written notice at least 30 days
          prior to the intended termination date. Landlord may terminate the tenancy by giving written notice as provided by law. Such notices may be
          given on any date.
   ☐ **B.** **Lease:** and shall terminate on (date) _____ at _____ ☐ AM/ ☐ PM.
          Tenant shall vacate the Premises upon termination of the Agreement, unless: **(i)** Landlord and Tenant have extended this Agreement in
          writing or signed a new agreement; **(ii)** mandated by local rent control law; or **(iii)** Landlord accepts Rent from Tenant (other than past due
          Rent), in which case a month-to-month tenancy shall be created which either party may terminate as specified in paragraph 2A. Rent shall
          be at a rate agreed to by Landlord and Tenant, or as allowed by law. All other terms and conditions of this Agreement shall remain in full
          force and effect.

3. RENT: "Rent" shall mean all monetary obligations of Tenant to Landlord under the terms of the Agreement, except security deposit.
   A. Tenant agrees to pay $ _____ per month for the term of the Agreement.
   B. Rent is payable in advance on the **1st (or** ☐ _____ **) day** of each calendar month, and is delinquent on the next day.
   C. If Commencement Date falls on any day other than the day Rent is payable under paragraph 3B, and Tenant has paid one full month's Rent in
       advance of Commencement Date, Rent for the second calendar month shall be prorated and Tenant shall pay 1/30th of the monthly rent per day
       for each day remaining in prorated second month.
   D. PAYMENT: Rent shall be paid by ☐ personal check, ☐ money order, ☐ cashier's check, or ☐ other _____ , to
       (name) _____ (phone) _____ at
       (address) _____ , (or
       at any other location subsequently specified by Landlord in writing to Tenant) (and ☐ if checked, rent may be paid personally, between the hours
       of _____ and _____ on the following days _____). If any payment
       is returned for non-sufficient funds ("NSF") or because tenant stops payment, then, after that: **(i)** Landlord may, in writing, require Tenant to pay
       Rent in cash for three months and **(ii)** all future Rent shall be paid by ☐ money order, or ☐ cashier's check.
   E. Rent payments received by Landlord shall be applied to the earliest amount(s) due or past due.

4. SECURITY DEPOSIT:
   A. Tenant agrees to pay $ _____ as a security deposit. Security deposit will be ☐ transferred to and held by the
       Owner of the Premises, or ☐ held in Owner's Broker's trust account.
   B. All or any portion of the security deposit may be used, as reasonably necessary, to: **(i)** cure Tenant's default in payment of Rent (which includes
       Late Charges, NSF fees or other sums due); **(ii)** repair damage, excluding ordinary wear and tear, caused by Tenant or by a guest or licensee of
       Tenant; **(iii)** clean Premises, if necessary, upon termination of the tenancy; and **(iv)** replace or return personal property or appurtenances.
       SECURITY DEPOSIT SHALL NOT BE USED BY TENANT IN LIEU OF PAYMENT OF LAST MONTH'S RENT. If all or any portion of the
       security deposit is used during the tenancy, Tenant agrees to reinstate the total security deposit within five days after written notice is delivered to
       Tenant. Within 21 days after Tenant vacates the Premises, Landlord shall: **(1)** furnish Tenant an itemized statement indicating the amount of any
       security deposit received and the basis for its disposition and supporting documentation as required by California Civil Code § 1950.5(g); and **(2)**
       return any remaining portion of the security deposit to Tenant.
   C. Security deposit will not be returned until all Tenants have vacated the Premises and all keys returned. Any security deposit returned
       by check shall be made out to all Tenants named on this Agreement, or as subsequently modified.
   D. No interest will be paid on security deposit unless required by local law.
   E. If the security deposit is held by Owner, Tenant agrees not to hold Broker responsible for its return. If the security deposit is held in Owner's
       Broker's trust account, **and** Broker's authority is terminated before expiration of this Agreement, **and** security deposit is released to someone
       other than Tenant, **then** Broker shall notify Tenant, in writing, where and to whom security deposit has been released. Once Tenant has been
       provided such notice, Tenant agrees not to hold Broker responsible for the security deposit.

5. MOVE-IN COSTS RECEIVED/DUE: Move-in funds made payable to _____
   shall be paid by ☐ personal check, ☐ money order, or ☐ cashier's check.

Category	Total Due	Payment Received	Balance Due	Date Due
Rent from _____				
to _____ (date)				
*Security Deposit				
Other _____				
Other _____				
Total				

*The maximum amount Landlord may receive as security deposit, however designated, cannot exceed two months' Rent for unfurnished premises, or
three months' Rent for furnished premises.

Tenant's Initials (_____) (_____)   Landlord's Initials (_____) (_____)

© 2015, California Association of REALTORS®, Inc.

LR REVISED 12/15 (PAGE 1 OF 6)

RESIDENTIAL LEASE OR MONTH-TO-MONTH RENTAL AGREEMENT (LR PAGE 1 OF 6)

EQUAL HOUSING
OPPORTUNITY

Phone: Fax:

Premises: _____   Date: _____

6. LATE CHARGE; RETURNED CHECKS:
   A. Tenant acknowledges either late payment of Rent or issuance of a returned check may cause Landlord to incur costs and expenses, the exact amounts of which are extremely difficult and impractical to determine. These costs may include, but are not limited to, processing, enforcement and accounting expenses, and late charges imposed on Landlord. If any installment of Rent due from Tenant is not received by Landlord within **5 (or ☐ _____) calendar days** after the date due, or if a check is returned, Tenant shall pay to Landlord, respectively, an additional sum of $ _____ or _____ % of the Rent due as a Late Charge and $25.00 as a NSF fee for the first returned check and $35.00 as a NSF fee for each additional returned check, either or both of which shall be deemed additional Rent.
   B. Landlord and Tenant agree that these charges represent a fair and reasonable estimate of the costs Landlord may incur by reason of Tenant's late or NSF payment. Any Late Charge or NSF fee due shall be paid with the current installment of Rent. Landlord's acceptance of any Late Charge or NSF fee shall not constitute a waiver as to any default of Tenant. Landlord's right to collect a Late Charge or NSF fee shall not be deemed an extension of the date Rent is due under paragraph 3 or prevent Landlord from exercising any other rights and remedies under this Agreement and as provided by law.

7. PARKING: (Check A or B)
   ☐ A.   Parking is permitted as follows: _____
   _____
   The right to parking ☐ is ☐ is not included in the Rent charged pursuant to paragraph 3. If not included in the Rent, the parking rental fee shall be an additional $ _____ per month. Parking space(s) are to be used for parking properly licensed and operable motor vehicles, except for trailers, boats, campers, buses or trucks (other than pick-up trucks). Tenant shall park in assigned space(s) only. Parking space(s) are to be kept clean. Vehicles leaking oil, gas or other motor vehicle fluids shall not be parked on the Premises. Mechanical work or storage of inoperable vehicles is not permitted in parking space(s) or elsewhere on the Premises.
   OR ☐ B.   Parking is not permitted on the Premises.

8. STORAGE: (Check A or B)
   ☐ A.   Storage is permitted as follows: _____
   The right to separate storage space ☐ is, ☐ is not, included in the Rent charged pursuant to paragraph 3. If not included in the Rent, storage space fee shall be an additional $ _____ per month. Tenant shall store only personal property Tenant owns, and shall not store property claimed by another or in which another has any right, title or interest. Tenant shall not store any improperly packaged food or perishable goods, flammable materials, explosives, hazardous waste or other inherently dangerous material, or illegal substances.
   OR ☐ B.   Except for Tenant's personal property, contained entirely within the Premises, storage is not permitted on the Premises.

9. UTILITIES: Tenant agrees to pay for all utilities and services, and the following charges: _____ .
   except _____, which shall be paid for by Landlord. If any utilities are not separately metered, Tenant shall pay Tenant's proportional share, as reasonably determined and directed by Landlord. If utilities are separately metered, Tenant shall place utilities in Tenant's name as of the Commencement Date. Landlord is only responsible for installing and maintaining one usable telephone jack and one telephone line to the Premises. Tenant shall pay any cost for conversion from existing utilities service provider.

10. CONDITION OF PREMISES: Tenant has examined Premises and, if any, all furniture, furnishings, appliances, landscaping and fixtures, including smoke detector(s).
   (Check all that apply:)
   ☐ A.   Tenant acknowledges these items are clean and in operable condition, with the following exceptions: _____
   _____
   ☐ B.   Tenant's acknowledgment of the condition of these items is contained in an attached statement of condition (C.A.R. Form MIMO).
   ☐ C.   **(i)** Landlord will Deliver to Tenant a statement of condition (C.A.R. Form MIMO) ☐ within **3 days** after execution of this Agreement; ☐ prior to the Commencement Date; ☐ within **3 days** after the Commencement Date.
   (ii) Tenant shall complete and return the MIMO to Landlord within **3 (or ☐ _____) days** after Delivery. Tenant's failure to return the MIMO within that time shall conclusively be deemed Tenant's Acknowledgement of the condition as stated in the MIMO.
   ☐ D.   Tenant will provide Landlord a list of items that are damaged or not in operable condition within **3 (or ☐ _____) days** after Commencement Date, not as a contingency of this Agreement but rather as an acknowledgement of the condition of the Premises.
   ☐ E.   Other: _____

11. MAINTENANCE USE AND REPORTING:
   A. Tenant shall properly use, operate and safeguard Premises, including if applicable, any landscaping, furniture, furnishings and appliances, and all mechanical, electrical, gas and plumbing fixtures, carbon monoxide devices and smoke alarms, and keep them and the Premises clean, sanitary and well ventilated. Tenant shall be responsible for checking and maintaining all carbon monoxide detectors and any additional phone lines beyond the one line and jack that Landlord shall provide and maintain. Tenant shall immediately notify Landlord, in writing, of any problem, malfunction or damage with any item including carbon monoxide devices and smoke alarms on the property. Tenant shall be charged for all repairs or replacements caused by Tenant, pets, guests or licensees of Tenant, excluding ordinary wear and tear. Tenant shall be charged for all damage to Premises as a result of failure to report a problem in a timely manner. Tenant shall be charged for repair of drain blockages or stoppages, unless caused by defective plumbing parts or tree roots invading sewer lines.
   B. ☐ Landlord ☐ Tenant shall water the garden, landscaping, trees and shrubs, except: _____
   _____ .
   C. ☐ Landlord ☐ Tenant shall maintain the garden, landscaping, trees and shrubs, except: _____
   _____ .
   D. ☐ Landlord ☐ Tenant shall maintain _____
   E. Landlord and Tenant agree that State or local water use restrictions shall supersede any obligation of Landlord or Tenant to water or maintain any garden, landscaping, trees or shrubs pursuant to 11B, 11C, and 11D.
   F. Tenant's failure to maintain any item for which Tenant is responsible shall give Landlord the right to hire someone to perform such maintenance and charge Tenant to cover the cost of such maintenance.
   G. The following items of personal property are included in the Premises without warranty and Landlord will not maintain, repair or replace them: _____
   _____

Tenant's Initials (_____) (_____)   Landlord's Initials (_____) (_____)

RESIDENTIAL LEASE OR MONTH-TO-MONTH RENTAL AGREEMENT (LR PAGE 2 OF 6)
Produced with zipForm® by zipLogix 18070 Fifteen Mile Road, Fraser, Michigan 48026   www.zipLogix.com

EQUAL HOUSING OPPORTUNITY

Premises: _____ Date: _____

12. **NEIGHBORHOOD CONDITIONS:** Tenant is advised to satisfy him or herself as to neighborhood or area conditions, including schools, proximity and adequacy of law enforcement, crime statistics, proximity of registered felons or offenders, fire protection, other governmental services, availability, adequacy and cost of any wired, wireless internet connections or other telecommunications or other technology services and installations, proximity to commercial, industrial or agricultural activities, existing and proposed transportation, construction and development that may affect noise, view, or traffic, airport noise, noise or odor from any source, wild and domestic animals, other nuisances, hazards, or circumstances, cemeteries, facilities and condition of common areas, conditions and influences of significance to certain cultures and/or religions, and personal needs, requirements and preferences of Tenant.

13. **PETS:** Unless otherwise provided in California Civil Code §54.2, no animal or pet shall be kept on or about the Premises without Landlord's prior written consent, ☐ except as agreed to in the attached Pet Addendum (C.A.R. Form PET).

14. ☐ (If checked) **NO SMOKING:** No smoking of any substance is allowed on the Premises or common areas. If smoking does occur on the Premises or common areas, (i) Tenant is responsible for all damage caused by the smoking including, but not limited to stains, burns, odors and removal of debris; (ii) Tenant is in breach of this Agreement; (iii) Tenant, guests, and all others may be required to leave the Premises; and (iv) Tenant acknowledges that in order to remove odor caused by smoking, Landlord may need to replace carpet and drapes and paint the entire premises regardless of when these items were last cleaned, replaced, or repainted. Such actions and other necessary steps will impact the return of any security deposit. The Premises or common areas may be subject to a local non-smoking ordinance.

15. **RULES/REGULATIONS:**
    A. Tenant agrees to comply with all Landlord rules and regulations that are at any time posted on the Premises or delivered to Tenant. Tenant shall not, and shall ensure that guests and licensees of Tenant shall not, disturb, annoy, endanger or interfere with other tenants of the building or neighbors, or use the Premises for any unlawful purposes, including, but not limited to, using, manufacturing, selling, storing or transporting illicit drugs or other contraband, or violate any law or ordinance, or commit a waste or nuisance on or about the Premises.
    B. **(If applicable, check one)**
       ☐ 1. Landlord shall provide Tenant with a copy of the rules and regulations within _____ days or _____ .
       OR ☐ 2. Tenant has been provided with, and acknowledges receipt of, a copy of the rules and regulations.

16. ☐ (If checked) **CONDOMINIUM; PLANNED UNIT DEVELOPMENT:**
    A. The Premises are a unit in a condominium, planned unit development, common interest subdivision or other development governed by a homeowners' association ("HOA"). The name of the HOA is _____ . Tenant agrees to comply with all HOA covenants, conditions and restrictions, bylaws, rules and regulations and decisions ("HOA Rules"). Landlord shall provide Tenant copies of HOA Rules, if any. Tenant shall reimburse Landlord for any fines or charges imposed by HOA or other authorities, due to any violation by Tenant, or the guests or licensees of Tenant.
    B. **(Check one)**
       ☐ 1. Landlord shall provide Tenant with a copy of the HOA Rules within _____ days
       or _____ .
       OR ☐ 2. Tenant has been provided with, and acknowledges receipt of, a copy of the HOA Rules.

17. **ALTERATIONS; REPAIRS:** Unless otherwise specified by law or paragraph 29C, without Landlord's prior written consent, **(i)** Tenant shall not make any repairs, alterations or improvements in or about the Premises including: painting, wallpapering, adding or changing locks, installing antenna or satellite dish(es), placing signs, displays or exhibits, or using screws, fastening devices, large nails or adhesive materials; **(ii)** Landlord shall not be responsible for the costs of alterations or repairs made by Tenant; **(iii)** Tenant shall not deduct from Rent the costs of any repairs, alterations or improvements; and **(iv)** any deduction made by Tenant shall be considered unpaid Rent.

18. **KEYS; LOCKS:**
    A. Tenant acknowledges receipt of (or Tenant will receive ☐ prior to the Commencement Date, or ☐ _____):
       ☐ _____ key(s) to Premises,   ☐ _____ remote control device(s) for garage door/gate opener(s),
       ☐ _____ key(s) to mailbox,   ☐ _____ ,
       ☐ _____ key(s) to common area(s), ☐ _____ .
    B. Tenant acknowledges that locks to the Premises ☐ have, ☐ have not, been re-keyed.
    C. If Tenant re-keys existing locks or opening devices, Tenant shall immediately deliver copies of all keys to Landlord. Tenant shall pay all costs and charges related to loss of any keys or opening devices. Tenant may not remove locks, even if installed by Tenant.

19. **ENTRY:**
    A. Tenant shall make Premises available to Landlord or Landlord's representative for the purpose of entering to make necessary or agreed repairs, (including, but not limited to, installing, repairing, testing, and maintaining smoke detectors and carbon monoxide devices, and bracing, anchoring or strapping water heaters), decorations, alterations, or improvements, or to supply necessary or agreed services, or to show Premises to prospective or actual purchasers, tenants, mortgagees, lenders, appraisers, or contractors.
    B. Landlord and Tenant agree that 24-hour written notice shall be reasonable and sufficient notice, except as follows: (1) 48-hour written notice is required to conduct an inspection of the Premises prior to the Tenant moving out, unless the Tenant waives the right to such notice. (2) If Landlord has in writing informed Tenant that the Premises are for sale and that Tenant will be notified orally to show the premises (C.A.R. Form NSE), then, for the next 120 days following the delivery of the NSE, notice may be given orally to show the Premises to actual or prospective purchasers. (3) No written notice is required if Landlord and Tenant orally agree to an entry for agreed services or repairs if the date and time of entry are within one week of the oral agreement. (4) No notice is required: **(i)** to enter in case of an emergency; **(ii)** if the Tenant is present and consents at the time of entry; or **(iii)** if the Tenant has abandoned or surrendered the Premises.
    C. ☐ (If checked) Tenant authorizes the use of a keysafe/lockbox to allow entry into the Premises and agrees to sign a keysafe/lockbox addendum (C.A.R. Form KLA).

20. **SIGNS:** Tenant authorizes Landlord to place FOR SALE/LEASE signs on the Premises.

21. **ASSIGNMENT; SUBLETTING:** Tenant shall not sublet all or any part of Premises, or assign or transfer this Agreement or any interest in it, without Landlord's prior written consent. Unless such consent is obtained, any assignment, transfer or subletting of Premises or this Agreement or tenancy, by voluntary act of Tenant, operation of law or otherwise, shall, at the option of Landlord, terminate this Agreement. Any proposed assignee, transferee or sublessee shall submit to Landlord an application and credit information for Landlord's approval and, if approved, sign a separate written agreement with Landlord and Tenant. Landlord's consent to any one assignment, transfer or sublease, shall not be construed as consent to any subsequent assignment, transfer or sublease and does not release Tenant of Tenant's obligations under this Agreement.

Tenant's Initials (_____) (_____)   Landlord's Initials (_____) (_____)

Premises: _____ Date: _____

22. JOINT AND INDIVIDUAL OBLIGATIONS: If there is more than one Tenant, each one shall be individually and completely responsible for the performance of all obligations of Tenant under this Agreement, jointly with every other Tenant, and individually, whether or not in possession.

23. ☐ **LEAD-BASED PAINT (If checked):** Premises were constructed prior to 1978. In accordance with federal law, Landlord gives and Tenant acknowledges receipt of the disclosures on the attached form (C.A.R. Form FLD) and a federally approved lead pamphlet.

24. ☐ **MILITARY ORDNANCE DISCLOSURE:** (If applicable and known to Landlord) Premises are located within one mile of an area once used for military training, and may contain potentially explosive munitions.

25. ☐ **PERIODIC PEST CONTROL:** Landlord has entered into a contract for periodic pest control treatment of the Premises and shall give Tenant a copy of the notice originally given to Landlord by the pest control company.

26. ☐ **METHAMPHETAMINE CONTAMINATION:** Prior to signing this Agreement, Landlord has given Tenant a notice that a health official has issued an order prohibiting occupancy of the property because of methamphetamine contamination. A copy of the notice and order are attached.

27. MEGAN'S LAW DATABASE DISCLOSURE: Notice: Pursuant to Section 290.46 of the Penal Code, information about specified registered sex offenders is made available to the public via an Internet Web site maintained by the Department of Justice at www.meganslaw.ca.gov. Depending on an offender's criminal history, this information will include either the address at which the offender resides or the community of residence and ZIP Code in which he or she resides. (Neither Landlord nor Brokers, if any, are required to check this website. If Tenant wants further information, Tenant should obtain information directly from this website.)

28. POSSESSION:

    A. Tenant is not in possession of the Premises. If Landlord is unable to deliver possession of Premises on Commencement Date, such Date shall be extended to the date on which possession is made available to Tenant. If Landlord is unable to deliver possession within **5 (or** ☐ _____ **) calendar days** after agreed Commencement Date, Tenant may terminate this Agreement by giving written notice to Landlord, and shall be refunded all Rent and security deposit paid. Possession is deemed terminated when Tenant has returned all keys to the Premises to Landlord.

    B. ☐ Tenant is already in possession of the Premises.

29. TENANT'S OBLIGATIONS UPON VACATING PREMISES:

    A. Upon termination of this Agreement, Tenant shall: **(i)** give Landlord all copies of all keys or opening devices to Premises, including any common areas; **(ii)** vacate and surrender Premises to Landlord, empty of all persons; **(iii)** vacate any/all parking and/or storage space; **(iv)** clean and deliver Premises, as specified in paragraph C below, to Landlord in the same condition as referenced in paragraph 10; **(v)** remove all debris; **(vi)** give written notice to Landlord of Tenant's forwarding address; and **(vii)** _____.

    B. All alterations/improvements made by or caused to be made by Tenant, with or without Landlord's consent, become the property of Landlord upon termination. Landlord may charge Tenant for restoration of the Premises to the condition it was in prior to any alterations/improvements.

    C. Right to Pre-Move-Out Inspection and Repairs: (i) After giving or receiving notice of termination of a tenancy (C.A.R. Form NTT), or before the end of a lease, Tenant has the right to request that an inspection of the Premises take place prior to termination of the lease or rental (C.A.R. Form NRI). If Tenant requests such an inspection, Tenant shall be given an opportunity to remedy identified deficiencies prior to termination, consistent with the terms of this Agreement. **(ii)** Any repairs or alterations made to the Premises as a result of this inspection (collectively, "Repairs") shall be made at Tenant's expense. Repairs may be performed by Tenant or through others, who have adequate insurance and licenses and are approved by Landlord. The work shall comply with applicable law, including governmental permit, inspection and approval requirements. Repairs shall be performed in a good, skillful manner with materials of quality and appearance comparable to existing materials. It is understood that exact restoration of appearance or cosmetic items following all Repairs may not be possible. **(iii)** Tenant shall: **(a)** obtain receipts for Repairs performed by others; **(b)** prepare a written statement indicating the Repairs performed by Tenant and the date of such Repairs; and **(c)** provide copies of receipts and statements to Landlord prior to termination. Paragraph 29C does not apply when the tenancy is terminated pursuant to California Code of Civil Procedure § 1161(2), (3) or (4).

30. BREACH OF CONTRACT; EARLY TERMINATION: In addition to any obligations established by paragraph 29, in the event of termination by Tenant prior to completion of the original term of the Agreement, Tenant shall also be responsible for lost Rent, rental commissions, advertising expenses and painting costs necessary to ready Premises for re-rental. Landlord may withhold any such amounts from Tenant's security deposit.

31. TEMPORARY RELOCATION: Subject to local law, Tenant agrees, upon demand of Landlord, to temporarily vacate Premises for a reasonable period, to allow for fumigation (or other methods) to control wood destroying pests or organisms, or other repairs to Premises. Tenant agrees to comply with all instructions and requirements necessary to prepare Premises to accommodate pest control, fumigation or other work, including bagging or storage of food and medicine, and removal of perishables and valuables. Tenant shall only be entitled to a credit of Rent equal to the per diem Rent for the period of time Tenant is required to vacate Premises.

32. DAMAGE TO PREMISES: If, by no fault of Tenant, Premises are totally or partially damaged or destroyed by fire, earthquake, accident or other casualty that render Premises totally or partially uninhabitable, either Landlord or Tenant may terminate this Agreement by giving the other written notice. Rent shall be abated as of the date Premises become totally or partially uninhabitable. The abated amount shall be the current monthly Rent prorated on a 30-day period. If the Agreement is not terminated, Landlord shall promptly repair the damage, and Rent shall be reduced based on the extent to which the damage interferes with Tenant's reasonable use of Premises. If damage occurs as a result of an act of Tenant or Tenant's guests, only Landlord shall have the right of termination, and no reduction in Rent shall be made.

33. INSURANCE: Tenant's or guest's personal property and vehicles are not insured by Landlord, manager or, if applicable, HOA, against loss or damage due to fire, theft, vandalism, rain, water, criminal or negligent acts of others, or any other cause. **Tenant is advised to carry Tenant's own insurance (renter's insurance) to protect Tenant from any such loss or damage.** Tenant shall comply with any requirement imposed on Tenant by Landlord's insurer to avoid: **(i)** an increase in Landlord's insurance premium (or Tenant shall pay for the increase in premium); or **(ii)** loss of insurance.

34. WATERBEDS/PORTABLE WASHERS: Tenant shall not use or have waterbeds on the Premises unless: **(i)** Tenant obtains a valid waterbed insurance policy; **(ii)** Tenant increases the security deposit in an amount equal to one-half of one month's Rent; and **(iii)** the bed conforms to the floor load capacity of Premises. Tenant shall not use on the Premises ☐ Portable Dishwasher ☐ Portable Washing Machine.

35. WAIVER: The waiver of any breach shall not be construed as a continuing waiver of the same or any subsequent breach.

Tenant's Initials (_____) (_____)   Landlord's Initials (_____) (_____)

Premises: _____ Date: _____

36 **NOTICE:** Notices may be served at the following address, or at any other location subsequently designated:
Landlord: _____ Tenant: _____

37. **TENANT ESTOPPEL CERTIFICATE:** Tenant shall execute and return a tenant estoppel certificate delivered to Tenant by Landlord or Landlord's agent within **3 days** after its receipt. Failure to comply with this requirement shall be deemed Tenant's acknowledgment that the tenant estoppel certificate is true and correct, and may be relied upon by a lender or purchaser.

38. **REPRESENTATION**
   A. TENANT REPRESENTATION; OBLIGATIONS REGARDING OCCUPANTS; CREDIT: Tenant warrants that all statements in Tenant's rental application are accurate. Landlord requires all occupants 18 years of age or older and all emancipated minors to complete a lease rental application. Tenant acknowledges this requirement and agrees to notify Landlord when any occupant of the Premises reaches the age of 18 or becomes an emancipated minor. Tenant authorizes Landlord and Broker(s) to obtain Tenant's credit report periodically during the tenancy in connection with the modification or enforcement of this Agreement. Landlord may cancel this Agreement: **(i)** before occupancy begins; **(ii)** upon disapproval of the credit report(s); or **(iii)** at any time, upon discovering that information in Tenant's application is false. A negative credit report reflecting on Tenant's record may be submitted to a credit reporting agency if Tenant fails to fulfill the terms of payment and other obligations under this Agreement.
   B. LANDLORD REPRESENTATIONS: Landlord warrants that, unless otherwise specified in writing, Landlord is unaware of **(i)** any recorded Notices of Default affecting the Premise; **(ii)** any delinquent amounts due under any loan secured by the Premises; and **(iii)** any bankruptcy proceeding affecting the Premises.

39. **MEDIATION:**
   A. Consistent with paragraphs B and C below, Landlord and Tenant agree to mediate any dispute or claim arising between them out of this Agreement, or any resulting transaction, before resorting to court action. Mediation fees, if any, shall be divided equally among the parties involved. If, for any dispute or claim to which this paragraph applies, any party commences an action without first attempting to resolve the matter through mediation, or refuses to mediate after a request has been made, then that party shall not be entitled to recover attorney fees, even if they would otherwise be available to that party in any such action.
   B. The following matters are excluded from mediation: **(i)** an unlawful detainer action; **(ii)** the filing or enforcement of a mechanic's lien; and **(iii)** any matter within the jurisdiction of a probate, small claims or bankruptcy court. The filing of a court action to enable the recording of a notice of pending action, for order of attachment, receivership, injunction, or other provisional remedies, shall not constitute a waiver of the mediation provision.
   C. Landlord and Tenant agree to mediate disputes or claims involving Listing Agent, Leasing Agent or property manager ("Broker"), provided Broker shall have agreed to such mediation prior to, or within a reasonable time after, the dispute or claim is presented to such Broker. Any election by Broker to participate in mediation shall not result in Broker being deemed a party to this Agreement.

40. **ATTORNEY FEES:** In any action or proceeding arising out of this Agreement, the prevailing party between Landlord and Tenant shall be entitled to reasonable attorney fees and costs, collectively not to exceed $1,000 (or $_____), except as provided in paragraph 39A.

41. **C.A.R. FORM:** C.A.R. Form means the specific form referenced or another comparable form agreed to by the parties.

42. **OTHER TERMS AND CONDITIONS; SUPPLEMENTS:** ☐ Interpreter/Translator Agreement (C.A.R. Form ITA);
   ☐ Keysafe/Lockbox Addendum (C.A.R. Form KLA); ☐ Lead-Based Paint and Lead-Based Paint Hazards Disclosure (C.A.R. Form FLD);
   ☐ Landlord in Default Addendum (C.A.R. Form LID) _____

   The following ATTACHED supplements are incorporated in this Agreement: _____

43. **TIME OF ESSENCE; ENTIRE CONTRACT; CHANGES:** Time is of the essence. All understandings between the parties are incorporated in this Agreement. Its terms are intended by the parties as a final, complete and exclusive expression of their Agreement with respect to its subject matter, and may not be contradicted by evidence of any prior agreement or contemporaneous oral agreement. If any provision of this Agreement is held to be ineffective or invalid, the remaining provisions will nevertheless be given full force and effect. Neither this Agreement nor any provision in it may be extended, amended, modified, altered or changed except in writing. This Agreement is subject to California landlord-tenant law and shall incorporate all changes required by amendment or successors to such law. This Agreement and any supplement, addendum or modification, including any copy, may be signed in two or more counterparts, all of which shall constitute one and the same writing.

44. **AGENCY:**
   A. CONFIRMATION: The following agency relationship(s) are hereby confirmed for this transaction:
   Listing Agent: (Print firm name) _____
   is the agent of (check one): ☐ the Landlord exclusively; or ☐ both the Landlord and Tenant.
   Leasing Agent: (Print firm name) _____
   (if not same as Listing Agent) is the agent of (check one): ☐ the Tenant exclusively; or ☐ the Landlord exclusively; or ☐ both the Tenant and Landlord.
   B. DISCLOSURE: ☐ (If checked): The term of this lease exceeds one year. A disclosure regarding real estate agency relationships (C.A.R. Form AD) has been provided to Landlord and Tenant, who each acknowledge its receipt.

45. ☐ **TENANT COMPENSATION TO BROKER:** Upon execution of this Agreement, Tenant agrees to pay compensation to Broker as specified in a separate written agreement between Tenant and Broker.

46. ☐ **INTERPRETER/TRANSLATOR:** The terms of this Agreement have been interpreted for Tenant into the following language: _____ . Landlord and Tenant acknowledge receipt of the attached interpreter/translator agreement (C.A.R. Form ITA).

Tenant's Initials (_____) (_____)   Landlord's Initials (_____) (_____)

Premises: _____   Date: _____

47. NOTICE OF RIGHT TO RECEIVE FOREIGN LANGUAGE TRANSLATION OF LEASE/RENTAL AGREEMENTS: California Civil Code requires a landlord or property manager to provide a tenant with a foreign language translation copy of a lease or rental agreement. If the agreement was negotiated primarily in Spanish, Chinese, Korean, Tagalog or Vietnamese. If applicable, every term of the lease/rental needs to be translated except for, among others, names, dollar amounts and dates written as numerals, and words with no generally accepted non-English translation.

48. OWNER COMPENSATION TO BROKER: Upon execution of this Agreement, Owner agrees to pay compensation to Broker as specified in a separate written agreement between Owner and Broker (C.A.R. Form LL or LCA).

49. RECEIPT: If specified in paragraph 5, Landlord or Broker, acknowledges receipt of move-in funds.

Landlord and Tenant acknowledge and agree Brokers: **(a)** do not guarantee the condition of the Premises; **(b)** cannot verify representations made by others; **(c)** cannot provide legal or tax advice; **(d)** will not provide other advice or information that exceeds the knowledge, education or experience required to obtain a real estate license. Furthermore, if Brokers are not also acting as Landlord in this Agreement, Brokers: **(e)** do not decide what rental rate a Tenant should pay or Landlord should accept; and **(f)** do not decide upon the length or other terms of tenancy. Landlord and Tenant agree that they will seek legal, tax, insurance and other desired assistance from appropriate professionals.

Tenant agrees to rent the Premises on the above terms and conditions.

Tenant _____   Date _____
Address _____   City _____   State ____ Zip _____
Telephone _____ Fax _____   E-mail _____
Tenant _____   Date _____
Address _____   City _____   State ____ Zip _____
Telephone _____ Fax _____   E-mail _____

☐ **GUARANTEE:** In consideration of the execution of this Agreement by and between Landlord and Tenant and for valuable consideration, receipt of which is hereby acknowledged, the undersigned ("Guarantor") does hereby: **(i)** guarantee unconditionally to Landlord and Landlord's agents, successors and assigns, the prompt payment of Rent or other sums that become due pursuant to this Agreement, including any and all court costs and attorney fees included in enforcing the Agreement; **(ii)** consent to any changes, modifications or alterations of any term in this Agreement agreed to by Landlord and Tenant; and **(iii)** waive any right to require Landlord and/or Landlord's agents to proceed against Tenant for any default occurring under this Agreement before seeking to enforce this Guarantee.

Guarantor (Print Name) _____
Guarantor _____   Date _____
Address _____   City _____   State ____ Zip _____
Telephone _____ Fax _____   E-mail _____

Landlord agrees to rent the Premises on the above terms and conditions.

Landlord _____ Date _____   Landlord _____ Date _____

Address _____
Telephone _____ Fax _____   E-mail _____

REAL ESTATE BROKERS:

A. Real estate brokers who are not also Landlord under this Agreement are not parties to the Agreement between Landlord and Tenant.

B. Agency relationships are confirmed in paragraph 44.

C. COOPERATING BROKER COMPENSATION: Listing Broker agrees to pay Cooperating Broker (Leasing Firm) and Cooperating Broker agrees to accept: **(i)** the amount specified in the MLS, provided Cooperating Broker is a Participant of the MLS in which the Property is offered for sale or lease or a reciprocal MLS; or **(ii)** ☐ (if checked) the amount specified in a separate written agreement between Listing Broker and Cooperating Broker.

Real Estate Broker (Listing Firm) _____   CalBRE Lic. # _____
By (Agent) _____   CalBRE Lic. # _____ Date _____
Address _____   City _____   State ____ Zip _____
Telephone _____ Fax _____   E-mail _____

Real Estate Broker (Leasing Firm) _____   CalBRE Lic. # _____
By (Agent) _____   CalBRE Lic. # _____ Date _____
Address _____   City _____   State ____ Zip _____
Telephone _____ Fax _____   E-mail _____

Published and Distributed by:
REAL ESTATE BUSINESS SERVICES, INC.
a subsidiary of the California Association of REALTORS®
525 South Virgil Avenue, Los Angeles, California 90020

Reviewed by _____ Date _____

Rent and Security Deposits

Rent is payment for the use of a property, generally under a lease agreement. The rent becomes due at the end of the term, unless otherwise agreed upon in the lease. If the rent is not paid when due, the tenant may be evicted. Rent received by the owner is taxable in the year received. Frequently rent adjustments on commercial leases are tied to increases in the **Consumer Price Index** for Urban Wage Earners and Clerical Workers (CPI-W).

In addition to the first month's rent, most leases require security deposits. A **security deposit** is money given to a landlord to prepay for any damage that might occur to a property during a lease term that is more than just normal wear and tear. Effective January 1, 2005, a landlord may not require tenants to pay rent in cash except if the tenant has defaulted on the rent. If the landlord first gives a tenant written notice that the rent must be paid in cash, the landlord can only require up to three payments to be paid in cash.

The maximum deposit allowed on an unfurnished property may not exceed the amount of two months' rent. The maximum deposit allowed on a furnished property is not more than the amount of three months' rent. A security deposit also includes any charges imposed at the beginning of the tenancy to reimburse the landlord for costs associated with processing a new tenant, other than application screening fees.

> Example: If rent on an unfurnished, 2-bedroom apartment is $900 per month and the landlord charged the tenant a $20 general processing fee, the maximum the landlord could collect up front is $2,700. The landlord can charge $900 for the first month's rent, $1,800 for the security deposit and nothing for the general processing fee because it is considered part of the security deposit.

The law is specific on the handling of residential security deposits. A security deposit must be refundable. The landlord has 21 days after the tenant has moved out to return all unused portions of the security deposit, with a written statement showing how the remainder was used (to clean, repair damage, replace windows, etc.). [C.C. §1950.5(g)]. A landlord may only deduct from the security deposit the cleaning cost "necessary to return the unit to the same level of cleanliness it was in at the beginning of the tenancy." A landlord who keeps deposits without reason for more than 3 weeks after the tenant has moved may be subject to twice the amount of the security deposit in statutory damages in addition to actual damages. [C.C. §1950.5(l)].

Responsibilities of a Landlord

In every lease the law implies a promise on the part of the lessor to the quiet enjoyment and possession of the property by the lessee during the term of the lease. In exchange for rent, a landlord gives up the use and possession of the property to a tenant.

Landlord's Duties and Responsibilities

- A landlord guarantees that health and safety codes are being met. With residential property, a landlord is usually liable for injuries occurring as a result of unsafe conditions in common areas, such as hallways, stairwells, or surrounding grounds. There is an **implied warranty of habitability** from the landlord to the tenant that the property will be maintained to meet bare living requirements.

- Periodic inspection of the property is allowed by a landlord, who must give reasonable notice of intent to enter, and then only during normal business hours. Twenty-four hours is considered reasonable notice. Some rental agreements only require a four-hour notice of entry to be given by the landlord. All leases are not the same and should be read carefully by both landlord and tenant before signing.

- A landlord must obey federal and state fair housing laws.

- California renters under month-to-month leases must be given 30-day notices to move out. The tenant does have recourse if the **eviction** is unfair, based on fair housing laws, or if the eviction is retaliatory. A **retaliatory eviction** is an eviction that occurs in revenge for some complaint made by the tenant.

- Tenants have the right to a **Pre-Move-Out Inspection** of the rental unit, no earlier than two weeks prior to the termination of the tenancy. The landlord provides to the tenant a written notice of the right to inspect the premises within a reasonable time. The landlord also informs the tenant of his or her right to be present at the inspection. If no agreement can be made for the inspection time, the landlord must give the tenant written notice 48 hours prior of the time of inspection and then may proceed with the inspection whether the tenant is there or not. Based on the inspection, the landlord must give the tenant an itemized statement listing of any proposed repairs or cleaning. The cost of the cleaning and repairs is the basis for deductions taken from the security deposit.

- The landlord has 21 days after the tenant has moved out to return all unused portions of the security deposit, with a written statement showing how the remainder was used.

Responsibilities and Rights of a Tenant

In return for the payment of rent, a tenant has certain obligations and rights.

Tenant's Duties and Responsibilities:

- A tenant must pay the rent when it is due.

- A tenant must give proper written notice before moving out, unless there is an agreement stating otherwise. The notice is based on the number of days between rent payments. For example, a tenant who pays monthly must give 30-days written notice or weekly at least 7-days written notice.

- A tenant may not interfere with the rights of other tenants.

- If there is a repair problem involving the tenant's health, welfare, or safety, the landlord has a duty to make needed repairs. If the landlord refuses, under the law, a tenant may spend up to one-month's rent to make repairs, and subtract the amount from the rent. The tenant may do this only two times in any 12-month period. A landlord may not retaliate by eviction or raising the rent for 180 days after this rent offset is used by the tenant to make lawful repairs. If the landlord does not correct the problem, the tenant may abandon the premises and break the lease.

Review - Landlord & Tenant Responsibilities

Landlord Must:
- provide habitable dwelling units.
- give 24-hours notice before entering.
- obey fair housing laws.
- give a 30-day written notice to the tenant before ending a month-to-month tenancy.
- return deposit within 21 days after tenant moves out.

Tenant Must:
- pay rent when due.
- give 30-days notice before ending month-to-month tenancy.
- not interfere with the rights of other tenants.

Tenant May:
- make needed repairs twice yearly and deduct from rent.

Transfer of a Lease

If the lease does not prohibit it, a lessee (tenant) may assign or sublease his or her interest in the property to another person.

Assignment

An **assignment** is the transfer of the entire leasehold estate to a new person, called an **assignee**. The original lessee (**assignor**) steps out of primary responsibility for the lease and a new lessee (assignee) becomes responsible to the landlord for all the terms of the original rental agreement.

> Example: Brad leases a two-bedroom apartment from Al for 1 year but only lives there for 6 months until he is transferred. Melissa accepts Brad's offer of assignment of his lease and moves into the apartment when Brad moves out. Melissa is responsible directly to the landlord (Al) who also collects the rent. Brad no longer has any interest in the lease.

Sublease

A **sublease** transfers possession of a leased property to a new person called the **sublessee**. The original tenant, who is now the **sublessor**, is still primarily liable for paying the rent to the owner. The sublessee is liable only to the sublessor. This type of lease is called a **sandwich lease**.

> Example: Bob leases a two-bedroom apartment at $1,000 per month on a 2 year lease from Al. He lives there for 6 months until he is transferred and still has 18 months left on the lease. Bob knows the transfer is temporary and wants to return to his apartment. Tom accepts Bob's offer to sublease the apartment for one year at $1,200 per month. Since Tom's sublease is with Bob, not the landlord, he sends his rent check to Bob each month. Bob pays rent of $1,000 to his landlord, Al. Bob is still responsible for his original agreement with the lessor and keeps his interest as lessee in the property. Bob holds a **sandwich lease** or a position in between the original lessor (Al) and the sublessee (Tom).

Termination of a Lease

The majority of leases end by the expiration of the agreed-upon lease term or by mutual agreement between the landlord and tenant. Other ways to terminate a lease are destruction of the premises, breach of conditions by either lessor or lessee, or eviction. For example, if a landlord fails to make needed repairs to property after repeated requests by the tenant, the tenant is considered constructively evicted and the tenant may terminate the lease. **Constructive eviction** is an implied eviction in which the landlord's act or omission justifies the immediate departure of the tenant. A sale of the property during the term of the lease does not usually terminate the lease.

When a tenant voluntarily gives up a lease before the expiration of its term, it is known as **surrender**. The tenant gives up any rights of possession, and has surrendered the property back to the landlord. If the landlord accepts the surrender, the tenant is no longer liable for rent. Sometimes a tenant just moves out or abandons the premises without doing a formal surrender. In this instance, the landlord has the option of demanding the balance of the rent due or rent due until the landlord finds another tenant.

The Eviction Process

The landlord has one legal remedy to remove a tenant—the eviction process using an **unlawful detainer action** or **action in ejectment**.

The landlord must use this court process to evict the tenant and not give in to frustration about the delinquent or remiss tenant by committing unlawful acts, such as changing the locks or bullying the tenant with threats of bodily harm.

Illegal Self-Help Remedies

- The landlord cannot turn off utilities, change the locks, remove outside doors or windows, or remove the tenant's personal property. If the landlord does any of the preceding, he or she will be liable for the actual damages of the tenant, plus $100 per day that it continues. [C.C. §789.3]. Under the right of replevin, a tenant has the legal right to recover personal property unlawfully taken by the landlord.
- The landlord cannot use threats or menacing conduct to interfere with the tenant's quiet enjoyment of the premises. The landlord is liable for $2,000 for each violation. [C.C. §1940.2].

The eviction process follows three main steps: (1) serving an eviction notice to terminate the rental agreement, (2) obtaining a judgment against the tenant in an unlawful detainer action, and (3) evicting the tenant by the sheriff under a writ of possession.

Eviction Notice

Simply violating the terms of the rental agreement does not actually terminate the agreement. To terminate the rental agreement, the landlord must serve the tenant an eviction notice (3-day notice) for cause asking the tenant to conform. A **three-day notice** instructs the tenant to either leave the rental unit or comply with the terms of the rental agreement within the three-day period. The 3-day notice gives the tenant **3 days** to pay the rent or take whatever action is required to cure the breach of the rental agreement. If the tenant fails to pay (or take the other action to cure the breach—e.g., to remove a non-permitted pet) within the 3 days, then the tenancy is terminated immediately, and the owner can proceed to court without further delay.

If the tenant fails to pay rent, the owner gives the tenant a **3-Day Notice to Pay Rent or Quit.** For breach of any conditions other than failure to pay rent, the owner uses a **3-Day Notice to Cure or Quit.**

Unlawful Detainer Action

An **unlawful detainer action** is a lawsuit to remove an unlawful holdover tenant (e.g. after the expiration of a 3-day or 30-day notice) and return the rental unit to its owner. The landlord may file an unlawful detainer action in the municipal court if a tenant ignores or fails to respond to the notification to pay or quit. This document lists the charges against the tenant, who then has 5 calendar days to respond after being served; otherwise, a default hearing is set.

Writ of Possession

A writ of possession is granted by the court to the landlord if the tenant does not move out or answer the lawsuit. A **writ of possession** is the legal document issued by the court commanding the tenant to leave the premises within five days. The 5 days begin to run once the sheriff, marshal, or registered process server posts the writ of possession on the property. Upon expiration of the 5 days, the sheriff physically removes the tenant and gives the landlord possession.

At this time, the landlord may remove personal property of the tenant and change the locks. The landlord must store any belongings left behind by the tenant after the eviction for 30 days, charging the tenant a reasonable storage fee. After that time, a public sale may be held and the proceeds used by the owner to pay costs of storage and sale. Any balance remaining after payment of these costs must be returned to the tenant.

> ### Review - Termination of a Lease
> - Expiration of the Term
> - Mutual Agreement
> - Violations of Terms and Conditions
> - Destruction of the Premises
> - Eviction

NOTICE OF TERMINATION OF TENANCY
(C.A.R. Form NTT, Revised 11/12)

To: _____ ("Tenant")
and any other occupant(s) in possession of the premises located at: (Street Address) _____
_____ (Unit/Apartment #)_____
(City) _____ (State) _____ (Zip Code) _____ ("Premises").

CHECK THE BOX THAT APPLIES. CHECK ONE BOX ONLY.

1. ☐ The tenancy, if any, in the Premises is terminated **60 days** from service of this Notice, or on _____ (whichever is later).

OR 2. ☐ **You have, or another tenant or resident has, resided in the Premises for less than one year.** Your tenancy, if any, in the Premises is terminated **30 days** from service of this Notice, or on _____ (whichever is later).

OR 3. ☐ **All of the following apply.** Your tenancy, if any, in the Premises is terminated **30 days** from service of this Notice, or on _____ (whichever is later).

    A. Landlord has entered into a contract to sell the Premises to a natural person(s);

  AND **B.** Purchaser intends to reside in the Premises for at least one year following the termination of the tenancy in the Premises;

  AND **C.** Landlord has established an escrow with an escrow company licensed by the Department of Corporations, Department of Insurance or a licensed Real Estate Broker;

  AND **D.** Escrow was opened 120 or fewer days prior to the delivery of this Notice;

  AND **E.** Title to the Premises is separately alienable from any other dwelling unit (i.e., it is a single-family unit or condominium);

  AND **F.** Tenant has not previously been given a notice of termination of tenancy.

OR 4. ☐ Tenant is a beneficiary of, and the tenancy is subject to, a government agency rental housing assistant program. The tenancy, if any, in the premises is terminated 90 days from service of this notice

or on _____ (whichever is later).

If you fail to give up possession by the specified date, a legal action will be filed seeking possession and damages that could result in a judgment being awarded against you.

Buyer's Initials (_____) (_____)   Seller's Initials (_____) (_____)

NTT REVISED 11/12 (PAGE 1 OF 2)

Reviewed by _____ Date _____

NOTICE OF TERMINATION OF TENANCY (NTT PAGE 1 OF 2)

Agent:	Phone:	Fax:	Prepared using zipForm® software
Broker:			

SUMMARY

In California, most real estate agents use the Residential Purchase Agreement and Joint Escrow Instructions (purchase agreement). This agreement is an offer to purchase property. Once the seller agrees to the offer and the buyer is informed of the seller's acceptance, the **purchase agreement** is a legally binding contract that all parties must sign.

Termination of offer occurs when the buyer withdraws the offer before the seller accepts it, the time limit for offer expires, the buyer dies before the seller accepts the offer, or the seller gives the buyer a **counteroffer**.

A **lease (rental agreement)** is a contract between an owner (**lessor** or **landlord**) and a **lessee** (tenant). A **tenant** takes possession and use of a property in return for rent payment. Leases over one year must be in writing. There are three classifications of leases: types of real estate, length of term, or method of payment. Leases based on type of real estate include commercial leases, ground leases, proprietary leases, and residential leases. The length of time includes short-term and long-term leases. Methods of rent payment include gross, net, and percentage.

The responsibilities of a landlord include a guarantee that health and safety codes are met, periodic inspection of the property with reasonable notice of intent to enter, 30-day advance notice when ordering the tenant to vacate and obeying fair housing rules and regulations. A tenant's responsibilities include paying rent when due, giving proper notice before moving out, and not interfering with the rights of other tenants.

Leases are commonly terminated by the expiration of the lease term or by mutual agreement between the landlord and tenant. Other methods to terminate a lease include destruction of property, breach of conditions by either lessor or lessee or eviction. When a tenant voluntarily gives up a lease before the expiration of its term, the tenant **surrenders** the property.

The **eviction process** follows three main steps: (1) serving an eviction notice to terminate the rental agreement, (2) obtaining a judgment against the tenant in an unlawful detainer action, and (3) evicting the tenant by the sheriff under a writ of possession.

UNIT 6 REVIEW

Matching Exercise

Instructions: Write the letter of the matching term on the blank line before its definition. Answers immediately follow the Multiple Choice Questions.

Terms

A. assignee

B. assignment

C. counteroffer

D. CPI

E. deposit receipt

F. gross lease

G. ground lease

H. implied warranty of habitability

I. interim occupancy agreement

J. lease

K. leased fee estate

L. lessee

M. lessor

N. liquidated damages clause

O. net lease

P. option

Q. percentage lease

R. proprietary lease

S. rent

T. residential lease

U. retaliatory eviction

V. security deposit

W. sublease

X. time is of the essence clause

Y. unlawful detainer action

Definitions

1. _____ A clause in a contract that emphasizes punctual performance as a requirement of the contract.

2. _____ A contract between an owner and tenant.

3. _____ A contract to keep open, for a set period of time, an offer to purchase real property.

4. _____ A lease for only the land.

5. _____ A lease is used for single-family homes and duplexes.

6. _____ An eviction that occurs in revenge for some complaint made by the tenant.

7. _____ An index used for rent adjustments on commercial leases.

8. _____ Clause in a contract that allows parties to the contract to decide in advance the amount of damages to be paid, should either party breach the contract.

9. _____ Contract that acts as the receipt for earnest money given by the buyer to secure an offer, as well as being the basic agreement, between the buyer and seller.

10. _____ A lease used on co-op apartment buildings.

11. _____ An agreement used if a buyer takes possession of a property prior to close of escrow.

12. _____ Payment for the use of a property.

13. _____ The interest of the lessor.

14. _____ The transfer of the entire leasehold estate to a new person.

15. _____ The tenant pays an agreed-upon sum as rent, plus certain agreed-upon expenses per month (i.e., taxes, insurance, and repairs).

16. _____ The rejection of an original purchase offer and the submission of a new and different offer.

17. _____ The property will be maintained to meet bare living requirements.

18. _____ The person who owns the property and signs the lease to give possession and use to the tenant.

19. _____ The legal remedy to remove a tenant.

20. _____ Money given to a landlord to prepay for any damage that might occur to a property during a lease term that is more than just normal wear and tear.

▉ Multiple Choice Questions

Instructions: Circle your response and then check your response with the Answer Key that immediately follows the Multiple Choice Questions.

1. The statute of frauds requires that contracts for the sale of real estate must:
   a. be recorded.
   b. be in writing.
   c. be bilateral contracts.
   d. have a cash deposit.

2. What is the status of a contract during the period of time after a real estate sales contract is signed by both parties but before title actually passes? The contract is:

    a. unilateral.

    b. voidable.

    c. executory.

    d. interim.

3. Buyer Baker presented an offer to Seller Sam for the purchase of a 10-year-old home in a quiet neighborhood. Seller Sam made a counteroffer to buyer Baker. Under these circumstances, buyer Baker:

    a. is required to accept seller Sam's offer.

    b. does not have to accept the counteroffer, but is still obligated under his original offer.

    c. has no obligation under his original offer.

    d. is obligated to make a new offer to seller Sam, if the counteroffer is unacceptable.

4. Seller Chris listed a vacant lot with a broker at $111,400. Prospective buyer Jordan submitted an offer of $111,000 that was to expire in three days. The next day, Chris made a counteroffer of $111,200. When Jordan did not respond within the three-day period, Chris signed an acceptance of Jordan's $111,000 original offer and instructed the broker to deliver it to Jordan. Jordan told the broker that he had decided not to purchase the property, but Chris insisted they had a deal. Based on these circumstances, there is:

    a. a valid contract.

    b. no contract.

    c. an invalid contract.

    d. an enforceable contract.

5. Which of the following statements is correct regarding an option contract to purchase real estate?

    a. The optionor is not obliged to sell the property.

    b. The option is a bilateral contract.

    c. The consideration must be money in excess of $100.

    d. The optionee is not obligated to purchase the property.

6. As used in real estate law, the term tenancy is best described as:

    a. the landlord-tenant relationship.

    b. retention of rights as a remainderman.

    c. a tenant in a lease agreement.

    d. the interest of a person holding property by any right or title.

7.   If an owner grants possession of real property to another person for less than the owner's interest, it is known as a:

   a. periodic assignment.
   b. demise.
   c. lease.
   d. sale-leaseback.

8.   The maximum amount of security deposit a landlord may demand from a prospective tenant depends upon the:

   a. total number of tenants who plan to occupy the premises.
   b. number of children occupying the unit.
   c. term of the lease and whether the unit is furnished or unfurnished.
   d. economic competition from nearby properties.

9.   An unlawful detainer proceeding is most often taken by a:

   a. beneficiary.
   b. trustee.
   c. lessor.
   d. grantee.

10. A tenant may abandon a leased property and refuse to pay further rent if the landlord carries out a constructive eviction. Which of the following is considered to be a constructive eviction?

   a. With the tenant's permission, the landlord has shown the property to another party and has entered into negotiations with that party to lease the premises.
   b. After multiple requests by the tenant, the landlord failed to make needed major repairs and to maintain the property in the agreed-upon manner.
   c. The landlord altered the property to meet the needs of a new tenant.
   d. All of the above

11. When purchasing property, the amount of the buyer's earnest money deposit is determined by:

   a. state law based on the purchase price of the property.
   b. local custom and location of the property.
   c. agreement between buyer and broker.
   d. agreement between buyer and seller.

12. A prospective buyer made an offer and gave the seller's broker a $500 check as a deposit for the sale of a residence. Before the offer was given to the seller, the buyer contacted the broker and withdrew the offer. What should the broker do with the $500 check?

    a. Deposit it in escrow
    b. Return it immediately
    c. Hold it until the seller is notified
    d. Keep it to be reimbursed for out-of-pocket expenses

13. Mary's broker presented a full-price offer to purchase to Susan's home with a 45-day closing. Susan accepted the offer but changed the closing date from 45 days to 90 days because she needed more time. In this situation, buyer Mary is:

    a. not bound by the original offer she sent to Susan.
    b. bound by Susan's acceptance because she only changed the closing date.
    c. bound by the original offer with the original closing date.
    d. not bound by the original offer, but is bound by Susan's counteroffer.

14. Pat gives an option to James to purchase Pat's ranch. This option most clearly constitutes a(n):

    a. voluntary lien on Pat's ranch.
    b. offer to enter into a contract.
    c. fiduciary agreement.
    d. contract to keep an offer open.

15. If real property is subleased, the interest held by the sublessor is known as a(n):

    a. double lease.
    b. freehold lease.
    c. assignment.
    d. sandwich lease.

UNIT 6 ANSWER KEY

Answers – Matching

1.	X	5.	T	9.	E	13.	K	17.	H
2.	J	6.	U	10.	R	14.	B	18.	M
3.	P	7.	D	11.	I	15.	O	19.	Y
4.	G	8.	N	12.	S	16.	C	20.	V

Answers – Multiple Choice

1. **(b)**   According to the Statute of Frauds, to be enforceable, real estate contracts must be in writing. [Introduction]

2. **(c)**   Usually there are terms in the contract that must be met during the escrow period; therefore, the contract is considered executory until all the terms are completed and escrow closes. [Purchase Agreement]

3. **(c)**   If a seller rejects the offer and submits a counteroffer, the original offer automatically terminates. [Counteroffer]

4. **(b)**   Chris' counteroffer terminated the buyer's original offer. [Option]

5. **(d)**   The optionee (buyer) is not required to buy the property. If the optionee decides to exercise the option and buy the property, the optionor (seller) must sell. An option is a unilateral contract, and the option must have actual monetary consideration to be valid, but no specific amount is required. [Option]

6. **(d)**   Tenancy is the interest of a person holding property by any right or title. [Leases]

7. **(c)**   A lease is a contract for exclusive possession of property in consideration for rent. The owner is giving his bundle of right of possession to a tenant for a specific period. [Leases]

8. **(c)**   The maximum deposit allowed on an unfurnished property is not more than the amount of two months' rent. The maximum deposit allowed on a furnished property is not more than the amount of three months' rent. [Leases]

9. **(c)**   The lessor is the landlord. An unlawful detainer action is the legal remedy to remove a defaulting tenant. [Leases]

10. **(b)**   The premises are unsuitable for occupancy, and the landlord has not made any repairs, resulting in a constructive eviction. [Leases]

11. **(d)**   The buyer indicates the amount of the deposit in the offer. Then it is always negotiated by buyer and seller until the seller accepts the offer. There is no state law specifying the amount of the deposit. [Purchase Agreements]

12. **(b)** Until an offer is accepted by the seller, the buyer owns the funds, and the broker must obey the buyer's instructions. If the seller refuses the offer, the check is returned to the buyer. [Purchase Agreements]

13. **(a)** By changing the number of days for the closing, Susan created a counteroffer, therefore, the original offer automatically terminates. [Counteroffer]

14. **(d)** An option is a form of contract to keep an offer open. [Option]

15. **(d)** The original tenant has a lease. He or she becomes a sublessor upon subletting the lease to another tenant, called the sublessee. The original tenant/sublessor still owes rent to the owner and collects rent from the sublessee; therefore, the tenant is sandwiched between the owner and the sublessor (current tenant). [Leases]

Unit 7

INTRODUCTION

Caveat emptor, a Latin phrase meaning, let the buyer beware, is becoming a thing of the past. The buyer was put on notice to examine the property and buy it at his or her own risk. Now, several consumer protection laws place the responsibility of disclosing the condition of the property on the seller and the broker.

Unless exempt, when people sell their homes, or any 1-4 residential property, they must give the buyers several statutory disclosures and reports regarding the condition of the property and any matters known to seller affecting title, whether of record or not. **Statutory disclosures** are those that are required by statute or law. Additionally, there are optional disclosures and reports that the buyers or lender may require. Sometimes the sellers will need to fill out and sign a form; other times the sellers (or broker) give the buyers informational booklets.

As buying and selling of real property becomes more complex, so do the required disclosures. As a real estate agent, you will be required to guide all parties through the disclosure minefield.

Learning Objectives

After completing this Unit, you should be able to:

6A   indicate disclosures required in a real estate transfer.

6B   recall subdivision disclosures required by federal and state laws.

6C   name other disclosures pertinent to real estate transactions.

SELLER'S STATUTORY DISCLOSURES

The Purchase Agreement itemizes several statutory disclosures that the sellers must provide the buyers within specified timeframes. The listing agent must ensure that the sellers are aware of their obligations regarding these disclosures and the timeframes in which the disclosure must be given to the buyers. Delivery of these statutory disclosures is important because the buyers can cancel the Purchase Agreement if the sellers have not delivered the disclosures within the time specified in the Purchase Agreement.

As a result of the *Easton v. Strassburger* case, real estate agents must perform a visual inspection of the property and sellers must complete a Transfer Disclosure Statement.

Easton v. Strassburger

The case of *Easton v. Strassburger*, 152 C.A. 3d 90, is about a home built on a landfill that had not been properly compacted, but was listed for sale. The owner did not tell the listing broker about the landslide problem that had developed as a result of the poor engineering on the slope. The property was sold and the buyer suffered a substantial loss as a result of land slippage.

In a court action, the buyer proved that one of the listing agents noticed the netting that had been placed on the slope to keep it in place, and another agent had noticed an uneven floor in the house that had occurred as a result of the undisclosed soil problem. The court stated that the red flags should have indicated to the real estate agents there was a problem, and the problem should have been investigated. A **red flag** is something that alerts a reasonably observant person of a potential problem. Typically a red flag could include cracks in walls, foundations, and sidewalks; stains from leaks in the roof, and similar items.

The court ruled that a broker has the duty to inspect a property and disclose any material facts affecting its value. A broker is required to uncover any reasonably discoverable problems and tell all interested parties.

The *Easton v. Strassburger* case findings stated real estate agents could be liable for defects in property that they know about as well as defects that they should know about as a result of a visual investigation. All listing brokers of a residential property and any cooperating brokers must conduct a reasonably competent and diligent **visual inspection** of the property. Additionally, they must disclose to a prospective buyer all material facts that may affect value, desirability, and intended use of the property. [CC §2079].

The real estate agent does not have to inspect areas of the property that are not reasonably accessible, public records, and permits. If the property is a condominium, the real estate agent is responsible for inspecting the unit, not the common area.

The required certification of the visual inspection is contained in the Real Estate Transfer Disclosure Statement. Depending on the brokerage firm's practices, the listing agent also may need to complete an **Agent Visual Inspection Disclosure** form (AVID).

Transfer Disclosure Statement

The **Real Estate Transfer Disclosure Statement** (TDS) is a statutory disclosure that most sellers of residential property (1-4) must provide to prospective buyers.

Disclosing Material Facts

The TDS is a detailed statement telling what the seller knows about the condition of the property. The sellers must disclose, in writing, any and all known **material facts** that affect the value of their property whether the buyers ask or not. Even if a home is sold "as is" in its present condition, the seller must disclose any observable (**patent**) defects as well as any hidden (**latent**) defects. The term "**as is**" means that the seller is not going to fix any of the problems.

Material Facts that Could Affect Desirability and Value of a Property

- Age, condition, and any defects or malfunctions of the structural components and/or plumbing, electrical, heating, or other mechanical systems

- Presence of **window security bars**, with/without any quick-release safety release mechanisms on the bars

- Common walls, fences or driveways

- Easements or encroachments

- Room additions, structural alterations, repairs, replacements, or other changes, especially those made without required building permits

- Flooding, drainage, or soil problems on, near, or in any way affecting the property

Material Facts that Could Affect Desirability and Value of a Property (continued)

- Major damage to the property from fire, earthquake, or landslide

- Zoning violations, such as nonconforming uses or insufficient setbacks

- Homeowners' association obligations and deed restrictions or common area problems

- Citations against the property, or lawsuits against the owner or affecting the property

Sellers must disclose whether they are aware of the presence of substances, materials or products that may be an **environmental hazard** including—but not limited to—asbestos, formaldehyde, radon gas, lead-based paint, mold, fuel or chemical storage tanks, and contaminated soil or water on the property. There is always a little mold everywhere—in the air and on many surfaces. **Mold** is a fungus that reproduces by means of spores. Molds themselves are not toxic or poisonous. However, certain molds are toxigenic because they can produce toxins (called mycotoxins). Currently, standards for judging what is an acceptable quantity of mold have not been established to determine toxicity. Therefore, no special disclosure requirements are in effect for **toxic mold**. The California Department of Health Sciences has prepared a consumer booklet on mold, which is available online.

Toxic mold can generally be found
in kitchens and bathrooms.

Timing of the TDS

Usually the listing broker obtains the TDS at the time the listing is taken and provides a copy to a buyer before an offer to purchase the property is presented. If the real estate agent gives a copy of the disclosure statement to the buyer after the offer to purchase the property is presented, the buyer may terminate the contract by written notice to the seller within three days after receiving the disclosure statement. If the TDS is delivered to the prospective buyer after the required date, the buyer/transferee has 3 days after delivery in person or 5 days after delivery by deposit in the mail to terminate the offer or agreement to purchase. A written notice of termination must reach the seller/transferor or the seller's agent.

The seller, listing broker, and cooperating broker have the obligation to prepare and deliver the disclosure. If more than one real estate agent is involved in the transaction (unless otherwise instructed by the seller), the agent obtaining the offer is required to deliver the disclosure to the prospective buyer.

If the prospective buyer receives a report or an opinion prepared by a licensed engineer, land surveyor, geologist, structural pest control operator, contractor, or other expert (with a specific professional license or expertise), the liability of the seller and the real estate agents may be limited when making required disclosures. The overall intention is to provide meaningful disclosures about the condition of the property being transferred. A violation of the law does not invalidate a transfer; however, the seller may be liable for any actual damages suffered by the buyer.

Sellers Exempt from the TDS Requirements

Under California law, a seller of a residential property (1-to-4 units) must prepare and deliver a written residential transfer disclosure statement to the prospective buyer. This requirement extends to any transfer by: sale, exchange, installment land sale contract, lease-option, or ground lease coupled with improvements.

Transfers Exempt from the Disclosure Requirement

- Transfers from one co-owner to another
- Transfers to a spouse or another related person resulting from a dissolution of marriage, legal separation, or a property settlement agreement
- Transfers pursuant to a court order, foreclosure sale, or probate estate sale
- Transfers by the state controller for unclaimed property
- Transfers resulting from the failure to pay taxes
- Transfers from or to any governmental entity
- Transfers of the first sale of a newly constructed home in a subdivision, provided a copy of a public report is delivered to the purchaser

CALIFORNIA
ASSOCIATION
OF REALTORS®

REAL ESTATE TRANSFER DISCLOSURE STATEMENT
(CALIFORNIA CIVIL CODE §1102, ET SEQ.)
(C.A.R. Form TDS, Revised 4/14)

THIS DISCLOSURE STATEMENT CONCERNS THE REAL PROPERTY SITUATED IN THE CITY OF
_____ , COUNTY OF _____ , STATE OF CALIFORNIA,
DESCRIBED AS _____ .
THIS STATEMENT IS A DISCLOSURE OF THE CONDITION OF THE ABOVE DESCRIBED PROPERTY IN
COMPLIANCE WITH SECTION 1102 OF THE CIVIL CODE AS OF (date) _____ . IT IS NOT A
WARRANTY OF ANY KIND BY THE SELLER(S) OR ANY AGENT(S) REPRESENTING ANY PRINCIPAL(S) IN THIS
TRANSACTION, AND IS NOT A SUBSTITUTE FOR ANY INSPECTIONS OR WARRANTIES THE PRINCIPAL(S) MAY
WISH TO OBTAIN.

I. COORDINATION WITH OTHER DISCLOSURE FORMS

This Real Estate Transfer Disclosure Statement is made pursuant to Section 1102 of the Civil Code. Other statutes require disclosures, depending upon the details of the particular real estate transaction (for example: special study zone and purchase-money liens on residential property).

Substituted Disclosures: The following disclosures and other disclosures required by law, including the Natural Hazard Disclosure Report/Statement that may include airport annoyances, earthquake, fire, flood, or special assessment information, have or will be made in connection with this real estate transfer, and are intended to satisfy the disclosure obligations on this form, where the subject matter is the same:

☐ Inspection reports completed pursuant to the contract of sale or receipt for deposit.
☐ Additional inspection reports or disclosures: _____

II. SELLER'S INFORMATION

The Seller discloses the following information with the knowledge that even though this is not a warranty, prospective Buyers may rely on this information in deciding whether and on what terms to purchase the subject property. Seller hereby authorizes any agent(s) representing any principal(s) in this transaction to provide a copy of this statement to any person or entity in connection with any actual or anticipated sale of the property.

THE FOLLOWING ARE REPRESENTATIONS MADE BY THE SELLER(S) AND ARE NOT THE REPRESENTATIONS OF THE AGENT(S), IF ANY. THIS INFORMATION IS A DISCLOSURE AND IS NOT INTENDED TO BE PART OF ANY CONTRACT BETWEEN THE BUYER AND SELLER.

Seller ☐ is ☐ is not occupying the property.

A. The subject property has the items checked below: *

☐ Range	☐ Wall/Window Air Conditioning	☐ Pool:
☐ Oven	☐ Sprinklers	☐ Child Resistant Barrier
☐ Microwave	☐ Public Sewer System	☐ Pool/Spa Heater:
☐ Dishwasher	☐ Septic Tank	☐ Gas ☐ Solar ☐ Electric
☐ Trash Compactor	☐ Sump Pump	☐ Water Heater:
☐ Garbage Disposal	☐ Water Softener	☐ Gas ☐ Solar ☐ Electric
☐ Washer/Dryer Hookups	☐ Patio/Decking	☐ Water Supply:
☐ Rain Gutters	☐ Built-in Barbecue	☐ City ☐ Well
☐ Burglar Alarms	☐ Gazebo	☐ Private Utility or
☐ Carbon Monoxide Device(s)	☐ Security Gate(s)	Other _____
☐ Smoke Detector(s)	☐ Garage:	☐ Gas Supply:
☐ Fire Alarm	☐ Attached ☐ Not Attached	☐ Utility ☐ Bottled (Tank)
☐ TV Antenna	☐ Carport	☐ Window Screens
☐ Satellite Dish	☐ Automatic Garage Door Opener(s)	☐ Window Security Bars
☐ Intercom	☐ Number Remote Controls _____	☐ Quick Release Mechanism on
☐ Central Heating	☐ Sauna	Bedroom Windows
☐ Central Air Conditioning	☐ Hot Tub/Spa:	☐ Water-Conserving Plumbing Fixtures
☐ Evaporator Cooler(s)	☐ Locking Safety Cover	

Exhaust Fan(s) in _____ 220 Volt Wiring in _____ Fireplace(s) in _____
☐ Gas Starter _____ ☐ Roof(s): Type: _____ Age: _____ (approx.)
☐ Other: _____

Are there, to the best of your (Seller's) knowledge, any of the above that are not in operating condition? ☐ Yes ☐ No. If yes, then describe. (Attach additional sheets if necessary): _____

(*see note on page 2)
Buyer's Initials (_____)(_____)   Seller's Initials (_____)(_____)

TDS REVISED 4/14 (PAGE 1 OF 3)

Reviewed by _____ Date _____

EQUAL HOUSING OPPORTUNITY

REAL ESTATE TRANSFER DISCLOSURE STATEMENT (TDS PAGE 1 OF 3)

Agent:	Phone:	Fax:	Prepared using zipForm® software
Broker:			

Property Address: _____   Date: _____

B. Are you (Seller) aware of any significant defects/malfunctions in any of the following? ☐ Yes ☐ No. If yes, check appropriate space(s) below.

    ☐ Interior Walls ☐ Ceilings ☐ Floors ☐ Exterior Walls ☐ Insulation ☐ Roof(s) ☐ Windows ☐ Doors ☐ Foundation ☐ Slab(s)
    ☐ Driveways ☐ Sidewalks ☐ Walls/Fences ☐ Electrical Systems ☐ Plumbing/Sewers/Septics ☐ Other Structural Components
(Describe: _____)

If any of the above is checked, explain. (Attach additional sheets if necessary.): _____
_____

*Installation of a listed appliance, device, or amenity is not a precondition of sale or transfer of the dwelling. The carbon monoxide device, garage door opener, or child-resistant pool barrier may not be in compliance with the safety standards relating to, respectively, carbon monoxide device standards of Chapter 8 (commencing with Section 13260) of Part 2 of Division 12 of, automatic reversing device standards of Chapter 12.5 (commencing with Section 19890) of Part 3 of Division 13 of, or the pool safety standards of Article 2.5 (commencing with Section 115920) of Chapter 5 of Part 10 of Division 104 of, the Health and Safety Code. Window security bars may not have quick-release mechanisms in compliance with the 1995 edition of the California Building Standards Code. Section 1101.4 of the Civil Code requires all single-family residences built on or before January 1, 1994, to be equipped with water-conserving plumbing fixtures after January 1, 2017. Additionally, on and after January 1, 2014, a single-family residence built on or before January 1, 1994, that is altered or improved is required to be equipped with water-conserving plumbing fixtures as a condition of final approval. Fixtures in this dwelling may not comply with section 1101.4 of the Civil Code.

C. Are you (Seller) aware of any the following:

  1. Substances, materials, or products which may be an environmental hazard such as, but not limited to, asbestos, formaldehyde, radon gas, lead-based paint, mold, fuel or chemical storage tanks, and contaminated soil or water on the subject property . . . . ☐ Yes ☐ No

  2. Features of the property shared in common with adjoining landowners, such as walls, fences, and driveways, whose use or responsibility for maintenance may have an effect on the subject property . . . . ☐ Yes ☐ No

  3. Any encroachments, easements or similar matters that may affect your interest in the subject property . . . . ☐ Yes ☐ No

  4. Room additions, structural modifications, or other alterations or repairs made without necessary permits. . . . . . . ☐ Yes ☐ No

  5. Room additions, structural modifications, or other alterations or repairs not in compliance with building codes. . . . ☐ Yes ☐ No

  6. Fill (compacted or otherwise) on the property or any portion thereof . . . . ☐ Yes ☐ No

  7. Any settling from any cause, or slippage, sliding, or other soil problems . . . . ☐ Yes ☐ No

  8. Flooding, drainage or grading problems . . . . ☐ Yes ☐ No

  9. Major damage to the property or any of the structures from fire, earthquake, floods, or landslides . . . . ☐ Yes ☐ No

  10. Any zoning violations, nonconforming uses, violations of "setback" requirements . . . . ☐ Yes ☐ No

  11. Neighborhood noise problems or other nuisances . . . . ☐ Yes ☐ No

  12. CC&R's or other deed restrictions or obligations . . . . ☐ Yes ☐ No

  13. Homeowners' Association which has any authority over the subject property . . . . ☐ Yes ☐ No

  14. Any "common area" (facilities such as pools, tennis courts, walkways, or other areas co-owned in undivided interest with others) . . . . ☐ Yes ☐ No

  15. Any notices of abatement or citations against the property . . . . ☐ Yes ☐ No

  16. Any lawsuits by or against the Seller threatening to or affecting this real property, claims for damages by the Seller pursuant to Section 910 or 914 threatening to or affecting this real property, claims for breach of warranty pursuant to Section 900 threatening to or affecting this real property, or claims for breach of an enhanced protection agreement pursuant to Section 903 threatening to or affecting this real property, including any lawsuits or claims for damages pursuant to Section 910 or 914 alleging a defect or deficiency in this real property or "common areas" (facilities such as pools, tennis courts, walkways, or other areas co-owned in undivided interest with others) . . . . ☐ Yes ☐ No

If the answer to any of these is yes, explain. (Attach additional sheets if necessary.): _____
_____
_____

D. 1. The Seller certifies that the property, as of the close of escrow, will be in compliance with Section 13113.8 of the Health and Safety Code by having operable smoke detector(s) which are approved, listed, and installed in accordance with the State Fire Marshal's regulations and applicable local standards.

  2. The Seller certifies that the property, as of the close of escrow, will be in compliance with Section 19211 of the Health and Safety Code by having the water heater tank(s) braced, anchored, or strapped in place in accordance with applicable law.

Buyer's Initials (_____)(_____)

| Reviewed by _____ Date _____ |

TDS REVISED 4/14 (PAGE 2 OF 3)
    REAL ESTATE TRANSFER DISCLOSURE STATEMENT (TDS PAGE 2 OF 3)

Property Address: _____ Date: _____

Seller certifies that the information herein is true and correct to the best of the Seller's knowledge as of the date signed by the Seller.

Seller _____ Date _____

Seller _____ Date _____

III. AGENT'S INSPECTION DISCLOSURE
(To be completed only if the Seller is represented by an agent in this transaction.)

THE UNDERSIGNED, BASED ON THE ABOVE INQUIRY OF THE SELLER(S) AS TO THE CONDITION OF THE PROPERTY AND BASED ON A REASONABLY COMPETENT AND DILIGENT VISUAL INSPECTION OF THE ACCESSIBLE AREAS OF THE PROPERTY IN CONJUNCTION WITH THAT INQUIRY, STATES THE FOLLOWING:

☐ See attached Agent Visual Inspection Disclosure (AVID Form)
☐ Agent notes no items for disclosure.
☐ Agent notes the following items: _____
_____
_____
_____

Agent (Broker Representing Seller) _____ By _____ Date _____
                                          (Please Print)   (Associate Licensee or Broker Signature)

IV. AGENT'S INSPECTION DISCLOSURE
(To be completed only if the agent who has obtained the offer is other than the agent above.)

THE UNDERSIGNED, BASED ON A REASONABLY COMPETENT AND DILIGENT VISUAL INSPECTION OF THE ACCESSIBLE AREAS OF THE PROPERTY, STATES THE FOLLOWING:

☐ See attached Agent Visual Inspection Disclosure (AVID Form)
☐ Agent notes no items for disclosure.
☐ Agent notes the following items: _____
_____
_____
_____

Agent (Broker Obtaining the Offer) _____ By _____ Date _____
                                          (Please Print)   (Associate Licensee or Broker Signature)

V. BUYER(S) AND SELLER(S) MAY WISH TO OBTAIN PROFESSIONAL ADVICE AND/OR INSPECTIONS OF THE PROPERTY AND TO PROVIDE FOR APPROPRIATE PROVISIONS IN A CONTRACT BETWEEN BUYER AND SELLER(S) WITH RESPECT TO ANY ADVICE/INSPECTIONS/DEFECTS.

I/WE ACKNOWLEDGE RECEIPT OF A COPY OF THIS STATEMENT.

Seller _____ Date _____   Buyer _____ Date _____

Seller _____ Date _____   Buyer _____ Date _____

Agent (Broker Representing Seller) _____ By _____ Date _____
                                       (Please Print)   (Associate Licensee or Broker Signature)

Agent (Broker Obtaining the Offer) _____ By _____ Date _____
                                       (Please Print)   (Associate Licensee or Broker Signature)

SECTION 1102.3 OF THE CIVIL CODE PROVIDES A BUYER WITH THE RIGHT TO RESCIND A PURCHASE CONTRACT FOR AT LEAST THREE DAYS AFTER THE DELIVERY OF THIS DISCLOSURE IF DELIVERY OCCURS AFTER THE SIGNING OF AN OFFER TO PURCHASE. IF YOU WISH TO RESCIND THE CONTRACT, YOU MUST ACT WITHIN THE PRESCRIBED PERIOD.

A REAL ESTATE BROKER IS QUALIFIED TO ADVISE ON REAL ESTATE. IF YOU DESIRE LEGAL ADVICE, CONSULT YOUR ATTORNEY.

Published and Distributed by:
REAL ESTATE BUSINESS SERVICES, INC.
a subsidiary of the California Association of REALTORS®
525 South Virgil Avenue, Los Angeles, California 90020

Reviewed by _____ Date _____

EQUAL HOUSING OPPORTUNITY

TDS REVISED 4/14 (PAGE 3 OF 3)

REAL ESTATE TRANSFER DISCLOSURE STATEMENT (TDS PAGE 3 OF 3)

Local Option Real Estate Transfer Disclosure Statement

If there is some local condition, which may materially affect a buyer's use and enjoyment of residential property, an optional disclosure form may be required, called the **Local Option Real Estate Transfer Disclosure Statement (LORETDS)**. Residential properties in cities and counties throughout California are typically subject to specific local ordinances on occupancy, zoning and use, building code compliance, fire, health and safety code regulations, and land subdivision descriptions. The various requirements for compliance as well as who and what is affected should be disclosed to the prospective buyer of the property by the seller or the seller's agent and any agent acting in cooperation with such agent. For example, based on the Farm Practices Protection Act of 1996, many jurisdictions in the Central Valley have enacted Right to Farm ordinances to protect existing agricultural uses adjacent to new residential uses.

Supplemental Statutory and Contractual Disclosures Form

If the seller is required to provide a TDS to a buyer, he or she also must complete and provide a 4-page Seller Property Questionnaire or a 1-page Supplemental Statutory and Contractual Disclosures form. The **Supplemental Statutory and Contractual Disclosures** (SSD) lists many of the statutory disclosures that sellers are required to give to buyers. When the buyers sign and return this form, they acknowledge that they have received the statutory disclosures.

Disclosures Included on the SSD

- Death on the property
- Methamphetamine contamination or release of an illegal controlled substance on or beneath the property
- Industrial use zone location
- Military ordnance location
- Common interest homeowner's association
- Insurance claims affecting the property
- Matters affecting title of the property
- Undisclosed material facts or defects affecting the property

CALIFORNIA ASSOCIATION OF REALTORS®

SUPPLEMENTAL STATUTORY AND CONTRACTUAL DISCLOSURES
(C.A.R. Form SSD, Revised 11/09)

1. Seller makes the following disclosures with regard to the real property or manufactured home described as _____ , Assessor's Parcel No. _____ , situated in _____ , County of _____ , California, ("Property").

2. **THE FOLLOWING ARE REPRESENTATIONS MADE BY THE SELLER AND ARE NOT THE REPRESENTATIONS OF THE AGENT(S), IF ANY. THIS DISCLOSURE STATEMENT IS NOT A WARRANTY OF ANY KIND BY THE SELLER OR ANY AGENT(S) AND IS NOT A SUBSTITUTE FOR ANY INSPECTIONS OR WARRANTIES THE PRINCIPAL(S) MAY WISH TO OBTAIN. A REAL ESTATE BROKER IS QUALIFIED TO ADVISE ON REAL ESTATE TRANSACTIONS. IF SELLER OR BUYER DESIRE LEGAL ADVICE, CONSULT AN ATTORNEY.**

3. **Are you (Seller) aware of any of the following? (Explain any "yes" answers below.)**
   A. Within the last 3 years, the death of an occupant of the Property upon the Property. . . . . □ Yes □ No
   B. An Order from a government health official identifying the Property as being contaminated by methamphetamine. (If yes, attach a copy of the Order.) . . . . □ Yes □ No
   C. The release of an illegal controlled substance on or beneath the Property . . . . □ Yes □ No
   D. Whether the Property is located in or adjacent to an "industrial use" zone . . . . □ Yes □ No
   (In general, a zone or district allowing manufacturing, commercial or airport uses.)
   E. Whether the Property is affected by a nuisance created by an "industrial use" zone . . . . □ Yes □ No
   F. Whether the Property is located within 1 mile of a former federal or state ordinance location . . □ Yes □ No
   (In general, an area once used for military training purposes that may contain potentially explosive munitions.)
   G. Whether the Property is a condominium or located in a planned unit development or other common interest subdivision . . . . □ Yes □ No
   H. Insurance claims affecting the Property within the past 5 years . . . . □ Yes □ No
   I. Matters affecting title of the Property . . . . □ Yes □ No
   J. Material facts or defects affecting the Property not otherwise disclosed to Buyer . . . . □ Yes □ No
   Explanation, or □ (if checked) see attached; _____
   _____
   _____
   _____
   _____
   _____
   _____

4. Seller represents that the information herein is true and correct to the best of Seller's knowledge as of the date signed by Seller. Seller hereby authorizes any agent(s) representing any principal(s) in this transaction to provide a Copy of this statement to any person or entity in connection with any actual or anticipated sale of the Property.

   Seller _____ Date _____

   Seller _____ Date _____

5. By signing below, Buyer acknowledges Buyer has received, read, and understands this **Supplemental Statutory and Contractual Disclosures** form.

   Buyer _____ Date _____

   Buyer _____ Date _____

Published and Distributed by:
REAL ESTATE BUSINESS SERVICES, INC.
a subsidiary of the California Association of REALTORS®
525 South Virgil Avenue, Los Angeles, California 90020

SSD REVISED 11/09 (PAGE 1 OF 1)

Reviewed by _____ Date _____

EQUAL HOUSING OPPORTUNITY

SUPPLEMENTAL STATUTORY AND CONTRACTUAL DISCLOSURES (SSD PAGE 1 OF 1)

| Agent: | Phone: | Fax: | **Prepared using zipForm® software** |
| Broker: | | | |

Stigmatized Property

Real estate agents must be careful when making disclosures about stigmatized properties. A **stigmatized property**, as defined by NAR, is "a property that has been psychologically impacted by an event which occurred, or was suspected to have occurred, on the property, such event being one that has no physical impact of any kind". The most common properties associated with stigmatized property are those in which there have been murders, suicides, illness, or criminal activity.

Death

Neither the transferor (seller/lessor) nor the agent has to disclose the fact of any death that occurred on the property to the transferee if the death was more than 3 years before the transferee (buyer/lessee) made an offer to buy or lease the property. However, if a death occurs on a property within 3 years and the circumstances of that death are *material* (gruesome, offensive, or affected the reputation of the property), it must be disclosed. (Civil Code §1710.2) Since it is difficult to judge what is considered *material*, it is better to disclose a death if it occurred within the last 3 years and let the buyer decide if it is a material fact. Death of an occupant on the property may be disclosed on the SSD form.

AIDS/HIV

Owners and the agents do NOT have to disclose voluntarily that a person has or has died from Acquired Immune Deficiency Syndrome (AIDS). However, if the transferee (buyer/lessee) asks a direct question about a death on the property, the transferee should direct any specific questions to the transferor in writing.

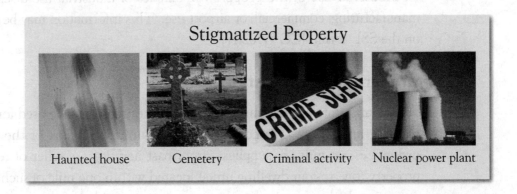

Stigmatized Property

Haunted house   Cemetery   Criminal activity   Nuclear power plant

Registered Sex Offenders (Megan's Law)

Every lease and sales contract is required to include a statutorily defined notice regarding the existence of public access to data base information regarding registered sex offenders in the neighborhood. Seller and brokers are not required to check the website (www.meganslaw.ca.gov). If a buyer wants more information, a broker should recommend that the buyer obtain information from the website during the buyer's inspection contingency period. Real estate licensees do not have expertise in this area.

Clean-up of Illegal Drug-Labs

No one wants a meth lab as a neighbor. The use and production of methamphetamine use may contaminate the property by hazardous chemicals. In the event a property is contaminated by an illegal controlled substance, the owner may receive **clean-up order** from the California Department of Toxic Substances Control (DTSC) or a local health officer. When selling or renting the property, the owner must give a copy of this order to the prospective buyer or tenant. The seller discloses this information by checking item 3.B and 3.C of the Supplemental Statutory and Contractual Disclosure (SSD) form and attaching the DTSC notice, if there is one.

If the owner knowingly and willfully fails to provide written notice to the buyer, the owner is liable for a civil penalty not to exceed $5,000 for each separate violation, in addition to any other damages provided by law.

Industrial Use Disclosure

The seller must disclose actual knowledge that the property is affected by or zoned for **industrial use of the property**. Examples of industrial use disclosure are manufacturing, commercial, or airport use. This information may be disclosed on the SSD form. [CC §1102.17].

Military Ordnance Location

Federal and state agencies have identified certain areas once used for military training and which may contain live ammunition as part of the **military ordnance**—or military supplies—from past activity. A seller of residential property (one-to-four dwelling units) located within one mile of such a hazard must give the buyer written notice as soon as possible before transfer of title. This obligation depends upon the seller having actual knowledge of the hazard. The location of military ordnance may be disclosed on the SSD form. [CC §1102.15].

Condominium/Planned Development Disclosure

If the property is a condominium, townhouse, or other property in a common interest subdivision, the seller must provide the buyer with copies of the governing documents, the most recent financial statements distributed, and other documents required by law or contract of the homeowners' association. This information should be affirmed on the **Homeowner Association Information Request** form.

Disclosure of Insurance Claims

Because the seller is required to disclose any known insurance claims on the property within the last 5 years, it is a good idea for sellers to order a **CLUE report**. CLUE is short for **Comprehensive Loss Underwriting Exchange**. This report shows any insurance claims that were made on the property within the past 5 years. The report includes the date of the claim, the name of the insurance company involved, policy number, claim number, address, cause of loss, amounts paid, status of the claim, and the name of the insured and the claimant.

Disclosure of Title Matters and Material Facts

The seller must disclose all known **title matters** to the buyer, even those not recorded. A seller (transferor) or real estate agent involved in the transaction must disclose any known material facts that affect the value or desirability of the property. Whether or not something is deemed material is determined by case law.

Natural Hazard Disclosure Statement

The Natural Hazard Disclosure Law of 1998, requires sellers to give buyers the **Natural Hazard Disclosure Statement** (NHD). The NHD warns prospective buyers that certain "hazards may limit their ability to develop the real property, to obtain insurance, or to receive assistance after a disaster." In addition to the usual Transfer Disclosure Statement, the agent must give the prospective buyer a separate Natural Hazard Disclosure Statement (NHD) if the residential property lies within any of six statutorily specified areas:

All sellers and their listing agents must determine and disclose to prospective purchasers if a parcel is in certain officially mapped natural hazard zones (geologic, flood, and fire).

The law prescribes the contents of the Natural Hazard Disclosure Statement including a checklist. The statement warns prospective buyers: "these hazards may limit your ability to develop the real property; to obtain insurance; or to receive assistance after a disaster". It also advises buyers and sellers that they "may wish to obtain professional advice regarding those hazards".

The disclosure must be made as soon as practicable before the transfer of title, unless the purchase contract provides for an earlier deadline. It is in the seller's and listing agent's best interest to disclose early because the buyer can annul the purchase contract during a certain period after getting the information. The rescission period is 3 days if the disclosures are hand-delivered or 5 days if the disclosures are mailed.

If the NHD report is prepared by a third-party expert on behalf of a seller or listing agent, additional notices, such as "Notice of Airport in Vicinity", "Notice of Right of Farm", and "Notice of Mining Operation" must be included in the report. [CA CC §1103.4(c)(1)(3)].

Special Flood Hazard Area (Zone "A" or "V")

Flood hazard boundary maps identify the general flood hazards within a community. They are also used in flood plain management and for flood insurance purposes. These maps, developed by the **Federal Emergency Management Agency** (FEMA) in conjunction with communities participating in the National Flood Insurance Program (NFIP), show areas within a **100-year flood boundary,** termed special flood zone areas. Also identified are areas between 100 and 500-year levels termed areas of moderate flood hazards and the remaining areas above the 500-year level termed areas of minimal risk.

A seller of property located in a special flood hazard area, or the seller's agent and/or any agent cooperating in the deal, must disclose to the buyer that federal law requires **Flood Disaster Insurance** as a condition of obtaining financing on most structures located in a special flood hazard area. Since the cost and extent of Flood Disaster Insurance coverage may vary, the buyer should contact an insurance carrier or the intended lender for additional information.

Areas of Potential Flooding

An **area of potential flooding in the event of a dam failure,** is an area designated on an **inundation map** prepared by the state Office of Emergency Services. If the property is on a list of properties posted at the County Public Works/Engineering Offices, Assessors Office, Water Agencies, or Planning Agency, the seller or listing broker must disclose this information to a prospective buyer. If the owner has received federal flood disaster assistance, the seller must tell the buyer to buy flood insurance. This is disclosed on the NHD.

CALIFORNIA ASSOCIATION OF REALTORS®

NATURAL HAZARD DISCLOSURE STATEMENT
(C.A.R. Form NHD, Revised 10/04)

This statement applies to the following property: _____

The transferor and his or her agent(s) or a third-party consultant disclose the following information with the knowledge that even though this is not a warranty, prospective transferees may rely on this information in deciding whether and on what terms to purchase the subject property. Transferor hereby authorizes any agent(s) representing any principal(s) in this action to provide a copy of this statement to any person or entity in connection with any actual or anticipated sale of the property.

The following are representations made by the transferor and his or her agent(s) based on their knowledge and maps drawn by the state and federal governments. This information is a disclosure and is not intended to be part of any contract between the transferee and transferor.

THIS REAL PROPERTY LIES WITHIN THE FOLLOWING HAZARDOUS AREA(S):

A SPECIAL FLOOD HAZARD AREA (Any type Zone "A" or "V") designated by the Federal Emergency Management Agency.
Yes _____   No _____   Do not know and information not available from local jurisdiction _____

AN AREA OF POTENTIAL FLOODING shown on a dam failure inundation map pursuant to Section 8589.5 of the Government Code.
Yes _____   No _____   Do not know and information not available from local jurisdiction _____

A VERY HIGH FIRE HAZARD SEVERITY ZONE pursuant to Section 51178 or 51179 of the Government Code. The owner of this property is subject to the maintenance requirements of Section 51182 of the Government Code.
Yes _____   No _____

A WILDLAND AREA THAT MAY CONTAIN SUBSTANTIAL FOREST FIRE RISKS AND HAZARDS pursuant to Section 4125 of the Public Resources Code. The owner of this property is subject to the maintenance requirements of Section 4291 of the Public Resources Code. Additionally, it is not the state's responsibility to provide fire protection services to any building or structure located within the wildlands unless the Department of Forestry and Fire Protection has entered into a cooperative agreement with a local agency for those purposes pursuant to Section 4142 of the Public Resources Code.
Yes _____   No _____

AN EARTHQUAKE FAULT ZONE pursuant to Section 2622 of the Public Resources Code.
Yes _____   No _____

A SEISMIC HAZARD ZONE pursuant to Section 2696 of the Public Resources Code.
Yes (Landslide Zone) _____   Yes (Liquefaction Zone) _____
No _____   Map not yet released by state _____

NHD REVISED 10/04 (PAGE 1 OF 2)

Buyer's Initials (_____) (_____)
Seller's Initials (_____) (_____)
Reviewed by _____ Date _____

EQUAL HOUSING OPPORTUNITY

NATURAL HAZARD DISCLOSURE STATEMENT (NHD PAGE 1 OF 2)

Agent:	Phone:	Fax:	Prepared using WINForms® software
Broker:			

Property Address: _____ Date: _____

THESE HAZARDS MAY LIMIT YOUR ABILITY TO DEVELOP THE REAL PROPERTY, TO OBTAIN INSURANCE, OR TO RECEIVE ASSISTANCE AFTER A DISASTER.

THE MAPS ON WHICH THESE DISCLOSURES ARE BASED ESTIMATE WHERE NATURAL HAZARDS EXIST. THEY ARE NOT DEFINITIVE INDICATORS OF WHETHER OR NOT A PROPERTY WILL BE AFFECTED BY A NATURAL DISASTER. TRANSFEREE(S) AND TRANSFEROR(S) MAY WISH TO OBTAIN PROFESSIONAL ADVICE REGARDING THOSE HAZARDS AND OTHER HAZARDS THAT MAY AFFECT THE PROPERTY

Signature of Transferor(s) _____ Date _____

Signature of Transferor(s) _____ Date _____

Agent(s) _____ Date _____

Agent(s) _____ Date _____

Check only one of the following:

☐ Transferor(s) and their agent(s) represent that the information herein is true and correct to the best of their knowledge as of the date signed by the transferor(s) and agent(s).

☐ Transferor(s) and their agent(s) acknowledge that they have exercised good faith in the selection of a third-party report provider as required in Civil Code Section 1103.7, and that the representations made in this Natural Hazard Disclosure Statement are based upon information provided by the independent third-party disclosure provider as a substituted disclosure pursuant to Civil Code Section 1103.4. Neither transferor(s) nor their agent(s) (1) has independently verified the information contained in this statement and report or (2) is personally aware of any errors or inaccuracies in the information contained on the statement. This statement was prepared by the provider below:

Third-Party Disclosure Provider(s) _____ Date _____

Transferee represents that he or she has read and understands this document. Pursuant to Civil Code Section 1103.8, the representations made in this Natural Hazard Disclosure Statement do not constitute all of the transferor's or agent's disclosure obligations in this transaction.

Signature of Transferee(s) _____ Date _____

Signature of Transferee(s) _____ Date _____

SURE TRAC The System for Success™

Published and Distributed by:
REAL ESTATE BUSINESS SERVICES, INC.
a subsidiary of the California Association of REALTORS®
525 South Virgil Avenue, Los Angeles, California 90020

Reviewed by _____ Date _____

NHD REVISED 10/04 (PAGE 2 OF 2)
NATURAL HAZARD DISCLOSURE STATEMENT (NHD PAGE 2 OF 2)

Very High Fire Hazard Zone

The seller must disclose if the property is located in a **Very High Fire Hazard Severity Zone** designated by the California Department of Forestry and Fire Protection. Properties in this zone are subject to property maintenance requirements, such as clearing brush and maintaining firebreaks. Generally, the CDF requires a 30-foot clearance area around dwellings per the Public Resources Code. This disclosure is made on the NHD.

Wild Land Fire Area

A property located in a Wildland Area may be subject to forest fires and other hazards. The seller must disclose the possibility of substantial fire risk in such **wild land areas** and that the land is subject to certain preventative requirements. Unless there is a cooperative agreement between the Department of Forestry and Fire Protection and a local county, city, or district, the Forestry Department is NOT obligated to provide fire protection services for any building or structure in the wild land area.

For areas that are the responsibility of the Department of Forestry and Fire Protection, the department produced maps identifying rural lands classified as **state responsibility areas**. In such an area, the state, as opposed to a local or federal agency, has the primary financial responsibility for the prevention and extinguishing of fires. Maps of State Responsibility Areas and any changes, including new maps produced every five years, are to be provided to planning agencies in the affected counties.

Earthquake Fault and Seismic Hazard Zones

Prompted by damaging earthquakes in northern and southern California, the State Legislature passed two laws to protect public safety from the effects of surface fault rupture and seismic hazards caused by earthquakes—the Alquist-Priolo Earthquake Fault Zoning Act (1972) and the Seismic Hazards Mapping Act (1990). The **Alquist-Priolo Earthquake Fault Zoning Act** prevents the construction of buildings for human occupancy on the surface trace of active faults. This Act addresses only the potential hazard of surface fault rupture and is not directed toward other hazards associated with earthquakes. The **Seismic Hazards Mapping Act** addresses non-surface fault rupture earthquake hazards, including liquefaction, lateral spreading, and seismically induced landslides.

Official Earthquake Fault Zones

These laws require the State Geologist to delineate various earthquake fault zones and seismic hazard zones. An **earthquake fault zone** is an area delineated by state officials to have an active fault within it and have the potential for surface rupture.

> Example: The 7.3 Landers earthquake (1992) created a 76 mile surface crack in the desert floor with as much as 18 feet of horizontal displacement and as much as 6 feet of vertical displacement. The surface fault rupture passed directly beneath/through a house in Landers, splitting it apart.

Seismic hazard zones are regulatory zones that the State has determined that a potential for liquefaction or earthquake-induced landslides may affect the property.

Example: Serious soil liquefaction occurred in the Marina District of San Francisco during the 7.1 Loma Prieta earthquake (1989). The displacement of the ground underlying the Marina District caused the vertical settlement and lateral displacement of buildings as well as the buckling of sidewalks, the cracking of asphalt pavement, and the rupture of underground pipes.

These potential hazards must be disclosed upon sale of the property and must be evaluated prior to obtaining a building or grading permit. The State Geologist prepares and issues appropriate maps that are distributed to all affected cities, counties, and state agencies for their use in planning decisions.

Disclosing Earthquake Hazards on the NHD

The fact that a property is located in an Earthquake Fault Zone or Seismic Hazard Zone must be disclosed to a potential buyer before the sales process is complete. This disclosure must be made on either the Natural Hazard Disclosure Statement (NHD) or the Local Option Real Estate Transfer Disclosure Statement (LORETDS).

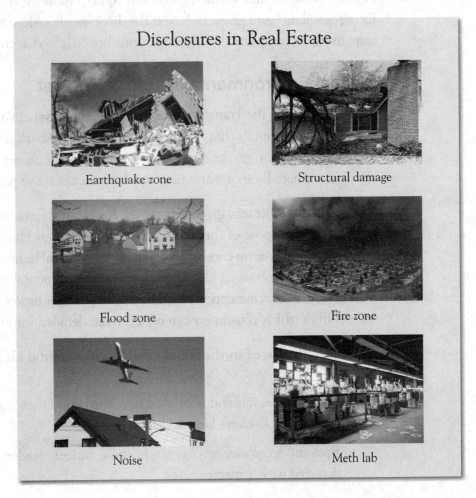

Disclosures in Real Estate

Earthquake zone

Structural damage

Flood zone

Fire zone

Noise

Meth lab

Provide Informational Booklets

Depending on the age and type of construction of the property, sellers can receive limited legal protection by providing buyers with booklets titled *Residential Environmental Hazards, Protect Your Family from Lead in Your Home, Home Energy Rating System,* and the *Homeowner's Guide to Earthquake Safety.* Some booklets are mandatory and some are voluntary. They may be provided to the buyers as four separate booklets or real estate licensees who are members of the California Association of REALTORS® can provide the *Combined*

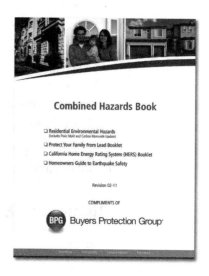

Hazards Book to their sellers to give to prospective buyers. The **Combined Hazards Book** includes all four booklets. By giving buyers this *Combined Hazards Book,* the disclosure requirement is met. Remember, even though the listing or selling agent gives the buyers the disclosure booklets, the sellers are still responsible to complete all disclosure forms honestly and accurately.

Residential Environmental Hazards Booklet

When completing the Transfer Disclosure Statement, sellers must disclose any substances or materials that may be an environmental hazard such as asbestos, formaldehyde, radon gas, lead-based paint, mold, fuel or chemical storage tanks, and contaminated soil or water that may be present on the property.

In addition, the seller may give the buyer the **Residential Environmental Hazards** booklet. The purpose of the Residential Environmental Hazards booklet is to help educate and inform consumers about environmental hazards that may affect real property. The booklet identifies common environmental hazards, describes their risks, discusses mitigation techniques, and provides lists of publications and sources from which consumers can obtain more detailed information.

Hazards Discussed in the Residential Environmental Hazards Booklet

- **Asbestos:** A mineral fiber used in construction materials, which has been found to cause lung and stomach cancer.

- **Radon:** A colorless gas known to cause cancer. Radon can be detected with a spectrometer.

- **Lead**: A mineral that causes major health problems.

- **Formaldehyde**: A chemical organic compound found in building materials, which may be a carcinogen.

- **Hazardous waste**: Materials—chemicals, explosives, radioactive, biological—whose disposal is regulated by the Environmental Protection Agency (EPA).

- **Household hazardous waste**: Consumer products such as paints, cleaners, stains, varnishes, car batteries, motor oil, and pesticides that contain hazardous components.

The booklet is not required, but by giving the booklet to the buyer, the seller and real estate broker are not required to provide any additional information concerning common environmental hazards. However, if the seller or agent has actual knowledge of environmental hazards on or affecting the subject property, that information must be disclosed on the TDS form.

Protect Your Family from Lead in Your Home Booklet

The Residential Lead-Based Paint Hazard Reduction Act of 1992 (Title X) became effective on September 6, 1996 for owners of property with four or fewer units. A **lead-hazard information brochure** (*Protect Your Family from Lead in Your Home*) and disclosure form (C.A.R. form FLD) must be provided to a buyer or lessee by a seller or landlord prior to becoming obligated under the contract. Also, the presence of any known lead-based paint must be disclosed.

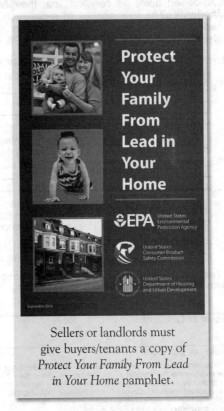

Sellers or landlords must give buyers/tenants a copy of *Protect Your Family From Lead in Your Home* pamphlet.

This disclosure pertains to residential housing built before 1978, called **target housing**, because the Act banned lead based paint for residential use in that year. Target housing does not include housing for the elderly or persons with disabilities, zero-bedroom dwellings such as studio apartments, short-term vacation housing, and foreclosures.

The seller, landlord, and real estate agent involved in the sale or rental of pre-1978 housing each have certain obligations under the law.

CALIFORNIA
ASSOCIATION
OF REALTORS®

LEAD-BASED PAINT AND LEAD-BASED PAINT HAZARDS DISCLOSURE, ACKNOWLEDGMENT AND ADDENDUM
For Pre-1978 Housing Sales, Leases, or Rentals
(C.A.R. Form FLD, Revised 11/10)

The following terms and conditions are hereby incorporated in and made a part of the: ☐ California Residential Purchase Agreement, ☐ Residential Lease or Month-to-Month Rental Agreement, or ☐ Other: _____ _____, dated _____ , on property known as: _____ ("Property") in which _____ is referred to as Buyer or Tenant and _____ is referred to as Seller or Landlord.

LEAD WARNING STATEMENT (SALE OR PURCHASE) Every purchaser of any interest in residential real property on which a residential dwelling was built prior to 1978 is notified that such property may present exposure to lead from lead-based paint that may place young children at risk of developing lead poisoning. Lead poisoning in young children may produce permanent neurological damage, including learning disabilities, reduced intelligent quotient, behavioral problems and impaired memory. Lead poisoning also poses a particular risk to pregnant women. The seller of any interest in residential real property is required to provide the buyer with any information on lead-based paint hazards from risk assessments or inspections in the seller's possession and notify the buyer of any known lead-based paint hazards. A risk assessment or inspection for possible lead-based paint hazards is recommended prior to purchase.

LEAD WARNING STATEMENT (LEASE OR RENTAL) Housing built before 1978 may contain lead-based paint. Lead from paint, paint chips and dust can pose health hazards if not managed properly. Lead exposure is especially harmful to young children and pregnant women. Before renting pre-1978 housing, lessors must disclose the presence of lead-based paint and/or lead-based paint hazards in the dwelling. Lessees must also receive federally approved pamphlet on lead poisoning prevention.

EPA'S LEAD-BASED PAINT RENOVATION, REPAIR AND PAINTING RULE: The new rule requires that contractors and maintenance professionals working in pre-1978 housing, child care facilities, and schools with lead-based paint be certified; that their employees be trained; and that they follow protective work practice standards. The rule applies to renovation, repair, or painting activities affecting more than six square feet of lead-based paint in a room or more than 20 square feet of lead-based paint on the exterior. Enforcement of the rule begins October 1, 2010. See the EPA website at www.epa.gov/lead for more information.

1. **SELLER'S OR LANDLORD'S DISCLOSURE**

    I (we) have no knowledge of lead-based paint and/or lead-based paint hazards in the housing other than the following:

    _____
    _____
    _____
    _____

    I (we) have no reports or records pertaining to lead-based paint and/or lead-based paint hazards in the housing other than the following, which, previously or as an attachment to this addendum have been provided to Buyer or Tenant:

    _____
    _____
    _____

    I (we), previously or as an attachment to this addendum, have provided Buyer or Tenant with the pamphlet *"Protect Your Family From Lead In Your Home"* or an equivalent pamphlet approved for use in the State such as *"The Homeowner's Guide to Environmental Hazards and Earthquake Safety."*

    For Sales Transactions Only: Buyer has 10 days, unless otherwise agreed in the real estate purchase contract, to conduct a risk assessment or inspection for the presence of lead-based paint and/or lead-based paint hazards.

    I (we) have reviewed the information above and certify, to the best of my (our) knowledge, that the information provided is true and correct.

    _____ _____
    Seller or Landlord   Date

    _____ _____
    Seller or Landlord   Date

    FLD REVISED 11/10 (PAGE 1 OF 2)

    Buyer's Initials (_____) (_____)

    Reviewed by _____ Date _____

    EQUAL HOUSING OPPORTUNITY

LEAD-BASED PAINT AND LEAD-BASED PAINT HAZARDS DISCLOSURE (FLD PAGE 1 OF 2)

Agent:	Phone:	Fax:	Prepared using zipForm® software
Broker:			

Property Address: _____ Date _____

2. LISTING AGENT'S ACKNOWLEDGMENT

Agent has informed Seller or Landlord of Seller's or Landlord's obligations under §42 U.S.C. 4852d and is aware of Agent's responsibility to ensure compliance.

I have reviewed the information above and certify, to the best of my knowledge, that the information provided is true and correct.

_____ By _____
(Please Print) Agent (Broker representing Seller or Landlord)   Associate-Licensee or Broker Signature   Date

3. BUYER'S OR TENANT'S ACKNOWLEDGMENT

I (we) have received copies of all information listed, if any, in 1 above and the pamphlet *"Protect Your Family From Lead In Your Home"* or an equivalent pamphlet approved for use in the State such as *"The Homeowner's Guide to Environmental Hazards and Earthquake Safety."* **If delivery of any of the disclosures or pamphlet referenced in paragraph 1 above occurs after Acceptance of an offer to purchase, Buyer has a right to cancel pursuant to the purchase contract. If you wish to cancel, you must act within the prescribed period.**

For Sales Transactions Only: Buyer acknowledges the right for 10 days, unless otherwise agreed in the real estate purchase contract, to conduct a risk assessment or inspection for the presence of lead-based paint and/or lead-based paint hazards; OR, (if checked) ☐ Buyer waives the right to conduct a risk assessment or inspection for the presence of lead-based paint and/or lead-based paint hazards.

I (we) have reviewed the information above and certify, to the best of my (our) knowledge, that the information provided is true and correct.

_____   _____
Buyer or Tenant   Date   Buyer or Tenant   Date

4. COOPERATING AGENT'S ACKNOWLEDGMENT

Agent has informed Seller or Landlord, through the Listing Agent if the property is listed, of Seller's or Landlord's obligations under §42 U.S.C. 4852d and is aware of Agent's responsibility to ensure compliance.

I have reviewed the information above and certify, to the best of my knowledge, that the information provided is true and correct.

_____ By _____
Agent (Broker obtaining the Offer)   Associate-Licensee or Broker Signature   Date

THIS FORM HAS BEEN APPROVED BY THE CALIFORNIA ASSOCIATION OF REALTORS® (C.A.R.). NO REPRESENTATION IS MADE AS TO THE LEGAL VALIDITY OR ADEQUACY OF ANY PROVISION IN ANY SPECIFIC TRANSACTION. A REAL ESTATE BROKER IS THE PERSON QUALIFIED TO ADVISE ON REAL ESTATE TRANSACTIONS. IF YOU DESIRE LEGAL OR TAX ADVICE, CONSULT AN APPROPRIATE PROFESSIONAL.

This form is available for use by the entire real estate industry. It is not intended to identify the user as a REALTOR®. REALTOR® is a registered collective membership mark which may be used only by members of the NATIONAL ASSOCIATION OF REALTORS® who subscribe to its Code of Ethics.

Published and Distributed by:
REAL ESTATE BUSINESS SERVICES, INC.
a subsidiary of the California Association of REALTORS®
525 South Virgil Avenue, Los Angeles, California 90020

Reviewed by _____ Date _____

EQUAL HOUSING OPPORTUNITY

FLD REVISED 11/10 (PAGE 2 OF 2)

LEAD-BASED PAINT AND LEAD-BASED PAINT HAZARDS DISCLOSURE (FLD PAGE 2 OF 2)

Seller/Landlord Obligations

Sellers or landlords must:

- give buyers/tenants *Protect Your Family From Lead in Your Home* pamphlet.

- disclose all known lead-based paint and lead-based paint hazards in the dwelling and provide buyers/tenants with any available reports.

- include standard warning language as an attachment to the contract or lease.

- complete and sign statements verifying completion of requirements.

- retain the signed acknowledgment for three years.

- give buyers a 10-day opportunity to test for lead (for sale transactions only).

Real Estate Agent Responsibilities

Real estate agents must ensure that:

- sellers/landlords are aware of their obligations.

- sellers/landlords disclose the proper information to buyers and tenants.

- leases and sales contracts include proper disclosure language and signatures.

- sellers give buyers the opportunity to conduct an inspection for 10 days or another mutually agreed-upon time.

Real estate agents must comply with the law if the seller or landlord fails to do so. However, the agent is not responsible if an owner conceals information or fails to disclose information.

Home Energy Rating System Booklet

Sellers and/or real estate agents may give the optional *Home Energy Rating System* informational booklet (**HERS booklet**) concerning the statewide home energy-rating program to buyers. The delivery of this booklet is not mandatory; however, the information in the booklet is deemed adequate to inform the buyer about the existence of a statewide home energy-rating program. If the HERS booklet is delivered to the buyer, then the seller or listing agent do not have to provide any additional information regarding energy rating.

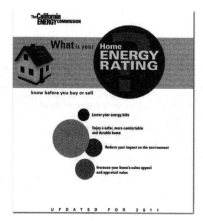

Homeowner's Guide to Earthquake Safety Booklet

Listing agents give their sellers copies of the *Homeowner's Guide to Earthquake Safety* booklet because known earthquake hazards must be disclosed by the seller whether the delivery of the *Homeowner's Guide to Earthquake Safety* booklet is mandatory or voluntary. [B&P Code §10149].

Mandatory Delivery – Pre 1960 Construction

A seller must deliver a copy of the *Homeowner's Guide to Earthquake Safety* booklet (developed by the Seismic Safety Commission) to the buyer if the home was built before 1960 or if the home is a masonry building with wood-frame floors or roofs built before January 1, 1975. Additionally, the seller must complete the Residential Earthquake Hazards Report (found at the back of the booklet) prior to giving the booklet to the buyer. Real estate licensees are required to provide sellers with copies of the *Homeowner's Guide to Earthquake Safety* booklet.

Requirement: *Homeowner's Guide to Earthquake Safety* Booklet

- Transfer of any real property with a residential dwelling built prior to January 1, 1960 and consisting of one-to-four units any of which are of conventional light-frame construction.

- Transfer of any masonry building with wood-frame floors or roofs built before January 1, 1975.

Voluntary Delivery – Sale of Any Real Property

If the buyer of real property receives a copy of the *Homeowner's Guide to Earthquake Safety*, neither the seller nor the agent is required to provide additional information regarding geologic and seismic hazards.

COMPLY WITH OTHER CONTRACT TERMS

Sellers are responsible for to make disclosures regarding certain tax issues, compliance with statewide and local retrofit ordinances, and requirements specified by the buyer's lender.

Mello-Roos Disclosure

Currently on purchase, property taxes are limited by Proposition 13 to a maximum of 1% of the assessed value of the property. The city, through the sale of municipal bonds, can include the cost and maintenance of infrastructure items in the property tax bill as a special assessment, exempt from the limitations of Proposition 13.

ANY CITY, CALIFORNIA

Mello Roos Disclosure Statement
Notice of Special Tax

Community Facilities District 20___-1
ABC Public Facilities Financing Agency
County of _____, State of California

To: The Prospective Purchaser of the Real Property Known as:

Address: Assessors Parcel Number:

_____

THIS IS A NOTIFICATION TO YOU PRIOR TO YOUR PURCHASING THIS
PROPERTY.

1. This property is subject to a special tax, which is in addition to the regular property
taxes and other charges and benefit assessments on the parcel. This special tax may not
be imposed on all parcels within the city or county where the property is located. If you
fail to pay this tax when due each year, the property may be foreclosed upon and sold.
The tax is used to provide public facilities or services that are likely to particularly
benefit the property. **You should take this tax and the benefits from the facilities and
services for which it pays into account in deciding to whether to buy this property.**

2. The maximum annual tax to which this property is subject is $_____ during the
20___ tax year and thereafter. The special tax will be levied each year until all of the
authorized facilities are built and all special tax bonds are repaid.

3. The authorized facilities which are being paid for by the special taxes, and by the
money received from the sale of bonds which are being repaid by the special taxes, are
set forth on Exhibit A attached hereto. These facilities may not yet have all been
constructed or acquired and it is possible that some may never be constructed or acquired.

4. The obligation to pay the special tax, attached to this property, was a condition
required in order to permit this property to be developed. The payment of tax is intended
to insure that there will be adequate capacity in the school district for the children that
may come from this property. However, the payment of the special tax does not
guarantee attendance at any particular school, nor does it guarantee attendance at a newly
constructed school. School attendance boundaries are set by the School Board and are
based on many criteria, only one of which is whether a property pays the special tax.

You may obtain a copy of the resolution of formation which authorized creation of the
community facilities district, and which specifies more precisely how the special tax is
apportioned and how the proceeds of the tax will be used, from the Comptroller of ABC
Public Facilities Financing Agency by telephoning (555) 123-4567. There may be a
charge for this document not to exceed the reasonable cost of providing this document.

I (we) acknowledge that I (we) have read this notice and received a copy of this
notice prior to entering into a contract to purchase or deposit receipt with respect
to the above-references property. I (we) understand that I (we) may terminate the
contract to purchase or deposit receipt within three days after receiving this notice
in person or within five days after it was deposited in the mail by giving written
notice of that termination to the owner, subdivider, or agent selling the property.

Date:

_____

The Mello-Roos Community Facilities Act of 1982 authorizes the formation of community facilities districts, the issuance of bonds, and the levying of special taxes, which will finance designated public facilities and services. A **Mello-Roos District** is an area where a special assessment is imposed on those real property owners within a Community Facilities District. Public services such as roads, sewers, parks, schools, and fire stations in new developments may be financed under this law.

A Mello-Roos lien is placed on each parcel in a new development by the developer to pay off municipal bonds issued to fund off-site improvements for the development. The developer must make the payments on the bond until the homes are sold, and then the new owners are responsible. Mello-Roos liens are a way a developer can make improvements and have each homeowner pay for them, without charging the improvements to property taxes.

Effective July 1, 1993, the seller of a property consisting of one-to-four dwelling units subject to the lien of a Mello-Roos community facilities district must make a good faith effort to obtain from the district a disclosure notice concerning the special tax and give a Notice of Special Tax to a prospective buyer. Exempt from this requirement are the various transfers listed earlier for the Transfer Disclosure Statement. According to the California Tax Data website, Mello-Roos information should be on the property tax bill. Mello-Roos funds are used to finance subdivision costs. The transferor (seller) of residential property (one-to-four units) is responsible to disclose if a property is subject to a Mello-Roos assessment. If the Notice of Special Tax is delivered to the buyer after a purchase agreement has been signed, the buyer has the right to terminate the agreement within three days of delivery in person, or five days after delivery by mail. The buyer must provide written notice of termination of the agreement to the seller or the seller's agent.

Prospective buyers must be told by real estate agents that a project is subject to a Mello-Roos special assessment because their tax bill will be higher than if they only paid property taxes without the special assessment. The listing agent does not have an affirmative duty to discover a special tax district or assessment not actually known to the agent. [CC 1102.6b (e)].

Notice of Supplemental Property Tax Bill

A seller or his or her agent must give prospective purchasers a **Notice of Supplemental Property Tax Bill** (C.A.R. Form SPT). The notice informs purchasers that county assessors revalue real property at the time the ownership of the property changes. Therefore, the buyer may receive one or two supplemental tax bills, depending on when escrow closes. CC §1102.6c].

**CALIFORNIA
ASSOCIATION
OF REALTORS®**

NOTICE OF YOUR "SUPPLEMENTAL" PROPERTY TAX BILL
(C.A.R. Form SPT, 10/05)

Name of Buyer(s) _____

Property Address _____

_____

Pursuant to Civil Code §1102.6c, Seller or his or her agent is providing this "Notice of Your 'Supplemental' Property Tax Bill":

"California property tax law requires the Assessor to revalue real property at the time the ownership of the property changes. Because of this law, you may receive one or two supplemental tax bills, depending on when your loan closes.

The supplemental tax bills are not mailed to your lender. If you have arranged for your property tax payments to be paid through an impound account, the supplemental tax bills will not be paid by your lender. It is your responsibility to pay these supplemental bills directly to the Tax Collector.

If you have any questions concerning this matter, please call your local Tax Collector's Office."

Buyer acknowledges Buyer has read, understands and has received a copy of this "Notice of Your 'Supplemental' Property Tax Bill".

Buyer _____ Date _____

Buyer _____ Date _____

Published and Distributed by:
REAL ESTATE BUSINESS SERVICES, INC.
a subsidiary of the California Association of REALTORS®
525 South Virgil Avenue, Los Angeles, California 90020

Reviewed by _____ Date _____

EQUAL HOUSING OPPORTUNITY

SPT 10/05 (PAGE 1 OF 1)
NOTICE OF YOUR SUPPLEMENTAL PROPERTY TAX BILL (SPT PAGE 1 OF 1)

Foreign Investment in Real Property

Both federal and state tax laws deal with foreign investment in U.S. real property. Buyers, their real estate agents, and the settlement agent are required to withhold a percentage of proceeds from the sale of property held by a foreign person. The buyer must find out if the seller is a foreigner, because if the seller is a foreigner, and the buyer fails to withhold the tax, the buyer, the real estate agent, and escrow officer may be held liable to pay the tax.

It is the buyer's responsibility for making sure the proper disclosures have been made and/or the proper funds have been set to comply with federal (FIRPTA) and California withholding laws. However, due to the potential liability, the escrow agent and real estate agent make sure this is done. All documents must be kept by the broker and the buyer for five years.

FIRPTA

The **Foreign Investment in Real Property Tax Act** of 1980 (FIRPTA) requires BUYERS of real property to withhold and send to the Internal Revenue Service (IRS) a percentage of the gross sales price if the seller of the real property is a foreign person. Currently, the tax is 15% on all real property. The IRS allows two exceptions from this 15% tax.

Exceptions Effective February 16, 2016

- If the sales price is $300,000 or less, AND the property will be used by the buyer as a residence, there is no tax and no money is withheld.

- If the sales price is between $300,001 and $1,000,000, AND the property will be used by the buyer as a residence, then a reduced rate of 10% of the sales price is withheld and remitted to the IRS.

However, withholding funds generally is not required when the seller provides a proper certificate of non-foreign status at closing called the **Seller's Affidavit of Non-foreign Status** including a U.S. taxpayer identification number.

Additionally, the withholding obligation may be reduced or eliminated when a **"withholding certificate"** is obtained through the IRS saying arrangements have been made for the collection of or exemption from the tax.

Due to the number of exceptions and other requirements relating to this law, it is recommended that the IRS be consulted. Sellers and buyers and the real estate agents involved who desire further advice should consult an attorney, CPA, or other qualified tax advisor.

CALIFORNIA
ASSOCIATION
OF REALTORS®

SELLER'S AFFIDAVIT OF NONFOREIGN STATUS AND/OR CALIFORNIA WITHHOLDING EXEMPTION
FOREIGN INVESTMENT IN REAL PROPERTY TAX ACT (FIRPTA)
AND CALIFORNIA WITHHOLDING LAW
(Use a separate form for each Transferor)
(C.A.R. Form AS, Revised 1/16)

Internal Revenue Code ("IRC") Section 1445 provides that a transferee of a U.S. real property interest must withhold tax if the transferor is a "foreign person." California Revenue and Taxation Code Section 18662 provides that a transferee of a California real property interest must withhold tax unless an exemption applies.

I understand that this affidavit may be disclosed to the Internal Revenue Service and to the California Franchise Tax Board by the transferee, and that any false statement I have made herein may result in a fine, imprisonment or both.

1. **PROPERTY ADDRESS** (property being transferred): _____ ("Property")
2. **TRANSFEROR'S INFORMATION:**
   Full Name _____ ("Transferor")
   Telephone Number _____
   Address _____
   (Use HOME address for individual transferors. Use OFFICE address for an "Entity" i.e.: corporations, partnerships, limited liability companies, trusts and estates.)
   Social Security No., or Federal Employer Identification No. _____
   For a corporation qualified to do business in California, California Corporation No. _____
   Note: In order to avoid withholding, IRC Section 1445 (b) requires that the Seller (a) provides this affidavit to the Buyer with the Seller's taxpayer identification number ("TIN"), or (b) provides this affidavit, including Seller's TIN, to a "qualified substitute" who furnishes a statement to the Buyer under penalty of perjury that the qualified substitute has such affidavit in their possession. A qualified substitute may be (i) an attorney, title company, or escrow company (but not the Seller's agent) responsible for closing the transaction, or (ii) the Buyer's agent.
3. **AUTHORITY TO SIGN:** If this document is signed on behalf of an Entity Transferor, THE UNDERSIGNED INDIVIDUAL DECLARES THAT HE/SHE HAS AUTHORITY TO SIGN THIS DOCUMENT ON BEHALF OF THE TRANSFEROR.
4. **FEDERAL LAW:** I, the undersigned, declare under penalty of perjury that, for the reason checked below, if any, I am exempt (or if signed on behalf of an Entity Transferor, the Entity is exempt) from the federal withholding law (FIRPTA):
   ☐ (For individual Transferors) I am not a nonresident alien for purposes of U.S. income taxation.
   ☐ (For corporation, partnership, limited liability company, trust and estate Transferors) The Transferor is not a foreign corporation, foreign partnership, foreign limited liability company, foreign trust or foreign estate, as those terms are defined in the Internal Revenue Code and Income Tax Regulations.
5. **CALIFORNIA LAW:** I, the undersigned, declare under penalty of perjury that, for the reason checked below, if any, I am exempt (or if signed on behalf of an Entity Transferor, the Entity is exempt) from the California withholding law.
   Certifications which fully exempt the sale from withholding:
   ☐ The total sales price for the Property is $100,000 or less.
   ☐ The Property qualifies as my principal residence (or the decedent's, if being sold by the decedent's estate) within the meaning of IRC Section 121 (owned and occupied as such for two of the last five years).
   ☐ The Property was last used as my principal residence (or the decedent's, if being sold by the decedent's estate) within the meaning of IRC Section 121 without regard to the two-year time period.
   ☐ The transaction will result in a loss or zero gain for California income tax purposes. (Complete FTB Form 593-E.)
   ☐ The Property has been compulsorily or involuntarily converted (within the meaning of IRC Section 1033) and Transferor intends to acquire property similar or related in service or use to be eligible for non-recognition of gain for California income tax purposes under IRC Section 1033.
   ☐ Transferor is a corporation (or an LLC classified as a corporation) that is either qualified through the California Secretary of State or has a permanent place of business in California.
   ☐ Transferor is a partnership (or an LLC that is not a disregarded single member LLC, classified as a partnership) and recorded title to the Property is in the name of the partnership or LLC. If so, the partnership or LLC must withhold from nonresident partners or members as required.
   ☐ Transferor is exempt from tax under California or federal law.
   ☐ Transferor is an insurance company, qualified pension/profit sharing plan, IRA or charitable remainder trust.
   Certifications which may partially or fully exempt the sale from withholding:
   ☐ The Property is being, or will be, exchanged for property of like kind within the meaning of IRC Section 1031.
   ☐ Payments for the Property are being made in installments, the transferor is a non-resident seller and withholding will be applied to each principal payment.
   ☐ As a result of the sale of the Property, Seller's tax liability, calculated at the maximum tax rate regardless of Seller's actual rate, will be less than the 3 1/3% withholding otherwise required. Seller will be required to sign a certification, under penalty of perjury, specifying the amount to be withheld. (Not to be used for sales closing prior to January 1, 2007)

By _____ Date _____
(Transferor's Signature) (Indicate if you are signing as the grantor of a revocable/grantor trust.)

_____   _____
Typed or printed name   Title (If signed on behalf of Entity Transferor)

Buyer's unauthorized use or disclosure of Seller's TIN could result in civil or criminal liability.

Buyer _____ Date _____
(Buyer acknowledges receipt of a Copy of this Seller's Affidavit)
Buyer _____ Date _____
(Buyer acknowledges receipt of a Copy of this Seller's Affidavit)

IMPORTANT NOTICE: An Affidavit should be signed by each individual or entity Transferor to whom or to which it applies. Before you sign, any questions relating to the legal sufficiency of this form, or to whether it applies to you or to a particular transaction, or about the definition of any of the terms used, should be referred to an attorney, certified public accountant, or other professional tax advisor, the Internal Revenue Service, or the California Franchise Tax Board.

© 1988-2016, California Association of REALTORS®, Inc. © 1988-2016, California Association of REALTORS®, Inc.

Published and Distributed by:
REAL ESTATE BUSINESS SERVICES, INC.
a subsidiary of the California Association of REALTORS®
525 South Virgil Avenue, Los Angeles, California 90020

Reviewed by _____ Date _____

AS 1/16 (PAGE 1 OF 2)
SELLER'S AFFIDAVIT OF NONFOREIGN STATUS AND/OR CALIFORNIA WITHHOLDING EXEMPTION (AS PAGE 1 OF 2)

Produced with zipForm® by zipLogix 18070 Fifteen Mile Road, Fraser, Michigan 48026   www.zipLogix.com   Phone: Fax:

Cal-FIRPTA

California law requires that if property is sold by a non-citizen of the United States or a resident of another state, the buyer must withhold 3 1/3% of the total sales price as state income tax and deliver the sum withheld to the State Franchise Tax Board. A buyer's failure to withhold and deliver the required sum may result in penalties.

Although the law requires buyers to withhold, they can request the escrow holder to handle the withholding to meet the Cal-FIRPTA requirements.

The escrow officer gives the Franchise Tax Board Form 593-C to the sellers to complete. If the sellers are exempt, no withholding is collected. However, if the sellers are not exempt the escrow holder collects the appropriate tax and sends it to the Franchise Tax Board.

Transactions Subject to the Law

- Seller shows an out-of-state address, or sale proceeds are to be disbursed to the seller's **financial intermediary**.

- Sales price exceeds $100,000.

- Seller does not certify that he or she is a California resident, or that the property being conveyed is his or her personal residence.

Transactions Exempt from the Law

- Sales price is $100,000 or less.

- Home is the seller's principal residence.

- Seller signs the Seller's Affidavit of Non-foreign Status and the Buyer's Affidavit of Residency for California.

Remember, both the buyer and escrow officer are responsible for making sure this law is observed. The paperwork is usually completed through escrow. For further information, contact the Franchise Tax Board at their website, www.ftb.ca.gov.

Retrofit Standards

Unless the property is exempt, the seller must comply with statewide **retrofit standards** including, but not limited to, installing operable smoke detectors, bracing water heaters, and notifying buyers whether carbon monoxide detectors are installed.

Water Heater Bracing Compliance

By the close of escrow, the sellers must conform to state and local laws regarding **water heater bracing** compliance. All residential water heaters must be braced, anchored, or strapped to resist falling due to earthquake motion.

The sellers must provide written certification to prospective buyers that the sellers have complied with the law. The seller may disclose this compliance on the Transfer Disclosure Statement or use the **Water Heater Statement of Compliance** form (WHSD). The buyers must acknowledge receipt of the form with their signatures and date.

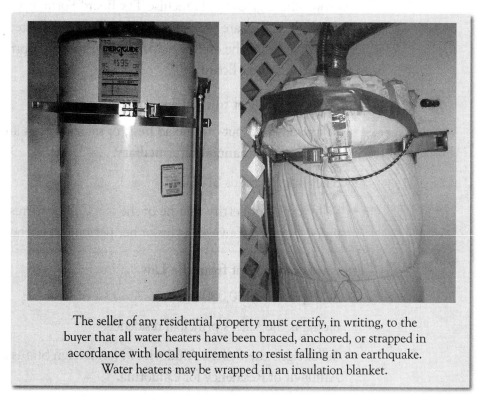

The seller of any residential property must certify, in writing, to the buyer that all water heaters have been braced, anchored, or strapped in accordance with local requirements to resist falling in an earthquake. Water heaters may be wrapped in an insulation blanket.

Operable Smoke Detector Compliance

By the close of escrow, the seller must also comply with state and local laws regarding **operable smoke detectors**. The seller must have a certification of having operable smoke detector(s) approved and listed by the State Fire Marshal installed in accordance with the State Fire Marshal's regulations and in accordance with applicable local ordinance(s) by signing and dating this form.

The Transfer Disclosure Statement includes a statement of compliance. However, when no TDS is used in the transaction, sellers may use the **Smoke Detector Statement of Compliance** form (WHSD). The buyers must acknowledge receipt of the form with their signatures and date.

CALIFORNIA
ASSOCIATION
OF REALTORS®

WATER HEATER AND SMOKE DETECTOR
STATEMENT OF COMPLIANCE
(C.A.R. Form WHSD, Revised 11/10)

Property Address: _____

NOTE: A seller who is not required to provide one of the following statements of compliance is not necessarily exempt from the obligation to provide the other statement of compliance.

WATER HEATER STATEMENT OF COMPLIANCE

1. **STATE LAW:** California Law requires that all new and replacement water heaters and existing residential water heaters be braced, anchored or strapped to resist falling or horizontal displacement due to earthquake motion. "Water heater" means any standard water heater with a capacity of no more than 120 gallons for which a pre-engineered strapping kit is readily available. (Health and Safety Code §19211d). Although not specifically stated, the statue requiring a statement of compliance does not appear to apply to a properly installed and bolted tankless water heater for the following reasons: There is no tank that can overturn; Pre-engineered strapping kits for such devices are not readily available; and Bolting already exists that would help avoid displacement or breakage in the event of an earthquake.
2. **LOCAL REQUIREMENTS:** Some local ordinances impose more stringent water heater bracing, anchoring or strapping requirements than does California Law. Therefore, it is important to check with local city or county building and safety departments regarding the applicable water heater bracing, anchoring or strapping requirements for your property.
3. **TRANSFEROR'S WRITTEN STATEMENT:** California Health and Safety Code §19211 requires the seller of any real property containing a water heater to certify, in writing, that the seller is in compliance with California State Law. If the Property is a manufactured or mobile home, Seller shall also file a required Statement with the Department of Housing and Community Development.
4. **CERTIFICATION:** Seller represents that the Property, as of the Close Of Escrow, will be in compliance with Health and Safety Code §19211 by having the water heater(s) braced, anchored or strapped in place, in accordance with those requirements.

Seller _____ Date _____
          (Signature)   (Print Name)

Seller _____ Date _____
          (Signature)   (Print Name)

The undersigned hereby acknowledges receipt of a copy of this document.

Buyer _____ Date _____
          (Signature)   (Print Name)

Buyer _____ Date _____
          (Signature)   (Print Name)

SMOKE DETECTOR STATEMENT OF COMPLIANCE

1. **STATE LAW:** California Law requires that (i) every single-family dwelling and factory built housing unit sold on or after January 1, 1986, must have an operable smoke detector, approved and listed by the State Fire Marshal, installed in accordance with the State Fire Marshal's regulations (Health and Safety Code §13113.8) and (ii) all used manufactured or mobilehomes have an operable smoke detector in each sleeping room.
2. **LOCAL REQUIREMENTS:** Some local ordinances impose more stringent smoke detector requirements than does California Law. Therefore, it is important to check with local city or county building and safety departments regarding the applicable smoke detector requirements for your property.
3. **TRANSFEROR'S WRITTEN STATEMENT:** California Health and Safety Code §13113.8(b) requires every transferor of any real property containing a single-family dwelling, whether the transfer is made by sale, exchange, or real property sales contract (installment sales contract), to deliver to the transferee a written statement indicating that the transferor is in compliance with California State Law concerning smoke detectors. If the Property is a manufactured or mobile home, Seller shall also file a required Statement with the Department of Housing and Community Development (HCD).
4. **EXCEPTIONS:** Generally, a written statement of smoke detector compliance is not required for transactions for which the Seller is exempt from providing a transfer disclosure statement.
5. **CERTIFICATION:** Seller represents that the Property, as of the Close Of Escrow, will be in compliance with the law by having operable smoke detector(s) (i) approved and listed by the State Fire Marshal installed in accordance with the State Fire Marshal's regulations Health and Safety Code §13113.8 or (ii) in compliance with Manufactured Housing Construction and Safety Act (Health and Safety Code §18029.6) located in each sleeping room for used manufactured or mobilehomes as required by HCD and (iii) in accordance with applicable local ordinance(s).

Seller _____ Date _____
          (Signature)   (Print Name)

Seller _____ Date _____
          (Signature)   (Print Name)

The undersigned hereby acknowledge(s) receipt of a copy of this Water Heater and Smoke Detector Statement of Compliance.

Buyer _____ Date _____
          (Signature)   (Print Name)

Buyer _____ Date _____
          (Signature)   (Print Name)

Published and Distributed by:
REAL ESTATE BUSINESS SERVICES, INC.
a subsidiary of the CALIFORNIA ASSOCIATION OF REALTORS®
525 South Virgil Avenue, Los Angeles, California 90020

Reviewed by _____ Date _____

WHSD REVISED 11/10 (PAGE 1 OF 1)

WATER HEATER AND SMOKE DETECTOR STATEMENT OF COMPLIANCE (WHSD PAGE 1 OF 1)

Agent:	Phone:	Fax:	Prepared using zipForm® software
Broker:			

CALIFORNIA
ASSOCIATION
OF REALTORS®

CARBON MONOXIDE DETECTOR NOTICE
(C.A.R. Form CMD, 4/12)

Property Address: _____

1. **INSTALLATION OF CARBON MONOXIDE DETECTORS:**
   A. **Requirements:** California law (Health and Safety Code sections 13260 to 13263 and 17296 to 17296.2) requires that as of July 1, 2011, all existing single-family dwellings have carbon monoxide detectors installed and that all other types of dwelling units intended for human occupancy have carbon monoxide detectors installed on or before January 1, 2013. The January 1, 2013 requirement applies to a duplex, lodging house, dormitory, hotel, condominium, time-share and apartment, among others.
   B. **Exceptions:** The law does not apply to a dwelling unit which does not have any of the following: a fossil fuel burning heater or appliance, a fireplace, or an attached garage. The law does not apply to dwelling units owned or leased by the State of California, the Regents of the University of California or local government agencies. Aside from these three owner types, there are **no other owner exemptions** from the installation requirement; it applies to all owners of dwellings, be they individual banks, corporations, or other entities. There is no exemption for REO properties.

2. **DISCLOSURE OF CARBON MONOXIDE DETECTORS:** The Health and Safety Code does not require a disclosure regarding the existence of carbon monoxide detectors in a dwelling. However, a seller of residential 1-4 property who is required to complete a Real Estate Transfer Disclosure Statement, (C.A.R. Form TDS) or a Manufactured Home and Mobile home Transfer Disclosure Statement (C.A.R. Form MHTDS) must use section II A of that form to disclose whether or not the dwelling unit has a carbon monoxide detector.

3. **COMPLIANCE WITH INSTALLATION REQUIREMENT:** State building code requires at a minimum, placement of carbon monoxide detectors in applicable properties outside of each sleeping area, and on each floor in a multi-level dwelling but additional or different requirements may apply depending on local building standards and manufacturer instructions. An owner who fails to install a carbon monoxide detector when required by law and continues to fail to install the detector after being given notice by a governmental agency could be liable for a fine of up to $200 for each violation. A transfer of a property where a seller, as an owner, has not installed carbon monoxide detectors, when required to do so by law, will not be invalidated, but the seller/owner could be subject to damages of up to $100, plus court costs and attorney fees. Buyer and Seller are each advised to consult with their own home inspector, contractor or building department to determine the exact location for installation of carbon monoxide detectors. Buyer is advised to consult with a professional of Buyer's choosing to determine whether the property has carbon monoxide detector(s) installed as required by law, and if not to discuss with their counsel the potential consequences.

4. **LOCAL REQUIREMENTS:** Some localities maintain their own retrofit or point of sale requirements which may include the requirement that a carbon monoxide detector be installed prior to a transfer of property. Therefore, it is important to check the local city or county building and safety departments regarding point of sale or retrofit requirements when transferring property.

The undersigned hereby acknowledge(s) receipt of a copy of this Carbon Monoxide Detector Notice.

Seller/Landlord _____ Date _____
             (Signature)   (Print Name)

Seller/Landlord _____ Date _____
             (Signature)   (Print Name)

Buyer/Tenant _____ Date _____
             (Signature)   (Print Name)

Buyer/Tenant _____ Date _____
             (Signature)   (Print Name)

R
E I
B N
S C Published and Distributed by:
      REAL ESTATE BUSINESS SERVICES, INC.
      a subsidiary of the California Association of REALTORS®
      525 South Virgil Avenue, Los Angeles, California 90020

CMD 4/12 (PAGE 1 OF 1)

Reviewed by _____ Date _____

EQUAL HOUSING
OPPORTUNITY

CARBON MONOXIDE DETECTOR NOTICE (CMD PAGE 1 OF 1)

Phone: _____ Fax: _____
Produced with zipForm® by zipLogix 18070 Fifteen Mile Road, Fraser, Michigan 48026 www.zipLogix.com

Carbon Monoxide Detector Compliance

The California Carbon Monoxide Poisoning Prevention Act of 2010 requires carbon monoxide detectors to be installed in every "dwelling unit intended for human occupancy" that contain a fossil fuel burning heater, appliance, or fireplace; or that have an attached garage. **Carbon monoxide** is an odorless gas produced whenever any fuel is burned. A **carbon monoxide detector** (CO detector) is a device similar to a smoke detector that signals detection of carbon monoxide in the air.

The Consumer Product Safety Commission recommends installing a CO detector in the hallway near every separate sleeping area of the home. Sellers notify buyers on the TDS whether the property has carbon monoxide devices installed. No separate compliance certification is required. If the property does not have carbon monoxide devices, the buyer may negotiate with the seller for their installation as a condition of sale.

Water-Conserving Plumbing Fixtures Disclosure

A law passed in 2010 (SB 407) requires residential and commercial properties built prior to January 1, 1994 to be retrofitted with water-conserving plumbing fixtures. **Water-conserving plumbing fixtures** include low-flow toilets, urinals, showerheads, and interior faucets.

Since 2014, any remodeling or building alterations requires the replacement of noncompliant plumbing fixtures. Effective 2017, sellers of single-family residences (2019 for sellers of multi-family residences) need to disclose whether the plumbing fixtures in their residences are water-conserving plumbing fixtures or noncompliant fixtures. [CA CC §1101].

Local Retrofit Ordinances

Many local governments impose energy retrofitting and disclosures as a condition of the sale of an existing home. The seller and/or agent should disclose to a prospective buyer the requirements of the various ordinances, as well as who is responsible for compliance.

Typical ordinances include conservation measures on new and/or existing homes including, but not limited to, installing low-flow toilets and showerheads, gas shut-off valves, tempered glass, constructing barriers around swimming pools and spas, and disclosing the **R-value** (resistance to heat loss) of the insulation that has been or will be installed in a remodel.

Real estate agents must know of these **local retrofit ordinances** in order to advise their clients of any additional conditions that must be met prior to the sale.

Pest Control Inspection and Certification Reports

The law does not require that a structural **pest control inspection** be performed prior to transfer of a real property. However, if required by the Purchase Agreement or by the lender, the seller or the seller's agent(s) must deliver to the buyer a copy of the report and written certification, prepared by a registered structural pest control company, regarding the presence or absence of wood-destroying organisms. The inspection report and written certification must be prepared and issued by a registered structural pest control company.

Typically the report is divided into two categories: part one identifies the portions of the property where existing damage, infection, or infestation are noted; and part two indicates the areas that may have impending damage, infection, or infestation. Lenders usually require that any infestation or damage discovered in part one of the report be corrected prior to close of escrow. The seller usually pays for the cost of correction. Since part two of the inspection report does not show actual infestation—just a potential, the seller is not obligated to correct it.

The **Structural Pest Control Inspection & Report Clearance** must be delivered before transfer of title and be reviewed/approved by the buyer. If more than one real estate broker is acting as the seller's agent, the broker who obtained the offer is responsible for delivery of the report in person or by mail, unless the seller directs otherwise in writing. The real estate broker responsible for delivery must retain a record for 3 years. [CA B&P §8519; CA CC §1099; Commissioner's Regulation 2905)]. Anyone can get a copy of the pest control report by requesting it from the Structural Pest Control Board and paying a fee.

OTHER DISCLOSURES

Staying informed is probably the most important task left to the real estate agent. Those who make continuing efforts to learn and stay current on the real estate industry will be the ones to successfully compete in the future. Two excellent sources of current information are the California Bureau of Real Estate and for members, the California Association of REALTORS® (www.car.org).

Disclosures Agents Make to Their Clients

Market Conditions Advisory

Real estate market conditions are fluid; therefore, no one can guarantee that prices will continue to move in a particular direction. The **Market Conditions Advisory** covers several important issues of concern to home buyers such as loan and appraisal contingencies, determine the offering price, and the current

**CALIFORNIA
ASSOCIATION
OF REALTORS®**

MARKET CONDITIONS ADVISORY
(C.A.R. Form MCA, Revised 11/11)

1. MARKET CONDITIONS: Real estate markets are cyclical and can change over time. It is impossible to predict future market conditions with accuracy. In a competitive or "hot" real estate market, there are generally more Buyers than Sellers. This will often lead to multiple buyers competing for the same property. As a result, in order to make their offers more attractive, some Buyers may offer more than originally planned or eliminate certain contingencies in their offers. In a less competitive or "cool" market there are generally more Sellers than Buyers, often causing real estate prices to level off or drop, sometimes precipitously. The sales price of homes being sold as foreclosures and short sales is difficult to anticipate and can affect the value of other homes in the area. Brokers, appraisers, Sellers and Buyers take these "distressed" property sales and listings into consideration when valuing property. In light of the real estate market's cyclical nature it is important that Buyers understand the potential for little or no appreciation in value, or an actual loss in value, of the property they purchase. This Advisory discusses some of the potential risks inherent in changing market conditions.

2. BUYER CONSIDERATIONS:

A. OFFERING PRICE: AS A BUYER, YOU ARE RESPONSIBLE FOR DETERMINING THE PRICE YOU WANT TO OFFER FOR A PROPERTY. Although Brokers may provide you with comparable sales data, generally from information published in the local multiple listing service, you should know that the reporting of this data is often delayed and prices may change, up or down, faster than reported sales indicate. All buyers should be sure they are comfortable with the price they are offering or the price they are accepting in a counter offer. You should be aware of and think about the following: **(i)** If your offer is accepted, the property's value may not increase and may even decrease. **(ii)** If your offer is accepted, you may have "Buyer's remorse" that you paid too much. **(iii)** If your offer is rejected there can be no guarantee that you will find a similar property at the same price. **(iv)** If your offer is rejected, you may not be satisfied that the amount you offered was right for you. Only you can determine that your offer was reasonable and prudent in light of the property and your circumstances.

B. NON-CONTINGENT OFFERS: Most residential purchase agreements contain contingencies allowing a Buyer within a specified period of time to cancel a purchase if: **(i)** the Buyer cannot obtain a loan; **(ii)** is dissatisfied with the property's condition after an inspection; or **(iii)** if the property does not appraise at a certain value. To make their offers more attractive, Buyers will sometimes write offers with few or no contingencies or offer to remove contingencies within a short period of time. In a "hot" market, sellers will sometimes insist that Buyers write offers with no contingencies. Broker recommends that Buyers do not write non-contingent offers and if you do so, you are acting against Broker's advice. However, if you do write a non-contingent offer these are some of the contractual rights you may be giving up:

(1) LOAN CONTINGENCY: If you give up your loan contingency, and you cannot obtain a loan, whether through your fault or the fault of your lender, and as a result, you do not or cannot purchase the property, you may legally be in default under the contract and required to pay damages or forfeit your deposit to the seller.

(2) APPRAISAL CONTINGENCY: If your lender's (or your own) appraiser does not believe the property is worth what you have agreed to pay for it, your lender may not loan the full amount needed for the purchase or may not loan any amount to all because of a low appraisal. As a result, if you do not purchase the property, and you have removed your appraisal contingency, you may legally be in default under the contract and could be required to pay damages to, or forfeit your deposit to, the Seller. The Seller is not obligated to reduce the purchase price to match the appraised value.

Buyer's Initials (_____) (_____)   Seller's Initials (_____) (_____)

Published and Distributed by:
REAL ESTATE BUSINESS SERVICES, INC.
a subsidiary of the California Association of REALTORS®
525 South Virgil Avenue, Los Angeles, California 90020

MCA REVISED 11/11 (PAGE 1 OF 2)

| Reviewed by _____ Date _____ |

MARKET CONDITIONS ADVISORY (MCA PAGE 1 OF 2)

Agent: _____ Phone: _____ Fax: _____ **Prepared using zipForm® software**
Broker: _____

condition of the marketplace (foreclosures, short sales, etc.). The Market Conditions Advisory form is used to document that a broker discussed market conditions with a buyer.

Notice Regarding the Advisability of Title Insurance

In an escrow for a sale (or exchange) of real property in which no title insurance is to be issued, the buyer (or both parties to an exchange) must receive and sign the following notice as a separate document in the escrow:

> **Important:** "In a purchase or exchange of real property, it may be advisable to obtain title insurance in connection with the close of escrow where there may be prior recorded liens and encumbrances which affect your interest in the property being acquired. A new policy of title insurance should be obtained in order to ensure your interest in the property that you are acquiring".

While the law does not expressly assign the duty, it is reasonable to assume that the escrow holder is obligated to deliver the notice. A real estate agent conducting an escrow also would be responsible for delivering the notice.

Broker Must Disclosure the Sales Price

A broker must inform both buyer and seller, in writing, the sale price on a property within one month of close of escrow. The Escrow Closing Statement meets this requirement.

Financing Disclosures

One of the purposes of financing disclosures is to help consumers become better shoppers for loan and settlement services. The required disclosures are given to borrowers at various times during the transaction. Some disclosures spell out the costs associated with the loan or the settlement, outline lender servicing and escrow account practices, and describe business relationships between settlement service providers.

> For example, the U.S. Department of Housing (HUD) requires lenders to provide a home inspection notice entitled **"For Your Protection: Get a Home Inspection"** to prospective borrowers who apply for an FHA loan for any residential property of one-to-four units.

The financing disclosures are discussed later in the course.

Subdivision Disclosures

Subdividers and developers are subject to laws designed to protect buyers when purchasing or leasing lots or parcels in new subdivisions.

Public Report of the Subdivided Lands Law

The **Subdivided Lands Law** is designed to protect buyers from fraud, misrepresentation, or deceit in the marketing of subdivided lots, parcels, units, and **undivided interests** in new subdivisions. This even applies to lands outside the state, if they are being marketed in California. Before any subdivision can be offered for sale in California, the Real Estate Commissioner must determine that the offering meets certain standards and issue a public report. The **public report** is a document disclosing all important facts about the property, its marketing and the financing of the subdivision. These disclosures may alert a potential buyer to any negative aspects in the subdivision (e.g., natural or environmental hazards, unusual costs, restrictions, easements, or financing arrangements). The public report must show that the subdivider (owner) can complete and maintain all improvements and that the lots or parcels can be used for the purpose for which they are being sold.

Preliminary Public Report

It can take many months for a developer to get project approval, once all the proper paperwork is submitted to the Commissioner. During that time, the developer may want to begin marketing the project while waiting for the final public report. By submitting a minimum application filing package, the developer can get a **preliminary public report**, which allows **taking reservations** for the project, but not accepting any non-refundable money or entering into any binding contracts until receiving the final public report from the Commissioner. Preliminary public reports have a one-year term and may be renewed.

Final Public Report

Before a subdivider can actually sell each lot in the project, he or she must give a copy of the Commissioner's **final public report** to the prospective buyer. The buyer signs a receipt for the report on a form approved by the Commissioner stating it has been read. The seller (subdivider) must keep a copy of the statement for 3 years. The subdivider must post a notice in the sales office that says that a copy of the public report must be given to any member of the public who asks for it. The public report is valid for 5 years with any material changes in the development reported to the Commissioner, who then can issue an amendment to the original report.

Violations - Penalties

Anyone who is found guilty of violating the Subdivided Lands Law is punishable by a maximum fine of $10,000; imprisonment for up to one year in the county jail or state prison; or by both fine and imprisonment. The district attorney of each county is responsible for prosecuting violators. In addition to possible fine and imprisonment, the Real Estate Commissioner may impose disciplinary actions for violations of the Subdivided Lands Law.

Interstate Land Sales Full Disclosure Act

The **Interstate Land Sales Full Disclosure Act** (ISLA) regulates land sales when there are two or more states involved. Subdividers must conform to this law if they have 25 or more lots in one state and want to sell them in another state. A **property report** must be given by the developer to each prospective buyer as a protection from less-than-truthful advertising in far-away places. Currently ISLA is regulated by the Bureau of Consumer Financial Protection (CFPB).

SUMMARY

Real estate agents are legally required to explain disclosures to their clients and customers. If real estate agents do not comply with California disclosure law, they become vulnerable to court action.

Real estate agents are responsible for documenting on the **Real Estate Transfer Disclosure Statement** (TDS) all visual and known defects found on the property. The buyer receives a copy of the TDS before the offer to purchase the property. If the buyer receives a copy of the TDS after the offer to purchase the property, the buyer has the option of terminating the contract within three days after receiving the statement.

Real estate agents also provide the buyer with written material to help educate and inform the consumer. Examples of written material are the **Natural Hazard Disclosure Statement**, *Protect Your Family From Lead in Your Home*, and *Homeowner's Guide to Earthquake Safety*. Once the buyer receives the printed material, the real estate agent is not obligated to provide additional information.

Local residential properties in cities and counties in California typically have zoning ordinances and building, health, and safety codes. These ordinances have an effect on a potential buyer's use and enjoyment of residential property. The seller or real estate agent may need to complete an optional form for local disclosures (the Local Option Real Estate Transfer Disclosure Statement). The buyer also receives a copy of this form from the seller or real estate agent.

UNIT 7 REVIEW

■ Matching Exercise

Instructions: Write the letter of the matching term on the blank line before its definition. Answers immediately follow the Multiple Choice Questions.

Terms

A. 100-year flood
B. as is
C. asbestos
D. caveat emptor
E. *Easton v. Strassburger*
F. earthquake fault zone
G. FIRPTA
H. formaldehyde

I. hazardous household waste
J. hazardous waste
K. lead
L. Mello-Roos District
M. mold
N. public report
O. radon

P. red flag
Q. stigmatized property
R. Subdivided Lands Law
S. target housing
T. Transfer Disclosure Statement (TDS)

Definitions

1. _____ Term stating the seller is not responsible for repairing any defect.

2. _____ Materials whose disposal is regulated by the EPA.

3. _____ Housing not exempt from the lead based paint disclosure.

4. _____ Something that alerts a reasonably observant person of a problem.

5. _____ Boundary indicating areas of special flood zone areas.

6. _____ Fungus that reproduces by means of spores.

7. _____ State law that protects buyers when buying homes in new subdivisions.

8. _____ Colorless, odorless, carcinogenesis gas that is detectable by a spectrometer.

9. _____ Detailed statement from the seller describing the condition of the property.

10. _____ Consumer products such as paints, cleaners, stains, varnishes, car batteries, motor oil, and pesticides that contain hazardous components.

11. _____ Special tax is imposed on real property owners within a Community Facilities District.

12. _____ Mineral fiber used in construction materials that causes cancer.

13. _____ An area delineated by state officials to have an active fault with the potential for surface rupture.

14. _____ Chemical organic, carcinogenesis compound found in building materials.

15. _____ Tax withholding requirement if the seller is a foreign person.

◻ Multiple Choice Questions

Instructions: Circle your response and then check your response with the Answer Key that immediately follows the Multiple Choice Questions.

1. The phrase "as is" in real estate refers to _____ conditions.
    a. habitable
    b. observable
    c. concealed
    d. any and all

2. A private seller advertises a single-family home for sale "as is". Since the seller is not using the services of a real estate broker, the seller:
    a. has met the legal requirement of caveat emptor by putting the term "as is" in the newspaper advertisement.
    b. is not obliged to disclose any defects in the property because the property is being sold "as is".
    c. must give a Real Estate Transfer Disclosure Statement to prospective buyers.
    d. is not obliged to give a Real Estate Transfer Disclosure Statement to prospective buyers.

3. All listing brokers must conduct a reasonably competent and diligent visual inspection of the property. Which items must be visually inspected?
    a. Condominium common area
    b. Permits held in the name of the condominium association
    c. Condominium unit
    d. All of these items must be visually inspected by a listing broker.

4. A Real Estate Transfer Disclosure Statement is required in the _____ of one-to-four residential units.
    a. sale
    b. lease
    c. foreclosure
    d. all of the above

5. During negotiations for the purchase of a house, the seller never informed the buyer that the house was served by a septic tank with a failed drainfield. Escrow closed and the buyer moved in. What recourse does the buyer have?

    a. Revoke the offer.

    b. Rescind the contract with the seller based on fraud.

    c. Rescind the contract with the broker.

    d. Sue the title company.

6. Regarding environmental hazards on the property, what is the seller required to do?

    a. Give a copy of the *Environmental Hazards* booklet to the buyer.

    b. Disclose any known environmental hazards to the buyer.

    c. Complete and give the Transfer Disclosure Statement to the buyer.

    d. The seller should do all of the above.

7. Seller Sam listed his newer ranch-style home built in 2002 with broker Bob. Regarding the lead based paint disclosure, Sam must:

    a. give the buyer the pamphlet, *Protect Your Family From Lead in Your Home*.

    b. complete statements verifying completion of the disclosure requirements.

    c. must give the buyers a 10-day opportunity to test for lead.

    d. do none of the above.

8. Broker Logan took a listing on a home. When filling out the NHD, which of the following would Logan not include?

    a. Flood hazard

    b. Seismic hazard

    c. Mold hazard

    d. Fire hazard

9. When a condominium is sold, the seller must, upon request, provide to the buyer:

    a. CC&Rs.

    b. bylaws.

    c. financial statements.

    d. all of the above

10. A broker took a listing on a property where a person died from AIDS. Does the broker have to disclose this information?

    a. Yes, the broker must disclose all material facts.

    b. No, the broker does not have to voluntarily disclose this information.

    c. Yes, but only if the death was within the previous three years.

    d. No, the law does not allow this disclosure to be made.

11. Which state law protects buyers from fraud, misrepresentation, or deceit in the marketing of subdivided lots, and undivided interests in new subdivisions?

    a. Megan's Law

    b. Interstate Land Sales Full Disclosure Act

    c. Subdivided Lands Law

    d. Mello-Roos Community Facilities Act

12. The Interstate Land Sales Full Disclosure Act regulates land sales of:

    a. 5 or more lots.

    b. 10 or more lots.

    c. 15 or more lots.

    d. 25 or more lots.

13. In the sale of real property, a copy of the structural pest control certification report, if requested, must be given to the:

    a. broker.

    b. escrow company.

    c. lender.

    d. buyer.

14. A pest-control company discovered no evidence of termite in a house offered for sale. But it did discover conditions that are likely to lead to infestation. The cost of correcting such conditions is:

    a. always paid by the seller.

    b. always paid by the buyer.

    c. split 50/50 by the seller and the buyer.

    d. paid by the buyer only if he or she wishes to have these conditions corrected.

15. All homes with a fossil fuel burning fireplace or an attached garage must:

    a. install carbon monoxide detectors.

    b. have braced water heaters.

    c. install operable smoke detectors.

    d. have water heater insulation blankets.

UNIT 7 ANSWER KEY

Answers – Matching

1. B	4. P	7. R	10. I	13. F
2. J	5. A	8. O	11. L	14. H
3. S	6. M	9. T	12. C	15. G

Answers – Multiple Choice

1. **(b)** A seller must disclose all known material facts to the buyer; however, an "as is" clause indicates that the seller will not be responsible for the cost of repairing any defect. [Seller's Statutory Disclosures]

2. **(c)** The seller of a 1-4 unit residential property must complete and give a Transfer Disclosure Statement to a prospective buyer. A seller can sell a home "as is" but must still disclose any defects. [Seller's Statutory Disclosures]

3. **(c)** The real estate agent does not have to inspect areas of the property that are not reasonably accessible, public records, and permits. If the property is a condominium, the real estate agent is responsible for inspecting the unit, not the common area. [Seller's Statutory Disclosures]

4. **(a)** The Transfer Disclosure Statement is required on a sale of 1-4 residential units Choice (b) is not correct, because it must be a lease with an option of purchase. [Seller's Statutory Disclosures]

5. **(b)** This is a material fact that should have been disclosed on page 1 of the TDS. If the offer had not been accepted, the buyer could revoke his offer. Once escrow closed, the buyer could rescind the sales contract based on fraud. [Seller's Statutory Disclosures]

6. **(d)** The seller or seller's agent should give a copy of the Environmental Hazards booklet to the buyer. Additionally, the seller must disclose any known environmental hazards on the TDS and give it to the buyer   [Provide Informational Booklets]

7. **(d)** The home was built in 2002, so there is no disclosure requirement. This disclosure pertains to residential housing built before 1978. [Provide Informational Booklets]

8. **(c)** Choices (a), (b), and (d) are included on the statement; mold is discussed on the Transfer Disclosure Statement. [Provide Informational Booklets]

9. **(d)** The owner must furnish CC&Rs, bylaws, and the most recent financial statements. [Seller's Statutory Disclosures]

10. **(b)** Neither the transferor (seller/lessor) nor the agent has to ever voluntarily disclose whether or not a person was afflicted with or died from AIDS. However, if the transferee (buyer/lessee) asks a direct question about a death on the property, the agent should direct the buyer to the seller. [Seller's Statutory Disclosures]

11. **(c)** The Subdivided Lands Law is designed to protect buyers from fraud, misrepresentation, or deceit in the marketing of subdivided lots, parcels, units, and undivided interests in new subdivisions. [Other Disclosures]

12. **(d)** The Interstate Land Sales Full Disclosure Act regulates land sales when there are two or more states involved. Subdividers must conform to this law if they have 25 or more lots in one state and want to sell them in another state. [Other Disclosures]

13. **(d)** The report is given to the buyer. Sometimes the question will have transferee (buyer) as the choice. [Comply with Other Contract Terms]

14. **(d)** The seller usually pays to have problems discovered in Part One of the report corrected. Any potential problems discovered in Part Two are usually paid for by the buyer, if he or she wants to correct the condition. [Comply with Other Contract Terms]

15. **(a)** Carbon monoxide detectors (CO detectors) must be installed in all dwelling units that contain a fossil fuel burning heater, appliance, or fireplace; or that have an attached garage. [Comply with Other Contract Terms]

Unit 8

INTRODUCTION

Escrow and title insurance are not required by law when transferring ownership to real property; however, they are extremely important. To determine if escrow and title insurance are needed, first decide how much your client can afford to lose. If the amount is relatively little, it may not be important to open an escrow. Obviously buying a home may be the most expensive purchase anyone will ever make; therefore, protections offered by escrow and title insurance are invaluable.

In the preceding units, you learned about ownership interests and real estate contracts, which usually lead to a transfer of that interest.

The process for the transfer of ownership is the subject of this Unit. In this Unit, you will learn about escrow principles and rules, the relationship of the escrow holder and real estate agent, designating the escrow holder, and title insurance.

Learning Objectives

After completing this Unit, you should be able to:

7A   recognize escrow rules and procedures.

7B   recall the purpose of title insurance and the types of policies.

7C   categorize types of legal descriptions for real property.

7D   determine tax issues in transferring real property.

ESCROW

For a large number of people, escrow is a mysterious, obscure process. They do not know what "going to escrow" means, or how you open an escrow. However, there is no real mystery about it. It is a period during which the paperwork required for the sale of real property is processed.

An **escrow** is a small and short-lived trust arrangement. In California, when ownership transfers from one person to another there is usually a neutral third party, called an **escrow agent,** handling the details of the sale. After the principals of a sale make an agreement, an agent normally opens escrow on their behalf.

An **escrow holder,** otherwise known as an escrow company, or some other eligible person, acts as a neutral agent of both buyer and seller. The escrow holder follows the directions of the principals, collects, and distributes documents and money as agreed upon in the purchase agreement.

If **escrow instructions** are drawn, they must reflect the understanding and agreement of the principals, who may not always be a buyer and seller, since transactions involving the sale of real estate are not the only kind that require the use of an escrow. Any time a neutral third party is needed to handle documents or money, such as leases, sales of personal property, sales of securities, loans, or mobile home sales, an escrow might be required. For the purpose of this unit, we will discuss escrow as it relates to the sale of real estate.

No one is required by law to use an escrow for any of the above transactions, including the sale of real property. However, when a buyer and seller reach an agreement about the sale of property, including terms and price, it is usually advisable to invite a neutral third party to handle the details of completing the agreement. If the contract is not handled by an outside professional whose business it is to conduct escrows, misunderstanding, or even criminal or innocent negligence, on the part of the principals could be the cause of loss to one or both parties.

After escrow is opened, it is the escrow holder's job to follow the buyer's and seller's instructions and request all parties involved to observe the terms and conditions of the contract. The escrow holder coordinates communication between the principals, the agents involved and any other professionals—such as the lender, title company, or pest control company, whose services are called for in the escrow instructions.

The principals trust that the escrow holder will carry out their wishes, and the escrow holder has a duty to be trustworthy, as the agent of both parties. As a neutral third party, the escrow holder does not make decisions for buyer or seller and may only operate at the direction of all parties to a transaction.

Designating the Escrow Holder

The escrow holder may be any disinterested third party and the choice of an escrow agent is always that of the buyer and seller. However, they probably do not have a relationship with an escrow agent and may rely on the advice of their real estate broker.

Basic Requirements for a Valid Escrow

Every sale escrow has two basic requirements to be valid: a binding contract between the buyer and seller and conditional delivery of transfer documents and funds to a neutral third party, e.g., escrow. The binding contract can be a purchase agreement, agreement of sale, exchange agreement, option, or mutual escrow instructions of the buyer and seller.

Binding Contract

The **binding contract** can be any legal agreement, such as a residential purchase agreement, exchange agreements, option agreements, or jointly executed bilateral or individually executed unilateral escrow instructions evidencing a mutual agreement of the buyer and the seller.

The California Association of REALTORS® Residential Purchase Agreement and Joint Escrow Instructions (purchase agreement) combines the strength of the offer to purchase and escrow instructions into one contract. Because the purchase agreement is the original agreement between the buyer and seller, it will reflect the mutual and agreed-upon desires of the parties when it becomes the actual escrow instructions. Any mutual changes are made using an addendum to the original contract rather than amendments to escrow instructions.

**CALIFORNIA
ASSOCIATION
OF REALTORS**®

PURCHASE AGREEMENT ADDENDUM No. _____
(May Also Be Used With Counter Offer)
(C.A.R. Form PAA, Revised 4/11)

This is an addendum to the ☐ California Residential Purchase Agreement, ☐ Counter Offer No. _____ , ☐ Other _____
_____ , ("Agreement"), dated _____ , on
property known as _____ ("Property"),
between _____ ("Buyer"),
and _____ ("Seller").
(The definitions in the California Residential Purchase Agreement are applicable to this Purchase Agreement Addendum.)

1. ☐ **CANCELLATION OF PRIOR SALE; BACK-UP OFFER** (If checked): This Agreement is in back-up position number _____ ,
   and is contingent upon written cancellation of any prior contracts and related escrows ("Prior Contracts") between Seller and other
   buyers. Seller and other buyers may mutually agree to modify or amend the terms of Prior Contracts. Buyer may cancel this
   Agreement in writing at any time before Seller provides Buyer Copies of written cancellations of Prior Contracts Signed by all parties
   to those contracts. If Seller is unable to provide such written Signed cancellations to Buyer by _____ (date),
   then either Buyer or Seller may cancel the Agreement in writing.
   A. **BUYER'S DEPOSIT CHECK** shall be: **(i)** held uncashed until Copies of the written cancellations Signed by all parties to the Prior
      Contracts are provided to Buyer; OR **(ii)** (if checked) ☐ immediately handled as provided in the Agreement.
   B. **TIME PERIODS** in the Agreement for Investigations, contingencies, covenants and other obligations **(i)** shall begin on the Day
      After Seller provides Buyer Copies of Signed cancellations of Prior Contracts; OR **(ii)** (if checked) ☐ all time periods shall begin
      as provided in this Agreement. However, if the date for Close Of Escrow is a specific calendar date, that date shall NOT be
      extended, unless agreed to in writing by Buyer and Seller.

2. ☐ **SELLER TO REMAIN IN POSSESSION AFTER CLOSE OF ESCROW** (If checked): This provision is intended for short-term
   occupancy (i.e. less than 30 Days). If occupancy is intended to be for 30 Days or longer, use Residential Lease After Sale (C.A.R.
   Form RLAS). **Note: Local rent control or other Law regarding tenant's rights may impact Buyer's and Seller's rights and
   obligations.**
   A. **TERM:** Seller to remain in possession of Property for _____ **Days** After Close Of Escrow (or ☐ _____).
      Seller has no right to remain in possession beyond this term and may be responsible for court awarded damages if Seller does
      remain.
   B. **COMPENSATION:** Seller agrees to pay Buyer (i) for the term specified in 2A, $ _____ per Day (or ☐
      _____), and (ii) a security deposit in the amount of $ _____ . Seller shall deposit
      such funds with escrow holder prior to Close Of Escrow or such funds shall be withheld from Seller's proceeds. At Close Of
      Escrow, compensation and security deposit will be released to Buyer (or ☐ held in escrow).
   C. **LATE CHARGE/NSF CHECKS:** If any payment from Seller to Buyer is required outside of escrow, and any such payment is not
      received by Buyer within **5 (or ☐ _____) Days** After date due, Seller shall pay to Buyer an additional sum of
      $ _____ as a Late Charge. If a check is returned for non-sufficient funds ("NSF"), Seller shall pay to
      Buyer $25.00 as an NSF charge. Seller and Buyer agree that these charges represent a fair and reasonable estimate of the costs
      Buyer may incur by reason of Seller's late or NSF payment. Buyer's acceptance of any Late Charge or NSF fee shall not
      constitute a waiver as to any default by Seller.
   D. **UTILITIES:** Seller agrees to pay for all utilities and services, and the following charges: _____
      _____ except _____ , which shall be paid for by Buyer.
   E. **ENTRY:** Seller shall make Property available to Buyer for the purpose of entering to make necessary or agreed repairs, or to
      supply necessary or agreed services, or to show Property to prospective or actual purchasers, tenants, mortgagees, lenders,
      appraisers or contractors. Buyer and Seller agree that 24 hours notice (oral or written) shall be reasonable and sufficient notice.
      In an emergency, Buyer may enter Property at any time without prior notice.
   F. **MAINTENANCE:** Seller shall maintain the Property, including pool, spa, landscaping and grounds, and all personal property
      included in the sale in substantially the same condition as on the date of Acceptance of the Agreement. Except as provided in the
      Agreement, Seller shall not make alterations to the Property without Buyer's written consent.
   G. **ASSIGNMENT; SUBLETTING:** Seller shall not assign or sublet all or any part of the Property, or assign or transfer the right to
      occupy the Property. Any assignment, subletting or transfer of the Property by voluntary act of Seller, by operation of Law or
      otherwise, without Buyer's prior written consent shall give Buyer the right to terminate Seller's right to possession.
   H. **SELLER'S OBLIGATIONS UPON DELIVERY OF POSSESSION:** Upon delivery of possession to Buyer, Seller shall deliver the
      Property in the condition and on the terms provided in the Agreement.
   I. **INSURANCE:** Seller's personal property (including vehicles) is not insured by Buyer, and, if applicable, owner's association,
      against loss or damage due to fire, theft, vandalism, rain, water, criminal or negligent acts of others, or any other cause. Seller is
      to carry Seller's own insurance to protect Seller from such loss.
   J. **WAIVER:** The waiver of any breach shall not be construed as a continuing waiver of the same or any subsequent breach.
   K. **OTHER TERMS AND CONDITIONS/SUPPLEMENTS:** _____
      _____
      _____

Buyer's Initials (_____) (_____)
Seller's Initials (_____) (_____)
Reviewed by _____ Date _____

**EQUAL HOUSING
OPPORTUNITY**

PURCHASE AGREEMENT ADDENDUM (PAA   PAGE 1 OF 2)

Agent:	Phone:	Fax:	Prepared using WINForms® software
Broker:			

Property Address: _____ Date: _____

3. ☐ **TENANT TO REMAIN IN POSSESSION** (If checked): Buyer shall take Property subject to the rights of existing tenants. Seller shall, within **7 (or** ☐ _____) **Days** After Acceptance, deliver to Buyer Copies of all: estoppel certificates sent to and received back from tenants; leases; rental agreements; and current income and expense statements ("Rental Documents"). Seller shall give Buyer written notice of any changes to existing leases or tenancies or new agreements to lease or rent ("Proposed Changes") at least **7 (or** _____) **Days** prior to any Proposed Changes. Buyer's approval of the Rental Documents and Proposed Changes is a contingency of the Agreement. Buyer shall, within **5 (or** ☐ _____) **Days** After receipt of Rental Documents or Proposed Changes remove the applicable contingency or cancel the Agreement. Seller shall transfer to Buyer, through escrow, all unused tenant deposits. No warranty is made concerning compliance with governmental restrictions, if any, limiting the amount of rent that can lawfully be charged, and/or the maximum number of persons who can lawfully occupy the Property, unless otherwise agreed in writing.

4. ☐ **SECONDARY OR ASSUMED LOAN** (If checked): Obtaining the secondary loan or assumption below, and Buyer's approval of such assumed financing, is a contingency of this Agreement. Buyer shall act diligently and in good faith to obtain the designated financing.

    A. ☐ **SECONDARY LOAN:**

        (1) The loan shall be conventional financing or, if checked, ☐ SELLER FINANCING, ☐ OTHER. The loan shall be at a fixed fixed rate not to exceed _____ %, or ☐ an adjustable rate loan with an initial rate not to exceed _____ %. Regardless of the type of loan, Buyer shall pay points not to exceed _____ % of the loan amount.

        (2) (i) Within **17 (or** ☐ _____) **Days** After Acceptance, Buyer shall, as specified in the Agreement, remove this contingency or cancel this Agreement.

        OR (ii) (If checked) ☐ secondary loan contingency shall remain in effect until the loan is funded.

    B. ☐ **ASSUMPTION OF EXISTING LOAN:**

        (1) Buyer will assume an existing note and deed of trust. Seller shall, within **5 (or** _____) **Days** After Acceptance, request from Lender, and upon receipt provide to Buyer, Copies of all applicable notes and deeds of trust, loan balances and current interest rates. Differences between estimated and actual loan balances shall be adjusted at Close Of Escrow by cash down payment. Impound accounts, if any, shall be assigned and charged to Buyer and credited to Seller. If this is an assumption of a VA Loan, the sale is contingent upon Seller being provided a release of liability and substitution of eligibility, unless otherwise agreed in writing.

        (2) (i) Within **17 (or** ☐ _____) **Days** After Acceptance, Buyer shall, as specified in the Agreement, remove this contingency or cancel this Agreement. However, if the assumed loan documents are not provided to Buyer within **7 Days After Acceptance,** Buyer has **5 (or** ☐ _____) **Days** After receipt of these documents, or the fixed time specified in 4B(2), whichever occurs last, to remove this contingency or cancel the Agreement.

        OR (ii) (If checked) ☐ assumed loan contingency shall remain in effect until the assumption is approved.

5. ☐ **COURT CONFIRMATION** (If checked): This Agreement is contingent upon court confirmation on or before _____ (date). If court confirmation is not obtained by that date, Buyer may cancel this Agreement in writing. Court confirmation may be required in probate, conservatorship, guardianship, receivership, bankruptcy or other proceedings. The court may allow open, competitive bidding, resulting in Property being sold to the highest bidder. Broker recommends that Buyer appear at the court confirmation hearing. Buyer understands that **(i)** Broker and others may continue to market the Property and **(ii)** Broker may represent other competitive bidders prior to and at the court confirmation.

By signing below Buyer and Seller acknowledge that each has read, understands, received a copy of and agrees to the terms of this Purchase Agreement Addendum.

Date _____   Date _____

Buyer _____   Seller _____

Buyer _____   Seller _____

Published and Distributed by:
REAL ESTATE BUSINESS SERVICES, INC.
a subsidiary of the California Association of REALTORS®
525 South Virgil Avenue, Los Angeles, California 90020

PAA REVISED 4/11 (PAGE 2 OF 2)

Reviewed by _____ Date _____

PURCHASE AGREEMENT ADDENDUM (PAA PAGE 2 OF 2)

An escrow is opened when a real estate agent brings the signed purchase agreement to the escrow holder, who makes a copy and accepts it by signing off in the required box in the document. The escrow holder should be concerned that the contract is complete, fully signed, and initialed before accepting it. The contract must be valid before becoming instructions for the escrow.

In addition to the purchase agreement as escrow instructions, an escrow holder will submit acceptance, or additional escrow instructions, for buyer and seller signatures. These instructions include any other terms that need to be agreed upon by buyer and seller to complete the escrow.

Conditional Delivery

A **conditional delivery** of transfer documents and funds, the second requirement for a valid escrow, means the seller will deliver a signed instrument of conveyance (e.g., grant deed) and the buyer and/or the lender will deliver to escrow whatever funds are required for the sale, per the contract. In addition, the escrow agent will hold the security for any loan (trust deed) conditionally until directed by the terms of the escrow. The escrow agent will keep documents and funds until all other terms of the escrow are completed, and then distribute them according to the expressed conditions of the escrow.

Sometime before the escrow closes, the seller will be asked to sign a grant deed conveying title to the buyer. Because the seller will sign over the ownership to the buyer before getting the money, the escrow holder is instructed to hold the signed deed until funds from the buyer are deposited in escrow and all the other terms of the escrow have been met. Conditional delivery of the grant deed has been made.

Toward the end of the escrow period, the buyer will be asked to sign a note and trust deed for the loan. The buyer is promising to pay back the money, using the property as security for the loan. Escrow has not closed, and the buyer does not own the house yet. Nor has the seller been given the promised money, but the note and trust deed are signed and deposited into escrow, conditionally, until all other terms have been met. At that time the money will be released by the lender to escrow.

Completed Escrow

Properly drawn and executed escrow instructions become an enforceable contract. An escrow is termed a "**completed escrow**" when all terms of the instructions have been met.

After the escrow has been completed and recorded, the buyer gets a grant deed, and the seller gets the money. The escrow closes shortly thereafter.

General Escrow Principles and Rules

Once escrow instructions or the purchase agreement as escrow instructions have been signed by the buyer and seller and returned to the escrow holder, neither party may unilaterally change the escrow instructions. Any changes must be made by mutual agreement between the buyer and seller.

The escrow agent does not have the authority to make changes in the contract upon the direction of either the buyer or seller, unless both agree to the change in the form of an amendment or addendum to the purchase agreement.

Also, it should be noted, the broker has no authority whatsoever to amend or change any part of the escrow

Escrow instructions must be understood by the principals to the escrow and must be mutually binding.

instructions without the knowledge of the principals. The written consent of both buyer and seller, in the form of an amendment to the original instructions or an addendum to the purchase agreement, must be given before any change may be made.

> Example: The Clarks and the Marshalls signed escrow instructions in June. The agreement reflected a sales price of $450,000, with $90,000 as a down payment. After signing the instructions, however, the buyers decided they only wanted to put $80,000 down, and told the escrow officer to change the instructions. An amendment was written for them to sign, and a copy sent to the sellers to sign.
>
> The buyers were disappointed when the Clarks did not want to change the contract and refused to sign the amendment. When the Marshalls wanted to back out, the escrow officer reminded them that they had a mutually binding legal agreement with the sellers. Neither side could change any part of the agreement, including terminating it, without the written agreement of the other.

As agent for both parties to an escrow, the escrow agent is in a position of trust. By operating as a dual agent, the escrow holder sits between the buyer and seller as a stakeholder with an obligation to both sides.

A Neutral Escrow Officer Must Observe Certain Rules

1. Escrow instructions must be understood by the principals to the escrow and must be mutually binding. Carefully written instructions or the offer to purchase are very clear about the agreement between the buyer and seller. Each party must understand his or her obligation to carry out the terms of the contract without assuming the escrow holder has any power to force compliance. The escrow holder may not act unless directed by the principals.

2. The escrow holder does not get personally involved in disagreements between the buyer and seller, nor act as a negotiator for the principals. Escrow instructions make each party's obligations and agreements clear, and it is up to the buyer and seller to keep the promises they each made in their agreement with the other.

3. An escrow agent usually is not an attorney. The escrow agent must advise anyone seeking legal advice to get counsel from a lawyer.

4. An escrow agent has a limited capacity as agent for buyer and seller and may only perform acts described in the contents of escrow instructions. While acting as a dual agent, the escrow officer must operate in the best interests of both parties, without special preference to either. The escrow agent may serve each principal after escrow closes, in dealing with his or her separate interests.

5. All parties must sign escrow instructions or the offer to purchase as escrow instructions for the contract to be binding. An escrow is officially open when both buyer and seller have signed the instructions and delivered them to escrow.

6. If separate escrow instructions are written, they must be clear and certain in their language. When there is a conflict between the signed instructions and the original agreement of the principals, the signed instructions will prevail as long as they reflect the intent of the parties.

7. All documents to be recorded must be sent to the title company in a timely manner (as quickly as possible), and all interested parties should receive copies of recorded documents.

8. Escrow instructions should specify which documents or funds the escrow holder might accept.

9. Overdrawn escrow trust accounts (debit balances) are prohibited by law.

10. Information regarding any transaction is held in trust by the escrow officer and may not be released to anyone without written permission of the principals.

11. An escrow holder has a duty to disclose to the principals any previously undisclosed information that might affect them. An amendment would be drawn at the direction of the buyer and seller to reflect any change as a result of new disclosures.

12. A high degree of trust and good customer service must be provided by an escrow holder.

13. An escrow holder must remain strictly neutral regarding the buyer's and the seller's interests.

14. Escrow records and files must be maintained daily. A systematic review of open escrow files will make sure no procedure has been overlooked, or time limit ignored.

15. Before closing an escrow, all files must be audited carefully.

16. All checks or drafts must have cleared before any funds may be released to the seller.

17. Escrow must close in a timely manner, according to the agreement between buyer and seller. A prompt settlement must be made to all principals.

What Each Party Does During the Escrow Process

The Seller

As soon as possible following the opening of escrow, the seller should furnish escrow with the following items:

- escrow instructions signed by the seller(s).
- executed deed to the buyer with the escrow holder.
- evidence of pest inspection and any required repair work.
- latest available tax and assessment bills and any other statements or bills which are to be prorated through escrow.
- other required documents, such as tax receipts, addresses of mortgage holders, insurance policies, equipment warranties, or home warranty contracts, etc.
- fire insurance policies, if they are to be assigned to the buyer.
- certificates or releases showing satisfaction of mechanic's liens, security agreements (chattel mortgages), judgments, or mortgages that are to be paid off through escrow.
- executed bill of sale covering any personal property to be conveyed to the buyer, together with an inventory of the items for the buyer's approval.

- assignment to buyer of all leases affecting the property.

- subordination or other agreement required by the purchase contract, to be approved by the parties through escrow.

Sellers should always keep copies of any documents and instruments they sign, deliver to, or receive from any party in the real estate transaction.

The Buyer

As soon as possible after the opening of escrow, the buyer should furnish the escrow holder with certain documents and information, and should review or inspect personally all of the following items:

- escrow instructions signed by all purchasers.

- deposit the funds required, in addition to any borrowed funds, to pay the purchase price with the escrow holder.

- arrange for any borrowed funds to be delivered to the escrow holder.

- deposit funds sufficient for escrow and closing costs.

- review and approve the preliminary report for the subject property to make sure that there are no items of record affecting the property that have not already been approved by the buyer.

- review and approve any Conditions, Covenants, and Restrictions affecting the property, whether of record or not.

- review and approve structural pest control and other reports to be delivered through escrow.

- confirm the terms of any mortgages or deeds of trust to be assumed by the buyer or those that will remain an encumbrance on the property.

- carefully review all new loan documents prior to signing.

- compare the terms of the purchase contract, escrow instructions, title report, and deed to make sure there are no discrepancies in the transaction documents.

- fulfill any other conditions specified in the escrow instructions.

- review and approve any items to be prorated in escrow.

- reinspect the property to determine that it is in the same condition as it was when the buyer made the purchase offer. Recheck for any undisclosed items that might affect the use of the property, such as: party walls, access roads to other properties, irrigation canals or ditches, common drives, or persons in occupancy or possession of the property, which the county records would not disclose.

Buyers should always keep copies of any documents and instruments they sign, deliver to, or receive from any party in the real estate transaction.

The Lender

A lender involved in the transfer is responsible to:

- deposit proceeds of the loan to the purchaser.
- direct the escrow holder on the conditions under which the loan funds may be used.

The Escrow Holder

The escrow holder follows the directions of the principals in the transaction and:

- opens the order for title insurance.
- obtains approvals from the buyer on title insurance report, pest, and other inspections.
- receives funds from the buyer and/or any lender.
- prorates insurance, taxes, rents, etc.
- disburses funds for title insurance, recordation fees, real estate commissions, lien clearance, etc.
- prepares a final statement for each party indicating amount to be disbursed for services and any further amounts necessary to close escrow.
- records deed and loan documents, and delivers the deed to the buyer, loan documents to the lender and funds to the seller, thereby closing the escrow.

Escrow Procedures

Escrow procedures vary according to local custom. For example, in Northern California title companies handle closings through escrow, whereas in Southern California escrow companies or banks conduct escrows. It is typical in Southern California for sellers to pay the title insurance premium and transfer tax and to split the escrow costs with the buyer.

Not only do escrow procedures differ between Northern and Southern California, they also vary somewhat from county to county. In spite of the differences, there are certain procedures that are followed during the regular course of all escrows.

Open Escrow

The person who usually opens escrow, if there is a real estate agent involved, is the selling agent. That person usually has an earnest money check that must be deposited into escrow or some other trust account no more than three business days after buyer and seller have signed the deposit receipt.

At the first opportunity, the real estate agent must take the buyer's check to the escrow officer to put it in a trust account. The agent then gives the escrow officer all the information needed to draw escrow instructions, or may give the escrow holder the original signed purchase agreement, which then becomes the escrow instructions. If instructions are being drawn, usually within a day or two, computer-generated instructions will be ready for the buyer and seller to sign. The instructions, as you recall, reflect the agreement between the buyer and seller as seen in the offer to purchase.

If there is no real estate agent involved, the principals may go to the escrow office and ask the escrow officer to prepare instructions according to their agreement.

Prepare Escrow Instructions

The escrow is officially opened when the escrow holder accepts the purchase agreement that has been signed by all parties to the escrow. When escrow instructions are drawn, the escrow holder prepares them on a computer-generated form, with details of the particular transaction completed in the blank spaces on the form. All parties sign identical instructions, with the exception of the commission agreement that is prepared for the seller to sign—if the seller in fact is paying the commission.

Buyer and seller sign the instructions, which are then returned to the escrow holder who follows the directions in the agreement to complete the escrow.

Imagine you are involved in the sale of your home. The following would probably be included in your escrow instructions or purchase agreement. In California, the purchase agreement becomes the escrow instructions.

1. **Purchase Price:** The **purchase price** is the amount of consideration the buyer and seller have agreed upon for the sale of the property.

2. **Terms:** The buyer and seller agree on how the buyer will purchase the property: cash, new loan, loan assumption, VA, or FHA loan, seller to carry a trust deed, trade, or any other special agreements provided in the contract between buyer and seller. This section describes the amount of the down payment and the terms of any loans for which the buyer will apply.

3. **Vesting**: The way title will be taken is called **vesting**. The buyer will take title in one of the following ways: sole ownership, joint tenancy, tenants in common, or tenancy in partnership. How the buyer will take title may be important for tax or inheritance purposes and the escrow holder must be directed how to draw the deed to reflect the wishes of the buyer.

4. **Matters of Record**: Buyer and seller may agree on some matter of record or, in other words, some matter that is recorded, affecting the property. It may be an easement, an existing street bond or a trust deed. An agreement may be made about who will be responsible for whatever exists as a recorded encumbrance on the title at the time of the sale.

5. **Closing**: Buyer and seller will agree on how long they want the escrow to last. They will mention a specific length of time for the escrow and instruct the escrow holder accordingly.

6. **Inspections**: Buyer and seller will agree on whether to have certain inspections of the property before the close of escrow, such as a pest control inspection, property inspection to identify any plumbing, electrical, or structural problems, and a soil inspection to check for slippage or unstable compaction. The buyer's approval of the reports will be a contingency of the sale and must be mentioned in the escrow instructions.

7. **Prorations**: The division of expenses and income between the buyer and seller as of the date of closing is known as **proration**. Some items that are prorated are taxes, rental deposits or income, and insurance premiums. The reason for prorations is that some payments may have been made by the seller for a time period beyond the agreed-upon date of closing of escrow, or the seller may be in arrears on taxes or insurance. The escrow holder debits or credits the seller or buyer, depending on the escrow closing date. Normally, proration is based on a 30-day month and a 360-day year. Examples of calculating proration are found in Appendix A.

8. **Possession**: The buyer and seller will have agreed on when the buyer can move into the house, and the escrow instructions must reflect their agreement on the date the buyer will take possession of the property. The close of escrow could be the date of possession, or sometimes the seller will rent the property back from the buyer after the close of escrow. In that case, a lease agreement should be signed and deposited in escrow.

9. **Documents**: The escrow holder will need to know which documents to prepare, have signed by the proper party, and record at the close of escrow. Usually, these will be a grant deed and a trust deed.

10. **Disbursements**: The escrow holder must settle the accounts of the buyer and seller according to the escrow instructions. At the close of escrow, each party receives a closing statement of costs and charges along with a final distribution of funds.

Order Title Search

The escrow officer, after escrow has been opened, orders a search of the title of the subject property. The title company searches the records for any encumbrances or liens against the property, checks to make sure the seller is the owner of record, and inspects the history of ownership, or chain of title. The purpose is to ensure that all transfers of ownership have been recorded correctly, there are no unexplained gaps, and there are no liens or encumbrances, which will not be released. After completing this search, the title company prepares a preliminary report. The **preliminary report** is an offer to issue a policy of title insurance covering a particular estate or interest in land subject to stated exceptions.

The buyer is allowed a certain number of days to approve this preliminary title report. Buyer approval is important to eliminate surprises regarding the title as the escrow progresses. The escrow holder should notify the buyer and seller if there is any difference in the preliminary report and the escrow instructions, by way of an addendum for information only.

As you recall, the escrow agent is a neutral party and only has the authority to do what is described in the escrow instructions. The escrow officer must wait for instructions about what to do next. The preliminary title report is the foundation for the title insurance policy insuring the buyer's title as instructed by the buyer and seller in the escrow instructions.

Example: The Clarks and the Marshalls instructed their escrow officer to order a preliminary title search. The Marshalls had three days to approve the report, as a contingency of the sale. When they examined it, however, they found there was a bond against the property for street repairs. They had not been aware of it.

The bond was a lien in the amount of $3,500. The buyers could not approve the preliminary title report until the issue was cleared up. An agreement about who would pay the bond had to be reached by the buyers and sellers, then new instructions given to the escrow officer, who would prepare an amendment for both parties' signatures, to indicate their agreement.

Request Demands and/or Beneficiary Statements

The escrow officer must also ensure that existing loans are paid off, or assumed, depending on the agreement of the buyer and seller. If the existing loan, or the seller's debt, is going to be paid off with proceeds from the sale, a demand from the lender holding the note and trust deed is needed, along with the unpaid principal balance and any other amounts that are due. The escrow officer requests a **demand for payoff** of a loan from the lender who holds a loan against the subject property. The exact amount of loans that are to be paid off must be known so the escrow officer's accounting will be correct at the close of escrow.

If an existing loan is going to be assumed, or taken subject to, a beneficiary statement is requested by the escrow holder from the lender. A **beneficiary statement** is a statement of the unpaid condition of a loan and describes the condition of the debt.

The escrow agent follows instructions about financing the property, and prepares any documents necessary for completing the escrow at the close. These might be a note and trust deed or assumption papers.

Example: The buyers are obtaining an adjustable loan for $360,000. The down payment will be $90,000, to make the purchase price of $450,000. The existing $250,000 loan on the property is held by UV Community Bank. The existing loan will be paid off when the buyer's new loan is funded, and the seller will get the remainder of $110,000 along with the down payment.

UV Community Bank is notified of the expected payoff and asked by the escrow officer to send a statement of the unpaid balance and condition of the existing loan. This is known as a request for demand for payoff.

Accept Reports

The parties to an escrow may request any number of reports about the condition of the property. The escrow holder is asked in the instructions to accept any reports submitted into escrow. These may include a structural pest control report (termite report), property inspection report, soil condition report, or environmental report. Any approval from the buyer or seller about a report is held in escrow until needed or given to the appropriate party at the close of escrow.

New Loan Instructions and Documents

Escrow accepts loan documents or instructions about financing the subject property and completes them as directed. The escrow agent gets the buyer's approval of and signature on loan documents, and receives and disburses loan funds as instructed.

Fire Insurance Policies

The parties to an escrow will have agreed on fire insurance policies and will instruct the escrow officer accordingly. The escrow holder will accept, hold, and deliver any policies and will follow instructions about transferring them. A lender will require fire insurance, and will expect the escrow holder and the buyer to be accountable for either a new policy or the transfer of an existing one.

Settlement

The escrow holder will be instructed by the buyer and seller about proration and other accounting to be done at the close of escrow. **Proration** is the adjustment of interest, taxes, insurance, etc., on a pro-rata basis as of the closing or agreed-upon date. Hazard insurance policies that are terminated prior to the expiration date at the request of the insured are subject to a short rate cancellation fee. A **short rate cancellation fee** is a fee (or penalty) charged to the person who cancels the insurance policy before it expires. The money returned is the unused premium minus administrative expenses. However, if the insurance company cancels the policy early, there is no penalty.

The escrow holder will prepare a settlement (closing) statement for all parties to the escrow. A **settlement statement** is a complete breakdown of all cash received, all charges and credits made, and all costs involved in the transaction. The statement shows how all closing costs and prepaid expenses are allocated between the buyer and seller. In most transactions, the seller pays for title insurance and any delinquent assessment liens that would show up as debits. If the seller prepaid the property taxes, he or she would expect to get the unused portion back, which would show up as a credit.

> ABC - **A**ssumption by the **B**uyer is a **C**redit

When a buyer assumes an existing loan, the assumption is shown on the closing statement as a debit to the seller and a credit to the buyer.

The borrower and lender will have agreed on impound accounts, and the escrow holder will be guided on how to handle the credits and debits. An **impound account** is a trust account set up for funds set aside for future, recurring costs relating to a property. After the escrow agent completes the accounting, the agent tells the buyer to deliver the down payment (usually a cashier's check is required), plus other escrow costs, to the escrow office.

> **Review - Prorations Normally Include**
> - Interest
> - Premiums on hazard (fire) insurance
> - Security deposits and rents (if the property is a rental)
> - Seller's current property taxes

At this time, the buyers sign the loan documents, and any other paperwork required for the financing is completed. If all is in order, the loan will be funded and the money sent to the escrow office along with the buyer's funds. Then the escrow may close.

Audit File

At the close of escrow, the escrow officer must examine each file to make sure all accounting has been accurate, and that escrow instructions have been followed. A **cash reconciliation statement** is completed by the escrow holder and closing statements are prepared for all principals.

Recording

The escrow holder records all transaction documents as instructed by the buyer and seller after a final check of the title company records to be sure nothing has changed since the preliminary title search was done. Then the title company will issue a policy of title insurance to insure the buyer's title. Documents that might require recording are the grant deed, trust deed, contract of sale, or option.

Closing the Escrow

Once all the terms and conditions of the instructions of both parties have been fulfilled, the last job of the escrow holder is to **close the escrow**. The escrow officer gives closing statements to buyer and seller, disburses all money, and delivers all documents to the proper parties after making sure all documents have been recorded by the title company. The seller gets a check for the proceeds of the sale minus escrow fees, real estate commissions, loan payoffs and all other costs of selling, and any pertinent documents; and the buyer gets a grant deed.

Termination of an Escrow

Full performance, by completion of the escrow, terminates the escrow. The authority to conduct an escrow is mutually given by the buyer and seller in the escrow instructions and may be terminated by mutual agreement. Neither party may end the escrow without the agreement of the other, in writing. Also, the escrow officer may not return any funds or documents to either party without agreement from all parties.

During escrow, the escrow officer is an agent for both buyer and seller, and must operate from the original escrow instructions. When they instruct the escrow agent to prepare an amendment canceling the escrow, a buyer and seller mutually end their agreement after they have both signed the amendment.

Rights and Obligations of the Parties to an Escrow

A buyer and a seller are known as principals in an escrow. The escrow holder is a neutral third party who is a dual agent for buyer and seller. A real estate agent is not a party to an escrow unless he or she is the buyer or the seller.

A buyer is the party purchasing the property and who will receive a deed conveying the title.

A seller is the owner of record who must deliver the title agreed upon in the contract.

An escrow agent is an impartial third party who collects all documents and money through the escrow and transfers them to the proper parties at the close of escrow.

An escrow agent may be a bank, savings and loan, title insurance company, attorney, real estate broker, or an escrow company. A real estate broker may act as an escrow agent in the course of a regular transaction for which a real estate license is necessary. The broker may conduct the escrow as a service only if he or she is the listing or selling broker to the subject sale.

Escrow Companies Must be Incorporated

The Commissioner of Business Oversight only licenses qualified corporations as escrow companies. An individual cannot be licensed as an escrow holder/ agent. A bond based upon predicted yearly average transactions and trust fund use must be furnished by an applicant for an escrow office license. A bond must be posted by all parties (officers, directors, trustees, and employees) having access to money or securities being held by the escrow company as safety against loss. Banks, savings and loans, title insurance companies, attorneys, and real estate brokers are exempt from Commissioner of Business Oversight licensing requirements.

Audit

An escrow company must keep accounts and records that can be examined by the Commissioner of Business Oversight. A yearly inspection prepared by an independent certified public accountant, describing operations, must be delivered to the Commissioner.

Prohibitions

- Referral fees may not be paid by an escrow company to anyone as a reward for sending business to them.

- Commissions may not be paid to a real estate broker until the closing of an escrow.

- Blank escrow instructions to be filled in after signing are not acceptable. Initials must be placed wherever there is a change or deletion.

- Information regarding an escrow may only be provided to parties of the escrow.

- Copies of escrow instructions must be provided to anyone signing them.

Agency

An escrow agent holds a limited agency, or authority. Any duties to be conducted must be mentioned specifically in escrow instructions or they are not authorized by the buyer and seller. The escrow holder must remain neutral, as the agent of both the buyer and seller, during the course of the escrow. After all conditions of the escrow have been met, the escrow officer is the agent of each of the parties in dealing with their individual needs.

Relationship of the Escrow Holder and the Real Estate Agent

No transaction can be completed without a good relationship between a broker and an escrow agent. The goodwill, positive guidance, and technical knowledge of an escrow officer have helped many brokers to get through an escrow, especially those new to the business.

After the real estate broker negotiates the sale, it is the job of the escrow agent to see that the agreements made by the parties are carried out. The broker and the escrow agent must check with each other regularly to make sure information is correct and to inform each other of how the escrow is progressing.

ASSURING MARKETABILITY OF TITLE

It is currently the general practice in California for buyers, sellers and lenders, as well as real estate brokers, to rely on title insurance companies for title information, title reports, and policies of title insurance. Title insurance that we use today grew from the need to protect real estate owners from challenges to their property titles. Under the old doctrine of caveat emptor (let the buyer beware) the buyer had the final responsibility to verify title of a property prior to purchasing it. As a result, many buyers ultimately lost their properties. The goal of title insurance companies is to ensure the clear, marketable title of property. **Marketable title** is one that a reasonable person would accept as clear and free from likely challenge. Over the years, determining marketable title has gone through several phases: abstract of title, certificate of title, guarantee of title, and finally title insurance.

Abstract of Title

Before reliable histories of properties came into existence, abstractors investigated the status of title to property. They searched available records and pertinent documents, and prepared an abstract of title. An **abstract of title** is a written summary of all useful documents discovered in a title search. The abstract of title together with an attorney's opinion of the documents appearing in the abstractor's chain of title was the source of our earliest basis for establishing marketable title. The **chain of title** is the public record of prior transfers and encumbrances affecting the title of a parcel of land.

Certificate of Title

Over time, the abstracts were accumulated along with references to the recorded information. Information regarding the property was organized in lot books and information affecting titles was organized in general indices. In time, these records became known as title plants. The abstract company used these title plants to supply interested parties with a **certificate of title**. This stated that the property was found to be properly vested in the present owner, subject to noted encumbrances.

Guarantee of Title

The next step was the **guarantee of title** under which the title insurance company provided written assurances (not insurance) about the title to real property, insuring against loss.

Title Insurance

Title insurance was created in response to the need for reliable assurance of title combined with an insurance against loss caused by errors in searching records and reporting the status of title. The title insurance company uses the **title plant** to conduct the most accurate search of the public records (county recorder, county assessor, county clerk and the federal land office) as possible to make sure the chain of title is correct. If there is a missing connection in a property's history or ownership, if a deed was recorded in error or is incomplete, it clouds the title.

When escrow is opened, the escrow officer requests a preliminary report from a title company. A **preliminary report** (prelim) is not a policy of title insurance but is only an offer to issue a policy of title insurance in the future for a specific fee. It shows encumbrances, liens or any other items of record that might affect ownership and it is used as the basis for the final title insurance policy. Since the prelim lists any liens affecting the property, it would show the existing seller's current loan or loans against the property. Therefore, the seller would appear as the trustor on the existing loan shown in the preliminary title report. Since all title insurance policies require legal descriptions, the prelim is the best source for the legal description of the property.

Any title problems that arise may be corrected during the escrow period so the new owner gets a clear title. The title company must determine insurability of the title as part of the search process that leads to issuance of a title policy. A marketable title is guaranteed because of title insurance, and a new owner is protected against recorded and unrecorded matters. If someone challenges the title, the title insurance company will defend the title and will pay losses that are covered under the policy.

ABC Title Company

PRELIMINARY REPORT

Order Number:

Title Officer:
Phone:
Fax No.:
E-Mail:
Escrow Officer:
Phone:
Fax No.:
E-Mail:
Borrower:
Owner:
Property:

In response to the above referenced application for a policy of title insurance, this company hereby reports that it is prepared to issue, or cause to be issued, as of the date hereof, a Policy or Policies of Title Insurance describing the land and the estate or interest therein hereinafter set forth, insuring against loss which may be sustained by reason of any defect, lien or encumbrance not shown or referred to as an Exception below or not excluded from coverage pursuant to the printed Schedules, Conditions and Stipulations of said Policy forms.

The printed Exceptions and Exclusions from the coverage of said Policy or Policies are set forth in Exhibit A attached. Copies of the Policy forms should be read. They are available from the office which issued this report.

Please read the exceptions shown or referred to below and the exceptions and exclusions set forth in Exhibit A of this report carefully. The exceptions and exclusions are meant to provide you with notice of matters which are not covered under the terms of the title insurance policy and should be carefully considered.

It is important to note that this preliminary report is not a written representation as to the condition of title and may not list all liens, defects, and encumbrances affecting title to the land.

This report (and any supplements or amendments hereto) is issued solely for the purpose of facilitating the issuance of a policy of title insurance and no liability is assumed hereby. If it is desired that liability be assumed prior to the issuance of a policy of title insurance, a Binder or Commitment should be requested.

Types of Title Insurance Policies

Policies of title insurance are commonly used throughout California, usually in the standardized forms prepared by the **California Land Title Association (CLTA)** or the **American Land Title Association (ALTA)**.

The main benefit of title insurance is that it extends protection against matters of record and many non-recorded types of risks, depending on the type of policy purchased. Two types of title insurance policies are normally used: Standard Policy of Title Insurance and Extended Coverage Policy.

Standard Title Insurance Policy

A standard title insurance policy is the type of policy usually issued to home buyers. No physical inspection of the property is required and the buyer is protected against all recorded matters, and certain risks such as forgery and incompetence. When preparing a standard title insurance policy, the title company does not do a survey or check boundary lines.

Standard Policy of Title Insurance

Losses Covered by Standard Title Policies

- Matters of record
- Off-record hazards, such as forgery, impersonation, or failure of a party to be legally competent to make a contract
- The possibility that a deed of record was not delivered with intent to convey title
- Losses that might arise from the lien of federal estate taxes, which becomes effective without notice upon death
- Expenses incurred in defending the title

Losses NOT Covered by Standard Title Policies

- Defects in the title known to the holder to exist at the date of the policy but not previously disclosed to the title insurance company
- Easements and liens that are not shown by public records
- Rights or claims of persons in physical possession of the land but whose claims are not shown by the public records
- Rights or claims not shown by public records but which can be discovered by physical inspection of the land
- Mining claims
- Reservations in patents or water rights
- Zoning ordinances

Extended Coverage Title Insurance Policy

All risks covered by a standard title insurance policy are covered by an **extended coverage title insurance policy,** as well as other insurance risks. These risks include unrecorded hazards such as outstanding mechanic's liens, unrecorded physical easements, facts a correct survey would show, certain water claims, and rights of parties in possession—including tenants and owners under unrecorded deeds.

Usually borrowers pay for an extended coverage title insurance policy for their lenders (typically called a **lender's title policy**). This policy insures lenders that they are receiving a lien, which will take priority over various interest and claims to the subject property. Most title insurance companies now offer an owner's extended coverage policy, which may be purchased at added cost.

Regulation of the Title Insurance Industry

Title insurance companies are controlled by the California Insurance Commissioner. Insurance rates are set by each company, not the state. Every title insurer must adopt a schedule of fees and charges for title policies and make it available to the public. In addition, each title insurance company must have a guarantee fund for the protection of title insurance policy holders on deposit with the Insurance Commissioner.

The title insurance premiums are a one-time fee and are not prorated in escrow. Title insurance remains in effect until the property is sold. If a property owner dies, the policy continues to protect the owner's heirs.

Title insurance companies are prohibited from paying any commission, rebate or other consideration as an incentive for title insurance business, escrow, or other title business. The **rebate law** requires title insurance companies to charge for preliminary reports and to make sincere efforts to collect for them. However, title insurance companies can still furnish the name of the owner of record and the record description of any parcel or real property without charge.

LAND DESCRIPTIONS

Exploring new land captured the imagination of the hardy individuals and families who opened up the U.S. frontier. As they moved west and improved the land on which they settled, these pioneers created a need for systematic property description.

A street address was adequate for social contacts and for delivering mail, but it was not precise enough to identify a particular property.

Today, a **legal description** is required before a deed may be recorded to transfer title to a new owner. There are three common ways to describe property: lot, block, and tract system; Public Land Survey system; and metes and bounds.

Review - Methods of Legal Descriptions
- Lot, Block, and Tract System
- Public Land Survey System
- Metes and Bounds

Lot, Block, and Tract System

Other names for the **lot, block, and tract system** are **lot and block system**, **subdivision system**, or **recorded map system.** It is the most convenient and easily understood method of land description. When developers divide parcels of land into lots, they are required by the California Subdivision Map Act to prepare and record a subdivision map or plat map. The subdivision map shows the location and boundaries of each separate new lot in the subdivision, and the map must be recorded in the county recorder's office. After the

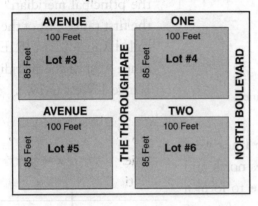

Lot 5: Block 8 of Clear Lake, recorded in Map Book 21, page 43 recorded in County Records.

subdivision map has been filed or recorded, it is public knowledge and is available to anyone. Each lot in a subdivision is identified by number, as is the block in which it is located; each lot and block is in a referenced tract. Recorded map descriptions of land are most likely to be found in cities where developers have planned communities and commercial growth areas.

U.S. Public Land Survey System

By the late 19th century, the U.S. government had established a system of land description for new territories, states, and other public lands. The **rectangular survey system**, also known as the **U.S. Public Land Survey System** (PLSS), uses imaginary lines to form a grid to locate land. North-south longitude lines, called **meridians**, and east-west latitude lines called **baselines**, intersect to form a starting point from which distances are measured.

In California there are three such starting points: the Humboldt Baseline and Meridian (Northwestern California), the Mt. Diablo Baseline and Meridian (Northeastern and Central California), and the San Bernardino Baseline and Meridian (Southern California).

California has three starting points: the Humboldt Baseline and Meridian, the Mt. Diablo Baseline and Meridian, and the San Bernardino Baseline and Meridian.

Range Lines

After establishing a starting point at the intersection of a chosen principal meridian and baseline, the government surveyors drew imaginary vertical lines called **range lines** every six miles east and west of the meridian to form columns called **ranges**. Each range was numbered either east or west of the principal meridian. For example, the first range east of the meridian was called Range 1 East (R1E), and the first range west of the meridian was called Range 1 West (R1W).

Imaginary **township lines** were drawn every six miles north and south of the baseline to form a horizontal row or **tier of townships**. These rows were numbered according to their distance from the baseline. For example, the first row of **townships** north of the baseline was called Township 1 North (T1N) and the first row of townships south of the baseline was called Township 1 South (T1S).

Township Lines

Thus, a grid of squares, called **townships**—each six miles by six miles (36 square miles)—appears. Townships run east-west in ranges and north-south in tiers.

Review - Township and Range
- Range Lines - every six miles east and west of meridian
- Township Lines - every six miles north and south of baseline

Each township is described by its location, relative to the intersection of the baseline and meridian we have just discussed. A particular township in the fourth tier north of the baseline and in the third range west of the meridian—with T for township and R for range—would be described as follows: T4N, R3W, San Bernardino Baseline, and Meridian.

The way to locate T4N, R3W is to start at the intersection of the baseline and meridian and count up (or north) four rows and then count to the left (or west) three rows.

You have learned how to use the intersection of the baseline and meridian as a starting point to locate a particular township. Now look at a township, which is divided into 36 sections, each measuring one mile by one mile. The sections are numbered, starting with section 1 in the northeast corner, and continuing in a snake-like manner to section 36 in the southeast corner. Each section is one mile by one mile and contains 640 acres. A section may then be divided further into quarter sections containing 160 acres each, and then divided into smaller and smaller parcels. These parcels are identified by their compass direction (NE, SE, NW, and SW).

Armed with this knowledge, a student may locate any size parcel, no matter how large or small, by simply dividing the section. Another important number for you to know is 5,280—the number of feet in a mile. You may be asked to calculate an answer on the state exam regarding linear feet around a section. (**Linear feet** refer to length rather than area.)

Review - U.S. Public Land Survey System
Baseline and Meridians in California

- Humboldt Baseline and Meridian
- Mt. Diablo Baseline and Meridian
- San Bernardino Baseline and Meridian

Facts About Townships and Sections

- Meridians run north and south
- Baselines run east and west
- Range lines run north and south, parallel to the principal meridian, every six miles
- Township lines run east and west, parallel to the baseline, every six miles
- Townships are six miles by six miles, 36 square miles
- Sections are one mile by one mile, 36 in each township and contain 640 acres
- 5,280 feet = one mile
- 43,560 square feet = one acre
- 640 acres = one square mile
- 16.5 feet = one rod
- Four miles = distance around a section/square mile

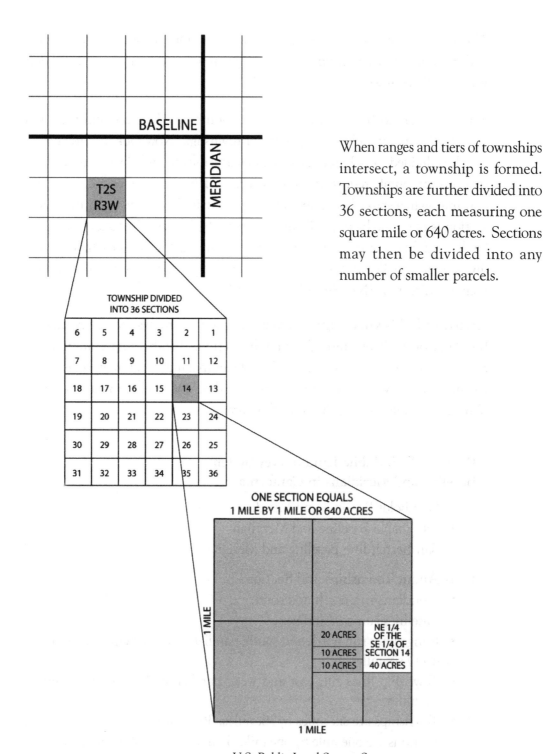

When ranges and tiers of townships intersect, a township is formed. Townships are further divided into 36 sections, each measuring one square mile or 640 acres. Sections may then be divided into any number of smaller parcels.

U.S. Public Land Survey System

Using the U.S. Public Land Survey System, a particular piece of property could be described as the Northeast quarter of the Southeast quarter of section 14, Township 2 South, Range 3 West. It is normally expressed as a legal description in abbreviated form: NE ¼ of the SE ¼ of the section 14, T2S, R3W. The quickest way to calculate the acreage contained within this description is to multiply the fractions by 640 acres (acres within a section). ¼ × ¼ × 640 = 40 acres.

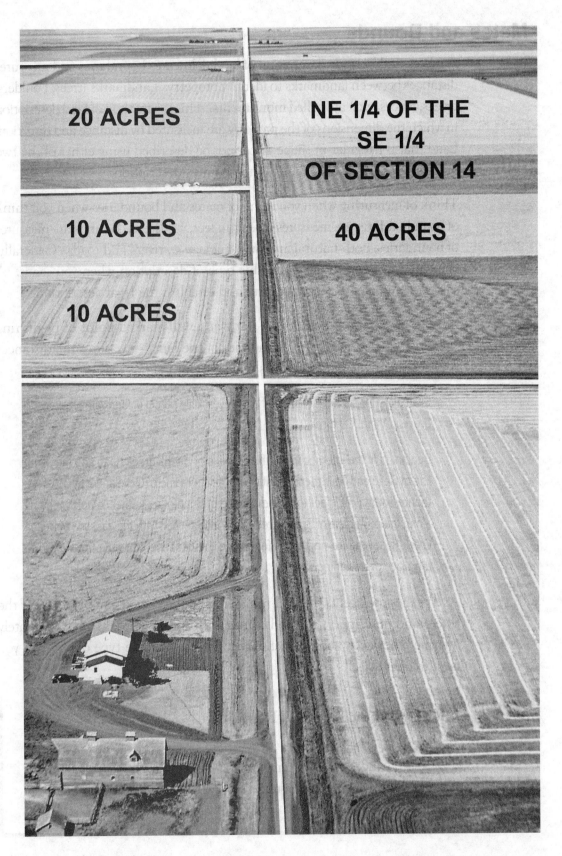

20 ACRES

NE 1/4 OF THE
SE 1/4
OF SECTION 14

10 ACRES

40 ACRES

10 ACRES

The U.S. Public Land Survey System is used for large rural tracts of land (farms).

Metes and Bounds

A **metes and bounds** description of land delineates boundaries and measures distances between landmarks to identify property. Landmarks (trees, boulders, creeks, fences, etc.) are called **monuments**. This is a method of land description in which the dimensions of the property are measured by distance and direction. Land that is irregular in shape or cannot be described using either of the two other methods may have a metes and bounds description.

Think of measuring when you think of metes and boundaries when you think of bounds. **Metes** are measures of length: feet, yards, etc. **Bounds** are measures of boundaries, both natural and man-made: e.g., rivers and roads. Generally, you will only need to recognize this type of description when you see it. A surveyor will measure the distances and establish the legal description.

A metes and bounds description starts at a well-marked **point of beginning** (POB), and—following the boundaries of the land—measures the distances between landmarks, then returns to the beginning.

> Example: Here is a description of an uneven, hilly parcel of land with an avocado grove in Vista, California:
>
> Beginning at the intersection of the east line of Buena Creek Road and the south line of Cleveland Trail; thence east along the south line of Cleveland Trail 300 feet; thence south 657.5 feet to the center line of Buena Creek; thence northwesterly along the center line of Buena Creek to its intersection with the east line of Buena Creek Road; thence north 325 feet along the east line of Buena Creek road to the place of beginning.

As a real estate agent, you will not be required to be an expert in any of the three land description methods. You will find it helpful to be adequately informed, however, about which method is used for the type of property you most frequently sell.

Review - Methods of Land Description

Method	Use
Section and Township Survey	Rural, undeveloped areas
Lot, Block, and Tract System	Urban areas, cities
Metes and Bounds	Irregular parcels of land

TAX ISSUES IN TRANSFERRING REAL PROPERTY

Most people have questions about taxes in a real estate transaction. It may not be apparent, but taxation is an indirect—yet important—factor in affecting the value of property. In this unit, we will see how taxes impact buying and selling. As a student, use this unit for general knowledge about real estate taxation; however, always refer your clients and customers to an expert for their own tax information as well as current tax laws.

Property Taxes

The idea of land taxation began in 1086 in England with the compilation of all land and resources into the *Doomsday Book* commissioned by William the Conqueror. Taxation was based on the notion that taxes should be assessed according to an owner's ability to pay. At that time, such an ability was reliably determined by how much and how good the owner's agricultural holdings were—since most people's income came almost entirely from products of their land. Therefore, land became the basis for determining the amount of tax imposed.

Proposition 13

As of June 1978, **Proposition 13** became the measure to use in assessing property in California. If there had been no change in ownership since March 1, 1975, the value of the property at that time was used as a starting point to assess the property (the initial full cash value). Under the new law, the maximum annual tax was limited to 1% of full cash value (market value). After that, a maximum increase of no more than 2% per year was allowed. Since June 1978, whenever property transfers to a new owner, it is re-assessed at 1% of fair market value, not necessarily the new sales price. Commonly, local taxes (approximately .25%) may be added to the 1% assessment.

Transfer of Ownership

Upon a change in ownership of real property unless the change is between spouses, a new assessment is made based on 1% of market value, which typically is the new purchase price. For example, if the sale price is $350,000, the new property tax would be $3,500. Any person buying real property is required to file a change-in-ownership statement with the county recorder or assessor. The change-in-ownership statement must be filed within 45 days of the change date. Failure to report a change results in a $100 penalty. A supplementary tax bill will be sent to the new owner, reflecting the change in taxes as of the date of transfer.

Proposition 60

Homeowners who are at least 55 years of age may sell their homes and transfer their present base-year property tax value to another home of equal or lesser value. Under Proposition 60, the new home must be in the same county. The base-year property value is whatever the value of the home was on March 1, 1975, or in the year they purchased the property after that time. Thus, they are allowed to continue with the original figure as their tax base, adding a maximum of 2% every year, to arrive at their tax bill, rather than be required to step up to 1% of the value of their new purchase.

Example: Mary and Mark bought their home in 1985 for $80,000 and it is currently valued at $310,000. Now that the kids are grown, the house is too big for them. They sold their home for $300,000 and purchased a smaller home in the same town for $250,000. The tax assessment on their original home was $102,400 at the time of the sale, and they were allowed to carry that to the new property because of Proposition 60. Instead of being taxed at 1% of the price of the new house ($250,000), their new tax bill was based on the assessed value of the one they sold.

Comparison of Mary and Mark's Tax Bills
- $250,000 x 1%= $2,500 tax bill
- $102,400 x 1%= $1,024 tax bill

Assessment and Collection of Taxes

Real property is taxed at the local level through ad valorem property taxes, special assessments and transfer taxes. **Ad valorem** means according to value.

Taxes are imposed on real or personal property to raise money so the government can carry out its general duties. All property within the locality of the taxing authority, whether it is the state or local government, will be taxed unless specifically exempt.

Decisions are carried out by officials during the process of assessing and collecting taxes. The following is a list of officials responsible for the correct taxation of real property.

Implementing the Job of Taxation

- County Board of Supervisors: determines the tax rate (limited to 1% of fair market value) plus any county bond debt or other assessments.

- City or County Auditor: maintains tax rolls (public records identifying parcels of land to be taxed, the owner and the assessed value.)

- City or County Assessor: assesses the value of all taxable property in the county yearly to establish the tax base and then mails out the tax bills. The annual assessments appear in the **Assessment Roll or Tax Roll**, a public record. Real property is assessed at 100% of fair market value. The tax bill identifies a property by an assessor's parcel number, which is not a legal description but is used for taxation purposes only.

- City or County Tax Collector: decides how much tax is to be paid by each property owner, depending on individual assessments. Land and improvements are assessed separately, but taxed at one rate.

- City Councils: sets property tax rates for cities.

- Assessment Appeals Board: appeals board for taxpayers' complaints about unfair taxation.

Tax Calendar

A **fiscal year**, or tax year, is used for tax purposes as compared to a **calendar year**. The fiscal or tax year starts on July 1 and goes through June 30 of the following year.

Taxation Time Line

Jan. 1	July 1	Nov. 1	Dec. 10	Feb. 1	Apr. 10	June 30
taxes become a lien	tax year starts	1st installment due	1st installment delinquent	2nd installment due	2nd installment delinquent	tax year ends

On January 1, preceding the tax year, property taxes become a lien on real property. The first installment is due November 1, but no later than December 10. The second installment is due February 1, but no later than April 10.

Property Taxes are Due
Mnemonic = NDFA

No	November 1	(1st installment due)
Darn	December 10	(delinquent after this date)
Fooling	February 1	(2nd installment due)
Around	April 10	(delinquent after this date)

Tax Sale

If a property owner does not pay the tax when it is due, the property is declared tax-defaulted and is then listed as a delinquent account by the tax collector. The property owner (or any interested party) may redeem the property from the tax collector by paying the total amount of all defaulted taxes. While the property is in a tax-defaulted status, the owner does not actually lose title and keeps possession for five years. If the taxes are not paid within that five-year period, a tax sale takes place, and the property may be sold at public auction to the highest bidder for cash. At that time, the owner loses possession and the buyer receives a **tax deed.**

Steps in a Tax Sale
1. June 8 Delinquent Tax List Published
2. Tax-Delinquent Property Status
3. Five-Year Redemption Period (Owner has Possession)
4. Unredeemed Property Deeded to State
5. Tax Collector Publishes Notice of Intent to Sell
6. Public Auction Tax Sale
7. Tax Deed to Buyer

Tax Exemptions

Homeowners' Exemption

A property owner may claim a **homeowners' exemption** in California on a residence that is both owned and occupied at 12:01 a.m. on January 1. Claims must be filed by February 15 following the change of ownership. If the prior owner claimed the homeowners' exemption, claim forms are mailed in the beginning of January for filing by February 15. The exemption reduces the assessed value by $7,000 and reduces the tax bill by at least $70.

It is the homeowner's responsibility to apply for the exemption. To receive the full exemption, the claim must be filed with the Assessor's office between January 1 and February 15, or within 30 days of a Notice of Supplemental Assessment. (A late filing is accepted from February 16 to December 10 for 80% of the exemption.) Your exemption automatically continues each year as long as you continue to own and occupy the property as your primary residence. It is the homeowner's responsibility to terminate the exemption when no longer eligible.

Example of a Homeowners' Exemption	
Assessed Value	$350,000.00
Minus Homeowner's Exemption	$ − 7,000.00
Taxable amount	$343,000.00

Veterans' Exemption

Another exemption available to some homeowners is the **veterans' exemption**. A resident of California who has been in the military during wartime is eligible to take a $4,000 tax exemption. If the resident takes the regular homeowners exemption, the veterans' exemption may not be taken on the same dwelling, but may be used for another property owned by the veteran.

Other Exemptions

Other tax exemptions are available for a variety of property owners. Certain senior citizens may qualify for tax relief. Churches, nonprofit organizations, and owners of timberlands, young orchards, or grapevines less than three years old may also qualify for tax exemptions.

Special Assessments

When specific improvements that benefit a certain area are needed—such as underground utilities, sewers or streets—**special assessments** are levied to pay for them. The difference between a special assessment and property taxes is that the latter are used to operate the government in general, whereas special assessments are used for specific local purposes. Special assessment liens are placed on the properties involved and usually paid at the same time as property taxes. The liens created by special assessments are equal in priority to general tax liens.

Street Improvement Act of 1911

One of the laws that empower cities and counties to levy a special assessment to repair streets is the **Street Improvement Act of 1911**. This act is used more than any other for street improvements in this state. Each owner is assessed for the improvement based on the front footage of the property. The amount of the assessment appears on the tax bill as a lien against the property. The assessment may be paid off at any time or paid in equal installments during the term of the bonds.

Mello-Roos Community Facilities Act of 1982

Mello-Roos covers a wide variety of community improvements, other than bond acts, for special assessments, such as streets and sewers. In some counties, Mello-Roos is on the tax bill, and in some other counties it is collected separately.

Documentary Transfer Tax

Documentary transfer tax is required whenever real property is transferred from one owner to another. In most cases, it is based on $.55 per $500 of purchase price, or $1.10 per $1,000 of purchase price. The money goes to local government, either city or county.

The full price of the property is taxed at the above rate if the sale is all cash, or if a new loan is involved, in which the seller gets all cash. The tax is levied only on the **equity** transferred (or consideration) if the buyer assumes an existing loan. The tax is usually paid through escrow or at the time the deed is recorded. Appendix A includes documentary transfer tax calculations.

> Example: If a buyer purchased a home for $100,000 assuming an existing loan of $50,000, the tax would be based on the $50,000 the buyer paid as a down payment, or the new money put into the transaction. $50,000 divided by $1,000 equals 50, therefore 50 times $1.10 equals $55.00 for the tax.

The county recorder places stamps on the recorded grant deed to indicate the amount of the documentary transfer tax paid. These are sometimes called doc stamps.

Tax Benefits of Homeownership

The federal government taxes individuals based on their earnings by means of a progressive income tax. In a progressive tax, the more you earn the higher your tax rate. The important consideration of a progressive tax is that the tax rate on which the taxpayer's obligation increases rises with additional levels of income brackets. One of the major reasons for buying real estate is to get relief from taxes.

The tax benefits of homeownership differ from those available to owners of investment property. The legal reduction of tax liability, otherwise known as tax shelter, is available to all owners of a primary residence as well as to a taxpayer owning investment property. However, different rules apply to each type of property and must be followed carefully to earn the desired tax shelter.

Personal Residence

Tax Deductions

Tax deductions are another way a homeowner can limit tax liability. **Tax deductions** are expenses that a taxpayer is allowed to deduct from taxable income. Certain expenses are deductible to homeowners, such as interest and property taxes on first and second homes. Deducting maintenance expenses, depreciation, and capital improvements is not allowed. New tax laws may or may not allow a deduction for the loss on the sale of a personal residence.

Review - Tax Deductions on Personal Residence

Deductible

1. Interest
2. Property taxes

Non-Deductible

1. Maintenance
2. Depreciation
3. Capital improvements

Sale of the Property

Individuals are generally permitted to exclude from taxable income up to $250,000 ($500,000 for married couples) of gain on the sale of their principal residence. To qualify, the taxpayer must have owned and used the property as a principal residence for at least two years during the five years prior to the sale or exchange. The exclusion is generally not allowed more than once every two years. Taxpayers who fail to meet either of these two-year requirements because of an employment change, health problems, or other unforeseen circumstances may be eligible for a partial exclusion, scaled back to the amount of time they did occupy the residence compared to the two-year requirement.

This exclusion replaces the rollover rules that have allowed taxpayers to defer all or part of the gain on a sale or exchange of a principal residence that is replaced with a new principal residence within a four-year period. In addition, the once-in-a-lifetime $125,000 exclusion on a sale of a principal residence for taxpayers age 55 and over has been replaced. The new exclusion rules are effective for sales or exchanges of a principal residence occurring after May 6, 1997. However, in certain circumstances taxpayers may elect to apply the old rules (i.e., the rollover, or the $125,000 exclusion).

Capital Gain or Loss

The cost of **capital improvements**, or physical improvements made to the property, such as the cosmetic addition of a new roof, swimming pool, or driveway, may not be deducted yearly, but may be added to the cost basis of the property when it is sold. The **cost basis** is usually the original purchase price of the property. When capital improvements are added to the original cost basis, the **adjusted cost basis** is the result.

The **taxable gain** generally is the difference between the purchase price plus capital improvements and the price when sold. Closing costs on the sale also may be subtracted from the sales price. The gain, or profit, after the $250,000 ($500,000) exclusion from the sale of a personal residence is then taxed according to current capital gains tax law.

Calculate Capital Gain on Sale of Personal Property

1. **Calculate the Adjusted Cost Basis of the Property**
   Add the cost of improvements and subtract the depreciation from the property.

Purchase price (cost basis)	$ 250,000
Add cost of improvements	+ 50,000
Adjusted cost basis	$ 300,000

2. **Calculate the Adjusted Selling Price of the Property**

Selling price	$ 400,000
Subtract the expenses of sale	− 24,000
Adjusted selling price	$ 376,000

3. **Calculate the Capital Gain (or loss)**

Adjusted selling price	$ 376,000
Subtract adjusted cost basis	− 300,000
Capital gain (or loss)	$ 76,000

HAZARD INSURANCE

Lenders require **hazard insurance** that covers the outstanding loan on the property. There are many casualty insurance companies that provide hazard insurance. In most cases, the lender is the loss payee on the policy and will receive the proceeds on a claim. The proceeds then will be used to pay for the repairs.

SUMMARY

Escrow is the deposit of paperwork and funds with a third party to process the sale of real property. An escrow is a small and short-lived trust arrangement. The **escrow holder** coordinates communications between the principals, the agents involved and other professionals (lender, title company, pest control company). Every escrow has two requirements to be valid: a binding contract between the buyer and seller and conditional delivery of transfer documents to a third party. Escrow companies must comply with the Real Estate Settlement Procedures Act (RESPA).

The California Association of REALTORS® Residential Purchase Agreement and Joint Escrow Instructions, seems to offer the best approach in the escrow process. The sales contract should incorporate the addendum (mutual changes by the buyer and seller). Escrow starts when a real estate agent brings the signed purchase agreement to the escrow holder. The escrow holder keeps all documents and funds until the terms of the escrow are completed. The escrow process is a time-consuming detailed process. Included in the escrow process is the title search. **Title insurance** companies search, gather public title records, analyze records, and issue policies of title insurance. There are two major types of title insurance policies available: the C.L.T.A. standard and the A.L.T.A. extended coverage. Consumers are responsible for all items not included in the title insurance coverage.

Closing costs are recurring and nonrecurring. The buyer prepays recurring closing costs to help offset expenses that will continue as long as the buyer owns the property. Nonrecurring closing costs are one-time charges paid upon escrow closing. The buyer and seller negotiate the payment of escrow fees, title insurance, and closing costs. Traditionally the buyer and seller are responsible for certain escrow closing costs. These traditions vary throughout California. Escrow and closing practices are also different between Northern and Southern California.

A **marketable title** is a title that a reasonable person would accept as clear and free from likely challenge. Title insurance is a contract that extends protection against risks depending on the type of policy purchased. An **American Land Title Association (A.L.T.A.)** owner's policy offers the same coverage as a standard policy with additional coverage.

UNIT 8 REVIEW

◻ Matching Exercise

Instructions: Write the letter of the matching term on the blank line before its definition. Answers immediately follow the Multiple Choice Questions.

Terms

A. abstract of title
B. ad valorem
C. assessment roll
D. beneficiary statement
E. calendar year
F. completed escrow
G. escrow

H. escrow holder
I. fiscal year
J. impound account
K. marketable title
L. metes and bounds
M. plat map
N. preliminary report

O. property taxes
P. proration
Q. section
R. special assessments
S. title insurance policy
T. vesting

Definitions

1. _____ Land description that delineates boundaries and measures distances between landmarks to identify property.

2. _____ Acts as a neutral agent of both buyer and seller.

3. _____ The way title will be taken.

4. _____ Begins on January 1 and continues through December 31 of the same year.

5. _____ Written summary of all useful documents discovered in a title search.

6. _____ A list of all taxable property showing the assessed value of each parcel; establishes the tax base.

7. _____ Taxes used to operate the government in general.

8. _____ An offer to issue a policy of title insurance in the future for a specific fee.

9. _____ A small and short-lived trust arrangement.

10. _____ Good or clear saleable title reasonably free from risk of litigation over possible defects.

11. _____ A Latin phrase meaning according to value.

12. _____ Starts on July 1 and runs through June 30 of the following year; used for real property tax purposes.

13. _____ All terms of the escrow instructions have been met.

14. _____ The division and distribution of expenses and/or income between the buyer and seller of property as of the date of closing or settlement.

15. _____ An area of land, one square mile, or 640 acres; 1/36 of a township.

16. _____ A trust account set up for funds set aside for future costs relating to a property.

17. _____ Map of a subdivision indicating the location and boundaries of individual lots.

18. _____ Taxes used for specific local purposes.

19. _____ An insurance policy that protects the insured against loss or damage due to defects in the property's title.

20. _____ A statement of the unpaid condition of a loan and describes the condition of the debt.

Multiple Choice Questions

Instructions: Circle your response and then check your response with the Answer Key that immediately follows the Multiple Choice Questions.

1. Escrow instructions must be:
    a. chartered.
    b. executed.
    c. notarized.
    d. recorded.

2. The reason for using an escrow when a deed of trust is conveyed is to:
    a. comply with the Civil Code.
    b. ensure that the conditions and instructions of the agreement are satisfied.
    c. allow for recordation of the deed.
    d. provide for third-party liability.

3. Which of the following best describes completed escrow?
    a. It is equivalent to a perfect escrow.
    b. The escrow holder has ceased being an agent for both parties.
    c. All escrow instructions have been carried out.
    d. All services of the escrow holder are involved.

4. Which of the following statements concerning escrow is correct?

   a. A perfect escrow exists when the buyer's closing statement and the seller's closing statement are exactly identical.

   b. In order for the escrow to be able to close, the buyer may be required to pay more than the amount stated in the escrow instructions.

   c. The amount in the final closing statement must be the same as the amount in the escrow instructions.

   d. None of the above

5. Which of the following statements regarding escrow procedures is correct?

   a. A broker may hold an escrow for compensation for other parties if the broker has no interest in the transaction.

   b. When the escrow requirements have been met, the escrow agency changes from being agent of both parties to an agent of each party.

   c. When the escrow holder is in possession of a binding contract between the buyer and seller, it is said to be a complete escrow.

   d. The escrow officer acts as an arbitrator of disputes between buyer and seller.

6. An escrow agent is authorized to:

   a. give the buyer advice about available financing.

   b. change the escrow instructions when asked to do so by the listing broker.

   c. call for funding of the buyer's loan.

   d. authorize a pest control company to make corrective repairs.

7. If an escrow holder receives pest control reports from two different companies, the escrow officer should:

   a. submit the estimate requiring the most work.

   b. contact both inspectors and determine which of the two reports should be accepted.

   c. contact the brokers to ask for instructions from the buyer and seller.

   d. contact the broker to ask for instructions from the seller.

8. Which of the following items would most likely appear as a credit in the seller's closing statement?

   a. Prepaid taxes

   b. Delinquent assessment lien

   c. An assumed loan

   d. Title insurance premium

9. If a buyer assumes an existing loan when purchasing a single-family residence, the settlement statement at close of escrow would show the assumption of the loan as:

    a. a debit to the buyer.

    b. a debit to the seller.

    c. a credit to the lender.

    d. neither a credit nor a debit.

10. How would a loan for the purchase of a residence appear on the buyer's closing statement?

    a. Credit to buyer, debit to seller

    b. Debit to buyer, credit to seller

    c. Credit to buyer

    d. Debit to buyer

11. Which of the following is regarded as a recurring cost in a closing statement?

    a. Escrow fees

    b. Recording fees

    c. Impound accounts

    d. Premiums for title insurance

12. A buyer who wishes to insure title to real property when it is purchased should secure a(n):

    a. guarantee of title.

    b. abstract of title.

    c. certificate of title.

    d. title insurance policy.

13. Which of the following title insurance policies protects against all risks?

    a. Standard policy

    b. Extended policy

    c. A.L.T.A. policy

    d. No policy insures against all risks.

14. When buying a home, a purchaser was given a grant deed and a standard policy of title insurance. Which of the following is warranted by the seller but is not covered by the standard policy of title insurance?

    a. The grantor is legally competent.

    b. The grantor actually signed the deed.

    c. The grantor has placed no undisclosed liens against the property.

    d. There are no forged deeds in the chain of title.

15. Which of the following is not covered by title insurance?
    a. A zoning ordinance, regulation, or plan
    b. Loss due to a missing signature of a spouse on a deed to community property
    c. Unpaid county property tax not shown in the policy
    d. Incompetence of a former seller

16. Which system of land description employs meridians and baselines?
    a. Metes and bounds
    b. Public Land Survey system
    c. Subdivision system
    d. Lot, block, and tract system

17. County governments levy taxes through:
    a. property taxes.
    b. special assessments.
    c. transfer taxes.
    d. all of the above.

18. An example of an ad valorem tax would be:
    a. income tax.
    b. estate tax.
    c. bridge toll.
    d. property tax.

19. How do special property tax assessments differ from annual property tax assessments?
    a. Annual assessments have priority over special assessments.
    b. Special assessments are imposed only by local authorities.
    c. Judicial foreclosure is required for unpaid special assessments.
    d. Special assessments provide for local improvements.

20. After a property is declared tax-defaulted for failure to pay property taxes, the occupant of the property:
    a. must vacate immediately.
    b. must pay rent to the State of California.
    c. may continue to reside on the property unhindered.
    d. is freed of tax obligations immediately.

UNIT 8 ANSWER KEY

Answers – Matching

1. L	5. A	9. G	13. F	17. M
2. H	6. C	10. K	14. P	18. R
3. T	7. O	11. B	15. Q	19. S
4. E	8. N	12. I	16. J	20. D

Answers – Multiple Choice

1. **(b)** One of the meanings of the term execute is to sign. An escrow is officially open when both buyer and seller have signed the instructions and delivered them to escrow. [Escrow]

2. **(b)** Escrow is not required. However, escrow, acting as a neutral third party helps to guarantee that all terms and conditions of the agreement are met. [Escrow]

3. **(c)** A perfect escrow is one for which all documents, funds, and instructions required to close escrow are completed and are in the hands of the escrow agent. A completed escrow is one in which all of the instructions have been satisfied. When an escrow is both perfect and complete, it is ready to close. Escrow is considered closed when the agent presents settlement statements to the buyer and seller, disburses escrow funds, and delivers all necessary documents. [Escrow]

4. **(b)** Closing costs are generally not included in escrow instructions. They are calculated just prior to closing and are included in the closing statement. [Escrow]

5. **(b)** During escrow, the escrow officer is a neutral third party who acts as an agent for both parties. At the close of escrow, the escrow officer becomes a single agent for each party. A broker may only act as an escrow in transactions in which he or she has an interest. The escrow officer delivers the deed to the buyer and the funds to the seller. [Escrow]

6. **(c)** Escrow agents may not offer legal advice, and may only act on written instructions from the parties to the escrow. Escrow agents write lenders of record for payoff amounts and funding. They accept pest control and similar reports, but cannot authorize any work. [Escrow]

7. **(c)** The escrow officer does not give advice; he or she waits for proper instructions from both parties' broker(s). [Escrow]

8. **(a)** A seller who prepays the taxes would expect to get the unused portion back, which would show up as a credit. In most transactions, sellers pay for title insurance and any delinquent assessment liens, which would show up as debits. The assumed loan is a debit to the seller and a credit to the buyer. [Escrow]

9. **(b)** Since the loan shifts from the seller to the buyer, the loan amount is debited against the seller and credited to the buyer. An assumed loan is shown as a credit to the buyer and a charge or debit to the seller. [Hint: ABC – Assumption by the Buyer is a Credit] If it were a NEW loan, only the buyer would be credited. [Escrow]

10. **(c)** Whenever a buyer has a loan (new or assumed) it is shown as a credit on the settlement statement. [Escrow]

11. **(c)** An impound account is a trust account set up for funds set aside for future, recurring costs relating to a property. It is used as needed. [Escrow]

12. **(d)** Title insurance insures and protects title to property. [Assuring Marketability of Title]

13. **(d)** No form of title insurance will insure against changes in zoning regulations. [Assuring Marketability of Title]

14. **(c)** As we learned previously, a grant deed offers an implied warranty that there are no undisclosed liens made by the grantor. A standard title insurance policy does not protect against undisclosed liens, although an extended policy would. [Assuring Marketability of Title]

15. **(a)** Generally, title insurance does not cover legislative regulations like zoning laws. [Assuring Marketability of Title]

16. **(b)** The Public Land Survey System uses imaginary lines to form a grid to locate land. North-south longitude lines, called meridians, and east-west latitude lines called baselines, intersect to form a starting point from which distances are measured. [Land Descriptions]

17. **(d)** Real property is taxed at the local level through ad valorem property taxes, special assessments, and transfer taxes. [Tax Issues in Transferring Real Property]

18. **(d)** Ad valorem means according to value. [Tax Issues in Transferring Real Property]

19. **(d)** Special assessments are spent on specific local improvements such as streets, sewers, sidewalks, parks, and water supply and treatment. Only owners who are affected by the improvements pay the assessment. [Tax Issues in Transferring Real Property]

20. **(c)** While the property is in a tax-defaulted status, the owner does not actually lose title and keeps possession for five years. [Tax Issues in Transferring Real Property]

Unit 9

INTRODUCTION

Imagine buying a house and being required to pay the total price in cash. With the average price of a single-family home being so high, buying a home would be unthinkable without the practical benefit of financing. By allowing a home-buyer to obtain a loan for the difference between the sales price and the down payment, real estate lenders have provided the solution to the problem of how property can be bought and sold without the requirement of an all-cash sale.

What began as a simple loan by a local bank—with an agreement that the borrower pay it all back in a timely manner—is now a complex subject. Buyers and sellers need to rely on experts to explain all the choices there are on financing the purchase or sale of property. You, as a real estate licensee, are one of the experts to whom they will turn.

Learning Objectives

After completing this Unit, you should be able to:

8A   distinguish between promissory notes and security instruments.

8B   differentiate between conventional and government-backed loans.

8C   determine the priority of recording.

8D   characterize types of loan programs.

PROMISSORY NOTES AND SECURITY INSTRUMENTS

When a loan is made, the borrower signs a promissory note, or note—as it is called, which states that a certain amount of money has been borrowed. The **promissory note**, then, is the evidence of the debt.

When money is loaned for financing real property, some kind of **collateral**, or security, is usually required of the borrower, as well as the promise to repay the loan. That means the lender wants some concrete assurance of getting the money back beyond the borrower's written promise to pay. The property being bought or borrowed against is used as the security, or collateral, for the debt. The lender feels more secure about making the loan if assured of the property ownership in case of default, or nonpayment, of the loan. Then the lender can sell it to get the loan money back.

In California, the most common **security instrument** for the note is a trust deed. After signing the promissory note, the borrower is required to **execute** (sign) a trust deed, which is the security guaranteeing loan repayment. The borrower (**trustor**) has possession of the property but transfers naked legal title of the property to a third party to hold as security for the lender in case of default on the loan. This process, known as **hypothecation**, allows a borrower to remain in possession of the property while using it to secure the loan. If the borrower does not make payments according to the terms of the agreement, he or she then loses the rights of possession and ownership. Hypothecation differs from a **pledge** because actual possession of pledged property is given to the lender. For example, in a pledge, personal property—such as stock certificates—is delivered to a lender, or jewelry is delivered to a pawnbroker. Once the loan is repaid, the personal property is returned to the borrower.

The lender holds the original promissory note and the trust deed until the loan is repaid. The trust deed allows the lender, in case of loan default, to order the third party to sell the property described in the deed.

Understanding Promissory Notes

A **promissory note** serves as evidence of the debt and is a written agreement between a lender and a borrower to document a loan. It is a promise to pay back a certain sum of money (the principal) at specified terms at an agreed-upon time. Sometimes it is called the note, a debt repayment contract, or more informally, it could be called an IOU.

A promissory note is a negotiable instrument. A **negotiable instrument** is a written unconditional promise or order to pay a certain amount of money at a definite time or on demand. A negotiable instrument is easily transferable from one person to another meaning it can be bought and sold. The most common type of negotiable instrument is an ordinary bank check. A check is an order to the bank to pay money to the person named. A promissory note is the same thing. It can be transferred by **endorsement** (signature), just like a check. If correctly prepared, it is considered the same as cash.

The **maker** is the person borrowing the money, or making the note. The note is a personal obligation of the borrower and a complete contract in itself, between the borrower and lender. The **holder** is the person loaning the money, or the one holding the note. A subsequent owner of the note is a **holder in due course** and is called the noteholder.

In order to be considered a negotiable instrument, however, the document must be consistent with statutory (legal) definition, and all of the following elements must be present.

Requirements for a Valid Promissory Note

- Unconditional written promise to pay a certain sum of money.
- Made by one person to another, both able to legally enter into a contract.
- Signed by the maker, or borrower.
- Payable on demand or at a definite time.
- Paid to bearer or to order.
- Voluntarily delivered by the borrower and accepted by the lender.

In addition to showing the amount borrowed, a promissory note sets the terms of the loan, such as the interest rate, the repayment plan, and an acceleration clause in the event of default. With that information, you can calculate the payments using a financial calculator, printed amortization schedule, or software.

Interest Rate

The interest charged on most real estate loans is **simple interest**—interest paid only on the principal owed. The interest rate stated in the note is called the **nominal** or **named rate**. The **effective interest rate** is the rate the borrower is actually paying, commonly called the annual percentage rate (APR). Lenders are compensated for their risk in the form of interest rates. If the lender thinks the borrower is a high risk, the lender will charge a higher interest rate for the privilege of borrowing the money. The lower the risk, the lower the rate.

Some promissory notes have a **fixed interest rate**, in which the interest rate and term do not change over the life of the loan. Others may include a fluctuating interest rate as well as changes in the payment over the life of the loan. Based on this, some loans are called fixed-rate loans and others adjustable rate loans.

Limits on Interest Rates — Usury

Usury is the charging of interest that is unreasonably high or beyond the legal limit set by the state. The California Usury Law makes a distinction between loans that are exempt from or covered by the law. Exempt loans include loans made by banks, savings and loans, and credit unions; real estate loans made directly or arranged by a mortgage loan broker; and seller carry back loans.

Under the California Usury Law, the interest rate on a loan made primarily for personal, family, or household purposes cannot exceed 10% per year. However, a loan used for home improvement or home purchase and all other loans made by a nonexempt lender are limited to the higher of 10% or 5% plus the discount rate charged by the San Francisco Federal Reserve Bank.

Types of Repayment Plans

A promissory note may stand alone as an unsecured loan or note, or it may be secured by either a trust deed or mortgage. The promissory note, however, is the prime instrument; and if there are conflicts in the terms of the note and trust deed or mortgage, generally the terms of the note are controlling. The promissory note terms create the basis for the repayment plan. There are several types of repayment plans, each with a different kind of obligation made clear by the terms of the note. The terms of the note include interest, repayment plan, and default. Some repayment plans are: (1) a single payment of principal and interest at the end of the loan term, (2) interest-only payments, (3) partially amortized with a balloon payment, and (4) fully amortized payments.

Single Payment of Principal and Interest

Some loans have no regular payments of interest and/or principal. Instead, the loan is paid off all at once, at a specified future date. This payment includes the entire principal amount and the accrued interest.

Interest-Only Payments

An interest-only loan offers consumers greater purchasing power, increased cash flow, and is a very popular alternative to traditional fixed-rate loans. The **interest-only loan** is also called a **straight loan** or **term loan**. It calls for regular interest payments during the term of the note. The interest rate is generally higher on a straight note and the principal does not decrease. A large payment is made at the end of the term to repay the principal and any remaining interest. This type of loan works well for people who only want to stay in a home for just a few years. If the borrower plans to live in the house for only three to five years, an interest-only loan may be the right choice. With a conventional 30-year mortgage, most of the payment is applied directly to the interest of the loan with very little applied to the principal. With an interest-only loan, the borrower will have a lower payment and have almost the same principal balance at the end of three to five years as if a conventional loan had been selected.

Amortized (Installment) Payments

Amortization is described as the liquidation of a financial obligation. With amortization, regular, periodic payments to include both interest and principal are made, which pay off the debt completely by the end of the term.

During the early amortization period, a large percentage of the monthly payment is used to pay the interest. As the loan is paid down, more of the monthly payment is applied to principal. A typical 30-year fixed-rate mortgage takes approximately 20 years to pay half of the original loan amount. For example, the balance on a $100,000 30-year fixed rate loan at 5% at the end of 20 years is $50,600. Typically, the longer the term of the loan, the lower the monthly payment. However, the total interest paid over the life of the loan will be higher.

Fixed-Rate Fully Amortized Note

A **fully amortized fixed-rate note** describes a loan with an interest rate that is fixed and payments that are level for the life of the loan. This type of note is the most common type with institutional lenders. It is characterized by regular, periodic payments of fixed amounts, to include both interest and principal, which pay off the debt completely by the end of the term.

> **Review - Two Features of Fixed-Rate Fully Amortized Loans**
> 1. Interest rate remains fixed for the life of the loan.
> 2. Payments remain level for the life of the loan and are structured to repay the loan at the end of the loan term.

Although the most common fixed-rate loans are 15-year and 30-year mortgages, there are also biweekly mortgages, which shorten the loan by calling for half the monthly payment every two weeks. Since there are 52 weeks in a year, the borrower makes 26 payments, or 13 months worth, every year.

Partially Amortized (Installment) Payments

This type of repayment schedule is used to create lower payments. The **partially amortized installment note** calls for regular, level payments on the principal and interest during the term of the loan. Since the loan does not fully amortize over the original term, there is still a remaining principal loan balance. The last installment, called a **balloon payment**, is much larger than any of the other payments because it includes all of the remaining principal and interest. Balloon payments can have extra risks because the borrower may need to refinance the property—possibly at higher interest rates.

Negative Amortization

There are loans that are not fully amortized. This occurs when the borrower makes lower payments than what should be made on a fully amortized loan. The difference between what should be paid and what is actually paid is added to the principal balance of the loan. This is called **negative amortization** and the principal increases instead of decreases.

Escrow No. _____   Title Order No. _____

INSTALLMENT NOTE - INTEREST INCLUDED
(Balloon Payment)

$ _____ _____ _____, California _____, 20____

FOR VALUE RECEIVED, we, or either of us, promise to pay in lawful money of the United States of America, to

_____
_____

or order, at place designated by payee, the principal sum of _____

_____ dollars,

with interest in like lawful money from _____, 20____ at _____ per cent
per annum on the amounts of principal sum remaining unpaid from time to time.

Principal and interest payable in _____ installments of _____

_____

or more each, on the _____ day of each and every _____ beginning on the

_____ day of _____, 20____ and continuing until _____

at which time the entire unpaid balance of principal and interest hereunder shall be due and payable.

Each payment shall be credited first on interest then due and the remainder of principal; and interest shall thereupon cease upon the principal so credited. Should default be made in payment of any installment of principal or interest when due the whole sum of principal and interest shall become immediately due at the option of the holder of this note. If action be instituted on this note I promise to pay such sum as the Court may fix as attorney's fees. This note is secured by a Deed of Trust in which the maker of this note is referred to as "Trustor".

THE FOLLOWING PARAGRAPH IS ONLY APPLICABLE ON ONE TO FOUR RESIDENTIAL UNITS:
This note is subject to Section 2966 of the Civil Code, which provides that the holder of this note shall give written notice to the Trustor, or his successor in interest, of prescribed information at least 90 and not more than 150 days before any balloon payment is due.

_____   _____

_____   _____

DO NOT DESTROY THIS NOTE
When paid, this note, with Deed of Trust securing same, must be surrendered to Trustee for cancellation before reconveyance will be made.

FD-30C (Rev. 4/94)   INSTALLMENT NOTE - INTEREST INCLUDED (BALLOON PAYMENT)

Adjustable Rate Mortgage (ARM)

Lenders have created nontraditional mortgage products, such as the adjustable-rate mortgage, which allow borrowers to qualify for larger loans and at the same time help maintain the lender's investment return. An **adjustable-rate mortgage** (ARM) is one whose interest rate is tied to a movable economic index. The interest rate in the note varies upward or downward over the term of the loan, depending on the agreed-upon index. To protect the borrower from wild swings in interest rates there is usually a limit on how much the interest rate can change on an annual basis, as well as a lifetime cap, or limit, on changes in interest rate.

A lender may offer several choices of interest rates, terms, payments, or adjustment periods to a borrower with an ARM. The initial interest rate, or **qualifying rate**, is determined by the current rate of the chosen index. Then, a **margin**, which might be anywhere from one-to-three percentage points, is added to the initial interest rate to determine the actual beginning rate the borrower will pay. The margin is maintained for the life of the loan and does not change. The interest rate may change, however, as the chosen index changes, depending on the economic conditions that lead it.

The borrower's payment will stay the same for a specified time, which might be six months or a year, depending on the agreement with the lender. At the agreed-upon time, the lender re-evaluates the loan to determine if the index has changed, either upward or downward, and calculates a new payment based on the changed interest rate plus the same margin. That will then be the borrower's payment until the next six months or year pass, and the loan will be reviewed again. The annual maximum increase is usually one to two percent while the lifetime cap is usually not allowed to go beyond five or six points above the starting rate.

Generally, adjustable-rate financing benefits the bankers because it allows for an inflow of extra cash during times of higher interest rates. In other words, the borrower's payments will increase because the interest rate will go up; therefore, more money will flow into the financial institution.

What is a Security Instrument?

A **security instrument** is a legal document given by the borrower to hypothecate the property to the lender as collateral for a loan, creating a security interest. The security interest allows certain assets of a borrower to be set aside so that a creditor can sell them if the borrower defaults on the loan. Proceeds from the sale of that property can be taken to pay off the debt. Security instruments are used to secure promissory notes.

The security instruments used to secure the interest for the lender are the deed of trust, mortgage, and contract for sale. In California and other states, deeds of trust are the principal instruments used to secure loans on real property. Mortgages accomplish the same thing as deeds of trust and are used in other states as security for real property loans. As you will learn, trust deeds and mortgages differ in the number of parties involved, statute of limitations, and transfer of title. In fact, the only thing trust deeds and mortgages have in common is that the property is used as security for the debt. You will hear the term mortgage used loosely in California, as in mortgage company, mortgage broker, and mortgage payment—but the mortgage referenced here usually refers to a deed of trust.

Deed of Trust

In California, the deed of trust (or trust deed) is the most commonly used security instrument in real estate finance. A **trust deed** is a security instrument that conveys title of real property from a trustor to a trustee to be held as security for the beneficiary for payment of a debt. The three parties to a trust deed are the borrower (**trustor**), lender (**beneficiary**), and a neutral third party called a **trustee**.

The trustor (borrower) signs the promissory note and the trust deed and gives them to the beneficiary (lender) who holds them for the term of the loan. Under the trust deed, the trustor has equitable title and the trustee has bare or **naked legal title** to the property.

Although bare legal title is conveyed using a trust deed it does not actually convey possession. Possession and equitable title remain with the borrower. **Equitable title** is the interest held by the trustor under a trust deed and gives the borrower the equitable right to obtain absolute ownership to the property when the terms of the trust deed are met.

The trustee, who has bare legal title, acts as an agent for the beneficiary and has only two obligations. The first is to foreclose on the property if there is a default on the loan, and the second is to reconvey the title to the borrower when the debt is repaid in full. When the debt is repaid in full, the beneficiary signs a **Request for Full Reconveyance** and sends it to the trustee requesting the trustee to reconvey title to the borrower. The trustee signs and records a **Deed of Reconveyance** to show the debt has been repaid and to clear the lien from the property. The trust deed is recorded at the close of escrow. A **fictitious trust deed** is a recorded trust deed containing details that apply to later loan documents.

Mortgage

Since its introduction in the early 1900s, the deed of trust virtually replaced the use of a note and mortgage when financing real estate. The promissory note shows the obligation of the debt, and the mortgage is a lien against the described property until the debt is repaid.

There are two parties in a mortgage: a **mortgagor** (borrower) and a **mortgagee** (lender). The mortgagor receives loan funds from a mortgagee and signs a promissory note and mortgage. Once signed by the borrower, both the note and mortgage are held by the lender until the loan is paid. Unlike a trust deed, under a mortgage both title and possession remain with the borrower.

Contract of Sale

The **contract of sale** is the financing instrument with many names. It may be called an installment sales contract, a contract of sale, an agreement of sale, a conditional sales contract, a contract for deed, or a land sales contract.

This is a contract in which the seller (**vendor**) becomes the lender to the buyer (**vendee**). The vendor pays off the original financing while receiving payments from the vendee on the contract of sale. The vendor and vendee's relationship is like that of a beneficiary and a trustor in a trust deed.

The buyer, (vendee) has possession and use of the property even though legal title is held by the seller (vendor). In a contract of sale, the vendor retains legal ownership of the property, and the vendee holds what is known as equitable title. When all the terms of the contract are met, the vendor will pass title to the vendee.

The vendor in a land contract may not use vendee's impound money for any other purpose without the consent of the payor (vendee). Land contracts are used in CalVet loans under the California Veterans Farm and Home Purchase Plan (discussed later in the unit). The state of California is the vendor who has legal title, and the veteran is the vendee who has equitable title.

> **Review - Interests Held under Equitable Title**
> - Trustor under a trust deed
> - Vendee under a contract for deed
> - Buyer of real property from the time the sales contract is signed, and earnest money is paid until the closing

Clauses Found in Finance Instruments

When a borrower signs a note promising to repay a sum, the lender usually will include some specific requirements in the note regarding repayment. In addition to the terms in the note, the trust deed lists several covenants (promises) regarding the relationship of the borrower and the lender. These special clauses are meant to protect the lender and the lender's interests.

Prepayment Clauses

The note usually includes a prepayment clause. A **prepayment clause** allows a borrower to pay off a loan early or make higher payments without paying a prepayment penalty. The prepayment is applied first to any accrued or unpaid interest and then to principal.

A **prepayment penalty** allows a lender to collect a certain percentage of a loan as a penalty for early payoff. When lenders make loans, they calculate their return over the term of the loan. If a loan is paid off early, the lender receives less interest and the return on investment is lower than planned. This is especially true on loans that carry higher interest rates. The lender charges a prepayment penalty to offset lost revenues resulting from early payoff. Prepayment penalties are not allowed on conforming, FHA, and VA loans.

Or More Clause

An **"or more clause"** allows a borrower to pay off a loan early, or make higher payments without penalty.

Lock-in Clause

A **lock-in clause** prohibits borrowers from paying off a loan in advance. It is not allowed on residential units of less than four units. In a land contract to purchase a home a lock-in clause may be ignored by the vendee (buyer).

Late Payments

Lenders may not impose a late charge on a payment until after the payment is 10 to 15 days late depending on the terms of the note.

Acceleration Clause

An **acceleration clause** allows a noteholder to call the entire note due, on occurrence of a specific event, such as default in payment, taxes or insurance, or sale of the property. A noteholder may use the acceleration clause to call the entire note due if the borrower does not pay the loan payments, the real property taxes or insurance premiums, or if the borrower sells the property. In order to pay off the outstanding loan, a noteholder will foreclose on the loan.

Default and Foreclosure

Foreclosure is the legal procedure used by lenders to terminate all rights, title, and interest of the trustor or mortgagor in real property by selling the property and using the sale proceeds to satisfy the liens of creditors.

There are two ways to foreclose: by trustee's sale and by judicial process. Any trust deed or mortgage with a **power-of-sale clause** may be foreclosed non-judicially by a trustee's sale or judicially by a court procedure. Without the power-of-sale clause, the only remedy a lender has is a judicial foreclosure by a court proceeding. Most trust deeds and mortgages in California include the power-of-sale clause, so the lender may choose either type of foreclosure method.

Foreclosure on Trust Deed by Trustee's Sale (Non-judicial)

Usually the lender or noteholder will elect to foreclose on the loan using the trustee's sale because it is the quickest and easiest method taking approximately four months. First, the beneficiary (lender) notifies the trustor (borrower) of default and requests the trustee to record a **notice of default**. Anyone who has recorded a **Request for Notice** must be notified of the default. The trustee must wait at least three months after recording the notice of default before advertising the trustee sale. Then the trustee advertises a Notice of Sale once a week for three weeks (21 days) and posts a notice of sale on the property.

As you can see the minimum time between recording the notice of default and the trustee sale is three months and 21 days. During this time the trustor may **reinstate** (bring current) the loan up to five business days prior to the trustee's sale. The trustee holds the sale and issues a **trustee's deed** to the highest bidder. A trustor has no right of redemption after the trustee sale.

Order Proceeds from Sale of the Property are Paid

1. Trustee's fees, costs, and expenses of the sale
2. Any tax and assessment liens that are due and owing
3. Trust deeds, mortgages, and mechanic's liens in their order of priority
4. Defaulting borrower

Sometimes the proceeds of the sale are not sufficient to satisfy the debt being foreclosed. If that happens, the noteholder may sue on the promissory note to obtain a deficiency judgment against the borrower. A **deficiency judgment** is a personal judgment against a borrower for the balance of a debt owed when the security for the loan is not sufficient to pay the debt. However, the noteholder cannot obtain a deficiency judgment against the trustor under a trustee sale.

RECORDING REQUESTED BY

WHEN RECORDED MAIL TO

NAME

ADDRESS

CITY

STATE&ZIP

Title Order No.   Escrow No.

SPACE ABOVE THIS LINE FOR RECORDER'S USE

REQUEST FOR NOTICE OF DELINQUENCIES
UNDER SECTION 2924e CIVIL CODE

In accordance with Section 2924e. California Civil Code. request is hereby made that a written notice of any or all delinquencies of four months or more. in payments of principal or interest on any obligation secured under the Deed of Trust recorded as Instrument Number: on:
Official Records of   County, California, loan number
Wherein   is the trustor, and describing land therein as:

1. The ownership or security interest of the requester, is the beneficial interest under that certain deed of trust recorded as instrument Number: on   of the Official Records of:
                    County, California.
Wherein   is the trustor.
2.   is the date on which the interest of the requester will terminate as evidenced by the maturity date of the note of the trustor in favor of the requester.
3.   is the name of the current owner of the security property described above.
4. The street address of the security property as described above is:

5. Said notice of delinquency and the amount thereof shall be sent to:

                                                        (Requester Beneficiary)
at
          (Address)   (City)

          (State)   (Zip)

Dated
                                        (Requester Beneficiary)

CONSENT BY TRUSTOR/OWNER

I _____ AUTHORIZE _____
          (Trustee)   (Senior Lienholder)
TO DISCLOSE IN WRITING TO _____
                              (Requesting Beneficiary)
NOTICE OF ANY AND ALL DELINQUENCIES OF FOUR MONTHS OR MORE, IN PAYMENT OF PRINCIPAL OR INTEREST ON ANY OBLIGATION SECURED BY THAT SENIOR LIEN MORE PARTICULARLY DESCRIBED AS INSTRUMENT NUMBER _____ RECORDED ON _____
IN OFFICIAL RECORDS OF _____COUNTY. CALIFORNIA.
DATED _____

Foreclosure by Court Proceeding (Judicial)

Default on a mortgage, unless the mortgage includes a power-of-sale clause, requires a court foreclosure. The mortgagee (lender) goes to court to start the foreclosure. The court issues a decree of foreclosure and an order of sale. After publication and posting of the sale notice, the court-appointed commissioner sells the property to the highest bidder and gives the buyer a Certification of Sale. After a court foreclosure sale on a mortgage, the mortgagor (borrower) gets to keep possession of the property and has one year to redeem the property by satisfying the loan in full including court costs and any interest unless the proceeds of the sale are sufficient to satisfy the secured indebtedness, then the redemption period is only 3 months. [CCP §729.030]. This is called statutory redemption. If after one year (or 3 months), the mortgagor does not redeem the property, a **sheriff's deed** is issued to the new buyer.

If a trust deed is foreclosed in court, it is treated like a mortgage and the trustor (borrower) may keep possession during the redemption period. Sometimes a lender with a trust deed may elect to foreclose by a court foreclosure. This may be the only way the beneficiary can obtain a deficiency judgment against the borrower.

Deficiency Judgments

As mentioned earlier, a deficiency judgment is a personal judgment against a borrower for the difference between the unpaid amount of the loan, plus interest, costs and fees of the sale, and the amount of the actual proceeds of the foreclosure sale. This means if the property sells for less than what is owed to the noteholder, the borrower will be personally responsible for repayment after the deficiency judgment is filed.

Deficiency Judgment Not Allowed

If a lender (beneficiary or mortgagee) chooses to foreclose a trust deed or mortgage with a power of sale using a trustee sale, no deficiency judgment is allowed if the proceeds do not satisfy the debt and all costs. Since trust deeds are used almost exclusively in California to secure loans, the only security for a beneficiary is the property itself. Any other personal assets of the borrower in default are protected from judgment under a trust deed.

Additionally a lender cannot get a deficiency judgment against a borrower if the loan is a purchase money loan secured by either a trust deed or a mortgage. Any loan made at the time of a sale, as part of that sale, is known as a **purchase-money loan**. This includes first trust deeds, junior loans used to purchase the property, and seller carry-back financing. A seller is said to **carry back** when the seller extends credit to a buyer by taking a promissory note executed by the buyer and secured by a trust deed on the property being purchased as a part of the purchase price.

Deficiency Judgment Permitted

A deficiency judgment is allowed on hard money loans. A **hard money loan** is one made in exchange for cash, as opposed to a loan made to finance the purchase of a home. Typically, a hard money loan refers to junior loans used to take money out for consumer purchases, home equity loans, debt consolidation, and even a refinance.

Alienation Clause

The **alienation** or **due-on-sale clause** is a type of acceleration clause. A lender or noteholder may call the entire note due if the original borrower transfers (alienates) ownership of the property to someone else. If the note contains an **acceleration clause** (due on sale), the trust deed must mention this clause in order to enforce the contract. This clause protects the lender from an unqualified, unapproved buyer taking over a loan. Justifiably, the lender fears possible default, with no control over who is making the payments.

Usually a lender will want the existing loan paid off if a property owner transfers the property to someone else. However, under certain circumstances, a property owner may transfer responsibility for the loan to the buyer when he or she sells the property to another party. A buyer may assume an existing loan, or may buy a property subject to an existing loan.

Loan Assumption

An **assumption clause** allows a buyer to assume responsibility for the full payment of the loan with the lender's knowledge and consent. When a property is sold, a buyer may assume the existing loan. Usually with the approval of the lender, the buyer takes over primary liability for the loan, with the original borrower secondarily liable if there is a default. What that means is that even though the original borrower is secondarily responsible, according to the loan assumption agreement, no actual repayment of the loan may be required of that person.

The original borrower (seller) can avoid any responsibility for the loan by asking the lender for a **substitution of liability (novation)**, relieving the seller of all liability for repayment of the loan. In most cases, a buyer assumes an existing loan with the approval of the underlying lender. However, an **alienation clause** in the note would prevent a buyer from assuming the loan.

Subject To

A buyer may also purchase a property subject to the existing loan. A **subject to** clause allows a buyer to take over a loan, making the payments without the knowledge or approval of the lender. The original borrower remains responsible

Escrow No. _____   Title Order No. _____

(DUE ON SALE CLAUSE)

$ _____, California _____, 20_____

_____ after date, for value received

I promise to pay to _____

_____ or order, at

_____

the sum of _____ DOLLARS

with interest from _____ until paid at the

rate of _____ per cent per annum, payable _____

_____

_____

Principal and interest payable in lawful money of the United States of America. should default be made in payment of interest when due the whole sum of principal and interest shall become immediately due at the option of the holder of this note and after said breach, said obligation shall continue to accrue interest at the rate of _____% per annum. If action be instituted on this note I promise to pay such sum as the Court may fix as Attorney's Fees. This note is secured by a Deed of Trust of even date herewith.

In the event the herein described property or any part thereof, or any interest therein which has been given as security for the payment of this obligation is sold, agreed to be sold, conveyed or alienated by the Trustor, or by the operation of the law or otherwise, all obligations secured by this instrument, irrespective of the maturity dates expressed therein, at the option of the holder hereof and without demand or notice shall immediately become due and payable.

_____   _____

_____   _____

_____   _____

DO NOT DESTROY THIS NOTE

When paid, this note, if secured by Deed of Trust, must be surrendered to Trustee for cancellation before reconveyance will be made.

FD-30G (Rev. 2/95)   STRAIGHT NOTE (DUE ON SALE CLAUSE) for the loan, even though the buyer takes title and makes the payments. In this case, also, the property remains the security for the loan. In the case of default, the property is sold and the proceeds go to the lender, with no recourse to the original buyer other than the foreclosure going against the borrower's credit.

When a buyer takes a property subject to the existing loan, the underlying lender may not always be informed. The buyer simply starts making the payments and the seller hopes he or she is diligent and does not default.

The occurrence of subject to sales is relative to economic and market conditions. In a real estate market where there are more buyers than sellers (a seller's market) a homeowner does not need to sell subject to his or her loan. When money is tight and interest rates high and sellers are wondering where all the buyers are, a subject to sale might be a seller's only option.

> ### Review - Notes, Trust Deeds, and Mortgages
> - A note is the evidence of a debt.
> - A trust deed or mortgage, even though it is the security for the debt, is still only an incident of the debt.
> - A trust deed or mortgage must have a note to secure, but a note does not need a trust deed or mortgage to stand alone.
> - If there is a conflict in the terms of a note and the trust deed or mortgage used to secure it, the provisions of the note will control.
> - If a note is unenforceable, the presence of a trust deed will not make it valid.

CONVENTIONAL AND GOVERNMENT-BACKED LOANS

All loans can be classified according to their loan terms and whether they have government backing. First, as we have already learned, all of the various loans are classified by their terms—fixed rate loans, adjustable-rate loans, and their combinations. Second, loans are classified by whether they have government backing—conventional or government loans. Some lenders specialize in only conventional conforming loans, whereas full service lenders offer a wide selection of loan programs including conventional, government-sponsored FHA and VA loans, and non-conforming loans.

Conventional Loans

A **conventional loan** is any loan made by lenders without any governmental guarantees. The basic protection for a lender making conventional loans is the borrower's equity in the property. A low down payment will mean greater risk for the lender and a higher interest charged to the borrower. Conventional loans may be conforming or non-conforming.

Conforming Loans

Conforming loans have terms and conditions that follow the guidelines set forth by Fannie Mae and Freddie Mac. These loans are called "A" paper loans, or prime loans, and can be made to purchase or refinance homes (one-to-four residential units). Fannie Mae and Freddie Mac guidelines establish the maximum loan amount, borrower credit and income requirements, down payment, and suitable properties. Fannie Mae and Freddie Mac announce new loan limits every year. Currently, the general conforming loan limit for a single-family home is $424,100. This limit is reviewed annually and, if needed, modified to reflect changes in the national average price for single-family homes. The loan limit on second mortgages is $212,050. To get the current loan limits, visit the Fannie Mae website at www.fanniemae.com.

Private Mortgage Insurance (PMI)

Conventional lenders usually require private mortgage insurance (PMI) on low down payment loans for protection in the event that the homeowner fails to make his or her payments. **Private mortgage insurance** protects the lender against financial loss if a homeowner stops making mortgage payments. When the loan exceeds 80% of the value of the property, lenders usually require private mortgage insurance on conventional loans. Usually borrowers pay for this insurance as part of the monthly payment. A small number of companies provide this insurance.

Non-Conforming Loans

Sometimes either the borrower's creditworthiness or the size of the loan does not meet conventional lending standards. These are called **non-conforming loans** and include jumbo loans and subprime loans.

Jumbo Loans

Loans that exceed the maximum loan limit set by Fannie Mae and Freddie Mac are called **jumbo loans**. Because jumbo loans are not funded by these government-sponsored entities, they usually carry a higher interest rate and some additional underwriting requirements.

Trust Deed	Mortgage Contract
1. Number of Parties (3) **Trustor:** Borrower who conveys title to trustee who holds as a security for debt. **Beneficiary:** Lender who holds original note and trust deed during life of the debt. **Trustee:** Receiver of naked legal title who conveys it when debt is paid or will sell if foreclosure is necessary.	**1. Number of Parties (2)** **Mortgagor:** Borrower retains title but gives lender a lien on the property as security. **Mortgagee:** Lender who holds the mortgage.
2. Title: Conveyed to trustee with trustor retaining equitable possession of the property.	**2. Title:** Held by mortgagor together with possession.
3. Statute of Limitations: The security for debt is held by trustee, rights of creditor are not ended when statute runs out on the note.	**3. Statute of Limitations:** Foreclosure is barred if no action is taken within four (4) years of delinquency on the note.
4. Remedy for Default: Foreclosure can be instituted through trustee's sale or court foreclosure. (Court foreclosure follows mortgage foreclosure procedure #7.)	**4. Remedy for Default:** Court foreclosure is usually the only remedy.
5. Right of Redemption: When the title has been sold by trustee at trustee's sale no right or statutory redemption exists.	**5. Right of Redemption:** Mortgagor has up to one (1) year to redeem the property after court foreclosure called statutory redemption.
6. Satisfaction: The beneficiary sends a request for full reconveyance to the trustee with the original note and trust deed. Upon payment of fees, the trustee issues a reconveyance deed which must be recorded.	**6. Satisfaction:** Upon final payment and on demand, the mortgagee signs the certificate that the debt is satisfied. Then the certificate or release is recorded.

Trust Deed (cont.)	**Mortgage Contract** (cont.)
7. Foreclosure by Trustee's Sale:	**7. Foreclosure by Court:**
Beneficiary notifies the trustee of default. The trustee notifies the trustor and records the notice. Anyone who has recorded the Request for Notice for Default must also be notified.	Court action is commenced by the mortgagee. The court issues a decree of foreclosure and an order of sale. A court appointed commissioner sells to the highest bidder after the publication and posting of the sale notice.
The trustee waits at least three (3) months. During the three (3) month period, the trustor can reinstate the loan. Then the trustee advertises a notice of sale once a week for three weeks (21 days) and posts a notice on the property.	The certificate of sale is issued. Mortgagor has one (1) year to redeem the property and remains in possession for that year. If sale proceeds satisfy the debt, court costs, and interest then the mortgagor has only three (3) months to redeem the property.
Trustor can now invade the three (3) week advertising period and can reinstate the loan up to five (5) business days prior to the trustee's sale.	If a trust deed is foreclosed in court, it is treated like a mortgage contract, and trustor remains in possession during the redemption period.
The trustee conducts the sale and issues a trustee's deed to the highest bidder.	A sheriff's deed is issued after one (1) year.
8. Deficiency Judgment:	**8. Deficiency Judgment:**
No deficiency judgment is available if the foreclosure is by trustee's sale.	A deficiency judgment is available in a court foreclosure.

9. No deficiency judgment is available on a purchase-money trust deed or mortgage.

Subprime Loans

Loans that do not meet the borrower credit requirements of Fannie Mae and Freddie Mac are called **subprime loans** or "B" and "C" paper loans as opposed to "A" paper conforming loans. Subprime loans are offered to borrowers that may have recently filed for bankruptcy or foreclosure, or have had late payments on their credit reports. Their purpose is to offer temporary financing to these applicants until they can qualify for conforming "A" financing. Due to the higher risk associated with lending to borrowers that have a poor credit history, subprime loans typically require a larger down payment and a higher interest rate.

Prior to 1990, it was very difficult for anyone to obtain a mortgage if he or she did not qualify for a conventional FHA or VA loan. Many borrowers with bad credit are good people who honestly intended to pay their bills on time. Catastrophic events such as the loss of a job or a family illness can lead to missed or late payments or even foreclosure and bankruptcy. Subprime loans were developed to help higher risk borrowers obtain a mortgage.

Government Participation in Real Estate Finance

There are two federal agencies and one state agency that help make it possible for people to buy homes they would never be able to purchase without government involvement. The two federal agencies that participate in real estate financing are the Federal Housing Administration (FHA) and the Veterans Administration (VA). The California Farm and Home Purchase Program, or CalVet loan, is a state program that helps eligible veterans.

Federal Housing Administration (FHA)

The FHA program, a part of HUD (U.S. Department of Housing and Urban Development) since 1934, has caused the greatest change in home mortgage lending in the history of real estate finance. The FHA was established to improve the construction and financing of housing. The main purpose of the FHA program has been to promote homeownership. Secondary results include setting minimum property requirements and systemizing appraisals. An appraiser would be reprimanded if he or she did not use FHA guidelines when preparing appraisals for FHA loans. Additionally, an appraiser who intentionally misrepresents the value on FHA loan appraisals, which subsequently cause a loss, could be fined and face legal action.

The FHA does not make loans; rather, it insures lenders against loss. Loans are made by authorized lending institutions, such as banks, savings banks, and independent mortgage companies. As long as FHA guidelines are used in funding the loan, the FHA, upon default by the borrower, insures the lender against loss. If the borrower does default, the lender may foreclose and the FHA will pay cash up to the established limit of the insurance.

The lender is protected, in case of foreclosure, by charging the borrower a fee for an insurance policy called **Mutual Mortgage Insurance** (MMI). The insurance requirement is how the FHA finances its program. The premium may be financed as part of the loan or paid in cash at the close of escrow.

The borrower applies directly to the FHA-approved lender (mortgagee), not the FHA, for a loan. FHA does not make loans, build homes, or insure the property. A buyer who would like to purchase a home with FHA financing would apply to an FHA-approved mortgagee (lender) who would then request a **conditional commitment** from FHA. Once the lender determines that the borrower and site qualify for the program, the lender submits a firm commitment request to the FHA.

The FHA guidelines encourage homeownership by allowing 100% of the down payment to be a gift from family or friends and by allowing closing costs to be financed to reduce the up-front cost of buying a home. The down payment on FHA loans varies with the amount of the loan.

Interest rates are determined by mutual agreement between the borrower and the lender—they are not set by the Federal Reserve Board. Sometimes a borrower will pay points to the lender to increase the lender's yield and compensate the lender for the difference between FHA interest rates (which tend to be low) and conventional interest rates. **Points** are a percentage of the loan amount paid to the lender when negotiating a loan. The borrower must make monthly payments. The FHA does not allow a borrower to make semi-monthly or semi-annual payments.

The FHA maximum loan amounts vary from one county to another. It is important that the total loan amount, including financed closing costs, not exceed the maximum limit set by the FHA for the county in which the property is located. There are no income limits on FHA loans and an FHA loan will be based on the selling price when it is lower than the appraisal.

There are no alienation and prepayment penalty clauses allowed in FHA loans. Any qualified resident of the United States may obtain an FHA loan as long as the property will be the borrower's principal residence and is located in the United States.

The FHA insures a variety of types of loans. For example, borrowers can get qualified for an FHA loan before a builder starts construction, enabling both borrower and builder to count on the completion of the transaction.

Popular FHA Loan Programs

Section 203(b) Residential Loan

The FHA 203(b) loan offers financing on the purchase or construction of owner-occupied residences of one-to-four units. This program offers 30 year, fixed-rate, fully amortized, mortgages with a down payment requirement as low as 3.5%, allowing financing of up to 96.5% of the value of the home. FHA has mortgage limits that vary from county to county. Their website, https://entp.hud.gov/idapp/html/hicostlook.cfm, provides the current FHA mortgage limits for several areas.

Section 203(k) Rehabilitation Loan

A purchase rehabilitation loan (purchase rehab) is a great option for buyers who are looking to improve their property immediately upon purchase. This mortgage loan provides the funds to purchase your home and the funds to complete your improvement project all in one loan, one application, one set of fees, one closing, and one convenient monthly payment.

A purchase rehab loan could be used for a variety of improvements, such as: adding a family room or bedroom, remodeling a kitchen or bathroom, performing general upgrades to an older property, or even completing a total tear-down and rebuild.

Section 245(a) Graduated Payment Mortgage

A **graduated payment mortgage** (GPM) has a monthly payment that starts out at the lowest level and increases at a specific rate. Payments for the initial years cover only part of the interest due, with the unpaid amount added to the principal balance. After a specified time, the loan is recalculated, with the new payments staying the same from that point on. With this loan, the interest rate is not adjustable and does not change during the term of the loan. What actually changes is the amount of the monthly mortgage payment. A GPM is structured for buyers who expect to be earning substantially more after a few years and can commit to higher future payments.

Energy Efficient Mortgage

The Energy Efficient Mortgages Program (EEM) helps homebuyers or homeowners save money on utility bills by enabling them to finance the cost of adding energy-efficiency features to new or existing housing. The program provides mortgage insurance for the purchase or refinance of a principal residence that incorporates the cost of energy efficient improvements into the loan. Due to the anticipated energy conservation savings, lenders can be more flexible with underwriting guidelines.

Section 255 Home Equity Conversion Mortgages

Home Equity Conversion Mortgages (HECM) are a type of reverse annuity mortgages. It is a program for homeowners who are 62 and older who have paid off their mortgages or have only small mortgage balances remaining. The program has three options for homeowners: (1) borrow against the equity in their homes in a lump sum, (2) borrow on a monthly basis for a fixed term or for as long as they live in the home, or (3) borrow as a line of credit.

The borrower is not required to make payments as long as the borrower lives in the home. The loan is paid off when the property is sold. FHA collects an insurance premium from all borrowers to provide mortgage coverage, which will cover any shortfall if the proceeds from the sale of the property are not sufficient to cover the loan amount. Senior citizens are charged a modest percentage of the home's value as an initial payment plus a small percentage on the loan balance each year. These amounts are usually paid by the mortgage company and charged to the borrower's principal balance. FHA's reverse mortgage insurance makes this program less expensive to borrowers than the smaller reverse mortgage programs run by private companies without FHA insurance.

VA Loan

The **Department of Veterans Affairs** (VA) does not make loans. It guarantees loans made by an approved institutional lender, much like the FHA. Both programs were created to assist people in buying homes when conventional loan programs did not fit their needs. There are two main differences between the two government programs: (1) only an eligible veteran may obtain a VA loan, and (2) the VA does not require a down payment up to a certain loan amount, which means qualified veterans, could get 100% financing. As with FHA loans, alienation or prepayment penalty clauses are not allowed in VA loans.

VA loans are made by a lender, such as a mortgage company, savings and loan or bank. The VA's guaranty on the loan protects the lender against loss if the payments are not made, and is intended to encourage lenders to offer veterans loans with more favorable terms. The amount of guaranty on the loan depends on the loan amount and whether the veteran used some entitlement previously.

VA Loan Process

A veteran must possess a **Certificate of Eligibility**, which is available from the Veteran Administration, before applying for a VA loan. The certificate will show the veteran's entitlement or right to obtain the loan.

When a veteran finds a house he or she wants to purchase, a VA-approved conventional lender will take the loan application, and the veteran's Certificate of Eligibility and process the loan according to VA guidelines. The lender will request the VA to assign a licensed appraiser to determine the reasonable value for the property. A **Certificate of Reasonable Value** (CRV) will be issued. A loan may not exceed the value established by the CRV appraisal. Once the loan has closed, it is sent to the VA for guaranty. The Certificate of Eligibility is annotated to show how much of the entitlement has been used and will be returned to the veteran.

A veteran may get another VA loan, if the prior VA loan is paid off and the property sold. A VA loan may be assumed by a nonveteran buyer, upon approval by the VA. If a veteran sells his or her property and allows the buyer to assume the existing VA loan, he or she cannot get another VA loan until the buyer who assumed the VA loan has paid it off. If a VA loan is foreclosed and there is a loss, the veteran cannot have eligibility be restored until the loss has been repaid in full.

Fees and Closing Costs

Although a veteran can get 100% financing, he or she will be required to pay a funding fee for a first-time use. The funding fee for second time users who do not make a down payment is higher because the veteran has already had a chance to use the benefit once.

The lender may charge reasonable closing costs that may not be included in the loan. The closing costs may be paid by the buyer (veteran) or the seller. Typical closing costs include Certificate of Reasonable Value, credit report, loan origination fee, discount points, title insurance, and recording fees. The VA allows the veteran to pay reasonable discount points on a refinance or a purchase. No commissions, brokerage fees, or buyer broker fees may be charged to the veteran.

California Veteran Loans (CalVet)

The **California Department of Veterans Affairs** administers the **CalVet loan** program to assist California veterans in buying a home or farm. Unlike other government financing, the CalVet program funds and services its own loans. Funds are obtained through the sale of State General Obligation Bonds and Revenue Bonds.

An eligible veteran (includes a 17-year old veteran) applies for the loan and makes loan payments directly to the Department of Veterans Affairs. Upon application for a CalVet loan and approval of the borrower and property, the Department of Veterans Affairs purchases the property from the seller, takes title to the property, and sells it to the veteran on a **contract of sale**. The Department holds legal title, with the veteran holding equitable title, until the loan is paid off and all the terms of the contract are met.

There are no discount points charged on a CalVet loan. The veteran has an obligation to apply for life insurance, with the Department of Veterans Affairs as beneficiary, to pay off the debt in case of the veteran's death.

PRIORITY OF RECORDING

Priority is the order in which documents are recorded and is determined by the date stamped in the upper right-hand corner of the document by the county recorder. If there are several trust deeds recorded against a property, no mention will be made about which one is the first, second, third, or fourth trust deed. A person inquiring about the priority of the deeds should look at the time and date the deed was recorded.

First and Junior Trust Deeds

The trust deed recorded first against a property is called a **first trust deed**. All others are junior loans. A **junior trust deed** is any loan recorded after the first trust deed, secured by a second, third or subsequent trust deed. Secondary or junior financing is another way to finance a property, either at the time of a sale, or afterward. The interest rates are usually higher because there is a greater risk of default on a junior loan. The beneficiary of a junior loan should record a Request for Notice of Default in order to be notified if the borrower defaults on a prior loan.

VA Department of Veterans Affairs

VA LOAN SUMMARY SHEET

1. VA'S 12-DIGIT LOAN NUMBER

2. VETERAN'S NAME *(First, middle, last)*

3. VETERAN'S SOCIAL SECURITY NUMBER	**4. GENDER OF VETERAN** *(Check one)* ☐ MALE ☐ FEMALE	**5. VETERAN'S DATE OF BIRTH** *(mm/dd/yyyy)*

6A. ETHNICITY

☐ NOT HISPANIC OR LATINO

☐ HISPANIC OR LATINO

6B. RACE *(May select more than one)*

☐ AMERICAN INDIAN OR ALASKAN NATIVE   ☐ ASIAN   ☐ BLACK OR AFRICAN AMERICAN

☐ NATIVE HAWAIIAN OR PACIFIC ISLANDER   ☐ WHITE   ☐ UNKNOWN

7. ENTITLEMENT CODE *(01 to 11, from VA Certificate of Eligibility)*	**8. AMOUNT OF ENTITLEMENT AVAILABLE** *(From VA Certificate of Eligibility)*

9. BRANCH OF SERVICE *(Check one)*
☐ 1. ARMY   ☐ 2. NAVY   ☐ 3. AIR FORCE   ☐ 4. MARINE CORPS   ☐ 5. COAST GUARD   ☐ 6. OTHER

10. MILITARY STATUS *(Check One)*
☐ 1. SEPARATED FROM SERVICE   ☐ 2. IN SERVICE

11. FIRST TIME HOME BUYER *(Check one)*

☐ YES   ☐ NO | This means a veteran who has not previously purchased a home, either by cash, assumption, or new financing. |

12. LOAN PROCEDURE *(Check one)*

☐ AUTOMATIC   ☐ AUTO-IRRRL   ☐ VA PRIOR APPROVAL

13. PURPOSE OF LOAN *(Check one)*
☐ 1. HOME (INCLUDES MH ON PERMANENT FOUNDATION)   ☐ 2. MANUFACTURED HOME   ☐ 3. CONDOMINIUM
☐ 4. ALTERATIONS/IMPROVEMENTS   ☐ 5. REFINANCE

14. LOAN CODE *(Check one)*
☐ 1. PURCHASE   ☐ 2. IRRRL (STREAMLINE REFINANCE)   ☐ 3. REGULAR *("Cash-out")* REFINANCE
☐ 4. MANUFACTURED HOME REFINANCE   ☐ 5. REFINANCING OF CONSTRUCTION LOAN, LAND SALE CONTRACT OR LOAN ASSUMED AT HIGHER RATE OF INTEREST *(*Maximum guaranty on these loans is $36,000)*

15. PRIOR LOAN TYPE *(Note: Must be completed if Regular ("Cash-out") Refinance is selected in Item 14)*
☐ 1. FHA-FIXED   ☐ 2. FHA-ARM/HARM   ☐ 3. CONVENTIONAL-FIXED   ☐ 4. CONVENTIONAL-ARM/HARM
☐ 5. CONVENTIONAL-INTEREST ONLY   ☐ 6. VA-FIXED   ☐ 7. VA-ARM/HARM   ☐ 8. OTHER

16. TYPE OF MORTGAGE *(Check one)*

☐ 0. REGULAR FIXED PAYMENT   ☐ 1. GPM-NEVER TO EXCEED NOV   ☐ 2. OTHER GPMs
☐ 3. GEM   ☐ 4. TEMPORARY BUYDOWN   ☐ 5. HYBRID ARM   ☐ 6. ARM

17. TYPE OF HYBRID-ARM *(NOTE: Must be completed if Hybrid Arm is selected in Item 16)*
☐ 3/1   ☐ 5/1   ☐ 7/1   ☐ 10/1

18. TYPE OF OWNERSHIP *(Check one)* ☐ 1. SOLE OWNERSHIP *(VETERAN & SPOUSE OR VETERAN ONLY)* ☐ 2. JOINT - 2 OR MORE VETERANS ☐ 3. JOINT - VETERAN/NON-VETERAN	**19. CLOSING DATE** *(mm/dd/yyyy)*

20. PURCHASE PRICE *(N/A for Refinance Loans)*	$

21. REASONABLE VALUE *(For IRRRLs - If appraisal has not been done, loan amount of prior VA loan)*	$

22. ENERGY IMPROVEMENTS *(Check all applicable boxes)*

☐ NONE   ☐ INSTALLATION OF SOLAR HEATING/COOLING

☐ REPLACEMENT OF A MAJOR SYSTEM   ☐ ADDITION OF A NEW FEATURE

☐ INSULATION, CAULKING, WEATHER-STRIPPING, ETC.   ☐ OTHER IMPROVEMENTS | $ |

23. LOAN AMOUNT	(Purchase - Purchase Price or RV (lesser) + Funding Fee) (Refi - Max 90% LTV + Funding Fee) (IRRRL - Old Loan Payoff + All Closing Costs)	$

24. PROPERTY TYPE *(Check one)*

☐ NEITHER   ☐ PUD   ☐ CONDOMINIUM

25. APPRAISAL TYPE *(Check one)*

☐ IND - SINGLE PROPERTY-IND APPRAISAL   ☐ ONE - MASTER CRV CASE (MCRV)   ☐ LAPP - LENDER APPRAISAL

☐ MBL - MANUFACTURED HOME   ☐ HUD - CONVERSION   ☐ PMC - PROP. MGMT. CASE

VA FORM NOV 2008   **26-0286**   SUPERSEDES VA FORM 26-0286, AUG 2006, WHICH WILL NOT BE USED.

26. TYPE OF STRUCTURE *(Check one)*
- [ ] 1. CONVENTIONAL CONSTRUCTION
- [ ] 2. SINGLEWIDE M/H
- [ ] 3. DOUBLEWIDE M/H
- [ ] 4. M/H LOT ONLY
- [ ] 5. PREFABRICATED HOME
- [ ] 6. CONDOMINIUM CONVERSION

27. PROPERTY DESIGNATION *(Check one)*
- [ ] 1. EXISTING OR USED HOME, CONDO, M/H
- [ ] 2. APPRAISED AS PROPOSED CONSTRUCTION
- [ ] 3. NEW EXISTING - NEVER OCCUPIED
- [ ] 4. ENERGY IMPROVEMENTS

28. NO. OF UNITS *(Check one)* | **29. MCRV NO.**
- [ ] SINGLE
- [ ] TWO UNITS
- [ ] THREE UNITS
- [ ] FOUR OR MORE

30. MANUFACTURED HOME CATEGORY *(Check one)*
- [ ] 0. OTHER - NOT M/H
- [ ] 1. M/H ONLY (RENTED SPACE)
- [ ] 2. M/H ONLY (VETERAN-OWNED LOT)
- [ ] 7. M/H ON PERMANENT FOUNDATION

31. PROPERTY ADDRESS

32. CITY	**33. STATE**	**34. ZIP CODE**	**35. COUNTY**

36. LENDER VA ID NUMBER	**37. AGENT VA ID NUMBER** *(If applicable)*	**38. LENDER LOAN NUMBER**

FOR LAPP CASES ONLY

39. LENDER SAR ID NUMBER

40. GROSS LIVING AREA *(Square Feet)*	**41. AGE OF PROPERTY** *(Yrs.)*	**42. DATE SAR ISSUED NOTIFICATION OF VALUE** *(mm/dd/yyyy)*

43. TOTAL ROOM COUNT	**44. BATHS** *(No.)*	**45. BEDROOMS** *(No.)*

46. IF PROCESSED UNDER LAPP, WAS THE FEE APPRAISER'S ORIGINAL VALUE ESTIMATE CHANGED OR REPAIR RECOMMENDATIONS REVISED, OR DID THE SAR OTHERWISE MAKE SIGNIFICANT ADJUSTMENTS?
- [ ] YES *(If "Yes," there must be written justification by fee appraiser and/or SAR)*
- [ ] NO

INCOME INFORMATION *(Not Applicable for IRRRLs)*

47A. LOAN PROCESSED UNDER VA RECOGNIZED AUTOMATED UNDERWRITING SYSTEM
- [ ] YES
- [ ] NO *(If "Yes," Complete Item 47B and 47C)*

47B. WHICH SYSTEM WAS USED? | **47C. RISK CLASSIFICATION**
- [ ] 01. LP
- [ ] 02. DU
- [ ] 03. PMI AURA
- [ ] 04. CLUES
- [ ] 05. ZIPPY
- [ ] 1. APPROVE
- [ ] 2. REFER

48. CREDIT SCORE *(Enter the median credit score for the veteran only)*

49. LIQUID ASSETS	$
50. TOTAL MONTHLY GROSS INCOME *(Item 31+Item 38 from VA Form 26-6393)*	$
51. RESIDUAL INCOME	$
52. RESIDUAL INCOME GUIDELINE	$

53. DEBT- INCOME RATIO *(If Income Ratio is over 41% and Residual Income is not 120% of guideline, statement of justification signed by underwriter's supervisor must be included on or with VA Form 26-6393)* %

54. SPOUSE INCOME CONSIDERED | **55. SPOUSE'S INCOME AMOUNT** *(If considered)*
- [ ] YES
- [ ] NO *(If "Yes," Complete Item 55)* $

DISCOUNT INFORMATION *(Applicable for All Loans)*

56. DISCOUNT POINTS CHARGED	% OR	$
57. DISCOUNT POINTS PAID BY VETERAN	% OR	$

58. TERM *(Months)*	**59. INTEREST RATE**	**60. FUNDING FEE EXEMPT**
	%	[ ] Y - EXEMPT [ ] N - NOT EXEMPT

FOR IRRRLS ONLY

61. PAID IN FULL VA LOAN NUMBER

62. ORIGINAL LOAN AMOUNT	**63. ORIGINAL INTEREST RATE**
$	%

64. REMARKS

VA FORM 26-0286, NOV 2008

Subordination Clause

A **subordination clause** is used to change the priority of a financial instrument. A lender agrees to give up priority to later loans. Remember, the priority of a trust deed is fixed by the date it is recorded: the earlier the date, the greater the advantage. When a note and trust deed includes a subordination clause, a new, later loan may be recorded, and because of the subordination clause, assume a higher priority. This clause is used mainly when land is purchased for future purposes of construction that will require financing. The lender on the new financing would want to be in first position to secure his or her interest, so the trust deed on the land would become subordinate to a new loan on the structure when the new loan was funded and recorded. Typically, the subordination clause benefits the trustor (borrower).

LOAN PROGRAMS

Traditionally, fixed-rate loans were the only choice offered by commercial banks and savings and loans for a home buyer. Over the past few years, lending institutions have been deregulated allowing them to offer consumers new solutions to credit demands. **Deregulation** is a process in which financial institutions that formerly had been restrained in their lending activities by the law, are allowed to compete freely for profits in the marketplace. Controls on lending practices still exist, but loans can now be marketed competitively by all lending institutions. As a result of deregulation the distinction between commercial and savings banks has practically been eliminated.

Because there are different kinds of lenders and different kinds of borrowers who are in need of credit to buy homes, there is no single type of financing that fits everyone. In an attempt to offer alternatives to consumers, lenders have developed nontraditional mortgage products. A **nontraditional mortgage product** is any loan other than a fixed-rate, 30-year, fully amortized loan.

Secondary Financing (Junior Loans)

Secondary financing or a **junior loan** is a loan secured by a trust deed or mortgage on a property, other than first-trust deed. One way to get the needed financing is for the buyer to obtain a secondary loan through an outside source, such as a mortgage lender, private investor or even the seller of the property. Junior loans take advantage of built-up equity in a property. **Equity** is defined as the difference between the value of the property and any outstanding loans or the initial down payment. Assuming there is enough equity, a homeowner can apply for a cash loan for any purpose. Being a homeowner can be advantageous, especially if there is built up equity in a house, townhouse, duplex, or condominium. The equity can pay for home improvements, bill consolidation, or college tuition. Typical junior loans include home equity loans, home equity lines of credit, and seller financing.

Home Equity Loan

In a **home equity loan,** the borrower gets the entire loan balance at one time. It is a fixed-rate second mortgage with principal and interest payments remaining the same over the life of the loan.

A lender uses strict standards about the amount of equity required in a property before loaning money, and particularly for a junior loan. The reason is simple. All a lender wants is to get his or her money back in a timely manner, along with the calculated return on the investment. Care must be taken in case of a decrease in the value of the subject property, to make sure there is enough of a margin between the total amount owed and the value of the property. If the lender has to sell the property at a foreclosure sale, he or she will be assured of getting the money back. By only loaning up to 75%-90% of the property value, the lender leaves some room for loss.

The priority of the loan will depend on what other instruments are recorded ahead of it, but it will be known as a hard money loan (subject to state laws) and will be secured by a deed of trust or mortgage against the property.

> Example: Michael's home was appraised at $400,000, with a $250,000 first trust deed recorded against it. Michael wants a $65,000 home equity loan. To determine whether to make the loan, the lender adds the amount owed to the amount desired in the loan to determine the percentage that would be encumbered by the existing first trust deed, and the desired second trust deed. If the lender would only loan up to 80% of the appraised value of the property, would Michael get his loan? (Of course, Michael does get his loan because he has enough equity in the property to qualify).

Home Equity Line of Credit

With a **home equity line of credit** (HELOC), the borrower takes money as it is needed—up to the credit limit. It has a low starting interest rate, with a variable monthly rate based on outstanding balance. More and more lenders are offering home equity lines of credit. By using the equity in their home, borrowers may qualify for a sizable amount of credit, available for use when and how they please, at an interest rate that is relatively low. Furthermore, under the California tax law—depending on each borrower's specific situation—he or she may be allowed to deduct the interest because the debt is secured by their home.

What is a home equity line of credit?

A home equity line is a form of revolving credit in which a borrower's home serves as collateral. Because the home is likely to be a consumer's largest asset, many homeowners use their credit lines only for major items, such as education, home improvements, or medical bills and not for day-to-day expenses.

With a home equity line, a borrower will be approved for a specific amount of credit—the credit limit—meaning the maximum amount, he or she can borrow at any one time.

Many lenders set the credit limit on a home equity line by taking a percentage (75%-90%) of the appraised value of the home and subtracting the balance owed on the existing mortgage. In determining the borrower's actual credit line, the lender also will consider his or her ability to repay, by looking at income, debts, and other financial obligations, as well as a borrower's credit history.

Home equity plans often set a fixed time during which a homeowner can borrow money, such as 10 years. When this period is up, the plan may allow the borrower to renew the credit line. But in a plan that does not allow renewals, a borrower will not be able to borrow additional money once the time has expired. Some plans may call for payment in full of any outstanding balance. Others may permit a borrower to repay over a fixed time, for example 10 years.

Once approved for the home equity plan, usually a borrower will be able to borrow up to the credit limit whenever he or she wants. Typically, a borrower will be able to draw on the credit line by using special checks, or under some plans, borrowers can use a credit card.

Interest Rate Charges and Plan Features

Home equity plans typically involve variable interest rates rather than fixed rates. A variable rate must be based on a publicly available index (such as the prime rate published in some major daily newspapers or a U.S. Treasury bill rate); the interest rate will change, mirroring fluctuations in the index. To figure the interest rate that the borrower will pay, most lenders add a margin of one or two percentage points to the index value. Because the cost of borrowing is tied directly to the index rate, it is important to find out what index and margin each lender uses, how often the index changes, and how high it has risen in the past.

How will the borrower repay the home equity plan?

Before entering into a plan, a borrower should consider how to repay any money that is borrowed. Some plans set minimum payments that cover a portion of the principal (the amount borrowed) plus accrued interest. But, unlike the typical installment loan, the portion that goes toward principal may not be enough to repay the debt by the end of the term. Other plans may allow payments of interest alone during the life of the plan, which means that the borrower pays nothing toward the principal. If the homeowner borrows $10,000, he or she will owe that entire sum when the plan ends.

Whatever the payment arrangements during the life of the plan—whether the borrower pays some, a little, or none of the principal amount of the loan—when the plan ends the borrower may have to pay the entire balance owed, all at once. He or she must be prepared to make this balloon payment by refinancing it with the lender, by obtaining a loan from another lender, or by some other means.

If a homeowner is thinking about a home equity line of credit, he or she also might want to consider a more traditional second mortgage loan. This type of loan provides a fixed amount of money repayable over a fixed period. Usually the payment schedule calls for equal payments that will pay off the entire loan within that time.

Seller Financing - 2nd Trust Deed

Another common source for secondary financing of a sale is the seller. If the seller is going to be the lender, he or she agrees to carry back, or act as a banker, and make a loan to the buyer for the needed amount. That loan is secured by a trust deed, in favor of the seller, recorded after the first trust deed. In a seller carryback loan, the seller acts as the beneficiary and the buyer is the trustor.

When a seller carries the paper on the sale of his or her home, it is also called a **purchase-money loan**, just like the loan made by an outside lender. If a seller receives a substantial amount from the proceeds of a first loan, plus the buyer's down payment, it may be in the seller's interest to carry a second trust deed—possibly for income or to reduce tax liability by accepting installment payments.

Example: Sam made an offer on a house owned by Gary, who accepted an offer of $375,000 with $37,500 as the down payment. The buyer qualified for a new first loan in the amount of $318,750, and asked Gary to carry a second loan in the amount of $18,750 to complete the purchase price.

When the seller extends credit in the form of a loan secured by a second deed of trust, the note may be written as a straight note, with interest-only payments, or even no payments. Or it could be an installment note with a balloon payment at the end, or fully amortized note with equal payments until it is paid off. The term of the loan is decided by the buyer and seller. The instructions of the buyer and seller regarding the seller financing are usually carried out through escrow.

If a trust deed held by the seller is sold to an outside party, usually a mortgage broker, the note and trust deed will be discounted. **Discounting a note** is selling a note for less than the face amount or the current balance. Even though the seller receives a reduction in value by the mortgage broker, it is one way a seller can get cash out of a trust deed that was carried back.

Example: Bob and Todd owned a house together as investors. After several years, they put the house on the market for $550,000 and hoped to get a full-price offer so they could go their separate ways with the profit from the house.

After a short time, they did get a full-price offer. The buyer offered to put $110,000 down, get a $385,000 new first loan and asked Bob and Todd to carry $55,000 for five years, as a second trust deed. Bob and Todd would have turned the offer down if their agent had not suggested they accept and sell the second trust deed after the close of escrow. Even though it would be discounted, it was one way they could get most of the cash out of their investment.

If the second trust deed was sold at a discounted 20%, or $11,000, Bob and Todd would end up with $55,000, less $11,000, or $44,000. In that way they would get the cash out of the sale, though they would be netting less than they originally planned because of the discount. They followed their agent's suggestion, and were satisfied with the result.

Whenever there is seller financing in a real estate transaction, the law requires the buyer and seller to complete a **Seller Financing Disclosure Statement**. It gives both the seller and buyer all the information needed to make an informed decision about using seller financing to complete the sale.

The seller can see from the disclosure whether the buyer has the ability to pay off the loan by looking at the buyer's income, and whether the buyer has a good credit history. The buyer can see what the existing loans are, as well as such things as due date and payments on existing loans that would be senior to the loan in question.

Seller Financing - All-Inclusive Trust Deed (AITD)

The **all-inclusive trust deed (AITD)**, or **wraparound mortgage**, is a type of seller financing. In general, only assumable loans (FHA and VA loans) can be part of an AITD. An AITD (wraparound mortgage) wraps an existing loan with a new loan, and the borrower makes one payment for both. In other words, the new trust deed (the AITD) includes the present encumbrances, such as first, second, third, or more trust deeds, plus the amount to be financed by the seller.

The AITD is a junior loan and subordinate to existing encumbrances because the AITD is created later. This means any existing encumbrances have priority over the AITD, even though they are included, or wrapped, by the new all inclusive trust deed.

The AITD does not disturb any existing loan(s). The seller, as the new lender, keeps making the payments while giving a new increased loan at a higher rate of interest to the borrower. The amount of the AITD includes the unpaid principal balance of the existing (underlying) loan, plus the amount of the new loan being made by the seller. The borrower makes payment on the new larger loan to the seller, who in turn makes payment to the holder of the existing underlying loan. The new loan wraps around the existing loan.

A seller usually will carry back an all-inclusive trust deed at a higher rate of interest than the underlying trust deed, thereby increasing the yield. The seller continues to pay off the original trust deed from the payments on the wraparound, while keeping the difference. This type of financing works best when the underlying interest rate is low and the seller can then charge a higher rate on the wrapped loan.

WRAPAROUND MORTGAGE RIDER

Rider and addendum to Security Instrument dated_____, _____

The attached security instrument is a wraparound mortgage/deed of trust subordinate to a certain mortgage/deed of trust dated _____, _____, executed in favor of _____ and currently held by_____ in the original principal amount of $_____, which was recorded on the _____day of _____, _____ in the county records of _____ County, State_____ as follows:

Book:_____
Page: _____
Libor: _____
Reception: _____
Date: _____

Borrower agrees to comply with all the terms and conditions of the above described mortgage including, but not limited to, those concerning taxes and insurance, other than with respect to the payment of principal or interest due under said mortgage. If Borrower herein shall fail to comply with all the terms, provisions and conditions of said mortgage so as to result in a default thereunder (other than with respect to payments of principal or interest due), that failure on the part of Borrower herein shall constitute a default under this security instrument and shall entitle the lender, at its options, to exercise any and all rights and remedies given this security instrument in the event of a default under this security instrument.

If the lender hereunder shall default in making any required payment of principal or interest under the above described mortgage or deed of trust, the Borrower shall have the right to advance funds necessary to cure that default and all funds so advanced by Borrower shall be credited against the next installment of principal and interest due under the Note secured by this security instrument.

_____   _____
Borrower   Borrower

Other Types of Loans

Today, many nontraditional mortgage programs are available to serve consumers.

Unsecured Loan

Some consumers, who need a small loan to fix the car, buy a new appliance, or take a trip are choosing a closed-end, unsecured loan instead of using their credit cards or getting a home equity loan. An **unsecured loan** is one in which the lender receives a promissory note from the borrower, without any security for payment of the debt, such as a trust deed or mortgage. The only recourse is a lengthy court action to force payment. This is truly the traditional IOU.

Open-End Loan

An **open-end loan** is essentially a revolving line of credit. An additional amount of money may be loaned to a borrower in the future under the same trust deed. The effect is to preserve the original loan's priority claim against the property with this open-end loan.

Package Loan

A loan on real property secured by more than the land and structure is known as a **package loan**. It includes fixtures attached to the building (appliances, carpeting, drapes, air conditioning) and other personal property.

Blanket Loan

A trust deed or mortgage that covers more than one parcel of property may be secured by a **blanket loan**. It usually contains a **partial release clause** that provides for the release of any particular parcel upon the repayment of a specified part of the loan. Commonly, it is used in connection with housing tracts, or construction loans. When a house is sold in a subdivision, the partial release clause is signed releasing that parcel from the blanket construction loan. A **deed of partial reconveyance** is recorded to show that the obligation has been met.

Another use of a blanket loan is for a homeowner to buy or build a new home, even if the current home still needs to be sold. In this instance, a blanket loan would cover both homes—the current property as well as the property being built or purchased. The result is making one monthly payment instead of two and eliminating the uncertainty of buying or building a home and selling a home at the same time. A blanket loan will save money and eliminate the inconvenience of obtaining a swing loan.

High-Cost Mortgages

A **high-cost mortgage** is a mortgage that has interest rates or costs that exceed a certain level. There are certain requirements for high-cost mortgages. Since the rules for these loans are contained in Section 32 of Regulation Z, they are called **Section 32 Mortgages**. The rules do not cover loans to buy or build a home, reverse mortgages, or home equity lines of credit (which are similar to revolving credit accounts). Since 2014, HOEPA rules include most types of mortgage loans secured by a consumer's principal dwelling, including purchase money mortgage loans, refinances, closed-end home-equity loans, and open-end credit plans (i.e., home-equity lines of credit, or HELOCs). Reverse mortgages and construction loans would still be excluded.

Banned Features on High-Cost Mortgages

- Balloon payments unless permitted by law
- Negative amortization
- Financing points and fees
- Most prepayment penalties

Higher-Priced Mortgage Loans

As defined by the Truth in Lending Act, Section 226.35, a **higher-priced mortgage loan** is a closed-end mortgage loan secured by the consumer's principal dwelling with an APR that exceeds the average prime offer rate for a comparable transaction. This definition pertains to home purchase loans—not to construction loans, bridge loans with a term of 12 months or less, reverse mortgage, or home equity lines of credit.

Higher-priced mortgage loans are subject to restrictions regarding repayment, prepayment penalties, and escrow accounts.

Repayment Ability. The loan cannot be based solely on the value of the property without regard to the borrower's repayment ability.

Prepayment Penalties. A loan may not include a prepayment penalty unless it is limited to the first two years of the loan.

Escrow Accounts. Lenders must establish an escrow account for payment of property taxes and premiums for mortgage-related insurance required by the creditor (i.e., hazard, liability, or mortgage insurance) when the loan is a first lien that secures the borrower's principal dwelling. Condominium units and cooperatives are exempt from this requirement if the homeowners' association maintains a master policy to insure all units.

Swing (Bridge) Loan

A **swing loan** (also called interim or bridge loan) is a temporary loan made on a borrower's equity in his or her home. It is usually a short-term loan that is due in six (6) months or when the borrower's home sells, whichever occurs sooner. It is used when the borrower has purchased another property, with the present home unsold, and needs the cash to close the sale of the new home. The new loan is secured by a trust deed or mortgage against the borrower's home. Usually there are no payments, with interest accruing during the term of the loan. When the borrower's home sells, the swing loan plus interest is repaid, through escrow, from the proceeds of the sale.

Swing loans can be risky depending on the current real estate market. In a fast-paced real estate market, it is usually safe to assume that the home will sell within several months if it is priced right. However, if the market is stagnant, it could take longer than six (6) months to sell and the borrower would have to pay the carrying costs on two homes.

Pledged Account Mortgage

A **pledged account mortgage** (PAM) is a loan made against security, such as money held in a savings account or a certificate of deposit. When a borrower has a large amount of money in a savings or thrift account, one way he or she can use that to an advantage is to **pledge** the account as security for a lender. Another version enables the borrower to get 100% financing if a relative (or more than one relative) agrees to pledge a savings account or Certificate of Deposit as collateral for the loan. A benefit of this loan program is that the person who pledges the money continues to earn interest. When the borrower has sufficient equity in the property, the pledge money is returned.

The lender will require a certain ratio of the loan amount to the balance in the account, and the borrower must keep that amount in the account for a specified length of time. The lender may release the pledge account when the property has acquired enough equity to qualify under normal loan-to-value ratios.

Shared Appreciation Mortgage

A **shared appreciation mortgage** (SAM) is a loan in which the lender offers a below-market interest rate in return for a portion of the profits made by the homeowner when the property is sold. The holding period (usually three to five years) and the percentage of shared equity are spelled out in the loan agreements.

Rollover Mortgage

The **rollover mortgage** (ROM) is a loan in which the unpaid balance is refinanced typically every five years at then current rates. This is good for the borrower and bad for the lender if interest rates are falling, and bad for the borrower and good for the lender if interest rates are rising.

Renegotiable Rate Mortgage

A **renegotiable rate mortgage** is a loan in which the interest rate is renegotiated periodically. The loan may be either a long-term loan with periodic interest rate adjustments, or a short-term loan that is renewed periodically at new interest rates, but based on a long-term mortgage. There is a maximum interest rate fluctuation of 5% over the term of the loan. [CC §1916.8].

Construction Loans

Construction financing comprises two phases—the construction phase and completion. An interim loan is a short-term loan to finance construction costs, such as the building of a new home. The lender advances funds to the borrower as needed while construction progresses. Since it is a high-risk loan it has a higher interest rate. Upon completion of the construction, the borrower must obtain permanent financing or pay the construction loan in full. The permanent loan that pays off a construction loan is called a **takeout loan**. Interim construction loans are usually made by commercial banks, whereas standby commitments and takeout loans are arranged by mortgage companies for large investors, such as insurance companies.

Do not confuse a takeout loan with a forward-takeout commitment (also called a standby commitment). A **forward-takeout commitment** is just a very expensive letter that promises to deliver a takeout loan in the future if the property is built according to plans and specifications and leased at the target rental rate. Typically, a forward-takeout commitment costs a developer one-to-two points, plus at least one additional point if the loan eventually funds. However, the borrower does not have to take the loan.

SUMMARY

Real estate financing in California is focused on promissory notes and deeds of trust. Promissory notes include interest only payments (straight notes or term loan) or payments of principal and interest (installment payments). The **promissory note** is a written agreement between a lender and a borrower to document a loan. This agreement also serves as evidence of the debt. The most popular promissory notes are the fully amortized installment note, adjustable-rate loans, and fixed-interest rate loans.

In California, real estate loans are secured primarily by a deed of trust. A **deed of trust** is a financial instrument consisting of a trustor (borrower), trustee (titleholder), and a beneficiary (lender). The deed of trust is the security guaranteeing loan repayment. Upon repayment of a loan, the trustee transfers **title back to the trustor.** If the trustor neglects to pay on the loan, the **trustee can foreclose** on the property by a trustee's sale.

Promissory notes and deeds of trust may also include special clauses that give a general description of the duties and responsibilities of the trustor. The most common clauses are acceleration and alienation.

Loans can be classified as fixed-rate loans, adjustable-rate loans, and/or combinations of the two. In addition, loans are classified as either conventional or government loans. A **conventional loan** is produced by lenders without any governmental guarantee. A **conforming loan** follows the regulations set by Fannie Mae and Freddie Mac. Loans that do not conform to conventional lending standards are called **non-conforming loans** (examples are **jumbo** and **subprime loans**). Popular government loans include Federal Housing Administration (FHA), Veterans Administration (VA), and CalVet.

Loan programs in general are varied and fit different kinds of borrowers who need credit to buy homes. Popular secondary financing loans are **junior loans, home equity loans** and **home equity line of credit.**

UNIT 9 REVIEW

Matching Exercise

Instructions: Write the letter of the matching term on the blank line before its definition. Answers immediately follow the Multiple Choice Questions.

Terms

A. acceleration clause

B. adjustable-rate mortgage

C. alienation clause

D. amortization

E. assumption clause

F. beneficiary

G. blanket loan

H. collateral

I. conforming loans

J. conventional loan

K. discounting a note

L. endorsement

M. equitable title

N. fictitious trust deed

O. mortgagee

P. mortgagor

Q. nominal or named rate

R. promissory note

S. purchase-money loan

T. renegotiable rate mortgage

U. standby commitment

V. takeout loan

W. trust deed

X. vendee

Y. vendor

Definitions

1. _____ Any loan made by lenders without any governmental guarantees.

2. _____ Selling a note for less than the face amount or the current balance.

3. _____ The lender under a mortgage.

4. _____ The interest held by the trustor under a trust deed.

5. _____ Any loan made at the time of a sale, as part of that sale.

6. _____ Recorded trust deed containing details that apply to later loan documents.

7. _____ Loan in which the interest rate is renegotiated periodically.

8. _____ The permanent loan that pays off a construction loan.

9. _____ The interest rate stated in the note.

10. _____ The seller under a contract of sale (land contract).

11. _____ A clause in a loan document describing certain events that would cause the entire loan to be due.

12. _____ The evidence of the debt.

13. _____ A clause in a loan document that would allow the lender to call the entire loan due upon the sale of the property.

14. _____ A note whose interest rate is tied to a movable economic index.

15. _____ A letter that promises to deliver a takeout loan in the future.

16. _____ The liquidation of a financial obligation.

17. _____ The borrower under a mortgage.

18. _____ The lender under a deed of trust.

19. _____ Something of value given as security for a debt.

20. _____ A security instrument that conveys naked legal title of real property.

Multiple Choice Questions

Instructions: Circle your response and then check your response with the Answer Key that immediately follows the Multiple Choice Questions.

1. A promissory note:
    a. is security for a trust deed.
    b. is evidence of a debt.
    c. must be recorded.
    d. is collateral for the loan.

2. All of the following are negotiable instruments except a(n):
    a. personal check.
    b. promissory note.
    c. installment note.
    d. trust deed securing a promissory note.

3. Which of the following statements is correct regarding effective interest rate and nominal interest rate?

    a. The effective interest rate is slightly above the average rate in the marketplace; the nominal interest rate is slightly below.

    b. The effective interest rate is the rate actually paid by the borrower; the nominal interest rate is the rate named in the note.

    c. The effective interest rate is the rate named in the contract; the nominal interest rate is the average rate in the marketplace.

    d. None of the above

4. If the payments on a loan financing a real estate purchase are insufficient to service the debt, the result will be:

    a. a smaller balloon payment.

    b. negative amortization.

    c. positive cash flow.

    d. default on the debt.

5. Which of the following will necessarily involve a balloon payment?

    a. Fully amortized loan

    b. Partially amortized loan

    c. Variable rate loan

    d. Fixed rate loan

6. When compared to a 25-year amortized loan, a 30-year amortized loan has:

    a. less interest over the term of the loan.

    b. more principal over the term of the loan.

    c. higher monthly payments of principal and interest.

    d. lower monthly payments of principal and interest.

7. Which of the following statements best defines a mortgage loan?

    a. A loan secured by a mortgage on real estate

    b. Any means of creating a trusteeship

    c. An unsecured loan in which the mortgage itself serves as collateral

    d. None of the above

8. In a deed of trust, the power of sale in the event of default is given from the:

    a. beneficiary to the trustee.

    b. buyer to the seller.

    c. trustor to the trustee.

    d. trustee to the beneficiary.

9. A power of sale or trustee's sale foreclosure of a deed of trust:
    a. is similar to a court foreclosure.
    b. prohibits a deficiency judgment.
    c. allows for no reinstatement period.
    d. gives the trustor rights of redemption.

10. Mortgages and trust deeds are different in all of the following respects, except:
    a. parties.
    b. security.
    c. statute of limitations.
    d. title.

11. In the case of a contract of sale, the best analogy for the financial relationship of the parties is:
    a. landlord-tenant.
    b. beneficiary-trustor.
    c. optionor-optionee.
    d. grantor-grantee.

12. Adding an acceleration clause to a note would:
    a. not make the note less negotiable.
    b. be of no benefit to the holder.
    c. make the note nonnegotiable.
    d. greatly limit the negotiability of the note.

13. Foreclosure of a deed of trust may be accomplished either by court action or by power of sale. Foreclosure by court action:
    a. is not a remedy available in California.
    b. prohibits a deficiency judgment.
    c. usually establishes a right-of-redemption period.
    d. is identical to foreclosure by trustee sale.

14. When real property subject to a mortgage is foreclosed judicially, the mortgagor may remain in possession of the property for what maximum amount of time after the foreclosure of the sale?
    a. 30 days
    b. 90 days
    c. 180 days
    d. one year

15. A broker sells a property and negotiates a first loan from a bank and a second loan from a seller. The broker would record a Request for Notice of Default for the protection of the _____ loan.

    a. beneficiary of the first
    b. beneficiary of the second
    c. trustor of the first
    d. trustee of the first

16. Buyer Taylor purchases a home from seller Sanders and agrees to assume an existing conventional loan. The lender agrees to the assumption and signs a substitution of liability. Under these circumstances:

    a. Taylor becomes primarily responsible for the loan, and Sanders remains liable as a surety.
    b. Sanders remains primarily responsible for the loan, and Taylor becomes secondarily liable.
    c. Sanders is relieved from all liability.
    d. the loan may not be secured by a purchase-money deed of trust.

17. The main purpose of the FHA was to:

    a. help stabilize the housing market.
    b. promote homeownership by insuring home loans.
    c. raise building standards on a national basis.
    d. provide a source of home-loan funds at low rates.

18. For an FHA insured loan, the interest rate is:

    a. set by market conditions.
    b. set by the FHA.
    c. determined by agreement between the borrower and lender.
    d. set by the borrower only.

19. Rose, a prospective home buyer, asked Steve at ABC Real Estate Brokerage Company to help her get FHA financing. The broker would most likely contact:

    a. a mutual mortgage insurer.
    b. the Federal Reserve Bank
    c. the Federal Housing Administration.
    d. an approved mortgagee.

20. One of the special features of VA financing is that:

    a. the down payment cannot exceed 3% of the assessed value.

    b. the down payment varies with the property value.

    c. the down payment is determined by the CRV.

    d. there is no down payment if the selling price does not exceed the CRV.

21. Which of the following statements is not correct regarding land contracts?

    a. The buyer has equitable ownership of the property.

    b. The buyer has possession of the property.

    c. The seller has legal title of the property.

    d. The seller is known as the vendee.

22. A deed of trust and note are given to a seller to finance the purchase of vacant land. The buyer intends to place a short-term construction loan on the land. Such a deed of trust is most likely to include a(n) _____ clause.

    a. subrogation

    b. or more

    c. subordination

    d. prepayment

23. Which of the following is true regarding a hard-money second deed of trust?

    a. It is a real property purchase loan.

    b. It has the highest possible lien priority.

    c. Through this type of deed, equity in real property is the collateral for a cash loan.

    d. It cannot be used to purchase personal property.

24. Mike borrowed money from Robert. As security for the loan, Mike gave Robert a trust deed covering six separate parcels of previously unencumbered real property that Mike owned. Such a trust deed would be regarded as a(n) _____ trust deed.

    a. blanket

    b. subordinated

    c. all-inclusive

    d. purchase-money

25. Which of the following terms are most nearly identical?

    a. Takeout loan/deficit financing

    b. Takeout loan/interim loan

    c. Construction loan/take-out loan

    d. Construction loan/interim loan

UNIT 9 ANSWER KEY

Answers – Matching

1. J	5. S	9. Q	13. C	17. P
2. K	6. N	10. Y	14. B	18. F
3. O	7. T	11. A	15. U	19. H
4. M	8. V	12. R	16. D	20. W

Answers – Multiple Choice

1. **(b)** A promissory note is evidence of the debt. [Promissory Notes & Security Instruments]

2. **(d)** A negotiable instrument is a written unconditional order to pay a certain amount of money at a definite time or on demand. The trust deed is not a negotiable instrument. [Promissory Notes & Security Instruments]

3. **(b)** The interest rate stated in the note is called the nominal or named or face rate. The effective interest rate is the rate the borrower actually pays. [Promissory Notes & Security Instruments]

4. **(b)** Negative amortization means that a portion of the interest is not paid each month. This portion is added to the unpaid principal. [Promissory Notes & Security Instruments]

5. **(b)** Partial amortization means that a large (balloon) payment will be due at the end of the loan term. [Promissory Notes & Security Instruments]

6. **(d)** The longer the term of the loan, the lower the monthly payments. Since interest will be paid for a longer period, the total financing costs over the life of the loan would be higher. [Promissory Notes & Security Instruments]

7. **(a)** The mortgage or trust deed on the real property acts as security for the repayment of the loan. [Promissory Notes & Security Instruments]

8. **(c)** The buyer is the trustor and gives the power of sale to the trustee. [Promissory Notes & Security Instruments]

9. **(b)** A trustee's sale is a non-judicial sale. In a trustee's sale, no deficiency judgments are permitted on purchase money loans. [Promissory Notes & Security Instruments]

10. **(b)** The only thing they have in common is that they are both security for the promissory note. [Promissory Notes & Security Instruments]

11. **(b)** The vendor (seller) is financing the buyer (vendee) just as the lender (beneficiary) finances the buyer (trustor). [Promissory Notes & Security Instruments]

12. **(a)** Most promissory notes have acceleration clauses, which have no affect on the negotiability of the note. [Promissory Notes & Security Instruments]

13. **(c)** A judicial foreclosure has a redemption period in which the borrower may buy back the property. [Promissory Notes & Security Instruments]

14. **(d)** The mortgagor may remain in possession for up to one year after the foreclosure sale, but must pay rent. [Promissory Notes & Security Instruments]

15. **(b)** The beneficiary of the second loan is a junior lien holder who could be wiped out by a senior lien foreclosure. A Notice of Default gives the junior beneficiary time to protect his or her interest. [Promissory Notes & Security Instruments]

16. **(c)** If a loan is assumed with the lender's approval, the buyer becomes the principal debtor. [Promissory Notes & Security Instruments]

17. **(b)** The FHA's purpose is to promote affordable housing for low and moderate-income families. [Conventional & Government Loans]

18. **(c)** Even though interest rates are market driven, the borrower and lender agree to the interest rate. [Conventional & Government Loans]

19. **(d)** FHA insures loan made by FHA approved mortgagees (lenders). [Conventional & Government Loans]

20. **(d)** A veteran may purchase a home with no down payment provided the selling price is less than the Certificate of Reasonable Value (CRV) (appraisal) and the veteran is eligible to borrow under the VA program [Conventional & Government Loans]

21. **(d)** Choices (a), (b), and (c) are correct. The seller is called the vendor. [Promissory Notes & Security Instruments]

22. **(c)** A mortgage or deed of trust may contain a subordination clause stating that the lien created will have a lesser priority to a specified existing or future lien. Construction lenders will require that their loan is secured by a lien first in priority, so a subordination clause is essential for prior liens. [Priority of Recording]

23. **(c)** A hard-money mortgage is one given to a borrower in exchange for cash as opposed to one given to finance a specific real estate purchase. [Promissory Notes & Security Instruments]

24. **(a)** A blanket mortgage is a voluntary lien placed over more than one parcel. A blanket deed of trust is one secured by several distinct properties or lots. [Loan Programs]

25. **(d)** A construction loan (interim loan) is eventually replaced by a long-term loan called a take-out loan. [Loan Programs]

Lending Institutions

Unit 10

INTRODUCTION

In the previous Unit we discussed promissory notes, security instruments, and types of loans. Now we will direct our attention to the banking system, the primary and secondary mortgage markets, and the intricacies of obtaining a loan.

Learning Objectives

After completing this Unit, you should be able to:

8E   specify functions of the Federal Reserve System.

8F   recall regulations pertaining to financial institutions.

8G   recognize participants in the primary and secondary mortgage markets.

8H   name the steps in the underwriting process.

8I   recall required disclosures in financing.

THE IMPORTANCE OF REAL ESTATE FINANCE

At the center of nearly all real estate transactions is some kind of financing. Without an understanding of how real property is financed, the developer, the contractor, the real estate professional, and the property manager would find themselves out of a job. Most sellers would not be able to sell, because most buyers would be financially unable to pay cash, or unwilling to purchase unless a large part of the purchase price could be borrowed.

The purchase of a home is generally the largest acquisition consumers make in their lifetime. Most consumers do not have the financial wherewithal to purchase a home outright and must obtain a real estate loan to finance the transaction.

As we have seen, the national economy is circular in nature; financial markets are circular in nature as well. The circle starts with the Federal Reserve System and ends with a consumer obtaining a loan from a regulated institution.

THE FEDERAL RESERVE SYSTEM

The **Federal Reserve Bank System** (the Fed) is the nation's central bank and acts as the **banker's bank**. The Fed's primary purpose is to regulate the flow of money and credit, and to promote economic growth with stability. The Fed develops national monetary policy and shares responsibility with the 12 Federal Reserve banks for applying that policy and setting money supply goals.

In addition to serving as the banker's bank, the Federal Reserve System acts as banker for the U.S. Government. Federal Reserve Banks maintain accounts for the U.S. Treasury, process government checks, postal money orders and U.S. Savings bonds, and collect federal tax deposits.

Structure of the Federal Reserve System

The Federal Reserve System consists of a seven-member **Board of Governors** (BOG) headquartered in Washington, D.C., and a network of 12 Federal Reserve Banks (FRBs) located in major cities throughout the United States. For the purpose of carrying out these day-to-day operations of the Federal Reserve System, the nation has been divided into 12 Federal Reserve Districts. California is part of District 12, with the Federal Reserve Bank in San Francisco and four Federal Reserve Branches located in Los Angeles, Portland, Salt Lake City, and Seattle.

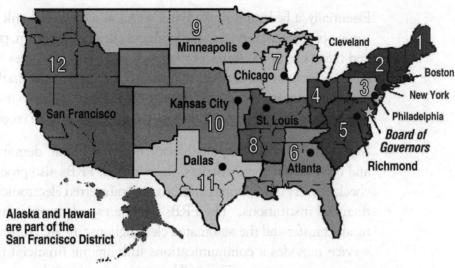

The 12 Federal Reserve Districts

Board of Governors

The primary responsibility of the Board of Governors of the Federal Reserve System is to formulate monetary policy. **Monetary policy** refers to the actions taken by the Fed to influence the availability and cost of money and credit as a means of promoting national economic goals. Additionally they have the responsibility to supervise the Federal Reserve Banks. Supervising banks generally means one of three duties: establishing safe banking practices, protecting consumers in financial transactions, and ensuring the stability of U.S. financial markets by acting as lender of last resort. The common goal of all three duties is to minimize risk in the banking system.

Federal Reserve Banks

Federal Reserve Banks are the operating arms of the central bank. They serve other lending institutions, the U.S. Treasury and, indirectly, the public. A **Federal Reserve Bank** (FRB) is often called the banker's bank, storing currency and coin, and processing checks and electronic payments. The 12 Federal Reserve Banks supervise state-chartered commercial banks, the companies that own banks (bank holding companies) and international organizations that do banking business in the United States.

The Federal Reserve is charged with the critical task of providing a safe and efficient method of transferring funds throughout the banking system. Reserve banks and their branches carry out this mission, offering payment services to all financial institutions in the United States, regardless of size or location. Hand in hand with that mission is the obligation to improve the payment system by encouraging efficiency and technological advances.

Essentially, a Federal Reserve Bank serves as a bankers' bank, offering a wide variety of payment services. It distributes currency and coin, processes checks, and offers electronic forms of payment. The Fed competes with the private sector in its financial services to foster competition in the marketplace, and to promote innovation and efficiency in the payment system. It does not seek to make a profit from its participation; it sets prices only to recover costs.

Regional FRBs are responsible for meeting public demand for currency and coin within their districts. In addition, FRBs also process commercial checks. Every day billions of dollars are transferred electronically among U.S. financial institutions. The FRBs provide two electronic payment services: funds transfer and the automated clearinghouse, or ACH. The funds transfer service provides a communications link among financial institutions and government agencies. The ACH provides a nationwide network to exchange paperless payments among financial institutions and government agencies. The ACH accommodates a wide range of recurring corporate and consumer transactions, such as payroll deposit, electronic bill payment, insurance payments, and Social Security disbursements.

Federal Open Market Committee

The **Federal Open Market Committee (FOMC)** is the most important monetary policy-making body of the Federal Reserve System. It is responsible for developing policies to promote economic growth, full employment, and stable prices. The FOMC makes key decisions regarding the conduct of open market operations-purchases and sales of U.S. government and federal agency securities.

How Does the Fed Implement Monetary Policy?

In an effort to avoid the peaks and valleys of the business cycle that cause liquidity and credit crises, the Fed monitors changing economic conditions and applies appropriate controls. The Fed influences the supply of money and credit available, thus controlling the behavior of lenders and borrowers. These controls are far reaching, often affecting interest rates, jobs, and economies worldwide. To accomplish its goals, the Fed uses three basic tools: (1) **reserve requirements**, (2) **setting the discount rates**, and (3) **open market operations**.

Reserve Requirements

All member banks must set aside a certain percentage of their deposits as a reserve. The reserve is money that the banks cannot lend. The Board of

Governors sets the reserve requirements. The Board increases or decreases the amount of money in circulation by raising or lowering reserve requirements for member banks. When the Board requires a larger reserve, the banks have less to lend, thus interest rates increase while borrowing and spending decrease. When the board lowers the reserve requirement, the banks have more money to lend, so interest rates may decrease, and borrowing and spending increase. Through its discount window, the Fed lends money to banks so that a shortage of funds at one institution does not disrupt the flow of money and credit in the entire banking system. Typically, the Fed makes loans to satisfy a bank's unanticipated needs for short-term funds. But the Fed also makes longer-term loans to help banks manage seasonal fluctuations in their customers' deposit or credit demands.

Discount Rate

A bank that needs to increase its reserve requirements would borrow money directly from the Federal Reserve Bank at the discount rate. A decrease in the interest rate allows more bank borrowing from the Fed. Bank borrowing increases money available for lending. Raising the discount rate produces less money available for lending to the consumer.

Open Market Operations

The **Federal Open Market Committee** (FOMC) of the Fed also buys and sells government securities, typically existing bonds, to influence the amount of available credit. The open market operations process is the most flexible and widely used technique for expanding or slowing the economy.

To stimulate or expand the economy, the Fed buys government securities from the public. This increases the bank's cash, which increases the money supply and lowers interest. This causes more money to be available in the banks to lend. To slow down the economy, the Fed sells government securities to the public. This reduces the banks' cash, tightens up the money supply, increases interest rates, and creates a **tight money market**.

REGULATION AND REFORM

During the Great Depression, the **Glass-Steagall Act** was passed that prohibited commercial banks from collaborating with full-service brokerage firms or participating in investment banking activities. In addition, before deregulation in the early 1980s, lending institutions were restricted on their activities, such as what interest rates they could pay on their deposits and where branches could be set up. **Deregulation** is a process whereby regulatory restraints are gradually relaxed. The first indication of a problem came in the late 1970s, when savers began to take their money out of savings and loan associations (S&Ls) and put it into investments that paid a higher rate of interest. This process, called **disintermediation**, began due to uncontrolled inflation, causing interest rates to increase dramatically. The regulated S&Ls were restricted by law from offering competitive interest rates. Therefore, depositors moved their money out of the S&Ls and put it into higher paying government securities, corporate bonds, and money market funds.

Many people felt that the government should remove the strict banking regulations and let them compete on the open market. In fact, this was the belief during both the Carter and Reagan administrations.

The **Depository Institutions Deregulation and Monetary Control Act** (DIDMCA) of 1980 had sweeping changes, one of which was to raise deposit insurance from $40,000 to $100,000. It also permitted savings and loans to offer a much wider range of services than ever before. The deregulatory measures allowed S&Ls to enter the business of commercial lending, trust services, and non-mortgage consumer lending.

The **Garn-St. Germain Depository Institutions Act** of 1982 completed the process of giving expanded powers to federally chartered S&Ls and enabled them to diversify their activities. Also in 1982, the Alternative Mortgage Transaction Parity Act (AMTPA) allowed lenders to originate adjustable-rate mortgages, and mortgages with balloon payments and negative amortization. Many S&Ls moved away from their traditional low-risk residential lending practices and began making higher-risk loans. Some S&Ls engaged in large-scale real estate speculation leading to the financial failure of over 500 institutions during the 1980s. Finally in 1989, the Federal Savings and Insurance Corporation (FSLIC), the insurer who provided a recovery fund for depositors in the event of an S&L failure, did not have enough funds to bail out the failing S&Ls, became insolvent and also failed.

The inevitable legislative backlash to the behavior of the savings and loan industry was the **Financial Institutions Reform, Recovery, and Enforcement Act** of 1989 (FIRREA). Under FIRREA, the Office of Thrift Supervision and the Housing Finance Board were authorized to oversee the S&L regulation responsibilities. The Federal Deposit Insurance Corporation (FDIC) now insures deposits in all federally chartered banks and savings institutions up to $250,000 per depositor, per insured bank. The Dodd-Frank Act of 2010 made the $250,000 permanent.

The **Gramm-Leach-Bliley Act** of 1999 (GLBA) repealed part of the Glass–Steagall Act prohibiting banks from affiliating with securities firms. This allowed commercial banks, investment banks, insurance companies, and securities firms to consolidate. Additionally, it created a new "financial holding company" that could engage in insurance and securities underwriting activities. In the same year, Fannie Mae eased the credit requirements to encourage banks to make home loans to borrowers whose credit was not good enough to qualify for conventional loans. In addition, in 2000, HUD required Fannie Mae to allocate 50% of its business to low-and moderate-income families.

The perfect storm of record low interest rates, abandonment of mortgage under-writing standards, subprime loans, and out-right mortgage fraud combined to create a housing bubble that burst in 2006. The plunge in home sales led to a huge increase in foreclosures of subprime mortgages. By 2007, many subprime lenders filed a Chapter 11 bankruptcy or closed. Even large mortgage lenders, such as Countrywide Financial, and investment banks, such as Bear Sterns, were not immune to the meltdown. By the summer of 2008, the financial institutions were in a state of chaos and reported billions of dollars in losses.

In 2008, the **Housing and Economic Recovery Act** (HERA) was passed to stimulate the housing market. It also established the **Federal Housing Finance Agency** (FHFA). On September 7, 2008, Fannie Mae and Freddie Mac were placed under the conservatorship of the FHFA in an attempt to stabilize the floundering mortgage markets.

In 2010, the federal **Dodd-Frank Wall Street Reform and Consumer Protection Act** (Dodd-Frank Act) was enacted into law as a response to the financial turbulence and recession in the late 2000s. It is making changes to financial regulatory agencies and affects almost every aspect of the nation's financial services industry. The Dodd-Frank Act established the Consumer Financial Protection Bureau (Bureau or CFPB) and authorized it to regulate consumer financial products and services and enforce seventeen "inherited" consumer protection laws. The Bureau recodified and republished the inherited regulations under Chapter X of Title 12 of the Code of Federal Regulations. For example, RESPA (24 CFR 3500) no longer is enforced by HUD; it is renumbered as 12 CFR 1024 and is enforced by the CFPB.

THE MORTGAGE MARKET

The real estate lending industry has grown substantially over the past years. In fact, the total real estate debt in the country is the largest in the world, second only to the debt of the U.S. government. Consumers use money and credit to develop and acquire real property. Real estate mortgage financing is made up of the institutions that create and purchase instruments of finance, and the markets in which they are transferred.

The residential real estate lending industry is comprised of two distinct markets— the primary mortgage market and the secondary mortgage market.

Primary Mortgage Market

The **primary mortgage market** is the market in which lenders make mortgage loans by lending directly to borrowers. Participants in the primary mortgage market sell loans in the secondary mortgage market to replenish their funds.

Lenders that make real estate loans are known as financial intermediaries. As the word intermediary indicates, these financial institutions stand between the suppliers and users of credit. As a liaison, the **financial intermediary** combines funds from many sources (individual savers, short-term or long-term investors) and adapts them into loans for the consumer. This process is called **intermediation**.

All mortgage lenders are financial intermediaries, even though they are not all depository institutions. A **depository institution** is one that accepts deposits in the form of savings accounts, and makes loans using their depositors' monies. These loans are carefully regulated by law because they consist of other peoples' money. Mortgage bankers do not accept deposits from savers so they are non-depository institutions. They make mortgage loans by using their own funds or by borrowing from lenders, and then selling the loans they originate.

Lenders are also classified as institutional lenders and non-institutional lenders. Institutional lenders are depository institutions. Non-institutional lenders are non-depository institutions.

Institutional Lenders

An **institutional lender**, as a depository, such as a commercial bank, accepts deposits that are then pooled to be invested in various ways, including trust deeds and mortgages. Institutional lenders receive most of their deposits from household savings (savings of individual investors). The main job of institutional lenders is to transfer money from the people who invest money to those who want to borrow it.

They make their money by lending money at a higher interest rate than what they pay their depositors or pay to borrow from the Fed. On mortgages, the lender receives the interest as well as the origination fees and points expressed as a percentage, called **mortgage yield**.

Institutional lenders include commercial banks, thrifts, credit unions, and life insurance companies. Although most people do their personal banking at commercial banks, thrifts, or credit unions, few know that they are different kinds of financial institutions, with similar banking services but operating under different regulations.

Commercial Banks

Commercial banks are the all-purpose lenders whose real estate loans represent only a portion of their overall activity. They make the widest range of loans, including loans for buying real estate, home equity loans, business loans, and other short-term loans. The major type of lending activity funded by commercial banks is for short-term (6-to-36 months) construction loans, even though they do make other types of loans as well. Typically though, a commercial bank will make short-term, or interim, loans to finance construction. Long-term, take-out loans may be available after a construction loan is paid off. Commercial banks rely on the creditworthiness of and experience with the borrower to assure repayment of the loan. When dealing with commercial loans, a borrower deposits funds with the bank in order to induce the lender into making a loan. This is known as a **compensating balance**.

Thrifts

Thrifts are the largest single resource for residential mortgage credit. Types of thrifts include savings and loan associations (S&Ls), savings banks, and mutual savings banks. Any thrift can be owned either as a mutual organization or as a stock institution. Deposits for both institutions are insured by the Federal Deposit Insurance Corporation (FDIC).

Mutual ownership means that all the depositors share ownership in the savings and loan or bank, which is managed by a board of trustees. The depositors (investors) in S&Ls, savings banks or mutual savings banks are paid dividends on their share of the earnings of the organization. Mutual organizations issue no stock. On the other hand, if the institution is organized as a stock institution, investors can purchase stock through their stockbroker. A stock institution is managed by a board of directors who represent the stockholders of the bank.

Savings & Loan Associations

Traditionally, **savings and loan institutions** (S&Ls) have played a major role in the economy by pooling the savings of individuals to fund residential mortgages. The first customers of S&Ls were depositors as well as borrowers, and as their customer base grew, the S&L associations became a primary source of loans to finance homebuilding. Deregulation in the early 1980s allowed the S&Ls

Banks are authorized to make mortgage loans.

to participate in a wide range of investment opportunities. Within less than 10 years, 20% of S&Ls were insolvent, 20% were marginal, and only 60% were financially sound. This led to many S&L failures and for others to change their charters to savings banks.

Savings Banks

Savings banks have been described as distinctive types of thrift institutions, behaving sometimes like commercial banks and sometimes like S&Ls. While savings banks are authorized to make mortgage loans, most specialize in consumer and commercial loans.

As mentioned previously, many financially troubled savings and loan associations were issued federal savings bank charters in an attempt to keep the S&Ls out of bankruptcy. By switching to the federal charters the new savings banks could offer their depositors the safety of deposit insurance under Federal Deposit Insurance Corporation—the same as commercial banks.

Mutual Savings Banks

When lending institutions were being established in the first part of the 19th century, the average income worker was ignored mostly due to their lack of extra funds to invest or save. **Mutual savings banks** were established to encourage savings by people who did not have a large amount of disposable income left after their living expenses, but who did want to invest in their future.

Initially, mutual savings banks were state-chartered, mutual organizations relying on their customers' savings to provide all the capital they needed to be successful. They did not sell stock in the company to shareholders. Recently, mutual savings banks were permitted to change their charter from mutual ownership to become federally chartered stock institutions that issue stock to raise capital. These institutions operate similarly to savings and loan associations and are located primarily in the northeastern section of the United States.

Credit Unions

A **credit union** is an association whose members usually have the same type of occupation. The members join for mutual benefit by saving money in their own bank and receiving better interest rates. Both secured and unsecured loans are made at rates lower than other lenders can offer. Because of the low overhead and other costs of doing business, credit unions are a growing source of funds for consumers. They are supervised by the National Credit Union Association Board (NCUAB) and deposits are insured by the federally insured National Credit Union Share Insurance Fund. Credit unions are limited by their charters to providing services for members of a particular organization, such as employees of fire departments, utilities, corporations or other specific group.

Insurance Companies

Insurance companies are major suppliers of money for large commercial loans to developers and builders. Commercial real estate is a good, long-term investment for insurance companies because of the long time-line of their investment goals. They usually do not make construction loans, but make take out loans on large properties. For example, a developer who wants a long-term $3,000,000 loan to purchase and rehabilitate an existing shopping center would borrow the money from an insurance company.

Loans made by insurance companies have low interest rates and the lowest loan-to-value ratio. Usually loans are made through loan correspondents (mortgage companies) who negotiate and service the loans.

They do not usually get involved with the single home residential market, but can buy loans from mortgage companies and invest in Ginnie Mae government insured or guaranteed loans. Life insurance companies, in particular, receive regular periodic payments from customers in return for assurance that any loss would be covered if certain described events occur for which the customer is insured.

Non-Institutional Lenders

In addition to institutional lenders, there is another group of lenders referred to as **non-institutional lenders**. Non-institutional lenders are non-depository institutions and do not take deposits. They are private lenders that invest their own funds or borrowed funds. This group includes private individuals, mortgage companies, and investment companies, as well as others—like pension funds and title companies.

Private Individuals

Private individuals (sellers) are the major source of junior loans. The most common way to create a junior loan is by sellers carrying back a trust deed on the sale of their own homes. Usually, private loans are short term, with the main focus of the lender being the safety of the loan, and a high return on the investment.

Mortgage Companies

A **mortgage company**, which is also known as a **mortgage banker**, is a company whose principal business is the origination, closing, funding, selling, and servicing of loans secured by real property. Since they are not depository institutions, they lend their own or money borrowed from warehouse lenders to fund loans. Since mortgage companies do not have depositors, they use short-term borrowing called a warehouse line or warehouse line of credit. A **warehouse line** is a revolving line of credit extended to a mortgage company from a warehouse lender to make loans to borrowers.

The mortgage banker often acts as a mover of funds from an area of the country with an abundance of money to be loaned, to another area that is capital deficient. The biggest role of mortgage companies, however, is to originate and service loans that they package and sell. After loans are originated, a mortgage company might retain the loans in the lender's portfolio or may package and sell them to an investor. The sale of these loan packages provides added capital the mortgage company can use to make more loans to be packaged and sold, thus repeating the cycle.

A mortgage company prefers loans that are most readily sold in the secondary market, such as FHA, VA, or conventional mortgages. Therefore, the mortgage banker is careful to follow guidelines established by those who will be buying the loans.

Do not confuse mortgage bankers with mortgage brokers. A **mortgage broker** is a third party originator (TPOs)—not a lender. Mortgage brokers coordinate the loan process between the borrower and the lender and charge an origination fee to provide this service to the borrower. Mortgage brokers qualify borrowers, take applications, and send completed loan packages to the lender. The lender approves and underwrites loans and funds them at closing. The mortgage broker does not service the loan and has no other concern with it once it is funded.

Real Estate Investment Trust

A real estate investment trust, or REIT, is a company that owns operates income-producing real estate or engages in financing real estate. REITs generally fall into three categories: equity REITs, mortgage REITs, and hybrid REITs. Equity REITs typically own and operate income-producing real estate. Mortgage REITs provide money to real estate owners and operators either directly in the form of mortgages or indirectly through the acquisition of mortgage-backed securities. Hybrid REITs generally are companies that use the investment strategies of both equity REITs and mortgage REITs.

To qualify as a REIT, a company must have the bulk of its assets and income connected to real estate investment and must distribute at least 90% of its taxable income in the form of dividends to shareholders. In addition, a REIT must have a minimum of 100 shareholders invest at least 75% of its total assets in real estate assets and cash.

The REIT itself does not pay taxes on its profits, but individual members of the trust are taxed, at their own tax rates, on the dividends distributed to them.

Non-Financial Institutions

Non-financial institutions, as you have read, are non-depository institutions. Universities, pension funds, trust departments of banks and title companies are all non-financial institutions and all hold real estate loans as investments.

Secondary Mortgage Market

In contrast to the primary mortgage market, in which lending institutions make mortgage loans directly to borrowers, the **secondary mortgage market** is for buying and selling existing mortgages from the primary mortgage market or from each other. Participants in the secondary mortgage market do not originate loans.

The secondary mortgage market can be seen as a resale marketplace for loans—in which existing loans are bought and sold. The secondary mortgage market exists because of the need, by thrifts and other financial institutions, to have the ability to sell their assets quickly when they need more money, particularly in a market in which consumers are demanding more home loans. This important market is the foundation of the lending process and an essential part of our national economy's health. The secondary market's main function is to get the money to primary lenders by buying their existing mortgages. The primary lenders then have more cash with which to make new loans. These loans are then sold in the secondary market, continuing the cycle of putting money back into the primary market. America's secondary mortgage market attracts capital from around the world to finance a wide range of mortgage products designed specifically to make homeownership affordable and accessible. No other country has a comparable secondary market.

Participants in the secondary market who purchase existing mortgages buy them with funds they have acquired by issuing bonds or other types of debt instruments. The mortgages they buy are used as security for those debt instruments. The **debt instruments**, known as **mortgage-backed securities**, are collateralized by the mortgages that have been bought in the secondary market. These mortgage-backed securities also are bought and sold in the secondary market.

The original source of the funds used to buy the mortgage-backed securities is investors who purchase the securities from the secondary market agency or company. That agency then uses the funds from the investor to buy more mortgages—for example, from a thrift or mortgage banker. The originators of the loans use the funds they receive from the sale of the loan to originate more mortgage loans. Consumers and the entire economy benefit by the investors supplying the funds that end up, eventually, as home loans to consumers.

Participants in the Secondary Mortgage Market

There are two major participants in the secondary mortgage market: (1) the Federal National Mortgage Association (Fannie Mae) and (2) the Federal Home Loan Mortgage Corporation (Freddie Mac). Both Fannie Mae and Freddie Mac are congressionally chartered, shareholder-owned corporations commonly known as government-sponsored enterprises. A **government-sponsored enterprise (GSE)** is a financial services corporation created by the United States Congress.

The **housing GSEs** are Fannie Mae, Freddie Mac, and the Federal Home Loan Banks (FHLBs). The housing GSEs are critical in providing liquidity, stability, and affordability to the mortgage market, particularly for long-term, fixed-rate mortgages. Fannie Mae and Freddie Mac purchase conforming loans from lenders (e.g., banks, thrifts, and mortgage companied) in the primary market who then use the proceeds to finance more mortgages. Fannie Mae and Freddie Mac securitize the mortgages they purchased and issue mortgage-backed securities (MBS) that are sold to investors in the capital markets. The FHLBs provide advances and other financial products to support their members' affordable housing activities.

The housing GSEs are regulated by the **Federal Housing Finance Agency** (FHFA), an independent regulatory agency that was established by the Federal Housing Finance Reform Act of 2007. Each year FHFA sets the limit of the size of a conforming loan, which is based on the October-to-October changes in mean home price.

Fannie Mae

Fannie Mae does not lend money directly to homebuyers. Initially, it was authorized to buy and sell FHA-insured loans from lenders, but VA-guaranteed loans were added in 1944. This secondary market for the FHA and VA loans helped make sure that affordable mortgage money was available for people in communities all across America and helped fuel the housing boom in the 1950s. Its role was expanded in 1972, when Fannie Mae was permitted to buy and sell conventional mortgages. Through the years, Fannie Mae has consistently been one of the nation's largest sources of financing for home mortgages.

Fannie Mae supports the secondary mortgage market by issuing mortgage-related securities and purchasing mortgages. Fannie Mae buys loans from lenders who conform to Fannie Mae guidelines and, by doing so, puts mortgage money back into the system so lenders can make more loans. **Mortgage-backed securities** (MBS) are pools of mortgages used as collateral for the issuance of securities in the secondary market. MBS are commonly referred to as **pass-through securities** because the principal and interest of the underlying loans are passed through to investors.

Freddie Mac

Freddie Mac's mission is to provide liquidity, stability, and affordability by providing secondary mortgage support for conventional mortgages originated by thrift institutions. Since its inception, Freddie Mac has helped finance one out of every six homes in America.

Freddie Mac links Main Street to Wall Street by purchasing, securitizing, and investing in home mortgages. Freddie Mac conducts its business by buying mortgages that meet the company's underwriting and product standards from lenders. The loans are pooled, packaged into securities, guaranteed by Freddie

Mac, and sold to investors such as insurance companies and pension funds. This provides homeowners and renters with lower housing costs and better access to home financing.

Federal Home Loan Banks

The **Federal Home Loan Banks** (FHLBanks) are 11 regional cooperative banks that lending institutions use to finance housing and economic development in their communities. Created by Congress, the FHLBanks have been one of the largest, private sources of funding for community lending in the U.S. for more than eight decades. They provide stable, on-demand, low-cost funding to financial institutions (not individuals) for home mortgage loans, small business, rural, agricultural, and economic development lending.

Approximately 7,400 lenders are members of the FHLBanks. Banks, thrifts, credit unions, community development financial institutions and insurance companies are all eligible for membership. Members, ranging in size from some of the largest financial institutions in the world to banks with just a single branch, do business throughout the United States.

With their members, the FHLBanks represents the largest collective source of home mortgage and community credit in the United States.

Ginnie Mae

Ginnie Mae is a government-owned corporation within the Department of Housing and Urban Development (HUD). Ginnie Mae was created in 1968 when the Federal National Mortgage Association was split into Fannie Mae and Ginnie Mae. Fannie Mae's focus is to support the secondary market for conventional loans and Ginnie Mae's is to support the market for FHA, VA, and other loans.

Unlike Fannie Mae and Freddie Mac, Ginnie Mae does not buy or sell pools of loans. Ginnie Mae does not issue mortgage-backed securities (MBS). Instead, Ginnie Mae guarantees investors the timely payment of principal and interest on MBS backed by federally insured or guaranteed loans—mainly loans issued by the FHA and the VA. In fact, the FHA insures approximately two-thirds of the loans backing Ginnie Mae securities.

In contrast to the MBS issued by Fannie Mae and Freddie Mac, all Ginnie Mae securities are explicitly backed by the full faith and credit of the U.S. Government. This is because Ginnie Mae is a wholly-owned government corporation.

The Mortgage Market Cycle

GETTING A LOAN (UNDERWRITING)

Getting a loan is an integral part of the real estate transaction since very few people have the amount of ready cash to buy a home with no financing. The first step in getting a loan is for the borrower to fill out a loan application. Once the lender has the borrower's completed application the underwriting process can begin. Simply put, **underwriting** is the process of evaluating a borrower's risk factors before the lender will make a loan.

The lender will determine the ability of a borrower to pay the loan and determine if the value of the property is sufficient to repay the loan in the event of a default by the borrower. The purpose of underwriting is to determine if the borrower and the property meet the minimum standards established by the primary lender and the secondary market investor. Once both the borrower and the property qualify, the loan process continues until it closes.

Loan Application

The underwriting process begins with the borrower filling out a loan application and gathering the documents needed by the lender. Usually the lender will ask for three monthly bank statements, the two most recent pay stubs, two year's previous tax returns, and proof of any investments. Once received the lender will verify the information and order an appraisal in order to qualify the property.

Qualifying the Borrower

Several risk factors are taken into consideration when evaluating a borrower for a loan, such as the borrower's debt-to-income level, employment history, type of property, and assets. The lender will order a credit report, which will show the borrower's payment history, balance of outstanding debt, credit history, number of credit inquiries, and types of credit held. The most important being the payment and credit history.

Credit Report

The lender requests a **credit report** from one of the credit reporting agencies Experian®, Equifax®, or TransUnion™. These companies research the credit records of consumers and memorialize the findings in a factual credit report. They have access to databases that store credit information on most consumers in the country. Additionally, they search the public records for derogatory items that may have been filed against a consumer, such as judgments, bankruptcies, and liens. The credit report indicates a credit score for the loan applicant. Credit scores only consider the information contained in the credit profile. They do not consider income, savings, down payment amount, or demographic factors—like gender, nationality, or marital status.

Credit scoring is an objective, statistical method that lenders use to quickly assess the borrower's credit risk. The score is a number that rates the likelihood that a borrower will repay a loan.

Past delinquencies, derogatory payment behavior, current debt level, length of credit history, types of credit, and number of inquiries are all considered in credit scores. Establishing a good track record of making payments on time will raise the credit score, but late payments will lower the score.

Scores range from 350 (high risk) to 850 (low risk). There are a few types of credit scores; the most widely used are **FICO**® scores, which were developed by Fair Isaac & Company, Inc. The FICO® scores run from 350 to 620 for the applicants who are late in paying bills and between 700 to above 800 for those applicants who always pay bills on time.

Under the Fair Credit Reporting Act, a person who has been denied credit, housing, or employment may receive a free copy of his or her credit report by contacting one of the credit reporting agencies directly.

Qualifying the Property

The lender's first line of defense in getting repaid on the loan is the borrower's creditworthiness. However, the underlying security for the loan is the property; therefore, an accurate valuation of the property is important. The lender will require an appraisal to determine fair market value of the property prior to making a loan. Once the appraised value is determined, the lender will calculate the loan amount. Most lenders want an 80% loan-to-value ratio. **Loan-to-value** is the percentage of appraised value to the loan. An 80% loan would require the borrower to make a 20% down payment. Loans made with less than a 20% down payment will require mortgage insurance.

The difference between the appraised value and the loan is called **equity.** Therefore, property is purchased with **equity funds** (down payment) and **debt** (loan funds).

Electronic Underwriting Credit Report and Evaluation

The mortgage industry uses electronic underwriting systems that predict multiple-risk factors in a loan application. The most widely used automated underwriting systems are Fannie Mae's **Desktop Underwriter®** and Freddie Mac's **Loan Prospector** ®. Fannie Mae offers its lenders electronic loan processing with its Desktop Underwriter system. Users receive an analysis of the borrower's credit, estimate of the property's value, and an opinion of the risk involved. This information is prepared from the data submitted on the loan application and is available in a matter of minutes. The use of a common automated underwriting standard will simplify the electronic mortgage application process and reduce its cost.

DISCLOSURES IN FINANCING

Since 1968, credit protections have multiplied rapidly. The concepts of fair and equal credit have been written into laws that prohibit unfair discrimination in credit transactions, require that consumers be told the reason when credit is denied, let borrowers find out about their credit records, and set up a way for consumers to settle billing disputes.

Each law was meant to reduce the problems and confusion about consumer credit, which—as it became more widely used in our economy—also grew more complex. Together, these laws set a standard for how individuals are to be treated in their financial dealings.

Uniform Residential Loan Application

This application is designed to be completed by the applicant(s) with the Lender's assistance. Applicants should complete this form as "Borrower" or "Co-Borrower," as applicable. Co-Borrower information must also be provided (and the appropriate box checked) when ☐ the income or assets of a person other than the Borrower (including the Borrower's spouse) will be used as a basis for loan qualification or ☐ the income or assets of the Borrower's spouse or other person who has community property or similar rights pursuant to applicable state law will not be used as a basis for loan qualification, but his or her liabilities must be considered because the spouse or other person who has community property or similar rights and the Borrower resides in a community property state, the security property is located in a community property state, or the Borrower is relying on other property located in a community property state as a basis for repayment of the loan.

If this is an application for joint credit, Borrower and Co-Borrower each agree that we intend to apply for joint credit (sign below):

Borrower _____   Co-Borrower _____

I. TYPE OF MORTGAGE AND TERMS OF LOAN			
Mortgage Applied for: ☐ VA ☐ USDA/Rural Housing Service ☐ FHA ☐ Conventional ☐ Other (explain):		Agency Case Number	Lender Case Number

Amount $	Interest Rate %	No. of Months	**Amortization Type:**	☐ Fixed Rate ☐ Other (explain): ☐ GPM ☐ ARM (type):

II. PROPERTY INFORMATION AND PURPOSE OF LOAN	
Subject Property Address (street, city, state & ZIP)	No. of Units
Legal Description of Subject Property (attach description if necessary)	Year Built

Purpose of Loan ☐ Purchase ☐ Refinance ☐ Construction ☐ Construction-Permanent ☐ Other (explain):	Property will be: ☐ Primary Residence ☐ Secondary Residence ☐ Investment

Complete this line if construction or construction-permanent loan.

Year Lot Acquired	Original Cost	Amount Existing Liens	(a) Present Value of Lot	(b) Cost of Improvements	Total (a + b)
	$	$	$	$	$

Complete this line if this is a refinance loan.

Year Acquired	Original Cost	Amount Existing Liens	Purpose of Refinance	Describe Improvements	☐ made ☐ to be made
	$	$			

Title will be held in what Name(s)	Manner in which Title will be held	Estate will be held in: ☐ Fee Simple ☐ Leasehold (show expiration date)

Source of Down Payment, Settlement Charges, and/or Subordinate Financing (explain)

III. BORROWER INFORMATION

Borrower				Co-Borrower			
Borrower's Name (include Jr. or Sr. if applicable)				Co-Borrower's Name (include Jr. or Sr. if applicable)			
Social Security Number	Home Phone (incl. Area code)	DOB (mm/dd/yyyy)	Yrs. School	Social Security Number	Home Phone (incl. Area code)	DOB (mm/dd/yyyy)	Yrs. School
☐ Married ☐ Separated ☐ Unmarried (include single, divorced, widowed)		Dependents (not listed by Co-Borrower) no. ages		☐ Married ☐ Separated ☐ Unmarried (include single, divorced, widowed)		Dependents (not listed by Borrower) no. ages	
Present Address (street, city, state, ZIP) ☐ Own ☐ Rent __No. Yrs.				Present Address (street, city, state, ZIP) ☐ Own ☐ Rent __No. Yrs.			
Mailing Address, if different from Present Address				Mailing Address, if different from Present Address			

If residing at present address for less than two years, complete the following:

Former Address (street, city, state, ZIP) ☐ Own ☐ Rent __No. Yrs.				Former Address (street, city, state, ZIP) ☐ Own ☐ Rent __No. Yrs.			

IV. EMPLOYMENT INFORMATION

Borrower			Co-Borrower		
Name & Address of Employer ☐ Self Employed		Yrs. on this job	Name & Address of Employer ☐ Self Employed		Yrs. on this job
		Yrs. employed in this line of work/profession			Yrs. employed in this line of work/profession
Position/Title/Type of Business		Business Phone (incl. area code)	Position/Title/Type of Business		Business Phone (incl. area code)

If employed in current position for less than two years or if currently employed in more than one position, complete the following:

Name & Address of Employer ☐ Self Employed		Dates (from - to)	Name & Address of Employer ☐ Self Employed		Dates (from - to)
		Monthly Income $			Monthly Income $
Position/Title/Type of Business		Business Phone (incl. area code)	Position/Title/Type of Business		Business Phone (incl. area code)
Name & Address of Employer ☐ Self Employed		Dates (from - to)	Name & Address of Employer ☐ Self Employed		Dates (from - to)
		Monthly Income $			Monthly Income $
Position/Title/Type of Business		Business Phone (incl. area code)	Position/Title/Type of Business		Business Phone (incl. area code)

V. MONTHLY INCOME AND COMBINED HOUSING EXPENSE INFORMATION						
Gross Monthly Income	Borrower	Co-Borrower	Total	Combined Monthly Housing Expense	Present	Proposed
Base Empl. Income*	$	$	$	Rent	$	
Overtime				First Mortgage (P&I)		$
Bonuses				Other Financing (P&I)		
Commissions				Hazard Insurance		
Dividends/ Interest				Real Estate Taxes		
Net Rental Income				Mortgage Insurance		
Other (before completing, see the notice in "describe other income," below)				Homeowner Assn. Dues		
				Other:		
Total	$	$	$	Total	$	$

   *   **Self Employed Borrower(s) may be required to provide additional documentation such as tax returns and financial statements.**

Describe Other Income   *Notice:* **Alimony, child support, or separate maintenance income need not be revealed if the Borrower (B) or Co-Borrower (C) does not choose to have it considered for repaying this loan.**

B/C		Monthly Amount
		$

VI. ASSETS AND LIABILITIES

This Statement and any applicable supporting schedules may be completed jointly by both married and unmarried Co-Borrowers if their assets and liabilities are sufficiently joined so that the Statement can be meaningfully and fairly presented on a combined basis; otherwise, separate Statements and Schedules are required. If the Co-Borrower section was completed about a non-applicant spouse or other person, this Statement and supporting schedules must be completed about that spouse or other person also.

Completed ☐ Jointly ☐ Not Jointly

ASSETS Description	Cash or Market Value	Liabilities and Pledged Assets. List the creditor's name, address, and account number for all outstanding debts, including automobile loans, revolving charge accounts, real estate loans, alimony, child support, stock pledges, etc. Use continuation sheet, if necessary. Indicate by (*) those liabilities, which will be satisfied upon sale of real estate owned or upon refinancing of the subject property.		
Cash deposit toward purchase held by:	$	**LIABILITIES**	Monthly Payment & Months Left to Pay	Unpaid Balance
List checking and savings accounts below		Name and address of Company	$ Payment/Months	$
Name and address of Bank, S&L, or Credit Union				
		Acct. no.		
Acct. no.	$	Name and address of Company	$ Payment/Months	$
Name and address of Bank, S&L, or Credit Union		Acct. no.		
Acct. no.	$	Name and address of Company	$ Payment/Months	$
Name and address of Bank, S&L, or Credit Union				
		Acct. no.		
Acct. no.	$	Name and address of Company	$ Payment/Months	$
Name and address of Bank, S&L, or Credit Union				
		Acct. no.		
Acct. no.	$	Name and address of Company	$ Payment/Months	$
Stocks & Bonds (Company name/number & description)	$			
		Acct. no.		
Life insurance net cash value	$	Name and address of Company	$ Payment/Months	$
Face amount: $				
Subtotal Liquid Assets	$	Acct. no.		
Real estate owned (enter market value from schedule of real estate owned)	$	Alimony/Child Support/Separate Maintenance Payments Owed to:	$	
Vested interest in retirement fund	$			
Net worth of business(es) owned (attach financial statement)	$	Job-Related Expense (child care, union dues, etc.)	$	
Automobiles owned (make and year)	$			
Other Assets (itemize)	$			
		Total Monthly Payments	$	
Total Assets a.	$	**Net Worth (a minus b)** $	**Total Liabilities b.**	$

Schedule of Real Estate Owned (If additional properties are owned, use continuation sheet.)

Property Address (enter S if sold, PS if pending sale or R if rental being held for income)		Type of Property	Present Market Value	Amount of Mortgages & Liens	Gross Rental Income	Mortgage Payments	Insurance, Maintenance, Taxes & Misc.	Net Rental Income
			$	$	$	$	$	$
	Totals		$	$	$	$	$	$

List any additional names under which credit has previously been received and indicate appropriate creditor name(s) and account number(s):

Alternate Name	Creditor Name	Account Number

VII. DETAILS OF TRANSACTION		VIII. DECLARATIONS				
		If you answer "Yes" to any questions a through i, please use continuation sheet for explanation.	Borrower		Co-Borrower	
			Yes	No	Yes	No
a. Purchase price	$					
b. Alterations, improvements, repairs						
c. Land (if acquired separately)		a. Are there any outstanding judgments against you?	☐	☐	☐	☐
d. Refinance (incl. debts to be paid off)		b. Have you been declared bankrupt within the past 7 years?	☐	☐	☐	☐
e. Estimated prepaid items		c. Have you had property foreclosed upon or given title or deed in lieu thereof in the last 7 years?	☐	☐	☐	☐
f. Estimated closing costs		d. Are you a party to a lawsuit?	☐	☐	☐	☐
g. PMI, MIP, Funding Fee		e. Have you directly or indirectly been obligated on any loan of which resulted in foreclosure, transfer of title in lieu of foreclosure, or judgment?	☐	☐	☐	☐
		(This would include such loans as home mortgage loans, SBA loans, home improvement loans, educational loans, manufactured (mobile) home loans, any mortgage, financial obligation, bond, or loan guarantee. If "Yes," provide details, including date, name, and address of Lender, FHA or VA case number, if any, and reasons for the action.)				
h. Discount (if Borrower will pay)		f. Are you presently delinquent or in default on any Federal debt or any other loan, mortgage, financial obligation, bond, or loan guarantee?	☐	☐	☐	☐
		If "Yes," give details as described in the preceding question.				
i. **Total costs** (add items a through h)		g. Are you obligated to pay alimony, child support, or separate maintenance?	☐	☐	☐	☐
j. Subordinate financing		h. Is any part of the down payment borrowed?	☐	☐	☐	☐

VII. DETAILS OF TRANSACTION (cont'd)			VIII. DECLARATIONS (cont'd)				
k.	Borrower's closing costs paid by Seller		i.	Are you a co-maker or endorser on a note?	☐ ☐	☐ ☐	
l.	Other Credits (explain)		j.	Are you a U.S. citizen?	☐ ☐	☐ ☐	
			k.	Are you a permanent resident alien?	☐ ☐	☐ ☐	
m.	Loan amount (exclude PMI, MIP, Funding Fee financed)		l.	**Do you intend to occupy the property as your primary residence?** If "Yes," complete question m below.	☐ ☐	☐ ☐	
n.	PMI, MIP, Funding Fee financed		m. in	Have you had an ownership interest in a property in the last three years?	☐ ☐	☐ ☐	
o.	Loan amount (add m & n)			(1) What type of property did you own–principal residence (PR), second home (SH), or investment property (IP)?	___	___	
p.	Cash from/to Borrower (subtract j, k, l & o from i)			(2) How did you hold title to the home– by yourself (S), jointly with your spouse or jointly with another person (O)?	___	___	

IX. ACKNOWLEDGMENT AND AGREEMENT

Each of the undersigned specifically represents to Lender and to Lender's actual or potential agents, brokers, processors, attorneys, insurers, servicers, successors and assigns and agrees and acknowledges that: (1) the information provided in this application is true and correct as of the date set forth opposite my signature and that any intentional or negligent misrepresentation of this information contained in this application may result in civil liability, including monetary damages, to any person who may suffer any loss due to reliance upon any misrepresentation that I have made on this application, and/or in criminal penalties including, but not limited to, fine or imprisonment or both under the provisions of Title 18, United States Code, Sec. 1001, et seq.;   (2) the loan requested pursuant to this application (the "Loan") will be secured by a mortgage or deed of trust on the property described in this application; (3) the property will not be used for any illegal or prohibited purpose or use;   (4) all statements made in this application are made for the purpose of obtaining a residential mortgage loan; (5) the property will be occupied as indicated in this application; (6) the Lender, its servicers, successors or assigns may retain the original and/or an electronic record of this application, whether or not the Loan is approved; (7) the Lender and its agents, brokers, insurers, servicers, successors, and assigns may continuously rely on the information contained in the application, and I am obligated to amend and/or supplement the information provided in this application if any of the material facts that I have represented herein should change prior to closing of the Loan; (8) in the event that my payments on the Loan become delinquent, the Lender, its servicers, successors or assigns may, in addition to any other rights and remedies that it may have relating to such delinquency, report my name and account information to one or more consumer reporting agencies;   (9) ownership of the Loan and/or administration of the Loan account may be transferred with such notice as may be required by law; (10) neither Lender nor its agents, brokers, insurers, servicers, successors or assigns has made any representation or warranty, express or implied, to me regarding the property or the condition or value of the property; and (11) my transmission of this application as an "electronic record" containing my "electronic signature," as those terms are defined in applicable federal and/or state laws (excluding audio and video recordings), or my facsimile transmission of this application containing a facsimile of my signature, shall be as effective, enforceable and valid as if a paper version of this application were delivered containing my original written signature.

<u>Acknowledgement</u>.   Each of the undersigned hereby acknowledges that any owner of the Loan, its servicers, successors and assigns, may verify or reverify any information contained in this application or obtain any information or data relating to the Loan, for any legitimate business purpose through any source, including a source named in this application or a consumer reporting agency.

Borrower's Signature	Date	Co-Borrower's Signature	Date
X		X	

X. INFORMATION FOR GOVERNMENT MONITORING PURPOSES

The following information is requested by the Federal Government for certain types of loans related to a dwelling in order to monitor the lender's compliance with equal credit opportunity, fair housing and home mortgage disclosure laws. You are not required to furnish this information, but are encouraged to do so. The law provides that a lender may not discriminate either on the basis of this information, or on whether you choose to furnish it. If you furnish the information, please provide both ethnicity and race. For race, you may check more than one designation. If you do not furnish ethnicity, race, or sex, under Federal regulations, this lender is required to note the information on the basis of visual observation and surname if you have made this application in person. If you do not wish to furnish the information, please check the box below. (Lender must review the above material to assure that the disclosures satisfy all requirements to which the lender is subject under applicable state law for the particular type of loan applied for.)

BORROWER	CO-BORROWER
☐ I do not wish to furnish this information	☐ I do not wish to furnish this information
Ethnicity: ☐ Hispanic or Latino ☐ Not Hispanic or Latino	**Ethnicity:** ☐ Hispanic or Latino ☐ Not Hispanic or Latino
Race: ☐ American Indian or Alaska Native ☐ Asian ☐ Black or African American ☐ Native Hawaiian or Other Pacific Islander ☐ White	**Race:** ☐ American Indian or Alaska Native ☐ Asian ☐ Black or African American ☐ Native Hawaiian or Other Pacific Islander ☐ White
Sex: ☐ Female ☐ Male	**Sex:** ☐ Female ☐ Male

To be Completed by Interviewer This application was taken by: ☐ Face-to-face interview ☐ Mail ☐ Telephone ☐ Internet	Interviewer's Name (print or type)	Name and Address of Interviewer's Employer
	Interviewer's Signature	Date
	Interviewer's Phone Number (incl. area code)	

CONTINUATION SHEET/RESIDENTIAL LOAN APPLICATION

Use this continuation sheet if you need more space to complete the Residential Loan Application. Mark **B** for Borrower or **C** for Co-Borrower.	Borrower:	Agency Case Number:
	Co-Borrower:	Lender Case Number:

I/We fully understand that it is a Federal crime punishable by fine or imprisonment, or both, to knowingly make any false statements concerning any of the above facts as applicable under the provisions of Title 18, United States Code, Section 1001, et seq.

Borrower's Signature	Date	Co-Borrower's Signature	Date
X		X	

Consumer Credit Protection Act

The **Consumer Credit Protection Act** of 1968—which launched Truth in Lending disclosures—was landmark legislation. For the first time, creditors had to state the cost of borrowing in a common language so that the consumer could figure out what the charges are, compare the costs of loans, and shop for the best credit deal.

Truth in Lending Act

The **Truth in Lending Act** (TILA), Title I of the Consumer Credit Protection Act, is aimed at promoting the informed use of consumer credit by requiring disclosures about its terms and costs. The TILA is intended to enable the customer to compare the cost of a cash transaction with the cost of a credit transaction and to see the difference in the cost of credit among different lenders. Its purpose is to assure a meaningful disclosure of credit terms.

In general, the law applies to all real estate loans for personal, family, or household purposes; to lenders who offer credit or help arrange credit; and to the advertising of most credit offerings. TILA applies to real estate loans that are secured by the borrower's principal dwelling. TILA defines a **dwelling** as a 1-4 residential structure , individual condominium unit, cooperative unit, mobile home, and trailer, if it is used as a residence. Real estate loans that are exempt from the TILA include credit extended primarily for business, commercial, or agricultural purposes, or credit extended to other than a natural person. Additionally, loans over $25,000 that are not real estate loans are exempt.

Regulation Z

Regulation Z implements the Federal Truth in Lending Act. [12 CFR §1026]. A creditor must furnish certain disclosures to the consumer before a contract for a loan is made. A **creditor** includes a lender (person or company) who regularly makes real estate loans; who extends credit for loans secured by a dwelling; and the credit extended is subject to a finance charge or is payable in more than four installments, excluding the down payment.

Disclosures

In 2008, Regulation Z was amended by the Mortgage Disclosure Improvement Act (MDIA). The purpose of the MDIA is to ensure that consumers receive cost disclosures early in the mortgage process.

In 2015, The Consumer Financial Protection Bureau (CFPB) adopted the TILA-RESPA Rule (TRID) creating the Loan Estimate and the Closing

Disclosure that are provided to BORROWERS for closed-end mortgage loan transactions. The Loan Estimate provides borrowers with good-faith estimates of credit costs and transaction terms. The **Closing Disclosure** contains the actual terms and costs of the transaction. The TRID rule applies to most closed-end residential mortgages, construction-only loans, and loans secured by vacant land or by 25 or more acres. Creditors are required to provide borrowers with a Loan Estimate at the time the borrower completes the application for a mortgage loan or within 3 business days after receiving an application. Neither the lender nor anyone else may charge a fee, other than a reasonable fee for obtaining the consumer's credit history, until after the borrower has received this disclosure.

Finance Charge and Annual Percentage Rate

TILA requires lenders to disclose the important terms and costs of their loans, including the annual percentage rate, finance charge, the payment terms, and information about any variable-rate feature. The **finance charge** is the dollar amount the credit will cost, and, as a condition to obtaining credit, is composed of any direct or indirect charges. Those include interest, loan fees, finder fees, credit report fees, insurance fees, and mortgage insurance fees. [§1026.4(b)]

IN REAL ESTATE loans, the finance charge does NOT include fees for appraisals or credit reports, title insurance, notary services, or for preparing loan-related documents, such as deeds or mortgages. [§1026.4(c)(7)]. The **annual percentage rate (APR)** is the relative cost of credit expressed as a yearly rate. It is the relationship of the total finance charge to the total amount financed, expressed as a percentage.

Regulation Z requires that the following **material disclosures** must be displayed to allow consumers ease of comparison. [§1026.18].

- **Amount financed** - *The amount of credit provided to you or on your behalf.*
- **Finance charge** - *The dollar amount the credit will cost you.*
- **Annual Percentage Rate** - *The cost of your credit expressed as a yearly rate.*
- **Total of payments** - *The amount you will have paid when you have made all the scheduled payments.*
- **Payment schedule** - The number, amount, and timing of payments.
- **Name of the lender**/creditor making the disclosure.

In addition to the previously mentioned disclosure, the regulation also requires disclosures regarding due-on-sale clauses, prepayment penalties, late payment charges, description of the property, insurance requirements, and loan assumptions.

Advertising

The Truth in Lending Act also establishes disclosure standards for advertisements that refer to certain credit terms. If the annual percentage rate (APR) is disclosed, no more disclosures are required. If the APR is not stated, then all the specifics of all credit terms must be disclosed. An advertisement that discloses the number of payments must also disclose the amount or percentage of down payment, number of payments, amount of any payments, the finance charge, interest rate, property description, etc. In fact, if the interest rate is stated, it must also disclose the APR. Ads that would require complete disclosure would include "No money down" or "100% financing".

Right of Rescission

The **right to rescind** (cancel) a real estate loan applies to most consumer credit loans (hard money loans) or refinance loans. Loans used for the purchase or construction of the borrower's personal residence (purchase money loans) have no right of rescission. The lender must provide a written rescission disclosure to every borrower who is entitled to rescind. When the right of rescission applies, the borrower has a right to rescind the agreement until midnight of the third business day after the promissory note is signed. According to TILA, for purposes of rescission and the 3-day or 7-day waiting period, a **business day** is defined as all calendar days except Sundays and legal public holidays.

Adjustable Rate Loan Disclosure

A lender offering adjustable rate residential mortgage loans must provide prospective borrowers with a copy of the most recent CFPB publication, which provides information about adjustable rate loans. The title is *Consumer Handbook on Adjustable Rate Mortgages*. The publication must be given to the borrower upon request of the prospective borrower, or when the lender first provides information concerning adjustable rate mortgages.

Real Estate Settlement Procedures Act

The federal **Real Estate Settlement Procedures Act (RESPA)** protects consumers by mandating a series of disclosures that prevent unethical practices by mortgage lenders. The disclosures must take place at various times throughout the settlement process.

RESPA applies to all federally related, 1-4 unit residential mortgage loans. These include most purchase loans, assumptions, refinances, property improvement loans, and equity lines of credit. The Consumer Financial Protection Bureau (CFPB) is responsible for enforcing RESPA.

Timing of Disclosures

The act requires lenders to give special disclosures and to use special procedures and forms for closing costs on most home loans. RESPA regulates specified disclosures at the time of the loan application and at or before the time of settlement or closing of escrow. When a potential homebuyer applies for a home loan, the lender must give the buyer a special information booklet, the Loan Estimate, and a Mortgage Servicing Disclosure Statement. The special information booklet, *Your Home Loan Toolkit*, contains consumer information on various real estate settlement services. The **Loan Estimate** summarizes key loan terms and gives an estimate of loan and closing costs. The lender is generally required to provide the Loan Estimate within 3 business days of the receipt of the borrower's loan application. Lenders must allow applicants to have a **7-business day waiting period** after mailing or delivering the Loan Estimate prior to closing the loan. The **Mortgage Servicing Disclosure Statement** states whether the lender intends to sell the real estate loan servicing immediately or in the future.

Lenders must ensure that BORROWERS receive the Closing Disclosure at least **3 business days before consummation** (the day the loan closes). The seller's Closing Disclosure must be provided to the seller **at or before consummation**. After closing, the loan servicer must deliver an **Annual Escrow Loan Statement** to the borrower.

The disclosure requirements are primarily the responsibility of the lender. Violators of this law can be penalized by up to one year in jail and/or a $10,000 fine.

Real estate brokers acting as mortgage brokers do not have to give borrowers a separate California-mandated mortgage loan disclosure statement in federally related loan transactions when the borrower receives a Loan Estimate and all disclosures required by the Truth in Lending Act.

Equal Credit Opportunity Act

The **Equal Credit Opportunity Act** (ECOA) ensures that all consumers are given an equal chance to obtain credit. This does not mean all consumers who apply for credit get it because factors, such as income, expenses, debt, and credit history are considerations for creditworthiness.

The law protects a borrower when dealing with any creditor who regularly extends credit, including banks, small loan and finance companies, retail and department stores, credit card companies, and credit unions. The ECOA bars discrimination based on characteristics such as the borrower's race, color, gender, or the race or national origin of the people in the neighborhood in which a borrower lives or wants to buy a home.

Borrowers are entitled to receive a copy of an appraisal report that they paid for in connection with an application for credit by submitting a written request for the report. The creditor must provide a copy of the appraisal promptly (generally within 30 days). [§1002.14].

Home Mortgage Disclosure Act

The federal **Home Mortgage Disclosure Act** of 1975 (HMDA) requires most mortgage lenders to gather data from borrowers who apply for loans. Its purpose is to determine whether lenders are serving their communities and to identify discriminatory lending patterns. To do this, HMDA tracks the type and amount of the loan, type of property with its location, and the borrower's ethnicity, race, gender, and income.

Fair Credit Reporting Act

The **Fair Credit Reporting Act (FCRA)** is one of the most important laws that protects consumer identity and credit information. It is designed to promote the accuracy, fairness, and privacy of the information collected and maintained by credit reporting agencies.

The Fair Credit Reporting Act establishes procedures for correcting mistakes on a person's credit record and requires that a consumer's record only be provided for legitimate business needs. It also requires that the record be kept confidential. If a consumer has been denied credit, a cost-free credit report may be requested within 30 days of denial.

Fair and Accurate Credit Transactions Act

The **Fair and Accurate Credit Transactions Act (FACTA)** of 2003 gives borrowers the right to see what is in their credit file and to have any errors corrected. If a lender refuses credit to a borrower because of unfavorable information in his or her credit report, a borrower has a right to get the name and address of the agency that keeps the report. FACTA allows consumers to request and obtain a free credit report once every 12 months from each of the three nationwide consumer-credit reporting companies—Equifax®, Experian®, and TransUnion™.

If a borrower notifies the bureau about an error, generally the bureau must investigate and resolve the dispute within 30 days after receiving the notice. The bureau contacts the creditor who supplied the data and removes any information that is incomplete or inaccurate from the credit file. If a borrower disagrees with the findings, he or she can file a short statement (100 words) in the record that gives the borrower's side of the story. All future reports to creditors must include this statement or a summary of its contents.

Red Flag Rules

Under the **FTC Red Flags Rules**, financial institutions and creditors must develop a written "Identity Theft Prevention Program" to detect, prevent, and mitigate identity theft in covered accounts. A **covered account** is any personal account, such as checking and savings accounts, credit card accounts, mortgage loans, automobile loans, margin accounts, and cell phone or utility accounts. The lender must create a list of warning signs—"red flags"—for possible identity theft. **Red flags** are suspicious patterns or practices or specific activities that indicate the possibility of identity theft. The law lists five categories of warning signs.

Categories of Red Flags

- Alerts, Notifications, & Warnings from a Credit Reporting Agency
- Suspicious Documents
- Suspicious Personal Identifying Information
- Suspicious Account Activity
- Notice from Other Sources

Financial Disclosures Required by California Law

It is federal policy to ensure fair housing by prohibiting discrimination based on race, color, religion, sex, national origin, marital status, age, or physical disabilities in connection with the sale, rental, construction, or financing of housing. Many state laws are passed to supplement federal legislation.

Housing Financial Discrimination Act of 1977

The Housing Financial Discrimination Act of 1977 (Holden Act) prohibits the discriminatory practice known as redlining. **Redlining** is an illegal lending policy of denying real estate loans on properties in older, changing urban areas, usually with large minority populations, because of alleged higher lending risks, without due consideration being given by the lending institution to the creditworthiness of the individual loan applicant.

The **Holden Act** encourages increased lending in neighborhoods where, in the past, financing has been unavailable. The major goal of the Holden Act is to ensure and increase the supply of safe and decent housing for creditworthy borrowers and to prevent neighborhood decay.

To ensure that prospective borrowers are aware of their rights under this law, lenders must give all applicants a Fair Lending Notice at the time of their loan application. The Fair Lending Notice must include the provisions of the Holden Act, be in at least 10-point type, and include the address where complaints may be filed. Additionally, the notice must be posted in a conspicuous location in the lender's place of business. [HSC §35800-35803].

Lender Compensation Disclosure

Commissioner's Regulation 2904 requires that all real estate licensees must disclose to their principals all compensation, or expected compensation, regardless of the form, time, or source of payment. The disclosure is required even if the broker does not handle the financing aspect of the transaction and it must be given to each party to the transaction before the transaction closes escrow.

Additionally, a real estate licensee may not receive compensation for referring customers to an escrow company, pest control firm, home inspection company, or title insurance company. Any compensation received would be considered commercial bribery.

Real Property Loan Law

The **Real Property Loan Law**, also referred to as the **Mortgage Loan Brokers' Law**, was enacted to curb a variety of lending abuses perpetrated by real estate brokers who engaged in loan transactions. The abuses included exorbitant commissions, inflated costs and expenses, short term loans with large balloon payments, and misrepresentations or concealments of material facts. [B&P Code §10240]

Article 7 applies to 1 to 4 residential properties that are secured directly or collaterally by sheltered loans. A **sheltered loan** is a first trust deed of LESS THAN $30,000 or a junior loan of LESS THAN $20,000. Article 7 limits the amount of commissions and costs that may be charged for arranging or making a sheltered loan.

Maximum Commissions for Sheltered Loans

1. First or senior loans:
    a. 5% of the principal of a loan of less than 3 years;
    b. 10% of the principal of a loan of 3 years or more;

2. Second or other junior loans:
    a. 5% of the principal of a loan of less than 2 years;
    b. 10% of the principal of a loan of at least 2 years but less than 3 years; and,
    c. 15% of the principal of a loan of 3 years or more.

For example, the maximum commission that the broker can charge for a $7,500 second trust deed with a 5-year term is 15%.

Maximum Costs and Expenses for Sheltered Loans

- Costs and expenses cannot exceed 5% of the original principal balance/amount of the loan or $390, whichever is greater, to a maximum of $700.

- The amount charged cannot exceed the actual costs and expenses paid, incurred or reasonably earned.

No balloon payment is allowed for loans on owner-occupied homes, in which a broker has been involved in the negotiation, if the term is 6 years or less. This requirement does not apply when a seller carries back a trust deed as part of the purchase price.

Mortgage Loan Disclosure Statement

A real estate broker who negotiates loans on behalf of borrowers or lenders, to be secured by liens on real property, must deliver a written disclosure called the **Mortgage Loan Disclosure Statement** (MLDS) to the borrower. It must be delivered within 3 business days of receipt of the borrower's written loan application, or before the borrower becomes obligated to complete the loan, whichever is earlier. If the loan is negotiated in Spanish, Chinese, Tagalog, Vietnamese, or Korean, the MLDS must be provided in that language.

The required statement must be in a form approved by the Real Estate Commissioner. The MLDS needs to disclose expected maximum costs and expenses of making the loan that are to be paid by the borrower, including fees for appraisal, escrow, credit report, title insurance, recording, and notary services. The MLDS form can be found at the CalBRE website.

In addition, the total amount of real estate commissions to be received by the broker for services performed in arranging the loan must be disclosed. These fees include points, loan origination fees, bonuses, rebates, premiums, discounts as well as other charges received by the real estate broker in lieu of interest in transactions in which the broker acts as the lender.

The MLDS must be signed by the borrower and the agent negotiating the loan. The broker negotiating the loan must keep a signed copy of the statement on file for 3 years.

A broker might not be required to provide the borrower with a MLDS for a federally regulated residential mortgage loan that exceeds the loan amounts in Article 7, if the Loan Estimate meets the requirements of and is compliant with the TILA-RESPA Integrated Disclosure Rule.

In order to satisfy the disclosure requirement, the Loan Estimate must include the broker's real estate license number and NMLS unique number, and include a clear and conspicuous statement on the face of the document stating that the "Loan Estimate" does not constitute a loan commitment.

Seller Financing Disclosure Statement

Some sellers help sell their homes by extending credit to the buyer in the form of seller carryback financing. This is usually in the form of a promissory note secured by a deed of trust. The requirement of a seller financing disclosure statement also applies to transactions by real property sales contracts and to leases with option-to-purchase provisions that transfer equitable title to the lessee.

To prevent abuses involving some of these seller assisted financing plans the state requires the arranger of credit to give the borrower a written disclosure. An **arranger of credit** is a person who is not a party to the transaction, but will be compensated for arranging the credit, negotiating the credit terms, completing the credit documents, and facilitating the transaction.

The arranger of credit must deliver a **Seller Financing Disclosure Statement** as soon as possible before the execution of any note or security document. The statement must be signed by the arranger of credit, the buyer, and the seller, who are each to receive a copy. The disclosure statement must include comprehensive

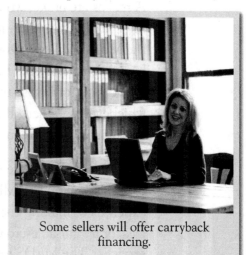

Some sellers will offer carryback financing.

information about the financing cautions applicable to certain types of financing, and suggestions of procedures that will protect the parties during the terms of the financing. [C.C.C. §2956 et. seq.]

The arranger of credit does not have to deliver a disclosure statement to a buyer or seller who is entitled to receive a disclosure under the regulations of the Federal Truth in Lending Act, Real Estate Settlement Procedures Act (RESPA), or a mortgage loan disclosure statement. [C.C.C. §2958].

SUMMARY

The **mortgage market** consists of primary markets (loan-originator sellers) and the secondary market (loan buyers). There are two divisions in the primary mortgage market—the institutional lenders and the non-institutional lenders. The **institutional lender** is a depository, such as a commercial bank. They receive most of their deposits from household savings or individual investors. The major type of lending activity funded by commercial banks is for short-term (six to thirty-six months) construction loans, even though they do make other types of loans as well. **Non-institutional lenders** are non-depositories and include private individuals, mortgage companies, investment companies, pension funds, and title companies. The primary market lenders make real estate loans and package them into mortgage pools to be sold to the customers in the secondary mortgage market. The **secondary mortgage market** is comparable to a resale marketplace for loans (in which existing loans are bought and sold).

Mortgage lenders are concerned about a customer's ability to repay a loan. Lenders use qualifying ratios with a review of the customer's credit report and net worth to screen potential borrowers. Security for the loan is the property. An appraisal of the property is made to obtain an accurate valuation.

Real Estate Laws require anyone negotiating a loan to provide a mortgage loan broker's statement to a prospective borrower, with information disclosing all important features of a loan to be negotiated for the borrower. Among these laws are the Consumer Credit Protection Act, Truth in Lending Act, **Regulation Z**, Adjustable-Rate Loan Disclosure, **Equal Credit Opportunity Act**, Lender Compensation Disclosure, and Seller Financing Disclosure Statement.

Any borrower who is denied credit must be told the reason why credit was denied, be given access to the credit report, and told how to challenge any disputed entries.

UNIT 10 REVIEW

Matching Exercise

Instructions: Write the letter of the matching term on the blank line before its definition. Answers immediately follow the Multiple Choice Questions.

Terms

A. APR
B. commercial banks
C. compensating balance
D. credit scoring
E. credit union
F. deregulation
G. disintermediation
H. Equal Credit Opportunity Act
I. FDIC
J. finance charge
K. Loan Estimate

L. loan-to-value
M. monetary policy
N. mortgage broker
O. mortgage companies
P. Mortgage Loan Disclosure Statement
Q. mortgage yield
R. mortgage-backed securities
S. pass-through securities
T. pledge
U. primary mortgage market

V. real estate investment trust
W. reconveyance deed
X. redlining
Y. secondary mortgage market
Z. security agreement
AA. tight money
BB. Truth in Lending Act
CC. underwriting
DD. warehousing

Definitions

1. _____ A statistical method lenders use to assess a borrower's credit risk.

2. _____ Lender whose principal business is the origination, closing, funding, selling, and servicing of loans secured by real property.

3. _____ Consumer-protection law passed to promote the informed use of consumer credit by requiring disclosures about its terms and costs.

4. _____ A company with a minimum of 100 shareholders that owns operates income-producing real estate or engages in financing real estate.

5. _____ The relative cost of credit expressed as a yearly percentage rate.

6. _____ Revolving line of credit extended to a mortgage company from a warehouse lender.

7. _____ Market in which lenders make mortgage loans directly to borrowers.

8. _____ Real estate licensee who is a third party originator.

9. _____ An economic situation in which the supply of money is limited, and the demand for money is high, as evidenced by high interest rates.

10. _____ A resale marketplace for mortgage loans.

11. _____ The percentage of appraised value to the loan.

12. _____ The process of evaluating a borrower's risk factors before the lender will make a loan.

13. _____ Corporation that insures deposits in all federally chartered banks and savings institutions up to $250,000 per depositor.

14. _____ A minimum credit balance that a bank requires a borrower to keep on deposit as a condition for granting a loan.

15. _____ Mortgage backed securities that pass through the principal and interest of the underlying loans to investors.

16. _____ Actions taken by the Fed to influence the availability and cost of money and credit as a means of promoting national economic goals.

17. _____ A discriminatory lending practice prohibited by the Holden Act.

18. _____ Federal act ensuring that all consumers have an equal chance to obtain credit.

19. _____ A process whereby regulatory restraints are gradually relaxed.

20. _____ Lender whose members usually have the same type of occupation.

21. _____ The total interest, fees, and points earned by the lender expressed expressed as a percentage.

22. _____ The dollar amount the credit will cost the borrower.

23. _____ Pools of mortgages used as collateral for the issuance of securities in the secondary market.

24. _____ Document that lists the charges the buyer is likely to pay at settlement.

25. _____ California-required statement that disclosed expected maximum costs and expenses of making the loan that are to be paid by the borrower.

▣ Multiple Choice Questions

Instructions: Circle your response and then check your response with the Answer Key that immediately follows the Multiple Choice Questions.

1. The most effective method for the Federal Reserve to create a "tight" money market is to:
    a. buy government bonds and increase the reserve requirement.
    b. sell government bonds and decrease the reserve requirement.
    c. buy government bonds and raise the discount rate.
    d. sell government bonds and raise the discount rate.

2. What federal agency insures deposits in all federally chartered banks and savings institutions?
    a. GLBA
    b. HUD
    c. FIRREA
    d. FDIC

3. The process of gradually relaxing regulatory restraints is called:
    a. disintermediation.
    b. deregulation.
    c. depreciation.
    d. none of the above

4. The type of lenders having the greatest percentage of its assets invested in residential real estate mortgages are:
    a. commercial banks.
    b. credit unions.
    c. life insurance companies.
    d. thrifts.

5. Which of the following lenders frequently uses a warehouse line to make loans to borrowers?
    a. FHA
    b. Mortgage companies
    c. Savings and loan associations
    d. VA

6. In the field of real estate financing, the term "secondary mortgage market" usually refers to:

    a. junior liens.

    b. secondary financing.

    c. unsecured financial instruments.

    d. the resale or transfer of existing trust deed loans.

7. The original purpose of Fannie Mae was:

    a. buying and selling FHA and VA loans in the secondary market.

    b. buying and selling conventional loans in the secondary market.

    c. buying FHA and VA loans in the primary market.

    d. selling FHA and VA loans in the primary market.

8. What shows the borrower's payment history, balance of outstanding debt, credit history, number of credit inquiries, and types of credit held?

    a. FICO score

    b. Credit score

    c. Loan application

    d. Credit report

9. The underlying security for the mortgage loan is the:

    a. creditworthiness of the borrower.

    b. loan-to-value.

    c. property.

    d. borrower's FICO score.

10. If only the annual percentage rate (APR) is disclosed in an advertisement for property, which additional disclosures must be made?

    a. The amount or percentage of the down payment

    b. The terms of repayment

    c. The amount of any finance charge

    d. No other disclosures are required

11. For a real estate loan, which of the following fees may not be included in the finance charge according to the federal Truth in Lending Act?

    a. Interest

    b. Finder's fees

    c. Buyer's points

    d. Appraisal fees

12. Which of the following statements violates the federal Truth in Lending Act?

    a. 3-bedroom, 2 bath, excellent FHA or VA financing available; total price $225,000

    b. 4-bedroom, 2 baths, easy terms; total price $225,000

    c. 3-bedroom, 2 bath, large lot, with 10% down; total price $225,000

    d. 3-bedroom, 3 bath, owner will help finance; total price $225,000

13. The Federal Real Estate Settlement Procedure Act of 1974 (RESPA) pertains to:

    a. all residential property.

    b. residential properties with 1-to-4 units.

    c. commercial properties only.

    d. agricultural property.

14. The Housing Financial Discrimination Act of 1977 prohibits the discriminatory practice known as:

    a. red flagging.

    b. red taping.

    c. redlining.

    d. red lighting.

15. The maximum commission that can be charged by a licensee for negotiating a second trust deed of $7,500 for a period of five (5) years is:

    a. 5%.

    b. 10%.

    c. 15%.

    d. unlimited because this loan is not regulated by Article 7.

UNIT 10 ANSWER KEY

Answers – Matching

1. D	6. DD	11. L	16. M	21. Q
2. O	7. U	12. CC	17. X	22. J
3. BB	8. N	13. I	18. H	23. R
4. V	9. AA	14. C	19. F	24. K
5. A	10. Y	15. S	20. E	25. P

Answers – Multiple Choice

1. **(d)**   A tight money market means the supply of money is relatively limited and the demand is high. Therefore, interest rates would generally increase. Selling government bonds takes money out of circulation as bonds are purchased. Raising the discount rate will mean less money will be borrowed and circulated. [Federal Reserve System]

2. **(d)**   The Federal Deposit Insurance Corporation (FDIC) now insures deposits in all federally chartered banks and savings institutions. [Regulation & Reform]

3. **(b)**   Deregulation is a process whereby regulatory restraints are gradually relaxed. Disintermediation occurs when savers take money out of S&Ls and put it into investments that pay a higher rate of interest. Depreciation is a loss in value from any cause. [Regulation & Reform]

4. **(d)**   Among institutional lenders, thrifts (savings and loan associations) provide the majority of home loans. [Mortgage Markets]

5. **(b)**   Since mortgage companies do not have depositors, they use short-term borrowing called a warehouse line or warehouse line of credit to make loans to borrowers. [Mortgage Markets]

6. **(d)**   The secondary mortgage market is for buying and selling existing mortgages from the primary mortgage market or from each other. Participants in the secondary mortgage market do not originate loans. [Mortgage Markets]

7. **(a)**   Fannie Mae was originally created to purchase FHA and VA loans in the secondary market. However, in recent years, Fannie Mae has also purchased conventional mortgages from approved lenders. [Mortgage Markets]

8. **(d)**   A credit report shows the borrower's payment history, balance of outstanding debt, credit history, number of credit inquiries, and types of credit held. [Underwriting]

9. **(c)**   The property is the underlying security for the mortgage loan. [Underwriting]

10. **(d)** It is correct to disclose just the APR and does not trigger the requirement for additional disclosures. [Disclosures in Financing]

11. **(d)** Regulation Z specifies the items that are not to be included in the finance charge for a real estate loan: seller's points, title fees, fees for preparing documents, notary charges, appraisal fees, and credit-report fees. [Disclosures in Financing]

12. **(c)** An ad must disclose all credit terms if it contains any one of the following four triggering terms: (1) the down payment, (2) the number, or term of payments, (3) the amount of any payment, or (4) the finance charge. In this case, the 10% down payment triggers the other disclosures. [Disclosures in Financing]

13. **(b)** RESPA applies to all federally related mortgage loans made by lenders for the sale or transfer of 1-4 unit residential dwellings. [Disclosures in Financing]

14. **(c)** The Housing Financial Discrimination Act prohibits redlining. [Disclosures in Financing]

15. **(c)** The Real Property Loan Law limits a licensee's commission to 15% where the loan term is three years or longer. [Disclosures in Financing]

Unit 11

INTRODUCTION

"How much do you think it is worth?" This may be the most frequently asked question in real estate. Every day a client or customer will ask about the fair price or fair rental for a property and an agent must be prepared to answer knowledgeably. Some of the most important services a listing agent can provide are to be familiar with how the worth of property is determined and to be able to explain it to the client.

Most homeowners know, within a range, the value of their homes. They probably are not aware they have used some of the same techniques the listing agent and the professional appraiser will use in determining the value of their home. For example, they may know the selling price of their neighbors' house, and the selling price of the house down the street. They have added to—or subtracted from—the value of their own house, depending on amenities, location and condition to come up with a pretty accurate value, if they are being honest with themselves. This Unit will examine the appraisal process and the methods used to determine property values so that you as an agent can answer when a client or customer asks the question, "How much do you think it is worth?"

This Unit discusses the appraisal process, the forces that influence value, principles of valuation, and approaches of appraising property. In addition, you will become familiar with appraisal licensing standards and professional appraisal organizations.

Learning Objectives

After completing this Unit, you should be able to:

9A   recall terms used to define appraisal and value.

9B   name the principles of valuation.

9C   identify steps in the appraisal process.

9D   specify the appraisal licensing standards and professional appraisal organizations.

DEFINITION OF APPRAISAL

An **appraisal** is an act or process of developing an opinion of value. [USPAP 2012-2013]. It usually is for a specific property's value on a given date. **Value** is the present worth of rights to future benefits that come from property ownership. An appraiser gives his or her opinion of value in a written statement called an **appraisal report**. It is the conclusion of the appraiser's research and analysis of all relevant data regarding the subject property.

Most of the time an objective and third-party opinion are needed to determine the value of real property. The professional appraiser because of training, experience, and ethics, is responsible for giving clients an objective opinion of value, reached without bias. An appraiser has a serious responsibility to be correct in evaluating data and not allow other factors to influence evaluation of a property. The appraiser must remember to be a neutral party, responding only to the forces affecting value and not to any other special interests who might want to influence his or her judgment.

> **Purpose of an Appraisal**
> - Transfer of property ownership
> - Financing and credit
> - Taxation
> - Insurance
> - Condemnation

An appraisal can be made for many different purposes. There are several reasons for determining the value of a particular property. The estimate of value may be different depending on the reason for ordering the appraisal. The condemnation value is going to be different from the taxation value, the insurance value, or the market value.

An appraiser must know what those differences are and how to estimate the value of a property based on the purpose for which it is being used.

The purpose of the appraisal is distinct from the intended use of the appraisal report. The **purpose of the appraisal** helps define how the appraisal process will be laid out. The **intended use** helps decide which report type is most appropriate for communicating the results of the process.

DEFINITION OF VALUE

Value or worth is the present and future anticipated enjoyment or profit from the ownership of property. It is the relationship between the thing desired and the purchaser. It is also the power of one commodity to attract other commodities in exchange.

Sometimes market price, cost, and market value are the same, but this is misleading. **Cost** represents expenses in money, labor, material, or sacrifices in acquiring or producing something. **Market price** is the actual sales price of the property, whereas the price for which the property should sell is its market value. Market value has very little to do with the original cost. Neither cost nor appreciation is considered an essential element of value.

The conditions of the sale affect the price, such as good financing or a forced sale. The circumstances of one buyer and one seller may affect the sale of a specific property, giving it its own value, apart from some other similar parcel. The job of an appraiser is to determine the special factors of a sale and assign a value based on each individual transaction.

> Example: Pamela and John wanted to buy their first house. They looked at several with their real estate agent and finally decided on one that was beyond their means. They made a hopeful, low offer. Unknown to them, the seller lost his job and was desperate to sell. He accepted their offer, which was well below market value.

In the above case, the sellers did not sell freely for market value, and the sales price only reflected their desperate situation, not the real value of the house.

Types of Value

The value of a parcel usually can be categorized by two basic types of value—market value and value in use.

Market Value

Real estate includes both land and anything belonging to the land, as well as rights or interests in that land. The price a property would bring if freely offered on the open market, with both a **willing buyer** and a **willing seller**, is known as **market value**, or **fair market value**. Market value is sometimes called the **objective value**, since it may be determined by actual data.

A property that is offered for sale as a result of default, foreclosure, bankruptcy, divorce, death or any other unusual circumstances cannot be said to be freely and willingly offered on the open market, and the sale price of such properties would not represent fair market value. An appraiser would take into account that there were special circumstances in those sales and would not use the price paid as a comparable measure of value.

> **Review - Fair Market Value**
> - Buyer and seller are operating in their own interest.
> - Buyer and seller are knowledgeable about the transaction and make careful decisions.
> - The property is available for a reasonable time on the open market.
> - The sale is for cash or trade or is specifically financed.
> - Normal financing, available to qualified borrowers, is used.

Value in Use

Value in use (also known as **utility value**) is the usefulness of the property to a specific user. For example, a six bedroom home may not be useful to a couple with no children. Features that add value to a property are called **amenities**. However, due to the subjective nature of the user's preference regarding amenities, value could actually decrease. This is called **subjective value**. For example, before listing a home, the owner remodeled the bathroom using her favorite color, lime green. If the prospective buyer also likes lime green, they may be willing to pay more for the home with the remodeled bathroom. However, a person who prefers neutral colors may overlook the value of the remodel and offer considerably less for the home or look for a lower priced, comparable property.

Elements to Create Value

The four elements of value that must be present for a property to have market value are demand, utility, scarcity, and transferability. **Demand** is the desire to buy or obtain a commodity. **Effective demand** is desire coupled with purchasing power. Demand and purchasing power available will affect the value of a property. **Utility** is the ability of a property to satisfy a need or desire, such as shelter, income, or amenities. **Functional utility** is the ability of a property to be useful and perform the function for which it is intended according to current market tastes and standards. The ultimate test of functional utility is marketability. **Scarcity** refers to the availability of a commodity in the marketplace. An oversupply diminishes value whereas an undersupply (or increased demand) increases value. **Transferability** means that title to the property is unclouded and marketable.

Each element by itself cannot create value. For example, something may be scarce, but if it has no utility there is no demand for it. Air has utility and may be in great demand, but is so abundant that it has no commercial value.

The appraiser must decide if there is a demand for a property, such as a high-rise residential building, or a low-cost housing project. Can it be used for the purpose it was intended, such as a family home or residential complex? How many projects like this one are there in the area? The fewer there are, the more value the subject property has. Is the title clear, and can the seller easily give ownership to a buyer?

As you can see, all of these factors are important in assigning a value to a property. An appraiser must hold each one up to the property in question to arrive at a correct estimate of value.

> **Mnemonic – DUST – Four Elements of Value**
>
> **D**emand
> **U**tility
> **S**carcity
> **T**ransferability

Forces Influencing Value

The essence of life is change, and real estate is not excluded from that force. Value is created, maintained, modified, and destroyed by the relationship of the following four forces: physical characteristics, economic influences, political or governmental regulations, and social ideals.

Physical Characteristics including Environmental Forces

Physical characteristics are also called external characteristics. This includes quality of conveniences; availability of schools, shopping, public transportation, churches; and similarity of land use. **Environmental forces** may be climate, soil, topography, oceans, and mountains.

Location: This may be the most important factor influencing value, as far as highest and best use. Another term used to describe where the physical location of property is **situs**.

Size: The use of a property may be determined by the width and depth of the land. A **depth table** is used to estimate the value of commercial properties.

Corner influence: Commercial properties benefit from more exposure, while residential parcels may lose privacy and incur higher maintenance costs from increased frontage.

Thoroughfare condition: Width of streets, traffic congestion, and condition of pavement affect the value of properties fronting on those streets. The term **front foot** defines the width of a property along a street.

Exposure: The south and west sides of business streets are usually preferred by shopkeepers because customers will seek the shady side of the street and window displays will not be damaged by the sun. The north and east sides are less desirable.

Orientation: Orientation is the placement of a building on its lot in relation to exposure to sun, prevailing wind, traffic, and privacy from the street.

Plottage increment: By putting several smaller, less-valuable parcels together, under one ownership through the process of **assemblage**, the value of the parcels will be increased.

Shape: Irregular-shaped lots are more difficult and expensive to develop.

Topography and soil: Construction costs will be affected by the terrain and soil condition. Limited irregularity in the contour is best for residential property.

Economic Influences

Economic forces influence value. Some of these forces are natural resources, industrial and commercial trends, employment trends, wage levels, availability of money and credit, interest rates, price levels, tax loads, regional and community economic base, new development, and rental and price patterns.

A blighted section of a city.

Blighted area: This refers to a section of a city, generally the inner city, where most of the buildings are run-down and the property values are extremely low.

Inflation: This is an unearned increment that affects property values. An **unearned increment** is an increase in real estate value that comes about from forces outside the control of the owner, such as a favorable shift in population.

Business climate: The presence of shopping areas, offices and medical suites as well as financial, wholesale, industrial, and other consumer-friendly businesses is important to establishing value.

Obsolescence: This may be caused by external or economic changes and decreases the usefulness of property or causes deterioration.

Political or Government Regulations

Some political forces that can affect value are: building codes, zoning laws, public health measures, fire regulations, rent controls, environmental legislation, and the community economic base.

Political or government regulations can affect value.

Directional growth: This is determined by how the area or city expands. Property in a growth area tends to increase in value.

Utility: The property's ability to be used for the purpose it was intended fulfills its utility. Building restrictions and zoning ordinances affect utility.

Building restrictions and zones: These may increase or depress values.

Social Ideals and Standards

Social ideals and standards can affect value. Population growth and decline, age, marriage, birth, divorce, and death rates, all combine to cause changes in social patterns. The study of population is called **demography**.

> **Review - Four Main Forces Influencing Value**
> **Mnemonic = PEPS**
>   Physical forces
>   Economic forces
>   Political forces
>   Social forces

PRINCIPLES OF VALUATION

Valuation is the process of estimating market value for real property as of a specific time. There are many valuation principles that interact to determine the final value of a piece of real estate. Not every property exhibits each principle; however, a real estate agent or professional appraiser must know the following basic principles of valuation before assigning value to any property.

Principle of Change

Cities and neighborhoods are always changing, and individual homes within those neighborhoods reflect that change. An appraiser must be aware of trends that affect the value of real estate. Economic, social, environmental, and governmental forces are always dynamic, causing changing values in real property.

Neighborhoods are dynamic and are always changing.

Neighborhood Life Cycle

All neighborhoods change. They start out as young dynamic areas, and eventually disintegrate in the process of passing years. All property goes through four distinct changes called a **neighborhood life cycle**: (1) growth (development), (2) maturity (stability), (3) old age (decline), and (4) revitalization (renaissance).

Growth, maturity, and decline are normal in all areas, and frequently the process can be reversed just as it reaches the last stages. For example, when a lovely neighborhood grows to be old and worn-out, young families may choose to move in and completely revitalize the neighborhood all over again with development.

Principle of Supply and Demand

Like all other marketable commodities, real estate is affected by supply and demand. The **principle of supply and demand** is almost universally recognized as being the first step in how market prices are determined. **Supply** refers to the total amount of a given type of property for sale or lease, at various prices, at any given point in time. **Demand** refers to the desire and ability to acquire goods and services through purchase or lease.

Increasing supply or decreasing demand will reduce the price in the market. A **buyer's market** is created because there is more supply than demand. Reducing supply or increasing demand will raise the price in the market. This creates a **seller's market** because there is more demand than supply. The less there is of something, the higher the cost; the more there is, the lower the cost.

If home prices decrease, the result will be an increase in the value of money because a given amount of money has more purchasing power. Basically, the home buyer gets more for his or her money.

Principle of Competition

Competition is another of the economic principles effecting valuation. Buyers compete with each other to purchase properties. Sellers compete with each other to attract buyers to their properties. When two or more prospective buyers are competing to obtain a particular property, the one giving the most attractive offer to a seller is the one most likely to prevail. In this case, buyers are in competition with one another to obtain a property. In order to attract prospective buyers, a seller must price his or her property competitively with other comparable offerings.

Principle of Substitution

The **principle of substitution** is the basis of the appraisal process. Explained simply, value is set by the cost of getting an equally desirable substitute. An owner cannot expect to sell for more than someone would ordinarily pay for a similar property, under similar conditions.

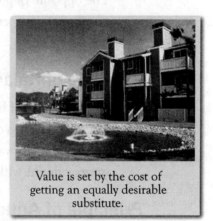

Value is set by the cost of getting an equally desirable substitute.

Principle of Conformity

The **principle of conformity** states that the more that structures are in harmony with one another, the more valuable each of those structures. A home's maximum value is realized when surrounding land uses are compatible and nearby homes are similar in design and size. This similarity is called conformity, and it upholds neighborhood values. Where there are mixed types of homes, unstable real estate values may occur.

Principle of Highest and Best Use

The highest and best use (HBU) of a property, more than anything else, is what determines its value. The **principle of highest and best use** is based on the reasonable use of real property at the time of the appraisal, which is

Multiple factors are involved in evaluating the highest and best use.

most likely to produce the greatest net return to the land and/or the building over a given period of time. The four tests to determine the HBU of a property are: (1) physically possible, (2) legally permitted, (3) economically feasible, and (4) maximally productive.

Interim use is a short-term and temporary use of a property until it is ready for a more productive highest and best use.

Principle of Progression

The **principle of progression** states that the value of an inferior property will be worth more because of the presence of greater-valued properties nearby.

Principle of Regression

The opposite of progression, the **principle of regression** states that the value of a superior property will be worth less because of the presence of lower-valued properties nearby.

Principle of Balance

The **principle of balance** states that real estate value is created and sustained when contrasting, opposing, or interacting elements are in a state of equilibrium. A careful mix of varying land use creates value. **Over-improvement** or **under-improvement** will cause imbalance.

Principle of Anticipation

The **principle of anticipation** expresses that value is created by the expectation of future benefits. An appraiser estimates the present worth of future benefits when he or she assigns a value based on anticipated returns.

Principle of Contribution

The **principle of contribution** is the worth of an improvement as well as what it adds to the entire property's market value, regardless of the actual cost of the improvement. An **improvement** is a valuable addition made to property to enhance value or extend useful remaining life.

A remodeled attic may not contribute its entire cost to the value of the property; but a new family room will increase the value of the house by more than the cost to build. This principle must be kept in mind by homeowners who want to change the character of their house in such a way that it no longer fits in the neighborhood. The cost of the improvement may not add to the value if the house is overbuilt for the area.

THE APPRAISAL PROCESS

At the end of an appraisal, an appraiser must be prepared to answer the following two questions:

"What is the highest and best use of the property?"

"What is this use worth?"

Professional appraisers have developed an orderly systematic method—known as the **appraisal process**—to arrive at an estimate of value.

Steps in the Appraisal Process

1. State the problem.

2. Gather the data needed and the sources.

3. Use the appraisal approaches to estimate value.

4. Reconcile the estimated values for the final value estimate.

5. Write the appraisal report.

State the Problem

The appraiser must know why the appraisal is necessary. He or she must identify and describe the property to be evaluated and indicate the purpose of the appraisal. Then the extent of ownership to be appraised must be identified. Rights affect value because they set the limits within which the property may be used, and the appraiser must know how the property is owned in order to determine the value of those rights. Is it a fee simple? Are there restrictions on use or possibly a life estate or co-ownership? The purpose of the appraisal will determine the types of information that will be gathered.

Purposes of an Appraisal

- Market value for a sale
- Value for mortgage loan purposes
- Value for insurance purposes
- Value for condemnation proceedings
- Value for inheritance purposes
- Value for Internal Revenue Service purposes
- Value for property tax purposes
- Value for liquidation purposes

Once the appraiser knows the purpose for the property evaluation, it is possible to move on to the next step.

Gather the Data

To determine the property's value, data can be obtained from government publications, newspapers, magazines, the Internet, and personal observation. There are two types of data: general and site specific.

General Data	Specific Data
Region	Location
Community	Lot type
Neighborhood	Legal
Market	Improvements (buildings)

Data should be gathered on population trends, income levels, and employment opportunities.

General Data

General data is information about the area where the property is located that affects the value of the property.

Regional Data

A region is a metropolitan area, such as San Francisco Bay, Southern California, or the Central Coast. **Regional data** is information about the region's economic health and amenities. Regional data can be gathered from monthly bank summaries, regional planning commissions, and government agencies. Governmental agencies, such as the Association of Bay Area Governments (ABAG) in the San Francisco Bay area, the San Diego Association of Governments (SANDAG), or the Southern California Association of Governments (SCAG) are also excellent sources for regional information.

Community Data

A community is the town or city where the property is located. **Community data** can be obtained from the Chamber of Commerce, City Planning Commission, city government agencies, banks, and real estate boards. As with the regional data, community data should be searched for information about the community's economic health and amenities.

Neighborhood Data

Neighborhood data concerning the neighborhood's condition and amenities can be obtained from personal inspections, real estate agents, or area builders. The appraiser notices the age and appearance of the neighborhood; any negative influences, such as physical or social hazards (rundown buildings, evidence of criminal activity); evidence of future development; and proximity to schools, businesses, recreation, and transportation.

The sales and listing prices of property in the neighborhood is the neighborhood's **market data**. It must be collected and analyzed. Sources for sales information are assessor's records and county recorder's office, title insurance companies, other property owners in the area, and the appraiser's own database.

Another factor that can affect value is the age of the buildings in the neighborhood. Information on structure age and other information regarding improvements can be gathered from the tax assessor's office, city building department, or personal inspection of the improvements.

Site Specific Data

Site **specific data** is information that has to do with the specific location being appraised. Appraisers rely on available market information, such as listings, offers, leases, and sales reports as the foundation of their appraisal methods.

Location

Even though the location of the neighborhood and city must be considered in any analysis of a specific site or plot of ground, the exact spot of the site itself is the most important factor in determining value. Since most sites are different sizes and in different locations, some are more desirable than others and should be evaluated separately from improvements for the highest and best use.

Types of Lots

The type of lot on which a property is located can affect its value.

A **cul-de-sac** lot is found at the end of a dead-end street. It is a street that has only one way in and out. This may be desirable because of the privacy and quietness, but the lot may be undesirable if oddly pie-shaped on the turn-around section of the street.

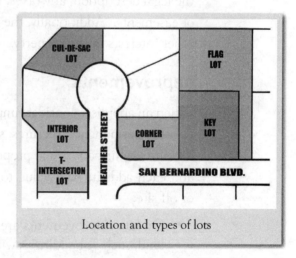

Location and types of lots

A **corner lot** is found at the intersection of two streets. It may be desirable because of its accessibility, but may also be noisy and expensive to maintain because of the increased frontage.

A **T-intersection lot** is one that is fronted head-on by a street. The noise and glare from headlights may detract from this type of lot.

An **interior lot** is one that is surrounded by other lots, with frontage on the street. It is the most common type lot and may be desirable or not, depending on other factors.

A **flag lot** looks like a flag on a pole. The pole represents the access to the site, which is usually located to the rear of another lot fronting a main street.

A **key lot**, so named because it resembles a key fitting into a lock, is surrounded by the backyards of other lots. It is the least desirable because of the lack of privacy.

> ### Review - Physical Factors of Site that Appraisers Consider
> - Shape of lot
> - Topography and soil conditions
> - Corner influence
> - Relation to surroundings
> - Availability of public utilities
> - Encroachments
> - Landscaping and subsurface land improvements
> - **Front foot** of a commercial property is usually the most valuable

Legal Data

An appraiser must evaluate all **legal data** connected with the site, including the legal description, any taxes, the zoning, general plan, and any restrictions or easements. Additionally, the appraiser needs to determine if there are any other interests in the property.

Improvements

When an appraiser considers improvements, it means looking at any buildings or other permanent structures, such as a fence, a swimming pool, a sauna, or a built-in whirlpool. Real property is divided into land and improvements, and each adds its own value to a site. Improvements can be either on-site or off-site:

- **On-site improvements** are structures permanently attached to the land, such as buildings, swimming pools, and fences.

- **Off-site improvements** are items in areas that border the site and add to its value, such as street lights, sidewalks, greenbelts, and curbs.

Decide on the Appraisal Approach

There are three main approaches to appraising property to arrive at a market value estimate: (1) sales comparison approach, (2) cost approach, and (3) income approach. The sales comparison approach depends on recent sales and listings of similar properties in the area and are evaluated to form an opinion of value.

The cost approach estimates the value of the land as if vacant and adds that to the depreciated cost of new improvements to determine an estimate of value for the entire property. The income or capitalization approach calculates the potential net income of the property considered and then capitalized into value.

> ### Review - Which Appraisal Approach to Use
> - Single-family homes   Sales comparison approach
> - New or unusual buildings   Cost approach
> - Rental properties   Income approach

Reconcile the Data

The final step in an appraisal is to examine the values derived by the various approaches. This process is called **reconciliation**.

In most appraisals, all three approaches will have something to add. Each approach is used independently to reach an estimated value. Many times an appraiser will use all three approaches to arrive at the market value of a property.

The appraiser gives each separate value a weight that is most compatible to the subject property. The appraiser decides which of the values is the most appropriate for the subject property, and uses that figure to determine the final estimate for the property in question.

Write The Appraisal Report

Appraisers report appraisal results using either of two reporting options—the Appraisal Report or the Restricted Appraisal Report. Each written appraisal report must be prepared according to the Uniform Standards of Professional Appraisal Practice (USPAP) standards.

When the intended users of the report include parties other than the client, the reporting option used must be the Appraisal Report. When the intended users do not include parties other than the client, the reporting option used is the Restricted Appraisal Report. The difference between the options is in the content and level of information provided.

An appraiser must be careful in deciding which type of reporting option to use. Appraisal standards set minimum requirements for the content and level of information in each type of report. The final report is presented in either a short-form or a narrative style. Appraisals are valid on the date that the appraiser signs and dates the appraisal report.

Appraisal Report

The **Appraisal Report** is the most commonly used report option. The Uniform Residential Appraisal Report (URAR) is an example of an Appraisal Report, which is used for most residential appraisals.

An Appraisal Report includes the identity of the client and any intended users (by name or type), the intended use of the appraisal, the real estate involved, the real property interest appraised, the purpose of the appraisal, and dates of the appraisal and of the report. It also describes work used to develop the appraisal, the assumptions, and limiting conditions, the information that was analyzed, the procedures followed, and the reasoning that supports the conclusions. The report states the current use of the real estate and the use reflected in the appraisal, the support for an appraiser's opinion of the highest and best use, and any departures from the Standards. It also includes a signed certification.

Restricted Appraisal Report

The **Restricted Appraisal Report** is the briefest presentation of an appraisal and contains the least detail. It covers the same categories as the Appraisal Report with a few differences. In this type of report, only the client is named because there are no other users and the use of the report is limited to the client. In addition, the report refers to the appraiser's workfile as the source of necessary additional information about the appraisal.

APPLY THE APPROACHES TO VALUE

As we have seen, an appraiser must apply the relevant approaches to value as part of the appraisal process. The approaches to value are the sales comparison approach, cost approach, and the income approach.

Sales Comparison Approach

The **sales comparison approach** is the one most easily and commonly used by real estate licensees. It is best for single-family homes or condominiums and vacant lots because sales information is readily available and easily compared. This approach uses the principle of substitution to compare similar properties.

As you recall, the principle of substitution states that a buyer will not pay more for a property than the cost of a similar one. The sales comparison approach takes the current selling price of a similar property and adjusts it for any differences to arrive at the market value for the subject property.

The appraiser will collect data on comparable properties (**comps**) that are as similar to the property in question as possible, in certain categories. **Comparables** are properties that are similar to a subject property and are used in the appraisal process. Typical categories include neighborhood location, size (comparable number of bedrooms/bathrooms as well as square footage), age, architectural style, financing terms, and the general price range.

The sales comparison approach is based on the idea that property is worth what it will sell for when there is no extra stress, if reasonable time is given to find a buyer. Because of this, the appraiser will research comparable sales to discover any special circumstances influencing those sales. Only those similar properties—sold on the open market, with approval of the seller, offered for a reasonable length of time—will be used for comparables. Also, if possible, only those properties that have sold within the past six months are selected. If the comparables are older than that, they are considered less reliable.

Features in either the property or the transaction itself are elements that can cause appraisals to vary. Estimates of value vary due to differences in the financing terms, time of the sale, sale conditions (**arm's length transaction**), location, physical features, and in any income that is derived from the property.

Thus, a price is found for each comparable property that should reflect its present value in the current market where the subject property is being sold. Those properties not as comparable are excluded, and greater weight is given to the comparable sales most like the property being appraised. By using judgment to reconcile the comparables, the appraiser arrives at the final estimate of value for the subject property, using the compatible comparables to show the value and price to be asked for the subject property.

Advantages of Sales Comparison Approach

- Most easily understood approach of valuation and most commonly used by real estate licensees.

- Easily applied for the sale of single-family homes.

- The sales comparison approach is best for single-family homes or condominiums and vacant lots.

Disadvantages of Sales Comparison Approach

- Finding enough recently sold similar properties to get comparable values.

- Correctly adjusting amenities to make them comparable to the subject property.

- Older sales unreliable with changing economic conditions.

- Difficulty in confirming transaction details.

Review - The Sales Comparison Approach Procedure
1. Find similar properties, select and verify data.
2. Select appropriate elements of comparison, adjust sales price of each comparable. (Adjustment is always made to the comparable, not the subject property.)
3. Adjust sales prices of comparables by subtracting the adjustment if the subject property is inferior to the comparable and by adding the adjustment if the subject property is superior.

Cost Approach

The **cost approach** looks at the value of the appraised parcel as the combination of two elements. These elements are: (1) the value of the land as if vacant, and (2) the cost to rebuild the appraised building as new on the date of valuation, less the accrued depreciation.

To determine the value of a property using the cost approach, first obtain the value of the land, then add the cost to build structure new, and then subtract any accrued depreciation. The cost approach tends to set the upper limit of value for a property. In other words, the most something would cost if it were built new. Using the principle of substitution, a person will not pay more for a substitute if he or she can get the subject property for less. In the cost approach, the substitute is the cost of reconstructing the present building new on vacant land.

The cost approach is used most often for appraising new buildings and special-purpose or unique structures. Depreciation on a new building is relatively easy to determine, whereas the cost approach is impractical with older buildings because of the difficulty in estimating depreciation. The cost approach is also used with buildings where it is difficult to find comparables because they are unique or one-of-a-kind, such as a church, fire station, or hospital.

Review - The Cost Approach Procedure

1. Estimate the value of the land as if it were vacant, using comparable land sales. (Principle of Substitution)

2. Estimate the replacement or reproduction cost of the existing building as of the appraisal date. **Replacement cost** is the cost of restoring a property to its previous condition or replacing it with something of like kind and quality. **Reproduction cost** is the cost of replacing the improvement with one that is the exact replica, having the same quality of workmanship, design, and layout.

3. Estimate the amount of accrued depreciation to the improvements.

4. Deduct the amount of the accrued depreciation from the replacement cost (new) to find the estimate of the depreciated value of the improvements.

5. Add the estimated present-depreciated value for the improvements to the value of the land. The result is an estimate of value for the subject property.

Occasionally, the cost approach is the only one an appraiser can use. If there have been no recent sales (such as during recession or when interest rates are too high), there will be no comparables for the sales comparison approach. If the subject is not an income-producing property, the income method (to be discussed next) cannot be used. So the cost method is a reliable way for an appraiser or real estate agent to determine the value of a property when all else fails.

Methods to Estimate the Cost of a New Building

To estimate the cost of building the structure new, an appraiser can use one of several methods, including square-foot, cubic-foot, quantity-survey, and the unit-in-place cost method.

An appraiser can use various methods to estimate the cost of a new building.

Square-Foot Method

The **square-foot method** is the most common, used by appraisers and real estate licensees to estimate the cost of construction. The size of the building in question is compared, by square foot, to other buildings with the same area. The building being appraised is compared with the most comparable standard building, and its cost per square foot is used for the subject property. This is the fastest way to estimate value using the cost method.

Cubic-Foot Method

The **cubic-foot method** is very similar to the square-foot method, but it takes height as well as area into consideration. The cubic contents of buildings are compared instead of just the square footage.

Quantity-Survey Method

This method is a detailed estimate of all labor and materials used in the components of a building. Items such as overhead, insurance, and contractor's profit are added to direct costs of building. This method is time-consuming but very accurate.

Unit-In-Place Cost Method

Cost of units in the building as installed is computed and applied to the structure cost. The total costs of walls in place, heating units, and roof are figured on a square-foot basis, including labor, overhead, and profit. This is the most detailed method of estimating value.

Depreciation

Depreciation means loss in value from any cause. It is usually measured by estimating the difference between the current cost to replace new and the estimated value of the property as of the date of appraisal.

The opposite of depreciation is **appreciation**, or an increase in value, usually as a result of inflation or some special supply and demand force relating to that specific property. Appreciation may balance the normal decrease of value due to depreciation.

All of the influences that reduce the value of a property below its cost new are included in the definition of depreciation.

Physical Deterioration

This type of depreciation can come from wear and tear, negligent care (sometimes called deferred maintenance), damage by dry rot or termites, or severe changes in temperature. This may or may not be curable.

Many things cause physical deterioration.

Functional Obsolescence

Functional obsolescence is depreciation that is attributable to an item or feature within the subject property that is no longer useful or functional. Poor architectural design and style can contribute to functional obsolescence, as can lack of modern facilities, out-of-date equipment, changes in styles of construction, changes in utility demand, and over-improvements. For instance, a four-bedroom house with only one bathroom might be considered functionally obsolete because most homes today have at least two bathrooms with many

Many older homes have features that contribute to functional obsolescence.

having one bath for each bedroom. It may or may not be curable. Over-improvements are features that are too large or of a higher quality than needed for a property. For example, building a 10,000 square foot home in the middle of a tract of homes ranging in size from 1,200 to 1,800 square feet in size is an example of an over-improvement.

Physical deterioration and functional obsolescence are further divided into two-sub categories of depreciation called curable and incurable.

Curable depreciation refers to a loss in value that is economically feasible to correct. In other words, the cost to fix the problem is less than the loss in value, so fixing the problem makes economic sense.

Incurable depreciation refers to items of depreciation that either are physically impossible to cure or are too expensive to be worth curing. If the cost to fix the problem exceeds the loss in value caused by the problem, then it does not make economic sense to repair it.

Economic Obsolescence

This type of depreciation occurs because of forces outside the property. Changes in the social or economic make up of the neighborhood, zoning changes, over-supply of homes, under-supply of buyers, recession, or legislative restrictions can cause economic obsolescence. It is usually incurable.

Depreciation for Appraisal Purposes

The book depreciation calculated by an accountant is not the depreciation considered by the appraiser, as we have seen.

The appraiser does not look at the owner's original cost to purchase but uses the cost to build new on the date of the appraisal as the basis for evaluation, using the cost approach. An appraiser subtracts the estimate of accrued actual (not book) depreciation on the building from the cost to build new.

As you recall, in using the cost approach, the value of the land and the value of the building (improvements) are determined separately, then added together to calculate the value of the entire property. So, the appraiser figures the actual depreciation on the building and subtracts it from the cost to construct the building new. The next step is to add that amount to the value given the land (using the principle of substitution from other land sales) to estimate the value of the whole parcel.

There are several ways to calculate accrued depreciation; however, for our purposes we will only discuss the straight-line (or age-life) method. It is the one most commonly used by real estate licensees and appraisers because it is easy to calculate, is used by the Internal Revenue Service, and is easily understood by the consumer.

Using the **straight-line method** to determine accrued depreciation, the appraiser assumes a building will decline in value the same amount each year, until nothing is left. For example, a property with an estimated effective age of 50 years would be said to depreciate at an equal rate of 2% per year (2% x 50 years equals 100% depreciation). In using this method of calculating accrued depreciation, the appraiser probably will not use the actual age of the building, rather the effective age, which is determined by its condition, not the number of years since it was built.

Actual age is the real age of a building. **Effective age** is not determined by the actual age of a building but by its condition and usefulness. **Economic life** is the estimated period over which a building may be profitably used. Economic life is usually shorter than physical (actual) life. For example, if the subject property was really 25 years old, but was as well maintained and would sell for as much as nearby 20-year-old properties, it would be said to have an effective age of 20 years.

Depreciation for Tax Purposes

Depreciation for income tax purposes is book depreciation, or a mathematical calculation of steady depreciation or loss, from the owner's original purchase price (**cost basis**). This allows the owner to recover the cost of investment over the **useful life** of the building. It is mathematically accrued annually and taken as an income tax deduction from the owner's gross income.

Many times, this deduction makes gross income a negative amount on paper. The building seems to be losing value, giving the owner a paper loss that can be offset against other income. This paper loss, or tax shelter, is why many people invest in income property.

Book value is the current value (for accounting purposes) of a property, calculated as the original cost plus **capital improvements** and minus accumulated or accrued depreciation of the improvement. Remember, this is used as an accounting method, not to be confused with actual depreciation of a building. Depreciation is allowed on buildings only, not on land. The depreciation, for accounting—or tax—purposes, is only a mathematical wasting away of the improvements. Property buyers have the least interest in an owner's book value.

In other words, the book value of a property may be calculated by adding the depreciated value of the improvement (the building) to the assigned value of the land. It is important to remember that book value and book depreciation are used only to figure income tax and are not particularly relevant to an appraiser.

Income Approach

The **income approach**, or **income-capitalization approach**, estimates the present worth of future benefits from ownership of a property. The value of the property is based on its capacity to continue producing an income. This approach is used to estimate the value of income-producing property (rentals), usually in combination with one or both of the other approaches. This approach is based mainly on the appraisal principles of comparison, substitution, and anticipation.

> **The value of the property is based on its capacity to continue producing an income.**

Contract rent, or the amount actually paid by a renter for use of the premises, may or may not be the same as economic rent, or the amount the rental could bring in an open market. An appraiser valuating a property looks at the economic rent, rather than the contract rent, in order to discover the fair income of the property. Properties are valued using both the income capitalization approach and gross rent multiplier approach.

Using Capitalization of Income

The process of calculating a property's present worth on the basis of its capacity to continue producing an income stream is called **capitalization**. Capitalization converts the future income stream into an indication of the property's present worth. Risk determines the capitalization rate to be used. The higher the perceived risk, the higher the capitalization rate. The appraiser evaluates the expected future income and expenses of a property using the income approach to determine its present value.

> **Formulas Used to Estimate the Value of an Income Property**
> NOI divided by the Cap Rate equals the Value of the Property.
> NOI divided by Value of Property equals Cap Rate.

The appraiser must determine the amount, reliability, and durability of the income stream. There are five basic steps.

Step 1. Calculate the Effective Gross Income

The **effective gross income** is the total annual income from the property minus any vacancy or rental losses. That includes rental income plus any other income generated by the property such as laundry room income or parking fees. Loss of income because of a vacant unit is known as the **vacancy factor**. The **vacancy rate** is the number of vacant units expressed as a percentage. Current market rents are used to determine the loss from the vacancy factor. **Market rent** is the rent the property should bring in the open market, while contract rent is the actual, or contracted, rent paid by the tenants. The appraiser uses the market rent in his or her calculations.

Calculation:

Gross scheduled annual income	$36,000
Subtract vacancy factor / rental loss	−3,600
Effective gross income	$32,400

Step 2. Determine Operating Expenses

Expenses are generally classified as being either fixed or variable. **Fixed expenses** include property taxes, insurance, and utilities. **Variable expenses** include management and maintenance.

> **Review - Operating Expenses**
> **Mnemonic = TIMMUR**
>
> Taxes
> Insurance
> Management
> Maintenance
> Utilities
> Reserves

Step 3. Calculate Net Operating Income

The **net operating income** (NOI) is the income after paying all expenses including a maintenance reserve. It does not include the principal and interest **(debt service)** paid on a loan.

Calculation:

Taxes	$1,920
Insurance	480
Management	2,400
Maintenance	1,000
Utilities	800
Reserves (roof, water heaters, etc.)	+ 800
Total expenses	$7,400
Effective gross income	$32,400
Subtract expenses	− 7,400
Net operating income	$25,000

4. Select a Capitalization Rate

The **capitalization rate**, more accurately called the **internal rate of return** (IRR) in the financial community, provides for the return of invested capital plus a return on the investment. The rate is dependent upon the return a buyer will demand before investing money in the property. The greater the risk of recapturing the investment price (making a profit), the higher the cap rate and the lower the price. The lower the risk, the lower the cap rate, and the higher the price of the property.

- The greater the risk, the higher the cap rate and the lower the price.
- The lower the risk, the lower the cap rate, and the higher the price.

Choosing a capitalization rate is the hardest part for appraisers using the income approach. Generally, a real estate agent will need further study and practice to use this approach to valuation. One way a capitalization rate can be determined is by a market analysis of similar income properties and using the same capitalization rate as those recent sales have. The net operating income is divided by the sales price to determine the cap rate used in each sale. Other methods of calculating a capitalization rate may be learned through additional study of appraisal.

Step 5. Calculate the Market Value

Calculate the market value by dividing the net operating income by the chosen cap rate.

Calculation:

Net Operating Income is $25,000 and the Cap Rate is 8%

$25,000 divided by .08 equals $312,500

Market value = $312,500

Using the Gross Rent Multiplier

Real estate licensees and appraisers use the **gross rent multiplier** to convert gross rent into market value. It is used for income-producing properties and is an easy way to get a rough estimate of the value of rental units.

Gross rent is income (calculated annually or monthly) received before any expenses are deducted. A gross rent multiplier, when multiplied by the total annual rents, will give a rough estimate of a property value that can then be compared with other like properties. Generally, gross multipliers will be somewhere between x5 and x10, depending on the market, the condition, and the location of the property.

In other words, a property with a gross annual income of $36,000, when multiplied by the current gross multiplier of 10, will be valued roughly at $360,000. So when you hear property values described as ten times gross, five times gross, or seven times gross, it means the value is shown by whatever multiplier is used, times the gross income. This is only a quick estimate of value, and does not take the place of a professional appraisal.

The reverse process can be used to calculate the gross multiplier, rather than the market value. The reason you might want to do that is to compare properties to see if they are priced right or are above or below market value. If you know that most rental properties are selling for around eight times the gross annual multiplier (eight times gross), simply divide the listed price by the gross income to arrive at the multiplier.

Calculation to find Gross Rent Multiplier

Listed price is $360,000 and the gross annual income is $ 36,000

Divide the list price by the gross annual income

$360,000 divided by $36,000 equals 10

Gross Rent Multiplier is 10

The gross rent multipliers of several income properties may be compared using the sales comparison approach to estimate their value. A gross rent multiplier can be stated on either an annual or a monthly basis.

APPRAISAL LICENSING STANDARDS

The Appraisal Foundation (TAF) is a non-profit organization that includes the Appraiser Qualifications Board, the Appraiser Standards Board, and the Appraisal Practices Board. The **Appraiser Qualifications Board** (AQB) establishes the minimum education, experience, and examination requirements an individual must meet in order to become a licensed or certified appraiser. The **Appraisal Standards Board** (ASB) develops, interprets, and amends the Uniform Standards of Professional Appraisal Practice (USPAP). The **Appraisal Practices Board** (APB) will identify and issue opinions on Recognized Valuation Methods and Techniques, which may apply to all disciplines within the appraisal profession.

In California, the **Bureau of Real Estate Appraisers** (BREA) licenses appraisers.

Types of Appraisal Licenses

There are four levels of real estate appraiser licensing in California:

1. Trainee License
2. Residential License
3. Certified Residential License
4. Certified General License

Each level requires a specific amount of education and experience, and each licensee must pass a state exam. Trainees must work under the supervision of a certified residential or general licensed appraiser. The types of structures that can be appraised are specified for each level. An appraisal on commercial property is conducted by a Certified General Appraiser. Continuing education is required to maintain the license.

Registered Appraisal Management Company

In 2009, the California Appraisal Management Company law was enacted requiring the registration of appraisal management companies with the Bureau of Real Estate Appraisers (BREA). The law also sets forth standards with which an appraisal management company must comply and provides enforcement authority to BREA.

CA B&P Code section 11302(d) defines an **appraisal management company** as any entity that satisfies all of the following conditions:

1. maintains an approved list containing 11 or more licensed or certified appraisers who are independent contractor or employs 11 or more licensed or certified appraisers who are employees;

2. receives requests for appraisals from one or more clients; and

3. for a fee, delegates appraisal assignments for completion by its independent contractor or employee appraisers.

PROFESSIONAL APPRAISAL ORGANIZATIONS

The major objective of these organizations is to make sure the members of the appraisal profession are knowledgeable and conform to a code of ethics and standards of professional appraisal practice. The main professional organization is the Appraisal Institute (AI). Members may hold the title of Member Appraisal Institute (MAI) or Senior Residential Appraiser (SRA).

Uniform Residential Appraisal Report   File

The purpose of this summary appraisal report is to provide the lender/client with an accurate, and adequately supported, opinion of the market value of the subject property.

<table>
<tr><td colspan="2">Property Address</td><td>City</td><td>State</td><td>Zip Code</td></tr>
<tr><td>Borrower</td><td>Owner of Public Record</td><td colspan="2">County</td><td></td></tr>
<tr><td colspan="5">Legal Description</td></tr>
<tr><td colspan="2">Assessor's Parcel #</td><td>Tax Year</td><td colspan="2">R.E. Taxes $</td></tr>
<tr><td colspan="2">Neighborhood Name</td><td>Map Reference</td><td colspan="2">Census Tract</td></tr>
<tr><td colspan="5">Occupant ☐ Owner ☐ Tenant ☐ Vacant   Special Assessments $ ☐ PUD   HOA $ ☐ per year ☐ per month</td></tr>
<tr><td colspan="5">Property Rights Appraised ☐ Fee Simple ☐ Leasehold ☐ Other (describe)</td></tr>
<tr><td colspan="5">Assignment Type ☐ Purchase Transaction ☐ Refinance Transaction ☐ Other (describe)</td></tr>
<tr><td colspan="5">Lender/Client   Address</td></tr>
<tr><td colspan="5">Is the subject property currently offered for sale or has it been offered for sale in the twelve months prior to the effective date of this appraisal? ☐ Yes ☐ No</td></tr>
<tr><td colspan="5">Report data source(s) used, offering price(s), and date(s).</td></tr>
</table>

I ☐ did ☐ did not analyze the contract for sale for the subject purchase transaction. Explain the results of the analysis of the contract for sale or why the analysis was not performed.

Contract Price $ Date of Contract   Is the property seller the owner of public record? ☐ Yes ☐ No   Data Source(s)

Is there any financial assistance (loan charges, sale concessions, gift or downpayment assistance, etc.) to be paid by any party on behalf of the borrower? ☐ Yes ☐ No
If Yes, report the total dollar amount and describe the items to be paid.

Note: Race and the racial composition of the neighborhood are not appraisal factors.

Neighborhood Characteristics			One-Unit Housing Trends			One-Unit Housing		Present Land Use %	
Location ☐ Urban	☐ Suburban	☐ Rural	Property Values ☐ Increasing	☐ Stable	☐ Declining	PRICE $(000)	AGE (yrs)	One-Unit	%
Built-Up ☐ Over 75%	☐ 25–75%	☐ Under 25%	Demand/Supply ☐ Shortage	☐ In Balance	☐ Over Supply			2-4 Unit	%
Growth ☐ Rapid	☐ Stable	☐ Slow	Marketing Time ☐ Under 3 mths	☐ 3–6 mths	☐ Over 6 mths	Low		Multi-Family	%
Neighborhood Boundaries						High		Commercial	%
						Pred.		Other	%

Neighborhood Description

Market Conditions (including support for the above conclusions)

Dimensions	Area	Shape	View
Specific Zoning Classification	Zoning Description		

Zoning Compliance ☐ Legal ☐ Legal Nonconforming (Grandfathered Use) ☐ No Zoning ☐ Illegal (describe)

Is the highest and best use of the subject property as improved (or as proposed per plans and specifications) the present use? ☐ Yes ☐ No If No, describe

Utilities	Public	Other (describe)		Public	Other (describe)	Off-site Improvements—Type	Public	Private
Electricity	☐	☐	Water	☐	☐	Street	☐	☐
Gas	☐	☐	Sanitary Sewer	☐	☐	Alley	☐	☐

FEMA Special Flood Hazard Area ☐ Yes ☐ No   FEMA Flood Zone   FEMA Map #   FEMA Map Date

Are the utilities and off-site improvements typical for the market area? ☐ Yes ☐ No If No, describe

Are there any adverse site conditions or external factors (easements, encroachments, environmental conditions, land uses, etc.)? ☐ Yes ☐ No If Yes, describe

General Description		Foundation		Exterior Description materials/condition		Interior materials/condition		
Units ☐ One ☐ One with Accessory Unit		☐ Concrete Slab ☐ Crawl Space		Foundation Walls		Floors		
# of Stories		☐ Full Basement ☐ Partial Basement		Exterior Walls		Walls		
Type ☐ Det. ☐ Att. ☐ S-Det./End Unit		Basement Area sq. ft.		Roof Surface		Trim/Finish		
☐ Existing ☐ Proposed ☐ Under Const.		Basement Finish %		Gutters & Downspouts		Bath Floor		
Design (Style)		☐ Outside Entry/Exit ☐ Sump Pump		Window Type		Bath Wainscot		
Year Built		Evidence of ☐ Infestation		Storm Sash/Insulated		Car Storage ☐ None		
Effective Age (Yrs)		☐ Dampness ☐ Settlement		Screens		☐ Driveway # of Cars		
Attic	☐ None	Heating ☐ FWA ☐ HWBB ☐ Radiant		Amenities	☐ Woodstove(s) #	Driveway Surface		
☐ Drop Stair	☐ Stairs	☐ Other	Fuel	☐ Fireplace(s) #	☐ Fence	☐ Garage # of Cars		
☐ Floor	☐ Scuttle	Cooling ☐ Central Air Conditioning		☐ Patio/Deck	☐ Porch	☐ Carport # of Cars		
☐ Finished	☐ Heated	☐ Individual	☐ Other	☐ Pool	☐ Other	☐ Att. ☐ Det. ☐ Built-in		

Appliances ☐ Refrigerator ☐ Range/Oven ☐ Dishwasher ☐ Disposal ☐ Microwave ☐ Washer/Dryer ☐ Other (describe)

Finished area above grade contains: Rooms   Bedrooms   Bath(s)   Square Feet of Gross Living Area Above Grade

Additional features (special energy efficient items, etc.)

Describe the condition of the property (including needed repairs, deterioration, renovations, remodeling, etc.).

Are there any physical deficiencies or adverse conditions that affect the livability, soundness, or structural integrity of the property? ☐ Yes ☐ No If Yes, describe

Does the property generally conform to the neighborhood (functional utility, style, condition, use, construction, etc.)? ☐ Yes ☐ No If No, describe

Uniform Residential Appraisal Report

File #

There are ___ comparable properties currently offered for sale in the subject neighborhood ranging in price from $ ___ to $ ___ .				
There are ___ comparable sales in the subject neighborhood within the past twelve months ranging in sale price from $ ___ to $ ___ .				

FEATURE	SUBJECT	COMPARABLE SALE # 1	COMPARABLE SALE # 2	COMPARABLE SALE # 3
Address				
Proximity to Subject				
Sale Price	$	$	$	$
Sale Price/Gross Liv. Area	$ sq. ft.	$ sq. ft.	$ sq. ft.	$ sq. ft.
Data Source(s)				
Verification Source(s)				

VALUE ADJUSTMENTS	DESCRIPTION	DESCRIPTION	+(-) $ Adjustment	DESCRIPTION	+(-) $ Adjustment	DESCRIPTION	+(-) $ Adjustment
Sale or Financing Concessions							
Date of Sale/Time							
Location							
Leasehold/Fee Simple							
Site							
View							
Design (Style)							
Quality of Construction							
Actual Age							
Condition							
Above Grade Room Count	Total Bdrms. Baths	Total Bdrms. Baths		Total Bdrms. Baths		Total Bdrms. Baths	
Gross Living Area	sq. ft.	sq. ft.		sq. ft.		sq. ft.	
Basement & Finished Rooms Below Grade							
Functional Utility							
Heating/Cooling							
Energy Efficient Items							
Garage/Carport							
Porch/Patio/Deck							
Net Adjustment (Total)		☐ + ☐ -	$	☐ + ☐ -	$	☐ + ☐ -	$
Adjusted Sale Price of Comparables		Net Adj. % Gross Adj. %	$	Net Adj. % Gross Adj. %	$	Net Adj. % Gross Adj. %	$

I ☐ did ☐ did not research the sale or transfer history of the subject property and comparable sales. If not, explain

My research ☐ did ☐ did not reveal any prior sales or transfers of the subject property for the three years prior to the effective date of this appraisal.
Data source(s)

My research ☐ did ☐ did not reveal any prior sales or transfers of the comparable sales for the year prior to the date of sale of the comparable sale.
Data source(s)

Report the results of the research and analysis of the prior sale or transfer history of the subject property and comparable sales (report additional prior sales on page 3).

ITEM	SUBJECT	COMPARABLE SALE # 1	COMPARABLE SALE # 2	COMPARABLE SALE # 3
Date of Prior Sale/Transfer				
Price of Prior Sale/Transfer				
Data Source(s)				
Effective Date of Data Source(s)				

Analysis of prior sale or transfer history of the subject property and comparable sales

Summary of Sales Comparison Approach

Indicated Value by Sales Comparison Approach $

Indicated Value by: Sales Comparison Approach $ Cost Approach (if developed) $ Income Approach (if developed) $

This appraisal is made ☐ "as is", ☐ subject to completion per plans and specifications on the basis of a hypothetical condition that the improvements have been completed, ☐ subject to the following repairs or alterations on the basis of a hypothetical condition that the repairs or alterations have been completed, or ☐ subject to the following required inspection based on the extraordinary assumption that the condition or deficiency does not require alteration or repair:

Based on a complete visual inspection of the interior and exterior areas of the subject property, defined scope of work, statement of assumptions and limiting conditions, and appraiser's certification, my (our) opinion of the market value, as defined, of the real property that is the subject of this report is
$ ___ , as of ___ , which is the date of inspection and the effective date of this appraisal.

Uniform Residential Appraisal Report

File #

ADDITIONAL COMMENTS

(blank lined comment area)

COST APPROACH TO VALUE (not required by Fannie Mae)

Provide adequate information for the lender/client to replicate the below cost figures and calculations.

Support for the opinion of site value (summary of comparable land sales or other methods for estimating site value)

ESTIMATED ☐ REPRODUCTION OR ☐ REPLACEMENT COST NEW	OPINION OF SITE VALUE .... = $	
Source of cost data	Dwelling Sq. Ft. @ $ .... =$	
Quality rating from cost service Effective date of cost data	Sq. Ft. @ $ .... =$	
Comments on Cost Approach (gross living area calculations, depreciation, etc.)		
	Garage/Carport Sq. Ft. @ $ .... =$	
	Total Estimate of Cost-New .... = $	
	Less Physical	Functional	External	
	Depreciation =$( )	
	Depreciated Cost of Improvements.................. =$	
	"As-is" Value of Site Improvements.................. =$	
Estimated Remaining Economic Life (HUD and VA only) Years	Indicated Value By Cost Approach .... =$	

INCOME APPROACH TO VALUE (not required by Fannie Mae)

Estimated Monthly Market Rent $ X Gross Rent Multiplier   = $ Indicated Value by Income Approach

Summary of Income Approach (including support for market rent and GRM)

PROJECT INFORMATION FOR PUDs (if applicable)

Is the developer/builder in control of the Homeowners' Association (HOA)? ☐ Yes ☐ No   Unit type(s) ☐ Detached ☐ Attached

Provide the following information for PUDs ONLY if the developer/builder is in control of the HOA and the subject property is an attached dwelling unit.

Legal name of project

Total number of phases   Total number of units   Total number of units sold

Total number of units rented   Total number of units for sale   Data source(s)

Was the project created by the conversion of an existing building(s) into a PUD? ☐ Yes ☐ No   If Yes, date of conversion

Does the project contain any multi-dwelling units? ☐ Yes ☐ No   Data source(s)

Are the units, common elements, and recreation facilities complete? ☐ Yes ☐ No   If No, describe the status of completion.

Are the common elements leased to or by the Homeowners' Association? ☐ Yes ☐ No   If Yes, describe the rental terms and options.

Describe common elements and recreational facilities

Uniform Residential Appraisal Report   File

This report form is designed to report an appraisal of a one-unit property or a one-unit property with an accessory unit; including a unit in a planned unit development (PUD). This report form is not designed to report an appraisal of a manufactured home or a unit in a condominium or cooperative project.

This appraisal report is subject to the following scope of work, intended use, intended user, definition of market value, statement of assumptions and limiting conditions, and certifications. Modifications, additions, or deletions to the intended use, intended user, definition of market value, or assumptions and limiting conditions are not permitted. The appraiser may expand the scope of work to include any additional research or analysis necessary based on the complexity of this appraisal assignment. Modifications or deletions to the certifications are also not permitted. However, additional certifications that do not constitute material alterations to this appraisal report, such as those required by law or those related to the appraiser's continuing education or membership in an appraisal organization, are permitted.

SCOPE OF WORK: The scope of work for this appraisal is defined by the complexity of this appraisal assignment and the reporting requirements of this appraisal report form, including the following definition of market value, statement of assumptions and limiting conditions, and certifications. The appraiser must, at a minimum: (1) perform a complete visual inspection of the interior and exterior areas of the subject property, (2) inspect the neighborhood, (3) inspect each of the comparable sales from at least the street, (4) research, verify, and analyze data from reliable public and/or private sources, and (5) report his or her analysis, opinions, and conclusions in this appraisal report.

INTENDED USE: The intended use of this appraisal report is for the lender/client to evaluate the property that is the subject of this appraisal for a mortgage finance transaction.

INTENDED USER: The intended user of this appraisal report is the lender/client.

DEFINITION OF MARKET VALUE: The most probable price which a property should bring in a competitive and open market under all conditions requisite to a fair sale, the buyer and seller, each acting prudently, knowledgeably and assuming the price is not affected by undue stimulus. Implicit in this definition is the consummation of a sale as of a specified date and the passing of title from seller to buyer under conditions whereby: (1) buyer and seller are typically motivated; (2) both parties are well informed or well advised, and each acting in what he or she considers his or her own best interest; (3) a reasonable time is allowed for exposure in the open market; (4) payment is made in terms of cash in U. S. dollars or in terms of financial arrangements comparable thereto; and (5) the price represents the normal consideration for the property sold unaffected by special or creative financing or sales concessions* granted by anyone associated with the sale.

*Adjustments to the comparables must be made for special or creative financing or sales concessions. No adjustments are necessary for those costs which are normally paid by sellers as a result of tradition or law in a market area; these costs are readily identifiable since the seller pays these costs in virtually all sales transactions. Special or creative financing adjustments can be made to the comparable property by comparisons to financing terms offered by a third party institutional lender that is not already involved in the property or transaction. Any adjustment should not be calculated on a mechanical dollar for dollar cost of the financing or concession but the dollar amount of any adjustment should approximate the market's reaction to the financing or concessions based on the appraiser's judgment.

STATEMENT OF ASSUMPTIONS AND LIMITING CONDITIONS: The appraiser's certification in this report is subject to the following assumptions and limiting conditions:

1. The appraiser will not be responsible for matters of a legal nature that affect either the property being appraised or the title to it, except for information that he or she became aware of during the research involved in performing this appraisal. The appraiser assumes that the title is good and marketable and will not render any opinions about the title.

2. The appraiser has provided a sketch in this appraisal report to show the approximate dimensions of the improvements. The sketch is included only to assist the reader in visualizing the property and understanding the appraiser's determination of its size.

3. The appraiser has examined the available flood maps that are provided by the Federal Emergency Management Agency (or other data sources) and has noted in this appraisal report whether any portion of the subject site is located in an identified Special Flood Hazard Area. Because the appraiser is not a surveyor, he or she makes no guarantees, express or implied, regarding this determination.

4. The appraiser will not give testimony or appear in court because he or she made an appraisal of the property in question, unless specific arrangements to do so have been made beforehand, or as otherwise required by law.

5. The appraiser has noted in this appraisal report any adverse conditions (such as needed repairs, deterioration, the presence of hazardous wastes, toxic substances, etc.) observed during the inspection of the subject property or that he or she became aware of during the research involved in performing this appraisal. Unless otherwise stated in this appraisal report, the appraiser has no knowledge of any hidden or unapparent physical deficiencies or adverse conditions of the property (such as, but not limited to, needed repairs, deterioration, the presence of hazardous wastes, toxic substances, adverse environmental conditions, etc.) that would make the property less valuable, and has assumed that there are no such conditions and makes no guarantees or warranties, express or implied. The appraiser will not be responsible for any such conditions that do exist or for any engineering or testing that might be required to discover whether such conditions exist. Because the appraiser is not an expert in the field of environmental hazards, this appraisal report must not be considered as an environmental assessment of the property.

6. The appraiser has based his or her appraisal report and valuation conclusion for an appraisal that is subject to satisfactory completion, repairs, or alterations on the assumption that the completion, repairs, or alterations of the subject property will be performed in a professional manner.

Uniform Residential Appraisal Report   File

APPRAISER'S CERTIFICATION: The Appraiser certifies and agrees that:

1. I have, at a minimum, developed and reported this appraisal in accordance with the scope of work requirements stated in this appraisal report.

2. I performed a complete visual inspection of the interior and exterior areas of the subject property. I reported the condition of the improvements in factual, specific terms. I identified and reported the physical deficiencies that could affect the livability, soundness, or structural integrity of the property.

3. I performed this appraisal in accordance with the requirements of the Uniform Standards of Professional Appraisal Practice that were adopted and promulgated by the Appraisal Standards Board of The Appraisal Foundation and that were in place at the time this appraisal report was prepared.

4. I developed my opinion of the market value of the real property that is the subject of this report based on the sales comparison approach to value. I have adequate comparable market data to develop a reliable sales comparison approach for this appraisal assignment. I further certify that I considered the cost and income approaches to value but did not develop them, unless otherwise indicated in this report.

5. I researched, verified, analyzed, and reported on any current agreement for sale for the subject property, any offering for sale of the subject property in the twelve months prior to the effective date of this appraisal, and the prior sales of the subject property for a minimum of three years prior to the effective date of this appraisal, unless otherwise indicated in this report.

6. I researched, verified, analyzed, and reported on the prior sales of the comparable sales for a minimum of one year prior to the date of sale of the comparable sale, unless otherwise indicated in this report.

7. I selected and used comparable sales that are locationally, physically, and functionally the most similar to the subject property.

8. I have not used comparable sales that were the result of combining a land sale with the contract purchase price of a home that has been built or will be built on the land.

9. I have reported adjustments to the comparable sales that reflect the market's reaction to the differences between the subject property and the comparable sales.

10. I verified, from a disinterested source, all information in this report that was provided by parties who have a financial interest in the sale or financing of the subject property.

11. I have knowledge and experience in appraising this type of property in this market area.

12. I am aware of, and have access to, the necessary and appropriate public and private data sources, such as multiple listing services, tax assessment records, public land records and other such data sources for the area in which the property is located.

13. I obtained the information, estimates, and opinions furnished by other parties and expressed in this appraisal report from reliable sources that I believe to be true and correct.

14. I have taken into consideration the factors that have an impact on value with respect to the subject neighborhood, subject property, and the proximity of the subject property to adverse influences in the development of my opinion of market value. I have noted in this appraisal report any adverse conditions (such as, but not limited to, needed repairs, deterioration, the presence of hazardous wastes, toxic substances, adverse environmental conditions, etc.) observed during the inspection of the subject property or that I became aware of during the research involved in performing this appraisal. I have considered these adverse conditions in my analysis of the property value, and have reported on the effect of the conditions on the value and marketability of the subject property.

15. I have not knowingly withheld any significant information from this appraisal report and, to the best of my knowledge, all statements and information in this appraisal report are true and correct.

16. I stated in this appraisal report my own personal, unbiased, and professional analysis, opinions, and conclusions, which are subject only to the assumptions and limiting conditions in this appraisal report.

17. I have no present or prospective interest in the property that is the subject of this report, and I have no present or prospective personal interest or bias with respect to the participants in the transaction. I did not base, either partially or completely, my analysis and/or opinion of market value in this appraisal report on the race, color, religion, sex, age, marital status, handicap, familial status, or national origin of either the prospective owners or occupants of the subject property or of the present owners or occupants of the properties in the vicinity of the subject property or on any other basis prohibited by law.

18. My employment and/or compensation for performing this appraisal or any future or anticipated appraisals was not conditioned on any agreement or understanding, written or otherwise, that I would report (or present analysis supporting) a predetermined specific value, a predetermined minimum value, a range or direction in value, a value that favors the cause of any party, or the attainment of a specific result or occurrence of a specific subsequent event (such as approval of a pending mortgage loan application).

19. I personally prepared all conclusions and opinions about the real estate that were set forth in this appraisal report. If I relied on significant real property appraisal assistance from any individual or individuals in the performance of this appraisal or the preparation of this appraisal report, I have named such individual(s) and disclosed the specific tasks performed in this appraisal report. I certify that any individual so named is qualified to perform the tasks. I have not authorized anyone to make a change to any item in this appraisal report; therefore, any change made to this appraisal is unauthorized and I will take no responsibility for it.

20. I identified the lender/client in this appraisal report who is the individual, organization, or agent for the organization that ordered and will receive this appraisal report.

Uniform Residential Appraisal Report   File

21. The lender/client may disclose or distribute this appraisal report to: the borrower; another lender at the request of the borrower; the mortgagee or its successors and assigns; mortgage insurers; government sponsored enterprises; other secondary market participants; data collection or reporting services; professional appraisal organizations; any department, agency, or instrumentality of the United States; and any state, the District of Columbia, or other jurisdictions; without having to obtain the appraiser's or supervisory appraiser's (if applicable) consent. Such consent must be obtained before this appraisal report may be disclosed or distributed to any other party (including, but not limited to, the public through advertising, public relations, news, sales, or other media).

22. I am aware that any disclosure or distribution of this appraisal report by me or the lender/client may be subject to certain laws and regulations. Further, I am also subject to the provisions of the Uniform Standards of Professional Appraisal Practice that pertain to disclosure or distribution by me.

23. The borrower, another lender at the request of the borrower, the mortgagee or its successors and assigns, mortgage insurers, government sponsored enterprises, and other secondary market participants may rely on this appraisal report as part of any mortgage finance transaction that involves any one or more of these parties.

24. If this appraisal report was transmitted as an "electronic record" containing my "electronic signature," as those terms are defined in applicable federal and/or state laws (excluding audio and video recordings), or a facsimile transmission of this appraisal report containing a copy or representation of my signature, the appraisal report shall be as effective, enforceable and valid as if a paper version of this appraisal report were delivered containing my original hand written signature.

25. Any intentional or negligent misrepresentation(s) contained in this appraisal report may result in civil liability and/or criminal penalties including, but not limited to, fine or imprisonment or both under the provisions of Title 18, United States Code, Section 1001, et seq., or similar state laws.

SUPERVISORY APPRAISER'S CERTIFICATION: The Supervisory Appraiser certifies and agrees that:

1. I directly supervised the appraiser for this appraisal assignment, have read the appraisal report, and agree with the appraiser's analysis, opinions, statements, conclusions, and the appraiser's certification.

2. I accept full responsibility for the contents of this appraisal report including, but not limited to, the appraiser's analysis, opinions, statements, conclusions, and the appraiser's certification.

3. The appraiser identified in this appraisal report is either a sub-contractor or an employee of the supervisory appraiser (or the appraisal firm), is qualified to perform this appraisal, and is acceptable to perform this appraisal under the applicable state law.

4. This appraisal report complies with the Uniform Standards of Professional Appraisal Practice that were adopted and promulgated by the Appraisal Standards Board of The Appraisal Foundation and that were in place at the time this appraisal report was prepared.

5. If this appraisal report was transmitted as an "electronic record" containing my "electronic signature," as those terms are defined in applicable federal and/or state laws (excluding audio and video recordings), or a facsimile transmission of this appraisal report containing a copy or representation of my signature, the appraisal report shall be as effective, enforceable and valid as if a paper version of this appraisal report were delivered containing my original hand written signature.

APPRAISER

Signature_____
Name _____
Company Name _____
Company Address_____
_____
Telephone Number _____
Email Address_____
Date of Signature and Report_____
Effective Date of Appraisal _____
State Certification # _____
or State License # _____
or Other (describe) _____ State # _____
State _____
Expiration Date of Certification or License _____

ADDRESS OF PROPERTY APPRAISED

_____
_____

APPRAISED VALUE OF SUBJECT PROPERTY $ _____
LENDER/CLIENT
Name _____
Company Name _____
Company Address_____
_____
Email Address_____

SUPERVISORY APPRAISER (ONLY IF REQUIRED)

Signature_____
Name_____
Company Name _____
Company Address_____
_____
Telephone Number _____
Email Address _____
Date of Signature _____
State Certification # _____
or State License # _____
State _____
Expiration Date of Certification or License _____

SUBJECT PROPERTY

☐ Did not inspect subject property
☐ Did inspect exterior of subject property from street
   Date of Inspection _____
☐ Did inspect interior and exterior of subject property
   Date of Inspection _____

COMPARABLE SALES

☐ Did not inspect exterior of comparable sales from street
☐ Did inspect exterior of comparable sales from street
   Date of Inspection _____

Freddie Mac Form 70 March 2005   Page 6 of 6   Fannie Mae Form 1004 March 2005

SUMMARY

There are several types of real estate appraisal licenses in California. The appraisal license or certificate is specific and independent from a real estate license.

An **appraisal** is an act or process of developing an opinion of value, usually for a specific property's value on a given date. Most appraisals are based on market value. **Market value** is the price a property would bring if freely offered on the open market, with both a willing buyer and a willing seller. Properties excluded from market value result from default, foreclosure, bankruptcy, divorce, and death.

The appraisal process is a series of four steps leading to a final value estimate: (1) stating the problem, (2) gathering data (general and specific), (3) deciding on the appraisal method, and (4) reconciling the data for final value estimate. Appraisal techniques include the cost approach, income approach, and sales comparison approach. The gross multiplier technique also determines estimated value.

Appraisal theory focuses on principles of value, which include change, substitution, supply and demand, highest and best use, progression, and competition.

Included in the appraisal process are the four elements for estimating value: **demand**, **utility**, **scarcity**, and **transferability** (DUST). After the value of the property is established, the appraiser reviews other forces, such as physical, economic, political, and social changes.

Another factor in the appraisal process is depreciation. **Depreciation** is a loss of value, and results from physical deterioration, functional obsolescence, and economic obsolescence. Classifications of depreciation are curable or incurable or as accrued or accrual for depreciation.

The final step in the appraisal process is the examination of the different values (reconciling). The appraiser decides which of the values is the most appropriate for the property. The final value conclusions are documented in an Appraisal Report or in a Restricted Appraisal Report.

UNIT 11 REVIEW

◼ Matching Exercise

Instructions: Write the letter of the matching term on the blank line before its definition. Answers immediately follow the Multiple Choice Questions.

Terms

A.	actual age	O.	economic rent	CC.	orientation
B.	amenities	P.	effective age	DD.	plottage increment
C.	appraisal process	Q.	effective demand	EE.	property
D.	appraisal report	R.	fair market value	FF.	reconciliation
E.	appraisal	S.	flag lot	GG.	replacement cost
F.	assemblage	T.	front foot	HH.	scarcity
G.	capitalization	U.	functional utility	II.	T-lot
H.	conformity	V.	improvements	JJ.	transferability
I.	contract rent	W.	interim use	KK.	utility value
J.	corner influence	X.	key lot	LL.	utility
K.	cost	Y.	location	MM.	vacancy factor
L.	cul-de-sac lot	Z.	market price	NN.	value
M.	depreciation	AA.	market rent		
N.	economic life	BB.	market value		

Definitions

1. _____ An act or process of developing an opinion of value.

2. _____ A lot that looks like a flag on a pole, which represents the access to the site; usually located to the rear of another lot fronting a main street.

3. _____ The increase in the value when several smaller parcels are combined together into one larger parcel.

4. _____ The power of goods or services to command other goods in exchange for the present worth of future benefits arising from property ownership.

5. _____ Desire coupled with purchasing power.

6. _____ When land uses are compatible and homes are similar in design and size, the maximum value is realized.

7. _____ Real age of a building.

8. _____ Features that add value to a property.

9. _____ The price the property would bring if freely offered on the open market with both a willing buyer and a willing seller.

10. _____ The rent a property should bring in the open market.

11. _____ The cost of replacing improvements with modern materials and techniques.

12. _____ Commercial properties benefit from more exposure on a corner lot.

13. _____ The ability of a property to satisfy a need or desire, such as shelter, income, or amenities.

14. _____ The placement of a building on its lot in relation to exposure to sun, prevailing wind, traffic, and privacy from the street.

15. _____ Age of a building determined by its condition and usefulness.

16. _____ The expenses in money, labor, material, or sacrifices in acquiring or producing something.

17. _____ An orderly systematic method to arrive at an estimate of value.

18. _____ Sometimes called the objective value.

19. _____ The process that can be employed to convert income to value.

20. _____ The availability or lack of availability of a commodity in the marketplace.

21. _____ The usefulness of the property to its owner. This is subjective value or the value given for personal reasons.

22. _____ Title to property must be marketable with an unclouded title.

23. _____ The estimated period over which a building may be profitably used.

24. _____ What a property actually sold for.

25. _____ Lot that is the least desirable due to the lack of privacy because it is surrounded by the back yards of other lots.

26. _____ A lot that is fronted head-on by a street; noise and glare from headlights may be detractors from this type of lot.

27. _____ This may be the most important factor influencing value.

28. _____ The ability of a property to be useful and perform the function for which it is intended according to current market tastes and standards.

29. _____ A lot found on a dead-end street with same way for ingress and egress.

30. _____ The final step in an appraisal is to examine the values derived by the various approaches.

31. _____ The process of putting several smaller less valuable lots together under one ownership.

32. _____ Any buildings or structures on a lot.

33. _____ Loss in value from any cause.

34. _____ Short-term and temporary use of a property until it is ready for a more productive highest and best use.

35. _____ The width of a property along a street.

▣ Multiple Choice Questions

Instructions: Circle your response and then check your response with the Answer Key that immediately follows the Multiple Choice Questions.

1. The "present and future anticipated enjoyment or profit from the ownership of property" is one definition of:
    a. economic function.
    b. economic necessity.
    c. effective public demand.
    d. value.

2. Market value of improved real property is least affected by:
    a. an open market.
    b. its exchange value.
    c. its objective value.
    d. the original cost of materials.

3.   What four elements that must be present for a property to have market value?

   a. Demand, depreciation, scarcity, and utility.
   b. Cost, demand, transferability, and utility.
   c. Cost, feasibility, scarcity, and utility.
   d. Demand, scarcity, transferability, and utility.

4.   The ultimate test of functional utility is:

   a. design.
   b. marketability.
   c. utility.
   d. maintenance costs.

5.   The term unearned increment most nearly means:

   a. an increase in value due to population increase.
   b. a decrease in value due to social forces rather than personal effort.
   c. a decrease of property taxes.
   d. depreciation.

6.   The commonality of blighted areas, inflation, and the business climate is that they are _____ forces the influence value.

   a. economic
   b. physical
   c. political
   d. social

7.   Which of the following appraisal approaches is based primarily on the principle of substitution?

   a. Cost approach
   b. Summation approach
   c. Sales comparison approach
   d. Income capitalization approach

8.   In a well-planned residential community, which of the following contributes most to the maintenance of value?

   a. Conformity to proper land-use objectives
   b. Deed restrictions
   c. Variances to permit the highest and best use of every parcel of land
   d. Prevention of major thoroughfare construction through the community

9. More than anything else, what determines the value of a property?
    a. Listing price
    b. Purchase price
    c. Highest and best use
    d. Closest comparable properties

10. In the sales comparison approach to appraisal, what is the most important as well as the most difficult step?
    a. Collection of data on comparable properties
    b. Analysis of data on comparable properties
    c. Adjustment of data to reflect differences between subject and comparable properties
    d. Establishing the correct unit of comparison

11. The sales comparison approach to appraisal would be least reliable:
    a. in an inactive market.
    b. in a neighborhood where the land uses are rapidly changing.
    c. when the comparables are in the same price range.
    d. when the comparables are located in another neighborhood.

12. An appraiser is using the sales comparison approach. A comparable property has an amenity that is not present in the subject property. The appraiser would therefore:
    a. add the value of the amenity to the subject property's value.
    b. subtract the value of the amenity from the comparable property's value.
    c. realize it does not matter because no two properties are exactly alike.
    d. list the value of the amenity separately.

13. Functional obsolescence would not include:
    a. eccentric design.
    b. items of surplus utility.
    c. lack of air conditioning.
    d. proximity to nuisances.

14. The major cause of loss of value of real property is usually due to:
    a. deterioration.
    b. passage of physical life.
    c. obsolescence.
    d. lack of maintenance.

15.   A building that is an improper improvement to its site is an example of:
    a.   curable physical obsolescence.
    b.   incurable physical obsolescence.
    c.   curable functional obsolescence.
    d.   incurable functional obsolescence.

16.   A 12-year-old building that has been maintained in excellent condition is given an age of 6 years by an appraiser. This would be known as its:
    a.   actual age.
    b.   economic life.
    c.   effective age.
    d.   physical life.

17.   When comparing the economic and physical life of a building, the economic life is usually:
    a.   equal.
    b.   longer.
    c.   shorter.
    d.   shorter or longer depending on the maintenance.

18.   Economic rent is best defined as the rent:
    a.   required to produce a suitable return for the owner.
    b.   generated by the property in a theoretically perfectly informed market.
    c.   agreed to by a lessor and lessee under the terms of a written lease.
    d.   received for comparable space in the competitive open market.

19.   The capitalization approach is based primarily on the appraisal concepts of:
    a.   change.
    b.   competition.
    c.   anticipation.
    d.   retribution.

20.   The effective annual gross income of a property is the difference between the annual gross income and:
    a.   vacancy factor and rent collection losses.
    b.   allowable expenses and depreciation.
    c.   capitalization rate.
    d.   administrative expenses and capital improvements.

21. When calculating the NOI, which of the following is not deducted from gross income?
    a. Maintenance expenses
    b. Management fees
    c. Mortgage interest
    d. Vacancy losses

22. To calculate accurately a gross rent multiplier, the appraiser needs _____ from comparable properties.
    a. net income and selling price
    b. original cost and the annual income
    c. annual rent and the selling price
    d. net income and the capitalization rate

23. Usually, an appraiser estimates the value of a property by using all three major approaches. To obtain a final estimate of value, the appraiser _____ the three indications of value.
    a. amortizes
    b. averages
    c. finalizes
    d. reconciles

24. When is the appraisal report valid?
    a. The date the appraiser inspects the property.
    b. The date the appraiser accepts the appraisal assignment.
    c. The date the appraiser signs the appraisal report.
    d. The date the intended user receives the appraisal report.

25. A person with a trainee license:
    a. may appraise small residential properties with no supervision.
    b. must work under the supervision of a certified appraiser licensee.
    c. must work under the supervision of an appraiser with a residential license.
    d. does not need supervision, but must work for an appraisal management company.

UNIT 11 ANSWER KEY

Answers – Matching

1. E	8. B	15. P	22. JJ	29. L
2. S	9. R	16. K	23. N	30. FF
3. DD	10. AA	17. C	24. Z	31. F
4. NN	11. GG	18. BB	25. X	32. V
5. Q	12. J	19. G	26. II	33. M
6. H	13. LL	20. HH	27. Y	34. W
7. A	14. CC	21. KK	28. U	35. T

Answers – Multiple Choice

1. **(d)** Value or worth is the present and future anticipated enjoyment or profit from the ownership of property. It is the relationship between the thing desired and the purchaser. It is also the power of one commodity to attract other commodities in exchange. [Definition of Appraisal and Value]

2. **(d)** The original cost of materials on improvement has little to do with current value. [Definition of Appraisal and Value]

3. **(d)** The four elements of value can be remembered by the mnemonic "DUST"—demand, utility, scarcity, and transferability. Cost is not one of the four elements to create value. [Definition of Appraisal and Value]

4. **(b)** Functional utility is the ability of a property to be useful and perform the function for which it is intended according to current market tastes and standards. [Definition of Appraisal and Value]

5. **(a)** An unearned increment is appreciation of a property through no effort of the property owner. [Definition of Appraisal and Value]

6. **(a)** Value is created, maintained, modified, and destroyed by the relationship of four forces: (1) physical characteristics, (2) economic influences, (3) political or governmental regulations, and (4) social ideals. [Definition of Appraisal and Value]

7. **(c)** Using the principle of substitution, value is set by the cost of acquiring an equally desirable substitute property. The sales comparison approach uses the principle of substitution to compare similar properties. [Principles of Valuation]

8. **(a)** Conformity upholds values in a neighborhood. [Principles of Valuation]

9. **(c)** The highest and best use (HBU) of a property, more than anything else, is what determines its value. [Principles of Valuation]

10. **(c)** One of the disadvantages of the sales comparison approach is correctly adjusting amenities to make them comparable to the subject property. [Appraisal Process]

11. **(a)** An inactive market would make it difficult to find enough similar comparable properties to obtain comparable values. Comparable properties can be included in the data from the same or similar neighborhoods. [Appraisal Process]

12. **(b)** An amenity is a feature that adds to the value of a property Adjustments are always made to the comparable, not the subject property. In this case, the value of the amenity is subtracted from the value of the comparable to arrive at the value of a subject property that lacks the amenity. [Appraisal Process]

13. **(d)** Functional obsolescence describes a factor arising from the property itself, as shown in choices (a), (b), and (c). The proximity to nuisances in choice (d) describes external or economic obsolescence. [Appraisal Process]

14. **(c)** Obsolescence includes both functional and economic (external) factors. Functional obsolescence may or may not be curable. Economic obsolescence is usually incurable. [Appraisal Process]

15. **(d)** An improper improvement or an improperly placed (oriented) structure are examples of functional obsolescence. This would be considered incurable if the cost to correct the problems is not economically feasible. [Appraisal Process]

16. **(c)** Actual age is the real age of a building. Effective age is not determined by the actual age of a building, but by its condition and usefulness. The effective age could be longer, shorter, or identical to the actual age. [Appraisal Process]

17. **(c)** Economic life is usually shorter than physical (actual) life. In many cases, the building may still be standing but is not producing any income. [Appraisal Process]

18. **(d)** Economic rent is the reasonable rental expectancy if the property were available for renting at the time of its valuation. [Appraisal Process]

19. **(c)** The principle of anticipation means that value is created by benefits anticipated from the property in the future. [Appraisal Process]

20. **(a)** Effective gross income is calculated by subtracting the vacancy factor and rent collection losses from the annual gross income. [Appraisal Process]

21. **(c)** The net operating income (NOI) is the income after paying all expenses including a maintenance reserve. It does not include the principal and interest (debt service) paid on a loan. [Appraisal Process]

22. **(c)** To calculate a gross rent multiplier, simply divide the sales price by the gross income (either annual or monthly). [Appraisal Process]

23. **(d)** The final step in the appraisal process is reconciliation (correlation) of the various estimates. An appraiser does not average the final estimates. [Appraisal Process]

24. **(c)** Appraisals are valid on the date that the appraiser signs and dates the appraisal report. [The Appraisal Report]

25. **(b)** Trainees must work under the supervision of a certified residential or certified general appraiser. [Appraisal Licensing Standards]

INTRODUCTION

Due to the rapid and continuing growth of cities and the movement of people into once quiet rural areas, the government has found itself in the real estate business. Such population changes have created problems, which have led to an increase in regulation.

The wide and varied range of problems includes ensuring adequate public facilities, such as schools and parks, preventing fraud and misrepresentation in the selling of subdivided real property, regulating lot design and physical improvements for the orderly and proper development of communities, and constructing streets, highways, and parking areas. Regulating airways over the land, providing a water supply, protecting life and property by means of police and firemen, maintaining clean air, mandating noise abatement, and providing sewage and waste disposal and utility services are also included in the range of problems.

When cities grow rapidly without design or control, problems are made worse, and the need for regulation and planning is greater. Communities try to ensure quality places to work and live by using the tools at hand: subdivision regulations, county and city master plans, zoning laws, and building codes.

In this Unit, you will examine the principles of land-use planning, development, and building.

Learning Objectives

After completing this Unit, you should be able to:

10A identify methods for government regulation of land use.

10B recognize procedures for land planning and development.

10C recall housing and construction regulations.

10D classify different construction and building styles.

GOVERNMENT REGULATION OF LAND USE

Continued urban growth and population increases overwhelm the existing infrastructure and place the burden of expanding public services in the hands of local, state, and federal agencies. As the demand for more schools, roads, hospitals, and public services increases, these agencies need to plan for and manage growth. Accommodating and managing this growth is accomplished through the legal powers of eminent domain and police power.

Eminent Domain

The Takings Clause of the Fifth Amendment to the Federal Constitution seems clear about the public use restrictions on the power of eminent domain. The power of **eminent domain** permits the government to take private property from an owner for the public good, paying fair market value (**just compensation**). Recently, cities, counties, and states have been extending the power of **eminent domain** to take private property, not for public use, but to benefit private groups. Instead of building a highway or school, they take the private property and sell it to private developers to build shopping centers, luxury residences, and factories.

The Michigan Supreme Court overturned the Poletown eminent domain ruling.

In 1981, Detroit used the power of eminent domain to take homes in the Poletown neighborhood, a well-kept, working-class neighborhood with more than 1,000 homes, 600 businesses, several churches, and a hospital. The only thing wrong with the neighborhood was that General Motors (GM) wanted the land to build a new assembly plant. GM threatened to take the plant out of Detroit if the city did not take the property by force. Using the excuse that the economic well-being of Detroit was dependent on the plant expansion, the city condemned and took the property under eminent domain and then sold it to General Motors. The Supreme Court of Michigan upheld this decision. However, in 2004, the Michigan Supreme Court was asked to "restore the constitutional protections, that ensure private property cannot be taken to benefit powerful interest groups at the expense of the less powerful." The Supreme Court voted unanimously to overturn the Poletown eminent domain ruling, 20 years after the neighborhood was razed.

In June 2005, the United States Supreme Court decided on the case of *Kelo v. City of New London*. The courts heard from a group of New London, Connecticut homeowners who did not want their homes razed in order to allow the building of a hotel, health club, and offices. The city wanted to build these new structures to complement a multi-million dollar research facility, recently built by Pfizer, the corporation. The court decided 5–4 to allow the neighborhood to be razed for the new structures. The majority opinion stated that the city had carefully planned for the economic development, which was not limited to new jobs and increased tax revenue. The minority opinion stated that the decision effectively deleted the words for public use from the Takings Clause of the Fifth Amendment.

Police Power

Police power is the power of the state to enact laws within constitutional limits to promote the order, safety, health, morals, and general welfare of our society. The power to pass such laws is given to the states by the United States Constitution and to each county and city in California by the State Constitution. Thus, all citizens of California benefit from this empowerment of government to regulate the law.

> The following excerpt from a United States Supreme Court case describes police power:
>
> *"The possession and enjoyment of all rights are subject to this power. Under it the state may prescribe regulations promoting the health, peace, morals, education and good order of the people, and legislate so as to increase the industries of the state, develop its resources and add to its welfare and prosperity."*

> *Police power does not give the state legislature authority to issue arbitrary laws that force unreasonable or unnecessary burdens on people or their property.*

Any laws made as a result of the exercise of police power must be necessary and proper for the protection of the public interest. Currently, the business of real estate is regulated and controlled by licensing real estate professionals; monitoring subdivisions; enforcing the numerous building, health, and safety codes; and determining growth with master plans and zoning. Almost every aspect of the real estate industry, from land use and development to sales and leasing of property, is controlled in some way under police power.

Police power, through legislation, promotes the general well-being of communities. Zoning in cities keeps neighborhoods free of objectionable businesses and limits the districts in which cemeteries, slaughterhouses, factories, and the like may be located. Setting speed limits and regulating liquor sales, prostitution, and gambling are other examples of police power. Additionally, city and county government prohibit the sale of adulterated or impure goods, handle waste disposal, and vaccinate schoolchildren. Businesses are required to meet state and federal health and safety laws.

Review - Government Control of Land Use
- Eminent Domain
- Police Power
  - General Plans
    - Zoning
    - Specific Plans
  - Subdivision Regulations
  - Building Codes
  - Health Codes

PLANNING AND DEVELOPMENT

In California, every city and county must adopt a comprehensive or **master plan**, known as a **General Plan**, for long-term physical development. Every General Plan must cover the development issues in the following seven major categories: land use, circulation, housing, conservation, open space, noise, and safety. Cities or counties located on the coast must also address coastal development and protection of natural resources and wetlands.

A General Plan is the basis of and sets the direction for a community's future development. All community development decisions, such as rezoning, subdivision map approvals, and public works projects are required to be consistent with the General Plan. The land use proposals outlined in a General Plan are implemented in many ways—zoning being the best known and most frequently used

Coastal communities must address the effects of development on natural resources.

tool. Additionally, General Plan land uses are carried out through specific plans, subdivision regulations, property tax incentives, land banking, and public finance measures, to name a few.

Zoning

The regulation of structures and uses of property within selected districts is known as **zoning**. Zoning ordinances are exercises of a city's or county's police power, and are upheld as long as they reasonably protect the public health, safety, and general welfare of an area. When the state uses police power, it is not required to compensate a property owner for any loss in property values as a result of the regulation, as it must do under the power of eminent domain.

Most cities and counties have ordinances that create land use districts or zones. A zoning ordinance does not duplicate the General Plan, even though both deal with land use. A **zoning ordinance** primarily implements the General Plan by regulating land use for individual projects, whereas the General Plan is more far-reaching and future-oriented. Each zone has a specific set of regulations that control the use of land, lot sizes, types of structures permitted, building heights, building setbacks, and density. There are zones for single-family residences, multi-family dwellings, commercial uses, industrial uses, and open space or agriculture land.

Symbols Used to Show Different Zoning Areas

- **A** - Agriculture
- **C** - Commercial
- **M** - Manufacturing
- **P** - Public Uses
  (like parking lots and parks)
- **R** - Residential

- **R1** - Single-family home
- **R2** - Duplex
- **R3** - Mulitiple residential units
- **R4** - Four units or higher
  density dwellings
- **PD** - Planned Development

A - Agriculture

C - Commercial

M - Manufacturing

P - Public Uses

R - Homes, other residences

R1 - Single-family home

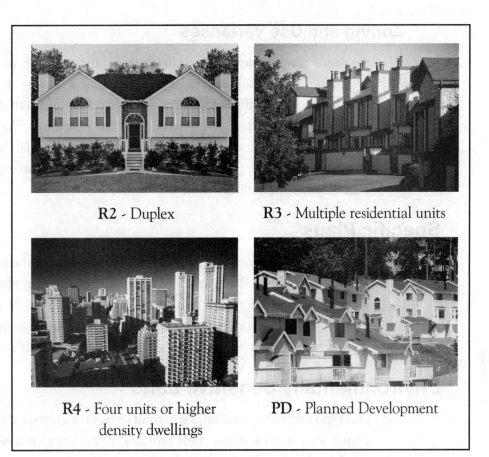

R2 - Duplex   R3 - Multiple residential units

R4 - Four units or higher density dwellings   PD - Planned Development

Each zone has a specific set of regulations.

Usually every district is zoned for different types of uses, known as permitted uses and conditional uses. **Permitted uses** meet the current use requirements within the district. **Conditional uses** do not meet the current use requirements but may be allowed by obtaining a special permit known as a conditional use permit. When an area is rezoned to another use, existing properties may retain the previous zoning under a **grandfather clause**. Such uses or structures are termed to be non-conforming. An owner who wants to use his or her property in a way that does not meet the current use requirements may be able to obtain a conditional use permit or a variance.

Conditional Use Permits

A **conditional use permit** allows a land use that may be incompatible with other uses existing in the zone. The use is allowed as long as the project owner complies with the conditions specified in the permit. If the owner does not comply with the conditions, the permit may be revoked. A conditional use permit runs with the land, and its provisions still apply even if there is a change in ownership.

Zoning and Use Variances

A city or county may allow a **variance**, or an exception to existing zoning regulations for special reasons. For example, if a lot has an irregular shape and does not meet the standard zoning for a side-yard setback, the owner is at a disadvantage when trying to develop the property. The owner may ask the city or county for a waiver or zoning variance, which would allow the property to be developed. In summary, a variance is simply a deviation from a development standard.

Specific Plans

After a General Plan is adopted, some cities and counties carry out the proposed land uses through a specific plan. A **specific plan** pertains to a particular development site or area of the General Plan. Since they pertain to just one specific project, they are able to consolidate many of the factors needed to develop a project and monitor the development costs.

Environmentally Sensitive Lands

Land and water areas containing natural features or ecological functions of such significance as to warrant their protection are considered **environmentally sensitive lands**. The public's desire to protect the natural environment is reinforced by federal and state laws, which require cities and counties to take into account environmental issues in arriving at planning decisions.

Local Coastal Programs

Under the **California Coastal Act**, 15 coastal counties and 58 cities, along with the state of California, have stewardship of the 1,100 miles of coast that stretches from Oregon to the border with Mexico. The **coastal zone** contains over 1.5 million acres of land and reaches from three miles at sea to an inland boundary that varies from a few blocks in urban areas to about five miles in less-developed areas.

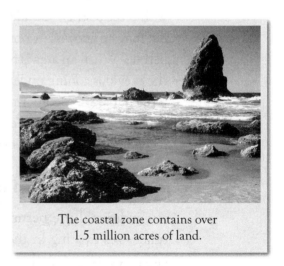

The coastal zone contains over 1.5 million acres of land.

Each city and county in the coastal zone must prepare Local Coastal Programs (LCPs), which adhere to the California Coastal Commission's strict standards for coastal development and protection. The LCPs are the basic planning tools used to review and decide permits for new development in coastal areas. Additionally, they protect the shoreline and environmentally sensitive habitats, determine ways to improve and expand existing ports, improve public access to the shoreline, and establish urban-rural boundaries to direct new development into areas with existing services to avoid wasteful urban sprawl and leapfrog development.

If property is located in the coastal zone, the owner or developer must apply for a coastal development permit (CDP) before any new construction can begin. Permits are routinely approved provided the projects comply with the Coastal Act policies and standards. In many areas, the California Coastal Commission retains permit authority over the coastal zone, and many local actions can be appealed up to the Coastal Commission.

Clean Water Act of 1977

The Clean Water Act (CWA) of 1977 regulates the discharge of pollutants into waters of the United States, including wetlands. **Wetlands** are areas where water covers the soil, or is present either at or near the surface of the soil all year or for varying periods during the year, including during the growing season. Wetlands can vary widely because of regional differences and are found from the tundra to the tropics and on every continent except Antarctica. There are two types of wetlands: **coastal wetlands** and **inland wetlands**.

Wetlands are areas where water covers the soil all year or for varying periods of time during the year.

Coastal or tidal wetlands are found along California's Pacific shoreline and estuaries. A **shoreline** is the intersection of the land with the water (mean high water line). An **estuary** is an area where seawater and freshwater mix. Inland wetlands are found in deltas, swamps, marshes, low-lying areas of lakes and ponds, and in floodplains along rivers and streams. A **floodplain** is the low land adjacent to a river, lake, or ocean.

Rangeland, Grazing Land, and Grassland Protection Act

In 2002 the Rangeland, Grazing Land, and Grassland Protection Act was passed to protect California's rangeland, grazing land, and grasslands. Its threefold program includes: (1) prevent the conversion of rangeland, grazing land, and grassland to nonagricultural uses; (2) protect livestock grazing areas; and (3) ensure continued wildlife, water quality, watershed, and open-space benefits to the State of California from livestock grazing.

Oak Woodlands Conservation Act

In 2001, the **California Oak Woodlands Conservation Program** was enacted to protect the oak woodlands from residential, commercial, and industrial development or conversion of the oak woodlands to intensive agricultural development. Since over 80% of the remaining oak trees are found on private property, this program offers landowners an opportunity to obtain funding to maintain and restore the oak woodlands. Additionally, the program is designed to help local governments implement oak conservation elements in local General Plans to achieve oak woodland protection.

Subdivision

A **subdivision** is the division of land into five or more lots for the purpose of sale, lease, or financing. Practically every place where people live has been subdivided at some time. All developments started as a large parcel of land that was divided up and sold to separate individuals. Sometimes the parcels were large enough to be subdivided repeatedly, creating a need for some control to make sure a desirable quality of life was protected.

Commonly, we think of a subdivision as a partition of a large piece of property into units designed for sale or lease for specific purposes. Usually, this is the case. The majority of subdivisions might be designated as lot and residential subdivisions. The parcels are meant to be sold to private individuals who plan to build homes on them or to speculators who will build houses on spec because they expect to sell them later. In most cases, the parcels are sold to a developer who will build multiple houses and sell the dwelling and lot as one package in a project that the developer will supervise. Some subdivisions are also developed for commercial purposes. A **commercial acre** is the area remaining from an acre of newly subdivided land after deducting the area devoted to streets, sidewalks, alleys, curbs, etc. It is also referred to as a **buildable acre**.

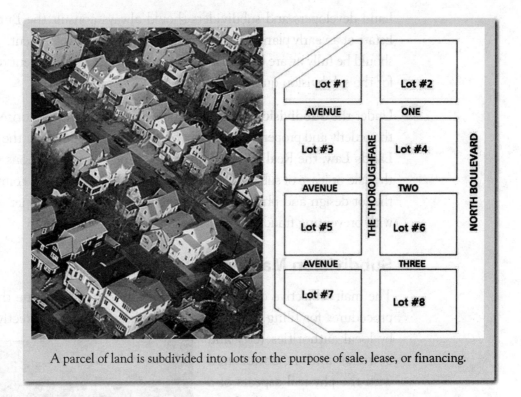

A parcel of land is subdivided into lots for the purpose of sale, lease, or financing.

Residential Subdivision Laws

There are two basic laws under which subdivisions are controlled in California—the **Subdivision Map Act** and the **Subdivided Lands Law**. To understand these two laws, it is important to know they were enacted for separate purposes. Different meanings of a subdivision were adopted in each law to achieve each of their objectives. However, both were created for the protection of the consumer.

> ### Review - Two Laws Control Subdivisions in California
> 1. Subdivision Map Act
> 2. Subdivided Lands Law

Complete compliance with all provisions of both subdivision laws is required in any subdivided development. Developers and their professional consultants must be thoroughly familiar not only with the provisions of state laws but also with specific provisions in local subdivision control ordinance in the community where the subdivision is being developed. In various local subdivision ordinances, there are many differences because of the great diversity in types of communities and conditions throughout California.

Land developers and subdividers should always consult the Bureau of Real Estate at an early planning stage in any subdivision development. A developer should be fully aware of the Real Estate Commissioner's current requirements for the subdivision qualification under consideration.

Under the **Subdivision Map Act,** the city or county is authorized to control the orderly and proper development of the community. Under the **Subdivided Lands Law,** the Real Estate Commissioner regulates conditions surrounding the sale or lease of subdivided real property while the city or county regulates the lot design and physical improvements. The Commissioner is concerned with preventing fraud and misrepresentation in selling.

Subdivision Map Act

The main objective of the Subdivision Map Act is to define the rules and procedures for filing maps to create subdivisions. It is directly controlled by local authorities (city and county) and is concerned with the physical aspects of a subdivision—such as building design, streets, and any adverse effects to the environment.

A subdivision is controlled by local authorities. They are concerned with building design, streets, and any adverse effects to the environment.

California has adopted the guidelines set forth by the **California Environmental Quality Act** (CEQA) to ensure that government agencies consider the environment prior to approving building projects. As a result, an environmental impact report may be required by authorities before issuing a building permit to private parties or prior to approving a subdivision tract map. An **environmental impact report** (EIR) is a study of how a development will affect the ecology of its surroundings. If it is determined that a proposed subdivision will have no adverse effect on the environment, the city or county prepares a **negative declaration** prior to making a decision on the project. A negative declaration is a written statement by the lead agency briefly describing the reasons that a proposed project, not exempt from the CEQA, will not have a significant effect on the environment and, therefore, does not require the preparation of an EIR.

Because of the Subdivision Map Act, the direct control of the kind and type of subdivisions to be allowed in each community and the physical improvements to be installed are left to local jurisdictions (city and county) within certain general limits specified in the act.

Subdivision Map Act has Two Major Objectives

The first is to coordinate the subdivision plans and planning, including lot design, water supply, street patterns, right-of-way for drainage and sewers, etc., with the community pattern and plan as laid out by the local planning authorities.

Every city and county is required by the Subdivision Map Act to regulate subdivisions for a final tract map (five or more lots) or parcel map (two to four lots).

The second objective is to ensure initial proper improvement of areas dedicated for public purposes by having the subdivider file subdivision maps, including public streets and other public areas, so that these necessities will not become an undue burden in the future for taxpayers in the community.

The Subdivision Map Act requires every city and county to regulate subdivisions for which a tentative and final tract map (for five-or-more lots), or a parcel map (for two-to-four lots), is required. A **tentative tract map** is a map of the proposed subdivision that is submitted to a planning commission for approval or disapproval. It is used to make sure that the improvements, such as lot layouts, sizes, and configurations; grading plans; traffic access and street alignments; storm drainage, sewers, and water facilities; and other project features have been designed to conform to city or county General Plans. A **final tract map** indicates any changes required by the planning commission and is recorded in the county where the property is located. A **parcel map** pertains to a parcel of land that will be subdivided into less than five parcels or units and shows land boundaries, streets, and parcel numbers.

In addition, the Act allows cities and counties to adopt laws for subdivisions for which no map is required. The diagram on the next page shows typical steps in subdivision procedure under the Act.

Basic Outline of Final Map Preparation and Approval

Preparation	*Approval*
Economic analysis of feasibility Locational analysis Physical survey of site	

Preliminary discussion with agencies having jurisdiction over subdivision, including question of environmental impact report.	On basis of preliminary conference subdivider obtains → requirements from local authorities, state agencies, title company, and financial source (lenders).

Subdivider prepares tentative tract map

Tentative map submitted for approval to:
1. local government
2. governmental loan insuring agency, e.g., FHA

Planning commission accepts map from subdivider and obtains approval from other → city or county offices. Copies forwarded to Bureau of Real Estate by applicant for Public Report.

Subdivider prepares final map and secures all necessary signatures (record owners, public utilities, public entities).

Final map submitted for approval to:
1. local government
2. governmental loan insuring agency

Officer designated in local ordinance accepts map from → subdivider and obtains approval from other city or county offices.

Approved map is recorded. Copy sent to Bureau of Real Estate by applicant for public report.

↓

Development is started.

Health and Sanitation

Every tentative tract map submitted must comply with health and sanitation regulations. Local **health officers** and local code enforcement officers enforce state and local health laws to ensure the sanitary condition of all housing.

Proper drainage, sewage disposal, and water supply are crucial health and sanitation considerations. The local health officers may determine if water is **potable** (safe to drink) or requires a percolation test. A **percolation test** is used to determine the ability of the land to absorb and drain water and is frequently used when installing septic systems. A **septic tank** is a sewage settling tank, which must be at least five feet away from the improvements. The sewage is converted into gas and liquids before the remaining waste is discharged by gravity into a leaching bed underground.

A septic tank is a sewage settling tank that is at least five feet from the improvement. Septic tanks are underground and covered.

To insure proper drainage the water table must be determined. The **water table** is the natural level where water will be found, either above or below the surface of the ground. **Percolating water** is underground water not flowing in a defined channel. A **defined channel** is any natural watercourse, even though dry during a good portion of the year. Local health officers have the authority to stop any development with problems in these areas.

> **Review - Subdivision Map Act**
> - Enforced by city or county authorities
> - Concerned with physical aspects of a subdivision

Subdivided Lands Law

The Subdivided Lands Law is directly administered by the Real Estate Commissioner. Its objective is to protect buyers of property in new subdivisions from fraud, misrepresentation, or deceit in the marketing of subdivided lots, parcels, units, and undivided interests.

The Real Estate Commissioner must issue a subdivision public report before any subdivision can be offered for sale in California. This even applies to lands outside the state, if they are being marketed in California.

The **public report** is a document disclosing all important facts about the marketing and financing of the subdivision. The public report must show that the subdivider (developer) can complete and maintain all improvements and that the lots or parcels can be used for the purpose for which they are being sold.

Before a developer can sell each lot in the project, he or she must give a copy of the Commissioner's final report to the buyer for approval. The buyer signs a receipt for the report stating it has been read. The seller (developer) must keep a copy of the statement for three years.

The public report is valid for five years, with any material changes in the development reported to the Commissioner, who then can issue an amendment to the original report.

RECEIPT FOR PUBLIC REPORT

The Laws and Regulations of the Real Estate Commissioner require that you as a prospective purchaser or lessee be afforded an opportunity to read the public report for this subdivision before you make any written offer to purchase or lease a subdivision interest or before any money or other consideration toward purchase or lease of a subdivision interest is accepted from you.

In the case of a preliminary subdivision public report you must be afforded an opportunity to read the report before a written reservation or any deposit in connection therewith is accepted from you.

In the case of a conditional subdivision public report, delivery of legal title or other interest contracted for will not take place until issuance of a final subdivision public report. Provision is made in the sales agreement and escrow instructions for the return to you of the entire sum of money paid or advanced by you if you are dissatisfied with the final public report because of a material change. (See Business and Professions Code §11012.)

DO NOT SIGN THIS RECEIPT UNTIL YOU HAVE RECEIVED A COPY OF THE REPORT AND HAVE READ IT.

I read the Commissioner's public report on _____
_____ [File Number]
_____
[Tract Number or Name]
I understand the report is not a recommendation or endorsement of the subdivision, but is for information only.

The issue date of the public report which I received and read is: _____

_____
Signature   Date
_____
Address

It can take many months for a developer to get project approval once all the proper paperwork is submitted to the Commissioner. During that time, the developer may want to begin marketing the project while waiting for the final report. By submitting a minimum application filing package, the developer can get a preliminary public report, which allows taking reservations for the project but not accepting any non-refundable money or entering into any binding contracts until receiving the final report from the Commissioner.

> **Review - Subdivided Lands Law**
> - Administered by Real Estate Commissioner
> - Concerned with protecting the public from fraud

As a student of real estate, sometimes it is difficult to sort out the differences between two very like-sounding laws. The following list comparing the Subdivision Map Act and the Subdivided Lands Law will help you compare the two laws.

> **Review - Comparison of Subdivision Laws**
>
> **Subdivision Map Act**
> - Two or more lots or parcels
> - Lots must be adjacent to each other
> - No exemption for 160 acres and larger parcels
> - Administered by local authorities
> - No public report needed
>
> **Subdivided Lands Law**
> - Five or more lots or parcels
> - Parcels need not be adjacent
> - 160 acres and selected larger parcels are exempt
> - Administered by Real Estate Commissioner
> - Requires a final public report

Commercial Subdivisions

The **Commercial and Industrial Common Interest Development Act** of 2013 provides for the creation and regulation of commercial and industrial common interest developments. Many provisions of the new law are patterned after provisions in the Davis-Stirling Common Interest Development Act for residential properties, including association governance, operating rules, and property use and maintenance. [Cal. Civil Code §§6500, et seq.]

Types of Subdivisions

Due to the scarcity of land suitable for subdividing, the subdivision process has become more sophisticated, often resulting in higher land prices and new types of subdivisions. The legislature recognized this trend and has enacted laws to regulate such developments, including planned neighborhoods, community apartment houses, condominiums, limited-equity housing cooperatives, and undivided interest subdivisions. These projects do not follow the traditional subdivision model as being the simple division of a large piece of land into smaller parcels for the construction of individual homes. Typically, there are three types of subdivisions: standard subdivisions, common interest developments, and undivided interest development.

Standard Subdivision

A **standard subdivision** is a land division with no common or mutual rights of either ownership or use among the owners of the parcels created by the division. This type of subdivision is a typical tract of single-family homes on individual lots.

Land Project

Subdivisions located in sparsely populated areas (fewer than 1,500 registered voters within the subdivision or within two miles of its boundaries), made up of 50 parcels or more, are known as **land projects**. In the past, it appeared that these projects had been sold more on the intense promotion of alleged benefits than on the actual value of the project. There was a need for legislation to regulate these sales.

The Real Estate Commissioner was given the authority to oversee sales in land projects to make sure the consumer was protected. The law now allows a buyer 14 days after signing a contract to purchase property in a land project to rescind the offer, with a full refund of any money paid. This gives the buyer time to investigate the project and decide, unpressured, whether he or she still wants to go through with the purchase, and whether it was represented accurately or not.

Common Interest Developments

A **common interest development** (CID) combines the individual ownership of private dwellings with the shared ownership of common facilities of the entire project. The common facilities can range from roads and water systems to clubhouses, swimming pools, golf courses and even stables and private airport facilities. The CID provides a system of self-governance through a community association, sometimes called a **homeowners' association**. The association has the authority to enforce special rules called CC&Rs (Covenants, Conditions, and Restrictions) and to raise money through regular and special assessments. Restrictions on lots in a new subdivision would be found in a recorded declaration of restrictions. Common interest developments vary both in physical design and legal form. The following CIDs are all considered subdivisions and under the control of the subdivision laws: condominiums, planned developments, stock cooperatives, community apartment projects, and timeshare projects.

Upon sale of an existing common-interest development, a buyer must be provided:

1. a copy of the Conditions, Covenants and Restrictions (CC&Rs), articles of incorporation, association by-laws, governing documents, and a current financial statement on the homeowners' association.

2. written notification of any known pending special assessments, claims, or lawsuits against the seller or the homeowners' association.

3. a statement showing whether the seller's account with the homeowners' association is paid up-to-date.

Condominiums

A **condominium** consists of a separate fee interest in a particular specific space (the unit), plus an undivided interest in all common or public areas of the development. All owners are allowed to use any of the facilities in the common area. Each unit owner has a deed, separate financing, and pays the property taxes for his or her unit.

> **Review – Condominiums**
> - Fee simple ownership to living unit
> - Undivided interest in land and common areas
> - Separate property tax bill, deed, deed of trust
> - Operations controlled by elected governing board

Planned Developments

A **planned development** (previously called planned unit development) is a planning and zoning term describing land not subject to conventional zoning requirements. It allows clustering of residences or other characteristics of the project, which differ from normal zoning. In a planned development subdivision, the owner has title to the unit and land under it, together with membership in an association that owns common area. Sometimes the owners of separate interests also have an undivided interest in the common area. The planned development is popular in suburban and rural areas. Owners have private ownership of their individual homes and lots but share the ownership of the common features. Shared facilities can include private roadways, water systems, septic systems, parks and open space, ponds and lakes, airport landing strips, trails, and ocean access. Some planned developments even share the ownership of forests and agricultural lands, which produce income for the community.

Stock Cooperatives

A corporation formed for the purpose of owning property is known as a **stock cooperative**. Each stockholder is given the use of a living unit and any amenities and community recreational facilities, with the building being owned by the corporation.

In a community apartment project, a buyer receives an undivided interest in the land coupled with the right of exclusive occupancy of one of the apartments in the project.

Timeshare Ownership

Timesharing is a favorite way to have an interest in a building, with the right to occupy limited to a specific time period. This type of ownership is popular in resorts and other desirable areas where people like to vacation once or twice a year but do not need the right of possession the rest of the time.

Undivided Interest

In an **undivided interest**, the land itself is not divided—just the ownership. The buyer receives an undivided interest in a parcel of land as a tenant in common with all the other owners. All owners have the nonexclusive right to the use and occupancy of the property. A recreational vehicle park with campground and other leisure-time amenities is an example.

REGULATION OF HOUSING AND CONSTRUCTION

The housing and construction industries in California are regulated by three laws: the State Housing Law, local building codes, and the Contractors' State License Law.

In addition, through the role of federal home building financing programs, both FHA and VA financing impose housing and construction regulations. It is critical in a subdivision with FHA or VA participation that the developer consults with those and any other appropriate agencies. These programs require, as a prerequisite to participation, that the house involved meet Minimum Property Requirements (MPRs). In some instances, MPRs are more demanding than either the State Housing Law or local building codes. An example of MPRs is the FHA 7-feet-6 inch minimum requirement for residential ceiling height.

State Housing Law

The **State Housing Law** (Health and Safety Code Section 17910, et seq.) outlines the minimum construction and occupancy requirements for dwellings.

Local building inspectors enforce the construction regulations while local health officers enforce the occupancy and sanitation regulations. One way of enforcing the construction regulations is by the issuance of a **building permit**. In order to issue a building permit, the building inspector reviews and approves plans, specifications, plot plan, and accompanying exhibits for a proposed project. All new construction rehabilitation or remodeling projects must have a building permit issued by the local building inspector prior to beginning any work. **Rehabilitation** is the restoration of a property to its former or improved condition without changing the basic design or plan. **Remodeling** changes the basic design or plan of the building to correct deficiencies.

Local Building Codes

In 1970, the California Legislature made the Uniform Housing Code, **Uniform Building Code** (UBC), Uniform Plumbing Code, Uniform Mechanical Code, and National Electric Code the applicable building codes for the entire state. Local government still has the power to set requirements for local zoning, local fire zones, building setbacks, side and rear yards, and property lines. Whenever there is a conflict between public restrictions (e.g., zoning) and private restrictions, the more restrictive of the two must be followed.

Currently, factory-built housing must be built to the standards of the most recent editions of the uniform building codes. Local government has the power to supervise and regulate on-site installation of factory-built housing.

Contractors' State License Law

In order to protect California consumers, contractors are licensed in California under the **Contractors' State License Law**. Contractors must meet certain experience and knowledge qualifications and must post a bond or cash deposit to the state of California for the benefit of anyone damaged by the contractor. Except for minor work not exceeding $500, a valid California Contractor's License is required for the license category in which the contractor is to work. Currently there are 42-different types of contractor licenses, including general and specialty contractors. General building contractors usually oversee projects and coordinate the specific subcontractors for a job. Specialty contractors or subcontractors usually are hired to perform a single job.

A contractor may have his or her license suspended or revoked if the contractor abandons a project, diverts funds, departs from plans and specifications, violates work safety provisions, violates building codes and regulations, or breaches the contract.

CONSTRUCTION AND BUILDING STYLES

Unless a real estate licensee works for a builder/developer or specializes in new home sales, it is not usually necessary to know the details of home construction, installation methods, or the price and quality of building materials. However, a licensee should be familiar with architectural styles, types of roofs, styles of windows, parts of a building, typical exterior materials, and different types of heating/cooling systems (HVAC). Additionally, a licensee should be able to answer questions about current insulation standards for roofs, walls, and window systems that prevent excess sun infiltration for homes in the area.

Terms Relevant to Energy Efficiency

Insulation

Material inserted into walls and ceilings to help keep the heat inside the home in the winter and outside the home in the summer. Insulation's resistance to heat is measured by the R-value.

R-Value

The R-value is a rating that measures how well insulation resists heat loss. When the R-value is higher, the insulation is better. New homes have minimum insulation requirements and the R-value rating of the insulation used in the homes must be disclosed.

Energy Efficient Ratio (EER)

A measurement of the efficiency of energy; used to determine the effectiveness of appliances.

British Thermal Unit (BTU)

A measurement that calculates heat; the amount of heat needed to raise one pound of water one degree Fahrenheit.

Many home buyers express common concerns about the condition of the soil on which the house is built because it can affect the stability of the foundation. Filled or compacted ground and expansive soil frequently cause foundation damage. **Compaction** refers to extra soil that is added and compressed to fill in the low areas or raise the level of the parcel. Clay soils are generally classified as **expansive soil**. This means that a given amount of clay will tend to expand (increase in volume) as it absorbs water and it will shrink (lessen in volume) as water is drawn away. **Adobe** is one of the most expansive of the clay soils. **Backfill** is soil that is used to fill in holes or support a foundation. It is also used to fill in trenches and around excavations.

Parts of a Building

Common terms used in building:

1. **Anchor Bolt**
   Attaches mud sill to foundation; embedded in concrete foundation

2. **Bracing**
   Diagonal board nailed across wall framing to prevent sway

3. **Building Paper**
   Waterproof paper used between sheathing and roof covering

4. **Closed Sheathing**
   Foundation for exterior siding; boards nailed to studding

5. **Crawlspace**
   A crawlspace is the area or space between the ground and floor joists used to access plumbing and electrical connections beneath the house. For FHA loans, the minimum crawlspace is 18 inches.

6. **Cripple**
   Stud above window or door headers, or below windowsills

7. **Eaves**
   Part of roof that hangs over the exterior walls

8. **Fire Stop**
   Boards nailed between studs to block the spread of fire in the walls

9. **Flashing**
   Sheet metal or other material that keeps water from seeping into a building.

10. **Footing**
    A footing is an extended part of foundation at the base or bottom of a foundation wall, pier, or column.

11. **Foundation**
    Base of house; usually concrete

12. **Header**
    The horizontal, load-bearing board over a doorway or window opening

13. **Joists**
    Parallel boards supporting floors or ceilings (The boards supporting them are girders, beams, or bearing walls.)

14. **Mud Sill**

    The lowest part of the frame of a house. It is fastened with bolts to the foundation and supports the upright studs of the frame. **Redwood** is frequently used because of its high resistance to termites. **Subterranean termites**, ant-like insects that eat wood, are the most destructive.

15. **Open Sheathing**

    Boards nailed to rafters to form foundation for roof

16. **Rafters**

    Slanted boards of a roof that are designed to support the roof boards and shingles. To strengthen the load-bearing factor of a roof, the rafters should be placed closer together.

17. **Ridge Board**

    Highest structural part of a frame building

18. **Sill**

    Horizontal board along the bottom of a window or door

19. **Sole Plate**

    A board (usually 2" x 4") on which wall and partition studs rest. Support for studs

20. **Studs**

    Vertical, supporting 2"x 4" boards in the walls spaced 16" on center

Parts of a Building

Other Building - Development Terms

Bearing wall: A wall that supports a vertical load as well as its own weight.

Board foot (144 cubic inches): A measurement of lumber equal to the volume of a board 12" x 12" x 1".

Conduit: A flexible pipe in which electrical wiring is installed.

Deciduous: Plants and trees that lose their leaves seasonally in the fall.

Drywall: Gypsum panels used in place of wet plaster to finish the inside of buildings.

Elevation sheet: A drawing that shows front and side exterior views of a building as it will be when finished.

Foundation plan: A drawing that shows foundation, sub-floors, footing, and pier placement.

Kiosk: A freestanding small booth, such as a jewelry store in a mall.

Linear foot: A measurement of length, rather than area (square foot) or volume (cubic foot).

Party wall: A wall erected on the line between two adjoining properties, which are under different ownership, for the use of both parties.

Residential ceiling height measurements: Minimum = 7.5 feet; Normal = 8 feet

Schematics: Preliminary drawings and sketches by an architect, such as site plans and elevations.

Setback: The distance a building must be set back from the street, property line, or curb; usually determined by local building code. A **side-yard setback** is the distance a building must be set back for the lot line at the side of the property.

Shopping centers' population requirements:
   Neighborhood shopping center (5,000-10,000 population required)
   Major shopping center or mall (50,000-100,000 population required)

Wainscoting: The bottom portion of a wall that is covered with wood siding; the top part is treated with another material.

Walk-up: An apartment of more than one story with no elevator.

Water-pressure test: Water pressure can be tested by turning on all faucets and flushing all toilets at the same time.

Roof Types

A licensee should know the most desirable roof pitches and be able to distinguish a hip roof from a gable roof. The **pitch** of a roof is its incline or rise. The steeper the pitch of a roof, the longer its life expectancy. A **gable roof** has a pitched roof with two sloping sides. A **gambrel roof**, typically seen in Dutch colonial architecture, is a curbed roof, with a steep lower slope with a flatter one above. A **hip roof** is a pitched roof with sloping sides and ends (all four sides).

Additionally a licensee should know the types of roofing materials that are permitted or required (in fire hazard areas, for example) in the community. Roof types are determined by the direction, steepness, and number of roof planes.

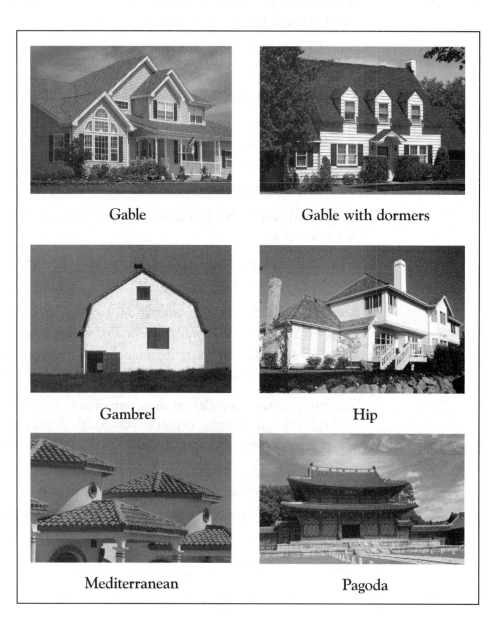

Gable

Gable with dormers

Gambrel

Hip

Mediterranean

Pagoda

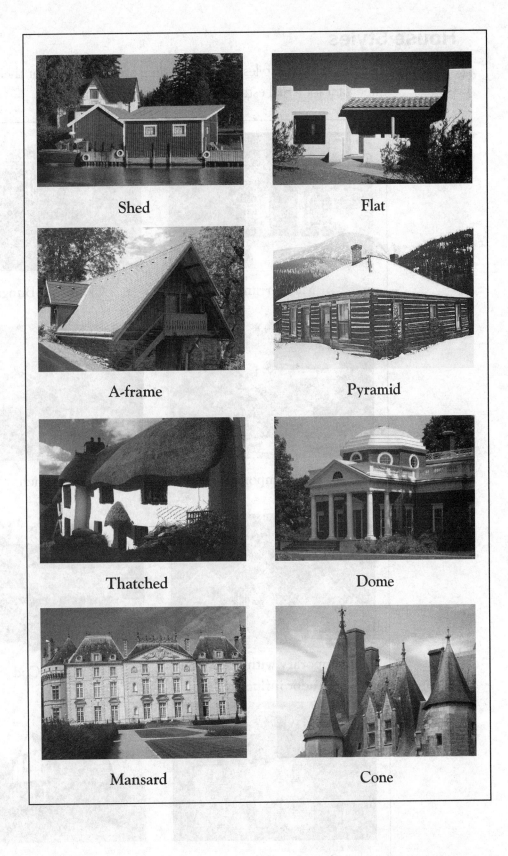

Shed

Flat

A-frame

Pyramid

Thatched

Dome

Mansard

Cone

House Styles

Traditional house styles used in building are interesting for their variety and important for a real estate agent to know.

Mediterranean

California Bungalow

Contemporary

Ranch

Contemporary with traditional Tudor influence

Cape Cod

Georgian Colonial

Tudor Revival

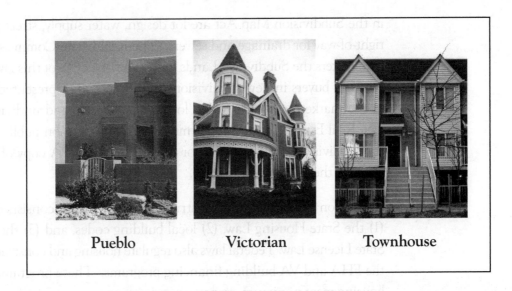

Pueblo   Victorian   Townhouse

SUMMARY

Land use is regulated and controlled through government agencies, private regulations, and direct public ownership of land. The government can acquire property by the power of **eminent domain** through **condemnation** proceedings from a private owner for public use. This power can extend beyond the federal government down to public agencies. When the government acquires property by eminent domain, the property owner is reimbursed for fair market value. Property owners displaced by federal condemnation are assisted in relocation.

Police power is the right of the state to create laws that regulate property use for the protection of the public interest. The state is not required to compensate the owner for any resulting loss in property due to police power.

A **master plan** is used to develop cities. The primary form of land-use regulation is zoning. Property owners who want to use property for nonconforming use must seek a conditional use permit or zoning variance. Each city and county in the coastal zone must prepare Local Coastal Programs to comply with the California Coastal Commission's strict standards for coastal development and protection.

A subdivision is the division of land into lots for the purpose of sale, lease, or financing. There are two basic laws that control subdivisions in California—the **Subdivision Map Act** and the **Subdivided Lands Law**. Local authorities administer the Subdivision Map Act. The objectives of the Subdivision Map Act are: (1) to coordinate the subdivision plans and planning and (2) to ensure initial proper improvement of areas dedicated for public purposes by filing detailed subdivision maps to avoid problems for future taxpayers. Included in the Subdivision Map Act are lot design, water supply, street patterns, and right-of-way for drainage and sewers. The Real Estate Commissioner directly administers the Subdivided Lands Law. The objective of this law is to protect property buyers in new subdivisions from fraud, misrepresentation, or deceit in the marketing of subdivided lots, parcels, units, and undivided interests. The Real Estate Commissioner must issue a subdivision public report before the subdivision can be offered for sale in California. A copy of this report is given to the buyer upon request.

Regulation of housing and construction in California consists of three laws: (1) the State Housing Law, (2) local building codes, and (3) the Contractor's State License Law. Federal laws also regulate housing and construction through the FHA and VA building financing programs. These programs require that housing meet minimum property requirements.

UNIT 12 REVIEW

Matching Exercise

Instructions: Write the letter of the matching term on the blank line before its definition. Answers immediately follow the Multiple Choice Questions.

Terms

A. backfill	M. final tract map	Y. setback
B. bearing wall	N. General Plan	Z. Subdivided Lands Law
C. board foot	O. linear foot	
D. BTU	P. parcel map	AA. subdivision
E. CID	Q. party wall	BB. Subdivision Map Act
F. condemnation	R. percolating water	CC. tentative tract map
G. conduit	S. percolation test	DD. variance
H. deciduous	T. planned development	EE. wainscoting
I. drywall	U. police power	FF. water-pressure test
J. EER	V. potable	GG. water table
K. EIR	W. R-value	HH. wetlands
L. eminent domain	X. schematics	II. zoning

Definitions

1. _____ The division of land into five or more lots for the purpose of sale, lease, or financing.

2. _____ A measurement of length, rather than area (square foot) or volume (cubic foot).

3. _____ A wall that supports a vertical load as well as its own weight.

4. _____ Underground water not flowing in a defined channel.

5. _____ The regulation of structures and uses of property within selected districts.

6. _____ Plants and trees that lose their leaves seasonally in the fall.

7. _____ Map showing a parcel of land that will be subdivided into less than five parcels or units and shows land boundaries, streets, and parcel numbers.

8. _____ The right of the government to take private property from an owner, for public use, paying fair market value.

9. _____ The natural level at which water will be found, either above or below the surface of the ground.

10. _____ Fresh water that is safe and agreeable for drinking.

11. _____ Water pressure can be tested by turning on all faucets and flushing all toilets at the same time.

12. _____ Measurement of lumber equal to the volume of a board 12"x12"x1" (144 cubic inches).

13. _____ Gypsum panels used in place of wet plaster to finish the inside of buildings.

14. _____ Measurement of the efficiency of energy; used to determine the effectiveness of appliances.

15. _____ Test used to determine the ability of the land to absorb and drain water and is frequently used when installing septic systems.

16. _____ Areas where water covers the soil, or is present either at or near the surface of the soil all year or for varying periods of time during the year, including during the growing season.

17. _____ Measurement that calculates heat; the amount of heat needed to raise one pound of water one degree Fahrenheit.

18. _____ Common-interest development combining the individual ownership of private dwellings with the shared ownership of common facilities of the entire project.

19. _____ State law protecting purchasers of property in new subdivisions from fraud, misrepresentation, or deceit in the marketing of subdivided property.

20. _____ Flexible pipe in which electrical wiring is installed.

21. _____ Exception granted to existing zoning regulations for special reasons.

22. _____ Soil that is used to fill in holes or support a foundation-bearing wall.

23. _____ Preliminary drawings and sketches by an architect, such as site plans and elevations.

24. _____ Map of the proposed subdivision that is submitted to a planning commission for approval or disapproval.

25. _____ Study of how a development will affect the ecology of its surroundings.

26. _____ Rating that measures how well insulation resists heat.

27. _____ The law that authorizes a city or county to control the orderly and proper development of the community.

28. _____ Wall erected on the line between two adjoining properties, which are under different ownership, for the use of both parties.

29. _____ The distance a building must be set back from the street; usually determined by local building code.

30. _____ The proceeding to exercise the power of eminent domain.

Multiple Choice Questions

Instructions: Circle your response and then check your response with the Answer Key that immediately follows the Multiple Choice Questions.

1. What is the power of the government to take private property for public use?
   a. Littoral
   b. Severance
   c. Riparian
   d. Eminent domain

2. A grandfather clause:
   a. is a change in zoning.
   b. is an example of downzoning.
   c. permits continuation of a nonconforming use.
   d. is an inheritance right to property.

3. A builder is allowed to make a change in construction that does not conform to the local building code. This is an example of:
   a. rezoning.
   b. a variance.
   c. a conditional-use permit.
   d. a restriction.

4. The intersection of the land with the water at the mean high-water line describes:
   a. wetlands.
   b. a shoreline.
   c. a floodplain.
   d. an estuary.

5. The division of land into 5 or more lots for the purpose of sale, lease, or financing is called a:
   a. land project.
   b. timeshare.
   c. tentative map.
   d. subdivision.

6. The law giving the city or county authority to control the orderly and proper development of the community is called the:
   a. Subdivided Lands Law.
   b. State Housing Law.
   c. Subdivision Map Act.
   d. Contractors' State License Law.

7. Under the Subdivided Lands Law, property can be subdivided into a minimum of _____ interest(s).
   a. one
   b. two
   c. four
   d. five

8. Waters that seep from the ground, arising from an indeterminable source, are known as _____ water.
   a. riparian
   b. percolating
   c. littoral
   d. appropriated

9. The purpose of a percolation test is to determine the:
   a. quality and potability of the water.
   b. acidity of the water.
   c. capacity of the soil to absorb water.
   d. location of any abandoned wells.

10. Which of the following statements is incorrect?

    a. State Housing Law has minimum construction requirements for houses.

    b. State building inspectors enforce the construction regulations.

    c. Local building inspectors enforce the construction regulations.

    d. Local health officers enforce the occupancy and sanitation regulations.

11. The main purpose of the Uniform Building Code is to:

    a. provide for the health, safety, and property rights of the public.

    b. provide construction data useful for scheduling.

    c. indicate prevailing sizes used to calculate construction costs.

    d. do none of the above.

12. The restrictions for a subdivision state that the minimum lot size is 10,000 square feet. Local zoning ordinances state that the minimum is 13,000 square feet. In this case, if the developer is subdividing one acre, which would prevail?

    a. Restrictions

    b. Zoning ordinances

    c. Whichever recorded first

    d. The county planning commission will decide the matter.

13. If a local building code is more stringent than a state code or the UBC:

    a. the stricter code prevails.

    b. contractors may choose between them.

    c. state or federal codes always take precedence over local codes.

    d. the local codes always take precedence.

14. The R-value is a rating that measures:

    a. how well insulation resists heat.

    b. the efficiency of energy; used to determine the effectiveness of appliances.

    c. the amount of heat needed to raise one pound of water one degree Fahrenheit.

    d. insulation.

15. The soil that is used to fill in holes or support a foundation is called:

    a. expansive soil.

    b. compaction.

    c. backfill.

    d. adobe.

16. For FHA loans, the minimum crawlspace is _____ inches.
    a. 12
    b. 18
    c. 24
    d. 36

17. Which of the following is not part of the foundation?
    a. Anchor bolts
    b. Footing
    c. Mud sill
    d. Ridge board

18. A freestanding small booth, such as a jewelry stand or a newsstand is known as a:
    a. joist.
    b. joint.
    c. kiosk.
    d. walk-up.

19. Drawing that shows front and side exterior views of a building as it will be when finished is called:
    a. a foundation plan.
    b. an elevation sheet.
    c. plot plan.
    d. none of the above

20. The words, gambrel, hip, gable, and flat refer to:
    a. styles of houses.
    b. types of conduit.
    c. types of insulation.
    d. types of roofs.

UNIT 12 ANSWER KEY

Answers – Matching

1. AA		7. P		13. I		19. Z		25. K
2. O		8. L		14. J		20. G		26. W
3. B		9. GG		15. S		21. DD		27. BB
4. R		10. V		16. HH		22. A		28. Q
5. II		11. FF		17. D		23. X		29. Y
6. H		12. C		18. E		24. CC		30. F

Answers – Multiple Choice

1. **(d)**   Eminent domain is the government's right to acquire property for the public good and for a public purpose. [Government Regulation of Land Use]

2. **(c)**   A grandfather clause allows a prior use to continue despite subsequent changes in zoning. [Planning and Development]

3. **(b)**   A variance is a special exception to the building code. [Planning and Development]

4. **(b)**   A shoreline is the intersection of the land with the water (mean high water line). Wetlands are areas where water covers the soil, or is present either at or near the surface of the soil all year or for varying periods during the year, including during the growing season. A floodplain is the low land adjacent to a river, lake, or ocean. An estuary is where seawater and fresh water mix together. [Planning and Development]

5. **(d)**   The division of land into five or more lots for the purpose of sale, lease, or financing is a subdivision. Subdivisions located in sparsely populated areas of California, made up of 50 parcels or more is a land project. A timeshare is a type of subdivision. A tentative map is a map of the proposed subdivision that is submitted to a planning commission for approval or disapproval. [Planning and Development]

6. **(c)**   The Subdivision Map Act authorizes cities and counties to control the orderly and proper development of the community. The Real Estate Commissioner regulates the sale or lease of subdivided real property under the Subdivided Lands Law. Contractors are licensed in California under the Contractors' State License Law. The State Housing Law outlines the minimum construction and occupancy requirements for dwellings. [Planning and Development]

7. **(d)**   The Subdivided Lands Law applies to a subdivision of five or more parcels. [Planning and Development]

8. **(b)**   Percolating water is underground water not flowing in a defined channel. [Planning and Development]

9. **(c)** A percolation test is used to determine the ability of the land to absorb and drain water, and is frequently used when installing septic systems. [Planning and Development]

10. **(b)** State Housing Law outlines the minimum construction and occupancy requirements for dwellings. Local building inspectors enforce the construction regulations while local health officers enforce the occupancy and sanitation regulations. [Regulation of Housing and Construction]

11. **(a)** Government regulations' purpose is always to protect the public. [Regulation of Housing and Construction]

12. **(b)** The zoning is more restrictive because it allows fewer lots to be developed by the subdivider. An acre is 43,560 SF. 43,560 SF divided by 10,000 SF = 4.36 or 4 lots per acre. 43,560 SF divided by 13,000 SF = 3.35 or 3 lots per acre. [Regulation of Housing and Construction]

13. **(a)** A stricter local code will take precedence over state or federal building codes. (UBC = Uniform Building Code) [Regulation of Housing and Construction]

14. **(a)** The R-value is a rating that measures how well insulation resists heat. [Construction and Building Styles]

15. **(c)** Backfill is soil that is used to fill in holes or support a foundation. Compaction refers to extra soil that is added and compressed to fill in the low areas or raise the level of the parcel. Expansive soil is soil that expands and shrinks. Adobe is one of the most expansive of the clay soils. [Construction and Building Styles]

16. **(b)** Crawl space is the area or space between the ground and floor joists. For FHA loans, the minimum crawl space is 18 inches. [Construction and Building Styles]

17. **(d)** The ridge board is the highest part of a frame building. [Construction and Building Styles]

18. **(c)** A kiosk is a freestanding small booth, such as a jewelry stand or a newsstand in a mall. Joists are boards supporting floors or ceilings. [Construction and Building Styles]

19. **(b)** An elevation sheet is a drawing that shows front and side exterior views of a building, as it will be when finished. A foundation plan is drawn to scale showing foundation, sub-floors, footing, and pier placement. A plot plan (map) shows the location of improvements on the lot. [Construction and Building Styles]

20. **(d)** These are all types of roofs. Roof types are determined by the direction, steepness, and number of roof planes. [Construction and Building Styles]

Real Estate Brokerage

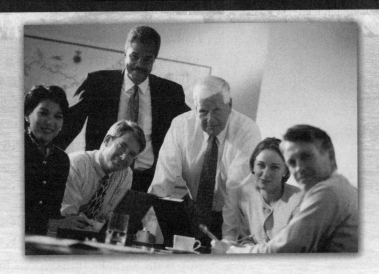

Unit 13

INTRODUCTION

So far, you have studied the regulation of real estate and the legal, financial, economic, and political aspects of real estate practice. Now you have reached the Unit in which you will see how a real estate brokerage works. This section examines the business and practical aspects of a brokerage and the real estate business in general.

We also will discuss how licensees must conduct themselves ethically. Know this well, for it could mean the difference between a successful real estate career and none at all.

Learning Objectives

After completing this Unit, you should be able to:

11A   recognize the types of real estate brokerages and the activities in which they engage.

11B   identify deciding factors a new licensee uses to select a brokerage.

11C   indicate the importance of prospecting, advertising, and marketing.

11D   recognize ethical and legal behavior expected of real estate licensees.

THE REAL ESTATE BROKERAGE BUSINESS

People commonly refer to a firm where real estate agents work as a real estate agency, but the firm is actually a real estate brokerage. The term **brokerage** generally means an activity involving the sale of something through an intermediary who negotiates the transaction for payment. In the case of a real estate brokerage, the product is real property, with the broker as negotiator and agent of the principal, expecting a commission at the end of the negotiation.

A licensed broker creates this business to bring together parties (brokering) who want to make transactions in real estate. The broker who creates the firm is the broker-owner of the real estate brokerage and sets all the policies of the firm.

A broker who creates a firm is the broker-owner of the real estate brokerage.

But a broker does not have to own a brokerage firm to be in business—a broker can even work from home.

Types of Brokerage Ownership

A real estate broker may set up the brokerage in a variety of ways, such as sole proprietorship, partnership, corporation, or Limited Liability Company (LLC).

Sole Proprietorship

A **sole proprietorship** is an unincorporated business owned by one individual. Since it is owned and operated by one person, it is used frequently to set up a real estate brokerage office. The owner is personally and fully liable for all business debts. This means that personal property could be taken to pay business debts. The broker reports all debts and reports any income or loss directly on his or her personal income tax return.

Partnership

A **partnership** is a form of business in which two or more persons join their money and skills in conducting the business. The Bureau of Real Estate does not issue partnership licenses. However, a partnership may perform acts for which a real estate broker license is required, as long as every partner has a real estate broker license. Just like a sole proprietorship, the broker-owners of a partnership are jointly and severally liable for all business debts. **Joint and several liability** is a legal term used in reference to a debt, in which each debtor is responsible for the entire amount of the debt. Partnerships file an annual information tax return. All partnership income, expenses, gains, and losses pass through to the individual partners and are reported on their personal income tax returns.

A partnership is made up of two or more people.

Corporation

A **corporation** is a legal entity whose rights in business are similar to that of an individual. It exists indefinitely and has centralized management in a board of directors. Its shareholder liability is limited to the amount of the individual investment and its corporate stocks are freely transferred. If permitted by its articles of incorporation, a corporation may take title to real estate. Due to its **indefinite duration**, a corporation may not hold title as a joint tenant. The profit of a corporation is taxed to the corporation when earned, and then is taxed to the shareholders when distributed as dividends. This creates a double tax.

S-Corporation

The **S corporation** is a corporation that operates like a corporation but is treated like a partnership for tax purposes. It avoids the double tax feature of a corporation because any gains and losses pass directly to the shareholders.

Limited Liability Company

A **limited liability company** (LLC) is an alternative business entity that has characteristics of both corporations and limited partnerships. Owners of LLCs are referred to as members. The LLC offers its members the advantage of limited personal liability (like a corporation) and a choice of how the business will be taxed. Members can choose for the LLC to be taxed as a separate entity (like a corporation) or as a partnership-like entity in which profits are passed through to partners and taxed on their personal income tax returns.

Broker's Responsibilities

When a broker opens a brokerage and employs licensees, he or she must follow various state laws and abide by the Commissioner's Regulations.

Maintain an Office

An active broker must maintain an office in California (home office is acceptable) to transact business and display licenses. [B&P §10162]. A broker may conduct business only at the address listed on his or her license. However, a broker may open more than one location but must apply for and receive an additional branch office license for each location. Only a licensed broker—not a salesperson—can have branch offices. If a broker employs associate licensees, the licenses are held by the broker until canceled or until the salesperson leaves the broker. The broker's license and those of his or her associate licensees must be available for inspection by the Commissioner in the broker's main office, not a branch office. [B&P §10160].

Follow Proper Procedure When Employing Salespeople

A broker must have written agreements with his or her sales associates, whether licensed as a salesperson or as a broker-associate. The agreement must be dated and signed by the parties and cover material aspects of the relationship between the parties, including supervision of licensed activities, duties, and compensation. [Reg. 2726].

When a real estate broker employs or terminates a salesperson, the broker must notify the Commissioner immediately in writing, typically within 5 days. The broker can inform the CalBRE by using the Salesperson Change Application or complete the notice through the eLicensing System. The broker must notify the Commissioner if a salesperson or associate-broker transfers his or her license to another broker. [Reg. 2752]. The broker must return the license certificate to the salesperson or broker associate within 3 business days following the transfer. [Reg. 2753]. If an associate licensee is fired for cause, the broker must immediately send the Commissioner a certified written statement of facts of the termination. [B&P §10178]. The license of the employing broker will not be suspended or revoked unless the Commissioner determines that the broker had guilty knowledge of the salesperson's violations of the law. [B&P §10179].

To change the information on a license, the salesperson crosses out the name of the former broker on the face of the license and types or writes (in ink) the name of the new employing broker on the reverse side, and dates and initials the license. [B&P §10161.8]. Then he or she gives it to the new employing broker to display in the broker's main office.

Also, as you recall, since a salesperson represents his or her broker in all operations, listings belong to the broker and not to the salesperson. When a salesperson leaves the employ of a particular broker, any listings he or she has will remain with that broker. The reason is that the seller's listing contract is with the broker, not the sales associate who took the listing (unless the broker happens to be the listing agent). This is a common source of confusion because sales associates may want to take their listings with them to a new broker. However, the law says the listings stay with the original broker.

Maintain Valid Real Estate Licenses

Everyone (broker and all sales associates) performing activities requiring a real estate license for compensation must have a valid real estate license. [B&P Code §10130]. Therefore, the broker should monitor the expiration dates and license status of their salespersons and broker associates on the Bureau of Real Estate's website. Even though a license has not expired, it could be suspended or revoked during the license term because the licensee has back child support payments, delinquent tax liabilities, unpaid recovery fund payouts, or has been barred from holding any position of employment in the real estate industry.

The Commissioner can bar or suspend any licensed or unlicensed persons from any position of employment with, or management or control of, a real estate business. The term "**bar**" means to prohibit or exclude from. The debarment or suspension can be placed if the Commissioner finds that the person was convicted of, or plead nolo contendere to, any crime or was held liable in any civil action if the crime involved dishonesty, fraud, or deceit. A debarred person cannot engage in any real estate-related business activity on the premises where a real estate salesperson or real estate broker is conducting business. [B&P Code §10087 and Reg. 2960].

If a license has expired, the sales associate cannot perform any licensed real estate activities until the license has been renewed. The late renewal period (**grace period**) simply allows the licensee to renew on a late basis without retaking the examination. It does not allow the licensee to conduct licensed activity during the late renewal period.

It is unlawful for a broker to employ or compensate (directly or indirectly) any person for performing licensed activity unless that person is a licensed broker, or a salesperson licensed to the broker. [B&P Code §10137]. A salesperson may not accept compensation for licensed activity except from his or her employing broker. [B&P Code §10137]. It is a misdemeanor for a person or an escrow holder to pay compensation to a broker unless the broker presents evidence that he or she was properly licensed at the time the compensation was earned. [B&P Code §10138].

Supervise Sales Associates

A broker must exercise reasonable supervision of his or her associate licensees (both sales associates and broker associates). To do this, the broker must establish policies and procedures for their sales associates to follow. [Reg. 2725].

Activities that Need a Broker's Supervision

- Handling transactions requiring a real estate license.
- Reviewing documents which may have a material effect upon the rights or obligations of a party to the transaction.
- Filing, storage, and maintenance of such documents.
- Handling of trust funds.
- Advertising of any service for which a license is required.
- Familiarizing salespersons with the requirements of federal and state laws relating to the prohibition of discrimination.

Brokers may have other brokers and salespersons help them supervise the activities of the associate licensees provided the brokers do not relinquish their overall responsibility for supervising the salespersons licensed to them. [Reg. 2725].

A broker can designate a broker-associate or a salesperson with 2 years of experience within the last 5 years to manage an office and supervise non-licensed employees. There must be a written agreement between the broker and broker-associate or salesperson with respect to the delegation of responsibility. [Reg. 2724].

Retain Records

A licensed broker must retain the records of a real estate transaction at the main office for 3 years. This includes copies of all listings, purchase agreements, canceled checks, trust account records, correspondence, email, and other documents that are part of the transaction. The requirement does not include electronic messages of an **ephemeral nature** such as text messages, instant messages, or tweets. [Civil Code §1624(d)]. The retention period starts from the date of the closing of the transaction or from the date of the listing if the transaction is not consummated. [B&P Code §10148].

Handle Trust Funds

Real estate brokers and salespeople, in their capacity as agents, receive money from people, usually in the form of a check to be used in a real estate transaction. The law is very clear about how these funds, called trust funds, should be handled. When an agent receives funds on behalf of someone else, a fiduciary duty is created to the owner of the funds. Agents must handle, control, and account for these trust funds according to specific legal guidelines. Noncompliance with the law can result in unfavorable business consequences. A license can be suspended or revoked for improper handling of trust funds, and an agent can be held financially responsible for damages occurring because of inept, negligent, or criminal actions regarding trust funds.

What are Trust Funds?

First of all, a licensee must be able to identify trust funds and distinguish them from non-trust funds. **Trust funds** are money, or anything of value, received from the buyer by an agent on behalf of a seller. Examples of trust funds are cash, a check used as a deposit for a purchase, or a personal note made payable to the seller. Do not confuse other monies such as commissions, general operating funds, and rents and deposits from broker-owned real estate with trust funds. The licensee has a fiduciary responsibility to the owners of the funds entrusted to his or her care. The funds can only be used for purposes authorized by the funds' owners and the licensee must maintain accurate, complete, lawful, and up-to-date records.

Proper Handling of Trust Funds

When a broker or salesperson receives trust funds from a principal in connection with the purchase or lease of real property, the transaction begins. Trust funds must be placed into the hands of the owner of the funds, into a neutral escrow depository, or into a lawful trust account no later than 3 business days following receipt of the funds by the broker or the broker's salesperson.

The only exception is when a check is received from an offeror in connection with an offer to purchase or lease real property. A deposit check may be held uncashed by the broker until acceptance of the offer under certain conditions. A broker may hold a deposit check uncashed if the check is not made out to the broker, or if the offeror (buyer) has given written instructions that the check may not be deposited or cashed until acceptance of the offer. Additionally, the offeree (seller) must be informed before or at the time the offer is presented for acceptance that the check is being held uncashed.

It is very important to remember that after acceptance of the offer, unless otherwise directed, the check must be placed no later than three business days into a neutral escrow depository, into the broker's trust fund bank account or into the hands of the offeree if expressly authorized in writing by both the offeror and offeree. A neutral depository is an escrow business conducted by someone who is a licensed escrow holder.

Before the seller accepts an offer, the buyer owns the funds, and they must be handled according to the buyer's instructions. After the seller accepts the offer, the funds must be handled according to instructions from both the buyer and seller.

Examples of Trust Funds Handled as Instructed

- An offeror's check held uncashed by the broker before an offer is accepted may be held uncashed after acceptance only upon written authorization from the offeree.

- The offeror's check may be given to the offeree only if both expressly authorize it in writing.

- All or part of an offeror's deposit may not be refunded by an agent or subagent of the seller without the express written permission of the offeree to make the refund.

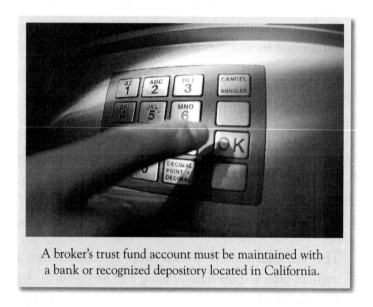

A broker's trust fund account must be maintained with a bank or recognized depository located in California.

Commingling

Trust funds may not be commingled (mixed) with funds belonging to the broker. **Commingling** is strictly prohibited by real estate law and may be punished by revocation or suspension of a real estate license.

Examples of Commingling

- Personal or company funds are deposited into the trust fund bank account. This violates the law even if separate records are kept.

- Trust funds are deposited into the licensee's general or personal bank account rather than into the trust fund account.

- Commissions, fees, or other income earned by the broker and collected from the trust account are left in the trust account for more than 25 days from the date they were earned.

A broker may keep up to $200 of personal funds in the trust fund account to pay for bank charges or service fees related to the trust account. When receiving commissions or other earned payment from the trust fund account, the broker may not use those moneys to pay bills or other expenses directly from the trust account. Rather, a check to the broker must be written first and deposited in a personal account for personal use.

A Broker's Trust Fund Account Must Meet These Requirements.

- It must be designated as a trust account in the name of the broker as trustee.
- It must be maintained with a bank or recognized depository located in California.
- It may not be an interest-bearing account for which prior written notice can be required for withdrawal of funds, except for certain instances.
- Withdrawals from a trust account may be made upon the signature of one or more specified persons.

Who Can Withdraw Funds from a Trust Account?

- The broker in whose name the account is maintained.
- The designated broker-officer if the account is in the name of a corporate broker.
- An individual specifically authorized in writing by the broker or a salesperson licensed to the broker.
- An unlicensed employee of the broker, if specifically authorized in writing by the broker, and if the employee is covered by a fidelity bond at least equal to the maximum amount of the trust fund to which the employee has access at any time.

CALIFORNIA
ASSOCIATION
OF REALTORS®

TRUST BANK ACCOUNT RECORD FOR ALL TRUST FUNDS DEPOSITED AND WITHDRAWN
(C.A.R. Form TAA, Revised 11/07)

Broker: _____

Address: _____

DATE	DEPOSIT (Received From)	OR	WITHDRAWAL (Paid To)	AMOUNT	BALANCE
					Forward from previous page $
	Name: _____ ☐ check ☐ cash ☐ ___ For: _____		Name: _____ Check # _____ For: _____	$	$
	Name: _____ ☐ check ☐ cash ☐ ___ For: _____		Name: _____ Check # _____ For: _____	$	$
	Name: _____ ☐ check ☐ cash ☐ ___ For: _____		Name: _____ Check # _____ For: _____	$	$
	Name: _____ ☐ check ☐ cash ☐ ___ For: _____		Name: _____ Check # _____ For: _____	$	$
	Name: _____ ☐ check ☐ cash ☐ ___ For: _____		Name: _____ Check # _____ For: _____	$	$
	Name: _____ ☐ check ☐ cash ☐ ___ For: _____		Name: _____ Check # _____ For: _____	$	$
	Name: _____ ☐ check ☐ cash ☐ ___ For: _____		Name: _____ Check # _____ For: _____	$	$
	Name: _____ ☐ check ☐ cash ☐ ___ For: _____		Name: _____ Check # _____ For: _____	$	$
	Name: _____ ☐ check ☐ cash ☐ ___ For: _____		Name: _____ Check # _____ For: _____	$	$
	Name: _____ ☐ check ☐ cash ☐ ___ For: _____		Name: _____ Check # _____ For: _____	$	$

SAMPLE

TAA REVISED 11/07 (PAGE 1 OF 1)

Reviewed by _____ Date _____

EQUAL HOUSING OPPORTUNITY

TRUST BANK ACCOUNT RECORD FOR ALL TRUST FUNDS DEPOSITED AND WITHDRAWN (TAA PAGE 1 OF 1)

Agent: Broker:	Phone:	Fax:	Prepared using zipForm® software

Measure Profitability

Real estate brokerage firms are in business to provide a service and to be profitable. The owner of the firm needs to know how much money is available to operate the business. Additionally, the broker needs to know how much each sales associate must produce to cover office expenses. Two quick ways the broker can determine profitability are the company dollar and the desk cost.

The **company dollar** is the amount a broker has left after all commissions have been paid. The **desk cost** shows how much each sales associate must earn to cover expenses. It is calculated by dividing the total operating expenses of the firm by the number of licensed sales associates. A profit margin for the broker is not included as an operating expense.

Employment Relationships

Employment status refers to the relationship between a salesperson and his or her broker—as an employee or self-employed. The compensation earned depends primarily on the salesperson's employment status. Generally, salespeople classified as employees earn a salary and salespeople categorized as self-employed earn a commission. Often, new self-employed licensees negotiate a 50/50 commission split with their broker.

Remember that in order to receive compensation from a real estate transaction, you must have a real estate license, and you must be supervised by a licensed real estate broker. Also, you can only accept compensation from your employing broker.

As a salesperson or broker-salesperson, you are classified as self-employed for some purposes and as an employee for others. Whether a person is an employee or is self-employed is critical when it comes to such important issues as federal income tax, Social Security, unemployment tax liability, pension eligibility, and many other matters.

The classification of a salesperson as an employee or as self-employed has significant tax consequences for brokers and associate-licensees alike.

Example: An employing broker must withhold income taxes, withhold and pay Social Security and Medicare taxes, and pay unemployment tax on wages paid to an employee. However, brokers do not generally have to withhold or pay any taxes on payments to self-employed workers.

When reporting income to the Internal Revenue Service (IRS), the broker will use IRS form W-2 for employees and IRS Form 1099 for self-employed individuals (independent contractors and statutory nonemployees).

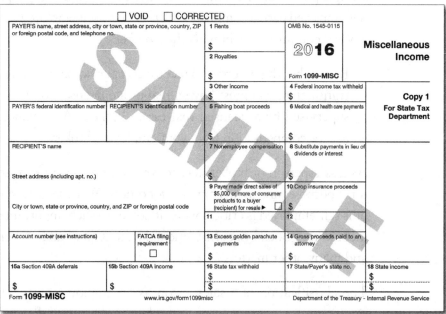

Legal Status of a Licensed Salesperson

For purposes of California real estate law and regulations, a salesperson or broker-salesperson is considered an employee of the broker. This is because the broker is required by law to supervise the activities of the salesperson. However, the broker must have a written independent contractor agreement with each of his or her associate-licensees. This agreement allows the associate-licensees to be self-employed.

The broker-associate licensee employment relationship is viewed in this manner only by the license law; not by other agencies. For all other purposes, associate-licensees are considered self-employed.

IRS Classifications

An associate licensee (real estate salesperson or broker-salesperson) is not considered an employee for federal income tax purposes—nor does the IRS consider real estate licensees independent contractors. In fact, since 1982, real estate licensees have been classified by the IRS as **statutory nonemployees**.

The IRS Code recognizes four types of individuals that a company can make payments to in return for services—independent contractor, statutory employee, statutory nonemployee, and employee.

Independent Contractor

The general rule used by the IRS is that an individual is an independent contractor if the payer has the right to control or direct only the **result** of the work and not what will be done or how it will be done. The IRS describes independent contractors as doctors, dentists, veterinarians, lawyers, accountants, contractors, subcontractors, public stenographers, or auctioneers who participate in an independent trade, business, or profession in which they offer their services to the public. **Real estate licensees are not listed**.

Statutory Nonemployee

Licensed real estate agents are classified by the IRS as **statutory nonemployees**. The statutory nonemployee classification was created in 1982. That is why many brokers are unaware that their associate-licensees are classified as statutory nonemployees by IRS definition rather than as independent contractors.

If an employing broker and real estate salesperson meet the following tests, the broker is **not treated as an employer** and the salesperson is **not treated as an employee** for federal income tax purposes.

Tests Used to Determine Statutory Nonemployee Status

- The salesperson or broker-salesperson must be duly licensed;
- The salesperson or broker-salesperson must be compensated on the basis of the number of sales closed and commissions earned—not on the basis of the number of hours worked; and
- There must be a written contract between the broker and the salesperson providing that the salesperson will not be treated as an employee for federal tax purposes. 26 USC §3508

Statutory nonemployees are treated as *self-employed* for all federal tax purposes, including income and employment taxes. Therefore, they must pay the full amount of Social Security and Medicare taxes, and not just a matching amount. Statutory nonemployees receive 1099s (instead of a W-2 form) and must file a Schedule C to report their income and expenses. Additionally, they must make quarterly estimated tax payments. This does not necessarily increase the tax burden, unless payments are underestimated or late. Fortunately, as a self-employed person, a salesperson or broker-salesperson has business deductions for various expenses that are not available to employees.

Statutory Employee

According to common-law rules, some independent contractors are treated as employees by statute (statutory employees) if they are in certain categories.

Employee

Under common-law rules, anyone who performs services for a company is the company's employee (**common-law employee**) if the company can control what will be done and how it will be done.

Review - Real Estate Salesperson and Real Estate Broker-Associate

- Person holding a salesperson or broker license and is employed by a real estate broker, for pay, to perform real estate activities
- Agent of the broker—not the buyer or the seller
- Employed and supervised by the broker, under real estate license law
- Self-employed for income tax purposes

Employment Agreement

The real estate law requires that every broker must have a written **employment agreement** with each of his or her salespeople, whether they are licensed as a salesperson or as a broker under a broker-associate arrangement. Although the employment agreement does not have to be on a form approved by the Commissioner, it must cover the important aspects of the employment relationship, including supervision of licensed activities, licensee's duties, and the compensation arrangement. In addition, in order to protect the self-employed status of the associate-licensees, it must also include the required language as previously discussed. Even though the IRS legally defines the associate-licensees as statutory non-employees, the C.A.R. employment agreement most commonly used is still called an Independent Contractor Agreement.

CALIFORNIA
ASSOCIATION
OF REALTORS®

INDEPENDENT CONTRACTOR AGREEMENT
WITHOUT ARBITRATION
(Between Broker and Associate-Licensee)
(C.A.R. Form ICA-NA, 4/15)

This Agreement, dated _____, is made between _____
_____ ("Broker") and
_____ ("Associate-Licensee").

In consideration of the covenants and representations contained in this Agreement, Broker and Associate-Licensee agree as follows:

1. **BROKER:** Broker represents that Broker is duly licensed as a real estate broker by the State of California, ☐ doing business as _____ (firm name), ☐ a sole proprietorship, ☐ a partnership, or ☐ a corporation. Broker is a member of the _____ Association(s) of REALTORS®, and a participant to the _____ Multiple Listing Service(s). Broker shall keep Broker's license current during the term of this Agreement.

2. **ASSOCIATE-LICENSEE:** Associate-Licensee represents that: **(i)** he/she is duly licensed by the State of California as a ☐ real estate broker, ☐ real estate salesperson, and **(ii)** he/she has not used any other names within the past five years, except _____. Associate-Licensee shall keep his/her license current during the term of this Agreement, including satisfying all applicable continuing education and provisional license requirements.

3. **INDEPENDENT CONTRACTOR RELATIONSHIP:**
    A. Broker and Associate-Licensee intend that, to the maximum extent permissible by law: **(i)** This Agreement does not constitute an employment agreement by either party; **(ii)** Broker and Associate-Licensee are independent contracting parties with respect to all services rendered under this Agreement; and **(iii)** This Agreement shall not be construed as a partnership.
    B. Broker shall not: **(i)** restrict Associate-Licensee's activities to particular geographical areas, or **(ii)** dictate Associate-Licensee's activities with regard to hours, leads, open houses, opportunity or floor time, production, prospects, sales meetings, schedule, inventory, time off, vacation, or similar activities, except to the extent required by law.
    C. Associate-Licensee shall not be required to accept an assignment by Broker to service any particular current or prospective listing or parties.
    D. Except as required by law: **(i)** Associate-Licensee retains sole and absolute discretion and judgment in the methods, techniques, and procedures to be used in soliciting and obtaining listings, sales, exchanges, leases, rentals, or other transactions, and in carrying out Associate-Licensee's selling and soliciting activities; **(ii)** Associate-Licensee is under the control of Broker as to the results of Associate-Licensee's work only, and not as to the means by which those results are accomplished; **(iii)** Associate-Licensee has no authority to bind Broker by any promise or representation; and **(iv)** Broker shall not be liable for any obligation or liability incurred by Associate-Licensee.
    E. Associate-Licensee's only remuneration shall be the compensation specified in paragraph 8.
    F. Associate-Licensee who only performs as a real estate sales agent, shall not be treated as an employee for state and federal tax purposes. However, an Associate-Licensee who performs loan activity shall be treated as an employee for state and federal tax purposes unless the activity satisfies the legal requirements to establish an independent contractor relationship.
    G. The fact the Broker may carry workers' compensation insurance for Broker's own benefit and for the mutual benefit of Broker and licensees associated with Broker, including Associate-Licensee, shall not create an inference of employment. (Workers' Compensation Advisory: Even though a Real Estate salesperson may be treated as independent contractors for tax and other purposes, the California Labor and Workforce Development Agency considers them to be employees for workers' compensation purposes. According to that Agency: **(i)** Broker must obtain workers' compensation insurance for a real estate salesperson and **(ii)** Broker, not a Real Estate sales person, must bear the cost of workers' compensation insurance. Penalties for failure to carry workers' compensation include, among others, the issuance of stop-work orders and fines of up to $1,000 per agent, not to exceed $100,000 per company.)

4. **LICENSED ACTIVITY:**
    A. All listings of property, and all agreements, acts or actions for performance of licensed acts, which are taken or performed in connection with this Agreement, shall be taken and performed in the name of Broker. Associate-Licensee agrees to and does hereby contribute all right and title to such listings to Broker for the benefit and use of Broker, Associate-Licensee, and other licensees associated with Broker.
    B. Broker shall make available to Associate-Licensee, equally with other licensees associated with Broker, all current listings in Broker's office, except any listing which Broker may choose to place in the exclusive servicing of Associate-Licensee or one or more other specific licensees associated with Broker.

Broker's Initials (_____)   Associate-Licensee's Initials (_____)

ICA-NA 4/15 (PAGE 1 OF 4)

INDEPENDENT CONTRACTOR AGREEMENT (ICA-NA PAGE 1 OF 4)

C. Associate-Licensee shall provide and pay for all professional licenses, supplies, services, and other items required in connection with Associate-Licensee's activities under this Agreement, or any listing or transaction, without reimbursement from Broker except as required by law.

D. Associate-Licensee shall work diligently and with his/her best efforts to: **(i)** sell, exchange, lease, or rent properties listed with Broker or other cooperating Brokers; **(ii)** solicit additional listings, clients, and customers; and **(iii)** otherwise promote the business of serving the public in real estate transactions to the end that Broker and Associate-Licensee may derive the greatest benefit possible, in accordance with law.

E. Associate-Licensee shall not commit any unlawful act under federal, state or local law or regulation while conducting licensed activity. Associate-Licensee shall at all times be familiar, and comply, with all applicable federal, state and local laws, including, but not limited to, anti-discrimination laws and restrictions against the giving or accepting a fee, or other thing of value, for the referral of business to title companies, escrow companies, home inspection companies, pest control companies and other settlement service providers pursuant to the California Business and Professions Code and the Real Estate Settlement Procedures Acts (RESPA).

F. Broker shall make available for Associate-Licensee's use, along with other licensees associated with Broker, the facilities of the real estate office operated by Broker at _____ and the facilities of any other office locations made available by Broker pursuant to this Agreement.

G. **PROHIBITED ACTIVITIES:** Associate-Licensee agrees not to engage in any of the following Real Estate licensed activities without the express written consent of Broker:
☐ Property Management; ☐ Loan Brokerage ☐ Business Brokerage; ☐ _____
☐ _____
However, if Associate-Licensee has a Real Estate Broker's License, Associate-Licensee may nonetheless engage in the following prohibited activity(ies) only: _____ provided that (1) such prohibited activities are not done under the Broker's License, (2) no facilities of Broker (including but not limited to phones, fax, computers, and office space) are used for any such prohibited activities, (3) Associate-Licensee shall not use any marketing, solicitation or contact information that include Broker's name (including business cards) for such prohibited activities, (4) Associate-Licensee informs any actual or intended Principal for whom Associate-Licensee performs or intends to perform such prohibited activities the name of the broker under whose license the prohibited activities are performed, and (5) if Associate-Licensee is performing other permitted licensed activity for that Principal under Broker's license, then Associate-Licensee shall inform any actual or intended Principal for whom the prohibited activities are performed that the prohibited activities are not performed under Broker's license.

5. **PROPRIETARY INFORMATION AND FILES:**
A. All files and documents pertaining to listings, leads and transactions are the property of Broker and shall be delivered to Broker by Associate-Licensee immediately upon request or termination of this Agreement.
B. Associate-Licensee acknowledges that Broker's method of conducting business is a protected trade secret.
C. Associate-Licensee shall not use to his/her own advantage, or the advantage of any other person, business, or entity, except as specifically agreed in writing, either during Associate-Licensee's association with Broker, or thereafter, any information gained for or from the business, or files of Broker.

6. **SUPERVISION:** Associate-Licensee, within 24 hours (or ☐ _____) after preparing, signing, or receiving same, shall submit to Broker, or Broker's designated licensee: **(i)** all documents which may have a material effect upon the rights and duties of principals in a transaction; **(ii)** any documents or other items connected with a transaction pursuant to this Agreement in the possession of or available to Associate-Licensee; and **(iii)** all documents associated with any real estate transaction in which Associate-Licensee is a principal.

7. **TRUST FUNDS:** All trust funds shall be handled through the Broker's trust account and in compliance with the Business and Professions Code, and other applicable laws.

8. **COMPENSATION:**
A. **TO BROKER:** Compensation shall be charged to parties who enter into listing or other agreements for services requiring a real estate license:
☐ as shown in "Exhibit A" attached, which is incorporated as a part of this Agreement by reference, or
☐ as follows: _____
_____
Any deviation which is not approved in writing in advance by Broker, shall be: (1) deducted from Associate-Licensee's compensation, if lower than the amount or rate approved above; and, (2) subject to Broker approval, if higher than the amount approved above. Any permanent change in commission schedule shall be disseminated by Broker to Associate-Licensee.

B. **TO ASSOCIATE-LICENSEE:** Associate-Licensee shall receive a share of compensation actually collected by Broker, on listings or other agreements for services requiring a real estate license, which are solicited and obtained by Associate-Licensee, and on transactions of which Associate-Licensee's activities are the procuring cause, as follows:
☐ as shown in "Exhibit B" attached, which is incorporated as a part of this Agreement by reference, or
☐ other: _____
_____

Broker's Initials (_____) Associate-Licensee's Initials (_____)

© 2015, California Association of REALTORS®, Inc.
ICA-NA 4/15 (PAGE 2 OF 4)

INDEPENDENT CONTRACTOR AGREEMENT (ICA-NA PAGE 2 OF 4)

C. **PARTNERS, TEAMS, AND AGREEMENTS WITH OTHER ASSOCIATE-LICENSEES IN OFFICE:** If Associate-Licensee and one or more other Associate-Licensees affiliated with Broker participate on the same side (either listing or selling) of a transaction, the commission allocated to their combined activities shall be divided by Broker and paid to them according to their written agreement. Broker shall have the right to withhold total compensation if there is a dispute between associate-licensees, or if there is no written agreement, or if no written agreement has been provided to Broker.

D. **EXPENSES AND OFFSETS:** If Broker elects to advance funds to pay expenses or liabilities of Associate-Licensee, or for an advance payment of, or draw upon, future compensation, Broker may deduct the full amount advanced from compensation payable to Associate-Licensee on any transaction without notice. If Associate-Licensee's compensation is subject to a lien, garnishment or other restriction on payment, Broker shall charge Associate-Licensee a fee for complying with such restriction.

E. **PAYMENT: (i)** All compensation collected by Broker and due to Associate-Licensee shall be paid to Associate-Licensee, after deduction of expenses and offsets, immediately or as soon thereafter as practicable, except as otherwise provided in this Agreement, or a separate written agreement between Broker and Associate-Licensee. **(ii)** Compensation shall not be paid to Associate-Licensee until both the transaction and file are complete. **(iii)** Broker is under no obligation to pursue collection of compensation from any person or entity responsible for payment. Associate-Licensee does not have the independent right to pursue collection of compensation for activities which require a real estate license which were done in the name of Broker. **(iv)** Expenses which are incurred in the attempt to collect compensation shall be paid by Broker and Associate-Licensee in the same proportion as set forth for the division of compensation (paragraph 8(B)). **(v)** If there is a known or pending claim against Broker or Associate-Licensee on transactions for which Associate-Licensee has not yet been paid, Broker may withhold from compensation due Associate-Licensee on that transaction amounts for which Associate-Licensee could be responsible under paragraph 14, until such claim is resolved. **(vi)** Associate-Licensee shall not be entitled to any advance payment from Broker upon future compensation.

F. **UPON OR AFTER TERMINATION:** If this Agreement is terminated while Associate-Licensee has listings or pending transactions that require further work normally rendered by Associate-Licensee, Broker shall make arrangements with another associate-licensee to perform the required work, or Broker shall perform the work him/herself. The licensee performing the work shall be reasonably compensated for completing work on those listings or transactions, and such reasonable compensation shall be deducted from Associate-Licensee's share of compensation. Except for such offset, Associate-Licensee shall receive the compensation due as specified above.

9. **TERMINATION OF RELATIONSHIP:** Broker or Associate-Licensee may terminate their relationship under this Agreement at any time, with or without cause. After termination, Associate-Licensee shall not solicit: **(i)** prospective or existing clients or customers based upon company-generated leads obtained during the time Associate-Licensee was affiliated with Broker; **(ii)** any principal with existing contractual obligations to Broker; or **(iii)** any principal with a contractual transactional obligation for which Broker is entitled to be compensated. Even after termination, this Agreement, inclusive of Paragraph 12, shall govern all disputes and claims between Broker and Associate-Licensee connected with their relationship under this Agreement, including obligations and liabilities arising from existing and completed listings, transactions, and services.

10. **AUTOMOBILE:** Associate-Licensee shall maintain automobile insurance coverage for liability and property damage in the following amounts $ _____ / $ _____ . Broker shall be named as an additional insured party on Associate-Licensee's policies. A copy of the endorsement showing Broker as an additional insured shall be provided to Broker.

11. **PERSONAL ASSISTANTS:** Associate-Licensee may make use of a personal assistant, provided the following requirements are satisfied. Associate-Licensee shall have a written agreement with the personal assistant which establishes the terms and responsibilities of the parties to the employment agreement, including, but not limited to, compensation, supervision and compliance with applicable law. The agreement shall be subject to Broker's review and approval. Unless otherwise agreed, if the personal assistant has a real estate license, that license must be provided to the Broker. Both Associate-Licensee and personal assistant must sign any agreement that Broker has established for such purposes.

12. **AGREEMENT TO MEDIATE DISPUTES:**
    (1) Broker and Associate-Licensee agree to timely notify the other person and mediate all disputes and claims between them arising from or connected in any way with this Agreement before resorting to   arbitration or court action.
    (2) If any dispute or claim is not resolved through mediation, or otherwise, Broker and Associate-Licensee may mutually agree to submit disputes involving commissions for property transactions to binding arbitration by the procedures and rules set forth in the California Code of Ethics and Arbitration Manual, a copy of which is available at the following link: www.car.org/legal/calarbrules/.

Broker's Initials (_____)   Associate-Licensee's Initials (_____)

13. **OFFICE POLICY MANUAL:** If Broker's office policy manual, now or as modified in the future, conflicts with or differs from the terms of this Agreement, the terms of the office policy manual shall govern the relationship between Broker and Associate-Licensee.

14. **INDEMNITY AND HOLD HARMLESS; NOTICE OF CLAIMS:**
   A. Regarding any action taken or omitted by Associate-Licensee, or others working through, or on behalf of Associate-Licensee in connection with services rendered or to be rendered pursuant to this Agreement or real estate licensed activity prohibited by this agreement: **(i)** Associate-Licensee agrees to indemnify, defend and hold Broker harmless from all claims, disputes, litigation, judgments, awards, costs and attorney fees, arising therefrom and **(ii)** Associate-Licensee shall immediately notify Broker if Associate-Licensee is served with or becomes aware of a lawsuit or claim regarding any such action.
   B. Any such claims or costs payable pursuant to this Agreement, are due as follows:
   ☐ Paid in full by Associate-Licensee, who hereby agrees to indemnify and hold harmless Broker for all such sums, or
   ☐ In the same ratio as the compensation split as it existed at the time the compensation was earned by Associate-Licensee ☐ Other: _____
   Payment from Associate-Licensee is due at the time Broker makes such payment and can be offset from any compensation due Associate-Licensee as above. Broker retains the authority to settle claims or disputes, whether or not Associate-Licensee consents to such settlement.

15. **ADDITIONAL PROVISIONS:** _____
   _____

16. **DEFINITIONS:** As used in this Agreement, the following terms have the meanings indicated:
   A. "Listing" means an agreement with a property owner or other party to locate a buyer, exchange party, lessee, or other party to a transaction involving real property, a mobile home, or other property or transaction which may be brokered by a real estate licensee, or an agreement with a party to locate or negotiate for any such property or transaction.
   B. "Compensation" means compensation for acts requiring a real estate license, regardless of whether calculated as a percentage of transaction price, flat fee, hourly rate, or in any other manner.
   C. "Transaction" means a sale, exchange, lease, or rental of real property, a business opportunity, or a manufactured home, which may lawfully be brokered by a real estate licensee.

17. **ATTORNEY FEES:** In any action, proceeding, or arbitration between Broker and Associate-Licensee arising from or related to this Agreement, the prevailing Broker or Associate-Licensee shall be entitled to reasonable attorney fees and costs.

18. **ENTIRE AGREEMENT:** All prior agreements between the parties concerning their relationship as Broker and Associate-Licensee are incorporated in this Agreement, which constitutes the entire contract. Its terms are intended by the parties as a final and complete expression of their agreement with respect to its subject matter, and may not be contradicted by evidence of any prior agreement or contemporaneous oral agreement. This Agreement may not be amended, modified, altered, or changed except by a further agreement in writing executed by Broker and Associate-Licensee.

Broker:

_____
(Brokerage firm name)
By _____
Its ☐ Broker/ ☐ Office manager (check one)

_____
(Print name)

_____
(Address)

_____
(City, State, Zip)

_____
(Telephone)   (Fax)

Broker's Initials (_____)

Associate-Licensee:

_____
(Signature)

_____
(Print name)

_____
(Address)

_____
(City, State, Zip)

_____
(Telephone)   (Fax)

Associate-Licensee's Initials (_____)

Reviewed by _____ Date _____

ICA-NA 4/15 (PAGE 4 OF 4)

INDEPENDENT CONTRACTOR AGREEMENT (ICA-NA PAGE 4 OF 4)

The agreement shall be dated and signed by both parties and both the salesperson and the broker must keep copies of it for three years after termination of employment. A salesperson can only be paid by his or her employing broker. He or she cannot receive compensation or referral fees from a lender, developer, or seller.

Workers' Compensation Insurance

For federal and state income tax purposes, sales associates are considered self-employed. However, due to their employee status under the license law, a broker must provide workers' compensation coverage to all sales associates as well as any non-licensee employees of the firm. Compliance with workers' compensation insurance requirements is enforced by the Employment Development Department (EDD). Failure to provide workers' compensation coverage for their real estate sales agents could result in fines up to $100,000.

CHOOSING A BROKERAGE

Hopefully you have selected your brokerage with great care and for the right reasons. The new broker should be available to give guidance and problem-solving advice and should be trained, confident, informed, and up-to-date on developments in the real estate industry. The broker's professional advice should come from knowledge and experience. Also, the sales associates in the office should be full-time professionals. They too should be trained, confident, informed, and up-to-date. Most importantly, they should be honest and straightforward with clients, co-brokers, business contacts, and each other.

A brokerage should have a large inventory of in-house listings.

If you have selected your new office carefully, the brokerage will have a big inventory of in-house listings in all price ranges and a great deal of referral business. The main points you are looking for are ethical business practices, training, and of course, the commission split.

Ethical Business Practices

You should look for a company that adheres to legal and ethical business practices. Since your livelihood will depend on the integrity of your employing broker's license, it is imperative to choose a brokerage firm that follows all legal and ethical business practices. If the Bureau of Real Estate suspends or revokes your employing broker's license, you will have to immediately transfer your license to another broker or stop working.

Your prospective broker will ask you many questions during your employment interview. Before accepting an offer to join a brokerage firm, you should be prepared to ask a few of your own. Of course, you will ask the usual questions about the working environment, benefits, items provided by the brokerage, and items you will have to pay for. Additionally, you should ask questions regarding the trust fund account, handling the transaction paperwork, availability of errors and omissions insurance, advertising policies, and adherence to fair housing practices.

Training

Training is something else to look for when selecting a brokerage. A new salesperson may get good, indifferent, or no training, depending on the company. Firms who are more selective of their salespeople tend to judge their potential and think of them as valuable additions to their staff, to be trained and treated with respect.

Most real estate companies provide extensive training.

Most real estate companies do provide extensive sales training, as well as on-the-job training, with the broker accompanying new agents to their first appointments. Remember, the broker is responsible for everything a salesperson does, and does not want anyone making costly mistakes—in money and/or reputation.

Commission Split

More than likely, you will be paid on a commission basis. A **commission** is a fee for services rendered usually based on a certain percentage of the sales price of a property. The amount is not set by law and must be decided between the employing broker and each employed sales associate. You, as a sales associate, will receive your share of the commission from your broker when a transaction for which you are responsible closes. It will be based on the **commission split** agreement you have with your broker. Your split will be a certain percentage of the commission that comes to the brokerage from your sales.

Usually, a new agent can count on a 50-50 split at first. That means the broker gets 50% and you get 50% of the commission on any sale you make. For example, if the agreed-upon commission split is 50-50, and the commission paid to the brokerage on one of your sales was $6,000, the broker gets $3,000, and you get $3,000. Usually commissions will be cash, but they can be anything agreed upon by the listing broker and the principal.

The escrow agent disburses the commissions to the broker(s) at the close of escrow. The commission paid to your brokerage is probably one-half the total commission paid if there is an agent from another brokerage involved. That is the normal split between a selling broker and listing broker.

How Commissions are Paid

A home sold for $425,000, with a 6% commission paid by the seller: ABC Real Estate Company was the listing broker, and EFG Real Estate Company was the selling broker. Individual agents for each company were on a 50-50 split with their brokers.

1. Commission equals $425,000 × 6% or $25,500
2. $25,500 divided by 2 brokerage firms equals $12,750 to each broker
3. $12,750 split 50/50 between broker and agent equals $6,375 to broker and $6,375 to salesperson

ACTIVITIES OF A REAL ESTATE BROKERAGE

The activities of a brokerage are varied and can be divided into five separate areas: securing listings, finding buyers, negotiating transactions, arranging financing, and closing transactions. You should understand the basics of the real estate business. In fact, you should know more than your clients and customers about your chosen area. The people you call will rely on your expertise to help them buy or sell property. Real estate agents are licensed and are expected to have a certain degree of product knowledge about the business. Become an expert in your area and your community. Keep up with current real estate trends.

Every salesperson performs the various brokerage activities in the course of pursuing a career in real estate.

> **Brokerage Activities Performed by Licensees**
> - Prospecting for listings
> - Selling and marketing the properties
> - Negotiating transactions between buyers and sellers
> - Arranging financing
> - Closing transactions

Prospecting for listings and selling properties are the main activities of a real estate brokerage. There is also a major amount of paperwork such as filling out forms, keeping track of listings, opening escrows, completing loan applications, ordering special reports, and keeping records of prospects. The agent who does not keep adequate records or who does not complete paperwork will not be in the business long.

Prospecting

A newly licensed salesperson will spend the majority of his or her time prospecting. Prospecting is an excellent way to market yourself to the community and let them know you are in the real estate business. As with any business, success in real estate depends upon your effectiveness in prospecting for new clients. **Prospecting** is the process of identifying potential customers. The majority of sales associates prospect by cold calling or sending text through mailings, faxes, or e-mails. **Cold calling** is the practice of making unsolicited calls to people you do not know in order to get new business.

Anytime real estate solicitation involves the use of the telephone, cell phone, fax, or e-mail, the sales associate must comply with applicable federal and state do-not-call and CAN-SPAM laws. You may still call, fax, and e-mail potential clients, but you must follow certain procedures.

Do-Not-Call and Do-Not-Fax Rules

The federal **do-not-call** rules are forcing real estate agents to try new methods of prospecting. We will discuss prospecting using the telephone, cell phone, fax, and e-mails.

Telephone and Cell Phone Calls

In general, both real estate licensees and unlicensed assistants may make cold calls providing the calls are made only between 8:00 a.m. and 9:00 p.m. Additionally, callers must introduce themselves, state the purpose of the call, and give the company's name, address, and phone number. If a person asks to be put on a do-not-call list, include his or her name on the company list. These calling restrictions do not apply if the person is already your client, if you have written permission to call them, or if you have a personal relationship with them.

Autodialers (automatic telephone dialing systems) are generally used for placing computerized or prerecorded messages. An **autodialer** refers to equipment that can generate and dial telephone or cell phone numbers randomly or sequentially. Using an autodialer is an acceptable business practice provided you follow a few simple rules. First, the autodialer cannot place calls after 9:00 p.m. and before 8:00 a.m. Secondly, if a salesperson or broker uses an autodialer, the call must be connected to a live sales associate within two seconds after the recorded greeting has finished.

Autodialer calls must connect to a live sales associate within two seconds after the recorded greeting has finished.

Violating the do-not-call rules can be very expensive. The broker of a salesperson who violates the FCC rules could be fined up to $16,000 per violation. Each call may be considered a separate violation.

How would a newly licensed real estate salesperson develop a clientele and get referrals if he or she is prevented from making cold calls? To build your business, mail flyers or postcards offering a free Comparative Market Analysis (CMA). Include a response card asking for telephone and cell phone numbers and permission to call them. The written permission exempts you from the do-not-call requirements. Another example would be to obtain permission from potential buyers by using an open house registry list. Tell them that by signing the registry and including phone numbers or an e-mail address, they are giving permission for you to call them with market updates and relevant property information.

Faxing Advertisements

Along with the do-not-call rules, the FCC adopted **do-not-fax rules** as well. Real estate agents are not exempt from these rules. In fact, as of January 1, 2005, real estate agents are no longer allowed to fax flyers advertising the availability of real estate services or property data sheets offering a real property for sale without prior written permission from the person receiving the fax. Bottom line, the advertisements may be mailed, downloaded from your website, or hand-delivered, but they generally cannot be faxed.

Once you have written permission to fax advertising material to a person, the fax must include the date and time it is sent; name of the person or company sending the message; and telephone number of the sending fax machine. Violating the do-not-fax rules carries the same penalties as violations of the do-not-call rules.

CAN-SPAM Act of 2003

The **CAN-SPAM Act** of 2003 became effective on January 1, 2004 and regulates commercial e-mail messages. The CAN-SPAM Act defines a **commercial e-mail message** as "any electronic mail message the primary purpose of which is the commercial advertisement or promotion of a commercial product or service." E-mails sent as part of an ongoing commercial transaction, called **transactional e-mail messages**, are excluded from the Act. An e-mail sent to a client concerning an existing listing or sales transaction is a transactional e-mail message and is exempt from the rules.

Types of Transactional E-mail Messages

- Facilitating or confirming an existing commercial transaction
- Giving notice about product updates or upgrades
- Providing notice about certain changes in a subscription, membership, account, or loan
- Providing warranty information, product recall information, or safety or security information with respect to a commercial product or service used or purchased by the recipient
- Providing information directly related to an employment relationship in which the recipient is currently involved

Unsolicited e-mail messages sent by a real estate agent to people on a mailing list for the purpose of offering that agent's services is a **commercial e-mail message**.

> ## Items Required in a Commercial E-mail Message
> - A legitimate return e-mail and a physical postal address
> - A clear and conspicuous notice of the recipient's opportunity to opt-out or decline to receive any future messages
> - Opt out mechanism active for at least 30 days after the transmission of the message
> - Clear and conspicuous notice that the message is an advertisement or solicitation

The penalties for violating the CAN-SPAM Act rules vary. They depend on the nature and severity of the violation and include monetary fines and imprisonment up to a maximum of five years. However, unlike the do-not-call and do-not-fax rules, there is no specific private right of action for consumers to pursue e-mail violations.

Marketing and Advertising

Successful real estate businesses pay careful attention to advertising and marketing the firm. Typically, the marketing and advertising effort is done through use of television, radio, Internet websites, and printed pieces such as company brochures, property flyers, newspapers, and real estate magazines.

Real estate companies need to be careful when advertising their services and the property they are selling. They need to be aware of both the legal and ethical restrictions on advertising to avoid liability. Real estate advertising is regulated in any medium, including, but not limited to, newspapers, flyers, business cards, e-mails, faxes, radio, and television.

Advertising Guidelines

Real estate advertising is regulated by state and federal agencies that expect real estate companies to be truthful when advertising property or services. Legally, licensees may be held liable for fraud, intentional misrepresentation, or negligent misrepresentation if they make material false statements or material omissions in any medium of advertising.

Advertising guidelines help real estate agents avoid penalties and possible suspension or loss of license. Avoid any advertising in which the advertisement can be interpreted a number of different ways. Avoid half-truths, inflated claims, and ambiguous or superlative terms. Example: Both the phrases "Fast Loans" and "Low Rates" are ambiguous because they do not explain how fast is fast and how low is low.

Name and License Status

A real estate broker or firm must disclose its **license status** in all advertising. Anytime a broker advertises real estate services, a term such as broker, agent, or licensee (or the abbreviations bro. or agt.) must be included in the advertisement. This requirement applies to all real estate licensees, both brokers and salespeople.

A real estate licensee must disclose his or her **eight-digit license identification** number on all solicitation materials and on real property purchase agreements when acting as an agent in those transactions. [B&P Code §10140.6 & Reg. 2773]. However, if the solicitation materials also include the name the salesperson's employing broker, the license number of the employing broker does not need to be included on the solicitation materials. **Solicitation materials** include business cards, stationery, websites owned or controlled by the licensee, advertising fliers, and other promotional materials designed to solicit a professional relationship between the licensee and a consumer. Solicitation material does not include promotional materials (e.g., refrigerator magnets), advertisements in print or electronic media (e.g., radio, cinema and television ads, and the opening section of streaming video and audio), and "For Sale" signs.

Real estate agents may use the term "free" and similar terms in their advertising—provided that all terms governing availability of the offered product or service are clearly disclosed at the same time. It is not unethical or illegal for real estate agents to offer premiums or prizes to induce sellers and buyers to do business with them. A real estate licensee may not advertise an illegal real estate lottery.

When mortgage loan brokers advertise on the radio or television or in printed ads, they must include the license under which the loan would be made or arranged. In addition, every licensed real estate broker must display his or her own eight-digit CalBRE license number on all advertisements soliciting borrowers. The following statements show the correct way to advertise.

Correct Advertising

Real estate broker, California Bureau of Real Estate, License #

California Bureau of Real Estate, Real Estate Broker, License #

Use of Words

Real estate ads should not have words that state or imply a preference or limitation with regard to race, color, religion, handicap, sex, familial status, or national origin. Some words are clearly objectionable whereas other words and phrases are neutral and will create no liability. For example, stating "housing for older persons" is acceptable providing that the property being rented is an age-qualified residence.

Advertisements should not describe the housing, residents, neighbors, or neighborhood in racial or ethnic terms (Hispanic community, racially integrated neighborhood, or Chinese businesses nearby). However, phrases such as gated complex, desirable neighborhood, or parks and schools nearby would be acceptable.

Advertisements should not contain an explicit preference for or against a specific religion. However, the ad may state houses of worship nearby. It is permissible to use secularized symbols relating to religious holidays such as Santa Claus, Easter Bunny, or St. Valentine's Day. Additionally, holiday phrases such as "Merry Christmas", "Happy Chanukah", or "Eid Mubarak" are acceptable under the federal Fair Housing Act.

Advertisements for single-family homes or apartments should not state "male only" or "female only". However, terms such as "mother-in-law suite", "bachelor apartment", and "master bedroom" are acceptable and are commonly used to physically describe housing units.

Advertisements should not discriminate based on handicap (i.e., no wheelchairs). Advertisements containing descriptions of properties (great view or walk-in closets), services or facilities (jogging trails), or neighborhoods (walk to bus stop) are acceptable. It is also appropriate to advertise accessibility features, such as a wheelchair ramp.

Advertisements may not contain limitations on the number or ages of children or state a preference for adults, couples, or singles. However, advertisements describing the properties (two bedroom, cozy, family room), services and facilities (no bicycles allowed), or neighborhoods (quiet streets) are acceptable.

Court Cases Regarding Advertising Practices

There have not been a large number of court cases that illustrate advertisements using offensive phrases.

Saunders v. General Services Corporation: This large real estate company located in Richmond, Virginia was fined $12,800 for using white models almost exclusively in the company's advertising materials.

Housing Rights Center v. Donald Sterling Corporation: In Los Angeles, California, several tenants sued their landlord, the Donald Sterling Corporation, because the landlord preferred Korean tenants over non-Korean tenants. The landlord actively discouraged other ethnic groups from moving into the apartment buildings. The lawsuit was based on the name of the apartment buildings. For example, the "Mark Wilshire Towers" was renamed the "Korean World Towers" and another building was renamed to include the word Korean. A Federal District Court told the Donald Sterling Corporation that they could not use the word Korean in the names of the buildings and had to stop demanding information about national origin in rental applications.

Penalties

A licensed real estate salesperson or broker who engages in false or misleading advertising is subject to imprisonment in the county jail for up to six months and penalties as high as $2,500 per violation, or both. A licensee may also face suspension or revocation of his or her license.

Real Estate Signs

The ability to display real estate signs has some protection under the United States and California Constitutions as a form of free speech. Even so, a city, county, or private entity, such as a homeowners' association, may regulate the size of signs and how they are displayed.

Sign Regulations

- A city or county may ban all signs on publicly owned property.
- A city or county cannot ban signs on privately owned property.
- A city or county may impose reasonable restrictions on the time, place, and manner of displaying signs regardless of whether it is on privately or publicly owned property.

In fact, private real estate signs may be banned completely from public property. However, a homeowners' association or CC&Rs cannot prohibit private owners from displaying real estate signs on their own property. The signs must be reasonably located, in plain view of the public, of reasonable dimensions and design, and used to advertise the property for sale or lease or to advertise directions to the property. The real estate sign may include the owner's name or the agent's name, along with address and telephone number.

Joining Trade and Professional Organizations

A **trade association** is a voluntary nonprofit organization of independent and competing business units engaged in the same industry or trade, formed to help solve industry problems, promote progress, and enhance service.

A **real estate board** or association is made up of members who share an interest in the business of real estate. Usually, members who join a local association of realtors automatically become members of the California Association of REALTORS® (C.A.R.) and the National Association of REALTORS® (NAR). C.A.R. performs the same function as NAR, but on the state level. The purpose of a real estate association is to bring together people in the real estate business, encourage professional conduct, protect the public from irresponsible licensees, and do anything in its power to upgrade the reputation and dignity of the real estate business.

A member of NAR is known as a **REALTOR®** and must follow NAR's rules and the Code of Ethics. **Ethic**s is a set of principles or values by which an individual guides his or her own behavior and judges that of others. The professional behavior set forth in real estate law is a course that a licensee must follow. By observing the code of ethics, members of local, state, and national trade associations promote **goodwill** and harmony, and further the interests of the real estate industry as well as the public.

You can review a copy of the NAR Code of Ethics at www.realtor.org.

Major Real Estate-related Trade Associations

- **Association of Commercial Real Estate (ACRE)**
  PO Box 1437
  Fair Oaks, CA 95628
  www.acre.org

- **California Association of Business Brokers**
  4747 N. First Street, Suite 140
  Fresno, CA 93726
  www.cabb.org

- **California Association of Community Managers, Inc.**
  23461 South Pointe Drive, Suite 200
  Laguna Hills, CA 92653
  www.cacm.org

- **California Association of Mortgage Professionals**
  1022 G Street
  Sacramento, CA 95814
  www.thecampsite.org

- **California Association of REALTORS®**
  525 South Virgil Avenue
  Los Angeles, CA 90020
  www.car.org

- **California Building Industry Association**
  1215 K Street, Suite 1200
  Sacramento, CA 95814
  www.cbia.org

- **California Mortgage Association**
  2520 Venture Oaks Way, Suite 150
  Sacramento, CA 95833
  www.californiamortgageassociation.com

- **California Mortgage Bankers Association**
  555 Capitol Mall, Suite 440
  Sacramento, CA 95814
  www.cmba.com

FAIR HOUSING LAWS

As the most populous state in the nation, it is not surprising that California is also the most culturally diverse. In fact, it has been multicultural since its beginning. California's continual attraction has brought an ever-increasing population growth of immigrants including minorities. Home ownership has always represented prosperity and the American way of life. Minorities account for over 40% of first-time homebuyers; therefore, it is good business for real estate agents to help everyone obtain the goal of home ownership.

Decent, safe, affordable housing is the goal of fair housing laws. Although much progress has been made, housing discrimination still affects people of all races, ethnicities, national origins, and religions. Women, people with disabilities, and families with children may also face barriers to their fair housing rights.

Real estate licensees must not only be aware of federal and state fair housing laws and issues, but must also apply this knowledge daily. By learning the fair housing laws, including advertising guidelines, your job will be made easier.

Federal Laws

1866 Civil Rights Act

This federal law prohibits discrimination based on race in all property transactions. However, it was basically ignored until 1968.

1968 U.S. Supreme Court Case of Jones v. Mayer

Jones v. Mayer prohibits discrimination based on race by upholding the 1866 Civil Rights Act and the 13th Amendment to the U.S. Constitution prohibiting slavery.

Fair Housing Act

Title VIII of the Civil Rights Act of 1968 and the Fair Housing Amendments Act of 1988, taken together, constitute the **Fair Housing Act**. In leasing or selling residential property, the Civil Rights Act of 1968 expanded the definition of discrimination to include not only race, but color, religion, sex, and national origin. The Fair Housing Amendments Act of 1988 further broadened the definition to include handicap status and familial status.

The Fair Housing Act requires businesses, such as real estate brokers and real estate lenders, to display the **Equal Housing Opportunity Poster** that depicts the equal housing logo. A copy of the poster is available from HUD or from one of various commercial vendors. Failure to display the poster at all or to display the most recent version can be used as prima facie evidence of discrimination by someone alleging that a brokerage has violated the Fair Housing Act. [Title 24, Part 110].

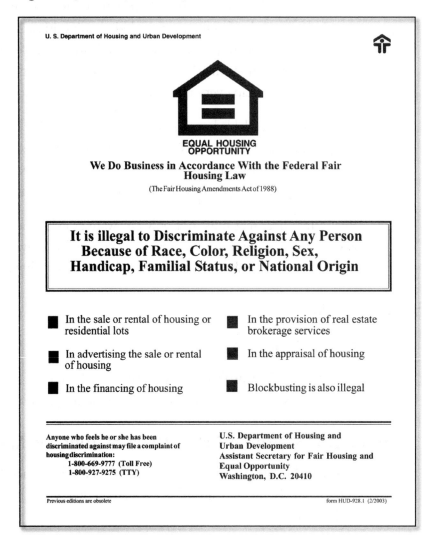

Specifically, the Fair Housing Act provides protection against the following discriminatory housing practices if they are based on race, sex, religion, color, handicap, familial status, or national origin.

Actions Prohibited by the Fair Housing Act

- Refusing to rent housing
- Refusing to sell housing
- Treating applicants differently from one another for housing
- Treating residents differently from one another in connection with terms and conditions

- Advertising a discriminatory housing preference or limitation
- Providing false information about the availability of housing
- Harassing, coercing, or intimidating people from enjoying or exercising their rights under the act
- Blockbusting: persuading an owner to sell or rent housing by saying that people of a particular race, religion, etc., are moving into the neighborhood
- Imposing different loan terms for purchasing, constructing, improving, repairing, or maintaining a residence
- Denying use of, or participation in, real estate services such as brokers' organizations or multiple-listing services

Protection for People with Disabilities

The **Americans with Disabilities Act** (ADA) protects anyone with a handicap and includes mental illness, AIDS, blindness, hearing impairment, mental retardation, and mobility impairment. A handicap is defined as any physical or mental impairment that substantially limits one or more major life activities; having a record of such an impairment; or being regarded as having such an impairment.

Housing for Older Persons

In response to the concerns of senior citizens residing in retirement communities, Congress provided exemptions for housing for older persons, which meets certain criteria.

Senior Citizen Housing Exemptions

- The housing is provided under a state or federal program specifically designed and operated to assist the elderly.
- The housing is intended for and solely occupied by people 62 years or older.
- The housing is intended and operated for occupancy by at least one person 55 years or older in each unit.
- 80% of the units are occupied by at least one person 55 years or older.
- The housing has significant facilities and services to meet the physical or social needs of older persons.
- The policies and procedures demonstrate the intent to provide housing for persons 55 years or older.

Federal Policy on Real Estate Advertising

The Federal Fair Housing Law states in part "... it shall be unlawful to make, print, or publish, or cause to be made, printed, or published any notice, statement, or advertisement, with respect to the sale or rental of a dwelling that indicates any preference, limitation, or discrimination based on race, color, religion, sex, handicap, familial status, or national origin, or any intention to make any such preference, limitation or discrimination."

All advertising media, advertising agencies, and other persons who use advertising with respect to the sale, rental, or financing of dwellings are required to take care that their words, phrases, symbols, and visual aids do not signal a prohibited preference or limitation.

All residential real estate advertising should contain the equal housing opportunity logotype and slogan. The logotype should be sufficiently large or visible to be noticed and understood. When the size of the logotype is so small that the facial features (ethnicities) of the people are not clearly distinguishable, then it is too small. The logotype should be a clear sign or symbol of welcome to all potentially qualified buyers or renters regardless of race, color, etc.

Human models in photographs, drawings, or other graphic techniques may not be used to indicate exclusiveness because of race, color, religion, sex, handicap, familial status, or national origin. If models are used in display advertising campaigns, they should be clearly definable as reasonable representation of majority and minority groups in the metropolitan area, both sexes and—when appropriate—families with children. Models, if used, should portray persons in an equal social setting and indicate to the public that the housing is open to all without regard to race, color, religion, sex, handicap, familial status, or national origin, and is not for the exclusive use of one such group.

Use of the HUD advertising criteria will be considered by the HUD General Counsel in deciding if there is reasonable cause to believe that the Fair Housing Act has been violated.

Enforcement of the Fair Housing Act

Any complaints must be filed with the Department of Housing and Urban Development (HUD). The Fair Housing Act gives HUD the authority to hold administrative hearings unless one of the parties elects to have the case heard in U.S. District Court and to issue subpoenas. The Administrative Law Judge in these proceedings can issue an order for relief, including actual damages, injunctions, or other equitable relief and penalties.

The penalties are less for a first violation and more for the third violation and those thereafter. The penalties are paid to the federal government. The damage payments go to the proven victims.

The act adds criminal penalties of fines and imprisonment as sanctions against people who willfully fail to give information and evidence or willfully give false information in a fair-housing investigation or proceeding.

California Laws

California has enacted several laws and regulations to complement the Federal Fair Housing laws. However, California includes other protected classes to complement the protections of the federal law.

Protected Class	Federal Fair Housing Protections	California Fair Housing Protections
Race	X	X
Color	X	X
National Origin	X	X
Religion	X	X
Sex	X	X
Disability	X	X
Familial Status	X	X
Age		X
Ancestry		X
Genetic Information		X
Marital Status		X
Medical Condition		X
Sexual Orientation		X
Source of Income		X

California Fair Employment and Housing Act

The **California Fair Employment and Housing Act** (FEHA) is derived from an earlier law (**Rumford Act**) that dealt specifically with prohibiting discrimination in the sale, rental, or financing of practically all types of housing. Currently, FEHA covers both housing and employment discrimination.

The protections under FEHA are broader than the federal law because FEHA applies to certain kinds of discrimination that are not covered by federal law. FEHA provides protection from harassment or discrimination in housing based on race, color, religion, sex, national origin, disability, familial status, age, ancestry, marital status, sexual orientation, medical condition, or source of income.

Violations are reported to the state Department of Fair Employment and Housing.

Unruh Civil Rights Act

The **Unruh Civil Rights Act** (enacted in 1959) covers illegal discrimination in all business establishments—including real estate companies. The act specifically outlaws discrimination in housing and public accommodations based on sex, race, color, religion, ancestry, national origin, disability, medical condition, marital status, or sexual orientation. [C.C. §51(b)]. It is particularly important for real estate licensees to be aware of the discriminatory practices of steering, blockbusting, and redlining. **Steering** is the illegal practice of only showing buyers property in certain areas. **Blockbusting**, or causing **panic selling**, is the illegal practice of telling people that property values in a neighborhood will decline because of a specific event, such as the purchase of homes by minorities. **Redlining** is the illegal use of a property's location to deny financing.

Important Provisions in the Unruh Act

§ 51   This is the primary provision of the law stating that business establishments cannot discriminate based on certain categories.

§ 51.2   Business establishments cannot discriminate in the sale or rental of housing based upon age, with the exception of senior housing (62 or older).

§ 51.8   Prohibits a franchisor from discrimination in the granting of franchises. In effect, it prohibits the equivalent of redlining in the granting of franchises just as the law prohibits redlining in other areas of the real estate business.

§ 53   Outlaws restrictive racial covenants and other covenants that attempt to bar the transfer of real property based on anything that would constitute discrimination under §51.

Housing Financial Discrimination Act

The **Housing Financial Discrimination Act** (Holden Act) prohibits all financial institutions from discriminating in real estate loan approvals based on the geographic location, the neighborhood, or any other characteristic of the property. In particular, redlining—the practice of disapproving real estate loans in economically or physically blighted areas—is forbidden unless it can be proved to be based on sound business practice. Violations may be reported to the state Secretary for Business and Transportation, who must act on the complaint within 30 days.

California Civil Code (Section 54-55.1)

This section of the Civil Code prohibits discrimination in the rental, leasing, or sale of housing accommodations to the blind, visually handicapped, deaf, or otherwise physically disabled. It also precludes restrictions on seeing-eye dogs and signal dogs from no pet clauses.

Commissioner's Regulations

The California Real Estate Commissioner has made it very clear that a person's real estate license will be restricted, suspended, or revoked for any violation of the fair housing laws. The Commissioner regulates all aspects of the real estate transaction from prospecting for listings through the closing of the transaction. In fact, every conceivable activity is regulated.

Activities Prohibited by Regulation 2780

- Refusing to list and show properties to selected people
- Processing some applications more slowly than others
- Stating to some people that property is not available when it is
- Using special codes on applications
- Actively discouraging other licensees from working with minorities
- Charging more for the cleaning or security deposit to some applicants
- Assisting other licensees to discriminate

Regulation 2781 Prohibits Blockbusting

Licensees are prohibited from creating fear, alarm, or transmitting written or oral warnings regarding the present or prospective entry of one or more persons of another race, color, sex, religion, ancestry, marital status, or national origin into an area or neighborhood.

SUMMARY

A real estate brokerage business consists of a broker who may employ one or more salespeople or other brokers. The salespeople (or brokers) are considered employees of the broker. However, for tax purposes, they are considered self-employed. The broker-officer relationship enables a brokerage to be incorporated. A brokerage may be a **sole proprietorship**, a **partnership**, a **corporation**, or a **limited liability company** (LLC).

The modern real estate brokerage office is constantly changing as a result of the advances in technology. Real estate salespeople and brokers are no longer restricted to working in the office. With the advances of technology, new laws are created to protect consumers. Some of these laws involve CAN-SPAM and do-not-call lists.

Professional conduct is important in maintaining a brokerage's reputation. There are real estate license laws and regulations that govern the professional conduct of brokers and salespeople. Many real estate brokerages are members of professional real estate organizations and follow their ethical standards.

Trust fund handling is regulated by real estate law. Trust funds cannot be commingled with funds belonging to the broker. However, a broker may keep up to $200 of personal funds in the trust fund account to pay for bank charges or service fees related to the trust account.

Real estate is also regulated by the fair housing laws. Federal and state laws prohibit discrimination in housing and business establishments. The Civil Rights Act of 1968 and 1988 amendments are federal laws that prohibit housing discrimination. California has two anti-discrimination laws: the Unruh Civil Rights Act and the California Fair Housing Act (Rumford Act).

UNIT 13 REVIEW

◗ Matching Exercise

Instructions: Write the letter of the matching term on the blank line before its definition.
Answers immediately follow the Multiple Choice Questions.

Terms

A. Americans with
  Disabilities Act

B. blockbusting

C. brokerage

D. California Fair
  Employment and
  Housing Act

E. CAN-SPAM laws

F. cold calling

G. commercial e-mail
  message

H. commission

I. commingle

J. company dollar

K. corporation

L. DBA

M. desk cost

N. do-not-call

O. employee

P. ethics

Q. fictitious business name

R. Housing Financial
  Discrimination Act

S. independent contractor

T. joint and several
  liability

U. *Jones v. Mayer*

V. limited liability
  company

W. partnership

X. prospecting

Y. redlining

Z. S corporation

AA. sole proprietorship

BB. steering

CC. trust funds

DD. Unruh Civil Rights
  Act

Definitions

1. _____ Money received by a broker to be used in a real estate transaction.

2. _____ Any electronic mail message whose primary purpose is the commercial
advertisement or promotion of a commercial product or service.

3. _____ Making unsolicited calls to unknown people to get new business.

4. _____ A legal term used in reference to a debt or a judgment for negligence,
in which each debtor or each judgment defendant is responsible for the
entire amount of the debt or judgment.

5. _____ A legal entity whose rights in business are similar to that of an individual.

6. _____ Business name that does not include the last name of the owner.

7. _____ A case prohibiting racial discrimination by upholding the 1866 Civil
Rights Act and the 13th Amendment to the U.S. Constitution.

8. _____ A set of principles or values by which an individual guides his or her own behavior and judges that of others.

9. _____ The process of identifying potential customers.

10. _____ An alternative business entity that has characteristics of both corporations and limited partnerships.

11. _____ Federal and state regulations regarding unsolicited phone calls.

12. _____ State law that prohibits discrimination by businesses.

13. _____ A person who is hired to do work for another person but who is not an employee of that person.

14. _____ The illegal use of a property's location to deny financing.

15. _____ A fee for services rendered usually based on a certain percentage of the sales price of a property.

16. _____ The amount a broker has left after all commissions have been paid.

17. _____ A business that is owned and operated by one person.

18. _____ State law that prohibits discrimination in the sale, rental or financing of practically all types of housing.

19. _____ Profitability measure calculated by dividing the total operating expenses of the firm by the number of licensed sales associates.

20. _____ Someone who is under the control and direction of a broker.

21. _____ The illegal practice of telling people that property values in a neighborhood will decline because minorities purchase the homes.

22. _____ A corporation that operates like a corporation but is treated like a partnership for tax purposes.

23. _____ Federal and state law regulating commercial e-mail messages.

24. _____ Federal law passed in 1990 that prohibits discrimination against individuals with disabilities.

25. _____ Another name for a fictitious business or trade name.

Multiple Choice Questions

Instructions: Circle your response and then check your response with the Answer Key that immediately follows the Multiple Choice Questions.

1. Which statement is correct regarding a real estate brokerage business?

  a. A real estate broker may open a real estate brokerage in his or her name.

  b. The Real Estate Commissioner does not allow a fictitious business name to be used for a real estate brokerage.

  c. The broker may have only one office.

  d. The ownership of the brokerage must be as a corporation.

2. All of the following businesses can get a California real estate broker license, except a(n):

  a. sole proprietorship.

  b. partnership.

  c. corporation.

  d. S corporation.

3. Which of the following business entities would be subject to double taxation?

  a. S corporation

  b. Limited liability company

  c. Partnership

  d. Corporation

4. The amount a broker has left after all commissions have been paid is called the:

  a. desk cost.

  b. profit.

  c. company dollar.

  d. brokerage cost.

5. Which of the following statements is incorrect?

  a. The real estate license law considers a licensed salesperson an employee of the broker.

  b. For federal income tax purposes, the salesperson is considered an employee.

  c. Except for purposes of supervision under the license law, a salesperson is self-employed.

  d. The broker must pay workers' compensation for both clerical workers and sales associates.

6. Which of the following statements is correct regarding the basic tests used to determine statutory nonemployee status?

    a. The salesperson must have a valid California real estate license.

    b. The salesperson must be compensated on the basis of the number of sales closed and commissions earned—not on the basis of the number of hours worked.

    c. There must be a written contract between the employing broker and the salesperson specifying that the salesperson will not be treated as an employee for both federal and California tax purposes.

    d. All of the statements are correct.

7. Which statement is incorrect regarding the broker/salesperson employment agreement?

    a. The real estate law requires that every broker must have a written agreement with each of his or her salespeople.

    b. The employment agreement must be on a form approved by the Commissioner.

    c. Both parties must sign the employment agreement.

    d. After termination of employment, both broker and salesperson must keep copies of it for three years.

8. Even though sales associates are considered self-employed for federal and state income tax purposes, a broker must provide Workers' Compensation insurance for:

    a. all clerical workers.

    b. all sales associates.

    c. both (a) and (b).

    d. neither (a) nor (b).

9. When a salesperson transfers his or her license to another broker, the listings obtained by the salesperson:

    a. may be taken to the new broker.

    b. will be divided evenly between the old and new broker.

    c. will remain with the original broker.

    d. belong to the salesperson who may decide how to divide them.

10. Ben just took a listing on a three-bedroom fixer-upper home located in an area with very good schools. Although it is a mixed neighborhood, it is primarily Malaysian. He's eager to sell the home and wrote the following ads. Which of the ads best follows acceptable advertising guidelines?

    a. "This is the best home in the neighborhood in a good school district."

    b. "Nice fixer, located by parks and good schools with three-bedrooms for the family."

    c. "Clean, bright, and move-in ready for the right family."

    d. "Beautiful home near parks, looking for Malaysian family."

11. A commercial e-mail message is an e-mail sent to:

    a. facilitate or confirm an existing commercial transaction.

    b. give notice about product updates or upgrades.

    c. provide notice about certain changes in a subscription, membership, account, or loan.

    d. offer the real estate agent's services to an unknown person.

12. Which of the following items must be included in a commercial e-mail message?

    a. Clear and conspicuous identification that the message is an advertisement or solicitation

    b. Valid and conspicuous physical postal address of the sender

    c. Clear and conspicuous notice that the recipient may opt out of further commercial e-mail messages from the sender

    d. All of the above

13. Under the do-not-call rules, when may a real estate licensee make cold calls?

    a. Only between 8:00 a.m. and 9:00 p.m.

    b. Never

    c. Anytime

    d. Only between 9:00 a.m. and 6:00 p.m.

14. Which of the following statements regarding advertising is correct?

    a. A real estate broker or firm must disclose its licensed status in all advertising.

    b. Anytime a broker advertises real estate services, a term such as broker, agent, licensee (or the abbreviations bro. or agt.) must be included in the advertisement.

    c. A salesperson may not use his or her name and telephone number in an advertisement without including the broker's name.

    d. All of the statements are correct.

15. Real estate ads should not have words that state or imply a preference with regard to race, color, religion, handicap, sex, familial status, or national origin. Of the following phrases, which would be unacceptable?

    a. Gated community

    b. Parks nearby

    c. No Scientologists or Hare Krishnas

    d. Houses of worship nearby

16. Which of the following statements is incorrect regarding real estate signs?
    a. A homeowners' association can prohibit private owners from displaying real estate signs on their own property.
    b. A city or county may ban all signs on publicly owned property.
    c. A city or county cannot completely ban signs on privately owned property.
    d. A city or county may impose reasonable restrictions on the time, place, and manner of displaying signs regardless of whether it is on privately or publicly owned property.

17. Which of the following would not be considered trust funds?
    a. Cash
    b. Check
    c. Commission
    d. Personal note made payable to the seller

18. A broker may keep up to _____ of personal funds in the trust fund account to pay for bank charges or service fees related to the trust account.
    a. $100
    b. $200
    c. $300
    d. $400

19. The illegal practice of telling people that property values in a neighborhood will decline because of a specific event, such as the purchase of homes by minorities is called:
    a. blockbusting.
    b. steering.
    c. redlining.
    d. panicking.

20. The California law that prohibits discrimination in the sale, rental or financing of practically all types of housing is called the:
    a. Holden Act.
    b. Housing Financial Discrimination Act.
    c. California Fair Employment and Housing Act.
    d. Unruh Civil Rights Act.

UNIT 13 ANSWER KEY

Answers – Matching

1. CC	6. Q	11. N	16. J	21. B
2. G	7. U	12. DD	17. AA	22. Z
3. F	8. P	13. S	18. D	23. E
4. T	9. X	14. Y	19. M	24. A
5. K	10. V	15. H	20. O	25. L

Answers – Multiple Choice

1. **(a)** A real estate broker may open a real estate brokerage in his or her name, or a fictitious business name. The broker may have multiple locations and take ownership in a variety of ways, such as sole proprietorship, partnership, corporation, or limited liability company (LLC). [Definition of Brokerage]

2. **(b)** The Bureau of Real Estate does not issue real estate partnership licenses. [Definition of Brokerage]

3. **(d)** Corporations are subject to double taxation. [Definition of Brokerage]

4. **(c)** The company dollar is the amount a broker has left after all commissions have been paid. The desk cost shows how much each sales associate must earn to cover expenses. It is calculated by dividing the total operating expenses of the firm by the number of licensed sales associates. [Definition of Brokerage]

5. **(b)** The license law considers a salesperson an employee, For income tax purposes, the IRS classifies real estate licensees as statutory nonemployees. [Definition of Brokerage]

6. **(d)** The three answers correctly list the three requirements. [Definition of Brokerage]

7. **(b)** The employment agreement does not have to be on a form approved by the Real Estate Commissioner. [Definition of Brokerage]

8. **(c)** Due to their employee status, a broker must provide workers compensation coverage to all sales associates as well as any non-licensee employees of the firm. [Definition of Brokerage]

9. **(c)** The sales associates are employees of the broker, and as we have learned, all listing contracts are between the seller and the broker, not the sales associate who took the listing. When a salesperson leaves the employ of a particular broker, any listings he or she has will remain with that broker. [Activities of a Real Estate Brokerage]

10. **(b)** Choices (a), (c), and (d) used half-truths, inflated claims, and ambiguous or superlative terms. [Marketing & Advertising]

11. **(d)** A commercial e-mail message is "any electronic mail message, the primary purpose of which is the commercial advertisement or promotion of a commercial product or service." E-mails sent as part of an ongoing commercial transaction, called transactional e-mail messages, are excluded from the Act. [Prospecting]

12. **(d)** All must be included in a commercial e-mail. [Prospecting]

13. **(a)** Under the Do Not Call rules, real estate licensees or unlicensed assistants may make cold calls provided that the calls are only made between 8:00 a.m. and 9:00 p.m. [Prospecting]

14. **(d)** All statements are correct: Choice (a) – B&P Code Section 10140.5. Choice (b) – B&P 10140.6 & Reg. 2770.1. Choice (c) – Reg. 2770. [Marketing & Advertising]

15. **(c)** Singling out one faith to the exclusion of others is discriminatory. [Marketing & Advertising]

16. **(a)** A homeowners' association or CC&Rs cannot prohibit private owners from displaying real estate signs on their own property. The signs must be reasonably located, in plain view of the public, of reasonable dimensions and design, and used to advertise the property for sale or lease, or to advertise directions to the property. [Marketing & Advertising]

17. **(c)** Trust funds are money, or anything of value, received from the buyer by an agent on behalf of a seller, such as: cash, a check used as a deposit for a purchase, or a personal note made payable to the seller. Do not confuse other monies such as commissions, general operating funds, and rents and deposits from broker-owned real estate with trust funds. [Handling Trust Funds]

18. **(b)** Only $200 of personal funds may be in the trust fund account. [Handling Trust Funds]

19. **(a)** Blockbusting or panic selling is illegal. Steering is the illegal practice of showing clients property in only certain areas. Redlining is the illegal use of a property's location to deny financing. [Fair Housing]

20. **(c)** The California Fair Employment and Housing Act (Rumford Act) prohibits discrimination in the sale, rental or financing of housing. Housing Financial Discrimination Act (Holden Act) prohibits discrimination in real estate lending. The Unruh Civil Rights Act covers discrimination in business. [Fair Housing]

Real Estate Specialization

Unit 14

INTRODUCTION

Usually the majority of real estate transactions take place in the residential market. Most licensees start out in real estate offices that specialize in selling homes, spending most of their time prospecting for listings on homes and buyers to buy them. After a time, the licensee may decide to specialize and become an expert in only one particular area of real estate, such as appraisal, property management, mortgage brokerage, commercial real estate, mobile-home brokerage, or business opportunities.

We have discussed lending, appraisal, development, and residential sales in other parts of this text. This Unit examines the detailed special knowledge and capability required in mobilehome sales, business opportunity brokerage, investment, property management, probate sales, and revitalization.

Learning Objectives

After completing this Unit, you should be able to:

11E   recall areas of real estate in which licensees may specialize.

MOBILEHOME BROKERAGE

Due to the increased need for affordable housing and the relative low cost to build, manufactured housing has become a major source of the residential housing supply. The United States Census Bureau reports that mobilehomes make up 7% of the total housing stock.

A mobilehome is a factory-built home manufactured prior to June 15, 1976.

What is the difference between a mobilehome and a manufactured home? A **mobilehome** is a factory-built home manufactured prior to June 15, 1976, constructed on a chassis and wheels, and designed for permanent or semi-permanent attachment to land. In the past, mobilehomes were known as trailers and were used mainly as a second, traveling home. **Manufactured homes** are homes built in a factory after June 15, 1976 and must conform to the federal Manufactured Home Construction and Safety Standards (HUD code). The federal standards regulate manufactured housing design and construction, strength and durability, transportability, fire resistance, energy efficiency, and quality. The HUD Code also sets performance standards for the heating, plumbing, air conditioning, thermal, and electrical systems of the home. It is the only federally regulated national building code. Each home or segment of a home is labeled with a red tag that is the manufacturer's guarantee the home was built to conform to the HUD code. Manufactured homes are built on a non-removable steel chassis and transported to the building site on their own wheels.

Today many manufactured homes are attached to a permanent foundation, and are considered real property.

Today many manufactured homes are attached to a permanent foundation, and are considered real property. Once transported from the factory to a permanent lot, very few are ever moved again. They are built in 8-, 10- and 12-foot widths, and up to 60 feet in length, making them expensive and difficult to move once they are put in place. When two or more sections are put together side by side, the result is an extra-large residence. Onsite additions, such as garages, decks and porches, often add to the attractiveness of manufactured homes and must be built to local building codes.

For the purpose of our discussion, we will refer to both mobilehomes and manufactured homes as mobilehomes.

Mobilehomes as Personal or Real Property

Because mobilehomes are manufactured in a factory, they are personal property, and remain personal property unless they have been converted into real property. The Department of Housing and Community Development (HCD) registers and licenses mobilehomes, and must be notified by anyone acquiring or releasing an interest in mobilehomes within 10 days after a sale. A copy of the registration will then be provided to all lien holders. Both the buyer and seller must sign a certificate of title. A **certificate of title** transfers ownership of a mobilehome owned as personal property. If the mobilehome is real property, a **clearance of tax liability** must be signed by the county tax collector.

A mobilehome is considered real property when it is attached to a permanent foundation.

Transforming a Mobilehome to Real Property

1. A building permit must be acquired.

2. The mobilehome must be set on a permanent foundation.

3. A recorded document must be filed stating that the mobilehome has been placed on a foundation. This typically is done by the local building department.

4. A certificate of occupancy must be obtained.

After transforming a mobilehome to real property, the Department of Housing and Community Development (HCD) must cancel the registration. Then, ownership of the mobilehome is recorded with the county recorder and taxed as real property.

If an owner wants to move a mobilehome after it has become real property, anyone who has an interest in it must approve. Thirty days before moving it, the owner must notify the HCD as well as the local tax assessor. The mobilehome becomes personal property once again and returns to the unsecured property tax rolls after the owner obtains a new registration or transportation permit from the HCD or DMV.

Mobilehome Parks

A **mobilehome park** is any area or tract of land where two or more mobilehome lots are rented or leased or held out for rent or lease to accommodate manufactured homes or mobilehomes used for human habitation.

The rental of lots in a mobilehome park is regulated by the state Department of Housing and Community Development (HCD).

Failure on the part of a real estate agent to become familiar with the rules and regulations of a mobilehome park could result in a cancelled sale, bad feelings, or even a lawsuit. The mobilehome's desirability to a buyer may be affected by the rules of the park. The real estate agent must disclose all known facts.

For example, many parks have a minimum age requirement that at least one of the buyers must be age 55 or over. There may be strict rules about animals, where they may be kept, and how they must be supervised when outside. Most mobilehome parks require buyers to sign a copy of the rules and agree to comply with them. At the time, the licensee accepts the mobilehome listing, a copy of the park's rules and regulations should be obtained.

Whenever a buyer takes title to a mobilehome, a new rental agreement must be negotiated with the owner of the mobilehome park. The new tenant (mobilehome owner) of the park must be approved by the owner and must agree to all terms of the park's rules and regulations.

Mobilehome Sales by Real Estate Agents

Only licensed mobilehome dealers can sell new mobilehomes. However, a person with a valid real estate broker or sales license may sell mobilehomes, which have been registered with HCD and placed in an established mobilehome park or have been installed on a foundation system. Additionally, real estate licensees can sell or lease a mobilehome if it is on a lot where its presence has been authorized for a total and uninterrupted period of at least one year. [B&P Code 10131.6(a)]

Real estate licensees must learn and follow the laws pertaining to selling mobilehomes that are personal property. They must be sure that the certificate of ownership or certificate of title of the mobilehome is endorsed, dated, and delivered to the new owner. It is unlawful for any real estate licensee to advertise or represent a mobilehome as a new mobilehome or that it can be transported on California highways if the mobilehome does not meet all of the requirements of Vehicle Code §24000. A real estate licensee must stop advertising that a mobilehome is for sale or lease within 48 hours after receiving notice that the mobilehome is no longer available.

Review - Approved Activities for Licensees

- Sales of new mobilehomes are restricted to specially licensed dealers.
- A real estate agent may sell any mobilehome that has been classified as real property. It may be listed and sold in the same manner as any other residence.
- A real estate agent may sell any mobilehome that has been registered with HCD and placed in an established mobilehome park.
- All sales must be reported by the licensee to the Department of Housing and Community Development (HCD) within 10 days.

Marketing Mobilehomes

The mobilehome park cannot prohibit For Sale signs within the mobilehome park. Mobilehomeowners, or their agents, have the right to display For Sale signs and For Rent signs if the mobilehome park management permits renting in the park.

The signs can be displayed in the window of the mobilehome on the side or front of the mobilehome facing the street. Signs can be at least 24" wide and 36" high and can state the name, address, and telephone number of the mobilehomeowners or their agents. Additionally, folders containing leaflets, which provide information on the mobilehome for sale or rent, may be included on the sign.

MANUFACTURED HOME AND MOBILEHOME:
TRANSFER DISCLOSURE STATEMENT
(C.A.R. Form MHTDS, Revised 11/10)

THIS DISCLOSURE STATEMENT CONCERNS THE MANUFACTURED HOME OR MOBILEHOME (HEREAFTER REFERRED TO AS "HOME") LOCATED AT _____ IN THE CITY OF _____ , COUNTY OF _____ , STATE OF CALIFORNIA,

DESCRIBED AS _____ .

| Year | Make | Serial #(s) | HCD Decal # or Equivalent |

THIS STATEMENT IS A DISCLOSURE OF THE CONDITION OF THE ABOVE-DESCRIBED HOME IN COMPLIANCE WITH SUBDIVISION (b) OF SECTION 1102 OF THE CIVIL CODE AND SECTIONS 18025 AND 18046 OF THE HEALTH AND SAFETY CODE AS OF _____ .
DATE

IT IS NOT A WARRANTY OF ANY KIND BY THE LAWFUL OWNER OF THE MANUFACTURED HOME OR MOBILEHOME WHO OFFERS THE HOME FOR SALE (HEREAFTER THE SELLER), OR ANY AGENT(S) REPRESENTING ANY PRINCIPAL(S) IN THIS TRANSACTION, AND IS NOT A SUBSTITUTE FOR ANY INSPECTIONS OR WARRANTIES THE PRINCIPAL(S) MAY WISH TO OBTAIN. AN "AGENT" MEANS ANY DEALER OR SALESPERSON LICENSED PURSUANT TO PART 2 (COMMENCING WITH SECTION 18000) OF THE HEALTH AND SAFETY CODE, OR A REAL ESTATE BROKER OR SALESPERSON LICENSED PURSUANT TO DIVISION 4 (COMMENCING WITH SECTION 10000) OF DIVISION 13 OF THE BUSINESS AND PROFESSIONS CODE.

I
COORDINATION WITH OTHER DISCLOSURES & INFORMATION

This Manufactured Home and Mobilehome Transfer Disclosure Statement is made pursuant to Article 1.5 (commencing with Section 1102) of Chapter 2 of Title 4 of Part 4 of Division 2 of the Civil Code. Other statutes require disclosures, or other information may be important to the prospective buyer, depending upon the details of the particular transaction (including, but not limited to, the condition of the park in which the manufactured home or mobilehome will be located; disclosures required or information provided by the Mobilehome Residency Law, Section 798 of the Civil Code et seq.; the mobilehome park rental agreement or lease; the mobilehome park rules and regulations; and park and lot inspection reports, if any, completed by the state or a local enforcement agency).

Substituted Disclosures: The following disclosures have or will be made in connection with this transfer, and are intended to satisfy the disclosure obligations of this form, where the subject matter is the same:
☐ Home inspection reports completed pursuant to the contract of sale or receipt for deposit.
☐ Additional inspection reports or disclosures: _____
_____

II
SELLER'S INFORMATION

The Seller discloses the following information with the knowledge that even though this is not a warranty, prospective buyers may rely on this information in deciding whether, and on what terms, to purchase the subject Home. Seller hereby authorizes any agent(s), as defined in Section 18046 of the Health and Safety Code, representing any principal(s) in this transaction to provide a copy of this statement to any person or entity in connection with any actual or anticipated sale of the Home.

THE FOLLOWING ARE REPRESENTATIONS MADE BY THE SELLER(S) AND ARE NOT THE REPRESENTATIONS OF THE AGENT(S), IF ANY, AS DEFINED IN SECTION 18046 OF THE HEALTH AND SAFETY CODE. THIS INFORMATION IS A DISCLOSURE AND IS NOT INTENDED TO BE PART OF ANY CONTRACT BETWEEN THE BUYER AND THE SELLER.

Seller ☐ is ☐ is not occupying the Home.

A. The subject Home includes the items checked below which are being sold with the Home:

☐ Range	☐ Wall/Window Air Conditioning	☐ Pool:
☐ Oven	☐ Sprinklers	☐ Child Resistant Barrier*
☐ Microwave	☐ Public Sewer System	☐ Pool/Spa Heater:
☐ Dishwasher	☐ Septic Tank	☐ Gas ☐ Solar ☐ Electric
☐ Trash Compactor	☐ Sump Pump	☐ Water Heater:
☐ Garbage Disposal	☐ Water Softener	☐ Gas ☐ Solar ☐ Electric
☐ Washer/Dryer Hookups	☐ Patio/Porch Decking	☐ Water Supply:
☐ Rain Gutters	☐ Porch Awning	☐ City ☐ Well ☐ Private Utility or
☐ Burglar Alarms	☐ Built-in Barbecue	Other _____

(Continued on page 2)

Buyer's Initials (_____) (_____)   Seller's Initials (_____) (_____)

MHTDS REVISED 11/10 (PAGE 1 OF 3)

| Reviewed by _____ Date _____ |

MANUFACTURED HOME TRANSFER DISCLOSURE STATEMENT (MHTDS PAGE 1 OF 3)

Home Address: _____   Date: _____

☐ Carbon Monoxide Device(s)
☐ Smoke Detector(s)
☐ Fire Alarm
☐ TV Antenna
☐ Satellite Dish
☐ Intercom
☐ Central Heating
☐ Central Air Conditioning
☐ Evaporator Cooler(s)

☐ Gazbo
☐ Security Gate(s)
☐ Garage:
☐ Attached ☐ Not Attached ☐ Carport Awning
☐ Automatic Garage Door Opener(s)*
☐ Number Remote Controls _____
☐ Private Sauna
☐ Private Hot Tub/Spa:
☐ Locking Safety Cover*

☐ Gas Supply:
☐ Utility ☐ Bottled Propane (Tank)
☐ Earthquake Resistant Bracing System
☐ Window Screens
☐ Window Security Bars
☐ Quick Release Mechanism on Bedroom Windows*

Exhaust Fan(s) in _____   220 Volt Wiring in _____   Fireplace(s) in _____
☐ Gas Starter _____   ☐ Roof(s): Type: _____   Age: _____   (approx.)
☐ Other: _____

*Installation of a listed appliance, device, or amenity is not a precondition of sale or transfer of the home. The carbon monoxide device, garage door opener, or child-resistant pool barrier may not be in compliance with the safety standards relating to, respectively, carbon monoxide device standards of Chapter 8 (commencing with Section 13260) of Part 2 of Division 12 of, automatic reversing device standards of Chapter 12.5 (commencing with Section 19890) of Part 3 of Division 13 of, or the pool safety standards of Article 2.5 (commencing with Section 115920) of Chapter 5 of Part 10 of Division 104 of, the Health and Safety Code. Window security bars may not have quick-release mechanisms in compliance with the 1995 edition of the California Building Standards Code.

Are there, to the best of your (Seller's) knowledge, any of the above that are not in operating condition? ☐Yes ☐No. If yes, then describe. (Attach additional sheets if necessary): _____

B. Are you (the Seller) aware of any significant defects/malfunctions in any of the following in connection with the Home? ☐ Yes ☐No. If yes, check appropriate space(s) below:
☐ Interior Walls, ☐ Ceilings, ☐ Floors, ☐ Exterior Walls, ☐ Insulation, ☐ Roof(s), ☐ Windows, ☐ Doors, ☐ Home Electrical Systems, ☐ Plumbing, ☐ Porch or Deck, ☐ Porch Steps & Railings, ☐ Other Steps & Railings, ☐ Porch Awning, ☐ Carport Awning, ☐ Other Awnings, ☐ Skirting, ☐ Home Foundation or Support System, ☐ Other Structural Components (Describe: _____
_____)

If any of the above is checked, explain. (Attach additional sheets if necessary.): _____
_____

C. Are you (the Seller) aware of any of the following:
1. Substances, materials, or products which may be an environmental hazard, such as, but not limited to, asbestos, formaldehyde, radon gas, lead-based paint, or chemical storage tanks on the subject home interior or exterior. . . . . ☐Yes ☐No
2. Room additions, structural modifications, or other alterations or repairs made without necessary permits. . . . . ☐Yes ☐No
3. Room additions, structural modifications, or other alterations or repairs not in compliance with applicable codes. . . . . ☐Yes ☐No
4. Any settling from slippage, sliding or problems with leveling of the home or the foundation or support system . . . . ☐Yes ☐No
5. Drainage or grading problems with the home, space or lot. . . . . ☐Yes ☐No
6. Damage to the home or accessory structures being sold with the home from fire, flood, earthquake, or landslides. . . . . ☐Yes ☐No
7. Any notices of abatement or citations against the home or accessory structures being sold with the home. . . . . ☐Yes ☐No
8. Any lawsuits by or against the seller threatening to or affecting the home or the accessory structures being sold with the home, including any lawsuits alleging any defect or deficiency in the home or accessories sold with the home. . . . . ☐Yes ☐No
9. Neighborhood noise problems or other nuisances . . . . ☐Yes ☐No
10. Any encroachment, easement, nonconforming use or violation of setback requirements with the home, accessory structures being sold with the home, or space. . . . . ☐Yes ☐No

If the answer to any of these is yes, explain. (Attach additional sheets if necessary): _____
_____

D. 1. The Seller certifies that the property, as of the close of escrow, will be in compliance with Section 13113.8 of the Health and Safety Code by having operable smoke detector(s) which are approved, listed, and installed in accordance with the State Fire Marshal's regulations and for used manufactured or mobilehomes, in compliance with Manufactured Housing Construction and Safety Act (Health and Safety Code §18029.6) as required by Department of Housing and Community Development and applicable local standards.
   2. The Seller certifies that the property, as of the close of escrow, will be in compliance with Section 19211 of the Health and Safety Code by having the water heater tank(s) braced, anchored, or strapped in place in accordance with applicable law.

Seller certifies that the information herein is true and correct to the best of the Seller's knowledge as of the date signed by the Seller.

Seller _____   Date _____

Seller _____   Date _____

MHTDS REVISED 11/10 (PAGE 2 OF 3)

Buyer's Initials (_____) (_____)

Reviewed by _____ Date _____

EQUAL HOUSING OPPORTUNITY

MANUFACTURED HOME TRANSFER DISCLOSURE STATEMENT (MHTDS PAGE 2 OF 3)
Produced with zipForm® by zipLogix 18070 Fifteen Mile Road, Fraser, Michigan 48026   www.zipLogix.com

Home Address: _____ Date: _____

III
AGENT'S INSPECTION DISCLOSURE
(To be completed only if the Seller is represented by an Agent in this transaction.)
THE UNDERSIGNED, BASED ON THE ABOVE INQUIRY OF THE SELLER(S) AS TO THE CONDITION OF THE HOME AND BASED ON A REASONABLY COMPETENT AND DILIGENT VISUAL INSPECTION OF THE ACCESSIBLE AREAS OF THE HOME IN CONJUNCTION WITH THAT INQUIRY, STATES THE FOLLOWING:

☐ See attached Agent Visual Inspection Disclosure (AVID Form)
☐ Agent notes no items for disclosure.
☐ Agent notes the following items: _____
_____
_____
_____

Agent
Representing Seller _____ By _____ Date _____
　　　　　　　　　(Please Print)　　　　　　　　　　　　　　　(Signature)

IV
AGENT'S INSPECTION DISCLOSURE
(To be completed only if the agent who has obtained the offer is other than the Agent above.)
THE UNDERSIGNED, BASED ON A REASONABLY COMPETENT AND DILIGENT VISUAL INSPECTION OF THE ACCESSIBLE AREAS OF THE HOME, STATES THE FOLLOWING:

☐ See attached Agent Visual Inspection Disclosure (AVID Form)
☐ Agent notes no items for disclosure.
☐ Agent notes the following items: _____
_____
_____
_____

Agent
Representing Buyer _____ By _____ Date _____
　　　　　　　　　(Please Print)　　　　　　　　　　　　　　　(Signature)

V
BUYER(S) AND SELLER(S) MAY WISH TO OBTAIN PROFESSIONAL ADVICE AND/OR INSPECTIONS OF THE HOME AND TO PROVIDE FOR APPROPRIATE PROVISIONS IN A CONTRACT BETWEEN THE BUYER(S) AND SELLER(S) WITH RESPECT TO ANY ADVICE/INSPECTIONS/DEFECTS.

I/WE ACKNOWLEDGE RECEIPT OF A COPY OF THIS STATEMENT.

Seller _____ Date _____　Buyer _____ Date _____

Seller _____ Date _____　Buyer _____ Date _____

Agent
Representing Seller _____　By _____ Date _____
　　　　　　　　(Please Print)　　　　　　　　　　　　(Signature)
Agent
Representing Buyer _____　By _____ Date _____
　　　　　　　　(Please Print)　　　　　　　　　　　　(Signature)

VI
SECTION 1102.3a OF THE CIVIL CODE PROVIDES A PROSPECTIVE BUYER WITH THE RIGHT TO RESCIND THE PURCHASE OF THE MANUFACTURED HOME OR MOBILEHOME FOR AT LEAST THREE DAYS AFTER DELIVERY OF THIS DISCLOSURE, IF DELIVERY OCCURS AFTER THE SIGNING OF AN OFFER TO PURCHASE. IF YOU WISH TO RESCIND THE CONTRACT, YOU MUST ACT WITHIN THE PRESCRIBED PERIOD.

A MANUFACTURED HOME OR MOBILEHOME DEALER OR A REAL ESTATE BROKER IS QUALIFIED TO PROVIDE ADVICE ON THE SALE OF A MANUFACTURED HOME OR MOBILEHOME. IF YOU DESIRE LEGAL ADVICE, CONSULT YOUR ATTORNEY.

Published and Distributed by:
REAL ESTATE BUSINESS SERVICES, INC.
a subsidiary of the California Association of REALTORS®
525 South Virgil Avenue, Los Angeles, California 90020

Reviewed by _____ Date _____

MHTDS REVISED 11/10 (PAGE 3 OF 3)
MANUFACTURED HOME TRANSFER DISCLOSURE STATEMENT (MHTDS PAGE 3 OF 3)

HOUSEBOAT LIVING

Houseboats are a common sight in Richardson Bay in Sausalito—and have been since the late 1900s. A **houseboat** is basically a barge that is designed and equipped for use as a dwelling. Initially they were used as summer retreats for wealthy San Francisco and Marin families. During the sixties,

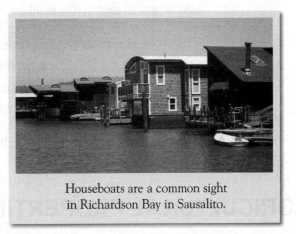

Houseboats are a common sight in Richardson Bay in Sausalito.

they became lawless floating neighborhoods running along the west shore north from Sausalito. Regulation of the houseboats increased to solve the problems of pollution and safety and now they are a colorful addition to the Tiburon shoreline. Those that are permanently attached to city utilities are considered real houses.

Houseboats range from one-to-three bedrooms. Most have just one bathroom, but a few of the more expensive homes have two or three.

TIMESHARE PROPERTIES

A **timeshare** is the common ownership of a single piece of property by an association of people with each owner having the exclusive right to

Timeshares are frequently purchased as a vacation investment.

occupy a unit for a specified period each year. Timeshares are usually for specific blocks of time per year. In addition to the one-time purchase price, timeshare owners pay an annual fee for property management and maintenance. Timeshares are usually resort-type subdivisions created with the intention of selling them to people who want a retirement home or second vacation home.

Timeshares are frequently purchased as a vacation investment because the cost of owning a good timeshare is less than renting comparable hotel accommodations year after year. Another advantage is the ability to trade vacations with other timeshare owners through exchange programs and travel to destinations all over the world.

The most common type of timeshare is a resort condominium (which can range from a studio with a partial kitchen, all the way up to a five-bedroom unit with a full kitchen and luxury amenities). Other less-common timeshare accommodations include hotel rooms, houseboats, and even motor homes.

In order to sell timeshares in California, a person must have a California real estate license.

AGRICULTURAL PROPERTIES

Agriculture is an essential part of economy of California. The economic impact of the agriculture value chain (production through distribution) in California exceeds $300 billion annually and employs over 2 million individuals.

Agricultural property is defined as property zoned for use in farming, including the raising of crops and livestock. A **farm** produces plant and animal products like grains, milk, eggs, and meat. A **ranch** is land that is used for grazing livestock. **Livestock** includes domestic animals (cattle, horses, sheep, etc.) that are used for food, breeding, or draft purposes. Farms and

Agriculture plays an important role in the economy of California.

ranches include improvements, such as structures, buildings, fixtures, fences, and water rights attached to the land.

There is a tendency for many individuals to invest in small farms, ranches, and vineyards as hobbies as is seen in the wine grape growing regions. Sometimes this is referred to as the gentleman farmer syndrome. Some buyers are looking for working farms, recreational ranches, or horse properties, while others are developers looking to buy land for subdivisions.

Regardless of the purpose, real estate licensees who specialize in agricultural and rural properties need to become familiar with the carrying capacity of the land and soils when dealing with farms and ranches. The **carrying capacity** refers to the number of animal units or tonnage of crops per acre that the land can support. In addition, a general knowledge of local farming practices, climate, hydrology, and soils would be useful when marketing agricultural properties.

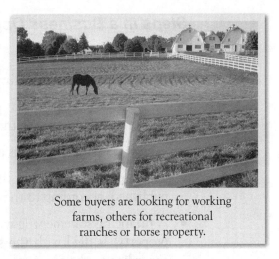

Some buyers are looking for working farms, others for recreational ranches or horse property.

BUSINESS OPPORTUNITY BROKERAGE

A **business opportunity** is any type of business that is for lease or sale. It also includes the intangible but salable asset of **goodwill**, which is the expectation of the continued patronage of an existing business. The sale of a business is considered to be the sale of personal property; and the rules about the transfer of chattels are applied. A real estate broker, as well as both buyer and seller, should be aware of the application of the bulk transfer laws on the sale of a business.

A licensee, in the course of the usual business opportunity sale, may become involved in the sale of shoe stores, bars, hotels, and bookstores. Stock, fixtures, and goodwill almost always will be included in the sale of a business. A licensee must be aware of certain legal demands, however, that might not be required in the sale of other types of non-business properties. The sale of a business opportunity may be negotiated by anyone holding a real estate license.

In dealing with the sale of a business, a real estate agent usually will be dealing with three elements: the real property or a lease, the personal property or the inventory and equipment, and the goodwill or the reputation enjoyed by the business. Each of the three elements in the sale is worth value and must be considered when listing a business opportunity.

> ### Review - Elements of the Sale of a Business
> - Lease or Real Property
> - Inventory
> - Goodwill

The sale of a business requires special knowledge and experience by a real estate agent, and the steps involved in the sale can be complicated. All sales do not include the same order of events, but the following is a general outline of the normal course of a business opportunity sale.

Steps in a Business Opportunity Sale

- The business is listed.

- A special business opportunity deposit receipt is completed when a buyer is found.

- The offer is presented to the seller by the broker for approval.

- Escrow is opened if offer is acceptable.

- Creditors are notified of the sale and a notice of intended bulk sale is published, according to the requirements of the Bulk Sales Act.

- A financing statement (a written notice of a creditor's interest in personal property) is filed with the secretary of state and/or the recorder's office, according to the requirements of the Uniform Commercial Code (UCC).

- If a liquor license is part of the sale, the required forms are filed with the Department of Alcoholic Beverage Control (ABC).

- Arrangements for the assignment or transfer of the lease are made with the landlord.

- Copies of the seller's permit and a tax clearance receipt are obtained from the Board of Equalization, according to the Sales and Use Tax Law. The buyer then is protected from liability from any unpaid sales tax that the seller might owe.

- Information about employee's salaries, benefits, and unemployment insurance tax is noted.

- An inventory is taken of stock, fixtures, and any other personal property that will be transferred by the sale and the seller executes a bill of sale, which transfers ownership of all personal property belonging to the business.

- At the close of escrow, buyer and seller receive closing statements.

Regulating the Sale of a Business Opportunity

There are certain legal requirements that must be met in the sale of a business. In order to complete the transaction, a real estate agent must understand the requirements of the Uniform Commercial Code, the Bulk Transfer Act, California Sales and Use Tax Regulations, and the Alcoholic Beverage Control Act.

Uniform Commercial Code

Whenever money has been borrowed for the sale of a business opportunity, it follows that someone has a security interest in the personal property belonging to the business. These transactions are regulated by the **Uniform Commercial Code (UCC)** Divisions 6 and 9.

Bulk Sales

Bulk sales, or the sale of a substantial part of the inventory of a business, are regulated by Division 6 of the UCC. The purpose of the Bulk Transfer Act is to protect the creditors of a person who sells a business. When a business is sold and most or all of the inventory, supplies, and other materials are transferred with the sale, public notice must be given.

Twelve business days before the transfer, notice of the sale must be filed with the county recorder, published in a local newspaper in the county where the business is located, and delivered to the county tax collector.

The above requirements give fair warning of the business inventory's sale to possible creditors. Any bulk sale that takes place without complying with the requirements of the **bulk transfer law** is considered valid between the buyer and seller but fraudulent and void against creditors. Therefore, the buyer is liable to creditors who hold valid claims based on transactions or events occurring before the bulk transfer sale.

Security Transactions in Personal Property and Fixtures

Division 9 of the Uniform Commercial Code (UCC) sets out the requirements for regulating security transactions in personal property and fixtures. The documents used are the promissory note, the security agreement, and the financing statement.

When money is borrowed, a **promissory note** is signed, just as in the financing of non-business property. The note is the evidence of the debt. At the same time, the borrower executes a security agreement that gives the lender an interest in the personal property. A **security agreement** is the document commonly used to secure a loan on personal property, much as a trust deed secures a loan on real property. The security agreement creates a lien on personal property, including fixtures. As you recall, personal property is something that is movable, and is not real property. Jewelry and bulk items—such as retail inventory, autos, and boats—are examples of personal property that might be used to secure a debt. The security agreement contains all the details of the agreement, and is the document that describes the obligation.

To protect, or perfect as it is called, the interest created by the security agreement, or prevent the security from being sold by someone else, a financing statement must be filed. The **financing statement** is merely the document used to record the debt; it is not actual evidence of the debt. By recording the financing statement, public notice of the security interest is given, and all parties are made aware of any interests in the property, much as a recorded trust deed gives public notice of a debt against a non-business property.

Once the interest created by the security agreement is perfected, the secured party's interest is protected against the debtor's other creditors. A financing statement must be filed with the secretary of state or in the county recorder's office giving public notice of the security interest created by the debt.

California Sales and Use Tax

The **Sales and Use Tax Law** protects a buyer from liability for unpaid sales tax owed by the seller. **Sales tax** is collected as a percentage of the retail sale of a product by a retailer. The owner of a retail business must obtain a **seller's permit** to collect the proper sales tax from customers and pay it to the State Board of Equalization, usually quarterly. A business owner who purchases tangible personal property for resale should obtain a **resale certificate**, so that any property purchased for resale is not subject to sales or use tax. Before assuming the ownership of a business, a buyer should obtain a copy of the seller's permit and a **tax clearance receipt** stating that the business is current on sales taxes from the State Board of Equalization.

Use tax is a tax imposed on the buyer who purchases goods from an out-of-state supplier for use in state. Sales and use tax are mutually exclusive, which means that a person will either pay sales tax or use tax, but not both.

Alcoholic Beverage Control Act

Whenever transfer of a liquor license is involved in a business opportunity sale, a buyer must not assume an automatic transfer of the liquor license. The **Department of Alcoholic Beverage Control** (ABC) issues liquor licenses and regulates the transfer of a liquor license from a seller to a buyer. A buyer must apply for the license and may be turned down for various reasons (e.g., criminal record). The cost of a liquor license varies from location to location. The fees associated with getting a liquor license usually have to do with the type of establishment and the population of the city.

> **Review - Codes and Laws Involved in the Sale of a Business**
> - Uniform Commercial Code
> - Bulk Transfer Act
> - California Sales and Use Tax Law
> - Alcoholic Beverage Control Act

California Gazette Classifieds

Public Notices

To place your ad, call 1-123-4567, ext. 8910 or Fax 1-111-2345

NOTICE OF PUBLIC SALE

NOTICE TO CREDITORS OF BULK SALE (SECS. 6104, 6105 U.C.C.) Notice is hereby given to creditors of the within named seller that a bulk sale is about to be made of the assets described below. The names and business addresses of the Seller are ABC INC. 1234 YERBA AVE., FULLERTON, CA 92800. The location in California of the chief executive office of the seller is: (If "same as above", so state) SAME AS ABOVE As listed by the seller, all other business names and addresses used by the seller within three years before the date such list was sent or delivered to the buyer are: (If "none", so state.) NONE. The names and business addresses of the buyer are TOM BANKS 12354 POPE STREET, LOS ANGELES, CA 90020. The assets to be sold are described in general as A BUSINESS INCLUDING FURNITURE, FIXTURE AND EQUIPMENT, GOODWILL, CORPORATION, AND TRADE NAME, LEASE, AND LEASEHOLD IMPROVEMENTS and are located at: 1234 YERBA AVE., FULLERTON, CA 92800. The business name used by the seller at that location is GOOD BUYS. The anticipated date of the sale/transfer is 12/28/2004 at the office of ABC Escrow, 12345 Brook Street, Westminster, CA 92600. This bulk sale IS subject to California Uniform Commercial Code Section 6106.2. If so subject, the name and address of the person with who claims may be filed is Tony Apellido. ABC Escrow, 12345 Brook Street, Westminster, CA 92600 and the last date for filing claims shall be 12/27/04, which is the business day before the sale date specified above. Dated: 10/27/04 /s/ TOM BANKS Published: Fullerton News October 29, 2004.

NOTICE TO CREDITORS OF BULK SALE AND OF INTENTION TO TRANSFER ALCOHOLIC BEVERAGE LICENSE (U.C.C. 6105 et seq. and B & P 24073 et seq.) Notice is hereby given that a bulk sale of assets and a transfer of alcoholic beverage license is about to be made. The names, Social Security or Federal Tax Numbers, and addresses of the Seller/Licensee are DEC INC.,18922 SAND AVENUE, HUNTINGTON BEACH, CA 92000. The business is known as OUR PLACE. The names, Social Security or Federal Tax Numbers, and addresses of the Buyer/Transferee are MICHAEL APELLIDO, 110 ASH BLVD., LOS OSOS, CA 94500, SS#123-00-1960. As listed by the Seller/Licensee, all other business names and addresses used by the Seller/Licensee within three years before the date such list was sent or delivered to the Buyer/Transferee are: (if none, so state.) NONE The Assets to be sold are described in general as: A BUSINESS INCLUDING FURNITURE, FIXTURES AND EQUIPMENT, GOODWILL, TRADE-NAME, LEASE AND LEASEHOLD IMPROVEMENTS and are located at: 18922 SAND AVENUE, HUNTINGTON BEACH, CA 92000. The kind of license to be transferred is: ON-SALE GENERAL EATING PLACE #11-112345 now issued for the premises located at: 18922 SAND AVENUE, HUNTINGTON BEACH, CA 92000. The anticipated date of the sale/transfer is 12/15/2004 at the office of ABC Escrow, 12345 Brook Street, Westminster, CA 92600. It has been agreed between the Seller/Licensee and the intended Buyer/Transferee, as required by Sec. 24073 of the Business and Professions Code, that the consideration for the transfer of the business and license is to be paid only after the transfer has been approved by the Department of Alcoholic Beverage Control. Dated: 10/15/04 DEC, INC. BY: PAT SMITH, Published: Beach Wave, November 4, 2004

Examples of a bulk sale published in a newspaper.

INVESTING IN REAL ESTATE

The main benefits of commercial real estate are appreciation, equity buildup, income, and tax benefits.

Why invest in Real Estate? With so many investment opportunities available, it is a valid question. Historically real property has shown a consistent growth in value and remains the best **hedge against inflation**. By owning assets that rise in value with inflation, e.g. real estate, you can beat inflation. Over the years, the value of real estate has appreciated considerably. If your objective is capital appreciation, then buying a promising piece of property in a promising neighborhood will help you achieve this. On the other hand, if you are looking for income, then buying a rental building can help provide regular income. Some investors purchase projects that are ready for occupancy, called **turnkey projects**.

The four main benefits of commercial real estate are: (1) appreciation, (2) equity buildup, (3) income, and (4) tax benefits.

Appreciation and Equity Buildup

The benefits of appreciation and equity buildup are available to the patient investor. **Appreciation** is an increase in property value with the passage of time. The increase in value of a mortgaged property generally accrues to the benefit of the trustor. The trustor is the owner and would benefit from this appreciation. This is called an **unearned increment**. In addition, payments made on a mortgage loan are like a monthly savings plan and build up equity. **Equity buildup** is the gradual increase of the borrower's equity in a property caused by amortization of loan principal.

Income

Most investors look for a return on their investment. Over the years many ask, "Which performs better, the stock market or real estate?" If we compare the Dow in 1980 at 830, to 2004 at 10,000 +/−, that's about a 1,100% gain. Home prices across the nation have increased by about 400% during the same time frame. This makes the stock market look pretty good. However, the comparison should be made on the basis of the cash actually invested and not just sale prices.

When a buyer invests a small down payment and obtains a loan to purchase property, he or she is using the lender's money to finance the sale. This is known as **leverage**—the use of borrowed capital to buy real estate, and is a process that permits the buyer to use little of one's own money and large amounts of someone else's. Now, let's go back to our comparison of the real estate investment to the stock market. Let's assume you made a 10% down payment on a $100,000 home in 1980. By 2004, if the home increased 400% it is now valued at $400,000. Your gain on the sale would be $310,000. This means your initial $10,000 investment grew to $310,000, which is a gain of about 3,000%, which is far better than the stock market. If you had invested the $10,000 in stocks, it would have grown to $110,000 in the same 24-year period.

As you can see, the use of leverage is appealing to both home buyers and real estate investors. The investor can use leverage to control several investments rather than just one, each purchased with a small amount of personal funds and a large amount of a lender's money. The investor can then earn a return on each property, therefore increasing the amount of yield on investment dollars.

Tax Benefits of Income Property Ownership

Another benefit of investing in real estate is the **tax benefits**. People considering the purchase of real property must examine the tax benefits and burdens of their purchase. Many times, the tax implications will seriously affect a sale and cause a buyer or seller to realize that—because of the taxes—full value of ownership may not be possible. What might look like a good deal could turn into a losing proposition after tax considerations.

The tax laws reward an investor for the financial risk taken and benefit the economy from the investment by allowing the taxpayer to reduce tax liability in numerous ways. As long as an investment is income producing, such as with an apartment building or commercial property, certain reductions in tax liability are allowed.

Depreciation

An investor may claim depreciation and other deductions, such as, mortgage interest, property taxes, insurance, management, maintenance, and utilities to reduce the tax bill. One of the most important tax benefits of income property ownership is the depreciation allowance. **Depreciation** is a tax advantage of ownership of income property.

Depreciation for tax purposes is not based on actual deterioration but on the calculated useful life of the property. The theory is that improvements, not land, deteriorate and lose their value. A building is thought to have a certain number of years in which it can generate an income, and after that, it is no longer considered a practical investment. The investor is compensated for the loss by being allowed to deduct a certain dollar amount each year based on the useful life of the property until, on paper at least, the property no longer has any value as an investment.

However, tax laws regarding depreciation change so often that it is advisable for the reader to check current Internal Revenue Service (IRS) rules for calculating depreciation.

A common method that one can use to determine the dollar amount per year that may be deducted is the **straight-line method,** by which the same amount is deducted every year over the depreciable life of a property. When using the straight-line method to calculate depreciation, the value of the improvements is divided by the depreciable life of the property to arrive at the annual depreciation that can be taken. Here is how it works:

Steps to Calculate Depreciation

1. Determine what the IRS allowance for the depreciable life of a residential income property is by checking current tax law. For our purposes let's assume it is 27 1/2 years.

2. Subtract the value of the land from the value of the property to determine the value of the building.

Value of property	$400,000
Subtract the value of land	−160,000
Value of building	$240,000

3. $240,000 divided by 27 1/2 years = $8,727 annual depreciation allowance.

Example: Jaime and Chris bought a four-plex at the beach and paid $600,000 for the property. The land was valued at 40% of the total investment, leaving 60% for the value of the improvements. How much depreciation could they claim each year when filing their income tax if they were allowed to depreciate the property over 27 1/2 years?

Step #1: Calculate the value of the improvements.
$600,000 x 60% (.60) = $360,000

Step #2 Divide the value of the improvements by the years.
$360,000 divided by 27 1/2 years = $13,091 allowable annual depreciation.

When Jaime and Chris sell the property, the amount depreciated over the years will be subtracted from their cost basis to determine their capital gain. Also, when the property is sold, the new owner is allowed to begin depreciating the building as if the building were new, based on the new sales price.

Capital Gains

The gain on an income-producing property is calculated much like that for a personal residence, except any depreciation that has been claimed over the years must be subtracted from the cost basis. This means the dollar amount that has been deducted for depreciation over the time of property ownership must be subtracted from the cost basis to arrive at the adjusted cost basis. The amount of taxable gain is then calculated by subtracting the adjusted cost basis from the selling price.

Unlike a primary residence where a certain amount of gain may be excluded from being taxed, taxes are owed on any profit made whenever income-producing property is sold. However, there are ways an investor may legally defer the gain to a later time. If an income property is sold at a loss, the loss may be deducted.

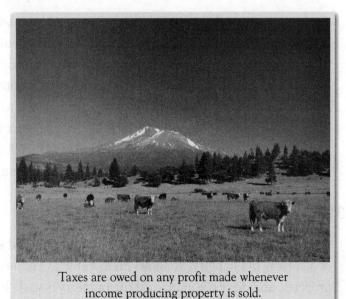

Taxes are owed on any profit made whenever income producing property is sold.

Calculate Capital Gain on the Sale of Income Property

1. Calculate the Adjusted Cost Basis of the Property

Add the cost of improvements and subtract the depreciation from the property.

Purchase price (cost basis)	$ 600,000
Add cost of improvements	+ 100,000
	$ 700,000
Subtract depreciation	− 75,000
Adjusted cost basis	$ 625,000

2. Calculate the Adjusted Selling Price of the Property

Selling price	$ 700,000
Subtract the expenses of sale	− 42,000
Adjusted selling price	$ 658,000

3. Calculate the Capital Gain (or Loss)

Adjusted selling price	$ 658,000
Subtract adjusted cost basis	− 625,000
Capital gain (or loss)	$ 33,000

Installment Sale

An **installment sale** is one in which payments are made by the buyer to the seller, over a period of more than one year. This is one way capital gain and the tax payments owed can be spread out over a period of time. Part of the tax liability can be deferred by the seller taking back a note and trust deed, or an All Inclusive Trust Deed (AITD) or contract of sale, with monthly payments. Only the amount of the gain that is collected in the tax year is taxable income, and the tax due on the rest can be deferred until collected. Once again, the reader should check current tax laws about installment sales.

1031 Tax-Deferred Exchange

The **1031 Exchange**, sometimes called a **tax-deferred exchange**, is a method of deferring tax liability. It allows an investor to exchange a property for a like property, and defer the gain until the property is sold. It is not really a tax-free exchange. The taxes are simply put off until a later date. The exchange can be simultaneous or non-simultaneous (deferred). The deferred exchange is often called a **Starker exchange**. In a Starker exchange, the investor must identify a replacement property within 45 days from the date the relinquished property is sold, and must go to settlement on the replacement property within 180 days from the previous sale. A two-party, simultaneous exchange seldom occurs because it is difficult to find two parties with properties of equal value who are willing to trade. Therefore, the Starker delayed-exchange, which allows the investor 45 days to locate and identify a replacement property, is used.

Most real property qualifies as like property, as long as it is held as an investment. It may be investment property (raw land), property held for the production of income (apartment or commercial building), or property used in a trade or business (an operating business). However, a personal residence would not qualify as a like property in an exchange with investment property.

If equities are not equal in two properties being exchanged, money or anything of value (cars, boats, stocks, furniture), other than like-kind property, may be put in by the investor who is trading up to balance the equities. This extra cash or non like-kind property put into an exchange is known as **boot**. The person who receives boot will be taxed on the net amount received up to any gain recognized from the exchange.

Example:

	Property A	Property B
Value	$400,000	$600,000
Less: Loans	− 50,000	− 200,000
Equity	$350,000	$400,000

To qualify for a tax-deferred exchange, Investor A needs to add $50,000 (boot) to the sale to make the equities match. Investor A would have no tax liability on the sale and Investor B would be taxed on the amount of the boot received in the year of the sale (if he or she realized a gain from the sale). If the amount of the boot exceeds the amount of the gain, tax liability is limited to the amount of the gain.

In calculating the gain on each property, the cost basis of the property being exchanged becomes the cost basis of the property being acquired, if no boot is given or received, and the cost basis follows the taxpayer through subsequent exchanges or sales. The profit or taxable gain is determined by subtracting the adjusted cost basis from the fair market value of the property. Tax-deferred exchanges can become very complicated. An accountant should be consulted before entering into the sale of a tax-deferred property. In this text, our discussion is mainly an overview of the subject. We recommend that you study the topic further if you find it of interest. As a real estate agent, never give tax advice. Always recommend that your clients and customers see a tax specialist for their special needs before making any decisions to purchase or sell property.

> **A personal residence does not qualify for a tax-deferred exchange.**

PROBATE SALES

Probate is the legal process to prove that a will is valid. Probate proceedings are held in the superior court to determine creditors' claims and beneficiaries' interests in an estate upon the owner's death. A **probate sale** is a court-approved sale of the property of a person who is deceased.

The purpose of a probate court is to discover any creditors of the deceased and pay them out of the estate of the person who died. After all debts are paid, anything of value that remains is distributed to the proper heirs, either according to a will or to the law of succession. The probate court sets the amount of commission when there is a real estate agent involved in the sale.

Estate property may be sold during the probate period at a public or private auction. An executor or administrator may list the property for up to 90 days with court permission. The court confirms the final sale and sets the broker's commission. The first offer must be for at least 90% of the appraised value and a subsequent offer at least 10% of the first $10,000 original bid, plus 5% of the remainder.

Sample Probate Bid	
Appraised value	$100,000
1. First bid: at least 90% of appraised value	$90,000
2. Second bid: at least 10% of first $10,000	$1,000
Plus 5% of the remainder ($80,000)	<u>$4,000</u>
Total minimum second bid required	$95,000

After court confirmation of a sale, usually normal escrow procedures are used to complete the transaction on the terms and conditions approved by the court.

Estate, Inheritance, and Gift Taxes

The **estate tax** is a federal tax on the "taxable estate" of a decedent's assets at the time of his or her death. All assets (e.g., real estate, stocks, bonds, bank accounts, retirement accounts, assets in a living trust, and sometimes life insurance) held by the decedent are included in determining the decedent's taxable estate. If the taxable estate is larger than the federal exemption, the estate must pay the applicable estate taxes before the assets can be fully distributed. Estate taxes are different from, and in addition to, probate expenses and final income taxes owed on the decedent's income received in the year of death.

California does not have an inheritance tax. An **inheritance tax** is a tax imposed on the privilege of inheriting property, paid by the person receiving the property.

A **gift tax** is a federal tax imposed on the transfer of property or other assets. Federal tax laws allow a donor to give up to a certain amount each year to any number of donees, with no gift tax due. When owed, the gift tax is paid by the donor.

DEVELOPERS REVITALIZE URBAN AMERICA

California communities are expressing a growing concern that the current development pattern of urban sprawl is not in the best interests of our cities, small towns, rural communities, and wilderness areas. **Urban sprawl** describes the unplanned and often haphazard growth of an urban area into adjoining areas. They are finding it economically unfeasible to abandon the existing infrastructure in the city, only to rebuild it further out. Developing further out from the commercial centers pollutes the air for entire regions as people drive further to their destinations. They question the wisdom of using up the open space and prime agricultural lands at the suburban fringe instead of filling in areas within the city and reusing the abandoned brownfields (contaminated property). As an alternative to sprawl, planners encourage and implement smart growth development practices that better serve the economic, environmental, and social needs of communities.

Smart Growth

Smart growth planning tries to reconcile the needs of development with the quality of life. Smart growth focuses on revitalizing older suburbs and older city centers. It usually has a greater mix of housing with commercial and retail uses. Where possible, it preserves open space and many other natural areas.

Principles of Smart Growth Planning

- Create a range of prices and types of housing using compact building designs to make the best use of the available land.

- Create walkable communities where people want to live, work, and play.

- Create communities that integrate mixed land uses into the planning.

- Preserve open space, farmland, and natural beauty.

- Encourage development in communities.

Types of Smart Growth

Typical smart growth plans the best ways to absorb growth without destructive traffic and pollution increases. It calls for mixed-use, higher-density, pedestrian-friendly, transit-oriented development. Some types of smart growth planning are mansionization, infill development, and brownfield development.

Mansionization

A new trend of home remodeling and construction is emerging in older neighborhoods with small-to-medium-sized homes. In many of these neighborhoods, developers and homeowners are tearing down the existing homes and building larger, more extravagant ones. The process, called **mansionization**, is a response to incredible land costs. In many of the older, built-out communities in California, land is valued as high as $1 million per acre or more.

This process has become popular with developers who want to balance the cost of construction with the cost of land. It is also popular with homeowners who cannot afford to buy the larger homes in expensive neighborhoods, but who can afford to purchase smaller homes and add on at a later time. However, in some communities residents claim that the houses are eyesores, out of character, and that they can depress property values.

In many older neighborhoods, developers and homeowners are tearing down the existing homes and building larger, more extravagant ones.

Some local planning commissions are trying to control mansionization by adopting a variety of restrictions on the design of homes, such as the size of side yards and the height and total square footage of a house. Many communities in California have adopted floor area ratios (FAR) in order to maintain the character of neighborhoods and to minimize the large, out-of-proportion monster homes. A **floor area ratio** (FAR) is a planning tool used to regulate a building's mass in relation to the size of its lot. The FAR is the ratio of the total building floor area to the total lot area and is determined by dividing the total floor area of a building by the area of the lot.

Infill Development

An **infill development** is simply the development of vacant parcels in existing urban and suburban areas. Development of this type typically brings the density of the area closer to that allowed by the existing zoning regulations. Industrial, commercial, and residential development projects can take advantage of land availability closer to urban centers. Infill developments not only keep green fields green; they are able to take advantage of proximity to a larger pool of potential employees, transportation, and utility infrastructures.

More cities and counties regulate development and restrict growth to preserve greenbelts and avoid suburban sprawl. This causes developers to consider infill development within existing neighborhoods and communities. In many areas it is easier to get the necessary building permits for infill development because these projects are considered more environmentally and urban friendly.

However, with more infill development taking place, there also has been a greater backlash toward such developments from neighboring residents, known as **NIMBY**, or the Not In My Backyard syndrome.

Brownfield Properties

A **brownfield** is an abandoned commercial or industrial site or under-utilized neighborhood where redevelopment is complicated by actual or perceived contamination. Traditionally, state governments have tried to cleanup and revitalize these sites under their State Superfund programs. The EPA's 2002 Brownfields Revitalization

Example of a brownfield

Act is a program designed to empower states to change the way contaminated property is perceived, addressed, and managed. It is estimated that there are more than 450,000 brownfield sites in the country. Cleaning up and reinvesting in these properties increases local tax base; facilitates job growth; utilizes existing infrastructure; takes development pressures off undeveloped, open land; and both improves and protects the environment.

Successful Land Revitalization in Hawthorne

The Lowe Enterprises Real Estate Group (Lowe) successfully redeveloped "The Exchange", a 104-acre mixed-use retail and industrial complex at a site in Hawthorne previously owned by Northrop Grumman. Since 1939, Northrop has manufactured military and commercial aircraft parts. The Hawthorne facility, which manufactured electronics for the defense industry, was closed at the end of 1997 leading to a loss of 530 jobs. A by-product of the manufacturing operations was hazardous wastes that contaminated soils and groundwater, creating a brownfield.

By solving the problems with the soil and groundwater contamination, Lowe was able to create 1,800,000 square feet of office, retail, and industrial space through renovation of existing buildings and new construction. An AT&T Internet data center was The Exchange's first tenant taking nearly a 300,000-square foot space.

The renovation and reuse of the old Northrop facility is economically revitalizing the Hawthorne community by creating hundreds of new jobs and generating tax revenue for the city.

PROPERTY MANAGEMENT

The management of a property on behalf of the owner is called **property management**. The main goal of property management is to protect the owner's investment as well as maximize the owner's return on that investment. The property manager takes over the mundane, day-to-day management of a property. Depending on the scope of the management contract, he or she will attract new tenants, retain existing tenants, collect rents, pay expenses, hire and supervise repairs, and maintain the property.

Any type of property may be managed—homes, duplexes, and apartment buildings, as well as large projects, such as office and industrial complexes and shopping centers.

Property managers are usually classified as individual property managers, building managers, and resident managers. The **individual property manager** is usually a real estate broker who owns his or her own company and manages properties for various owners. Some property managers work for a property management firm or for a corporation as an asset manager.

The **building manager** may be employed by a property manager or directly by an owner, and he or she usually manages a single, large building or office complex.

Resident managers are employed to manage an apartment building on either a part-time or full-time basis.

The Management Contract

The **management contract** shows the terms of the agreement between the owner and the property manager. The owner employs and authorizes the broker to perform the duties listed in the contract. The agreement should be a written contract, which clearly sets forth the responsibilities of both parties. The contract should include the terms and period of the contract, the policies pertaining to the management of the premises, management fees, and the authority and powers that are given by the owner to the agent.

Property managers need a basic understanding of the laws concerning real estate licensing, contracts, agency, fair housing, employment, property protection, and tenant/landlord relationships. However, the preparation of leases, tax reports, and other matters may involve legal and accounting expertise that should be sent to a legal or tax expert.

Management Fees

Management fees are negotiated between the owner and the property manager. They can be either a flat amount per month, a percentage of the gross rents collected, or a combination of the two. Property managers usually base their fees on a percentage of the gross rents collected. This may vary from 3% on large structures to as high as 20% on individual houses or small buildings. Property managers who also act as leasing agents will often receive additional compensation for the renewal of leases and for supervising major repairs or alterations.

CALIFORNIA
ASSOCIATION
OF REALTORS®

MOVE IN / MOVE OUT INSPECTION
(C.A.R. Form MIMO, Revised 11/07)

Property Address _____ Unit No. _____
Inspection: Move In _____ (Date) Move Out _____ (Date)
Tenant(s) _____

When completing this form, check the Premises carefully and be specific in all items noted. Check the appropriate box:
N- NEW   S - SATISFACTORY/CLEAN   O - OTHER   D - DEPOSIT DEDUCTION

	MOVE IN N S O	Comments	MOVE OUT S O D	Comments
Front Yard/Exterior				
Landscaping	☐☐☐		☐☐☐	
Fences/Gates	☐☐☐		☐☐☐	
Sprinklers/Timers	☐☐☐		☐☐☐	
Walks/Driveway	☐☐☐		☐☐☐	
Porches/Stairs	☐☐☐		☐☐☐	
Mailbox	☐☐☐		☐☐☐	
Light Fixtures	☐☐☐		☐☐☐	
Building Exterior	☐☐☐		☐☐☐	
Entry				
Security/Screen Doors	☐☐☐		☐☐☐	
Doors/Knobs/Locks	☐☐☐		☐☐☐	
Flooring/Baseboards	☐☐☐		☐☐☐	
Walls/Ceilings	☐☐☐		☐☐☐	
Light Fixtures/Fans	☐☐☐		☐☐☐	
Switches/Outlets	☐☐☐		☐☐☐	
Living Room				
Doors/Knobs/Locks	☐☐☐		☐☐☐	
Flooring/Baseboards	☐☐☐		☐☐☐	
Walls/Ceilings	☐☐☐		☐☐☐	
Window Coverings	☐☐☐		☐☐☐	
Windows/Locks/Screens	☐☐☐		☐☐☐	
Light Fixtures/Fans	☐☐☐		☐☐☐	
Switches/Outlets	☐☐☐		☐☐☐	
Fireplace Equipment	☐☐☐		☐☐☐	
Dining Room				
Flooring/Baseboards	☐☐☐		☐☐☐	
Walls/Ceilings	☐☐☐		☐☐☐	
Window Coverings	☐☐☐		☐☐☐	
Windows/Locks/Screens	☐☐☐		☐☐☐	
Light Fixtures/Fans	☐☐☐		☐☐☐	
Switches/Outlets	☐☐☐		☐☐☐	

Tenant's Initials (_____)(_____)   Tenant's Initials (_____)(_____)
Landlord's Initials (_____)(_____)   Landlord's Initials (_____)(_____)

MIMO REVISED 11/07 (PAGE 1 OF 5)

Reviewed by _____ Date _____

EQUAL HOUSING OPPORTUNITY

MOVE IN / MOVE OUT INSPECTION (MIMO PAGE 1 OF 5)

Agent:	Phone:	Fax:	Prepared using WINForms® software
Broker:			

Property Address: _____   Date: _____

	MOVE IN	MOVE OUT

Other Room _____
Doors/Knobs/Locks
Flooring/Baseboards
Walls/Ceilings
Window Coverings
Windows/Locks/Screens
Light Fixtures/Fans
Switches/Outlets

MOVE IN: N S O   Comments
MOVE OUT: S O D   Comments

Bedroom # _____
Doors/Knobs/Locks
Flooring/Baseboards
Walls/Ceilings
Window Coverings
Windows/Locks/Screens
Light Fixtures/Fans
Switches/Outlets
Closets/Doors/Tracks

Bedroom # _____
Doors/Knobs/Locks
Flooring/Baseboards
Walls/Ceilings
Window Coverings
Windows/Locks/Screens
Light Fixtures/Fans
Switches/Outlets
Closets/Doors/Tracks

Bedroom # _____
Doors/Knobs/Locks
Flooring/Baseboards
Walls/Ceilings
Window Coverings
Windows/Locks/Screens
Light Fixtures/Fans
Switches/Outlets
Closets/Doors/Tracks

Bedroom # _____
Doors/Knobs/Locks
Flooring/Baseboards
Walls/Ceilings
Window Coverings
Windows/Locks/Screens
Light Fixtures/Fans
Switches/Outlets
Closets/Doors/Tracks

SAMPLE

Tenant's Initials (_____)(_____)   Tenant's Initials (_____)(_____)
Landlord's Initials (_____)(_____)   Landlord's Initials (_____)(_____)

Copyright © 1982-2007, CALIFORNIA ASSOCIATION OF REALTORS®, INC.
MIMO REVISED 11/07 (PAGE 2 OF 5)

Reviewed by_____ Date_____

EQUAL HOUSING OPPORTUNITY

MOVE IN / MOVE OUT INSPECTION (MIMO PAGE 2 OF 5)

Property Address: _____ Date: _____

	MOVE IN				**MOVE OUT**			
	N	S	O	Comments	S	O	D	Comments

Bath #_____
Doors/Knobs/Locks
Flooring/Baseboards
Walls/Ceilings
Window Coverings
Windows/Locks/Screens
Light Fixtures
Switches/Outlets
Toilet
Tub/Shower
Shower Door/Rail/Curtain
Sink/Faucets
Plumbing/Drains
Exhaust Fan
Towel Rack(s)
Toilet Paper Holder
Cabinets/Counters

Bath #_____
Doors/Knobs/Locks
Flooring/Baseboards
Walls/Ceilings
Window Coverings
Windows/Locks/Screens
Light Fixtures
Switches/Outlets
Toilet
Tub/Shower
Shower Door/Rail/Curtain
Sink/Faucets
Plumbing/Drains
Exhaust Fan
Towel Rack(s)
Toilet Paper Holder
Cabinets/Counters

Bath #_____
Doors/Knobs/Locks
Flooring/Baseboards
Walls/Ceilings
Window Coverings
Windows/Locks/Screens
Light Fixtures
Switches/Outlets
Toilet
Tub/Shower
Shower Door/Rail/Curtain
Sink/Faucets
Plumbing/Drains
Exhaust Fan
Towel Rack(s)
Toilet Paper Holder
Cabinets/Counters

Tenant's Initials (_____)(_____)   Tenant's Initials (_____)(_____)
Landlord's Initials (_____)(_____)   Landlord's Initials (_____)(_____)

MIMO REVISED 11/07 (PAGE 3 OF 5)

Reviewed by_____ Date_____

MOVE IN / MOVE OUT INSPECTION (MIMO PAGE 3 OF 5)

Property Address: _____   Date: _____

| | **MOVE IN** | | | | **MOVE OUT** | | | |
| | N | S | O | Comments | | S | O | D | Comments |

Kitchen
Flooring/Baseboards
Walls/Ceilings
Window Coverings
Windows/Locks/Screens
Light Fixtures
Switches/Outlets
Range/Fan/Hood
Oven(s)/Microwave
Refrigerator
Dishwasher
Sink/Disposal
Faucet(s)/Plumbing
Cabinets
Counters

_____
_____

Hall/Stairs
Flooring/Baseboards
Walls/Ceilings
Light Fixtures
Switches/Outlets
Closets/Cabinets
Railings/Banisters

_____
_____

Laundry
Faucets/Valves
Plumbing/Drains
Cabinets/Counters

_____
_____

Systems
Furnace/Thermostat
Air Conditioning
Water Heater
Water Softener

_____
_____

Other _____

_____
_____
_____
_____
_____
_____
_____
_____

Tenant's Initials   (_____)(_____)   Tenant's Initials   (_____)(_____)
Landlord's Initials   (_____)(_____)   Landlord's Initials   (_____)(_____)

Reviewed by _____ Date _____

MOVE IN / MOVE OUT INSPECTION (MIMO PAGE 4 OF 5)

Property Address: _____ Date: _____

	MOVE IN				MOVE OUT			
	N	S	O	Comments	S	O	D	Comments

Garage/Parking
Garage Door ☐ ☐ ☐ _____ ☐ ☐ ☐ _____
Other Door(s) ☐ ☐ ☐ _____ ☐ ☐ ☐ _____
Driveway/Floor ☐ ☐ ☐ _____ ☐ ☐ ☐ _____
Cabinets/Counters ☐ ☐ ☐ _____ ☐ ☐ ☐ _____
Light Fixtures ☐ ☐ ☐ _____ ☐ ☐ ☐ _____
Switches/Outlets ☐ ☐ ☐ _____ ☐ ☐ ☐ _____
Electrical/Exposed Wiring ☐ ☐ ☐ _____ ☐ ☐ ☐ _____
Window(s) ☐ ☐ ☐ _____ ☐ ☐ ☐ _____
Other Storage/Shelving ☐ ☐ ☐ _____ ☐ ☐ ☐ _____

_____   _____

Back/Side/Yard
Patio/Deck/Balcony ☐ ☐ ☐ _____ ☐ ☐ ☐ _____
Patio Cover(s) ☐ ☐ ☐ _____ ☐ ☐ ☐ _____
Landscaping ☐ ☐ ☐ _____ ☐ ☐ ☐ _____
Sprinklers/Timers ☐ ☐ ☐ _____ ☐ ☐ ☐ _____
Pool/Heater/Equipment ☐ ☐ ☐ _____ ☐ ☐ ☐ _____
Spa/Cover/Equipment ☐ ☐ ☐ _____ ☐ ☐ ☐ _____
Fences/Gates ☐ ☐ ☐ _____ ☐ ☐ ☐ _____

_____   _____

Safety/Security
Smoke/CO Detector(s) ☐ ☐ ☐ _____ ☐ ☐ ☐ _____
Security System ☐ ☐ ☐ _____ ☐ ☐ ☐ _____
Security Window Bars ☐ ☐ ☐ _____ ☐ ☐ ☐ _____

_____   _____

Personal Property

_____   _____

Keys/Remotes/Devices
Keys _____   _____
Remotes/Devices _____   _____

☐ **Attached Supplement(s)** _____

THIS SECTION TO BE COMPLETED AT MOVE IN: Receipt of a copy of this form is acknowledged by:
Tenant _____ Date _____
Tenant _____ Date _____
New Phone Service Established? ☐ Yes ☐ No   New Phone Number _____
Landlord (Owner or Agent)_____ Date _____
Landlord _____
      (Print Name)

THIS SECTION TO BE COMPLETED AT MOVE OUT: Receipt of a copy of this form is acknowledged by:
Tenant _____ Date _____
Tenant _____ Date _____
Tenant Forwarding Address _____

Landlord (Owner or Agent)_____ Date _____
Landlord _____
      (Print Name)

Published and Distributed by:
REAL ESTATE BUSINESS SERVICES, INC.
a subsidiary of the CALIFORNIA ASSOCIATION OF REALTORS®
525 South Virgil Avenue, Los Angeles, California 90020

Reviewed by _____ Date _____

Functions of a Property Manager

In addition to the basic real estate knowledge of agency, contracts, fair housing, rentals, and leases, a property manager needs to know about business administration, marketing, insurance, repairs and maintenance, and taxes.

The property manager must be a jack-of-all trades because the duties are many and varied. Property managers have a dual responsibility to both the owner and the tenants. The owner wants the highest possible return from the property, and the tenants want the best value for their money. With this in mind, property managers must keep the properties rented at the highest market rent possible, implement reasonable safety measures, keep operational and other costs within budget, and preserve and enhance the physical value and prestige of the property. In addition, he or she must do all of this along with the legal requirements of managing his or her own business.

Reports to Owner

The owner relies on the information provided by the property manager about the profitability of his or her property. Therefore, the property manager must set up and maintain accurate records and send regular reports to the owner. In addition to the monthly accounting statement, a detailed annual statement should be prepared. Through the monthly and annual reports, both owner and property manager can assess the fluctuations of income and expense and formulate future rental and maintenance policies.

Managing Properties Subject to Rent Control

Rent control, or **rent stabilization**, is a collection of laws in some communities that limit or prohibit rent increases. They also limit the reasons for eviction. Typical provisions of rent stabilization regulations include: (1) control the amount that may be charged for a rental unit, (2) determine the amenities and services that are included as part of the rent, and (3) provide for only good cause evictions. These regulations work together so that the landlord cannot circumvent a rent limit by just evicting the tenant.

Rent control stabilizes rents and helps prevent unfair evictions.

Rent control has been in effect in a number of major cities for many years. The best-known example is New York City, which still uses the same rent controls from the 1940s. In 1979, two California cities, Berkeley and Santa Monica, imposed strict rent control ordinances. Shortly thereafter, more cities followed suit—including San Francisco, Los Angeles, West Hollywood, East Palo Alto, Beverly Hills, Hayward, Los Gatos, Oakland, Palm Springs, and San Jose. San Diego is the only major California city to go against the trend by rejecting rent control by a 2-to-1 vote in a 1985 referendum.

Review - California Cities with Rent Control

Berkeley	Los Angeles	San Francisco
Beverly Hills	Los Gatos	San Jose
East Palo Alto	Oakland	Santa Monica
Hayward	Palm Springs	West Hollywood

Stabilization of Rent

Although regulations differ from city to city, rents usually can only be raised once a year. The amount of the increase is decided by the Rent Stabilization Board of the city. The **Maximum Allowable Rent** (MAR) is the maximum legal rent that a landlord may charge for a controlled rental unit. Many of the rent control laws allow tenants to request rent decreases when landlords do not maintain their rental property or do not continue to provide housing services or amenities.

Lawful Evictions

Rent control laws are specific on tenant evictions. A **good cause eviction** includes failing to pay the rent, violating an important condition of the rental agreement, or causing a substantial nuisance.

A **no-fault eviction** is a type of lawful eviction in which the tenant is not at fault. This would include things like the owner wanting to occupy the apartment or get out of the rental housing business. Most no-fault evictions require the landlord to pay substantial relocation benefits to the displaced tenants.

A property manager or an owner of a rent-controlled property should consult an attorney whenever an eviction is necessary because there are specific legal requirements that must be followed.

Property Manager's Duties

Some of the specific duties a property manager must perform are:

- create rental schedule.
- merchandise the space.
- advertise vacancies through selected media.
- develop a tenant/resident relations policy.
- qualify and investigate a prospective tenant's credit.
- prepare and execute leases.
- collect the rent.
- review and pay bills.
- obtain and pay insurance premiums and taxes.
- create and supervise maintenance schedules and repairs.
- maintain proper records and make regular reports to the owner.
- comply with Fair Housing Laws.

Duties of a Property Manager with Employees

- Hire and keep personnel to staff the building(s).
- Instruct and supervise employees.
- Develop employee policies, including an Injury Prevention Plan.
- Set up payroll system for all employees.
- Comply with applicable federal, state, and local laws.
- Keep abreast of the times and competitive market conditions.

SUMMARY

Most people obtain a real estate license to sell homes; however, many other opportunities in real estate can be pursued. Licensees can specialize in mobilehome brokerage, business opportunity brokerage, **property management**, probate sales, real estate investment, and new areas of expertise, such as smart growth.

New fields of specialization or expertise are also emerging in real estate. One of these fields, **smart growth**, utilizes the city's existing infrastructure and redevelops rather than abandons property. An example of smart growth is the clean up and redevelopment of brownfields. Developers are now revitalizing urban America by redeveloping the industrial, commercial, and residential areas close to the urban center rather than focusing on **urban sprawl**.

UNIT 14 REVIEW

Matching Exercise

Instructions: Write the letter of the matching term on the blank line before its definition. Answers immediately follow the Multiple Choice Questions.

Terms

A. 1031 Exchange
B. agricultural property
C. appreciation
D. boot
E. brownfield
F. building manager
G. bulk sales
H. business opportunity
I. certificate of title
J. clearance of tax liability
K. Department of Alcoholic Beverage Control
L. depreciation

M. equity buildup
N. estate tax
O. financing statement
P. gift tax
Q. goodwill
R. hedge against inflation
S. houseboat
T. infill development
U. installment sale
V. leverage
W. management contract
X. mansionization
Y. manufactured home
Z. mobilehome park

AA. mobilehome
BB. probate sale
CC. promissory note
DD. resident manager
EE. sales tax
FF. security agreement
GG. seller's permit
HH. straight-line method
II. timeshare
JJ. turnkey project
KK. unearned increment
LL. Uniform Commercial Code
MM. urban sprawl
NN. use tax

Definitions

1. _____ A factory-built home manufactured prior to June 15, 1976, constructed on a chassis and wheels.

2. _____ Home built in a factory after June 15, 1976 that conforms to the federal Manufactured Home Construction and Safety Standards.

3. _____ Any area or tract of land where two or more lots are rented to accommodate manufactured homes or mobilehomes used for human habitation.

4. _____ Certificate signed by the county tax collector in mobilehome sales.

5. _____ A barge that is designed and equipped for use as a dwelling.

6. _____ Common ownership of a single piece of property by an association with each owner having the exclusive right to occupy a unit for a specified period each year.

7. _____ Property zoned for use in farming.

8. _____ Any type of business that is for lease or sale.

9. _____ The expectation of the continued patronage of an existing business.

10. _____ Code regulating security interests in personal property of businesses.

11. _____ The sale of a substantial part of the inventory of a business.

12. _____ The document commonly used to secure a loan on personal property.

13. _____ The document used to record the debt; it is not actual evidence of the debt.

14. _____ Tax collected as a percentage of the retail sales of a product, by a retailer.

15. _____ Permit used to collect sales tax from customers.

16. _____ Real property appreciation keeps pace or exceeds inflation rates.

17. _____ Projects that are ready for occupancy.

18. _____ An increase in property value with the passage of time.

19. _____ The increase in value of a mortgaged property generally accrues to the benefit of the trustor.

20. _____ The gradual increase of a borrower's equity in a property caused by amortization of loan principal.

21. _____ The use of borrowed capital to buy real estate.

22. _____ Tax advantage of ownership of income property.

23. _____ Depreciation method where the same amount is deducted every year over the depreciable life of a property.

24. _____ Sale in which payments are made, by the buyer, to the seller, over a period of more than one year.

25. _____ Tax-deferred exchange used to defer tax liability.

26. _____ Extra cash or non like-kind property put into an exchange.

27. _____ A court-approved sale of the property of a person who is deceased.

28. _____ Federal tax on the "taxable estate" of a decedent's assets at the time of death.

29. _____ The unplanned growth of an urban area into adjoining areas.

30. _____ Building larger, more extravagant homes older neighborhoods with small to medium-sized homes.

31. _____ The development of vacant parcels in existing urban and suburban areas.

32. _____ An abandoned commercial or industrial site or under-utilized neighborhood where redevelopment is complicated by actual or perceived contamination.

33. _____ Person employed by a property manager or directly by an owner, and who usually manages a single, large building or office complex.

34. _____ Person employed to manage an apartment building.

35. _____ Contract between the owner and the property manager.

Multiple Choice Questions

Instructions: Circle your response and then check your response with the Answer Key that immediately follows the Multiple Choice Questions.

1. A real estate licensee can sell:
    a. a new mobilehome.
    b. a one-year-old mobilehome.
    c. a mobilehome over 31 feet in length.
    d. any mobilehome with a deed.

2. Which of the following documents is used to transfer ownership of a mobilehome?
    a. Certificate of Title
    b. Deed
    c. DMV vehicle registration certificate
    d. Bill of sale

3. Timeshare properties are primarily designed for buyers looking for:
    a. income-producing real property.
    b. vacation property.
    c. a primary residence.
    d. agricultural property.

4. In a security transaction in personal property, the document used to perfect the security interest is called the:

    a. promissory note.

    b. security agreement.

    c. mortgage.

    d. financing statement.

5. In the sale of business opportunity, the Notice to Creditors of Bulk Transfer must be recorded at least how many days before the auction is to commence?

    a. 12 business days

    b. 14 business days

    c. 18 calendar days

    d. 21 calendar days

6. Which government agency issues liquor licenses to businesses?

    a. Franchise Tax Board (FTB)

    b. California Agency on Wine and Spirits (AWS)

    c. Department of Alcoholic Beverage Control (ABC)

    d. Liquor and Marijuana Dispensary Board (LMDB)

7. Which of the following provides an investor with the best hedge against inflation?

    a. An investment with high liquidity

    b. A high-risk, high-income deed of trust

    c. An income property that will maintain its value

    d. An investment with the characteristics of an annuity

8. When considering investment opportunities in real estate, a real estate investor would probably devote least attention to:

    a. protection against inflation.

    b. quantity and safety of annual income.

    c. quantity and safety of the initial capital outlay.

    d. liquidity of any capital invested.

9. Value that increases with the passage of time is called:

    a. cash flow.

    b. leverage.

    c. depreciation.

    d. appreciation.

10. Which of the following is the best example of leverage?
    a. Investing primarily personal funds
    b. Investing personal and borrowed funds equally
    c. Investing primarily borrowed funds
    d. Investing in properties with diminishing values

11. An appreciation in value of a mortgaged home generally accrues to the benefit of the:
    a. trustor.
    b. beneficiary.
    c. trustee.
    d. none of the above

12. All of the following would be considered boot, except:
    a. cash.
    b. antique furniture.
    c. vacant land in the outskirts of a large city.
    d. a commercial fishing boat.

13. In a probate sale, the amount of a commission to be paid a real estate agent is set by the:
    a. owner.
    b. executor.
    c. administrator.
    d. court.

14. As more cities and counties regulate development and restrict growth to preserve greenbelts and avoid suburban sprawl, developers are encouraged to develop vacant parcels in existing urban and suburban areas. This is called:
    a. greenbelt development.
    b. brownfield development.
    c. infill development.
    d. reurbanization.

15. A property manager should:
    a. protect the owner's investment.
    b. maximize the owner's return on the property.
    c. maintain accurate records and send regular reports to the owner.
    d. all of the above

UNIT 14 ANSWER KEY

Answers – Matching

1.	AA	8.	H	15.	GG	22.	L	29. MM
2.	Y	9.	Q	16.	R	23.	HH	30. X
3.	Z	10.	LL	17.	JJ	24.	U	31. T
4.	J	11.	G	18.	C	25.	A	32. E
5.	S	12.	FF	19.	KK	26.	D	33. F
6.	II	13.	O	20.	M	27.	BB	34. DD
7.	B	14.	EE	21.	V	28.	N	35. W

Answers – Multiple Choice

1. **(d)** A real estate licensee can sell a mobilehome classified as real property. [Mobilehome Brokerage]

2. **(a)** In general, a certificate of title is used to transfer ownership of a mobilehome. Ownership of a mobilehome classified as real property is transferred by a grant deed. [Mobilehome Brokerage]

3. **(b)** Timeshares are frequently purchased as a vacation investment because the cost of owning a good timeshare is less than renting comparable hotel accommodations year after year. [Timeshare Properties]

4. **(d)** To protect, or perfect, the interest created by the security agreement, or prevent the security from being sold by someone else, a financing statement must be filed. The financing statement is merely the document used to record the debt. [Business Opportunity Brokerage]

5. **(a)** This is one of many requirements of the Uniform Commercial Code, Division 6, relating to bulk sales. [Business Opportunity Brokerage]

6. **(c)** The Department of Alcoholic Beverage Control (ABC) issues liquor licenses and regulates the transfer of a liquor license from a seller to a buyer. A buyer must apply for the license and may be turned down for various reasons (e.g., criminal record). [Business Opportunity Brokerage]

7. **(c)** An income-generating property will create income as inflation rises. [Investing in Real Estate]

8. **(d)** The four main benefits of commercial real estate are: (1) appreciation, (2) equity buildup, (3) income, and (4) tax benefits. Real estate is not a liquid investment such as savings, stocks, or bonds. Therefore, liquidity would be less of a concern than the other variables. [Investing in Real Estate]

9. **(d)** Appreciation is an increase in the market value of an asset (e.g., real property), over, and above its value at the date when purchased. [Investing in Real Estate]

10. **(c)** Leverage means using primarily borrowed funds to increase buying power and, ideally, profits from investments. A large investment is controlled with a small amount of the investor's or borrower's own equity capital. [Investing in Real Estate]

11. **(a)** The trustor is the borrower (owner), beneficiary is the lender, and the trustee is the third party in a trust deed. Therefore, the trustor (owner) would benefit from an appreciation in the home's value. [Investing in Real Estate]

12. **(c)** Boot is money or anything of value (cars, boats, stocks, furniture) other than like-kind property that is put in by the investor who is trading up to balance the equities. [Investing in Real Estate]

13. **(d)** At the time the sale is confirmed, the court will set the amount of commission to be paid if there is a real estate agent involved. [Probate Sales]

14. **(c)** An infill-development is simply the development of vacant parcels in existing urban and suburban areas. [Developers Revitalize Urban America]

15. **(d)** The main goal of property management is to protect the owner's investment as well as maximize the owner's return on that investment. The property manager must maintain accurate records and send regular reports to the owner. [Property Management]

Unit 15

INTRODUCTION

Early real estate transactions were very simple. People transferred property ownership by exchanging symbolic lumps of dirt for something of value. As life became more complicated, however, there was a need for a more sophisticated way to transfer real property.

At the same time, the need emerged for some kind of regulation of the practice and the practitioners. Unethical people were taking advantage of the average citizen's lack of knowledge about real estate and the law.

The mission of the California Bureau of Real Estate (CalBRE) is to safeguard and promote the public interests in real estate matters through licensure, regulation, education and enforcement. As a licensee, you are regulated by CalBRE. The following discussion of CalBRE and its related activities serves as the foundation for your career as a real estate agent.

Learning Objectives

After completing this Unit, you should be able to:

12A   identify the steps for getting sarted in California real estate.

12B   recognize provisions of the Real Estate Law.

12C   identify the requirements for real estate licensing.

12D   specify actions that enforce the Real Estate Law.

12E   recall violations of the Real Estate Law.

THE REAL ESTATE LAW

California has long been a leader in real estate trends. As a matter of fact, the nation's first real estate licensing law was passed in California in 1917. In an attempt to create and maintain higher professional standards, and develop greater trust from the public in general, the real estate industry has supported legislation that protects consumer interests. As time went by, the law was codified and organized into two parts of the Business and Professions Code. Part 1 is titled "Licensing of Persons" and is called the **Real Estate Law**, which we will discuss in this Unit. Part 2 is titled "Regulation of Transactions" and is called the Subdivided Lands Law.

The Real Estate Law, sometimes referred to as the **license law**, is designed mainly for the protection of the public in real estate transactions where a licensee is involved. When you hear the term, "Real Estate Law", it means the law that affects the licensing and conduct of real estate brokers and salespeople. It must be seen separately from what is known as real property law, law of agency, contract law, or other legal aspects of real estate ownership and transfer.

> **Review - The Real Estate Law**
>
> The two main purposes are to protect:
>
> 1. consumers from loss because of dishonest and incompetent agents.
>
> 2. the good standing of ethical agents from the adverse publicity caused by unprincipled licensees.
>
> It pertains to the:
>
> 1. licensing of Real Estate Brokers and Salespeople.
> 2. conduct of Real Estate Brokers and Salespeople.

The Real Estate Commissioner

The **Real Estate Commissioner** (Commissioner), appointed by the Governor, determines administrative policy, and enforces the provisions of the Real Estate Law and the Subdivided Lands Law to ensure that the public is protected when dealing with licensees and when purchasing subdivided real property. To be appointed, the designee must have been a real estate broker for five years and actively engaged in the real estate business in California.

The Real Estate Law is not upheld in a court of law, but is enforced by the Real Estate Commissioner. One of the jobs not assigned to the Commissioner is settling commission disputes. That issue falls under the power of a court of law, and must be handled through an attorney if the parties involved cannot settle the matter agreeably.

Responsibilities of the Real Estate Commissioner

- Screen and qualify applicants for license
- Issue, restrict, suspend, or revoke real estate licenses
- Examine complaints against licensees
- Pursue formal action against licensees, where appropriate
- Monitor real property securities transactions
- Regulate prepaid rental listing services
- Regulate specific aspects of the sale of subdivisions

Real Estate Fund

All fees charged and collected from the licensing of persons or from the regulation of transactions are placed in the **Real Estate Fund**. The money is used by the Commissioner to carry out the provisions of the Real Estate Law. This includes running the Bureau of Real Estate and paying salaries to the Commissioner and his or her deputies, clerks, and assistants. Part of the fees collected in the Real Estate Fund is set aside into two separate accounts for education and for recovery.

Education and Research Account

The Commissioner may credit up to 8% of the fees collected into a separate account called the Education and Research Account. The **Education and Research Account** pays for the advancement of real estate education at California universities, California state colleges, and California community colleges. It also funds real estate research projects conducted by colleges or qualified associations.

Consumer Recovery Account

The **Consumer Recovery Account** is a separate account funded through collection of up to 12% of license fees collected. This fund assures the payment of otherwise non-collectable court judgments against licensees who have committed fraud, misrepresentation, deceit, or conversion of trust funds in a transaction. Under specific conditions of law, the person with a qualifying judgment may seek reimbursement from the Consumer Recovery Account for actual and direct loss to a statutory maximum. Currently the amount paid will be $50,000 per transaction, with a possible total aggregate maximum of $250,000 per licensee.

If the Commissioner pays a judgment on behalf of a broker or salesperson, the license is automatically suspended. A suspended license will only be reinstated after full reimbursement, plus interest, is repaid to the Recovery Fund.

REAL ESTATE LICENSING

Because real estate brokers and salespeople often act in an agency capacity, the state places strict requirements in the form of real estate licensing on those who wish to practice real estate.

Types of Real Estate Licenses

It is important for brokers and salespeople both to understand the obligations and restrictions of the different licenses that may be held. Any person who wants to engage in the real estate business and act as a real estate broker or real estate salesperson within the state of California must obtain a license from the Bureau of Real Estate (CalBRE).

Currently, CalBRE issues real estate broker and salesperson licenses for a 4-year period. A license obtained by fraud, misrepresentation, or deceit may undergo suspension by the Commissioner, without a hearing within 90 days after its issuance.

Real Estate Broker

A **real estate broker** is someone who holds a broker license issued by the Bureau of Real Estate. The license legally permits the broker to perform any acts for which a real estate license is required. In a real estate transaction, a broker is the **agent** of his or her principal.

A real estate broker is also an independent businessperson who can employ someone who holds a salesperson or a broker license. Any broker who places his or her license with an employing broker is a **broker associate** and must have a written employment agreement. These sales associates are agents of their employing broker—not the buyer/seller or the lessor/lessee. Therefore, brokers are legally responsible for all the business actions of their employees.

Individual Broker License

A real estate broker license allows a licensee to run a brokerage business under his or her own name or under a fictitious business name.

Fictitious Business Name

A licensed real estate broker may obtain a license with a **fictitious business name** (DBA-doing business as). The broker must apply to CalBRE and attach a certified copy of the Fictitious Business Name Statement that is filed with the county clerk. Filing a Fictitious Business Name Statement is good for 5 years from December 31st of the year filed. Each fictitious business name is an addition to the existing license, and it will expire at the same time as the license. [B&P §10159.5 and Reg. 2731]

Reasons Why the Commissioner Might Deny a License with a DBA

- The DBA is misleading or would constitute false advertising.
- The DBA implies a partnership or corporation when a partnership or corporation does not exist.
- The DBA includes the name of a real estate salesperson.
- The DBA is the name formerly used by a licensee whose license has since been revoked.

Branch Office License

A broker is authorized to conduct business only at the address listed on his or her license. A broker who maintains more than one place of business must apply for a **branch office license** for each location. The application for a branch office license must state the name of the person and the location of the place of business. [B&P §10163]

Partnership

CalBRE does not issue partnership licenses. A real estate business may be run as a partnership as long as every partner through whom the partnership acts is a licensed real estate broker. A salesperson may be employed by a broker who is a member of a partnership formed by written agreement and may work in any branch office managed by any one of the partners.

Corporate Real Estate License

A corporation may be licensed as a real estate broker as long as one officer of the corporation is a qualified real estate broker and acts as the corporation's responsible **designated broker-officer.** Salespeople may be employed by a corporate real estate broker as long as they are supervised by the designated broker-officer.

Real Estate Salesperson

A **real estate salesperson** is someone who holds a salesperson license issued by the Bureau of Real Estate. The salesperson must be employed by a real estate broker in order to perform any of the activities that require a license. A salesperson is an agent of his or her employing broker. **Real estate sales associate** is a term used to refer to employees of a broker.

A **salesperson license** is required for people employed as salespeople under the supervision of a licensed broker. A person may obtain a salesperson license even if he or she does not intend to be employed immediately by a broker. However, a salesperson without an employing broker may not perform acts requiring a license.

Mortgage Loan Originator License Endorsement

Since January 1, 2011, a Mortgage Loan Originator License Endorsement (**MLO Endorsement**) must be obtained before a real estate licensee can solicit or originate a loan application, or negotiate or offer to negotiate any residential mortgage loans. This is in compliance with the federal **Secure and Fair Enforcement for Mortgage Licensing Act (SAFE Act)**. The SAFE Act is intended to provide uniform national mortgage loan originator licensing standards, which will require minimum licensing and education. It is also designed to create a comprehensive national licensing database to enable government and consumers to track loan originators and help prevent fraud. Loan originators registered in the national database will be provided with a Unique Identifier number assigned to that licensee by the Nationwide Mortgage Licensing System and Registry.

The program to obtain the MLO Endorsement is administered by the National Mortgage License System and Registry (NMLSR). A licensee submits an application for the MLO Endorsement to the NMLSR, successfully completes the National and California-specific examinations, and submits fingerprints and credit report authorization to the NMSLR. In addition, 20 hours of pre-license education is required, but it does not have to be completed before taking the National or State examination components.

MLO endorsements will be issued annually and expire December 31st each year. The renewal requirements for a MLO license endorsement will include a renewal request filed electronically through the NMLSR, a renewal fee, and filing evidence of completion of 8 hours of annual continuing education (CE). The CE completed to renew a MLO license endorsement cannot be used to satisfy real estate CE requirements.

More information can be obtained from the CalBRE website or the NMLS Resource Center website at http://mortgage.nationwidelicensingsystem.org.

Restricted License

The Commissioner will sometimes issue a restricted license. A **restricted license** is a type of probationary license issued when a license has been suspended, revoked, or denied after a hearing. Typically, restrictions are placed by term (one month, three months, etc.), employment by a particular broker (for a salesperson), limitation to a certain type of activity, requiring detailed reports of each transaction, requiring the filing of a surety bond, or any combination.

If a real estate broker license is revoked or suspended by CalBRE, any salesperson licenses held by that broker are cancelled until the license is transferred to a new employing broker.

Review - License Facts:
- Brokers and salespeople are both licensees.
- Brokers are agents of the principal.
- Salespeople are agents of their broker (not the principal).
- A salesperson must be employed by a broker to be paid.
- A salesperson can only be paid by his or her employing broker.

When is a License Required?

Obtaining a real estate license is a prerequisite for performing real estate work. Specifically, unless someone is involved in the direct sale or purchase of property for him or herself, a real estate license is a prerequisite for performing real estate work. Under section 10131 of the Business and Professions Code, a real estate broker is someone who, for compensation, does perform or negotiates to perform one or more of the acts requiring a real estate license. A salesperson, if employed by a real estate broker, may also do any of the following activities.

Acts Requiring a Real Estate License

- Soliciting sellers
- Soliciting buyers
- Negotiating sales
- Negotiating leases
- Soliciting for tenants or rentals

- Negotiating sales contracts
- Negotiating loans
- Negotiating a promissory note secured by real property
- Negotiating exchanges

Unlicensed Person Penalties

No **unlicensed person** may receive payment for any act requiring a real estate license. The fine for paying a fee to an unqualified person is $100 for each offense. Prior to paying a commission, an escrow holder should require a broker to present evidence he or she is a regularly licensed real estate broker at the time such compensation is earned.

It is unlawful for any unlicensed person to pose as a real estate broker or salesperson or to advertise that he or she is a real

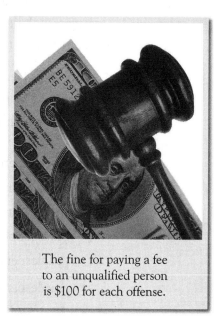

The fine for paying a fee to an unqualified person is $100 for each offense.

estate broker. The punishment for an individual falsely claiming to be a broker or salesperson is a fine or imprisonment up to six months, or both.

Exemptions to the License

Certain exemptions from licensing requirements are allowed. The following list shows many but not all of the people who are exempt from obtaining a real estate license.

Real Estate License Exemptions

- A person who deals only with his or her own property
- A corporation that performs any of the specified activities through one of its regular officers, who must receive no special compensation for doing so
- Anyone holding a duly executed power of attorney from the owner of property

- An attorney-at-law performing services in the regular course of business as an attorney
- Resident managers of apartment buildings and complexes or their employees
- Short-term (vacation) rental agents
- Employees of certain lending institutions
- Clerical employees of real estate brokers for specific, limited functions
- Licensed personal property brokers
- Any film location representative employed to arrange for the use of real property for photographic purposes
- Cemetery authorities
- Certain collectors of payments for lenders or on notes for owners in connection with loans secured directly or collaterally by liens on real property, provided such collectors annually meet exemption criteria
- Any receiver, trustee in bankruptcy or person acting under order of any court
- Any trustee selling under a deed of trust
- Lenders making loans guaranteed or insured by an agency of the federal government
- An employee of lending institutions, pension trusts, credit unions, or insurance companies, in connection with loans secured by liens on real property or a business opportunity
- Escrow agents collecting funds in connection with loans secured by liens on real property when the funds are deposited in the escrow agent's trust account

Steps in Getting a Real Estate License

Before an applicant for a real estate salesperson or broker license may obtain a license, he or she must fulfill certain real estate education requirements and then apply for and pass a real estate examination. After completing the education requirements and passing the examination, additional documentation is necessary when applying for the actual license.

Eligibility Requirements for Salesperson & Broker

Before applying for a broker or salesperson license, a prospective licensee must meet certain eligibility requirements.

Eligibility Requirements for Obtaining a License

- Be at least 18 years old
- Provide a social security or tax ID number
- Be honest and truthful
- Complete real estate course(s) as required by law
- Apply for and pass the state qualifying examination
- Apply for the license

Additional Requirements: Salesperson License

A salesperson must submit proof of completion of 3 approved real estate courses—Real Estate Principles, Real Estate Practice, and an elective course. A salesperson must be employed by a licensed broker to perform acts regulated by a salesperson license.

Additional Requirements: Broker License

An applicant for an original real estate broker license must meet specific education and experience standards. A broker candidate must complete 8 approved real estate courses. In addition, a broker candidate must also have 2 years of full-time licensed real estate experience within the past 5 years or the equivalent. Acceptable equivalents include a four-year degree with a major or minor in real estate from an accredited college.

Required Education

You must submit evidence, in the form of transcripts or certificates, that you have completed the statutory license courses. Courses may be taken from a CalBRE-approved private vocational real estate school or from a college that is accredited by the Western Association of Schools and Colleges or a comparable regional accrediting entity. Unless the California Real Estate Commissioner has granted prior approval, no private vocational real estate school outside California may grant credit for the required prelicense courses. The required number of hours for a statutory course is 45 hours if taken from a real estate school. If taken at an accredited college, a course for three-semester units or four-quarter units is acceptable.

Real Estate Courses	Salesperson	Broker
Real Estate Principles	Required	Elective
Real Estate Practice	Required	Required
Legal Aspects of Real Estate	Elective	Required
Real Estate Appraisal	Elective	Required
Real Estate Finance	Elective	Required
Real Estate Economics	Elective	Required
General Accounting	May waive RE Economics	May waive RE Economics
Business Law	Elective	Elective
Common Interest Developments	Elective	Elective
Computer Applications in RE	Elective	Elective
Escrows	Elective	Elective
Mortgage Loan Brokering/ Lending	Elective	Elective
Property Management	Elective	Elective
Real Estate Office Administration	Elective	Elective
Adv. Legal Aspects of Real Estate	Not allowed	Elective
Adv. Real Estate Appraisal	Not allowed	Elective
Adv. Real Estate Finance	Not allowed	Elective

Real Estate Examination

The purpose of the real estate license examination is to make sure consumers are protected in all transactions where they are to be represented by an agent. License applicants must have knowledge of the English language, including reading, writing, and spelling; and of arithmetical computations common to real estate and business opportunity practices.

The exam tests an applicant's general knowledge of real estate, appraisal, finance, forms, and other fundamentals of the industry. The subject matter covered in the examination is based on laws and procedures appropriate within California. The following lists of examination topics are for informational purposes and should not be considered totally comprehensive.

Topics Tested on the Real Estate License Examinations		
Area of Knowledge	Salesperson Exam	Broker Exam
Property Ownership and Land Use Controls	15%	15%
Laws of Agency	17%	17%
Valuation and Market Analysis	14%	14%
Financing	9%	9%
Transfer of Property	8%	8%
Practice of Real Estate and Mandated Disclosures	25%	25%
Contracts	12%	12%

Examination Rules and Grading		
	Salesperson	Broker
Time	3 ¼ hours	5 hours
Number of multiple-choice questions	150	200
Passing score	70%	75%

Applying for the Examination

The applications and fee schedule for both the sales and broker license examination can be obtained from the CalBRE website. A person has two years from the date the application is received to complete all qualifications and take the examination. After the two-year period, the application will expire and the applicant will have to resubmit everything again and pay another fee.

A person applying for the salesperson examination fills out the salesperson examination application and mails it to CalBRE along with the appropriate fee and proof of completion of three approved real estate courses—Real Estate Principles, Real Estate Practice, and an elective.

Once the application is processed, CalBRE will send notification of the examination date, time, and location. You can also check online at the CalBRE website to see if your examination has been scheduled.

An applicant who fails to pass the state exam may apply for reexamination any number of times by filing an application and paying the fee. The person must take the exam within 2 years or file a new application and pay a new fee.

Upon passing the state exam, the applicant may apply for the salesperson or broker license within one year of the examination date.

Applying for the License

After passing the state exam, the applicant may apply for the salesperson or broker license within one year of the examination date. Unless you are currently licensed as a salesperson or hold a real estate license that expired less than two years ago, there are other documents you will need to include with your license application. You will need to submit one set of classifiable fingerprints, provide a social security or tax ID number, and, if you are an out-of-state applicant, you must include an irrevocable Consent to Service of Process.

Fingerprint Requirements

An applicant for an original real estate license must submit one set of classifiable **fingerprints**. The fingerprints must be submitted electronically to the state Department of Justice (DOJ) using the Live Scan Program, which takes and transmits fingerprints to the DOJ and the Federal Bureau of Investigation (FBI). Social Security numbers are now required on examination applications so fingerprint results can be processed.

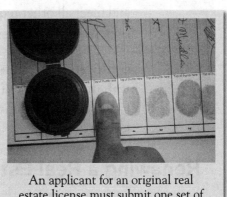

An applicant for an original real estate license must submit one set of classifiable fingerprints.

An original license will not be issued until a report from the DOJ and the FBI is received either stating that there is no criminal history or disclosing criminal history information, which then must be reviewed and evaluated. More information can be found on the CalBRE website.

Tax Identification Requirement

The Legislature finds that it is in the best interests of the State of California to allow people who are not lawfully present in the United States to obtain real estate licenses. [B&P code 135.5(a)]. Therefore, the California Bureau of Real Estate cannot deny licensure to an applicant based on his or her citizenship status or immigration status.

However, a real estate license applicant must provide his or her social security number, or if the applicant is a partnership, its federal employer identification number. [B&P Code 30(a)].

A licensee failing to provide the federal employer identification number, or the individual taxpayer identification number or social security number shall be reported by CalBRE to the Franchise Tax Board. [B&P Code30 (b)]. CalBRE cannot process an application for an initial license unless the applicant provides its federal employer identification number, or individual taxpayer identification number or social security number where requested on the application. [B&P Code 30(c)].

Out-of-State Applicants

A person does not have to live in California in order to become licensed in this state, but you must take the appropriate written examination in California and meet all other requirements. California has no reciprocity with any other state to allow a waiver of any of the requirements to obtain a license.

Out-of-state residents must file an irrevocable Consent to Service of Process with the California Bureau of Real Estate. Brokers must maintain a California business address if engaging in business in California, and salespeople must be licensed with a California broker if engaging in business in California.

Renewing a Real Estate License

In general, both types of licenses may be renewed by submitting the appropriate fee and application, along with evidence of completion of 45 hours of CalBRE-approved continuing education courses. Both broker and salesperson licenses are valid for four years and may be renewed at that time upon payment of a fee and evidence that the requirements for continuing education have been met.

Nonrenewal or Suspension - Delinquent Child Support

If there are delinquent child support payments, a four-year license will not be renewed or issued. The California Department of Child Support

Services prepares a list of people, called **obligors**, who owe child support payments. A child support obligor may be issued a 150-day temporary license. During the 150 days, a person must show CalBRE proof that the delinquency is cleared and that he or she has been removed from the list, so that a permanent license can be issued. In addition, a license may be suspended if a licensee's child support remains unpaid.

Nonrenewal or Suspension – Delinquent Tax List

The State Board of Equalization (BOE) and the Franchise Tax Board (FTB) provide CalBRE with **certified tax lists** that list the names of the top 500 **tax debtors** who owe $100,000 or more in delinquent taxes. If the name of an applicant for licensure or a real estate licensee is on either of the certified lists, CalBRE will send a preliminary notice to the applicant or licensee of its intent to withhold issuance or renewal of the license, or to suspend a current license. The notice advises the licensee that any license suspended due to delinquent taxes will remain suspended until CalBRE receives a release from the BOE or FTB to reinstate the license. However, CalBRE may issue a 90-day temporary license to an applicant whose name is on a certified list if the applicant is otherwise eligible for a license. [B&P Code §494.5]

e-Licensing Transactions

CalBRE now offers **eLicensing**, an interactive online system that lets you complete license renewal and change transactions via the Internet. The following list includes many of the available transactions.

eLicensing Transactions

- Online Registration with CalBRE
- Mailing Address Changes
- Broker Main Office Address Changes
- Salesperson Requests To Change Employing Broker
- Broker Certification Of Salesperson Employment
- Salesperson/Broker License Renewals
- Duplicate License Requests
- Examination Services

User-friendly features include customized menus, e-mail confirmations, status tracking of online transactions, and clear instructions. eLicensing is available on the CalBRE website.

Late Renewal

A real estate license that has expired may be renewed within 2 years of the expiration date. A **two-year grace period** for renewal is allowed as long as all real estate activity has ceased during that time and a late fee is paid at the time of renewal. There is no provision for an inactive license status. Two years after a license expires, all license rights lapse, and the person will have to go through the state examination process again to get another real estate license.

However, if a broker's license expires, all licensed activities of the broker must stop and all of the broker's salespeople (if any) are immediately placed in a non-working status. Any branch office licenses are cancelled. That means no listing, selling, showing, leasing, or any licensed activity between the date of license expiration and the date of late renewal. A commission may not be claimed without a valid license. Once the broker has renewed his or her license, all the salesperson licenses and branch office licenses must be reactivated.

When a salesperson is discharged for a violation of any of the provisions of the Real Estate Law, the employing broker must immediately file a certified written statement of the facts with the Commissioner.

Continuing Education

Each time brokers and salespeople renew their licenses—every 4 years—they must present evidence of completing the required continuing education (CE) courses within the four-year period immediately preceding license renewal.

Initial Renewal - Broker and Salesperson

Real estate brokers and salespeople renewing an original license for the first time must complete 45 clock hours of CalBRE-approved CE courses. The required courses are 3 hours each of Agency, Ethics, Fair Housing, Risk Management, and Trust Fund Handling. In addition, 30 more CE hours must be completed, of which 18 hours must be in the consumer protection category. The remaining clock hours required to complete the 45 hours of continuing education may be related to either consumer service or consumer protection courses. Beginning January 1, 2016, brokers must complete a 3-hour course in Management and Supervision as part of the 45-hour requirement.

STATE OF CALIFORNIA
DEPARTMENT OF REAL ESTATE
Serving Californians Since 1917

SALESPERSON RENEWAL APPLICATION

RE 209 (Rev. 6/09)

	DRE RECEIVED DATE

NOTE — Read pages 3–4 (general intructions, renewal info., mailing address,etc.,) before completing this application.

TO AVOID PENALTY — Renew on or before current license expiration date.

1. LICENSE I.D. NUMBER

2. RENEWAL STATUS (check appropriate box)
   ☐ ON TIME   ☐ LATE

RENEWAL FEE

ON TIME FEE | LATE FEE

CURRENT EXP. DATE | 2-YR LATE RENEWAL ENDS

COMMENT

3. **License Changes** — Changes indicated will be effective the date the application is received by DRE, if this application is filed before the current license expiration date.

   ☐ Change of Personal Name   ☐ Change of Mailing Address
   ☐ Change of Broker

4. WITHIN THE SIX-YEAR PERIOD PRIOR TO FILING THIS APPLICATION, HAVE YOU BEEN CONVICTED OF A MISDEMEANOR OR FELONY? CONVICTIONS EXPUNGED UNDER PENAL CODE SECTION 1203.4 MUST BE DISCLOSED. HOWEVER, YOU MAY OMIT TRAFFIC CITATIONS WHICH DO NOT CONSTITUTE A MISDEMEANOR OR FELONY. .... ☐ YES   ☐ NO

5. ARE THERE CRIMINAL CHARGES PENDING AGAINST YOU AT THIS TIME? .... ☐ YES   ☐ NO
   IF YES TO EITHER ITEM 4 OR 5, COMPLETE ITEM 17 ON PAGE 2.

6. WITHIN THE SIX-YEAR PERIOD PRIOR TO FILING THIS APPLICATION, HAVE YOU HAD A DENIED, SUSPENDED, RESTRICTED OR REVOKED BUSINESS OR PROFESSIONAL LICENSE (INCLUDING REAL ESTATE), IN CALIFORNIA OR ANY OTHER STATE? .... ☐ YES   ☐ NO

7. ARE THERE ANY LICENSE DISCIPLINARY ACTIONS PENDING AGAINST A BUSINESS OR PROFESSIONAL LICENSE YOU HOLD AT THIS TIME? ...... ☐ YES   ☐ NO
   IF YES, TO EITHER ITEM 6 OR 7, COMPLETE ITEM 18 ON PAGE 2.

8. DO YOU RESIDE IN CALIFORNIA? .... ☐ YES   ☐ NO
   IF NO, A CONSENT TO SERVICE OF PROCESS (RE 234) MUST BE ON FILE WITH DRE.

9. ON RENEWAL DATE, WILL YOU BE ENGAGED IN REAL ESTATE ACTIVITIES FOR WHICH A CALIFORNIA REAL ESTATE LICENSE IS REQUIRED? ...... ☐ YES   ☐ NO
   IF YES, BROKER MUST SIGN AND COMPLETE BROKER INFORMATION ON PAGE 2.

10. NAME – LAST | FIRST | MIDDLE

11. NEW PERSONAL NAME *(see page 3)* – LAST | FIRST | MIDDLE

12. MAILING ADDRESS – STREET ADDRESS OR POST OFFICE BOX **(Do not leave blank.)**

CITY | STATE | ZIP CODE

13. BIRTH DATE (Month/Day/Year) | 14. BUSINESS TELEPHONE *(Include area code)* | 15. RESIDENCE TELEPHONE *(Include area code)*

Salesperson Certification

I certify under penalty of perjury that the answers and statements given in this application are true and correct and that if licensed I will not violate any provisions of the Real Estate Law nor abuse the privileges of a real estate licensee. *I understand that if I fail to qualify for renewal for any reason or withdraw this application the Department of Real Estate cannot refund the fees remitted with this application.*

16. SIGNATURE OF SALESPERSON | DATE
》》》

FOR DRE USE ONLY

PROCESSOR NUMBER AND DATE PROCESSED | LICENSE EFFECTIVE DATE | LICENSE EXPIRATION DATE | COMMENTS/FORM LETTERS

VIOLATIONS

NOTE: Attach this sheet to renewal application before mailing/delivering to DRE.	SALESPERSON IDENTIFICATION NUMBER

CONVICTION DETAILS

"Convicted" as used in Item 4 includes a verdict of guilty by judge or jury, a plea of guilty, a plea of nolo contendere (i.e., "no contest"), or a forfeiture of bail in the courts (including military courts) of any state, commonwealth, possession or country. Convictions within the six-year period prior to filing this application must be disclosed, even if the plea or verdict was set aside, the conviction dismissed or expunged, or you have been pardoned.

17. DETAILED EXPLANATION OF ITEM 4 AND/OR 5.

COMPLETE ONE LINE FOR EACH VIOLATION AND PROVIDE EXPLANATION BELOW. IF YOU ARE UNABLE TO PROVIDE THIS INFORMATION, PROVIDE ALL THE REQUESTED INFORMATION YOU CAN OBTAIN, WITH AN EXPLANATION FOR THE MISSING INFORMATION. IF THE CONVICTION STATUS HAS BEEN SUBSEQUENTLY CHANGED OR REDUCED, NOTE THAT FACT IN THE AREA PROVIDED FOR ADDITIONAL INFORMATION.

ATTACHMENTS FOR ADDITIONAL INFORMATION: SPECIFY WHICH LINES YOU ARE REFERRING TO. *EACH ADDITIONAL SHEET MUST BE SIGNED BY APPLICANT AND EMPLOYING BROKER, IF APPLICABLE.*

* CODE SECTION VIOLATED (i.e., 1014, 484, ETC.)
** CODE VIOLATED (i.e., U.S. CODE, PENAL CODE, ETC.)
*** DISPOSITION (i.e., PROBATION, PAROLE, FINE, LENGTH OF TERM, etc.)

COURT OF CONVICTION (Name and Address)	ARRESTING AGENCY (Name and Address)	DATE OF CONVICTION	TYPE OF CONVICTION	* CODE SECTION VIOLATED	** CODE VIOLATED	*** DISPOSITION	CASE NUMBER
Example: Sacramento Cnty. 456 Main St., Sac	Sacramento City Police 123 Main St., Sac	2/20/87	☐ Felony ☒ Misdemeanor	484	Penal Code	6 months probation and $200 fine	1234
17A.			☐ Felony ☐ Misdemeanor				
17B.			☐ Felony ☐ Misdemeanor				

18. DETAILED EXPLANATION OF ITEM 6 AND/OR 7. IF NEEDED, EXPLANATION MAY BE PROVIDED BELOW.

18A. TYPE OF LICENSE	18B. LICENSE ID NO.	18C. LICENSE EXPIRATION DATE	18D. STATE
18E. ACTION (revoked, etc.)	18F. DATE OF ACTION	18G. DATE ACTION TERMINATED	18H. CODE SECTION VIOLATED

ADDITIONAL INFORMATION: SPECIFY AREAS YOU ARE REFERRING TO.

_____

_____

_____

_____

_____

19. SIGNATURE OF SALESPERSON, IF ITEM 17 OR 18 ABOVE IS COMPLETED	DATE
〉〉〉	

EMPLOYING BROKER INFORMATION

20. BROKER OR CORPORATION ID NUMBER	21. BROKER OR CORPORATION NAME (PRINT AS IT APPEARS ON LICENSE CERTIFICATE; NO DBA'S.)

22. BUSINESS TELEPHONE NUMBER (Include area code)	23. RESIDENCE TELEPHONE NUMBER (Include area code)

24. BROKER OR CORPORATION MAIN OFFICE ADDRESS — STREET ADDRESS, CITY, ZIP CODE

Broker Certification

I am aware of the provisions of Section 3700 of the Labor Code which require every employer to be insured against liability for workers' compensation. I certify that this salesperson is employed by me and there is a written agreement on file in my office in compliance with Section 2726 of the Regulations of the Real Estate Commissioner. (Refer to page 4.)

25. SIGNATURE OF BROKER OR LICENSED OFFICER	DATE
〉〉〉	

26. PRINTED NAME OF SIGNER ON LINE #25.

Subsequent Renewals - Broker and Salesperson

For subsequent renewals, all real estate brokers and salespersons must complete 45 clock hours of CalBRE-approved continuing education. The licensee may take EITHER the six mandatory 3-hour CE courses in Agency, Ethics, Fair Housing, Management and Supervision, Risk Management, and Trust Fund Handling OR one 8-hour Survey Course that covers the six mandatory subjects.

The balance of the required hours must include at least 18 hours of consumer protection topics. The remaining clock hours required to complete the 45 hours of continuing education may be related to either consumer service or consumer protection courses.

Initial Renewals - Broker and Salesperson			
Salesperson		**Broker**	
Course	Hours	Course	Hours
Agency	3	Agency	3
Ethics	3	Ethics	3
Fair Housing	3	Fair Housing	3
Risk Management	3	Risk Management	3
Trust Fund Handling	3	Trust Fund Handling	3
		Management and Supervision	3
Consumer Protection	18	Consumer Protection	18
Balance of CE Hours	<u>12</u>	Balance of CE Hours	<u>9</u>
Total Hours	45	*Total Hours*	45

Subsequent Renewals - Broker and Salesperson			
Choice A - 45 hrs		**Choice B - 45 hrs**	
Renewal Course	Hrs	Renewal Course	Hrs
Agency	3	Agency	0
Ethics	3	Ethics	0
Fair Housing	3	Fair Housing	0
Trust Fund Handling	3	Trust Fund Handling	0
Risk Management	3	Risk Management	0
Management and Supervision	3	Management and Supervision	0
Survey Course	0	Survey Course	8
Consumer Protection	18	Consumer Protection	18
Balance of CE Hours	<u>12</u>	Balance of CE Hours	<u>19</u>
Total Hours	45	*Total Hours*	45

ENFORCING THE REAL ESTATE LAW

The license law is only effective if it can be enforced. The Commissioner enforces the provisions of the Real Estate Law and has the power to restrict, suspend, or revoke a person's real estate license. The Commissioner also investigates people or firms who appear to be operating improperly, without benefit of a license, or who subdivide land without complying with the subdivision laws. If sufficient evidence of a violation is obtained, an **Order to Desist and Refrain** is issued, or a complaint is brought, and the parties are prosecuted in a court of competent jurisdiction.

The enforcement section of CalBRE investigates complaints against real estate brokers and salespersons. Any licensee found in violation of the law may be required to pay the costs associated with an enforcement action. The CalBRE website must disclose the status of every license issued, including information on accusations, suspensions and revocations. However, citations do not have to be disclosed. When the Commissioner investigates a complaint, which may involve criminal activities, it is the duty of the local district attorneys to prosecute all criminals in their respective counties.

> Only the Commissioner—not the courts—can restrict, suspend, or revoke a real estate license.

CalBRE handles simple complaints through its Advocacy Program, minor infractions by citations, and serious violations with a formal hearing.

Advocacy Program

A complaint that involves simple disputes or minor issues between consumers and licensees is usually handled by the **Advocacy Program** as an alternative to setting up formal investigations. Many of the issues that the enforcement advocates resolve involve a breakdown in communication between licensees and their principals. The types of cases handled through the Advocacy Program include small monetary disputes where there does not appear to be a violation of the Real Estate Law.

Types of Cases Handled by the Advocacy Program

- Consumers who needed copies of their documents and had been unable to secure a response.
- Consumers who needed assistance in contacting their agent or broker on a current transaction.

- Consumers who needed information that they had not been able to obtain from their agent for escrow, lenders, or inspectors.

- Consumers trying to cancel transactions or loans.

- Consumers who wanted to know where their earnest money was.

- Consumers who were asked to sign documents or do something they did not understand or did not feel is appropriate.

- Consumers having homeowner association issues while CalBRE still has jurisdiction over a subdivider.

- Licensees questioning whether offers have been presented to sellers, or to lenders in REO transactions.

Citations and Fines

The Commissioner can issue **citations and fines** to both licensees and unlicensed persons for minor violations of the Real Estate Law. The **citation** describes the basis of the complaint and contains an order to correct the violation and a reasonable time period in which to correct it. In addition, the Commissioner may assess an administrative fine not to exceed $2,500 per citation. If a broker or salesperson receives a citation and/or is assessed a fine, the Commissioner will not take other administrative discipline and the citation will not be reported as disciplinary action. If necessary, the Commissioner can apply to the appropriate superior court for an order to enforce the citation

However, if a licensee fails to comply with the terms of a citation or to pay an assessed fine, the Commissioner shall subject that person to further disciplinary action. Additionally, a license will not be renewed if the licensee has not complied with the terms of the citation or has not paid any assessed fines. [B&P Code 10080.9]

Formal Hearing Process

The Commissioner must follow the established legal procedures found in the Administrative Procedure Act to discipline licensees under the formal hearing process. Some violations may result in civil injunctions, criminal prosecutions, or substantial fines.

Investigation and Accusation

Usually an **investigation** of the actions of a licensee is based upon receipt of a verified written complaint from someone who believes a licensee, while acting as an agent, has wronged them. Investigations are made by CalBRE's

Enforcement and Audit Sections. The investigator takes statements from witnesses and the licensee and obtains and verifies documents. An informal conference may be called to determine the validity and seriousness of the complaint. If it appears that the complaint is of a serious nature and that a violation of law has occurred, an **accusation** is filed, and there may be a formal hearing, which could result in suspension or revocation of the license.

Formal Hearings

A **formal hearing** is held according to the Administrative Procedures Act. The accusation or statement of issues is served upon the affected licensee. In the hearing, the Commissioner is the complainant and brings the charges against the

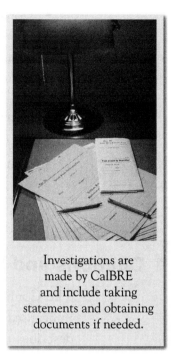

Investigations are made by CalBRE and include taking statements and obtaining documents if needed.

licensee. The licensee, known as the respondent, may appear with or without an attorney. The Commissioner's counsel presents the case to an administrative law judge who issues a proposed decision based upon the findings.

The Commissioner may accept, reject, or reduce the proposed penalty from the administrative law judge and makes an official decision. Sometimes the charges against the respondent (licensee) are dismissed, but if the charges are sufficiently serious, the license of the respondent is suspended or revoked. A person whose license has been revoked or suspended must wait one year until he or she can apply for reinstatement.

VIOLATIONS OF THE REAL ESTATE LAW

Real estate agents who make continuing efforts to learn and stay current on issues concerning the real estate industry should have successful careers. Real estate agents must be prepared to meet the duties and obligations required by law. If they do not comply, they may be subject to civil, criminal, and/or Bureau of Real Estate action and penalties. All around the country, courts and legislatures are continuing to hold real estate agents accountable for their activities. Increasingly, agents must know what and how to disclose—as well as when, where, why, by, and to whom. The uninformed real estate agent is highly vulnerable to court action in our consumer-oriented society.

The Real Estate Commissioner is empowered to adopt regulations to enforce the Real Estate Law. Duly adopted regulations become part of the California Code of Regulations and, in effect, have the force and authority of the law itself. Therefore, all licensees and prospective licensees should be thoroughly familiar with the Real Estate Commissioner's Regulations. They should be considered in conjunction with the law, as they specifically outline procedures directed and authorized by the statutes. The following is a partial listing of the Business and Professions Code sections that are of utmost importance to those who practice real estate.

The Business and Professions Code, Article 3, Section 10175 authorizes the Real Estate Commissioner to enforce the Real Estate Law. Upon grounds provided in this article and the other articles of this chapter, the license of any real estate licensee may be revoked or suspended in accordance with the provisions of this part relating to hearings.

Although most violations of Real Estate Law occur under sections 10176 and 10177 of the Business and Professions Code, we are including some of the other sections that need discussion and mention. Section 10176 refers to actions committed while conducting business under a real estate license. Section 10177 refers to circumstances when a licensee is not necessarily acting as an agent.

Section 10176: Violations When Acting as an Agent in a Real Estate Transaction

The Commissioner may upon his or her own motion, and shall upon the verified complaint in writing of any person, investigate the actions of any person engaged in the business or acting in the capacity of a real estate licensee within this state. He also may temporarily suspend or permanently revoke a real estate license at any time where the real estate licensee, in performing or attempting to perform any of the acts within the scope of this chapter, has been guilty of any of the following:

Section 10176(a)   Misrepresentation

Licensee made substantial misrepresentations. A **misrepresentation** is a false statement of fact.

Section 10176(b)   False Promise

Licensee made false promises. A **false promise** is an incorrect statement about what someone is going to do in the future.

Section 10176(c)   Continued Misrepresentation

Licensee pursued a continued and flagrant course of misrepresentation or making of false promises.

Section 10176(d)   Dual Agency

Licensee did not inform all principals that he or she was acting as agent for more than one party in a transaction.

Section 10176(e)   Commingling

Licensee commingled funds. **Commingling** is the mixing of the principal's funds with the broker's own money. **Conversion** is misappropriating and using principal's funds.

Section 10176(f)   Definite Termination Date

Licensee failed to specify a termination date on all exclusive listings relating to transactions for which a real estate license is required.

Section 10176(g)   Secret Profit

Licensee made a secret profit by failing to disclose the full amount of the licensee's compensation.

Section 10176(h)   Listing-Option

Licensee with both a listing and an option to buy on a property failed to inform the principal of the amount of profit the licensee would make and failed to obtain the written consent of the principal approving the amount of such profit, before the licensee exercised the option.

Section 10176(i)   Dishonest Dealing

Licensee engaged in activities that constitute fraud or dishonest dealing.

Section 10176(j)   Signatures of Prospective Purchasers

Licensee failed to obtain a written authorization to sell from a business owner before securing the signature of a prospective purchaser to any such agreement.

Section 10176(k)   Failing to Disburse Mortgage Funds

Licensee (when acting as a lender) failed to disburse funds in accordance with a commitment to make a mortgage loan that is accepted by the applicant.

Section 10176(l)   Delaying the Closing of a Mortgage Loan

Licensee intentionally delayed the closing of a mortgage loan for the sole purpose of increasing interest, costs, fees, or charges payable by the borrower.

Section 10176(m) Violating Other Laws

Licensee violated any part of the licensing law, if it occurs within the scope of that person's duties as a licensee.

10176.5(a) Real Estate Transfer Disclosure Statement Violations

Licensee willfully or repeatedly violated any of the provisions of the Transfer Disclosure Statement provisions.

Section 10177: Violations When Not Necessarily Acting as an Agent

The Commissioner may suspend or revoke the license of a real estate licensee, delay the renewal of a license of a real estate licensee, or may deny the issuance of a license to an applicant, who has done any of the following, or may suspend or revoke the license of a corporation, delay the renewal of a license of a real estate licensee, or deny the issuance of a license to a corporation, if an officer, director, or person owning or controlling 10% or more of the corporation's stock has done any of the following:

Section 10177(a) Obtaining a License by Fraud

Licensee or applicant made material misstatements of fact in an application for a license and in those instances where licenses have been procured by fraud, misrepresentation, or deceit.

Section 10177(b) Convictions

Licensee or applicant entered a plea of guilty or *nolo contendere* (no contest) or was found guilty of, or was convicted of a felony or a crime which involves moral turpitude and is substantially related to the qualifications, functions, or duties of a real estate licensee. **Moral turpitude** includes perjury, embezzlement, robbery, murder, and other base or vile acts.

Section 10177(c) False Designations

Licensees misrepresented and/or made false statements about their education, their special education, their credentials and professional designations.

Section 10177(d) Violations of Other Sections

Licensee willfully violated any of the other sections of the Real Estate Law, the Regulations of the Commissioner, and the subdivision laws.

Section 10177(e)   Misuse of Trade Name

Only active members of the National Association of REALTORS® may use the term REALTOR®. It is unlawful and unethical to misuse the terms REALTOR® and/or Realtist or any trade name or insignia of which the licensee is not a member.

Section 10177(f)   Conduct Warranting Denial of License

Licensee conducted himself or herself in a manner that would have warranted the denial of his or her application for a real estate license. This is a general section of the Real Estate Law. Almost any act involving a crime or dishonesty will fall within this section including the denial or suspension of a license issued by another government agency.

Section 10177(g)   Negligence or Incompetence

Licensee demonstrated negligence or incompetence while performing activities for which a real estate licensee is required.

Section 10177(h)   Failure to Supervise Salespersons

A broker is subject to disciplinary action if the broker, or the officer designated by a corporate broker licensee, fails to exercise reasonable supervision and control over the activities of the broker's salespeople.

Section 10177(i)   Misuse of Government Employment

Licensee misused government employment to gain access to records in a manner that violates the confidential nature of records.

Section 10177(j)   Dishonest Dealing

Licensee engaged in conduct which constitutes fraud or dishonest dealing.

Section 10177(k)   Restricted License Violation

Licensee violated any of the terms, conditions, restrictions, and limitations contained in any order granting a restricted license.

Section 10177(l)   Inducement of Panic Selling

Licensee solicited or induced the sale, lease, or the listing for sale or lease of residential property on the grounds of loss of value, increase in crime, or decline in the quality of schools due to the present or prospective entry into the neighborhood of people of another race, color, religion, ancestry, or national origin. This is also called **blockbusting** or **panic peddling**.

Section 10177(m)   Violation of Franchise Investment Law

Licensee violated provisions of the Franchise Investment Law or any regulations of the Corporations Commissioner Franchise Investment Law.

Section 10177(n)   Violation of Corporations Code

Licensee violated provisions of the Corporations Code or of the regulations of the Commissioner of Corporations relating to securities as specified by the Corporations Code.

Section 10177(o)   Failure to Disclose Conflict of Interest

Licensee failed to disclose to the buyer of real property, in a transaction in which the licensee is an agent for the buyer, the nature and extent of a licensee's direct or indirect ownership interest in that real property.

Section 10177(p)   Violation of Corporate Securities Law

Licensee violated provisions of the Corporate Securities Law (B&P Code, Article 6, §10237).

Section 10177(q)   Violation of Foreclosure Laws

Licensee violated or failed to comply with provisions of Civil Code, §2290 et. seq. that deal with foreclosures and mortgage foreclosure consultants.

Section 10177.1   Suspend a License Obtained by Fraud

Within 90 days of issuing a license, the Commissioner may without a hearing suspend the license of any person who procured the issuance of the license to himself by fraud, misrepresentation, deceit, or by the making of any material misstatement of fact in his application for such license.

Section 10177.2   Mobilehome Sales Violations

When dealing with mobilehomes/manufactured homes, a licensee could have his or her license suspended or revoked if he or she is found guilty of any of the following acts: committed fraud on an application for the registration of a mobilehome; did not deliver a properly endorsed certificate of ownership from the seller to the buyer; knowingly purchased or sold a stolen mobilehome; or gave the Department of Housing and Community Development a bad check.

Section 10177.3 Misrepresent Price Opinions

A real estate licensee must not knowingly or intentionally misrepresent the value of real property or provide an opinion of value of residential real property to a lender wherein the licensee has an economic interest in the property.

Section 10177.4 Referral of Customers for Compensation

A real estate licensee must not receive a commission, fee, or other consideration as compensation or inducement for referral of customers to any escrow agent, structural pest control firm, home protection company, title insurer, or controlled escrow company.

Section 10177.5 Fraud in a Civil Action

If a final judgment is obtained in a civil action against any real estate licensee upon grounds of fraud, misrepresentation, or deceit with reference to any transaction for which a license is required, the commissioner may, after hearing, suspend or revoke the license of such real estate licensee.

Other Violations

Sections 10137 & 10138 Employing or Paying an Unlicensed Person

A broker may not pay a commission to an unlicensed person, except to a broker of another state. A licensed salesperson may not accept compensation from anyone except his or her employing broker. The broker may be fined $100.

Section 10140 False Advertising

Real estate licensees who knowingly authorize or publish, distribute, or circulate any written statement that is false or fraudulent regarding subdivided lands or government patents, are guilty of a public offense. Punishment includes a $1,000 fine, imprisonment up to one year, or both. Additionally, real estate licensees may have their license revoked by the Commissioner.

Section 10140.5 Name of Broker

An advertisement offering to help a person file an application to purchase or lease government-owned land (State or Federal) must include the name of the broker and that he or she is a licensed California real estate broker.

Section 10140.6 Disclosure of Licensed Status in Advertising

Advertisements placed in newspapers, periodicals, mailers, or the like by real estate agents for any activity that requires a real estate license must also include a designation disclosing that the agent is performing acts that require a real estate license. [§10140.6 (a)]. The use of the terms broker, agent, REALTOR®, loan correspondent or the abbreviations "bro.", "agt.", or other similar terms or abbreviations is deemed sufficient identification to fulfill the designation requirement. [Reg. 2770.1].

A real estate licensee must disclose his or her eight digit license identification number and the unique identifier if the licensee is a MLO on all solicitation materials intended to be the first point of contact with consumers and on real property purchase agreements when acting as an agent in those transactions. Solicitation materials include items such as business cards, stationery, and advertising fliers, but exclude advertisements in print or electronic media and "for sale" signs. [§10140.6 (b) and Reg. 2773(a)].

Section 10141 Selling Price Disclosure

A broker must notify the buyer and the seller of the selling price within one month after completion of the sale. It is usually done by the escrow company.

Section 10141.5 Recording Trust Deed

A broker (or escrow company) must record a trust deed created on the sale of a property within one week of closing.

Section 10141.6 Notification of Escrow Activities

Real estate brokers who handle 5 or more escrows in a calendar year or whose escrow activities exceed $1 million in a calendar year must file a report with CalBRE. The report documents the number of escrows conducted and the dollar volume escrowed during the calendar year.

Section 10142 Delivery of Agreement

A broker must give a copy of any contract to the party signing it at the time that it is signed.

Section 10148 Document Retention

A broker must retain the following documents for 3 years from the date of the closing or, if the transaction is not closed, from the date of the listing: listings, deposit receipts, cancelled checks, trust records, disclosure documents, Mortgage Loan Disclosure Statements, correspondence, email, and other related documents. The requirement does not include electronic messages of an **ephemeral nature** such as text messages, instant messages, or tweets. [Civil Code §1624(d)]. The Bureau of Real Estate can suspend or revoke the license of any real estate licensee who knowingly destroys, alters, conceals, mutilates, or falsifies any of the documents that are required to be retained.

Section 10175.2(a)   Monetary Penalty in Lieu of Suspension

The Real Estate Commissioner may permit a real estate licensee to pay a monetary penalty to the department in lieu of an actual license suspension.

Section 10178   Broker Must Report Discharge of Salesperson for Violation

When any real estate salesperson is discharged by his or her employer for a violation of any of the provisions of the Real Estate Law, a certified written statement of the facts with reference thereto shall be filed forthwith with the Commissioner by the employer. If the employer fails to notify the Commissioner as required by this section, the Commissioner may temporarily suspend or permanently revoke the real estate license of the employer, in accordance with the provisions of this part relating to hearings.

Section 10182   Reinstatement Examination

As a condition to the reinstatement of a revoked or suspended license, the Commissioner may require the applicant to take and pass a qualifying examination.

Section 10185   Violations Are Misdemeanors

Any person, including officers, directors, agents, or employees of corporations, who willfully violates or knowingly participates in the violation of this division shall be guilty of a misdemeanor punishable by a fine not exceeding $10,000, imprisonment in the county jail not exceeding six months, or a fine and imprisonment.

SUMMARY

Real estate licensees must obey the Real Estate Law and the Regulations of the Real Estate Commissioner. The Real Estate Law, sometimes referred to as the **license law**, is designed mainly for the protection of the public in real estate transactions where a licensee is involved.

The **Real Estate Commissioner** and the Bureau of Real Estate (CalBRE) supervise the education, licensing, and conduct of real estate professionals. Real estate licensees involved in business opportunities need to be familiar with the Uniform Commercial Code.

The Commissioner enforces the provisions of the Real Estate Law and has the power to restrict, suspend, or revoke a person's real estate license.

UNIT 15 REVIEW

❑ Matching Exercise

Instructions: Write the letter of the matching term on the blank line before its definition. Answers immediately follow the Multiple Choice Questions.

Terms

A. 45 hours

B. accusation

C. Advocacy Program

D. branch offices

E. conversion

F. false promise

G. fictitious business name

H. license law

I. misrepresentation

J. obligors

K. panic peddling

L. REALTOR®

M. real estate broker

N. Real Estate Commissioner

O. Real Estate Law

P. Real Estate Recovery Fund

Q. real estate salesperson

R. restricted license

S. secret profit

T. two-year grace period

Definitions

1. _____ Another name for the Business and Professions Code, Part 1 entitled Licensing of Persons.

2. _____ Another term for the Real Estate Law.

3. _____ Person appointed by the governor to enforce the provisions of the Real Estate Law and the Subdivided Lands Law.

4. _____ Designation used by active member of NAR.

5. _____ Someone with real estate license who must be employed by a real estate broker in order to perform any of the activities that require a license.

6. _____ Hours needed for subsequent renewal of broker or salesperson license.

7. _____ Type of probationary license issued when a license has been suspended, revoked, or denied after a hearing.

8. _____ A person listed by Child Support Services as delinquent in paying child support.

9. _____ The period of time after a license that renewal is allowed, as long as all real estate activity has ceased during that time and a late fee is paid at the time of renewal.

10. _____ A separate account funded through collection of a fixed amount from each license fee.

11. _____ A false statement of fact.

12. _____ A false statement about what someone is going to do in the future.

13. _____ Misappropriating and using principal's funds.

14. _____ Undisclosed profit made by a broker at his or her principal's expense.

15. _____ CalBRE enforcement program that handles simple disputes.

Multiple Choice Questions

Instructions: Circle your response and then check your response with the Answer Key that immediately follows the Multiple Choice Questions.

1. Broker Larwin held an open listing to sell a house that provided for Larwin to receive a 6% commission. Larwin orally agreed to split the commission with Broker Porter if Porter found the buyer. Porter did so, but at close of escrow Larwin kept the entire commission. Under these circumstances, Porter:
    a. has recourse by means of a civil suit.
    b. has recourse under the Real Estate Law.
    c. has recourse under the Statute of Frauds.
    d. does not have a legal claim for a commission because Larwin had an open listing.

2. CalBRE regards a salesperson's relationship with a broker as a(n):
    a. employee.
    b. independent contractor.
    c. general partner.
    d. limited partner.

3. Someone places an advertisement for real estate services without listing a real estate license number. In fact, the person does not have a real estate license. Such an individual could be liable for prosecution by the:

    a. Bureau of Real Estate.

    b. local district attorney.

    c. office of the Attorney General.

    d. local law enforcement agencies.

4. Which of the following must have a current and valid California real estate license?

    a. A mortgage loan broker

    b. A resident manager of an apartment building

    c. A trustee conducting a trust deed foreclosure sale

    d. A short-term (vacation) rental agent

5. A broker must have a written contract with which of the following employees?

    a. Secretaries

    b. Janitorial service

    c. Brokers acting as salespeople who do not have their own office

    d. All of the above

6. If a real estate licensee is listed as an obligor by the California Department of Child Support Services, can he or she renew his or her real estate license?

    a. No, CalBRE revokes the license of anyone who owes child support.

    b. Yes, CalBRE is not concerned with the obligor list.

    c. No, whenever a person is listed as an obligor for delinquent child support, all licenses, including the driver license, are canceled.

    d. Yes, the licensee may be issued a 150-day temporary license.

7. A licensed salesperson gave notice of leaving the real estate brokerage office to the salesperson's employing broker. What, if anything, must the broker do with the salesperson's license?

    a. The broker leaves the license unmarked and gives it to the next broker who employs the salesperson.

    b. The broker returns the license to the salesperson and notifies the Real Estate Commissioner.

    c. The broker marks the license inactivated, returns it to the salesperson, and notifies the Real Estate Commissioner.

    d. The broker marks the license cancelled and mails it to the Real Estate Commissioner.

8. In the course of his or her duties, a real estate salesperson might prepare or sign documents or legal instruments that may have a material effect on the rights or obligations of those entering the transaction. The supervising broker must review, initial, and date these documents or instruments within five days or before the close of escrow. However, the broker may delegate these duties to a salesperson to review items prepared by other salespeople provided that the delegated salesperson has:

   a. been employed by that same broker for at least two years full time.
   b. been employed by that same broker for at least two years full time and has completed at least 18 units of college-level courses related to real estate.
   c. at least two years full-time experience as a real estate salesperson within the past five years.
   d. at least two years full-time experience as a real estate salesperson within the past five years and has completed at least 18 units of college-level courses related to real estate.

9. A broker holding an unrestricted license negotiated the sale of real estate. The broker defrauded the buyer during the sales transaction. The defrauded buyer brought a civil suit against the broker on grounds of fraud and was awarded a final judgment. The Real Estate Commissioner:

   a. may suspend the broker's license when the Commissioner receives a copy of the final judgment of the court.
   b. must wait to take action until the buyer files a formal complaint with the Commissioner.
   c. may suspend the broker's license until a formal hearing is convened.
   d. may hold a hearing but may not suspend or revoke the license until the hearing is concluded.

10. A broker assured a client that a loan could be found at 5% even though there were no such loans available. When it came time to sign the agreement, the rate offered was 7%. The buyer felt he had to accept the loan because he had already given notice at his apartment complex.

   a. The broker acted unethically.
   b. The broker acted illegally.
   c. The broker acted legally.
   d. The doctrine of caveat emptor applies.

11. By law, a broker must keep a copy of the deposit receipt for at least three years from:

   a. the first date on the deposit receipt.
   b. the closing of the transaction.
   c. the recording of the deed.
   d. whichever of the above is earliest.

12. Davis did not have a real estate license but negotiated a contract with Taylor to buy Taylor's 20-acre lot for $5,000/acre. Taylor accepted Davis' offer. During negotiations, Davis himself was offered $20,000/acre by a third party for the same 20 acres. Davis did not disclose this fact to Taylor and went ahead with the purchase. Davis later sold the 20 acres to the third party for $20,000/acre. Taylor subsequently learned that Davis resold the lot. Under these circumstances, an attorney will probably advise that:

    a. Taylor may rescind the contract if Taylor reimburses the third party for expenses incurred in the transaction.

    b. Taylor has no recourse against Davis.

    c. Taylor has a cause of action against Davis because Davis had special knowledge of the property that was not disclosed during the transaction.

    d. Taylor must show that the third party had knowledge of the realistic property value.

13. A licensed real estate salesperson regularly accepted a fee for every client she referred to a lender who signed up for a new mortgage loan. When her employing broker discovered this arrangement, the broker took two steps: (1) The broker fired the salesperson. (2) The broker explicitly warned the rest of the office not to engage in such practices. Who, if anyone, is liable for disciplinary action?

    a. No one. The Real Estate Law was not violated.

    b. Only the broker can be disciplined.

    c. Only the salesperson can be disciplined because the broker had no guilty knowledge of the offense.

    d. Both the salesperson and broker can be disciplined.

14. If an employing broker discharges a salesperson for violating a provision of the Real Estate Law, the broker:

    a. must notify the Real Estate Commissioner within three days of the termination of the salesperson.

    b. must telephone the Commissioner immediately.

    c. must notify the Commissioner immediately by mailing a certified written statement of the facts.

    d. is under no duty to inform the Commissioner.

15. Broker Kim, who is not a member of any trade organization, has been trying out a new advertising slogan: "A new breed of Realtor." This practice is:

    a. grounds for revocation or suspension of her real estate license.

    b. permissible, providing the word realtor is not capitalized.

    c. acceptable as long as she is not licensed in more than one state.

    d. a violation of the Fair Housing Laws.

16. What must a newly licensed salesperson include on his or her business cards?

    a. Eight digit license identification number
    b. Company website
    c. Email address
    d. Special designations

17. Broker Pat has a property listed for nine months without success. He believes the property is 10% overpriced, and he knows that major structural repairs are required. Pat writes and pays for the following advertisement to run in a local newspaper: "Charming 2 BDRM Victorian. Move in right away! Wait `til you see the price! Ready for you! Call Pat at 555-1212." What, if anything, is wrong with the advertisement?

    a. There is no asking price: Regulation Z was violated.
    b. It was unlawful because Pat knew structural work was required and the ad did not state this.
    c. It was unethical to advertise for overpriced property.
    d. The newspaper publisher would be liable for damages if anyone purchased the property as a result of the advertisement.

18. A complaint that involves simple disputes or minor issues between consumers and licensees is usually handled by:

    a. issuing a citation.
    b. involving the Advocacy Program.
    c. assessing a fine.
    d. holding a formal hearing.

19. A broker who holds a valid listing on a property places the following classified advertisement in the local newspaper: "FOR SALE: 3 bedroom, 2 bath home, swimming pool. $129,000. Phone 555-1234." What needs to be included in the ad?

    a. Email address
    b. Website
    c. Sales associates employed by the broker
    d. Broker or "bro"

20. After close of escrow, the actual selling price of the property must be disclosed to both buyer and seller within:

    a. 5 business days.
    b. 10 business days.
    c. 15 days.
    d. 1 month.

UNIT 15 ANSWER KEY

Answers – Matching

1. O		4. L		7. R		10. P		13. E
2. H		5. Q		8. J		11. I		14. S
3. N		6. A		9. T		12. F		15. C

Answers – Multiple Choice

1. **(a)** The Real Estate Commissioner regulates licensed activities. B&P Code Section 10071. Commission disputes are generally civil, not criminal, matters. [The Real Estate Law]

2. **(a)** According to B&P Code Section 10137, salespersons are always employees of their brokers and can only be paid by their brokers. [Real Estate Licensing]

3. **(b)** B&P Code Section 10139 covers penalties for unlicensed persons. The violation could be turned over to the local district attorney to determine whether to prosecute the case. [Real Estate Licensing]

4. **(a)** B&P Code Section 10131 lists activities for which a California real estate license is required--mortgage loan brokers being one of them. B&P Code Section 10133 lists those who are not required to have a license. [Real Estate Licensing]

5. **(c)** Commissioner's Regulation 1726 states, "Every real estate broker shall have a written agreement with each of his salespersons, whether licensed as a salesperson or as a broker under a broker-salesperson arrangement. [Real Estate Licensing]

6. **(d)** A child support obligor may be issued a 150-day temporary license. During the 150 days, a person must show CalBRE proof that the delinquency is cleared and that he or she has been removed from the list, so that a permanent license can be issued. [Real Estate Licensing]

7. **(b)** The broker must notify the Commissioner in writing and return the license certificate to the salesperson. B&P Code Section 10161.8d. [Real Estate Licensing]

8. **(c)** Commissioner's Regulation 2724 gives the experience requirements for delegation of a broker's responsibility and authority to a salesperson. A salesperson must have at least two years full-time experience as a salesperson licensee within the past 5 years (plus a written agreement with the broker regarding delegation). [Real Estate Licensing]

9. **(d)** A hearing is required before an unrestricted (standard) license can be suspended or revoked; no such protection is afforded a restricted license. B&P Code Sections 10100 & 10156.7(a). [Enforcing the Real Estate Law]

10. **(b)** The broker is guilty of misrepresentation and fraud. B&P Code Sections 10776(a), (b) and (i). [Violations of Real Estate Law]

11. **(b)** B&P Code Section 10148a requires the broker to keep records for 3 years. The obligatory retention period runs from the date the transaction is closed or from the date a listing is made if the transaction is not completed. [Violations of Real Estate Law]

12. **(b)** Since Davis is not a real estate licensee, he has no duty to disclose his profit. However, if Davis were licensed, the prohibition against secret (undisclosed) profit would apply. B&P Code Section 10176g. [Violations of Real Estate Law]

13. **(d)** The salesperson violated B&P Code Section 10176g by benefiting from a secret profit. The employing broker violated B&P Code Section 10177h by not exercising supervision over the activities of his or her salespersons. Additionally the broker violated B&P Code 10178 because he or she should have immediately notified the Commissioner of the firing. [Violations of Real Estate Law]

14. **(c)** B&P Code 10178 "When any real estate salesperson is discharged by his or her employer for a violation of any of the provisions of the Real Estate Law, a certified written statement of the facts with reference thereto shall be filed forthwith with the commissioner by the employer and if the employer fails to notify the commissioner as required by this section, the commissioner may temporarily suspend or permanently revoke the real estate license of the employer, in accordance with the provisions of this part relating to hearings." The code's term forthwith, means without delay, within a reasonable time under the circumstances, or at the first opportunity that arises. [Violations of Real Estate Law]

15. **(a)** Broker Kim violated B&P Code Section 10177e by misusing the REALTOR® trade name. This misrepresentation is grounds for disciplinary action by the commissioner. [Violations of Real Estate Law]

16. **(a)** A real estate licensee must disclose his or her eight digit license identification number on all solicitation materials—such as business cards. B&P Code 1014036. [Violations of Real Estate Law]

17. **(b)** The ad is misleading: The broker knows that major structural repairs are needed, so the property can hardly be described as being ready to move into. False advertising regarding any real estate is unlawful. B&P Code Section 10140. [Violations of Real Estate Law]

18. **(b)** A complaint that involves simple disputes or minor issues between consumers and licensees is usually handled by the Advocacy Program as an alternative to formal investigations. [Enforcing the Real Estate Law]

19. **(d)** B&P Code Section 10140.6 requires that the broker disclose his or her involvement in the sale, such as broker, agent, "bro.", "agt.", or other similar terms or abbreviations. [Violations of Real Estate Law]

20. **(d)** B&P Code Section 10141 requires that the broker notify the buyer and the seller of the selling price within one month after completion of the sale. It is usually done by the escrow company. [Violations of Real Estate Law]

A

Appendix

INTRODUCTION

This appendix will explain the basic mathematical procedures you will need to be successful in your new real estate career. Many people are intimidated by the word math, but in this case the concepts presented for your understanding are mainly a review of information you already possess—and probably use in your daily life. An understanding of the principles and formulas explained in this appendix will help you as a licensee in solving math problems you will meet everyday.

MATH

Learning Objectives

After completing this Appendix, you should be able to:

- calculate the selling price of a property.
- calculate the broker (any sales associate) split of a commission.
- calculate the original amount of a note.
- calculate the yield on a discounted trust deed purchase.
- prorate insurance in escrow.
- calculate documentary tax.
- calculate net operating income and property value.
- calculate a percentage of profit.
- calculate acreage in multiple parcels.

BASIC MATH PRINCIPLES

It is important to review math basics including terminology, decimals, percentages, measurements, conversions, and formulas before starting our study of how to solve various real estate problems.

Terminology

Decimal point	The period that sets apart a whole number from a fractional part of that number.
Divisor	A number by which another number is divided.
Dividend	A number to be divided by another number.
Interest	The charge for the use of money.
Principal	The amount of money borrowed.
Proration	The process of making a fair distribution of expenses, through escrow, at the close of the sale.
Rate	The percentage of interest charged on the principal.
Time	The duration of a loan.
Annual	Once per year
Semiannual	Twice per year at 6-month intervals
Biannual	Twice per year
Monthly	Every month
Bimonthly	Every 2 months
Semimonthly	Twice a month
1 year	For escrow and proration purposes, 360 days, 12 months, 52 weeks
1 month	For escrow purposes, 30 days

Decimals and Percentages

It will be beneficial to review the concept of decimals here before starting our study of how to solve various real estate problems. The period that sets apart a whole number from a fractional part of that number is called a **decimal point**. The value of the number is determined by the position of the decimal point.

Any numerals to the right of the decimal point are less than one. The 10th position is the first position to the right of the decimal point, the 100th position is the second to the right of the decimal point, the 1,000th position is the third to the right of the decimal point, and so forth.

The whole numerals are to the left of the decimal point. The units are in the first position to the left of the decimal point, the 10s in the second position to the left of the decimal point, the 100s in the third position to the left of the decimal point, the 1,000s in the fourth position to the left of the decimal point, and so forth.

Equivalent Amounts

Percentage	Decimal	Fraction
4 1/2%	0.045	45/1000
6 2/3%	0.0667	1/15
10%	0.10	1/10
12 1/2%	0.125	1/8
16 2/3%	0.1667	1/6
25%	0.25	1/4
33 1/3%	0.33	1/3
50%	0.50	1/2
66 2/3%	0.667	2/3
75%	0.75	3/4
100%	1.00	1/1

Converting Percentages to Decimals

Looking at a number expressed as a percentage, such as 10% or 20%, the decimal point is assumed to be on the right side of the number. Move the decimal point two places to the left to remove the percentage sign and add a zero if necessary.

Example:

6.0%	becomes	0.06
30.0%	becomes	0.30
2.3%	becomes	0.023
210.0%	becomes	2.10

Converting Decimals to Percentages

Reverse the above process to convert a number expressed as a decimal to a percentage; in other words, move the decimal point two places to the right.

Example:	0.02	becomes	2.0%
	0.57	becomes	57.0%
	0.058	becomes	5.8%
	9.02	becomes	902.0%

Addition of Decimal Numbers

All numbers must be in a vertical column when adding numbers with decimals. Always be sure to line up the decimals vertically.

Example:

$$\begin{array}{r} 902.360 \\ 2.053 \\ \text{Add}\quad 387.100 \\ \hline 1{,}291.513 \end{array}$$

Subtraction of Decimal Numbers

In subtracting numbers with decimals, the same process is used, making sure to line up the decimals vertically.

Example:

$$\begin{array}{r} 43{,}267.23 \\ \text{Subtract}\quad 235.10 \\ \hline 43{,}032.13 \end{array}$$

Multiplication of Decimal Numbers

After multiplying the numbers just as you would in a non-decimal problem, count the total number of decimal places in the numbers being multiplied and place the decimal point in the answer that many places from the right.

Example:

$$\begin{array}{r} 4.3270 \\ \text{Multiply}\quad 82.2000 \\ \hline 355.6794 \end{array}$$

Division of Decimal Numbers

The decimal point must be removed before solving the problem when there is a decimal in the **divisor**. Move the decimal point in the divisor to the right, then move the decimal point in the **dividend** the same number of places to the right. Add zeros to the dividend if it has fewer numerals than are needed to carry out this procedure. Put the decimal point in the answer directly above the new decimal point in the dividend.

Example: $840 \div .021 = 40,000$

$840,000 \div 21 = 40,000$

$$\begin{array}{r} \text{Quotient} \\ 40,000 \\ 21 \overline{\smash{)} 840,000} \\ \text{Dividend} \end{array}$$

Measurements

1 foot	12 inches
1 square foot	A unit of area equal to 1 foot by 1 foot square (144 square inches)
1 board foot	144 cubic inches (1 foot x 1 foot x 1 inch =144 cu. inches)
Square footage	The number of square feet of livable space in a home
Perimeter	The distance measured around the outside of a geometric shape
1 yard	36 inches or 3 feet
1 square yard	9 square feet
1 mile	5,280 feet or 320 rods
1 rod	16 ½ feet
1 acre	43,560 square feet

Conversions

Convert feet to inches:	multiply the number of feet by 12
Convert inches to feet:	divide the number of inches by 12
Convert yards to feet:	multiply the number of yards by 3
Convert feet to yards:	divide the number of feet by 3
Convert sq. feet to sq. inches:	multiple the number of sq. feet by 144
Convert sq. inches to sq. feet:	divide the number of square inches by 144
Convert sq. yards to sq. feet:	multiply the number of sq. yards by 9
Convert sq. feet to sq. yards:	divide the number of sq. feet by 9

Basic Real Estate Formulas

There are usually only three variables in any real estate problem—two things that are known and one that is unknown. One way to solve these types of problems is to imagine a circle divided into three sections. One third is labeled Made, one third is labeled Paid, and the last third is labeled Rate or Percentage.

Here are the 3 variations of the Made-Paid formula.
Made equals Paid times Rate
Paid equals Made divided by Rate
Rate equals Made divided by Paid

Use this simple way to solve most real estate math problems and look carefully at the circle until you grasp this easy concept.

- Made = Paid x Rate
- Paid = Made ÷ Rate
- Rate = Made ÷ Paid

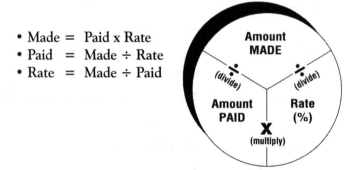

The circle concept for basic real estate formulas.

Whenever you have a math problem, one of these formulas probably can be used. You will always know two of the quantities and will be asked to find the third. From the information given in the problem, you must decide whether to multiply or divide the two numbers that you know in order to find the unknown third number.

When you are asked to find an amount resulting from an interest rate, it usually will be an annual number. Make sure you annualize, or convert any monthly figures to annual figures by multiplying the monthly figures by 12.

Some math problems will have a two-step solution. In other words, some process (add, subtract, multiply) will have to be performed either before or after the above formula can be applied. Use the circle concept as an easy way to solve the math problems included here. Once you know into which section of the circle your information fits, simply perform the math function indicated.

SOLVING REAL ESTATE PROBLEMS

The following problem-solving techniques are explained for the beginning math student or someone who has not used math techniques for quite some time and just needs a little practice to become proficient.

There are several ways any of the following examples may be solved, and we have attempted to be consistent in our explanations for the beginner. Some students will recognize the algebraic solutions presented, and will use their own techniques for solving the problems.

The math problems presented are similar to those you will experience in real life. Learn to recognize the type of problem, and the math solution it requires, and you will be proficient in your real estate career.

Here are several guidelines for you to follow to answer some of the most basic math questions you will need to solve.

The amount MADE, or earned income, is shown as "I" in the formulas. It stands for different types of **income**. For example: commission Income earned by a real estate agent, interest Income earned by the lender or investor and paid by the borrower, net operating Income from an income property, and earned Income from an investment. There are two dollar amounts in a problem: a small amount and a large amount. The amount MADE is the smaller of the two amounts. For example, the broker's commission on a property that sold for $200,000 is never going to be $300,000—that is larger than the sales price! On the following chart, the small "$" sign represents the smaller amount of money.

The amount PAID is also shown as "P" in the formulas. It stands for different types of amounts **paid**. For example, sales Price for a property, Principal amount of a loan, the Property value, or the amount Paid for an investment. The amount PAID is the larger of the two amounts because it represents the large amount that is paid or invested. On the following chart, the large "$" sign represents the larger amount of money.

The RATE is also shown as "**R**" in the formulas. The "R" stands for different percentage rates. Whenever you see a "%", it is referring to a **rate**. For example, commission Rate, interest Rate, capitalization Rate, and Rate of return.

MATH

Review – Solving Real Estate Problems		
$	$	%
MADE	PAID	RATE
I	P	R
Commissions — Commission Income	Sales Price	Commission Rate
Loans — Interest	Principal	Interest Rate
Appraisal — Net operating Income	Property value	Cap Rate
Investment — Earned Income	Amount Paid	Rate of Return
Selling Price — Increase	Purchase Price	Rate of Profit
Seller's Net — Net Income	Sales Price	Commission Rate

Commission Problems

- Paid = Selling Price of Property
- Made = Amount of Commission
- Rate = Commission Rate

The circle concept for commission problems.

Commission problems involve these three variables:

Made = I = $ = Amount of commission Income
Paid = P = $ = Selling Price of the property
Rate = R = % = Commission Rate

Formulas:

1. When the amount of selling price and the commission rate (%) are given and you are solving for the commission paid (smaller $), use:

   I = P x R   (Commission Income = Sales Price x % Rate)

2. When the commission income and commission rate are given and you are solving for sales price (larger $), use:

   P = I ÷ R (Sales Price = Commission Income ÷ % Rate)

3. When the commission income and the sales price are given and you are solving for % (commission rate) use:

   R = I ÷ P (% Rate = Commission Income ÷ Sales Price)

Practice Problem #1

The circle concept for Practice Problem #1.

Pat, a real estate salesperson, found a buyer for a $600,000 house. The seller agreed to pay a 6% commission on the sale to Pat's broker. Pat is on a 50-50 split with her broker. **What is the amount of her commission?**

Known: P (Sales Price, $) and R (Commission Rate %)

> P = $600,000
> R = 6% or 0.06

Unknown: I (Commission Income, $) What we do not know is the dollar amount of the commission paid to the salesperson Pat. First, the total commission paid to the broker must be calculated, then calculate the amount due Pat.

Formula: I = P x R, or Commission Income = Sales Price x Rate

> I = P x R
> I = $600,000 x 0.06
> I = $36,000 (Total commission income earned by the broker.)

Pat's commission = ½ of the total commission earned
Pat's commission = $36,000 ÷ 2
Pat's commission = $18,000

Practice Problem #2

The circle concept for Practice Problem #2.

Paul, a real estate broker, listed a parcel of land for $500,000, with a commission of 10%. A few days later he presented an offer which was 5% less than the listed price. The seller agreed to accept the price if the broker would reduce his commission by 15%. If Paul agrees to the seller's proposal, **how much will his commission be?**

Known: P (Sales Price, larger $) and R (Commission Rate, %)

P = $500,000 less 5% ($25,000) = $475,000

R = 10% less 15%

[First calculate 15% of 10% (0.15 x 0.10 = .0150), then subtract it from 10% (.10 - 0.015 = 0.085, or 8.5%]

Unknown: I (Commission Income, smaller $)

What we do not know is the amount of the commission income.

Formula: I = P x R, or Commission Income = Sales Price x Rate

I = P x R

I = $475,000 x 0.085

I = $40,375

Interest and Loan Problems

The charge for the use of money is called **interest**. The rate of interest that is charged will determine the total dollar amount of the payments. When money is borrowed, both the principal and interest must be repaid according to the agreement between the borrower and lender.

> **Review – Interest Terms**
> (P) Principal: dollar amount of money borrowed, loan amount
> (I) Interest: charge for the use of money
> (R) Rate: percentage of interest charged
> (T) Time: duration of loan

When using the Circle Formula to solve interest and loan problems, MADE is the dollar amount of interest, PAID is the principal amount of the loan, and RATE refers to the annual interest rate of the loan.

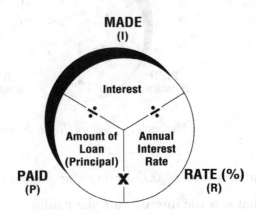

The circle concept for solving interest and loan problems.

Interest and loan problems involve these three variables:

$$\text{Paid} \;=\; P \;=\; \$ \;=\; \text{Principal}$$
$$\text{Made} \;=\; I \;=\; \$ \;=\; \text{Interest}$$
$$\text{Rate} \;=\; R \;=\; \% \;=\; \text{Interest Rate}$$

Formulas:

1. When the amount of principal and interest rate (%) are given and you are solving for amount of interest earned (smaller $), use:

$$I = P \times R \times T \quad (\text{Interest} = \text{Principal} \times \text{Rate} \times \text{Time})$$

2. When the interest income and interest rate are given and you are solving for the principal (larger $), use:

$$P = I \div (R \times T) \text{ [Principal = Interest} \div (\% \text{ Rate x Time)]}$$

3. When the interest income and the principal are given and you are solving for % (interest rate), use:

$$R = I \div (P \times T) \text{ [Rate = Interest} \div (\text{Principal x Time)]}$$

Practice Problem #3

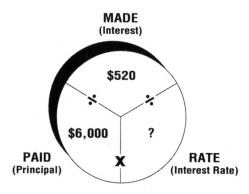

The circle concept for Practice Problem #3.

Ann borrowed $6,000 for one year and paid $520 interest.

What was the interest rate she paid?

Known: I (Interest Income), P (Principal), and T (Time)

P = $6,000 (Principal amount of loan)

I = $520 (Interest income bank made on the loan)

T = 1 year

Unknown: R (Interest Rate)

What we do not know is the interest rate Ann paid.

Formula: R = I ÷ (P x T), or Rate = Income ÷ (Principal x Time)

R = I ÷ (P x T)

R = $520 ÷ ($6,000 x 1)

R = $520 ÷ $6,000

R = 0.0867 or 8.67%

Practice Problem #4

The circle concept for Practice Problem #4.

If one month's interest is $50 on a five-year, straight interest-only note, and the interest rate on the note is 10% per year, **what is the amount of the loan?**

Known: I (Interest Income), R (Rate), and T (Time)

> I = $600 (Interest income bank made on the loan)
> ($50 per month x 12 months = $600)
>
> R = 10% or 0.10
>
> T = 1 year

Unknown: P (Principal)
What we do not know is the larger $ amount of the loan.

Formula: P = I ÷ (R x T), or Principal = Interest ÷ (Rate x Time)

> P = I ÷ (R x T)
> P = $600 ÷ (0.10 x 1)
> P = $600 ÷ 0.10
> **P = $6,000**

The majority of real estate loans are fully amortized, fixed rate loans. By using a calculator or mortgage tables, you can **calculate the monthly payment of principal (P) and interest (I).** If a lender has requested an impound account

> **Review - Monthly Loan Payment**
> **Mnemonic = PITI**
> Principal
> Interest
> Taxes
> Insurance

to collect taxes and insurance, the borrower will make monthly payments of principal (P), interest (I), property taxes (T), and hazard insurance (I).

Discounting Notes

As you recall, when someone buys a note at a discount, it means the buyer pays less than the dollar amount shown on the note, and the profit is the difference between what the buyer paid and the amount paid when the note is due. In other words, a certain amount is paid for the note, but a greater amount is received when the note is paid off.

When using the Made/Paid formula for discounting notes remember: (1) Made is the total interest payment plus the discount amount, (2) Paid is the original note amount less the discount amount, and (3) Rate is the rate of return on the investment. Before the rate of return can be determined, the dollar amount of profit made by the investor must be known.

Discounting note problems involve these three variables:

- Made = **I** = **$** = Income (Interest + discount)
- Paid = **P** = **$** = Amount **P**aid (Note amount less discount)
- Rate = **R** = **%** = **R**ate of return on investment

The circle formula for discounting notes.

Formulas:

1. When the amount of money paid and the rate of return are given and you are solving for income or profit, use:

   I = P x R (Income = Amount **P**aid x **R**ate)

2. When the income and rate of return are given and you are solving for the amount paid, use:

   P = I ÷ R   (Amount **P**aid = **I**ncome ÷ **R**ate)

3. When the income and the dollar amount invested are given and you are solving for %, use:

   R = I ÷ P   (**R**ate = **I**ncome ÷ Amount **P**aid)

Practice Problem #5

The circle formula for Practice Problem #5.

Ted signed a note for $3,000, in favor of (or owed to) a private lender, which is to be paid off in 12 months. He owes the $3,000 plus 9% interest when the note is due. An investor buys the note at a 20% discount. **What is the rate of return on the amount invested by the investor?**

Known: I (Income) and P (Amount Paid)

> I = Income (Calculate the interest and the discount)
> Interest = $3,000 x 0.09 = $270 (interest owed on due date).
>
> Discount = $3,000 x 0.20 = $600 (20% discount allowed investor)
>
> I = $870 ($270 + $600)
>
> P = Amount Paid (Calculate the discount and subtract from the amount of the note.)
> Discount = $3,000 x 0.20 = $600
>
> P = $2,400 ($3,000 – $600)

Unknown: Rate (Rate of Return on amount invested)

What we do not know is the rate (%).

Formula: R = I ÷ P or Rate = profit) ÷ Paid (invested):

> Rate = Profit ÷ Amount Invested
> Rate = $870 ÷ $2,400
> **Rate = 36.25%**

Capitalization Problems

- Paid = Value of Property
- Made = Annual Net Income or Loss
- Rate = Capitalization Rate

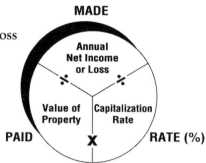

The circle concept for capitalization problems.

Capitalization problems involve these three variables:

Made = **I** = $ = Net Operating **I**ncome (NOI)
Paid = **P** = $ = Value of **P**roperty
Rate = **R** = % = Capitalization **R**ate (Cap **R**ate)

Formulas:

1. When the amount of value of the property and the cap rate (%)
   are given and you are solving for the NOI (smaller $), use:

   I = P x R (NOI = **P**roperty Value x Cap **R**ate)

2. When the NOI and capitalization rate are given and you are solving
   for the value of the property (larger $), use:

   P = I ÷ R (**P**roperty Value = NOI ÷ Cap **R**ate)

3. When the NOI and the property value are given and you are solving
   for % (capitalization rate), use:

   R = I ÷ P   (Cap **R**ate = NOI ÷ **P**roperty Value)

Practice Problem #6

The circle concept for Practice Problem #6.

A duplex brings in $600 per month per unit. Gail and Kevin are interested in buying the property as an investment, and need an investment rate (capitalization rate, or cap rate) of a 10% return. **What should Gail and Kevin pay for the duplex?**

Known: I (NOI) and Rate (Cap Rate)

> I = $600 per unit x 2 units = $1,200 net income per month
> $1,200 x 12 months = $14,400 annual net income

> R = 10% or 0.10

Unknown: P (Value of the Property)

What we do not know is what they should pay for the duplex.

Formula: P = I ÷ R, or Property value = NOI ÷ Cap Rate

> P = I ÷ R
> P = $14,400 ÷ 0.10
> P = $144,000

Practice Problem #7

• Paid = Amount Invested or Investment
• Made = Income or Profit Earned
• Rate = Rate of Return or Profit

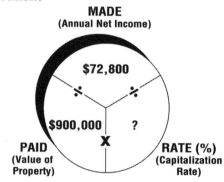

The circle concept for Practice Problem #7.

Kate paid $900,000 for an eight-unit apartment building. The gross income is $800 per month per unit, with expenses of $4,000 annually. **What capitalization rate (%) will Kate make on her investment?**

As you recall, net operating income, rather than gross income is used to calculate a capitalization rate. Therefore, the first step is to calculate the gross income and then subtract the annual expenses to arrive at the net operating income.

Gross Income = $800 per month x 8 units = $6,400 per /month x 12 months = $76,800 annual gross income.

Annual Expenses = $4,000

Net Operating Income = $76,800 - $4,000 = $72,800

Known: I (NOI) and P (Property value)

    I = $ 72,800
    P = $ 900,000

Unknown: R (Cap Rate)

What we do not know is the capitalization rate.

Formula: R = I ÷ P, or Cap Rate = NOI ÷ Property value

    R = I ÷ P
    R = $72,800 ÷ $900,000
    R = .081 or 8.1%

Investments

The circle concept for investments.

Investment problems involve these three variables:

Made = **I** = $ = **I**ncome or profit earned

Paid = **P** = $ = Amount **P**aid or invested in the **P**roperty

Rate = **R** = % = **R**ate of Return or Profit

Formulas:

1. When the amount of money invested and the rate (%) are given and you are solving for $ (smaller dollar amount) use:

    I = P x R   (Income = Amount Paid x Rate of Return)

2. When the income and rate of return are given and you are solving for $ (larger dollar amount) use:

    P = I ÷ R   (Amount Paid = Income ÷ Rate of Return)

3. When the income and the dollar amount invested are given and you are solving for % (percentage of rate of profit) use:

    R = I ÷ P   (Rate of Return = Income ÷ Amount Paid)

MATH

The circle concept for Practice Problem #8.

Steve has a savings account and wants to earn $100 per month in interest. If the account pays 4% interest, **how much should Steve keep in the account?**

Known: I (Income) and R (Cap Rate)

  I = $1,200 per year ($100 x 12 months)
  R = 4% or 0.04

Unknown: P (Amount Paid)
The amount of the investment is what we do not know.

Formula: P = I ÷ R, or Amount Paid = Income ÷ Rate

  P = $1,200 ÷ 0.04
  P = $30,000

Practice Problem #9

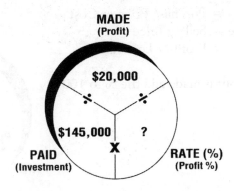

The circle concept for Practice Problem #9.

Mitch bought a house for $145,000. The house was later sold for $165,000.
What is the rate (%) of profit Mitch made on this sale?

Known: P (Amount Paid) and I (Income)

P = $145,000
I = $20,000 ($165,000 – $145,000)

Unknown: R (Rate)

The rate of profit is not known.

Formula: R = I ÷ P, Rate = Income ÷ Amount Paid

R = $20,000 ÷ $145,000
R = 0.138 or 13.8%

Cost and Selling Price Problems

- Paid = Purchase Price or Cost
- Made = Selling Price
- Rate = Profit or Loss Rate

If a profit is made add the % to 100%

The circle concept for cost and selling price problems.

Profit or Loss on Sales involves these three variables:

Made = I = $ = Increase in value

Paid = P = $ = Purchase price or original cost of **P**roperty

Rate = R = % = **R**ate of Return (profit or loss)

Formulas:

1. When the purchase price and the rate of return (%) are given and you are solving for the sales price (increase in value), use:

$$I = P \times R \,(\text{Increase} = \textbf{P}\text{urchase Price} \times \textbf{R}\text{ate})$$

2. When the sales price (increase in value) and rate of return are given and you are solving for the original purchase price, use:

$$P = I \div R \quad (\textbf{P}\text{urchase Price} = \textbf{I}\text{ncrease} \div \textbf{R}\text{ate})$$

3. When the sales price (increase in value) and the original purchase price are given and you are solving for % (rate of return), use:

$$R = I \div P \quad (\textbf{R}\text{ate} = \textbf{I}\text{ncrease} \div \textbf{P}\text{urchase Price})$$

This type of problem is easy to identify because you will be given a selling price and be asked to calculate the amount of profit or the cost before a profit. Sometimes determining the percentage to use can be confusing. Just remember that if a profit is made, add the % to 100%, and if a loss occurs, subtract the % from 100%.

Review – Calculating the Rate of Profit or Loss

When a profit is made add the % to 100%

(15% profit: 100% + 15% = 115% or 1.15)

When a loss occurs subtract the % from 100%

(20% loss: 100% - 20% = 80% or 0.80)

Practice Problem #10

The circle concept for Practice Problem #10.

Donna sold a rural cabin for $30,000, which allowed her to make a 20% profit. **What did she pay for the property?**

Known: I (Increase) and R (% Rate of profit)

I = $30,000 (Increase earned on the sale of the property. The amount actually earned is the smaller $ because it is the difference between the selling price and the original purchase price.)

R = 100% + 20% = 120% = 1.20

Unknown: P (Purchase Price)

What we do not know is the larger $ amount that she paid for the property.

Formula: P = I ÷ R, or Purchase price = Increase ÷ Rate

P = $30,000 ÷ 1.20

P = $25,000

We have determined that she paid $25,000 for the property and sold it for $30,000, which is an increase in value of $5,000 (the smaller $ amount). Is $5,000 a 20% profit? We can determine this by using the formula: $R = I \div P$. We know the increase in value is $5,000 and that she paid $25,000 for the property, so we divide $5,000 by $25,000 to get the rate of profit, which is 0.20 or 20%.

You may be asked to find the selling price or amount of a loan when the seller receives a net amount.

Practice Problem #11

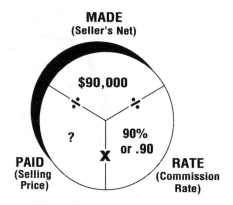

The circle concept for Practice Problem #11.

A farmer put his land on the market, wanting to net a certain amount. The real estate agent who found a buyer gave the farmer a check for $90,000, after deducting a 10% commission. **What was the selling price of the farm?**

Known – I (Net Income) and R (Commission Rate)

    I = $90,000 (Income made from sale)
    R = 100% – 10% = 90% or 0.90 (Commission rate)

Unknown – P (Selling Price)
What we do not know is the selling price of the farm.

Formula: P = I ÷ R, or Selling Price = Income ÷ Rate

    P = I ÷ R
    P = $ 90,000 ÷ 0.90
    P = $100,000 (Selling Price)

Proration

When property is bought and sold, there are certain expenses that are charged to each party. It is one of the jobs of escrow to credit and debit the buyer and seller correctly as of the closing date of escrow. **Proration** is the process of making a fair distribution of expenses, through escrow, at the close of the sale. For prorating purposes, use 30 days for a month and 360 days in a year.

Review - Proration

The Proration Process:

1. Determine the number of days to be prorated.

2. Calculate the cost per day.

3. Multiply the number of days by the cost per day.

4. Decide whether the item should be a credit or a debit to the seller or to the buyer.

5. Expenses that have been paid to some time after escrow closes, credit the seller and debit the buyer.

6. Expenses that will be due after the close of escrow, debit the seller and credit the buyer.

Common Expenses that usually are prorated:

- Property taxes
- Interest on assumed loans
- Fire and hazard insurance
- Rents

MATH

Practice Problem #12

Lynn sold her home on September 1, 2010. She has an existing loan of $200,000 on the house. The interest on the loan is 8%. Terry took over Lynn's loan with interest paid to August 15, 2010. Terry also assumed an existing three-year fire insurance policy for $360 per year, paid by Lynn until November 15, 2011. Lynn also owes property taxes of $1,900 for the year.

Calculate the following:

- Prorate interest, and who is credited or debited
- Prorate insurance, and who is credited or debited
- Prorate tax, and who is credited or debited

1. Prorate the interest:

August 15 to September 1 = 15 days

$200,000 x 8% = $16,000 annual interest

$ 16,000 ÷ 360 days in year = $44.44 per day

15 days x $44.44 per day = $666.60 interest

Credit the buyer and debit the seller.

2. Prorate the insurance:

September 1, 2010, through November 15, 2011 = 435 days

$360 ÷ 360 = $1.00 per day

435 days x $1.00 = $435

Credit the seller and debit the buyer.

3. Prorate the property taxes:

July 1 to September 1 = 60 days

$1,900 ÷ 360 = $5.27 per day

60 days x $5.27 = $316.66

Debit the seller and credit the buyer.

Documentary Transfer Tax

Each county, upon the transfer of property, may charge a documentary transfer tax. As you recall, the amount of the transfer tax is stamped in the upper right-hand corner of a recorded deed. The amount of the tax is based on $1.10 per $1,000 or $.55 per $500 of transferred value. When a sale is all cash, or a new loan is obtained by the buyer, the tax is calculated on the entire sales price. When an existing loan is assumed by a buyer, the tax is calculated on the difference between the assumed loan and the sales price.

Practice Problem #13

Denise sold her home for $250,000, with the buyer obtaining a new loan. **What is the amount of the documentary tax?**

Known – Sales Price and Tax Rate

Sales price = $250,000

The sale involves a new loan so the tax is based on entire sales price

Tax rate = $1.10 per $1,000

Unknown – Amount of Tax Due

What we do not know is the amount of the tax due.

Calculation – Tax Due = Sales Price ÷ $1,000 x $1.10

Tax due = $250,000 ÷ $1,000 = $250.00

Tax due = $250.00 x $1.10

Tax due = $275.00

MATH

Square Footage and Area Calculations

Occasionally you may be asked to solve problems about square footage. Square footage problems are fairly simple and can be solved easily using these simple formulas.

Area = Length x Width
Length = Area ÷ Width
Width = Area ÷ Length

The concept for square footage and area calculations.

As you recall, the way to determine the value of a building using the cost method is to measure the square footage (buildings are measured on the outside). Then check with a contractor to determine the standard cost to build per square foot. Multiply that cost by the square footage of the building to derive the cost to build new, or the upper limit of value.

> **Review - Basic Area Formulas**
>
> The Area of a Square = Length x Width
> The Area of a Rectangle = Length x Width
> The Area of a Right Triangle = Altitude x Base ÷ 2

Practice Problem #14

The concept for Practice Problem #14.

Fred owned four acres of land with a front footage of 500 feet along the street. **What is the depth of the land?**

Known – Area and Width

Area = 4 acres or 174,240 sq. ft. (43,560 sq. ft. per acre x 4 acres)
Width = 500 feet

Unknown – Length

What we do not know is the length (depth) of the parcel.

Formula – Length = Area ÷ Width

Length = 174,240 sq. ft. ÷ 500 feet
Length = 348.48 feet

All buildings are not square or rectangular and therefore may be irregular in shape. Always reduce the building to squares, rectangles and triangles, for which you know the formula to determine the square footage.

Practice Problem #15

Kelly and Sam bought a lot, with the intention of building a house on it. They needed to determine how much it would cost them to build the house. They were told by contractors the cost to build was $40 per square foot for a garage and $80 per square foot for a home.

Kelly and Sam had plans drawn for the house. They used the total square footage of the house and garage to figure the cost to build.

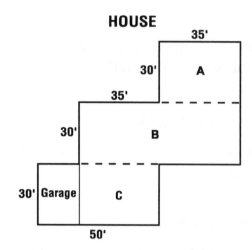

The concept for Practice Problem #15.

Known – Measurements of structure and cost per square foot.

Unknown – The cost to build the house and garage
To find the square footage of the house, divide the diagram into imaginary rectangles and use the formula: Area = Width x Length

1. Calculate the area of the house

Rectangle A = 35' x 30'	= 1,050 square feet
Rectangle B = 70' x 30'	= 2,100 square feet
Rectangle C = 30' x 35'	= 1,050 square feet
Area of house	**= 4,200 square feet**

2. Calculate the area of the garage

   Garage = 15' x 30' = 450 square feet

3. Calculate the cost to build the house and garage

   House: 4,200 square feet x $80 per square foot = $336,000
   Garage: 450 square feet x $40 per square foot = $18,000
   Total cost to build house and garage = $354,000

Appendix B
Websites Used in this Book

Entity	Website
California Apartment Association	http://www.caanet.org
California Association of REALTORS®	http://www.car.org
California Bureau of Real Estate Appraisers	http://www.orea.ca.gov
California Bureau of Real Estate	http://www.calbre.ca.gov
California Coastal Commission	http://www.coastal.ca.gov
California Dept. of Alcoholic Beverage Control	http://www.abc.ca.gov
California Dept. of Forestry and Fire Protection	http://www.fire.ca.gov
California Dept. of Insurance	http://www.insurance.ca.gov
California Dept. of Veterans Affairs	http://www.calvet.ca.gov
California Franchise Tax Board	http://www.ftb.ca.gov
California Housing & Community Development	http://www.hcd.ca.gov
California Property Tax Resources	http://calproptax.com
Dept. of Housing and Urban Development	http://www.hud.gov
Fannie Mae	http://www.fanniemae.com
Federal Emergency Management Agency	http://www.fema.gov
Freddie Mac	http://www.freddiemac.com
Ginnie Mae	http://www.ginniemae.gov
Mello-Roos Property Tax Information	http://www.californiataxdata.com
myFICO, a division of FairIsaac	http://www.myfico.com
National Association of Real Estate Brokers	http://www.nareb.com
National Association of REALTORS®	http://www.realtor.org
The Appraisal Institute	http://www.appraisalinstitute.org
The Federal Reserve System	http://www.federalreserve.gov
U.S. Internal Revenue Service	http://www.irs.ustreas.gov
U.S. Small Business Administration	http://www.sba.gov
Veterans Home Loan Guaranty Services	http://www.benefits.va.gov/homeloans
Western Manufactured Housing Communities Association	http://www.wma.org

WEBSITES

WEBSITES

Appendix C
Glossary

A.L.T.A. owner's policy
An owner's extended title insurance policy.

A.L.T.A. title policy
A type of title insurance policy issued by title insurance companies that expands the risks normally insured against under the standard type policy to include unrecorded mechanic's liens; unrecorded physical easements; facts a physical survey would not show; water and mineral rights; and rights of parties in possession, such as tenants and buyers under unrecorded instruments.

abandonment *(abandono)*
The obvious and intentional surrender of the easement.

abandonment of homestead *(abandono de casa)*
A legal document that proves a homestead was abandoned. An owner must file an abandonment of homestead on the old property in order to obtain a homestead on a new property.

abatement of nuisance
Extinction or termination of conduct or activity that interferes with use or enjoyment of property.

abrogation *(abrogación)*
(1)The rescission or annulling of a contract. (2) The revocation or repealing of a contract by mutual consent of parties to the contract, or for cause by either party to the contract. (Pronounced ab-ro-ga-tion)

abstract of judgment *(extracto del juicio)*
A summary of a court decision.

abstract of title *(titulo de sumario)*
Written summary of all useful documents discovered in a title search.

abstractor *(abstractor)*
A person who, historically, searches out anything affecting the title to real property and summarizes the information in the findings.

acceleration clause *(cláusula de aceleración)*
A clause in a loan document describing certain events that would cause the entire loan to be due.

acceptance *(aceptación)*
An unqualified agreement to the terms of an offer.

accession *(accesión)*
(1) The acquisition of title to additional land or to improvements as a result of annexing fixtures or as a result of natural causes such as alluvial deposits along the banks of streams by accretion. (2) A process by which there is an addition to property by the efforts of man or natural forces.

accretion *(aumento)*
A buildup of soil by natural causes on property bordering a river, lake, or ocean.

accrued
Accumulated over a period of time.

accrued depreciation *(depreciación acumulada)*
The difference between the cost to replace the property and the property's current appraised value.

acknowledgment *(reconocimiento)*
(1) A signed statement, made before a notary public, by a named person confirming the signature on a document and that it was made of free will. (2) A formal declaration to a public official (notary) by a person who has signed an instrument which states that the signing was voluntary.

acquisition *(adquisición)*
The act or process by which a person procures property.

acre
(1) A measure of land equaling 160 square rods, or 4,840 square yards, or 43,560 square feet. (2) A tract about 208. 71 feet square.

action
A lawsuit brought to court.

action in ejectment *(acción en el ejectment)*
(1) The legal remedy to remove a tenant. (2) Also known as unlawful detainer action.

actual age *(edad real)*
(1) The chronological age of a building. (2) Real age of a building.

actual authority *(autoridad real)*
Authority expressly given by the principal or given by the law and not denied by the principal.

actual notice *(aviso real)*
A fact, such as seeing the grand deed or knowing a person inherited a property by will.

ADAM E. LEE
The mnemonic for the eight ways to terminate an easement: Abandonment, Destruction, Adverse possession, Merger, Express agreement, Lawsuit, Estoppel, and Excessive use.

ad valorem *(el anuncio valoren)*
A Latin prefix meaning according to value. (Pronounced adva-lo-rem)

addendum
Additional documents attached to and made part of a contract.

adjustable rate mortgage *(hipoteca de tarifa adjustable)*
A note whose interest rate is tied to a movable economic index.

adjusted cost basis *(adjused base del coste)*
Original basis plus capital improvements and costs of the sale, less depreciation if income producing.

administrator *(administrador)*
A person appointed by the probate court to administer the estate of a deceased person. His or her duties include making an inventory of the assets, managing the property, paying the debts and expenses, filing necessary reports and tax returns, and distributing the assets as ordered by the probate court.

advance fees *(honorarios anticipados)*
A fee paid in advance of any services rendered. Sometimes unlawfully charged in connection with an illegal practice of obtaining a fee in advance for the advertising of property or businesses for sale, with no intent to obtain a buyer, by persons representing themselves as real estate licensees, or representatives of licensed real estate firms.

adverse possession *(posesión adversa)*
Acquiring title to property owned by someone else by continued possession and payment of taxes.

affirm *(afirme)*
(1) To conform, to aver, to ratify, to verify. (2) To make a declaration.

after-acquired title *(titulo despues-adquirido)*
Any benefits that come to a property after a sale must follow the sale and accrue to the new owner.

agency *(agencia)*
A legal relationship in which a principal authorizes an agent to act as the principal's representative when dealing with third parties.

agency coupled with an interest *(agencia juntada con un interés)*
An agent acquires an interest in the subject of the agency (the property).

agency relationship *(relación de la agencia)*
A special relationship of trust by which one person (agent) is authorized to conduct business, sign papers, or otherwise act on behalf of another person (principal). This relationship may be created by expressed agreement, ratification, or estoppel.

agent *(agente)*
A person who acts for and in the place of another, called a principal, for the purpose of affecting the principal's legal relationship with third persons.

agreement
A mutual exchange of promises (either written or oral). Although often used as synonymous with contract, technically it denotes mutual promises that fail as a contract for lack of consideration.

agreement of sale
(1) A contract for the sale of real property where the seller gives up possession, but retains the title until the purchase price is paid in full. (2) Also called contract for sale or land contract.

agricultural property
Property zoned for use in farming, including the raising of crops and livestock.

air rights *(derechos aéros)*
The rights in real property to the reasonable use of the air space above the surface of the land.

airspace *(espacio aéreo)*
The interior area which an apartment, office or condominium occupies. Airspace is considered real property to a reasonable height. For example, an owner or developer of condominiums may sell the airspace as real property.

alienate
(1) To transfer, convey, or sell property to another. (2) The act of transferring ownership, title, or interest.

alienation clause *(cláusula de enajenación)*
(1) A clause in a loan document that would allow the lender to call the balance of the loan due upon the sale of the property. (2) Also called the due-on-sale clause.

all-inclusive trust deed
A purchase money deed of trust subordinate to but still including the original loan.

alluvial deposit *(depósito alluvial)*
Sand or mud, carried by water and deposited on land.

alluvium *(alluvium)*
The gradual build-up of soil.

amenities *(amenidades)*
Features that add value to a property.

Americans with Disabilities Act
Federal law passed in 1990 that prohibits discrimination against individuals with disabilities.

amortization *(amortización)*
The liquidation of a financial obligation on an installment basis.

amortized loan *(préstamo amortizado)*
(1) A loan to be repaid, interest and principal, by a series of regular payments that are equal or nearly equal, without any special balloon payment prior to maturity. (2) Also called a level payments loan.

anchor bolt
(1) Attaches mud sill to foundation. (2) Embedded in concrete foundation.

annual *(anual/per annum)*
Once per year.

annual percentage rate
The relationship of the total finance charge to the total amount to be financed as required under the Truth-in-Lending Act.

anticipation, principle of
Affirms that value is created by anticipated benefits to be derived in the future.

appraisal *(avalúo)*
An act or process of developing an opinion of value. Usually for a specific property's value on a given date.

appraisal process
An orderly systematic method to arrive at an estimate of value.

appraisal report *(información de la evaluación)*
A written statement where an appraiser gives his or her opinion of value.

appraiser *(tasador)*
A person qualified by education, training and experience who is hired to estimate the value of real and personal property based on experience, judgment, facts, and use of formal appraisal processes.

appreciation *(aprecio)*
(1) An increase in the worth or value of property. (2) The increase in market value of real estate. (3) An increase in property value with the passage of time.

appropriation
The right to use water for a beneficial use by diverting surface water.

appurtenance
Anything used with the land for its benefit.

appurtenant
Belonging, appended or annexed to. Appurtenant items transfer with the land when property is sold.

architectural style
Generally the appearance and character of a building's design and construction.

arm's-length transaction
A transaction, such as a sale of property, in which all parties involved are acting in their own self-interest and are under no undue influence or pressure from other parties.

arranger of credit
A person who is not party to the real estate transaction, but will be compensated for arranging the credit, negotiating the credit terms, completing the credit documents, and facilitating the transaction.

articles of incorporation
An instrument setting forth the purposes, power and basic rules under which a private corporation is formed.

"as is"
Term stating the seller will not be responsible for the cost of repairing any defect.

asbestos
A mineral fiber used in construction which has been found to cause lung and stomach cancer.

assemblage *(ensambladura)*
The process of putting several smaller less valuable lots together under one ownership.

assessed value
Value placed on property by a public tax assessor as a basis for taxation.

assessment *(tasación)*
The valuation of property for the purpose of levying a tax or the amount of the tax levied.

assessment roll *(rodillo del gravamen)*
A list of all taxable property showing the assessed value of each parcel; establishes the tax base.

assessor
The official who has the responsibility of determining assessed values.

assignee *(cesionario)*
Party to whom a lease is assigned or transferred.

assignment *(asignación)*
The transfer of entire leasehold estate to a new person.

assignor *(transferidor)*
The person transferring a claim, benefit or right in property to another.

associate licensee
Another term used for a licensed real estate salesperson employed by a licensed real estate broker.

assumption clause *(cláusula de la asunción)*
A clause in a document that allows a buyer to take over the existing loan and agree to be liable for the repayment of the loan.

assumption fee *(honorarios de la asunción)*
A lender's charge for changing over and processing new records for a new owner who is assuming an existing loan.

assumption of mortgage *(asunción de la hipoteca)*
The taking of a title to property by a grantee wherein grantee assumes liability for payment of an existing note secured by a mortgage or deed of trust against the property, becoming a co-guarantor for the payment of a mortgage or deed of trust note.

attachment *(embargo)*
The process by which the court holds the property of a defendant pending outcome of a lawsuit.

attachment lien *(embargo preventivo del accesorio)*
(1) The process by which the court holds the real or personal property of a defendant as security for a possible judgment pending the outcome of a lawsuit. (2) Also known as writ of attachment.

attorney-in-fact *(abogado en hecho)*
(1) The person holding the power of attorney. (2) A competent and disinterested person who is authorized by another person to act in his or her place in legal matters.

avulsion *(avulsion)*
The sudden washing or tearing away of land by the action of water.

backfill *(relleno)*
Soil that is used to fill in holes or support a foundation.

balloon payment *(pago de globo)*
Under an installment loan, a final payment that is substantially larger than any other payment and repays the debt in full.

bankruptcy *(bancarrota)*
A court proceeding to relieve a person's or company's financial insolvency.

base and meridian
Imaginary lines used by surveyors to find and describe the location of public or private lands.

baseline *(linea de fondo)*
A survey line running east and west, used as a reference when mapping land.

beam
A long thick piece of wood, metal or concrete, used to support weight in a building.

bearing wall
A wall that supports a vertical load as well as its own weight.

bench mark *(marca de fija)*
Location indicated on a permanent marker by surveyors.

beneficiary *(beneficiario)*
The lender under a deed of trust.

beneficiary statement *(declaración del beneficiario)*
A statement of the unpaid balance of a loan and describes the condition of the debt.

bequeath *(legar)*
To convey real or personal property by will.

bequest
A gift of personal property by will. (See *legacy*)

bilateral contract *(contrato bilateral)*
An agreement in which each person promises to perform an act in exchange for another person's promise to perform.

bill of sale
A written agreement used to transfer ownership in personal property.

blanket loan *(préstamo cubre)*
A loan secured by several properties. The security instrument used can be a blanket deed of trust or a blanket mortgage.

blighted area *(area marchitada)*
A section of a city, generally the inner city, where a majority of the buildings are run-down, and the property values are extremely low.

blind advertising
Advertising that fails to disclose that the party is a licensee acting as an agent.

blind pool
A type of syndication where money is raised for unspecified properties that meet specific investment criteria.

blockbusting *(rompe cuadras)*
The illegal practice of telling people that property values in a neighborhood will decline because of a specific event, such as the purchase of homes by minorities.

board foot *(pie de tablero)*
A unit of measurement for lumber equal to the volume of the board: one foot wide, one foot long, one inch thick (144 cubic inches).

bona fide purchaser
Bona fide means good faith *(auténtico)*, so a bona fide purchaser is one who pays fair value for property in good faith, and without notice of adverse claims.

book value *(valor de la libro)*
The current value (for accounting purposes) of a property, calculated as the original cost, plus capital improvements, minus accumulated or accrued depreciation.

boot
Extra cash or non like-kind property put into an exchange.

bracing
Diagonal board nailed across wall framing to prevent sway.

breach of contract *(abertura del contrato)*
A failure to perform on part or all of the terms and conditions of a contract.

bridge loan
(1) A loan to bridge the gap between the termination of one mortgage and the beginning of another, such as when a borrower purchases a new home before receiving cash proceeds from the sale of a prior home. (2) Also known as a swing loan.

British Thermal Unit
(1) A measurement that calculates heat; the amount of heat needed to raise one pound of water one degree Fahrenheit. (2) Also known as BTU.

broker *(corredor)*
An agent who earns income by arranging sales and other contracts. A real estate broker is an individual licensed by the state of California to arrange the sale or transfer of interests in real property for compensation.

broker's trust fund account
An account set up by a broker; withdrawals from this account may be made only by the broker.

brokerage *(corretaje)*
An activity involving the sale of something through an intermediary who negotiates the transaction for payment.

brownfield
An abandoned commercial or industrial site or under-utilized neighborhood where redevelopment is complicated by actual or perceived contamination.

building manager
A person employed by a property manager or directly by an owner, and usually manages a single large building or office complex.

building paper
Waterproof paper used between sheathing and roof covering.

bulk transfer law
The law concerning any transfer in bulk (not a sale in the ordinary course of the seller's business).

bundle of rights
An ownership concept describing all the legal rights that attach to the ownership of real property.

Business and Professions Code
The statute regulating the conduct of real estate brokers and establishing the Bureau of Real Estate.

business opportunity
Any type of business that is for lease or sale.

buyer's agent
A broker employed by the buyer to locate a certain kind of real property.

C.L.T.A. standard policy
A policy of title insurance covering only matters of record.

calendar year
Starts on January 1 and continues through December 31 of the same year.

California Fair Employment and Housing Act
State law that prohibits discrimination in the sale, rental or financing of practically all types of housing.

California Land Title Association
A trade organization of the state's title companies.

CAL-VET Program
A program administered by the State Department of Veterans Affairs for the direct financing of farm and home purchases by eligible California veterans of the armed forces.

CAN-SPAM laws
Federal and state law regulating commercial e-mail messages.

capital *(capital)*
Money and/or property owned or used by a person or business to acquire goods or services.

capital gain
At resale of a capital item, the amount by which the net sale proceeds exceed the adjusted cost basis (book value). Used for income tax computations. Gains are called short or long term based upon length of holding period after acquisition. Usually taxed at lower rates than ordinary income.

capitalism
An economic system in which most of the economy's resources are privately owned.

capitalization *(capitalización)*
(1) The process that can be employed to convert income to value. (2) An economic system in which most of the economy's resources are privately owned.

capitalization rate *(tasa de capitalización)*
(1) The rate of interest which is considered a reasonable return on the investment, and used in the process of determining value based upon net income. It may also be described as the yield rate that is necessary to attract the money of the average investor to a particular kind of investment. (2) It is sometimes call the cap rate.

carryback financing
Financing by a seller who takes back a note for part of the purchase price.

cash flow
The net income generated by a property before depreciation and other non cash expenses.

caveat emptor *(caveat emptor)*
"Let the buyer beware".

CC&Rs
(See *covenants, conditions, and restrictions*)

certificate of eligibility
Issued by Department of Veterans Affairs; evidence of individual's eligibility to obtain VA loan.

certificate of reasonable value *(certificado del valor razonable)*
The Federal VA appraisal commitment of property value.

certificate of title *(certificado de título)*
A written opinion by an attorney that ownership of the particular parcel of land is as stated in the certificate.

chain of title *(cadena de título)*
A chronological history of property's ownership.

change, principle of
Holds that it is the future, not the past, which is of prime importance in estimating value. Change is largely the result of cause and effect.

chattel
Personal property.

chattel real
An item of personal property which is connected to real estate; for example, a lease.

chattels
(1) Personal property. (2) This term is sometimes used in law to describe any interest in real or personal property other than a freehold.

client *(cliente)*
The person who employs an agent to perform a service for a fee.

closed sheathing
Foundation for exterior siding; boards nailed to studding.

closing *(cierre)*
(1) Process by which all the parties to a real estate transaction conclude the details of a sale or mortgage. The process includes the signing and transfer of documents and distribution of funds. (2) Condition in description of real property by courses and distances at the boundary lines where the lines meet to include all the tract of land.

closing costs
The miscellaneous expenses buyers and sellers normally incur in the transfer of ownership of real property over and above the cost of the property.

closing statement
An accounting of funds made to the buyer and seller separately. Required by law to be made at the completion of every real estate transaction.

cloud on title
Any condition that affects the clear title of real property or minor defect in the chain of title which needs to be removed.

COALD
The mnemonic for the five duties an agent owes a principle: Care, Obedience, Accounting, Loyalty, and Disclosure.

Code of Ethics *(código de ética)*
A set of rules and principles expressing a standard of accepted conduct for a professional group and governing the relationship of members to each other and to the organization.

codicil
A change in a will before the maker's death.

cold calling
The practice of making unsolicited calls to people you do not know in order to get new business.

collateral
Something of value given as security for a debt.

color of title
That which appears to be good title but which is not title in fact.

commercial acre
(1) The area remaining from an acre of newly subdivided land after deducting the area devoted to streets, sidewalks, alleys, curbs, etc. (2) Also known as a buildable acre.

commercial e-mail message
Any electronic mail message whose primary purpose is the commercial advertisement or promotion of a commercial product or service.

commingling
The illegal practice of depositing client's funds in a broker's personal or general business account.

commission

A fee for services rendered usually based on a certain percentage of the sales price of a property.

commission split

The previously agreed upon division of money between a broker and sales-associate when the brokerage has been paid a commission from a sale made by the associate.

common area

An entire common interest subdivision except the separate interests therein.

common interest development

A common-interest development combining the individual ownership of private dwellings with the shared ownership of common facilities of the entire project.

common interest subdivision

Individuals owning a separate lot or unit, with an interest in the common areas of the entire project. The common areas are usually governed by a homeowners' association.

common law dedication

When a property owner implies through his or her conduct, the intent that the public use the land.

common law

A body of unwritten law that was developed in England from the general customs and usage that was adopted in the United States.

community property

All property acquired by a husband and wife during a valid marriage (excluding certain separate property).

community property with right of survivorship

A law allowed a husband and wife to hold title to their property.

compaction

Extra soil that is added and compressed to fill in the low areas or raise the level of the parcel.

company dollar

The amount a broker has left after all commissions have been paid.

comparable sales

(1) Sales which have similar characteristics as the subject property and are used for analysis in the appraisal process. (2) Commonly called comps, they are recent selling prices of properties similarly situated in a similar market.

comparative market analysis *(análisis del mercado comparativo o competitivo)*

A comparison analysis that real estate brokers use while working with a seller to determine an appropriate listing price for the seller's house.

comparison approach

(1) A real estate comparison method which compares a given property with similar or comparable surrounding properties. (2) Also called market comparison.

compensating balance

When a borrower deposits funds with the bank in order to induce the lender into making a loan.

competent

Legally qualified.

competition, principle of

Holds that profits tend to breed competition and excess profits tend to breed ruinous completion.

complete escrow

All terms of the escrow instructions have been met.

compound interest

Interest paid on original principal and also on the accrued and unpaid interest which has accumulated as the debt matures.

comps

A term used by real estate agents and appraisers to mean comparable properties.

concurrent ownership

(1) When property is owned by two or more persons or entities at the same time. (2) Also known as co-ownership.

condemnation

(1) The process by which the government acquires private property for public use, under its right of eminent domain. (2) The proceeding to exercise the power of the government to take private property from an owner for the public good, paying fair market value. (3) The proceeding to exercise the power of eminent domain.

condition

Condition similar to a covenant, a promise to do or not to do something. The penalty for breaking a condition is return of the property to the grantor.

condition precedent

A condition which requires something to occur before a transaction becomes absolute and enforceable; for example, a sale that is contingent on the buyer obtaining financing.

condition subsequent

A condition which, if it occurs at some point in the future, can cause a property to revert to the grantor. For example, a requirement in a grant deed that a buyer must never use the property for anything other than a private residence.

conditional use permit

Allows a land use that may be incompatible with other uses existing in the zone.

condominium *(condominio)*

A housing unit consisting of a separate fee interest in a particular specific space, plus an undivided interest in all common or public areas of the development. Each unit owner has a deed, separate financing and pays the property taxes for their unit.

conduit

A flexible pipe in which electrical wiring is installed.

conformity

When land uses are compatible and homes are similar in design and size, the maximum value is realized.

consideration

Something of value—such as money, a promise, property or personal services.

constructive fraud

A breach of duty legally declared fraudulent because it deceives others despite no dishonesty nor deceptive intent.

construction loan

An interim loan made to finance the actual construction or improvement on land. Funds are usually disbursed in increments as the construction progresses.

constructive eviction

Conduct by a landlord that impairs tenant's possession of the premises making occupancy hazardous.

constructive notice

Notice given by recording a document or taking physical possession of the property.

Consumer Credit Protection Act

A federal law that includes the Truth-in-Lending Law.

consumer goods

Goods sold or purchased primarily for personal, family, or household purposes.

contiguous

In close proximity.

contour

The surface configuration of land. Shown on maps as a line through points of equal elevation.

contract *(contrato)*

A legally enforceable agreement made by competent parties, to perform or not perform a certain act.

contract date

The date the contract is created. The contract is created when the final acceptance was communicated back to the offeror.

contract of sale *(contrato decompraventa)*

(1) A contract for the sale of real property where the seller gives up possession but retains title until the total of the purchase price is paid off. (2) Also called installment sales contract, a contract of sale, an agreement of sale, a conditional sales contract, or a land sales contract.

contract rent

The amount actually paid by a renter for use of the premises.

contribution, principle of

The worth of an improvement and what it adds to the entire property's market value, regardless of the actual cost of the improvement. Holds that maximum values are achieved when the improvements on a site produce the highest (net) return, commensurate with the investment.

conventional loan

Any loan made by lenders without any government guarantees (FHA insured or VA guaranteed).

conversion

The appropriation of property or funds belonging to another; as in a broker using a client's money.

convey

To transfer ownership or title.

conveyance *(escritura de traspaso)*

The transfer of title to land by use of a written instrument.

cooperating agent

A selling agent who assists another broker by finding a buyer.

cooperative

(1) Ownership of an apartment unit in which the owner has purchased shares in the corporation that holds title to the entire building. (2) A residential multi-family building.

corner influence

Commercial properties benefit from more exposure on a corner lot.

corner lot

A lot found at the intersection of two streets. It may be desirable because of its accessibility, but may also be noisy and expensive to maintain because of the increased frontage.

corporation *(corporación)*

A legal entity whose rights in business are similar to that of an individual.

correlation

(1) A step in the appraisal process involving the interpretation of data derived from the three approaches in value (cost, market and income) leading to a single determination of value. (2) Also frequently referred to as reconciliation.

cost

The expenses in money, labor, material or sacrifices in acquiring or producing something.

cost approach *(acer camiento del coste)*
An appraisal method whereby a value estimate of a property is derived by estimating the replacement cost of the improvements, deducting the estimated accrued depreciation, then adding the market value of the land.

cost basis
Original price paid for a property.

counteroffer *(contraoferta)*
(1) The rejection of an original offer that becomes a new offer. (2) The rejection of original purchase offer and the submission of a new and different offer.

covenant
A promise to do or not do certain things.

Covenants, Conditions, and Restrictions (CC&Rs)
Restrictions are placed on certain types of real property and limit the activities of owners. Covenants and conditions are promises to do or not to do certain things. The consequence for breaking those promises may either be money damages in the case of covenants, or the return of the property to the grantor, in the case of conditions.

crawlspace
Exterior or interior opening permitting access underneath a building, as required by building codes.

credit *(credito)*
A bookkeeping entry on the right side of an account, recording the reduction or elimination of an asset or an expense, or the creation of an addition to a liability or item of equity or revenue.

credit reporting agency
A company that researches the credit records of consumers and summarizes the findings in a factual credit report.

credit scoring
An objective, statistical method that lenders use to quickly assess the borrower's credit risk.

credit unions
An association whose members usually have the same type of occupation.

cripple
Stud above or below a window opening or above a doorway.

cubic-foot method
Similar to the square-foot method, except that it takes height as well as area into consideration. The cubic contents of buildings are compared instead of just the square footage.

cul-de-sac lot
A lot found on a dead-end street with the same way for ingress and egress.

curable depreciation
Items of physical deterioration and functional obsolescence which are customarily repaired or replaced by a prudent property owner.

customer
A prospective buyer of real estate; not to be confused with a property seller, who is the listing broker's client.

debt service
The sum of money needed for each payment period to amortize the loan or loans.

debtor *(deudor)*
A person who is in debt; the one owing money to another.

DEC
The mnemonic for the three disclosure requirements: Disclose, Elect, and Confirm.

deciduous
Plants and trees that lose their leaves seasonally in the fall.

decimal point
The period that sets apart a whole number from a fractional part of that number.

Declaration of Homestead
The recorded document that protects a homeowner from foreclosure by certain judgment creditors.

Declaration of Restrictions
A written legal document which lists covenants, conditions and restrictions (CC&Rs). This document gives each owner the right to enforce the CC&Rs.

dedication
The giving of land by its owner to a public use and the acceptance for such use by authorized officials on behalf of the public.

deed *(escritura de propiedad)*
A formal transfer by a party.

deed in lieu of foreclosure
A deed to real property accepted by a lender from a defaulting borrower to avoid the necessity of foreclosure proceedings by the lender.

deed of trust
(See *Trust Deed*)

deed restrictions *(limitaciones en la escritura)*
Limitations in the deed to a property that dictate certain uses that may or may not be made of the property.

GLOSSARY

default
Failure to pay a debt on a contract.

defeasible
Capable of being defeated. A defeasible estate is one that has a condition attached to the title, which if broken causes the termination of that estate.

deferred maintenance
Negligent, postponed, care of a building.

deficiency judgment
A judgment against a borrower for the balance of a debt owed when the security or the loan is not sufficient enough to pay the debt.

defined channel
Any natural watercourse, even if it is dry during a good portion of the year.

definite and certain
Precise acts to be performed are to be clearly stated.

delivery (of a deed)
The unconditional, irrevocable intent of a grantor immediately to divest (give up) an interest in real estate by a deed or other instrument.

demand *(demanda)*
The desire to buy or obtain a commodity.

demise
(1) To convey as an estate by will or lease. (2) To transmit by succession or inheritance.

demographics
Information from a variety of sources used to create a broad profile of any community.

demography *(demografía)*
The statistical study of human populations.

deposit receipt
Contract that acts as the receipt for earnest money given by the buyer to secure an offer, as well as being the basic agreement, between the buyer and seller.

depository institution
An institution that accepts deposits in the form of savings accounts, and makes loans using their depositors' monies.

depreciation *(depreciación)*
(1) Loss in value from any cause. (2) A tax advantage of ownership of income property.

depth table
A statistical table that may be used to estimate the value of the added depth of a lot.

deregulation
A process whereby regulatory restraints are gradually relaxed.

desk cost
(1) Profitability measure calculated by dividing the total operating expenses of the firm by the number of licensed sales associates. (2) Shows how much each sales associate must earn to cover expenses.

devise
A gift of real property by will.

directional growth
The location or direction toward which the residential sections of a city are destined or determined to grow.

discharge of contract
The cancellation or termination of a contract.

disclosure statement
The statement required by the Truth-in-Lending Law whereby a creditor must give a debtor a statement showing the finance charge, annual percentage rate, and other required information.

discount *(rebaja)*
(1) To sell a promissory note before maturity at a price less than the outstanding principal balance of the note at the time of sale. (2) Also an amount deducted in advance by the lender from the nominal principal of a loan as part of the cost to the borrower of obtaining the loan.

discount points
The amount of money the borrower or seller must pay the lender to get a mortgage at a stated interest rate. This amount is equal to the difference between the principal balance on the note and the lesser amount which a purchaser of the note would pay the original lender for it under market conditions. A point equals 1% of the loan.

discount rate
The interest rate that is charged by the Federal Reserve Bank to its member banks for loans.

discounting a note
Selling a note for less than the face amount or the current balance.

disintermediation
The process of depositors removing funds from savings.

dividend
A number to be divided by another number.

divisor
A number by which another number is divided.

do-not-call
Federal ad state regulations regarding unsolicited telephone calls.

doctrine of correlative-rights
Owner may use only a reasonable amount of the total underground water supply for his or her beneficial use.

documentary transfer tax

A state enabling act allowing a county to adopt a documentary transfer tax to apply on all transfers of real property located in the county. Notice of payment is entered on face of the deed or on a separate paper filed with the deed.

document *(documento)*

Legal instruments such as mortgages, contracts, deeds, options, wills, bills of sale, etc.

dominant tenement

The property that benefits from an easement.

downzoning

A zone change from a high density use to a lower density use. For example, a commercial zone to a light industrial zone.

drywall

Gypsum panels used in place of wet plaster to finish the inside of buildings.

dual agency

An agency relationship in which the agent acts concurrently for both principals in a transaction.

dual agent

A broker acting as agent for both the seller and the buyer in the same transaction.

due-on-sale clause

An acceleration clause granting the lender the right to demand full payment of the mortgage upon a sale of the property.

duress *(coerción)*

The use of force to get agreement in accepting a contract.

DUST

The mnemonic for Demand, Utility, Scarcity, and Transferability.

18-month conditional license

Initial license issued to real estate salesperson who has only completed the Real Estate Principles course.

earnest money *(adelanto)*

(1) Down payment made by a purchaser of real estate as evidence of good faith. (2) A deposit or partial payment.

easement

(1) An interest owned by one person in the land of another person, such as a right-of-way across a parcel of land. (2) The right to enter or use someone else's land for a specified purpose.

easement appurtenant

An easement that enhances land; usually a right-of-way.

easement by prescription

Created by continuous and uninterrupted use, by a single party, for a period of five years. The use must be against the owner's wishes and be open and notorious. No confrontation with the owner is required and property taxes do not have to be paid. The party wishing to obtain the prescriptive easement must have some reasonable claim to the use of the property.

easement in gross

An easement that is not appurtenant to any one parcel; for example, public utilities to install power lines.

eaves

The part of roof that hangs over the exterior walls.

economic age *(vida económica)*

Age of a building determined by its condition and usefulness.

economic life *(valor económica)*

(1) The estimated period over which a building may be profitably used. (2) Also known as effective life.

economic obsolescence

(1) A type of depreciation occurring because of forces outside the property. (2) Changes in the social or economic make-up of the neighborhood, zoning changes, over-supply of homes, under-supply of buyers, recession or legislative restrictions can cause economic obsolescence.

economic rent

What a leased property would be expected to rent for under current market conditions if the property were vacant and available for rent.

effective age

The age of a building based on its condition and usefulness.

effective demand

The desire coupled with purchasing power.

effective gross income

The amount of net income that remains after the deduction from gross income of vacancy and credit losses.

effective interest rate

The percentage of interest that is actually being paid by the borrower for the use of the money, distinct from nominal interest.

effective life

The estimated period over which a building may be profitably used.

egress

The right to exit from a property using an easement.

elevation sheet

Drawing that shows front and side exterior views of a building as it will be when finished.

emancipated minor
Someone who is legally set free from parental control/supervision.

emblements
Growing crops that are cultivated annually for sale.

eminent domain
(1) The right of the government to take private property from an owner, for the public good, paying fair market value. (2) Also known as condemnation or a taking.

employee
Someone who is under the control and direction of a broker.

encroachment
The unauthorized placement of permanent improvements that intrude on adjacent property owned by another.

encumbrance
An interest in real property that is held by someone who is not the owner.

energy efficient ratio
(1) A measurement of the efficiency of energy; used to determine the effectiveness of appliances. (2) Also known as EER.

Environmental Impact Report *(declaración de impacto ambiental)*
(1) A study of how a development will affect the ecology of its surroundings. (2) Also known as EIR.

Equal Credit Opportunity Act
Federal act to ensure that all consumers are given an equal chance to obtain credit.

equitable title
(1) The interest held by the trustor under a trust deed. (2) Selling a note for less than the face amount or the current balance.

equity
The difference between the appraised value and the loan.

equity buildup
The gradual increase of the borrower's equity in a property caused by amortization of loan principal.

equity of redemption
(1) The right of a debtor, before a foreclosure sale, to reclaim property that had been given up due to mortgage default. (2) Also known as the right of redemption.

erosion
The gradual wearing away of land by natural processes.

escheat
A legal process where property reverts to the state because the deceased left no will and has no legal heirs. The state must wait five years before trying to claim the property. (Pronounced es-cheat)

escrow *(en custodia de tercero persona)*
A small and short-lived trust arrangement.

escrow agent
The neutral third party holding funds or something of value in trust for another or others.

escrow holder
Acts as a neutral agent of both buyer and seller.

escrow instructions
Written directions, signed by a buyer and seller, detailing the procedures necessary to close a transaction and directing the escrow agent how to proceed.

estate
(1) The ownership interest or claim a person has in real property. (2) A legal interest in land; defines the nature, degree, extent and duration of a person's ownership in land.

estate at sufferance
A tenancy created when one is in wrongful possession of real estate even though the original possession may have been legal.

estate at will
The tenancy that may be ended by the unilateral decision of either party. There is no agreed upon termination date, and either party must give 30-days notice before ending the tenancy.

estate for life
A possessory, freehold estate in land held by a person only for the duration of his or her life or the life or lives of another.

estate for years
(1) A leasehold estate with a definite end date that must be renegotiated. (2) Commonly used for commercial leases.

estate from period to period
(1) A leasehold estate that is automatically renewed for the same term; a conveyance for an indefinite period of time. This does not need to be renegotiated upon each renewal. (2) Commonly a month-to-month rental.

estate in fee
(1) The most complete form of ownership of real property. (2) A freehold estate that can be passed by descent or by will after the owner's death. (3) Also known as estate of inheritance or fee simple estate.

estate of inheritance
(1) An estate which may descend to heirs. (2) Also known as perpetual estate.

estate tax
Federal tax on the transfer of assets owned by the estate of a person who has died.

estoppel

(1) A legal doctrine which prevents a person from denying something to be true or a fact which is contrary to previous statements made by that same person. (2) Also known as an implied or ostensible agency.

estuary

Where sea water and fresh water mix together.

et al

And others.

et ux

(1) Abbreviation for et uxor. (2) Means "and wife."

ethics

A set of principles or values by which an individual guides his or her own behavior and judges that of others.

eviction *(evicción)*

The legal process of removing a tenant from the premises for some breach of the lease.

eviction notice

Written notice from the landlord to the tenant requesting that he or she move out of the property within three days or meeting the landlord's requirements.

evidence of title

Proof of property ownership.

exclusive authorization and right-to sell listing

An exclusive contract where the seller must pay the listing broker a commission if the property is sold within the time limit by the listing broker, any other person, or even by the owner.

exclusive listing *(listado exclusivo)*

An exclusive contract where the seller must pay the listing broker a commission if any broker sells the property.

execute

(1) To perform or complete. (2) To sign.

executed contract

All parties have performed completely.

execution sale

The forced sale of a property to satisfy a money judgment.

executor/executrix *(albacea)*

A person named in a will to handle the affairs of a deceased person.

executory contract

A contract in which obligation to perform exists on one or both sides.

expedientes

Land grants recorded by the Mexican government in California.

expenses

Certain items which appear on a closing statement in connection with a real estate sale.

express agreement

A written agreement, usually in the form of a listing contract which authorizes the broker to represent the seller in finding a ready, willing, and able buyer.

express contract

Parties declare the terms and put their intentions in words, either oral or written.

extended policy

An extended title insurance policy.

external obsolescence

Any influence negatively affecting a property's value that falls outside of the specific property site (i.e., a property located under an airport flight pattern).

fair market value

(1) The price the property would bring if freely offered on the open market with both a willing buyer and a willing seller. (2) Also known as market value and objective value.

false promise

A false statement of fact.

Fannie Mae

Fannie Mae buys loans that conform to Fannie Mae guidelines from lenders, and, by doing so, puts mortgage money back into the system so lenders can make more loans.

farm

A specific geographical location in which an agent walks every month in order to obtain listings.

Federal Deposit Insurance Corporation (FDIC)

The Federal Deposit Insurance Corporation (FDIC) insures depositors for at least $250,000 per insured bank if a bank or thrift institution fails.

Federal Fair Housing Act

This law, amended in 1988, was created to provide fair housing throughout the United States.

Federal Housing Administration

A federal government agency that insures private mortgage loans for financing of homes and home repairs.

GLOSSARY

Federal Reserve System *(Systema de la Reserva Federal)*

The federal banking system of the United States under the control of a central board of governors (Federal Reserve Board) involving a central bank in each of twelve geographical districts with broad powers in controlling credit and the amount of money in circulation.

fee

See *estate in fee* or *fee simple absolute*.

fee simple

The greatest possible interest a person can have in real estate.

fee simple absolute

(1) The largest, most complete ownership recognized by law. (2) An estate in fee with no restrictions on its use. (3) Property transferred or sold with no conditions or limitations on its use.

fee simple defeasible

Also known as fee simple qualified.

fee simple estate

The most complete form of ownership.

fee simple qualified

(1) An estate in which the holder has a fee simple title, subject to return to the grantor if a specified condition occurs. (2) Also known as fee simple defeasible.

fictitious business name

(1) A business name other than the name of the person who has registered the business. (2) Also known as assumed name. (3) A name that does not include the last name of the owner in the name of the business. (4) Also known as DBA or doing business as.

fictitious trust deed

Recorded trust deed containing details which apply to later loan documents.

fiduciary

A relationship that implies a position of trust or confidence.

fiduciary duty

That duty owned by an agent to act in the highest good faith toward the principal and not to obtain any advantage over the latter by the slightest misrepresentation, concealment, duress of pressure.

fiduciary relationship

A relationship that implies a position of trust or confidence.

final tract map

A map indicating any changes required by the planning commission and is recorded in the county where the property is located.

finance charge

The dollar amount the credit will cost and is composed of any direct or indirect charge as a condition of obtaining credit.

financial intermediary

(1) An organization that obtains funds through deposits and then lends those funds to earn a return such as savings banks, commercial banks, credit unions and mutual savings banks. (2) Lenders that make real estate loans.

financing statement

(1) A written notice filed with the county recorder by a creditor who has extended credit for the purchase of personal property; establishes the creditor's interests in the personal property which is security for the debt. (2) A document used to record debt.

finder's fee

(1) Money paid to a person for finding a buyer to purchase a property or a seller to list property. (2) Also known as a referral fee.

fire stop

Boards nailed between studs to block the spread of fire in the walls.

first trust deed

A legal document pledging collateral for a loan (see *trust deed*) that has first priority over all other claims against the property except taxes and bonded indebtedness. This trust deed is superior to any other.

fiscal year

Starts on July 1 and runs through June 30 of the following year (used for real property tax purposes).

fixed rate full amortized loan

A loan with two distinct features. First, the interest rate remains fixed for the life of the loan. Second, the payments remain level for the life of the loan and are structured to repay the loan at the end of the loan term.

fixed rate loan

The most common type of loan. The principal and interest are calculated for the term of the loan. Payments are determined by dividing the total by the number of payments in the term of the loan. Regular payments of fixed amounts, to include both interest and principal are made. This payment pays off the debt completely by the end of the term.

fixture

(1) Personal property that has become affixed to real estate. (2) Real property that used to be personal property.

flag lot

A lot that looks like a flag on a pole. The pole represents the access to the site, which is usually located to the rear of another lot fronting a main street.

flashing
Sheet metal or other material that keeps the water from seeping into a building.

flood (100-year)
Boundary indicating areas of moderate flood hazards.

flood hazard boundary maps
Maps that identify the general flood hazards within a community.

floodplain
Low land adjacent to a river, lake or ocean.

floodwater
Water that overflows a defined channel.

footing
(1) The spreading part at the base of a foundation wall or pier. (2) A footing is an extended part of the foundation at the base or bottom of a foundation wall, pier or column.

forbearance
(1) Refraining from action by a creditor against a debt or after the debt has become due. (2) Forgiving a debt or obligation.

foreclosure
A legal procedure by which mortgaged property in which there has been default on the part of the borrower is sold to satisfy the debt.

foreclosure action
After a mechanic's lien is recorded, the claimant has 90 days to bring foreclosure action to enforce the lien. If he or she does not bring action, the lien will be terminated and the claimant loses the right to foreclose.

foreclosure sale
A sale where property is sold to satisfy a debt.

formaldehyde
A chemical organic compound found in building materials which may be a carcinogen.

foundation
The base of a house; usually concrete.

foundation plan
Drawing that shows foundation, sub-floors, footing, and pier placement.

franchise *(franquicia)*
A right or privilege awarded by law to operate a business using another company's name and products. In real estate, there are franchised brokerages such as Century 21® and ERA®.

fraud
An act meant to deceive in order to get someone to part with something of value.

Freddie Mac
A shareholder-owned corporation that purchases, secures, and invests in home mortgages.

freehold
The full use of real estate for an indeterminate time. It differs from leasehold, which allows possession for a limited time.

freehold estate
An estate in real property which continues for an indefinite period of time.

front foot
The width of a property on the side facing the street.

front money
The minimum amount of money necessary to initiate a real estate venture, to get the transaction underway.

frontage
The length of a property along a street.

fructus industriales
Crops produced by human labor such as lettuce and grapes.

fructus naturales
Naturally occurring plant growth such as grasses.

fully amortized note
A note that is fully repaid at maturity by periodic reduction of the principal.

functional obsolescence
A type of depreciation stemming from poor architectural design, lack of modern facilities, out-of-date equipment, changes in styles of construction, or changes in utility demand.

functional utility
The combined factors of usefulness with desirability.

gable roof
A pitched roof with two sloping sides.

gambrel roof
Typically seen in Dutch colonial architecture, is a curbed roof, with a steep lower slope with a flatter one above.

general agent
A person authorized by a principal to perform any and all tasks associated with the continued operation of a particular project.

general lien
A lien on all the property of a debtor.

general plan
A measurement of length, rather than area (square foot) or volume (cubic foot).

gift deed

Used to make a gift of property to a grantee, usually a close friend or relative.

gift tax

Tax that can be due when you give property or other assets to someone.

Ginnie Mae

An agency of HUD, which functions in the secondary mortgage market, primarily in social housing programs.

gold rush

A large migration of people to a newly discovered gold field.

good consideration

Gifts such as real property based solely on love and affection.

goodwill

An intangible, salable asset arising from the reputation of a business; the expectation of continued public patronage.

government survey

A method of specifying the location of parcels of land using prime meridians, base lines, standard parallels, guide meridians, townships, and sections.

grace period

An agreed-upon time after the payment of a debt is past due, during which a party can perform without being considered in default.

graduated payment mortgage

(1) A loan with partially deferred payments of principal at the start of the term, increasing as the loan matures. (2) Also known as the flexible rate mortgage.

grandfather clause

An expression used in law that permits the continuation of a use or business to proceed because the current law denies permission.

grant

(1) A technical legal term in a deed of conveyance bestowing an interest in real property on another. (2) The words convey and transfer have the same effect.

grant deed

A type of deed in which the grantor warrants that he or she has not previously conveyed the property being granted, has not encumbered the property except as disclosed, and will convey to the grantee any title to the property acquired later.

grantee

The person receiving the property, or the one to whom it is being conveyed.

grantor

The person conveying or transferring the property.

gratuitous agent

A person not paid by the principal for services on behalf of the principal, who cannot be forced to act as an agent, but who becomes bound to act in good faith and obey a principal's instructions once he or she undertakes to act as an agent.

gross domestic product

The measure of goods and services produced by the nation during any one calendar year.

gross income

Total income from property before any expenses are deducted.

gross income multiplier

A figure which, when multiplied by the annual gross income, will theoretically determine the market value. A general rule of thumb which varies with specific properties and areas (industrial and commercial).

gross lease

(1) A gross lease is also called a flat, fixed or straight lease. The tenant pays an agreed-upon sum as rent and the landlord pays any other expenses such as taxes, maintenance, or insurance. (2) The tenant pays an agreed-upon sum as rent, plus certain agreed-upon expenses per month (i.e., taxes, insurance and repairs).

gross national product (GNP)

The total value of all goods and services produced in an economy during a given period of time.

gross rent

Income (calculated annually or monthly) received from rental units before any expenses are deducted.

gross rent multiplier

A method used by real estate agents and appraisers to quickly convert gross-rent into market value. It is used for income-producing properties and is an easy way to get a rough estimate of the value of rental units.

ground lease

A lease for only the land.

ground rent

(1) Earnings of improved property credited to earnings of the ground itself after allowance is made for earnings of improvements. (2) Also called economic rent.

growing equity mortgage

A mortgage that has a fixed interest rate of increasing monthly payments.

guarantee of title

An assurance of clear title.

habendum clause

The *to have and to hold* clause which may be found in a deed.

handicap

Any physical or mental impairment which substantially limits one or more major life activities.

hard money loan

Any loan made on real property in exchange for cash.

hazard insurance

A property insurance policy that protects the owner and lender against physical hazards to property such as fire and windstorm damage.

hazardous household waste

Consumer products such as paints, cleaners, stains, varnishes, car batteries, motor oil, and pesticides that contain hazardous components.

hazardous waste

Materials—chemicals, explosives, radioactive, biological—whose disposal is regulated by the Environmental Protection Agency (EPA).

header

The horizontal, load-bearing, board over a doorway or window opening.

hedge against inflation

Real property appreciation keeps pace or exceeds inflation rates.

heir *(heredero)*

One who inherits property at the death of the owner or if the owner has died without a will (intestate).

highest and best use

An appraisal phrase meaning that use which at the time of an appraisal is most likely to produce the greatest net return to the land and/or buildings over a given period of time; that use which will produce the greatest amount of amenities or profit. This is the starting point for appraisal.

hip roof

A pitched roof with sloping sides and ends.

hold harmless clause

Protects the broker from incorrect information.

Holden Act

(1) A law designed primarily to eliminate discrimination in leading practices based upon the character of the neighborhood in which real property in located. (2) Also known as Housing Financial Discrimination Act of 1977. (See *redlining*)

holder

The party to whom a promissory note is made payable.

holder in due course

A person who has obtained a negotiable instrument (promissory note, check) in the ordinary course of business before it is due, in good faith and for value, without knowledge that it has been previously dishonored.

holographic will

Written in the maker's own handwriting, dated and signed by the maker.

home equity loan

A cash loan made against the equity in the borrower's home.

homeowners' association *(asociación de los dueños)*

A group of property owners in a condominium or other subdivision neighborhood, who manage common areas, collect dues, and establish property standards.

homeowners' exemption

A $7,000 tax exemption available to all owner-occupied dwellings.

homestead

A piece of land that is owned and occupied as a family home.

Hoskold Tables

A method used to value an annuity that is based on reinvesting capital immediately; used by appraisers to valuate income property.

houseboat

A barge that is designed and equipped for use as a dwelling.

housing inventory

Housing units that are available for sale or in the process of being made ready for sale.

HVAC

The mnemonic for Heating, Ventilation, and Air Conditioning.

hypothecation

A process which allows a borrower to remain in possession of the property while using it to secure a loan.

intestate *(intestado)*

Dying without leaving a will.

implied contract

An agreement shown by acts and conduct rather than written words.

implied warranty of habitability

The property will be maintained to meet bare living requirements.

impound account
A trust account set up for funds set aside for future costs relating to a property.

improvements *(hacer reformas)*
Valuable additions made to property to enhance value or extend useful remaining life.

income approach
Estimates the present worth of future benefits from ownership of a property.

independent contractor
A person who is hired to do work for another person but who is not an employee of that person.

infill development
The development of vacant parcels in existing urban and suburban areas.

inflation
The increase in the general price level of goods and services.

ingress
The right to enter onto a property using an easement.

inheritance tax
A tax levied by states on inherited property and paid by the person receiving the property.

injunction *(requerimiento judicial)*
A court order forcing a person to do or not do an act.

innocent misrepresentation
When a person unknowingly provides incorrect information.

installment note
A note which provides for a series of periodic payments of principal and interest, until amount borrowed is paid in full. This periodic reduction of principal amortizes the loan.

installment sales
Where payments are made, by the buyer, to the seller, over a period of more than one year.

institutional lenders
A financial intermediary, such as a savings and loan association, commercial bank, or life insurance company, which pools money of its depositors and then invests funds in various ways, including trust deed and mortgage loans.

instrument *(instrument)*
A formal legal document such as a contract, deed or will.

insurance company
Major supplier of money for large commercial loans to developers and builders.

interest *(interés)*
The charge for the use of money.

interest only loan
A straight, non-amortizing loan in which the lender receives only interest during the term of the loan and principal is repaid in a lump sum at maturity.

interest rate
The percentage charged for the use of money.

interim loan
A short-term, temporary loan used until permanent financing is available, e.g., a construction loan.

interim use
(1) When the highest and best use is expected to change. (2) A short-term and temporary use of a property until it is ready for a more productive highest and best use.

interior lot
A lot that is surrounded by other lots, with a frontage on the street. It is the most common type lot and may be desirable or not, depending on other factors.

intermediation
The process of transfer capital from those who invest funds to those who wish to borrow.

interpleader action
A court proceeding initiated by the stakeholder of property who claims no proprietary interest in it for the purpose of deciding who among claimants is legally entitled to the property.

intestate succession *(sucesión intestada)*
When a person inherits property as a result of someone dying without a will.

inverse condemnation
When a private party forces the government to pay just compensation, if the property value or use has been diminished by a public entity.

involuntary lien
When the owner does not pay taxes or the debt owed, a lien may be placed against his or her property without permission.

Inwood tables
Means by which an income stream can be converted into present value; used by appraisers to valuate income property.

irrigation districts
Quasi-political districts created under special laws to provide for water services to property owners in the district; an operation governed to a great extent by law.

joint and several liability

(1) A legal term used in reference to a debt or a judgment for negligence, in which each debtor or each judgment defendant is responsible for the entire amount of the debt or judgment. (2) An activity involving the sale of something through an intermediary who negotiates the transaction for payment.

joint tenancy

When two or more parties own real property as co-owners, with the right of survivorship.

joint venture *(contrato de asociación en participación)*

When two or more individuals or firms join together on a single project as partners.

joists

Parallel boards supporting floors or ceilings. The boards supporting them are girders, beams or bearing walls.

judgment

The final legal decision of a judge in a court of law regarding the legal rights of parties to disputes.

judgment lien

The final determination of the rights of parties in a lawsuit by the court.

judicial foreclosure

Foreclosure by court action.

junior mortgage

A second mortgage; one that is subordinate or has an inferior priority to the first mortgage.

junior trust deed

Any trust deed that is recorded after a first trust deed, whose priority is less than that first trust deed.

just compensation

Fair and reasonable payment due to a private property owner when his or her property is condemned under eminent domain.

key lot

A lot that resembles a key fitting into a lock, is surrounded by the back yards of other lots. It is the least desirable because of the lack of privacy.

kiosk

A free-standing small booth, such as a jewelry stand or a newsstand.

laches

Delay or negligence in asserting one's legal rights.

land

Includes airspace, surface rights, mineral rights, and water rights.

LAND

The mnemonic for the four elements of a valid lease: Length of time, Amount of rent, Names of parties, and Description of the property.

land contract

(1) A contract for the sale of real property where the seller gives up possession, but retains the title until the purchase price is paid in full. (2) Also known as a contract of sale or agreement of sale.

land project

Subdivisions located in sparsely populated areas (fewer than 1,5000 registered voters within the subdivision or within two miles of its boundaries), made up of 50 parcels or more.

landlocked

Property surrounded by other property with no access to a public road, street or alley.

landlord *(arrendador)*

(1) Lessor. (2) Property owner.

lateral support

The support which the soil of an adjoining owner gives to a neighbor's land.

lease *(arrendamiento)*

(1) A contract between owner, (lessor or landlord) and a lessee (tenant) which gives the tenant a tenancy. (2) Also known as a rental agreement. (3) A contract between an owner and tenant. (4) A movable document describing the temporary possession and use of the property.

leased-fee estate

The interest of the lessor in property.

leasehold

(1) An agreement, written or unwritten, transferring the right to exclusive possession and use of real estate for a definite period of time. (2) Also known as a rental agreement or lease.

leasehold estate

A tenant's right to occupy real estate during the term of the lease. This is personal property interest.

legacy

A gift of personal property by will.

legal description

(1) A land description recognized by law. (2) A description by which property can be definitely located by reference to government surveys or approved recorded maps.

legal title

Title that is complete and perfect regarding right of ownership.

lessee

(1) Tenant. (2) The one to whom property is rented or leased.

lessor

(1) Landlord. (2) Property owner. (3) The person who owns the property and signs the lease to give possession and use to the tenant.

less-than-freehold estate

(1) The lessee's interest. (2) An estate owned by a tenant who rents real property. (3) Also known as a leasehold estate.

leverage

Using a lender's money to finance a sale.

license *(licencia)*

(1) A permission granted by competent authority to engage in a bueinsss or occupation. (2) Permission to use a property, which may be revoked at any time.

license law

Another term for the Real Estate Law.

lien *(gravamen)*

(1) A claim on the property of another for the payment of a debt. (2) A legal obligation to pay.

LIEN$

The mnemonic for the dollar sign and to show that lien$ involve money.

life estate

An estate that is limited in duration to the life of its owner or the life of another designated person.

limited liability company (LLC)

An alternative business that has characteristics of both corporations and limited partnerships.

limited partnership

A partnership of at least one general partner and one limited partner.

linear foot

A measurement of length rather than area (square foot) or volume (cubic feet).

liquidated damages clause

Clause in a contract that allows parties to the contract to decide in advance the amount of damages to be paid, should either party breach the contract.

lis pendens

(1) A recorded notice that indicates pending litigation affecting title on a property. (2) Also called a pendency of action. (Pronounced lis pendenz)

listing

A contract between an owner of real property and an agent who is authorized to obtain a buyer.

listing agent

A broker who obtains a listing from a seller to act as an agent for compensation.

listing agreement

A written contract by which a principal, or seller, employs a broker to sell real estate.

littoral

Land bordering a lake, ocean or sea as opposed to land bordering a stream or river (running water). (Pronounced lit-to-ral)

loan assumption

A buyer assumes the existing loan when a property is sold. The buyer takes over primary liability for the loan, with the original borrower secondarily liable if there is a default.

loan-to-value ratio (LTV)

The percentage of appraised value to the loan.

lot, block and tract system

(1) A process where developers divide parcels of land into lots. Each lot in a subdivision is identified by number, as is the block in which it is located; each lot and block is in a referenced tract. This process is required by the California Subdivision Map Act. (2) Also known as lot and block system, subdivision system or recorded map system.

love and affection

Consideration used in a gift deed.

maker

The borrower who executes a promissory note and becomes primarily liable for payment to the lender.

management contract

A contract that shows the terms of the agreement between the owner and the property manager.

mansionization

A new trend of home remodeling and construction that is emerging in older neighborhoods with small to medium-sized homes.

manufactured home

A home built in a factory after June 15, 1976 and must conform to the U.S. government's Manufactured Home Construction and Safety Standards.

MARIA

The mnemonic for the five tests of a fixture: Method of attachment, Adaptation, Relationship of the parties, Intention, and Agreement of the parties.

market comparison approach

(1) An appraisal method using the principles of substitution to compare similar properties. (2) A means of comparing similar type properties, which have recently sold, to the subject property. (3) Also called market data approach.

market price

The price paid regardless of pressures, motives or intelligence.

market rent

The rent a property should bring in the open market.

market value *(valor de mercado)*

(1) The highest price a property would bring if freely offered on the open market, with both a willing buyer and a willing seller. (2) Sometimes called objective value.

marketable title

Good or clear saleable title reasonably free from risk of litigation over possible defects.

material fact

Any fact that would seem likely to affect the judgment of the principal in giving consent to the agent to enter into the particular transaction on the specified terms.

maximum allowable rent

The maximum legal rent that a landlord may charge for a controlled rental unit.

mechanic's lien *(gravamen de una constructora o de un constructor)*

A lien placed against a property by anyone who supplies labor, services, or materials used for improvements on real property and did not receive payment for the improvements.

median home price

The price that is middle value of a sample of sales with one-half of the sales below and one-half of the sales above the median home price.

megalopolis

A large densely populated metropolitan area consisting of a number of major urban areas and smaller surrounding cities.

Mello-Roos Act

Allows developers to make improvements (roads, parks, schools, fire stations) while making each homeowner pay for the improvements. These improvements are listed in the property taxes.

Mello-Roos District

An area where a special assessment is imposed on those real property owners within a Community Facilities District. Public services such as roads, sewers, parks, schools and fire stations in new developments may be financed under this law.

menace

Using the threat of violence to get agreement in accepting a contract.

meridian

A survey line running north and south, used as a reference when mapping land.

metes and bounds

Land description that delineates boundaries and measures distances between landmarks to identify property.

minerals

Land elements found beneath the ground such as gold and coal and owned as real property. Fugitive substances that are not solid such as oil or gas must be taken from the ground. Once these elements are taken from the ground, they become the personal property of whoever removed them.

mineral rights

The legal interest in the valuable items found below the surface of a property (i.e., gold and coal).

minor *(menor de edad)*

A person under 18 years of age.

misplaced improvements

Improvements on land which do not conform to the most profitable use of the site.

misrepresentation

(1) Making a false statement or concealing a material fact. (2) A false statement of fact.

mistake

(1) An agreement was unclear or there was a misunderstanding in the facts. Mistake does not include ignorance, incompetence or poor judgment. (2) An error or misunderstanding.

mnemonics

The following memory aids may be found alphabetically in this Glossary: ADAM E. LEE, COALD, DEC, DUST, LAND, LIEN$, MARIA, NDFA, NIMBY, PANCHO, PEPS, PETE, PITI, SCI, TIMMUR, T-TIP, and UPTEE.

mobilehome

A factory-built home manufactured prior to June 15, 1976, constructed on a chassis and wheels, and designed for permanent or semi-attachment to land.

mobilehome park

Any area or tract of land where two or more mobile home lots are rented or leased or held out for rent or leased to accommodate manufactured homes or mobilehomes used for human habitation.

GLOSSARY

monetary policy

The actions taken by the federal government to influence the availability and cost of money and credit as a means of promoting national economic goals.

money encumbrance

An encumbrance that affects the title.

month-to-month tenancy

A tenant rents property for a month at a time, under a periodic tenancy that continues for successive months until terminated by proper notice.

monument

A fixed landmark used in a metes and bounds land description.

mortgage *(hipoteca)*

A legal document used as security for a debt.

mortgage banker

A person whose principal business is the originating financing, closing, selling, and servicing of loans secured by real property for institutional lenders on a contractual basis.

mortgage loan disclosure statement

A statement that informs the buyer of all charges and expenses related to a particular loan.

mortgage yield

The amount received or returned from an investment expressed as a percentage.

mortgage-backed securities

Pools of mortgages used as collateral for the issuance of securities in the secondary market.

mortgagee *(acreedor hipotecario)*

The lender under a mortgage.

mortgagor *(deudor hipotecario)*

The borrower under a mortgage.

multiple-listing service

A cooperative listing service conducted by a group of brokers (usually members of a real estate association) to provide an inventory of all available properties in the area.

mutual assent

(1) An agreement between the parties in a contract. (2) The offer and acceptance of a contract.

mutual consent

(1) The offer by one party and acceptance by another party. (2) Also known as mutual assent or meeting of the minds.

mutual mortgage insurance

A fee for an insurance policy charged to the borrower to protect lender under an FHA loan, in the event of foreclosure on the property.

mutual rescission

When all parties to a contract agree to cancel an agreement.

mutual water company

A water company organized by or for water users in a given district with the object of securing an ample water supply at a reasonable rate; stock is issued to users.

naked legal title

Title lacking the rights and privileges commonly associated with ownership may be held by trustee under a trust deed.

narrative appraisal

A summary of all factual materials, techniques, and appraisal methods used by the appraiser in setting forth his or her value conclusion.

NDFA

The mnemonic for No Darn Fooling Around.

negative amortization

Occurs when monthly installment payments are insufficient to pay the interest, so any unpaid interest is added to the principal due.

negligent misrepresentations

Untrue statements made without facts to back them up.

negotiable

Capable of being negotiated, assignable or transferable in the ordinary course of business.

negotiable instrument

Any written instrument that may be transferred by endorsement or delivery.

net lease *(arrendamiento neto)*

The tenant pays an agreed-upon sum as rent, plus certain agreed-upon expenses per month (i.e., taxes, insurance and repairs).

net listing

An employment contract in which the commission is not definite. The broker receives all the money from the sale of the property that is in excess of the selling price set by the seller. The broker must disclose the selling price to both buyer and seller within 30 days after the transaction.

net operating income (NOI) *(ingreso neto de operación)*

The balance remaining after deducting gross receipts of all fixed expenses.

net worth

The value of all assets minus all liabilities.

neutral depository

An escrow business conducted by someone who is a licensed escrow holder.

NIMBY
The mnemonic for Not In My Backyard.

no fault eviction
A lawful eviction in which the tenant is not at fault. This includes whether the owner wants to occupy the apartment or to get out of the rental housing business.

no notice of completion
If the owner does not record a notice of completion when work is finished, all claimants have a maximum of 90 days from the day work was finished to record a mechanic's lien.

nominal interest rates
The interest rate that is named or stated in loan documents.

non-conforming use *(uso no conforme)*
Legal use of property that at one period was established and maintained at the time of its original construction but no longer conforms to the current zoning law.

notary public
A licensed public officer who takes or witnesses the acknowledgement.

note
An evidence of a debt.

notice of completion
A notice filed by the owner or general contractor after completion of work on improvements, limiting the time in which mechanic's liens can be filed against the property.

notice of default
A notice to a defaulting party that there has been a nonpayment of a debt.

notice of non-responsibility
When an owner discovers unauthorized work on the property, he or she must file a notice. This must be recorded and posted on the property to be valid. The notice states the owner is not responsible for work being done, and releases the owner from the liability for work done without permission.

notice of trustee's sale
Notice given, and published, that a trustee's sale will be held to sell a property to satisfy a debt.

notice to pay rent or quit
(1) A written notice from the landlord to the tenant informing him or her to move out of the property within three days or meet the landlord's requirements. (2) Also known as an eviction notice.

novation *(novación)*
The substitution by agreement of a new obligation for an existing one.

null and void
Of no legal validity or effect.

1 month
For escrow purposes, 30 days.

1 year
For escrow and proration purposes, 360 days, 12 months, or 52 weeks.

1031 exchange
(1) A method of deferring tax liability. (2) Also known as a tax-deferred exchange.

obligor
(1) One how is bound by a legal obligation. (2) A person, delinquent in paying child support, whose name is listed by the Child Support Services.

obsolescence *(obsolescencia)*
Loss in value due to reduced desirability and usefulness of a structure because its design and construction became obsolete; loss because old-fashioned and not in keeping with modern needs, with consequent loss of income. May be functional or economic.

offer
A presentation or proposal for acceptance to form a contract.

offer to purchase
The proposal made to an owner of property by a potential buyer to purchase the property under stated terms.

offeree
The party receiving an offer.

offeror *(oferente)*
The party making an offer.

open end loan
A loan where the borrower is given a limit up to which may be borrowed, with each advance secured by the same trust deed.

open house *(casa abierta)*
A common real estate practice of showing listed homes to the general public during established hours.

open housing law
Congress passed the Federal Fair Housing Act in April 1968 which prohibits discrimination in the sale of real estate because of race, color, or religion of buyers. Its amendment in 1988 added: Those physically and mentally handicapped and those children under 18 years of age.

open listing
A listing agreement that gives any number of brokers the right to sell a property.

open sheathing
Boards nailed to rafters to form foundation for the roof.

option *(opción)*

(1) A contract to keep open, for a set period of time. (2) An offer to purchase or lease real property.

optionee

The person who wants to purchase or lease (lessee) the property.

optionor

The person who owns the property (seller, lessor).

or more clause

A clause in a mortgage or trust deed that allows a borrower to pay it off early with no penalty.

orientation *(orientación)*

The placement of a building on its lot in relation to exposure to sun, prevailing wind, traffic, and privacy from the street.

ostensible agency

An agency relationship created by the actions of the parties rather than by an express agreement.

ownership

(1) The right of one or more persons to possess and use property to the exclusion of all others. (2) A collection of rights to the use and enjoyment of property.

ownership in severalty

Property owned by one person or entity.

package loan

A type of loan on real property used in home financing covering land, structures, fixtures, and other personal property.

PANCHO

The mnemonic for the six requirements for adverse possession: Possession, Adverse, Notorious, Continuous, Hostile, and Open.

paramount title

Title which is superior or foremost to all others.

parcel map

Map showing a parcel of land that will be subdivided into less than five parcels or units, and shows land boundaries, streets, and parcel numbers.

parol evidence rule

(1) Oral or written negotiations made prior to a dispute about an executed contract and brought forward to influence the executed contract. Parol mean oral or by word of mouth but in this case means any evidence outside of the written agreement. (2) Prohibits introducing any kind of outside evidence to change or add to the terms of deeds, contracts or other writing once they have been executed.

partial reconveyance

A clause in a trust deed or mortgage permitting the release of a parcel or part of a parcel from the lien of that security instrument. The release usually occurs upon the payment of a specified sum of money.

partially amortized note

A promissory note with a repayment schedule that is not sufficient to amortize the loan over its term.

partition action

A court action to divide a property held by co-owners.

partnership

A form of business in which two or more persons join their money and skills in conducting the business.

party wall

A wall erected on the line between two adjoining properties, which are under different ownership, for the use of both parties.

patent

The legal document that transmits real property from the state or federal government to a person.

PEPS

The mnemonic for the four forces influencing value: Physical characteristics, Economic Influences, Political (governmental) regulations, and Social ideals.

percentage lease

The tenant pays a percentage of gross monthly receipts in addition to a base rent.

percolating water

Underground water not flowing in a defined channel.

percolation test

Test used to determine the ability of the land to absorb and drain water and is frequently used when installing septic systems.

personal property

Anything movable that is not real property.

PETE

The mnemonic for four types of government controls: Police power, Eminent domain, Taxation, and Escheat.

physical deterioration

(1) A type of depreciation caused by wear and tear, negligent care, damage by dry rot or termites or severe changes in temperature. (2) Also known as deferred maintenance.

pier

A column of masonry used to support other structural members.

pitch

The slope, incline, or rise of a roof.

PITTI
The mnemonic for Principles, Interest, Taxes, and Insurance.

planned development
(1) A planning and zoning term describing land not subject to conventional zoning to permit clustering of residences or other characteristics of the project which differ from normal zoning. (2) Sometimes called a planned unit development (PUD).

planning commission
An agency of local government charged with planning the development, redevelopment or preservation of an area.

plat map
Map of a subdivision indicating the location and boundaries of individual lots.

pledge
The transfer of property to a lender to be held as security for repayment of a debt. The lender takes possession of property.

pledged savings account mortgage
A borrower has a large amount of money in a savings or thrift account, and uses this money to maintain the account as security for a lender. The lender requires a certain ratio of the new loan amount to the balance in the account. The borrower must keep that amount in the account for a specified length of time. The lender can release the pledge account when the property has acquired enough equity to qualify under normal loan-to-value ratios.

plottage increment
Putting several smaller, less valuable parcels together under one ownership to increase value of total property.

pocket listing
A list that is kept by the listing broker or salesperson, and is not shared with other brokers in the office or other multiple listing service members. This is discouraged by the real estate profession and is prohibited by many broker's offices.

points
Charges levied by the lender based on the loan amount. Each point equals 1% of the loan amount; for example, two points on a $100,000 mortgage is $2,000. Discount points are used to buy down the interest rate. Points can also include a loan origination fee, which is usually one point. (See *Discount Points*)

police power
The power of the state to enact laws within constitutional limits to promote the order, safety, health, morals and general welfare of our society.

potable water *(agua potable)*
Fresh water that is safe and agreeable for drinking.

power of attorney *(energía del abogado)*
A legal document that gives another person the legal authority to act on his or her behalf.

power of sale
A clause in a trust deed or mortgage that gives the holder the right to sell the property in the event of default by the borrower.

preliminary notice
A written notice that must be given to the owner within 20 days of first furnishing labor or materials for a job by anyone eligible to file a mechanic's lien.

preliminary title report
An offer to issue a policy of title insurance in the future for a specific fee.

prepaid items of expense
Prorations of prepaid items of expense which are credited to the seller in the closing escrow statement.

prepayment clause
A clause in a trust deed that allows a lender to collect a certain percentage of a loan as a penalty for an early payoff.

prepayment penalty
(1) Penalty for the payment of a note before it actually becomes due. (2) A fee or charge imposed upon a debtor who desires to pay off their loan before its maturity.

prescription
The process of acquiring an interest, not ownership, in a certain property.

price
What the property actually sold for.

prima facie
Latin meaning first sight, a fact presumed to be true until disproved.

primary mortgage market *(mercado de hipote primario)*
Lenders make mortgage loans by lending directly to borrowers.

principal
(1) In a real estate transaction, the one (seller) who hires the broker to represent him or her in the sale of the property. (2) The amount of money borrowed.

priority
The order in which deeds are recorded.

private grant
The granting of private property to other private persons.

private mortgage insurance *(seguro hipotecario privado)*
Mortgage guarantee insurance available to conventional lenders on the first part of a high risk loan.

GLOSSARY

private restrictions
Created at the time of sale or in the general plan of a subdivision.

pro rata
In proportion; according to a certain percentage or proportion of a whole.

probate
The legal process to prove a will is valid.

probate sale
A court-approved sale of the property of a deceased person.

procuring cause
A broker who produces a buyer ready, willing and able to purchase the property for the price and on the terms specified by the seller, regardless of whether the sale is completed.

progression, principle of
The worth of a lesser valued residence tends to be enhanced by association with higher valued residences in the same area.

promissory note *(nota promisoria)*
The evidence of the debt.

promulgate
To publish or make laws known.

property
Anything that may be owned and gained lawfully.

property management *(administración de propiedad)*
(1) A specialty in which real estate brokers manage homes and large real estate projects such as industrial complexes, shopping centers, apartment houses and condominiums. (2) The branch of the real estate business involving the marketing, operation, maintenance and day-to-day financing of rental properties.

property taxes
Taxes used to operate the government in general.

proprietary lease
The lease used in co-op apartment buildings.

prorate *(proratear)*
(1) The division and distribution of expenses and/or income between the buyer and seller of property as of the date of closing or settlement. (2) The process of making a fair distribution of expenses, through escrow, at the close of the sale.

prospecting
The process of identifying potential customers.

public dedication
When private property is intended for public use. There are three types of public dedication: common law dedication, statutory dedication, or deed.

public grant
The transfer of title by the government to a private individual.

Public Land Survey System (PLSS)
A land description method that uses imaginary lines to form a grid to locate land.

public record
(1) A document disclosing all important facts about the property, its marketing and the financing of the subdivision. (2) Also known as public report.

puffing
(1) A statement of opinion about property that is not factual. (2) Exaggerated comments or opinions not made as representations of fact, thus not grounds for misrepresentation.

pur autre vie
(1) For another's life. (2) A life estate created on the life of a designated person.

purchase money mortgage or trust deed
A trust deed or mortgage given as part or all of the purchase consideration for real property. In some states the purchase money mortgage or trust deed loan can be made by a seller who extends credit to the buyer of property or by a third party lender (typically a financial institution) that makes a loan to the buyer of real property for a portion of the purchase price to be paid for the property. In many states there are legal limitations upon mortgages and trust deed beneficiaries collecting deficiency judgments against the purchase money borrower after the collateral hypothecated under such security instruments has been sold through the foreclosure process. Generally no deficiency judgment is allowed if the collateral property under the mortgage or trust deed is residential property of four units or less with the debtor occupying the property as a place of residence.

Q

quantity survey method *(estudio de costas)*
A detailed estimate of all labor and materials used in the components of a building. Items such as overhead, insurance and contractor's profit are added to direct costs of building. This method is time consuming but very accurate.

quiet enjoyment
Right of an owner or tenant to the use of the property without interference from the acts or claims of third parties.

quiet title action
(1) A court proceeding to clear a cloud on the title of real property. (2) Also known as action to quiet title.

quitclaim deed
Transfers any interest the grantor may have at the time the deed is signed with no warranties of clear title.

radon

Colorless, odorless, gas that is a carcinogen detected by a spectrometer.

rafters

Slanted boards of a roof that are designed to support the roof boards and shingles. To strengthen the load bearing factor of a roof, the rafters should be placed closer together.

range

A land description used in the U.S. government survey system consisting of a strip of land located every six miles east and west of each principal meridian.

range lines

Government survey imaginary vertical lines six miles east and west of the meridian to form columns.

rate

The percentage of interest charged on the principal.

ratification

The approval of a previously authorized act, performed on behalf of a person, which makes the act valid and legally binding.

ratified

Approved after the fact.

ready, willing, and able buyer

A person who is prepared to enter into a purchase contract, really wants to buy, and meets the financing requirements of purchase.

real estate *(bienes raices)*

Land and whatever physical property is on it, including buildings and structures. Current usage makes the term real estate synonymous with real property.

Real Estate Advisory Commission

A 10-member commission to offer advice to the Commissioner on matters pertinent to the Bureau of Real Estate.

real estate agent

A broker licensed by the Bureau of Real Estate who negotiates sales for other people.

real estate broker

Someone holding a broker license issued by the Bureau of Real Estate and permitted by law to negotiate real estate transactions between principals to employ persons holding salesperson or broker licenses.

Real Estate Commissioner

A person appointed by the governor to determine administrative policy and enforce the provisions of the Real Estate Law and the Subdivided Lands Law.

Real Estate Investment Trust *(Fideicomiso de Inversiones en Bienes Raíces)*

A special arrangement under federal and state law whereby investors may pool funds for investments in real estate and mortgages and yet escape corporation taxes, profits being passed to individual investors who are taxed.

Real Estate Law

(1) The law that affects the licensing and conduct of real estate licensees. (2) Another name for the Business and Professions Code, Part 1 entitled Licensing of Persons.

Real Estate Recovery Fund

A separate account funded through collection of a fixed amount from each license fee. It was established to pay judgments against real estate licenses.

real estate salesperson

A person with a real estate license who must be employed by a real estate broker in order to perform any of the activities that requires a license.

Real Estate Settlement Procedures Act

A federal law requiring disclosure to borrowers of settlement (closing) procedures and costs by means of a pamphlet and forms prescribed by the United States Department of Housing and Urban Development.

real estate syndicate

An organization of investors usually in the form of a limited partnership who have joined together to pool capital for the acquisition of real property interests.

Real Estate Transfer Disclosure Statement

A document that the seller must provide to any buyer of residential property (one-to-four units).

real property *(biene inmueble)*

Land (air, surface, mineral, water rights), appurtenances and anything attached, and immovable by law. Also included in real property are the interests, benefits and rights inherent in owning real estate, i.e., the bundle of rights. Current usage makes the term real property synonymous with real estate.

real property loan law

Article 7 of Chapter 3 of the Real Estate Law under which a real estate licensee negotiating loans secured by real property within a specific range is required to give the borrower a statement disclosing the costs and terms of the loan and which also limits the amount of expenses and charges that a borrower may pay with respect to the loan.

real property sales contract

An agreement to convey title to real property upon satisfaction of specified conditions which does not require conveyance within one year of formation of the contract.

Realtist

A member of a national organization, generally composed of African-American real estate brokers, known as the National Association of Real Estate Brokers (NAREB).

REALTOR®

A real estate broker holding active membership in a real estate board affiliated with the National Association of REALTORS® (NAR)

reconciliation

(1) The adjustment process of weighing results of all three appraisal methods to arrive at a final estimate of the subject property's market value. (2) Also known as correlation.

reconveyance deed

Conveys title to property from a trustee back to the borrower (trustor) upon payment in full of the debt secured by the trust deed.

recording

The process of placing a document on file with a designated public official for public notice. This public official is usually a county officer known as the County Recorder who designates the fact that a document has been presented for recording by placing a recording stamp upon it indicating the time of day and the date when it was officially placed on file.

red flag

Something that alerts a reasonably observant person of a potential problem.

redemption period

A period of time established by state law during which a property owner has the right to recover real estate after a foreclosure or tax sale by paying the sales price plus interest and costs.

redlining

(1) The illegal lending policy of denying real estate loans on properties in older, changing urban areas, usually with large minority populations, because of alleged higher lending risks, without due consideration being given by the lending institution to the creditworthiness of the individual loan application. (2) The illegal use of a property's location to deny financing.

refinancing

Paying off an existing obligation and assuming a new obligation in its place. To finance anew, or extend or renew existing financing.

rehabilitation

The restoration of a property to its former or improved condition without changing the basic design or plan.

reinstate

To bring current and restore.

release clause

A provision found in many blanket mortgage or trust deeds enabling the borrower to obtain partial release from the loan of specific parcels.

reliction

When land covered by water becomes uncovered because of alluvial deposits along the banks of streams.

remodeling

Changes the basic design or plan of the building to correct deficiencies.

renegotiable rate mortgage

A type of loan in which the interest rate is renegotiated periodically.

rent *(alquiler)*

Payment for the use of a property, generally under a lease agreement.

rent control

(1) Laws in some communities that limit or prohibit rent increases. (2) Also known as rent stabilization.

rental agreement

Another name for lease.

replacement cost *(costo de reposición)*

The cost of replacing improvements with modern materials and techniques.

reproduction cost *(costo de reproducción)*

The current cost of building a replica of the subject structure, using similar quality materials.

request for notice

A notice that is sent, upon request, to any parties interested in a trust deed, informing them of a default.

rescission

Legal action taken to repeal a contract either by mutual consent of the parties or by one party when the other party has breached a contract.

resident manager

A person employed to manage an apartment building on a part or full-time basis.

residential ceiling height measurements

Minimum - 7.5 feet; normal - 8 feet

residential lease

A lease used for single-family homes and duplexes.

restricted license

A type of probationary license issued when a license has been suspended, revoked or denied after a hearing.

restriction

A limitation placed on the use of property and may be placed by a private owner, a developer or the government. It is usually placed on property to assure that land use is consistent and uniform within a certain area.

retaliatory eviction

An eviction that occurs in revenge for some complaint made by the tenant.

return

(1) Profit from an investment. (2) The yield.

reversionary interest

(1) The right of the landlord to reclaim the property. (2) A future interest.

revocation

The canceling of an offer to contract by the person making the original offer.

revoke

Recall and make void.

ridge board

The highest structural part of a frame building.

right of replevin

The tenant has a legal right to recover personal property unlawfully taken by the landlord.

right of survivorship

(1)The right of a surviving tenant or tenants to succeed to the entire interest of the deceased tenant. (2) The distinguishing feature of a joint tenancy.

riparian rights

The rights of a landowner whose land is next to a natural watercourse to reasonable use of whatever water flows past the property.

rollover mortgage

A loan that allows the rewriting of a new loan at the termination of a prior loan.

R-value

A rating that measures how well insulation resists heat.

S corporation

A corporation that operates like a corporation but is treated like a partnership for tax purposes.

safety clause

Protects the listing broker's commission, if the owner personally sells the property to someone who was show the property or made an offer during the term of the listing.

sale-leaseback

A financial arrangement where at the time of sale the seller retains occupancy by concurrently agreeing to lease the property from the purchaser. The seller receives cash while the buyer is assured a tenant and a fixed return on buyer's investment.

sales associate

(1) A licensed real estate salesperson or broker whose license is held by an employing licensed broker. (2) Also known as associate licensee.

sales contract

A contract by which buyer and seller agree to terms of a sale.

sales tax

Collected as a percentage of the retailing sales of a product, by a retailer, and forwarded to the State Board of Equalization.

sandwich lease

A lease agreement created when a tenant sublets the property to another person, thus creating a sublessor-sublessee relationship. The person in the sandwich is a lessee to the owner and a lessor to the sublessee.

satisfaction

Discharge of a mortgage or trust deed from the records upon payment of the debt.

savings and loan association

A lending institution created as a mutual organization or as a stock institution. Deposits are insured by the Federal Deposit Insurance Corporation (FDIC).

scarcity

(1) The availability of a commodity in the marketplace. (2) A lack of supply of some type of real property resulting in increased value when deman exceeds supply.

schematics

Preliminary drawings and sketches by an architect, such as site plans and elevations.

SCI

The mnemonic for three approaches to value: Sales comparison approach, Cost approach, and Income approach.

second trust deed

The evidence of a debt that is recorded after a first trust deed; a junior trust deed.

secondary mortgage market *(mercado de hipote secundaria)*

The buying and selling of existing mortgages.

secret profit

Undisclosed profit made by a broker at their principal's expense.

section

An area of land, one square mile, or 640 acres; 1/36 of a township.

security *(garantía)*

Evidence of obligations to pay money.

security agreement *(contrato de garantía)*

A document commonly used to secure a loan on personal property.

security deposit

Money given to a landlord to prepay for any damage other than just normal wear and tear.

security interest

The interest of a creditor (lender) in the property of a debtor (borrower).

seller's market

The market condition which exists when a seller is in a more commanding position as to price and terms because demand exceeds supply.

seller's permit

Allows a retailer to buy the product at wholesale prices without paying sales tax. The retailer must then collect the proper sales tax from customers and pay it to the State Board of Equalization.

selling agent

The broker who finds a buyer and obtains an offer for the real property.

semiannual

Twice per year at six month intervals.

semimonthly

Twice a month.

separate property

Property owned by a married person in his or her own right outside of the community interest, including property acquired by the spouse (1) before marriage, (2) by gift or inheritance, (3) from rents and profits on separate property, and (4) with the proceeds from other separate property.

septic tank

A sewage settling tank which must be at least five feet away from the improvements.

servicing loans

Supervising and administering a loan after it has been made. This involves such things as collecting the payments, keeping accounting records, computing the interest and principal, foreclosure of defaulted loans, and so on.

servient tenement

The property that is burdened by an easement.

setback

The distance a building must be set back from the property line, street, or curb usually determined by local building codes.

severalty

Ownership of real property by one person or entity.

shared appreciation mortgage

Lender and borrower agree to share a certain percentage of the appreciation in market value of the property.

sheriff's deed

A deed given to a buyer when property is sold through court-action in order to satisfy a judgment for money or foreclosure of a mortgage.

shoreline

The intersection of the land with the water (mean high water line).

short fund

When a home is sold and the homeowner's insurance policy is cancelled, the seller or owner of the policy receives a refund which is less than the credit they would receive if the buyer were to take over the existing homeowners' insurance.

side yard setback

The distance a building must be set back for the lot line at the side of the property.

sill (mud sill)

The lowest part of the frame of a house. It is fastened with bolts to the foundation and supports the upright studs of the frame.

simple interest

Interest computed on the principal amount of a loan only as distinguished from compound interest.

single agency

The representation of only one party in a real estate transaction.

sinking fund

A fund set aside from the income from property which, with accrued interest, will eventually pay for replacement of the improvements.

site

The position, situation or location of a piece of land in a neighborhood.

situs

A term used to describe the physical location of a property.

smart growth
Reconciling the needs of development with the quality of life. Smart growth focuses on revitalizing older suburbs and older city centers.

soil pipe
A pipe that carries waste from the house to the main sewer line.

Soldiers' and Sailors' Civil Relief Act (SSCRA)
A federal law designed to protect persons in the military service from loss of property when their ability to make the payment has been affected by their entering military service.

sole plate
(1) A board, usually 2" x 4", on which wall and partition studs rest. (2) A support for studs.

sole proprietorship
A business owned and operated by one person.

special agent
A person employed to perform a specific task.

special assessments
Taxes used for specific local purposes.

special power of attorney
A written instrument where a principal confers limited authority upon an agent to perform certain prescribed acts on behalf of the principal.

specific lien
A lien placed against a certain property, such as a mechanic's lien, trust deed, attachment, property tax lien or lis pendens.

specific performance
An action brought in a court to compel a party to carry out the terms of a contract.

specific plan
A particular development site or area of the general plan.

square-foot method
The most common method used by appraisers and real estate agents to estimate the cost of construction.

standard depth
Generally the most typical lot depth in the neighborhood.

standard policy
A policy of title insurance covering only matters of record.

standard subdivision
A land division with no common or mutual rights of either ownership or use among the owners of the parcels created by the division.

standby commitment
A letter that promises to deliver a takeout loan in the future.

State Housing Law
Outlines the minimum construction and occupancy requirements for dwellings.

statute of frauds
A state law which requires that certain contracts must be in writing to prevent fraud in the sale of land or an interest in land.

statute of limitations *(ley de prescripción)*
The period of time limited by statute within which certain court actions must be brought by one party against another.

statutory
Regarding laws created by the enactment of legislation as opposed to law created by court decisions.

steering
The illegal practice of only showing clients property in certain areas.

stigmatized property
(1) Property buyers or tenants may avoid for reasons unrelated to physical conditions or features. The most common are those in which there have been murders, suicides, or criminal activity. (2) Also known as psychologically impacted property.

stock cooperative
A corporation formed for the purpose of owning property.

straight-line depreciation
A method of depreciation under which improvements are depreciated at a constant rate throughout the estimated useful life of the improvement.

straight note
(1) A promissory note in which payments of interest only are made periodically during the term of the note, with the principal payment due in one lump sum upon maturity. (2) This may also be a note with no payments on either principal or interest until the entire sum is due.

Street Improvement Act of 1911
A law that empowers cities and counties to levy a special assessment to repair streets.

studs
Vertical supporting 2" x 4" boards in the walls spaced 16" on the center.

subagent
A broker delegated by the listing agent (if authorized by the seller) who represents the seller in finding a buyer for the listed property.

Subdivided Lands Law

A state law protecting purchasers of property in new subdivisions from fraud, misrepresentation or deceit in the marketing of subdivided property.

subdivision *(subdivisión)*

The division of land into five or more lots for the purpose of sale, lease, or financing.

Subdivision Map Act

The law that authorizes a city or county to control the orderly and proper development of the community.

subdivision system

Also known as a recorded map system.

subject to clause

A buyer takes over the existing loan payments, without notifying the lender. The buyer assumes no personal liability for the loan.

subjective value

Value given for personal reasons.

sublease *(subarrendamiento)*

Transfers less than the entire leasehold, with the original lessee being primarily liable for the rental agreement.

subleasee

The new person who has possession of a leased property.

sublessor

The original tenant of a leased property. They are still primarily liable for paying the rent to the owner for the sublease.

subordination clause

A clause in which the holder of a trust deed permits a subsequent loan to take priority.

subrogation *(subrogación)*

Replacing one person with another in regard to a legal right or obligation. The substitution of another person in place of the creditor, to whose rights he or she succeeds in relation to the debt. The doctrine is used very often where one person agrees to stand surety for the performance of a contract by another person.

substitution, principle of

Affirms that the maximum value of a property tends to be set by the cost of acquiring an equally desirable and valuable substitute property, assuming no cost delay is encountered in making the substitution.

succession

The legal transfer of a person's interest in real and personal property under the laws of descent.

supply and demand, principle of *(oferta y demanda)*

In appraising, a valuation principle stating that market value is affected by intersection of supply and demand forces in the market as of the appraisal date.

surplus productivity, principle of

The net income that remains after the proper costs of labor, organization, and capital have been paid, which surplus is imputable to the land and tends to fix the value thereof.

surrender

When a tenant voluntarily gives up a lease before the expiration of its term.

suspend

(1) Temporarily make ineffective. (2) The Real Estate Commisioner may suspend a real esate license for a violation of the licensing law.

swing loan

(1) A short-term loan used to enable the purchaser of a new property to buy that property on the strength of the equity from the property the purchaser is now selling. (2) Also known as a bridge loan.

syndicate

(1) Two or more individuals who come together for the business purpose of managing an investment. (2) Also known as a real estate syndicate.

takeout loan

The permanent loan that pays off a construction loan.

tax deed

A deed given to a successful bidder at a tax auction.

tax-deferred exchange

The trade or exchange of one real property for another without the need to pay income taxes on the gain at the time of trade.

tax delinquent property

Property that has unpaid taxes.

tax lien *(gravamen de tributación)*

When income or property taxes are not paid.

tax sale

Sale of property after a period of non-payment of taxes.

tenancy

(1) The interest of a person holding property by any right or title. (2) A mode or method of ownership or holding title to property.

tenancy in common

When two or more persons, whose interests are not necessarily equal, are owners of undivided interests in a single estate.

tenancy in partnership
Ownership by two or more persons who form a partnership for business purposes.

tenant *(arrendatorio)*
A renter.

tender
An offer by one of the parties to a contract to carry out his or her part of the contract.

tentative tract map
A map of the proposed subdivision that is submitted to a planning commission for approval or disapproval. It is used to make sure that the improvements, such as lot layouts, sizes, and configurations; grading plans; traffic access and street alighments; storm drainage, sewers, and water facilities; and other project features have been designed to conform to city or county general plans. The approval or disapproval of the planning commission is noted on the map. Therefore, a final map of the tract embodying any changes requested by the planning commission is required to be filed with the planning commission.

testate
A person who dies leaving a valid will.

testator / testatrix *(testador / testadora)*
A person who has made a will.

third party *(terceros)*
A person who may be affected by the terms of an agreement but who is not a party to the agreement.

tidelands
Lands that are covered and uncovered by the ebb and flow of the tide.

tight money
An economic situation in which the supply of money is limited, and the demand for money is high, as evidenced by high interest rates.

time
The duration of a loan.

timely manner
An act must be performed within certain time limits described in a contract.

time is of the essence clause
A clause in a contract that emphasizes punctual performance as an essential requirement of the contract.

timeshare project
A form of subdivision of real property into rights to the recurrent, exclusive use or occupancy of a lot, parcel, unit, or segment of real property, on an annual or some other periodic basis, for a specified period of time.

TIMMUR
The mnemonic for Taxes, Insurance, Management, Maintenance, Utilities, and Reserves.

T-intersection lot
A lot that is fronted head-on by a street. The noise and glare from headlights may be detractors from this type of lot.

title *(título)*
Evidence that the owner of land is in lawful possession.

title companies
Companies that perform a title search on the property and issue a title policy for the lender and the purchaser to ensure that there is a valid mortgage lien against the property and title is clear.

title insurance *(seguro de título)*
An insurance policy that protects the named insured against loss or damage due to defect in the property's title.

title plant
The storage facility of a title company in which it has accumulated complete title records of properties in its area.

title report
A report which discloses condition of the title, made by a title company preliminary to issuance of title insurance policy.

to let, to demise
These phrases mean the same as to rent.

topography
Nature of the surface of land; topography may be level, rolling, and mountainous.

tort
A violation of a legal right, or a civil wrong such as negligence, libel, or nuisance.

townhouse
One of a row of houses usually of the same or similar design with common side walls or with a very narrow space between adjacent side walls.

township *(municipio)*
A grid of squares-each six miles by six miles (36 square miles).

township lines
Imaginary lines drawn every six miles north and south of the base line to form a horizontal row or tier of townships.

trade association
A voluntary nonprofit organization of independent and competing business units engaged in the same industry or trade, formed to help solve industry problems, promote progress, and enhance service.

GLOSSARY

trade fixture

An item of personal property, such as a shelf, cash register, room partition or wall mirror, used to conduct a business.

transferability

The title must be marketable with an unclouded title.

trust account

An account separate and apart and physically segregated from broker's own funds, in which broker is required by law to deposit all funds collected for clients.

trust deed

A security instrument that conveys naked legal title of real property.

trust funds

Money or other things of value received from people by a broker to be used in real estate transactions.

trustee *(fideicomisario)*

Holds naked legal title to property as a neutral third party where there is a deed of trust.

trustee's deed

A deed given to a buyer of real property at a trustee's sale.

trustee's sale

The forced sale of real property, by a lender, to satisfy a debt.

trustor

The borrower under a deed of trust.

Truth in Lending Act *(ley de Veracidad en los Préstamos)*

(1) A federal law that requires borrowers to be informed about the cost of borrowing money. (2) Also known as Regulation Z.

T-TIP

The mnemonic for the four unities of joint tenancy: Time, Title, Interest, and Possession.

turnkey projects

Investors purchase projects that are ready for occupancy.

two-year grace period

A period of time after the expiration of a license that renewal is allowed as long as all real estate activity has ceased during that time and a late fee is paid at the time of renewal.

 U

underwriting

The process of evaluating a borrower's risk factors before the lender will make a loan.

undivided interest

The buyer receives an undivided interest in a parcel of land as a tenant in common with all the other owners.

undue influence

Using unfair advantage to get agreement in accepting a contract.

unearned increment

An increase in value to real estate that comes about from forces outside the control of the owners, such as a favorable shift in population.

unemployment rate

The percentage of the people classified as unemployed as compared to the total labor force.

unenforceable contract

A contract that was valid when made but either cannot be proved or will not be enforced by a court.

Uniform Commercial Code (UCC)

A code that establishes a unified and comprehensive method for regulation of security transactions in personal property.

unilateral contract *(contrato unilateral)*

A contract where a party promises to perform without expectation of performance by the other party.

unilateral rescission

Legal action taken to repeal a contract by one party when the other party has breached a contract.

unit-in-place method

Cost of units in the building as installed is computed and applied to the structure cost. The total costs of walls in place, heating units and roof are figured on a square-foot basis, including labor, overhead, and profit. This is the most detailed method of estimating value.

unity

Equal right of possession or undivided interest. For example, each tenant has the right to use the whole property. None of the owners may exclude any co-owner from the property, nor claim any portion of the property for exclusive use.

unjust enrichment

The situation where a person has received and keeps money or goods that belongs to another. A lawsuit may be necessary to get back the property.

unlawful detainer action

(1) The legal remedy to remove a tenant. (2) Also called an action in ejectment.

Unruh Civil Rights Act

State law that prohibits discrimination by businesses.

UPTEE

The mnemonic for the five ownership rights in the Bundle of Rights: Use, Possess, Transfer, Encumber, and Enjoy.

urban sprawl
The unplanned and often haphazard growth of an urban area into adjoining areas.

useful life
The time frame when an asset (e.g., a building) is expected to remain economical to the owner.

usury *(usura)*
The act of charging a rate of interest in excess of that permitted by law.

utility *(utilidad)*
The ability of a property to satisfy a need or desire, such as shelter, income or amenities.

utility value
The usefulness of the property to its owner.

vacancy factor
Loss of income because of a vacant unit.

VA loan
A loan made to qualified veterans for the purchase of real property wherein the Department of Veterans Affairs guarantees the lender payment of the mortgage.

valid
Legally binding

valid contract
(1) A binding and enforceable contract. (2) A document that has all the basic elements required by law.

valuable consideration
Each party to a contract must give up something to make the agreement binding.

valuation
The process of estimating market value.

value
(1) The present and future anticipated enjoyment or profit from the ownership of property. (2) Also known as worth.

variance *(variación)*
An exception granted to existing zoning regulations for special reasons.

vendee
The buyer under a contract of sale (land contract).

vendor
The seller under a contract of sale (land contract).

vested
Owned by.

vesting
The way title will be taken.

Veterans Exemption
Entitles a resident of California who has been in the military during wartime to take a $4,000 real estate tax emption. Because the Homeowners' Exemption of $7,000 is greater, most California veterans choose the Homeowners' Exemption.

void
An agreement which is totally absent of legal effect.

void contract
A contract that has no legal effect due to lack of capacity or illegal subject matter.

voidable
An agreement which is valid and enforceable on its face, but may be rejected by one or more of the parties.

voluntary lien
When an owner chooses to borrow money, using the property as security for the loan.

wainscoting
The bottom portion of a wall that is covered with wood siding; the top part is treated with another material.

waive
(1) To abandon. (2) To relinquish a right to enforce or require anything.

waiver
The relinquishment or refusal to accept a right.

walk-up
An apartment of more than one story with no elevator.

warehousing
The process of assembling into one package a number of mortgage loans, prior to selling them to an investor.

warranty deed
No longer used in California; a deed used to transfer title to property, guaranteeing that the title is clear and the grantor has the right to transfer it.

WASTO
The mnemonic for five ways to acquire or convey property: Will, Accession, Succession, Transfer, or Occupancy.

water
Water on the surface flowing in a stream or underground (percolating) is real property. If it is taken and bottled, then it becomes personal property.

water pressure test

Water pressure can be tested by turning on all faucets and flushing all toilets at the same time.

water table

The natural level at which water will be found, either above or below the surface of the ground.

wear and tear

Depreciation of an asset due to ordinary usage.

wetlands

Areas where water covers the soil, or is present either at or near the surface of the soil all year or for varying periods of time during the year, including the growing season.

will *(testamento)*

A written instrument whereby a person makes a disposition of his or her property to take effect after their death.

witnessed will

Will usually prepared by an attorney and signed by the maker and two witnesses.

wraparound loan

(1) A method of financing where a new loan is placed in a secondary position; the new loan includes both the unpaid principal balance of the first loan and whatever sums are loaned by the lender. (2) Sometimes called an All-Inclusive Trust Deed (AITD).

writ of execution

A legal document issued by a court forcing the sale of a property to satisfy a judgment.

writ of possession

A legal action granted by the court to the landlord if the tenant does not move out or answer a lawsuit.

"X"

A person who cannot write may execute a document by placing an "X" (his or her mark) where the signature is normally placed. Beneath the mark a witness then writes the person's name and signs his or her own name as a witness.

yield *(rédito)*

(1) The interest earned by an envestor or an investment (or by a bank on the money it has loaned). (2) Also called a return.

yield rate

(1) The yield expressed as a percentage of the total investment. (2) Also called rate of return.

zoning

The regulation of structures and uses of property within selected districts.

zoning ordinance

Regulates land use for individual projects.

Index

INDEX